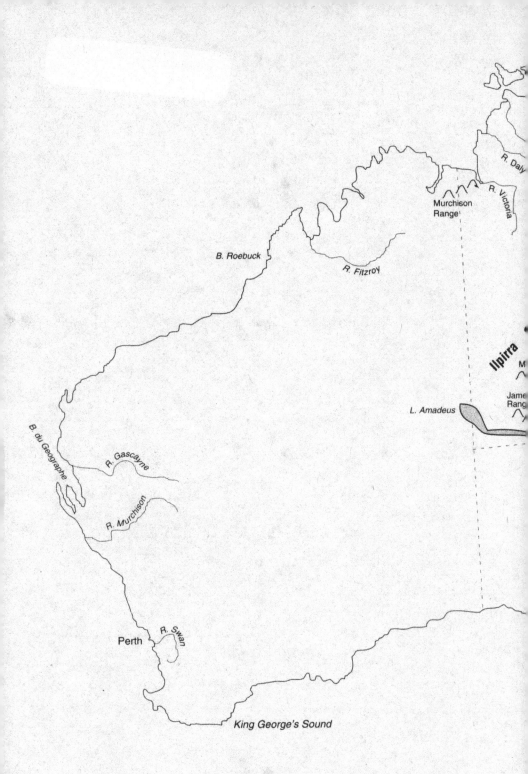

Ethnographic Map of Australia
(The names of Australian peoples appear in boldface type

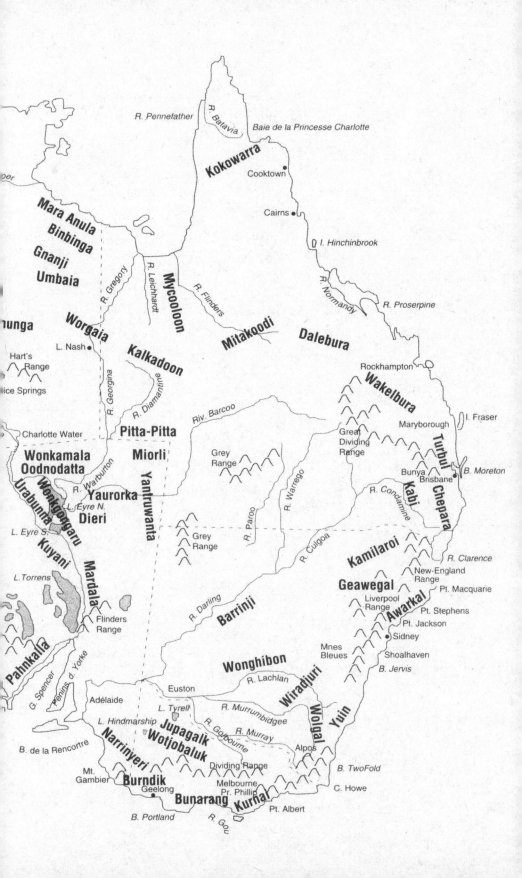

The Elementary Forms of

RELIGIOUS LIFE

The Elementary Forms of
RELIGIOUS LIFE

EMILE DURKHEIM

Translated and with an Introduction by
Karen E. Fields

THE FREE PRESS

The Free Press
A Division of Simon & Schuster Inc.
1230 Avenue of the Americas, New York, N.Y. 10020

printing number
20 19 18 17 16 15 14 13 12

Library of Congress Cataloging-in-Publication Data

Durkheim, Emile, 1858–1917.
    [Formes élémentaires de la vie religieuse. English]
    The elementary forms of religious life/ Emile Durkheim;
translated and with an introduction by Karen E. Fields.
      p. cm.
    Translation of: Les formes élémentaires de la vie religieuse.
    Includes index.
    ISBN: 978-0-02-907937-9
      II. Title.
    GN470.D813   1995
    306.6—dc20   94–41128
                                         CIP

This book was originally published as *Les Formes élémentaires de la vie religieuse: Le système totémique en Australie*, Paris, F. Alcan, 1912.

The endpaper art in this volume is based on a map that appeared in the French edition.

CONTENTS

INTRODUCTION
Subject of the Study:
Religious Sociology and the Theory of Knowledge 1

I. • Main subject of the book: analysis of the simplest known religion, to determine the elementary forms of religious life. • Why they are easier to arrive at and explain through primitive religions. 1

II. • Secondary subject: origin of the fundamental notions or categories of thought. • Reasons for believing their origin to be religious and consequently social. • How a means of regenerating the theory of knowledge can be seen from this point of view. 8

BOOK ONE: PRELIMINARY QUESTIONS
Chapter One: Definition of Religious Phenomena
and of Religion 21

The usefulness of a preliminary definition of religion; method to be followed in arriving at that definition. • Why the usual definitions should be examined first. 21

I. • Religion defined by the supernatural and the mysterious. • Criticism. The idea of mystery was not present at the beginning. 22

II. • Religion defined in relation to the idea of God or a spiritual being. Religions without gods. • Rites in deistic religions that imply no idea of deity. 27

III. • Search for a positive definition. • Distinction between beliefs and rites. Definition of beliefs. • First characteristic: bipartite division of things into sacred and profane. • Distinguishing traits of that division. • Definition of rites in relation to beliefs. • Definition of religion. 33

Chapter Six: Origins of These Beliefs (Continued):
The Notion of Totemic Principle, or Mana, and the Idea of Force 190

I. • The notion of force or totemic principle. • Its ubiquity. • Its simultaneously physical and moral character. 190

II. • Similar conceptions in other lower societies. • Gods in Samoa. • Wakan of the Sioux, orenda of the Iroquois, mana in Melanesia. • Relationships of these notions with totemism. • Arúnkulta of the Arunta. 193

III. • The logical priority of the notion of impersonal force over the various mythical personalities. • Recent theories that tend to accept this priority. 201

IV. • The notion of religious force is the prototype of the notion of force in general. 205

Chapter Seven: Origins of These Beliefs (Conclusion):
Origin of the Notion of Totemic Principle, or Mana 207

I. • The totemic principle is the clan, but the clan thought of in tangible form. 207

II. • General reasons society is capable of arousing the sensation of the sacred and the divine. • Society as an imperative moral power; the notion of moral authority. • Society as a force that raises the individual above himself. • Facts proving that society creates the sacred. 208

III. • Reasons peculiar to the Australian societies. • The two phases through which the life of these societies alternately passes: dispersal and concentration. • Great collective effervescence during the periods of concentration. Examples. • How the religious idea is born from that effervescence. Why the collective force was conceived of in totemic forms: The totem is the emblem of the clan. • Explanation of the principal totemic beliefs. 216

IV. • Religion is not a product of fear. • It expresses something real. • Its fundamental idealism. • That idealism is a general trait of collective mentality. • Why religious forces are external to their substrates. • On the principle *the part equals the whole.* 225

V. • Origin of the notion of emblem: use of emblems, a necessary condition of collective representations. • Why the clan has taken its emblems from the animal and plant kingdoms. 231

BOOK III: THE PRINCIPAL MODES
OF RITUAL CONDUCT

Chapter One: The Negative Cult and Its Functions: *The Ascetic Rites* 303

I. • The system of prohibitions • Magic and religious prohibitions. Prohibitions between sacred things of different kinds. Prohibitions between sacred and profane. • These last are the basis of the negative cult. • Principal types of these prohibitions; their reduction to two basic types. 303

II. • Observance of the prohibitions modifies the religious states of individuals. Cases in which that efficacy is especially apparent: ascetic practices. • Religious efficacy of pain. • Social function of asceticism. 313

III. • Explanation of the system of prohibitions: antagonism of the sacred and the profane; contagiousness of the sacred. 321

IV. • Causes of this contagiousness. • It cannot be explained by the laws of the association of ideas. • It arises because religious forces are external to their substrates. Logical interest of this property of the religious forces. 325

Chapter Two: The Positive Cult: *The Elements of the Sacrifice* 330
The Intichiuma ceremony in the tribes of central Australia. • Various forms it exhibits. 330

I. • The Arunta form. • The two phases. • Analysis of the first: visiting sacred places, spreading sacred dust, shedding blood, etc., to bring about the reproduction of the totemic species. 331

II. • Second phase: ritual eating of the totemic plant or animal. 338

III. • Interpretation of the ceremony as a whole. • The second rite consists of a communion meal. • Reason for that communion. 340

IV. • The rites of the first phase consist of offerings. • Analogies with sacrificial offerings. • Hence the Intichiuma contains the two elements of sacrifice. • Interest of these facts for the theory of sacrifice. 344

V. • On the alleged absurdity of the sacrificial offerings. • How they are explained: dependence of sacred beings on their worshippers. • Explanation of

CONCLUSION

ACKNOWLEDGMENTS

In preparing this translation I have incurred many debts: to the Woodrow Wilson International Center for a semester-long fellowship, the congenial effervescence of its staff and community of scholars, and for the quiet of my turret office in the Smithsonian Institution; to the University of Rochester for research support, both in dollars and in the kind sharing by specialists in many fields that is the heart of organic solidarity—classicist Kathryn Argetsinger, German Studies scholar Patricia Herminghouse, historians William J. McGrath and Morris A. Pierce, Indologist Douglas R. Brooks, philosophers Lewis W. Beck, Deborah Modrak, and George Dennis O'Brien, psychologist Craig R. Barclay, and most of all French scholar Andrée Douchin, who read my text alongside Durkheim's line by line and provided detailed critique; to colleagues elsewhere—Karen McCarthy Brown, Jay Demerath, Alexandre Derczansky, Barbara J. Fields, Terry F. Godlove, Gila Hayim, Winston A. James, Robert Jay, Robert Alun Jones, Edward Kaplan, Douglas A. Kibbee, Valentin Y. Mudimbe, James T. Richardson, Jan Vansina, Loïe Wacquant, and Robert Paul Wolff, for clarifying correspondence; to librarians Zdenek David and Ursula Heinen and to research assistants Nafiz Aksehirioglu, Antonia Balosz, Chad Birely, Lloyd Brown, Stephen Monto, and Samuel Tylor, for help with notes and references at the various stages of a long project; to Charlette W. Henry and Lela Sims-Gissendaner, staff of the Frederick Douglass Institute for African and African-American Studies, for practical solutions to the practical problems of preparing a manuscript; to Bruce Nichols, Celia Knight, and others of the Free Press editorial staff for their painstaking attention to the text's several languages.

I owe especially large debts to Ayala Gabriel, my colleague and friend, with whom I spent many hours of clarifying conversation about religion and much else; and to Moussa Bagate, my husband, who shared his general and scientifically specialized knowledge of French, and who shared, period.

ABBREVIATIONS

AA	*American Anthropologist*
AAAS	Australasian Association for the Advancement of Science
AMNH	*Memoirs of the American Museum of Natural History*
APS	*Proceedings of the American Philosophical Society*
ArA	*Archaeologia Americana*
AS	*Année sociologique*
BAAS	British Association for the Advancement of Science (Reports)
BAE	*Reports of the Bureau of American Ethnology*
CJ	*Cambrian Journal*
CNAE	*Contributions to North American Ethnology*
FR	*Fortnightly Review*
HLCAPS	*Transactions of the Historical and Literary Committee of the American Philosophical Society*
JA	*Journal asiatique*
JAI	*Journal of the Anthropological Institute of Great Britain and Ireland*
QGJ	*Queensland Geographical Journal*
RAM	*Records of the Australian Museum*
RCI	*Revue coloniale internationale*
RHR	*Revue de l'histoire des religions*
RIS	*Revista italiana di sociologia*
RMM	*Revue de morale et de métaphysique*
RNM	*Report of the U.S. National Museum*
RP	*Revue philosophique*
RSC	*Transactions of the Royal Society of Canada*
RSI	*Report of the Smithsonian Institution*
RSNSW	*Journal and Proceedings of the Royal Society of New South Wales*

RSSA	*Transactions of the Royal Society of South Australia*
RSV	*Transactions and Proceedings of the Royal Society of Victoria*
TICHR	*Transactions of the Third International Congress for the History of Religions*
VGJ	*Victorian Geographical Journal*
ZE	*Zeitschrift für Ethnologie*
ZV	*Zeitschrift für Völkerpsychologie*
ZDP	*Zeitschrift für Deutsche Philologie*

TRANSLATOR'S INTRODUCTION:

RELIGION AS AN EMINENTLY SOCIAL THING

> [W]hat I ask of the free thinker is that he should confront religion in the same mental state as the believer. . . . [H]e who does not bring to the study of religion a sort of religious sentiment cannot speak about it! He is like a blind man trying to talk about colour.
>
> Now I shall address the free believer. . . . Without going so far as to disbelieve the formula we believe in, we must forget it provisionally, reserving the right to return to it later. Having once escaped from this tyranny, we are no longer in danger of perpetrating the error and injustice into which certain believers have fallen who have called my way of interpreting religion basically irreligious. There cannot be a rational interpretation of religion which is fundamentally irreligious; an irreligious interpretation of religion would be an interpretation which denied the phenomenon it was trying to explain.[1]
>
> Emile Durkheim (1858–1917)

Easily the most striking feature of Emile Durkheim's 1912 masterpiece, *Les Formes élémentaires de la vie religieuse*, is his insistence that religions are founded on and express "the real." The most casual skim through the book's very first pages—even through the Contents—will reveal that insistence. And it is continually present, like a heartbeat. At the same time, however, as a reader might well mutter, the most striking feature of religions is that they are full to overflowing with spectacular improbabilities. As if anticipating that thought, Durkheim challenges it from the start: "There are no religions that are false." More than that: "If [religion] had not been grounded in the nature of things, in those very things it would have met resistance that it could not have over-

xvii

come."[2] A hostile reviewer writing in the *American Anthropologist* said flatly that Durkheim's "search for a reality underlying religion does not seem to rest on a firm logical basis."[3] Judgment about the logic of that search belongs to readers of Durkheim's greatest book, which I offer in its first full retranslation since Joseph Ward Swain's, in 1915.[4]

To gauge Durkheim's claim about the roots of religion in "the real," it will be necessary to follow an argument that is provocative through and through. Pressing that claim to its very limit, Durkheim announces that his case in point will be the totemic religions of Australia, with totemism's jarring identification of human beings and animals or plants—on its face, to readers in 1912, anything but a religious milieu with anything like credible roots in the real and, to some of them, not even a religious milieu. *Au contraire,* cautions Durkheim. Totemism qualifies as a religion; furthermore, all religions are "true after their own fashion," and all, including totemism, meet "needs" (*besoins*) that are part and parcel of human life.[5] Then or now, anyone encountering the first pages of *Formes* for the first time must wonder straightaway what he intends by "the real," or by "needs" built into the human makeup that religion fulfills. Here are claims likely to draw the religiously committed and the religiously uncommitted to the edge of their seats. From the start, it is clear that the questions Durkheim has set himself about religion concern the nature of human life and the nature of "the real." (From now on I drop the quotation marks around the phrase, noting that part of Durkheim's agenda in *Formes* is to apply his conception of the real to all social forms of existence. Philosophers in Durkheim's milieu were reworking the old polarity of appearance versus essence, as handled by Immanuel Kant. We can flash forward to Edmund Husserl, and again, regarding the social world specifically, from Husserl to Alfred Schutz.)

It is equally clear from the start that received ideas offer Durkheim few intellectual park benches along the route toward the answers. The opening chapters (Book One) define religion and totemism. They then demolish two earlier families of theory, animism and naturism, certain of whose received ideas about what is fundamental to religion still have a certain currency—for example, naturism's thesis that religion arises from human awe before the grandeur of the natural world. Gone there and then (to many, maddeningly) is religion as "ultimate concern" and as encounter with a power transcending the human, or with "the holy."[6] The middle chapters (Book Two) systematically examine what Durkheim calls *représentations collectives:* shared mental constructs with the help of which, he argues, human beings collectively view themselves, each other, and the natural world. Having adopted totemism as an especially challenging system of collective representations,

Durkheim develops a theory of how society constitutes itself, one that is simultaneously (and in his view, necessarily) a theory of how human mentality constitutes itself. That theory, in turn, encloses another, about those "unified systems" of *représentations* concerning nature and humanity that religions always contain.

The final chapters (Book Three) deal with forms of collective conduct that can be thought of as collective representations in action and, at the same time, as action that makes collective representations real in individual minds. Here are echoes of Marx, in *The German Ideology*, where reality is above all *done:* "Consciousness can never be anything else than conscious existence." As though hearing that echo, Durkheim cautions against understanding his thought as "merely a refurnishment of historical materialism."[7] In fact, his common ground with Marx on the subject of religion is far from negligible and yet far from total. For Durkheim, religions exist because human beings exist only as social beings and in a humanly shaped world. Religion is "an eminently social thing."[8]

In the Australians' world, as we come to know it through *Formes*, to have the clan name Kangaroo is not merely to postulate an amazing inner bond of shared essence with animals, whose inherent distinctness from humans is obvious. It is also to postulate a just as amazing inner bond of shared essence with other humans, by sharing a name. Human individuals are inherently distinct from one another, and so the potential for mutually recognized identity is far from obvious. On this subject, the early critical voice is unamazed, settling for well-worn park benches of thought: "The experience of all times and places teaches that the rapport of the *individual, as such,* with the *religious object* is of prime importance in *religious situations.*"[9] But Durkheim's challenge in *Formes* is to detect questions, not self-evidences, in phrases like "individual, as such," "religious object," and "religious situation." His expedition goes to a place where "[t]he kangaroo is only an animal like any other; but, for the Kangaroo people, it has within itself a principle that sets it apart from other beings, and this principle only exists in and through the minds of those who think of it." On that expedition, "in a philosophical sense, the same is true of any thing; for things exist only through representation."[10]

By many, usually benchless, routes through Australian ethnography, Durkheim brings us to what he intends by the real that human beings in general come to know through the distinctively human means of knowing. Those means begin, he argues, with human sociability. Society is the form in which nature produced humankind, and religion is reason's first harbor. In *Formes,* we meet the mind as a collective product and science as an offspring of religion. In those very processes of abstraction that enabled the Australian to imagine who he was by imagining his relationship with other Australians and with the natural world, we meet the beginning of abstract thought. And we meet the concept, ours via the social treasury of language, defined as "a beam that lights, penetrates, and transforms" sensation.[11] Durkheim's querying of the Australians and their totems is thus the point of departure for his investigation into distinctive traits of humankind: reason, identity, and community—three subjects that we tend neither to place under the heading "religion" nor to treat together. Few people today would end a sentence that begins, "Religion is . . ." in the way he does: ". . . above all, a system of ideas by which men imagine the society of which they are members and the obscure yet intimate relations they have with it."[12]

If Durkheim's sustained insistence on religions' basis in the real is the most striking feature of *Formes*, his provocative, sharp-witted mode of exposition comes a close second.[13] And if the book has a heartbeat about the nature of the real, it has a rhetorical body built to subvert received notions. As he admits in the Introduction, some readers were bound to find his approach "unorthodox."[14] He chose to explore huge questions about humankind in general via the stone-tool-using specificity of Aboriginal Australia, and his argument moves in ways that could not fail to scandalize many readers, on various grounds. We can begin to feel the specific texture of *scandale* if we consider another hostile reviewer's observation about the academically orthodox view of totemism, in a long article titled "Dogmatic Atheism in the Sociology of Religion." There we learn that totemism, "[a]s currently taught in Anglican universities, . . . appeared to fit with the providential mission of the Jews and the possibility of Christian revelation."[15] In other words, some scholars dealt with totemism by making it into a "Christianity in embryo." Being born and reared a Jew and the son of a rabbi, Durkheim lacked the nearsightedness that made totemism as embryonic Christianity seem a necessary lens. What is more, he doubtless had no investment in preserving high evolutionary rank for any religion at all. As a young man, he had rejected religious commitment outright, a fact to which the article's neon title alludes.

For the scholars referred to and addressed in that article, in any case, totemism was anything but well adapted to showing religion's roots in the real. It could be relegated to the category of magic, as the critic points out that Herbert Spencer did (which Durkheim disputed, since that amounted to disconnecting it from the real).[16] Or it could be adapted to that role if imagined with an arrow on it, pointing forward in an evolutionist sense to religions whose connections with the real seemed a priori more credible than totemism's. But there stood Durkheim, firing argument in two directions: claiming that religion would not have survived if it had not been grounded in the real and claiming to study religion in general by juxtaposing the allegedly lowest and highest. For many reasons, in that unself-consciously self-satisfied era, *Formes* must have been a shocker. Looking back, the French sociologist Raymond Aron described the immediate reaction to it in France as *violent*. Being highly sophisticated, Durkheim no doubt expected that. Notice the rhetorical sandpits in the quotations I used as an epigraph, taken from extemporaneous remarks he made in 1914 to the Union of Free Thinkers and Free Believers. Now picture the sinuous road to be traveled in any attempt to represent him in a comprehensive portrait as the great contributor to empirical science that he was.

Durkheim's commentators have often expressed dismay about the rhetorical mode in which *Formes* is written. Dominick LaCapra spoke of an "oceanic form of discourse" in a text "which has had the power to allure and repel at the same time."[17] Steven Lukes wrote of Durkheim's style that it "often tends to caricature his thought: he often expressed his ideas in an extreme or figurative manner."[18] I imagine that Talcott Parsons was reacting in part to some of those very qualities when he claimed, essentially, that in *Formes* Durkheim was feeling his way uneasily between the naiveté of positivism and something far smarter.[19] Raymond Aron disliked the book, said so in no uncertain terms (including the term "impiety"), and professed to be so unsure in his understanding of it that he deliberately included long sections of verbatim quotation, to enable more sympathetic readers to do better than he.[20] I will not tarry over those who, finding the posture of *Formes* enigmatic, respond by characterizing the book as mystical, metaphysical, and even theological, charges that must make Durkheim's soul shake its head. If it is true that he rejected not only religion but also his family's intention for him to become a rabbi, in his father's and grandfather's footsteps, he must have paid full fare for a secular voyage through the mysteries and commonplaces of life.[21] As far as I am concerned, it is sufficient to say that Durkheim was experimenting with ideas that deeply mattered to him, and there is every reason to imagine that he often ran up against the expressive limits of his medium. Up against those same limits, no less a sociological theorist than Talcott Parsons used the unsettling term "nonempirical reality."[22]

Durkheim's rhetoric is often remarked upon but generally not built into the systematic commentary about him.[23] Traditional accounts usually stop at saying sociology was a new science at the turn of the century, Durkheim one of those battling to define a tenable version of its subject matter and method, and his mode (alas) polemical. But if polemic in the midst of developing something new is stigmatized as antithetical to systematic thought, then the very notion of systematic thought is impoverished. Left unimagined is the sense of absorbing puzzles to be solved and a living sense of inspiration before it becomes "system." It is easy to see a calculated polemical edge in Durkheim's *Suicide*, where he tackles as a sociological puzzle an act that received notions even today hold to be quintessentially individual. Often noticed as well is the sinewy argument to be expected of a philosophically trained product of the Ecole normale supérieure, France's *crème de la crème* in higher education. But seldom imagined is what must have been the high humor of working against received ideas and toward fundamental truth. To miss those features is to miss the freshness of the work he did, at the time he was doing it: gone is the sense of experiment and excitement he shared with the many talented students he taught at the Sorbonne, and with the scholars who joined him in creating the celebrated journal *Année sociologique;* gone too is his wit on the page. If those elements are missed, *Formes* is by the same stroke uplifted as a classic and downgraded to a tome.

Durkheim breathed the air of turn-of-the-century Paris, a place that fizzed with experiments in artistic representation, and a time when philosophy, science, and art existed in nothing like today's isolation from one another.[24] Picasso painted his *Demoiselles d'Avignon* in 1907, launching cubism and, therewith, a new vocabulary for the art of the new century. It may turn out that illuminating connections can be drawn between Durkheim's transgressing the boundaries between "primitive" and "civilized" in the search for a vocabulary suited to comprehending, and then representing, the real, and Picasso's own encounters with those same boundaries as he reconceived perspective. To give attention to Durkheim's rhetorical leaps is not to show where he fell short as a systematic thinker; it is to amplify his voice and hear him better. In *Formes,* one of his tasks is to show how a kangaroo can be, at one and the same time, a powerful sacred being, a man or woman, and just a kangaroo—all in the real. His rhetorical tactics in representing these barely representable things are in themselves interesting to observe. That they have succeeded in some way accounts for the book's capacity over the years to motivate fruitful empirical work in a range of fields.

ANATOMY OF A CLASSIC

As a classic in the sociology and anthropology of religion, *Formes* is widely mentioned and characterized, if not so widely read. My purpose in undertaking a new translation is to re-present Durkheim's ideas about what he called the "religious nature of man" in the English of our own day while rendering Durkheim's French as faithfully as I can. I have undertaken this new translation at a time when the serious study of religion has finally begun to return to center stage in our culture, after an unfortunate hiatus of many decades. My hope is that this book will be more widely read and studied, and not only by sociologists and anthropologists or scholars of religion. American postmodernist theorizers of discursive practices and representations will recognize through *Formes* the Durkheimian pedigree of Michel Foucault.[25] Psychologists will repeatedly glimpse old and not-so-old ways of thinking about phenomena that the scientific study of memory, identity, language, and intelligence must be able to account for. Philosophers will find old problems interestingly tackled, if not necessarily solved.[26]

My hope for a broadened readership raises a larger question, about *Formes* in particular and the genus "classic" to which it belongs: Why read classics? Of late, that question and sundry answers to it have framed a sometimes poisonous debate over which ancestors should be so honored in memory. This conversation is largely impersonal, as short on "I's" as it is long on impersonal, puritanical "shoulds"; it is outspoken about discipline but inarticulate about individual pleasure, and mute as the grave about excitement. Like broccoli, classics are said to be good for one, even if swallowed unwillingly. My view is that dead ancestors should stay dead to us unless pleasure and excitement come from getting to know them. While in the midst of this project, I heard Wynton Marsalis, the virtuoso classical and jazz trumpeter, tell a cautionary tale of honesty about the point of classics and about the work involved in translating them for new audiences. His introduction to some new settings of old work by Duke Ellington brought out problems that both bedevil such work and inspire its product.

To begin with, Marsalis said, he was unenthusiastic about Ellington. His friend, the choreographer Garth Fagan, invited him to see a rehearsal performance set to an old piece by Ellington. A period piece, Marsalis thought. "That's just some boring old ballroom music. I know I *should* want to hear it but I don't." But Fagan pressed, sure about his rendering. Marsalis went, and then reconsidered: "Everybody said Ellington was great. But what made him so great? Nobody said. Well, that night, I understood." He, in turn, trumpeted some "old ballroom music" to us, his audience. As Fagan had interpreted to Marsalis, so Marsalis interpreted to his own audience, who were invited to discover Ellington's greatness, partly through the original work itself but also with Marsalis present as a "translator," with all the complexities that implies. It was Marsalis's "translation" that gave us access to the greatness of some out-of-style music, and irremediably so, for we had no access to the music except by hearing someone render it in sound (unless we decided to experience the music by sight, from Ellington's page). No two renderings could be the same. None could be exactly what Ellington meant. We cannot know exactly what he meant. The only certainty was that rendering the music freed it to win the audience over, or not to.

But what is true about music that begins its public life with popular audiences is not true about the high culture of old books. When that seems at stake, the answer to the question, "Why read classics?" too often hides behind the busy boredom of Ecclesiastes: "That which has been done is that which shall be done." I think otherwise. Every classic should be free to win the right to be read again with pleasure, not just to be set to labor as a captive servant of tradition, trapped in the highbrowed storage of a museum display. The case for studying old works now needs to be made now, partly through the manner of their presentation. If the classics really are good enough to keep reading, in spite of their age and flaws, then they are due the respect of being allowed to win their audience over. "Because they are classics" amounts to saying, "Because they are there." And that is the unhappy fate of captives in those Smithsonians of the mind that college reading lists can be, on permanent exhibition to pedants, connoisseurs, and cranky tourists, indiscriminately. Every schoolchild learns that Mount Everest was scaled "because it was there" and can understand from a distance what makes it "great." But the superlatives about great books are not the same. To know there, as a character of Zora Neale Hurston says, you have to go there. I have taken it to be my task, in retranslating this classic, not only to make the way straight to go there but to say why go there at all.

I recommend this classic in sociology for reading today, even though the ethnography is outdated, and the outlook upon gender quaint, because it presents the opportunity to encounter a dazzlingly complex soul whose burden of life animates the work. It is this same burden that animates great art. *Formes* has not only the steady brilliance of a classic but also a certain incandescence. It is like a virtuoso performance that is built upon but leaps beyond the technical limits of the artist's discipline, beyond the safe striving merely to hit the correct notes, into a felt reality of elemental truth. To read it is to witness such a performance. The illuminations are public, the performance personal.

Durkheim is usually remembered as the no-nonsense advocate of *science positive*—"positive[27] science"—in the study of social life, as a man who set out to rescue social science from undisciplined subjectivity, from philosophical argument that delicately minuetted with facts or touched them not at all, from parochial sentimentality, and from the naive individualisms of his time. But the argument of *Formes* is markedly personal in both rhetorical style and scientific substance, revealing a man who was far more than the hard-nosed opponent of the second-rate and the sentimental in social science (although he was that too). We hear the heartbeat of *Formes* in Durkheim's stunning theme throughout: that religious life (*la vie religieuse*) both expresses and constructs the logical life (*la vie logique*) of humankind. We hear it in the audacious claim he makes, ostensibly as a secondary issue but in fact throughout the book, that the elemental categories in which we think—time, space, number, cause, class, person, totality—have their origins in religious life.

It is gripping drama to see how a man of *science positive* could possibly make such claims, how he could go about arguing them in an era when science seemed to be dismembering religion, and most of all, why such a man would ever choose to. This drama is gripping for us still: The dispute between science and religion is at least as loud now as it was in his time. In the book, Durkheim's feet seem at one moment to be on the solid ground of immensely detailed scientific observation and at the next on the high wire of faith. But whose? His Aboriginal Australian subjects'? His contemporaries'? His own? Ours? We keep listening in order to find out which it is, when, in what, and in what capacity. People sleepwalk even in the company of the powerful, if they are uninteresting men and women of shallow dilemmas. Durkheim was an interesting man, because he had the capacity to sustain the manifold internal tension of his own ideas, and because he had a dilemma and a subject capable of earning prolonged attention.

Religion still arouses passionate interest, and passion too. If it is an opium of the oppressed, it is not only the opium that puts people to sleep but also the one that makes legions of people go to great lengths to get their own dose of it. If religion is incompatible with scientific rationality and secular political life, those conflicts are public and active ones, not the passive withering away into self-evident defeat that observers of right and left long imagined. Doom has not followed from religion's demonstrated setbacks in describing nature. Indeed, one cannot describe today's world without the collective identities that religions sustain: quietly worshipping churches in some places, churches militant in others. Religion is the steady, day-in-day-out reality of millions, their routine framework of everyday activity, their calm certainty of life and its steady, but sometimes racing, pulse.

In 1979, we watched as crowds shouting "*Allahu Akbar!*"—"God is great!"—destroyed the Iranian monarchy and consecrated Ruhollah Khomeini as Imam. In 1989, we saw the reconsecration of the People's House of Culture in Vilnius as the Cathedral of Vilnius, the replacement there of St. Casimir's bones after some forty years, and then the dignified filing past of Lithuanians reconstituting themselves as a religiously and ethnically defined nation-state. And who would have thought in 1912 that, three generations later in America, religion would be a hot button political topic, the object of undignified excitement, the locus of dispute over where the authoritative designation of where right conduct lies and must lie?[28] As a scholar and teacher, I advocate the dignified excitement of studying religion with discipline—and Durkheim's shuttling between *science positive* and the high wire of faith exemplifies a sort of discipline that we can cultivate.

Yet discipline cannot be the whole point. Works of genius ultimately are disrespected by being touted as mere calisthenics for the mind. They are diminished to the extent that, like aids to physical exercise, they become tools fitted to known tasks, captive servants of mental "training" in the school years. The improvisational high-wire mode of the unexpected is lost thereby and, with it, the special work and worth of genius. In the end, *Formes* would not be worth reading again and again if all it did was help us cultivate intellectual discipline in our attempts to understand what we call "religion." In fact it does much more. In this sometimes sober, sometimes high-wire, exploration of what he calls "the religious nature of man," Durkheim carries his readers beyond ordinary ideas about what religion is and does. We meet the man who could say, to the sober assent of believers down the ages, that "the man who has communed with his god . . . is *stronger*"[29] but who could also say, to the boisterous dissent of true believers down the ages, "There are no religions that are false." We meet the man who said both—and in a work of *science positive*.

AN ARCHAEOLOGY OF THE SOUL

Little is known about Durkheim's personal life. I will not repeat the tidbits here but instead refer readers to W. S. F. Pickering's and Steven Lukes's compilations of what is known, and portray the man as we meet him in Book One, Chapter 2, in his mode of virtuoso play—and display. There, in the posture of demolishing mistaken theory, he takes up one of religions' elemental *représentations collectives.* I propose that we make our acquaintance with him by observing how he acquaints us with the great nineteenth-century scholar of religion, Edward Burnett Tylor.

Tylor put forward a very influential theory about the origin of an idea that a great many peoples have developed and variously conceived of as a singular thing (*the* or *a* soul), or yet as a generic substance (soul, period),[30] immortal yet sometimes susceptible to annihilation, attached to persons yet migratory despite such attachments, intimately known yet almost impossible to describe, personal yet transmissible to objects and animals, ethereal yet powerful, and much else, but above all conceived as mysterious, contradictory, and hard to conceive. Introducing us to Tylor, the man of *science positive* introduces us to the idea of soul. In Chapter 8, Durkheim returns to soul at length, in a hauntingly beautiful construction of how human beings in the full dignity of reason might have come to postulate the idea of soul in order to theorize aspects of the real. In his view, those human beings were not, like St. Augustine, able to "believe precisely because it was absurd." He trained his heavy rhetorical guns against scholars whose logic entailed that they must have been able to do so.

By Durkheim's day, comparative studies on religion had long since revealed that soul, as a concept, is to be found virtually wherever religion is found. The question scholars asked themselves was why such an inherently confusing idea came to be such a widespread idea, even in societies nothing like those of the Australians. The existence of individual souls had to be accommodated even in the society inhabited by Descartes. And everywhere, accommodating their existence led to questions about where they might reside and about their relationship to those residences. Readers who remember their Descartes (who, of course, was at Durkheim's intellectual fingertips and those of his readers) will remember that, via his *Cogito, ergo sum*, the mind/body dualism, hence the soul/body dualism, was rooted in his search for that which cannot be doubted. Bear in mind, too, that Descartes conceived of a mechanics that held for all things that possessed "extension"—but not for God or soul, whose existence in the real included neither extension nor subordination to the laws of mechanics. Speculating about the soul's localization, Descartes postulated that it resides in the (still mysterious) pineal gland.

Durkheim addressed the matter of localization differently. Free from the hot breath of the Inquisition, as Descartes (1596–1650) was not, and freed also by his interpretive use of exotic materials, Durkheim repeated the solutions his Australian subjects gave the same empirical problem—for example, in many rituals, notably those conducted in the midst and aftermath of mourning. The practicalities of ritual doing localized the soul in certain organs and in the blood, which were thereby revealed, in his phrase, as "the soul itself seen from outside"[31] (a formulation that may have suggested to Durkheim's audience certain philosophers of antiquity).[32] The Australians' urge to localize the soul set them beside not only the Catholic Descartes but also the pagan Empedocles[33] and the Jewish writers of Leviticus and Deuteronomy (whom Durkheim cites), all solving it rather more like the Australians than like Descartes. By Tylor's more secularized day, the question was not merely where the soul might be but a more radical one that would surely have provoked the Inquisition into action: why people ever *imagined* any such thing. Tylor held that the idea arose from the universal but individual experience of dreaming. For Tylor, dreaming posed a theoretical problem that nagged nightly at earliest humanity's consciousness until it was solved with the invention of a double, or a soul. Demolishing this argument was the Durkheim who had already pronounced religious ideas to be grounded in and to express the real. The solution Tylor imputed to "primitives" failed that test.

After reviewing the merits of Tylor's enterprise, Durkheim proceeded to carry out an intellectual death of a thousand cuts. According to Tylor, the idea of the soul, or double, explained ecstasy, catalepsy, apoplexy, and fainting; illnesses and health, good fortune, bad fortune, special abilities, or anything else that departed slightly from the ordinary; and on down an expanding list applied to an expanding population of souls. Thus did an idea of great import for religions everywhere come to explain everything. Thus did the power of souls increase. And thus did Tylor's primitive man, having come up with the concept of soul to solve a merely speculative problem, finally end up as "a captive in this imaginary world, even though he is its creator and model."[34] Here is Durkheim's *coup de grâce:* "Even if the hypothesis of the double could satisfactorily explain all dreaming, and all dreaming could be explained in no other way, one would still have to say why man tried to explain it at all. . . . [H]abit easily puts curiosity to sleep."[35] Indeed, even if curiosity had been awake, dreaming would not by any stretch have posed the most obvious problem: "There was something incomprehensible in the fact that a luminous disc of such small diameter could be adequate to light the Earth—and yet, centuries went by before humanity thought of resolving that contradiction." So, why should humanity, especially Tylor's materially hard-pressed primitive humanity, have invented an idea fundamental to virtually all religions, in order to solve the nighttime puzzle of dreaming, a trivial puzzle by comparison with the one they bypassed in the light of day? Durkheim then moves on to stiletto Herbert Spencer's amendments to Tylor's theory. He ends on his point about the real:

> In the end, religion is only a dream, systematized and lived but without foundation in the real. . . . Indeed, whether, in such conditions, the term "science of religions" can be used without impropriety is questionable. . . . What sort of a science is it whose principal discovery is to make the very object it treats disappear?[36]

Returning in Chapter 8 to treat the idea of soul according to his own principle about the roots of religion in the real, Durkheim gives his argument a striking end and then a still more striking coda. The idea of soul, he concludes, actually was needed to solve a problem that the daytime course of social life forced human reason to confront: the indisputable reality that there is death, yet communities live on, and there is birth: "In sum, belief in the immortality of souls is the only way man is able to comprehend a fact that cannot fail to attract his attention: the perpetuity of the group's life."[37] Socially, he argued, it stood for that collective life; individualized, it stood for the social part of every human being, the human (as distinct from the animal) part. It is at once a discrete being and an ethereal substance, at once individual par excellence and yet social.[38]

In the coda, Durkheim's evocations of Leibniz and Kant begin far from ethnography, but close to us. Using their ideas, he reminds us that soul, however slippery as a concept, is something humankind has come to know very well from our experience of the real: "The idea of soul long was, and in part still is, the most universally held form of the idea of personality."[39] At the very end, therefore, we arrive at the notion of soul as an utterly indispensable daytime concept by which humankind has expressed a vivid sense of "person" characterized by discreteness and yet by continuity through time. Despite the analytical prickliness for *science positive* of this reality, to call its reality "nonempirical" would be odd.[40] After all, we do not ordinarily have something nonempirical in mind when we think of "person" as a physical body plus something more. At the same time, however, to tackle the soul as an empirical matter is alive with difficulties. Perhaps for this reason, Durkheim's attempt to set study of it into the frame of empirical scholarship has been almost completely ignored. So far as I am aware, the only recent scholarship that puts to use Durkheim's elegant reconstruction of soul on secular terrain of the real is Michel Foucault's, in *Discipline and Punish*.[41]

I suspect that this reconstruction of the soul from the raw material of real experience takes us close to the intuitional sources of Durkheim's work on religion. I suddenly felt those sources nearby me one hot August afternoon as I contended with the chapter on mourning rites (Book Three, Chapter 5), which is full of evidence from Australia about sin, the soul, and the things that happen to or are done about both. At one point, the *Book of Common Prayer* phrase "remission of sin" suddenly came unbidden from depths of the heard but dimly understood formulas of my own churchgoing childhood. It came to me in a flash that Durkheim's mind must have had strata of the same sort. Consider the *Modeh,* a prayer of thanks said from early childhood every morning, even before washing, by means of which Jews thank God for the return of the soul after its departure each night.[42] I suspect that, on an inherently elusive topic like soul, Durkheim's own personal archaeology, available consciously and unconsciously, enabled him to encounter religious notions other than as "a blind man trying to talk about colour." Consider this from Durkheim:

The soul is not merely distinct from its physical envelope, as the inside is from the outside. . . . [I]t elicits in some degree those feelings that are everywhere reserved for that which is divine. If it is not made into a god, it is seen at least as a spark of the divinity. This fundamental characteristic would be inexplicable if the idea of the soul was no more than a prescientific solution to the problem of dreams. Since there is nothing in dreaming that can awaken religious emotion, the same must be true of the cause that accounts for dreaming. However, if the soul is a bit of divine substance, it represents something within us that is other than ourselves.[43]

Now consider this passage by a Jewish authority of our own day:

To be sure, the world as a whole may be viewed as a divine manifestation, but the world remains as something else than God, while the soul of man, in its depths, may be considered a part of God. . . . [W]e speak of only an aspect of God, or of a divine spark, as constituting the essence of the inner life of man. . . . Every soul is thus a fragment of the divine light.[44]

Not to belabor a point that cannot be developed here, let me invite further study by noting that Durkheim analyzes Australian notions such as transmigration and an original fund of souls and that the passage just quoted from goes on to talk about *Knesset Israel*, "the pool in which all the souls in the world are contained as a single essence." If Durkheim's personal experience is part of *Formes* in this way and if religion's roots in the real preoccupy him, as I have shown they do, then we must take very seriously his remarks addressed to "free believers" about the injustice of anathematizing *Formes* as "irreligion." To make this point, however, is not to launch a silly search for correspondences between Durkheim's religious upbringing and his theorizing.[45] Rather, just as my own understandings of religion could unpredictably mediate my attempt to understand Durkheim, so too must his own early religious experience have given him an unavoidable—and yet invaluable— door into the subject of this work.

In justifying his methodological choice of studying totemism as a useful lens through which to study religion in general, Durkheim observes that sometimes "nature spontaneously makes simplifications."[46] Analogously, I suggest, Durkheim's own experience provided a "spontaneous simplification" that enabled him to move the topic of religion away from its capacity (or its confused and confusing incapacity) to give an account of the natural world, but instead to explore, and explore profoundly, its capacity to deliver a humanly shaped world to that very world's human shapers. As he says in the Conclusion, "[D]ebates on the topic of religion most often turn around and about on the question of whether religion can or cannot be reconciled with science. . . . But the believers—the men who, living a religious life, have a direct sense of what religion is made of—object that, in terms of their day-to-day experience, this way of seeing does not ring true. . . . Its true function is to make us act and to help us live."[47]

This once-practicing member of a tightly knit religious community who abandoned religion, but whose scientific work was enriched by the fact that certain core intuitions of religion did not abandon him, knew an off-the-mark theory of religion when he saw one. It is no surprise to find him scornful of writers who think they have undone religion merely by debunking its account of nature. To mix a metaphor, the human Kangaroo clan members we view through his lens had bigger theoretical fish to fry than the kangaroos leaping around them. And so it will not be Durkheim who discovers among the Australians "the thoroughgoing idiocy" that some authors ascribed to "primitives."[48] It will be Durkheim who again and again refutes that discovery, out of those same authors' own evidence.

But for my own chance encounter with a problem of translation, I would not have guessed the complex strata that underlie *Formes*. Most commentators walk back and forth on the ground directly above them. W. S. F. Pickering and Lewis A. Coser at least point out that those layers are down there and are important.[49] But consider Alvin Gouldner's stunning characterization of Durkheim's thought as "*Catholic* organicism."[50] And Aron, in his magisterial comparative portraiture of nineteenth-century masters, paints Durkheim first, ignoring the question of religious background altogether until he arrives at his second portrait, of Max Weber, a great sociologist of religion who, he observes, "belong[ed] to a profoundly religious family (although probably a nonbeliever himself)."[51] But it is Weber who called himself religiously "unmusical," while Durkheim told an audience that he was not blind to religions' color. In general, I found little confirmation for my own sense that Durkheim's religious background mattered in what he said and wrote.[52] Some writers apparently believe that truth can be arrived at from nowhere in particular, or from everywhere at once, and that the person is irrelevant. In the case of testing hypotheses, that view is doubtless correct. In the case of genius, however, it is self-contradictory. Creative genius is by its nature individual, and its sources are quintessentially personal.

INDIVIDUAL MINDS AND YET COLLECTIVE CONSCIOUSNESS: SOME KEY ARGUMENTS IN *FORMES*

Ordinarily my task would now be to render an account of Durkheim's intellectual world: the influences he inherited and passed on, the debates he waged with his contemporaries, the understandings he took for granted but that we cannot—in short, a world of texts into which *Formes* fits. There is, of course, such a world, but understanding it can be left for later without immediate loss to understanding the central arguments of *Formes*. One set of questions to be delved into elsewhere would certainly be Durkheim's conversations with Kant, about the problem of knowledge and about moral obligation, which merits a kind of attention that his traditional audience of sociologists and anthropologists has in general not given it; and so does his dialogue with Auguste Comte, a philosopher now remembered by most of us only via two or three canned characterizations—academic sound bites, so to speak.[53] Another would be the book's relation to the versions of psychology that represented the state of the art in Europe at the turn of this century.[54] Finally, there is a whole set of questions that are perennial and that have the same rewards as playing scales: whether *Formes* (like Durkheim's work generally) is or is not ahistorical[55]—and, in connection with that, does or does not belong to the miscellany of theoretical notions that came to be called functionalism.[56] I leave all those questions aside for now.

I note but leave aside controversies about the use Durkheim made of the Australian ethnography available in his time (and, to a lesser extent, Native American and others), on the grounds that even furious and emotional academic debates of the past are not always riveting, or especially enlightening, in the present. This is not to say that the ethnographic details can safely be skipped. As we learn right from the introduction, Durkheim intends that his own route through the Australian ethnography should lead to "man in general"—and "more especially," he says, "present-day man, for there is none other that we have a greater interest in knowing well." Totemism seemed to him a usefully simplifying case that would reveal "the religious nature of man . . . a fundamental and permanent aspect of humanity."[57] So although *Formes* displays his grasp of the ethnographies on totemism that were available to him, it is far less an investigation of how or why human beings come to imagine themselves as plants or animals than an investigation of how they come to imagine themselves as human beings. Since the fact jumps off the page that totemic communities must be imagined, their study enables us to grasp the same fact in relation to our own: To exist at all, all communities must be imagined. What his intellectual descendant Benedict Anderson has so well shown for large-scale twentieth-century anticolonial nationalism is also true of any face-to-face community and of the smallest Australian clan.[58] But clearly, no one today should read *Formes* if he or she is only interested in the religions of Australia.[59]

Finally, I will not repeat here what nearly three generations of critique have by now shown in great detail about where lie the shortcomings of *Formes* and of Durkheim's work more generally. I cannot do better than Steven Lukes's intellectual biography of Durkheim,[60] Robert Nisbet's analysis of his thought in its intellectual context,[61] or W. S. F. Pickering's close study of his sociology of religion,[62] to name only three quite different studies out of a long and often distinguished list. I make no attempt here to review the vast and growing literature. In addition, since I have made it my task to show why the book can still be read with excitement, I bypass many difficulties and legitimate qualifications. Instead, I focus on key bits and pieces of Durkheim's argument that are still immediately provocative, and that move through the world as canned characterizations of the book, part of an intellectual world *about* Durkheim's sociology of religion. After briefly considering the elements of his famous but contested definition of religion, let us turn to three such traditional academic sound bites, each of which has always implied potentially hostile queries: Durkheim's "equation" of religion and society, or God and society,[63] his use of collective concepts, and, foremost among those, his sacred/profane dichotomy.

This world *about* Durkheim contains a good deal of distortion, in part the legacy of Joseph Ward Swain's monumental 1915 translation. Distortions arise not only from inaccuracies in Swain's translating, but also from the challenges of an English text that discourages readers from tackling *Formes* under their own intellectual steam. Its difficult English invites reliance on interpretational clues from various "trots." If we follow the out-of-context bites to their intellectual places in *Formes* itself, however, we gain keys to the book as a whole. Some of the most persistently troublesome of those bites are found in Book Two, Chapter 7. There, the ideas of totemic principle and force are derived as outputs of collective life, that is, as outputs of the mechanisms by which collective life is produced. If those ideas did not exist, they or something quite like them would have to be invented. I will turn to this centrally important chapter of *Formes* after examining Durkheim's manner of defining his overall subject.

Religion Defined

Durkheim defines religion in Book One, Chapter 1:

> A religion is a unified system of beliefs and practices relative to sacred
> things, that is to say, things set apart and forbidden—beliefs and practices
> which unite into one single moral community called a Church, all those
> who adhere to them.[64]

Bear three points in mind. First, religion is not defined in terms of anything
that would turn a man of *science positive* away from observable phenomena, or
the real—not divinity, the otherworldly, the miraculous, or the supernatural.
Second, the phrase "unified system" postulates that religious beliefs and rites
are not hodgepodges but are internally ordered. Third, the objects of those
rites and beliefs acquire their religious status as sacred, or "set apart and forbidden," as a result of joint action by people who set them apart and who, by
the same stroke, constitute themselves a "moral community" or "a Church."
Once again, then, religion is social, social, social. In addition, the "moral" in
the term "moral community" specifies that the groups are not hodgepodges
either but are made up of individuals who have mutually recognized and recognizable identities that set them, cognitively and normatively, on shared
human terrain. Hence, the quality of sacredness exists in the real, and its creation is the observable product of collective doing. Here is one reason that
Durkheim found it attractive to handle rites analytically as being prior to beliefs.[65]

This definition foreshadows the organization of *Formes* as a whole. Book
Two examines totemic beliefs insofar as they seem to him jointly to constitute a "unified system" of core beliefs; at the same time it associates those beliefs with one kind of moral community, which Durkheim calls "social
organization based on clans."[66] Book Three examines those beliefs as they are
being collectively *done,* entering the real through the performance of rites. It
makes an analytical distinction between two moments of ritual doing that
typically occur simultaneously on the ground: differentiation, or doing that
creates the sacredness of people or things (negative rites, characterized by setting apart people and things, through the various procedures described), and
integration, or doing that takes place amid already sanctified people or things
(positive rites, characterized by the bringing together of sanctified things and
people, again by various procedures).[67]

The God/Society Equation

Virtually everyone who has encountered *Formes* is stopped dead when Durkheim says, "Is it not that the god and the society are one and the same?" From this passage has fallen the nugget that by "equating" the god with the society, Durkheim "reduces" the god to the society (sometimes revealingly shorthanded as God, capital "G," and society). Many discussions about the interpretation of *Formes* converge here, at his famous "equation." Now, if we go to the actual statement in the actual argument, we recover a fact that is sometimes lost sight of: Durkheim's question in that chapter is how it comes about that rationally constituted Australians ascribe power to totemic beings and indeed to symbolic representations of them. As usual, he seeks to find the basis of that in the real. His problem is not who, what, or how great the god is but how a science of religion can turn its beam of light on the religious object without "making it disappear." The argument surrounding the nugget will clarify:

> [The totem] expresses and symbolizes two different kinds of things. From one point of view, it is the outward and visible form of what I have called the totemic principle or god; and from another, it is also the symbol of a particular society that is called the clan. It is the flag of the clan, the sign by which each clan is distinguished from the others, the visible mark of its distinctiveness, and a mark that is borne by everything that in any way belongs to the clan: men, animals, and things. *Thus if the totem is the symbol of both the god and the society, is this not because the god and the society are one and the same?* How could the emblem of the group have taken the form of that quasi-divinity if the group and the divinity were two distinct realities? Thus the god of the clan, the totemic principle, can be none other than the clan itself, but the clan transfigured and imagined in the physical form of the plant or animal that serves as totem.[68]

Durkheim's question and his answer have tended to bring out curiously theological anxieties and reticences.

Suppose he had committed a "reduction."[69] Would it mean that some necessary thing is lost? If so, what? For certain believers, the answer obviously is that God, capital "G," is lost (and so is "the god," if we have in mind believers ecumenical enough to battle for the pagan Greeks' Zeus, say, or for those aspects of the emperor of mid-twentieth-century Japanese that went beyond the ordinarily human). But who is God that *secular* social scientists should take note of him?[70] For secular social scientists, or for men and women of *science positive*, religion cannot be altered by subtracting a supernatural being from it. Their methods begin from unbelief (professionally, not necessarily in terms of personal conviction) in anything that cannot in principle be observed by anyone who uses those methods. Through those methods of observation, people with God look exactly the same as people without God.[71] No supernatural realm or being is available to a (methodologically) unbelieving social scientist, who can claim access only to nature, not to supernature. To a believer, on the other hand, it is unclear that anyone else's supernatural realm is available. So unless sociology must be made consonant with theology, nothing necessary is lost. A reader now wondering whether the integrity of theology is thereby compromised has arrived on the fascinating and ambiguous spiritual territory promised by the quotations from Durkheim with which I began this Introduction. There is no need to resolve the question. To keep it open is to keep pace with an agile guide to this territory.

If, alternatively, we asked what necessary thing must be kept or added, some would argue that not God or gods but *belief* oriented to him or her, or to them, must be included.[72] For Durkheim, however, religion was "a fundamental and permanent aspect of humanity," though gods were not a fundamental and permanent aspect of religion. It thus followed that neither gods themselves nor beliefs about gods could be essential. What if we disagreed, insisting that *observed* believing was essential, contending something like this: If gods and the supernatural cannot be observed by scientific means, action oriented to them or presupposing belief in them can be. But if only belief in supernatural beings is the victim, then Durkheim has a powerful reply: Nothing durable is lost, for what is more fleeting or hard to observe than subjective belief? What is more open to derailment, from one moment to the next, whimsically or in the cold light of observable fact (recall those very things whose "resistance" religions "could not have overcome")? And besides, from the standpoint of the social scientist, believers in gods look exactly the same as unbelievers in gods—and exactly the same as people with beliefs in or about other things. The subjective is no handier than the supernatural, and but slightly more accessible. In those terms, we can begin to see the advantage in Durkheim's choice of observing religious ideas (*représentations,* the subject of Book Two) as being (observably) *done* (as *attitudes rituelles,* the subject of Book Three) and, hence, why even his exposition of *the ideas* (Book Two) resorts to slow-motion, set-piece depictions of totemic rites, giving them an almost you-are-there vividness.

As a way out of the predicament of evaporating tools, it might be tempting to accept belief as given, taking up the W. I. Thomases' famous sociological crutch: Whatever is believed in as real is real in its consequences. But to regard belief as a simple given is also to skirt the obvious question of how people come to treat something as real that to the unbelieving onlooker cannot be. The world of religion is full of improbable things: Christians' Immaculate Conception or their life from death; Aztecs' sunrises caused by human sacrifices; Lithuanians' gaining well-being from the bones of St. Casimir; Australians' black men who are also white cockatoos. And as Durkheim himself points out, deadpan, people look most like relatives and friends, not like plants or animals.[73] "Real in its consequences" quickly wears thin. Which consequences? What reality? If the faithful are thought of as rationally constituted human beings, what would cause them to fly in the face of what they can observe from moment to moment and year after year? And is our understanding advanced if we assume the religious faithful of all ages merely to be people who can be sold the Brooklyn Bridge, not just once but over and over again? Ultimately, then, to leave belief unexamined is to gain a mentally incompetent human.

Hence, once again, Durkheim's point about the real holds importance: A human institution that endures must necessarily be founded on something that anyone, not just those certifiably afflicted with "thoroughgoing idiocy," can accept as being really real—not just "believed in" as real and not just patronized as "believed in." The whole of Book One spectacularly demolishes theories of religion that want to be scientific but whose logic implies that religion's objects are unreal, and its subjects eternally open to being sold the Brooklyn Bridge.[74] How the objects of religion can be real for a secular social scientist is the question Durkheim asks his reader to explore with him. His point is not to diminish God but to lift into view the reality of God worshipped, the reality of the experience of God, and the rationality of those who experience God.

The Chapter 7 academic sound bite just picked apart belongs to an extended argument establishing that "religious forces are real forces," not mere figments of mythic or mystic belief. If we begin again, not at that memorable show-stopping line about the god and the society as being one but in its intellectual context within *Formes,* we need not hop around to avoid treading on the theological and metaphysical feet of social researchers and their subjects. To start, all we have to do is concede that sometimes the objects of religion strain the sense of what is real but do not necessarily lose the adherent for that reason. (Besides, for Durkheim, the very warp and woof of religions is something other than reality "as the senses show it to him."[75] And yet without this human imagining beyond reality as the senses show it, science would be impossible.) Religious conceptions that do strain credulity pose the question Durkheim tries to answer. His religious human is capable of noticing religion's empirical discrepancies. Even if it was true, as LaCapra has (I think, mistakenly) suggested, that Durkheim is on a "Thomist" mission of reconciling faith with reason, he would be doing so precisely because it is believing that is inherently problematic for the faithful.[76] Doing, on the other hand, is not; hence, yet another route to the priority Durkheim gives to rites over beliefs and its usefulness as a way of thinking about the persistence of beliefs that are nonsensical on their face.[77] But not only that: Since we speak of "Thomism," let us remember that Thomas Aquinas came centuries after Jesus's personal friend Thomas, whom the sophisticated faithful of antiquity passed down the ages as an eternal figment of religious life: doubt.[78] If religion could exist *only* on condition of being believed or even believable, its life would have had numbered days, speedily exhausted.

The line about the god and the society as one and the same can be thought about in yet another way. Consider the religious world into which God, or "the god," sent the Ten Commandments (Exodus 20). Note that the first five concern the relationship of humans to God, and the second five, that of humans to one another. Furthermore, the passage contains no invitation to regard either set as having a different or higher status than the other, as being obligatory in a way that the other is not—or, for that matter, as being separately conceived. In terms of that theological world, the conceptions of the god and of the society are inseparable. To say that "the god and the society are one and the same" is not necessarily to say any more than God did, speaking through Moses. It seems to me that *Formes* throughout has that world in view. If the point just made is at all contentious, and I have no doubt it is, then the contentiousness itself gives a point to Durkheim's strategy in choosing an exotic case.

The Case for a Simplifying Case

Let us now notice how Durkheim prepares the tool of using an exotic case to simplify. First, he assumes the Australians to be rationally constituted humans, as are their Parisian contemporaries. There is no question of one's being civilized and the other not, or of the two groups' having different mental constitutions. He presumes the Australians to hold the same title of "man" as Parisians do, and in the same right. "Man is man only because he is civilized," he says.[79] Therefore Australia is as good a place as any other for studying "the religious nature of man," and it has an advantage: Small-scale, stone-tool-using societies were "simple" and thus permitted a degree of clarity and distinctness in thinking that France did not. *Formes* exemplifies a single well-conducted experiment whose results may be put forward as holding for all cases that can be shown to be of the same kind. Furthermore, as Comte had said, "The simplest phenomena are the most general."[80] Boiled down to its constituent elements, religion in Australia is religion anywhere else. Second, in using ethnography to study religion, Durkheim follows exactly a procedure others had used in attacking religion: taking exotic facts to expose religion universally as delusion, fabrication, and the like. What is delusion and so on in religion among the naked "X's" is also delusion and so on in religion among the well-covered consumers of *haute couture*. But he then stands that procedure on its head, making Australia serve as a simple and, by the same stroke, a tough case for religion's roots in the real. Demonstrating the tough case will carry the easier one: What is true for the turn-of-the-century Australian will then be true for the turn-of-the-century Parisian.[81]

Durkheim uses the same rhetorical tactic in arguing the reality of "religious forces": taking the idea of *mana* or totemic principle as the truly tough case. What is shown to be true of the less credible real will be established for the more credible one. Before showing how this tough case also simplifies, however, I briefly digress, for there is one criticism against Durkheim's use of ethnography that can derail us if bypassed. Durkheim was wrong, it is said, to imagine that the societies and religions of Australia were "simple." Their ideas were as elaborate or sophisticated as anyone else's, and since those ideas were as much subject to historical development and change as anyone else's, he had a mistaken fantasy (shared with others in his time) that Australia's stone-tool users preserved in primitive form what must have existed at the dawn of humanity. Although he did not in fact think that,[82] such criticisms are nevertheless partly valid. Yet simplicity is not only a way of characterizing (or stigmatizing) things but also a way of setting problems with clarity—for example, physicists' calculating gravitational force under the (never true) assumption of a perfect vacuum. Since we easily understand why it is useful to simplify by assuming away the atmosphere, we can easily set aside as irrelevant someone's insistence that it is really there.[83] Similarly, rather than settle for the generous discovery that little about the Australians was simple, we do better to imagine what might have been complicating about the French.[84]

What might Durkheim have thought simplifying about looking as far afield from France as he did to investigate "the religious nature of man"? One answer surely was the uncontrollably vague, half-formulated notions that are characteristic of the familiar. (Think back to my contentious statement about the Ten Commandments.) If the discipline of ethnographic study is to uncover what is familiar in the strange, it is also to uncover what is strange about the familiar. From that angle, things Europeans vaguely "know" about the "power of God" look strange enough to make the exotic case of *mana* a usefully simplifying place to begin. Why is it, for example, that from within the Judeo-Christian tradition, even for thoroughly secular people, it is somehow less troublesome to speak about "the power of God" and mean a transcendental deity than to use the same phrase in respect to a physical object? To borrow Parsons's phrase again, both deity and *mana* should probably be classified together, as "nonempirical reality." Yet somehow, for no logical reason, it *feels* like a different matter to speak of a transcendent deity than to speak of *mana*, the totemic principle, or someplace in the real where objects speak with lips of wood and smite from painted pedestals (and inversely, where lips and smiting hands of flesh are alleged to be only human in appearance but superhuman in essence).

Think of how we read the encounter between the ancient Israelites and their enemies, the people of Ashdod, who built a towering god with feet of clay. That phrase "feet of clay" contains in itself, and takes as given, a complicated and complicating discourse about obviously misplaced (as opposed to well-placed) faith. And consider this: It is a transcendent God whose existence a long tradition in Western philosophy attempts to prove rationally, while living with the culturally given safety net that the failure of proof need not impose the conclusion that that God does not in fact exist.[85] If I am right about what we "know" culturally about the "power of God," even the most secular among us, in contrast to the ideas Durkheim explores (*mana, kwoth, orenda*, etc.), I have just turned up the volume of our own half-heard cultural Muzak, as it were, of an especially troublesome case for the real. Why should this be so? For the same reason that an "equation" of society and God should be troublesome for social scientists supposedly operating nontheologically. A moral equivalent to the material perfect vacuum was called for.

Conscience Collective

Mana, Durkheim says, is the "quasi-divine principle" immanent in things that gives power to certain plants or animals, *and to representations of them*. Before tackling it, he reminds his reader (in the last paragraph of the preceding chapter) that Comte, in calling the idea of force metaphysical, and metaphysics the direct descendant of theology, had already implied that the idea of force began in religion, from which it was borrowed first by philosophy and later by science. But Comte mistakenly concluded that, because of this ancestry, the idea of force had no objective counterpart in reality and thus would eventually disappear from science. To the contrary, however, the concept of force was alive and well in the modern science of Durkheim's day. In fact, the English term "vector" (which appeared in English in 1867) entered French (*vecteur*) in 1899, and Durkheim used the term "resultant" (a vector sum) to mean a social sum of individual forces. Therefore, in contrast to Comte, Durkheim "will show . . . that religious forces are real, no matter how imperfect the symbols with whose help they were conceived of. From this it will follow that the same is true for the concept of force in general."[86]

The reality of religious forces is to be found in the real experience of social life, according to Durkheim. Just as, in the case of soul, psychology sought a physical basis for what humankind had long since discovered in social life, so too force. Contrary to what Comte anticipated, by the end of the nineteenth century, the idea of force had completed its transit from religion, to metaphysics, to *science positive*. To appreciate Durkheim's context, note that cutting-edge work on the fundamental forces was being done no farther away than the laboratories of Marie and Pierre Curie. From 1906 on, Mme. Curie continued her work on radioactivity as a professor at the Sorbonne. Durkheim's account of rites is meant to seize the *idea* of force at its "birth," as he says. He found the birth of that idea in rites, at moments of collective *effervescence*, when human beings feel themselves transformed, and are in fact transformed, through ritual doing. A force experienced as external to each individual is the agent of that transformation, but the force itself is created by the fact of assembling and temporarily living a collective life that transports individuals beyond themselves. Those moments he conveys in a set piece drawn from ethnographic description.

Durkheim's set piece opens with the practical occupations of life suspended, the validity of ordinary rules adjourned, people dressed and painted to resemble one another and the animal or plant by which they name their shared identity, the objects around them "uniformed" in the same way, the whole taking place under a night sky, the scene dotted with firelight, and frenzy—a collective *effervescence*. Swept away, the participants experience a force external to them, which seems to be moving them, and by which their very nature is transformed. They experience themselves as grander than at ordinary times; they do things they would not do at other times; they feel, and at that moment really are, joined with each other and with the totemic being. They come to experience themselves as sharing one and the same essence—with the totemic animal, with its representation, and with each other. In addition, since a symbolic representation of the totemic being stands at the center of things, the real power generated in the assembly comes to be thought of as residing in the totemic object itself. Symbols of the totemic object extend the effects of the *effervescence* into life after the assembly is dispersed. Seen on objects, and sometimes on bodies, totemic representations of various kinds will fill the role of what would be called today a secondary stimulus—a reminder that reactivates the initial feelings, although more dimly.[87] Since the transformation cannot be done once and for all and fades despite the symbolic reminders, it must periodically be redone—hence, the cyclically repetitive performance of rites.

Through real experience, then, the participants come to ascribe power to sacred objects, that power having nothing to do with the physical characteristics of those objects. It is also through real experience that they arrive at the concept of force, but the real experience they have is that of human beings assembled—or to use Durkheim's abstract formulation, that of society's "concentrating" or "pulling itself together" and thus becoming a unity in the real. This depiction will no doubt seem contrived and mechanical at first glance and on that account may tempt discounting, until the historical memory it activates in us brings us to similar events that we ourselves know operated mechanically—uniformed, firelit, nighttime *effervescences* of the Nazis or the Ku Klux Klan, with individuals led to impute to themselves shared inborn essences and fabulous collective identities,[88] with symbolic reminders shaping everyday life afterward, and with individual doubt in large part not requiring physical violence to be overcome. The mechanism itself is neither good nor evil. If Durkheim is right that it is universal, then we should expect to find it, and do find it, from tattooed street gangs to the Salvation Army, from the habits of the convent to those of the exclusive club.

In all cases an outcome of joint doing, the real that comes into being in the rite, as Durkheim describes it, is independent of (but not necessarily exclusive of) individual belief. The power felt is real, and is felt not only in the physical being of humankind but also in its mental being—humankind's *conscience collective,* that is, in both "conscience" and "consciousness." Besides, its reality can be dramatically transforming. During the exaltation of the French Revolution, for example, "[w]e see the most mediocre or harmless bourgeois transformed . . . . into a hero or an executioner."[89] In undramatic times, it is undramatically transforming, as Durkheim says a few sentences later:

> There is virtually no instant of our lives in which a certain rush of energy fails to come to us from outside ourselves. In all kinds of acts that express the understanding, esteem, and affection of his neighbor, there is a lift that the man who does his duty feels, usually without being aware of it.[90]

What creates the transformation is a product of thought, but thought that cannot be accommodated by our usual vocabulary of mere individuals' thinking. It exists only in the mind; but if it exists in only one mind, it does not belong to what can be experienced *by any and everyone* as the real. We arrive by this route at Durkheim's superficially troublesome term *pensée collec-*

tive, "collective thought." It is in collective thought, built into the experience of social life, that the idea of a divinity to which human beings are subordinate gains its foothold in the real.

Yet—and this is a big "yet"—far from erasing the thought of individuals, collective thought is found nowhere else. Throughout Chapter 7 and indeed the whole of *Formes,* we find statements such as this, periodically inserted with teacherly repetition:

> [B]ecause society can exist only in and by means of individual minds, it must enter into us and become organized within us. That force thus becomes an integral part of our being and, by the same stroke, uplifts it and brings it to maturity.[91]

> [L]ike any other society, the clan can only live in and by means of the individual consciousnesses of which it is made. Thus, insofar as religious force is conceived of as embodied in the totemic emblem, it seems to be external to individuals and endowed with a kind of transcendence; and yet from another standpoint, and like the clan it symbolizes, it can be made real only within and by them."[92]

Durkheim has not postulated some outside mind hovering in the human midst. He is striving conceptually to represent aspects of the real that are readily observable but that cannot possibly be *there* to observe or represent at all, if the lone individual is our conceptual unit. To see those aspects of the real, let us turn now to sacredness, an extraordinary quality that ordinary objects acquire only within moral communities. Sacredness is eminently a *représentation collective,* eminently a feature of *pensée* and *conscience collectives.* As a quality of things—or, rather, as Durkheim insists, a quality superadded to things—sacredness can come to be its real self only within the domain of collective consciousness (that is, in the domain of conscience *and* of consciousness). Sacredness is an aspect of the real that exists only in the mind but cannot possibly exist as the real in only one mind.[93]

The Sacred/Profane Dichotomy

Over the years, it has proved easy to make heavier weather than need be of both *le sacré* and *la conscience collective.* W. E. H. Stanner's careful and respectful article on *Formes* called the sacred/profane dichotomy "unusable except at the cost of undue interference with the facts of observation."[94] Try as he might in his fieldwork, he said, he could not find it. If there is in fact nothing about the idea that connects us with our own sense of the real in a way that illuminates it, then Durkheim would rightly be patronized as the writer of a classic freighted with intractable concepts, to be suffered through and forgotten. But this classic suggests more interesting mental activity than the exercise involved in logically dissecting the term "sacred" itself. In any case, Lukes has already shown in detail its logical rough surfaces.[95] The sacred points to aspects of the real that were doubtless amazing to Durkheim, and that are still there in the social world to amaze us.

Consider first the biblical example of the Holy Ark. Reading at Exodus 25, we see it being made to exact specifications (two carved cherubim on top, the tablets inside, etc.), using materials collected from the community and manufactured in full view of all those present (and subsequently, all readers of the Bible). Thousands of years and miles from that biblical scene, we find very powerful sacred objects called *churingas* in the same state: "[E]ven among the Arunta, there are churingas that are made by the elders of the group, with the full knowledge of and in full view of everyone."[96] Whatever is added to make those objects' sacredness is, like soul, real but without extension. Jewish tradition wonderfully presents that feature by saying of the Ark that even though its dimensions were known, it "miraculously occupied no space in the Holy of Holies."[97] The real, yet nonphysical, characteristic we can observe in both cases cannot be the feature, or the creature, of an individual mind. In both cases, the physical characteristics of the things cannot possibly disclose what they are in the real. In Durkheim's words, "The sensations that the physical world evokes in us cannot, by definition, contain anything that goes beyond that world. From something tangible one can only make something tangible; from extended substance one cannot make unextended substance."[98]

At the same time, both objects' nonphysical reality is available to the individual mind only as it participates in mind both inside and outside itself. And because sacredness originates as it does, it is inherently impermanent and so must be added to the object again and again, just as it was originally: by collective human doing. Equally, because sacredness originates as it does, there necessarily is no unifying characteristic that is shared by everything designated as *sacré*, no all-purpose key to preordain the outcome of fieldwork. "Things so disparate cannot form a class [the sacred] unless a class can be marked by a property, its absence, and its contrary,"[99] Stanner wrote. By thinking in such terms, he created for himself the un-Durkheimian nightmare I will now indicate by moving from the Ark to other examples: Ayatollah Khomeini, the bones of St. Casimir, the louse, and Mt. Sinai.

Remember the tumultuous arrival in 1979 of Ruhollah Khomeini at Tehran airport, with a million people crowding to welcome him. During the evening news, the effervescence of that moment could be felt worldwide regardless of language and in every household of secularized America. Despite the haze of TV distance, the vocal flatness of TV correspondents, dissonant shouting in a language most Americans do not understand, and ritual gestures specific to the moral community Khomeini shared with the crowd, every viewer witnessed the elevation of Khomeini to sacredness. Before our eyes, Khomeini became something other than what he had been as he left Paris only hours before. That Khomeini's elevation was attached to a particular moral community was evidenced straightaway. He had put on sacredness *there,* but not everywhere—a moral distance marked in America by continuing to call "Ayatollah" a man who had gained, *there,* a higher title, "Imam," by acclamation. What was done could only have been done within a group of assembled faithful and could not be undone by individual doubt or unbelief. It was the real to anyone going to Iran then, no matter where they were coming from. Like the Ark, Khomeini's human measurements were known and the same as before; the beard, the turban, and the robes looked exactly as before, but the man was not the same as before. What was added belonged to the real, but it took up no space.

We have also witnessed the inverse process, in which the other crucial term, moral community, is created. In 1989, leaders of a newly independent territory of Lithuania returned relics said to be the bones of St. Casimir to the People's House of Culture, which they reconstituted and reconsecrated as the Cathedral of Vilnius. Lithuanians filed through the new cathedral and past the bones, participants in the birth of a nation. In this example, the sanctification preceded, and was a tool in, the construction of a new moral community, now added to (or superadded to) the already existing physical territory, population, and apparatus of statehood. To the possible objection that such community "always existed," the answer we find in the doing is the late-twentieth-century revival of old bones; the answer we find in *Formes* is that nothing that must be imagined "always exists," but must be continually re-imagined through human doing. This is just as true of moral community as it is of sacred objects. By the selfsame process, those dry bones were made to live again as the sacred objects they once had been.[100] They were resurrected in postcommunist Lithuania and rehabilitated from their lowly state for forty years as the dusty trove of the reactionary and the superstitious. The known physical characteristics and population of Lithuania were the same as before, but the moral community was not. What was added was objectively real, but it took up no space. Imagine the confusion many Americans would feel if asked to pay their respects to the bones.

Sacredness is not a quality inherent in certain objects, nor is it available to the unaided senses of just any individual human observer. It is a quality that objects acquire when they are, in the phrase from Durkheim's definition, "set apart and forbidden." They are made sacred by groups of people who set them apart and keep them bounded by specific actions; they remain sacred only so long as groups continue to do this. Humans acting collectively make and remake this quality of sacredness but then encounter it after the fact as if it had always been built into objects and was ready-made. In the religious vocabulary used within communities of faith, those things that have been sanctified, "set apart and forbidden," are intrinsically "holy"—and have always been. In the technical vocabulary developed in *Formes*, they are "sacred"—but made so by doing.[101] The same process can make a man or woman, a piece of cloth, a lizard, a tree, an idea or principle (anything, including excrement, which Durkheim slides into a footnote) into a sacred thing and the mandatory recipient of elaborated deference. Durkheim makes this point over and over again, hammering it home one last time in Book Three, Chapter 2. There we come upon ritual celebrations that center on, of all things, the louse.

Sacredness is not merely a set of peculiar relationships between people and certain designated objects. The very act that constitutes those peculiar relationships also relates a designated group of people to one another and sets them apart from others to whom they are not bound and who do not have the same relationship to designated physical objects. Turn the Thomases' formula around: Whatever is obviously real, given its obviously real consequences, tends to be accepted as real. Whatever power they acquire, and it can be quite considerable, is real power. Notice that there is no question of debunking native beliefs about that power as imaginary. To do so would be the same as saying that social life itself is merely imaginary and society itself changeable merely by an impulse to change one's mind. So far as sacred objects are concerned, the question is how to describe and explicate the nature of that power, which Durkheim posits as real.

"Power" in what sense and "real" in what sense may be observed in the following passage from Exodus (19), when Mount Sinai evolves by a set of human actions into a place where the power of God may "break forth upon" the people and destroy them:

> And the Lord said unto Moses, Go unto the people, and sanctify them to day and to morrow, and let them wash their clothes. . . . And thou shalt set bounds unto the people round about saying, Take heed to yourselves, that ye go not up into the mount, or touch the border of it: whosoever toucheth the mount shall be surely put to death. There shall not an hand touch it, but he shall surely be stoned, or shot through; whether it be beast or man, it shall

not live. . . . And Moses went down from the mount unto the people, and sanctified the people; and they washed their clothes. (Exodus 19:10, 12, 13)

Remember by what agency transgressors would be "stoned" or "shot through." As the people did their part, the mountain did its own, and by the "third day" of God's instructions to Moses, it had become enveloped in smoke and it quaked.

And the Lord said unto Moses, Go down, charge the people, lest they break through unto the Lord to gaze, and many of them perish. . . . And Moses said unto the Lord, The people cannot come up to mount Sinai: for thou chargedst us, saying, Set bounds about the mount and sanctify it. (Exodus 19:21, 23)

Notice that the biblical text explains natural power in natural terms (whoever violates the sacredness of the mountain will be "stoned," "shot through," or "surely put to death") but that the power of the mountain is not thereby explained away. The Bible writers presumably could see what we do in what they themselves wrote quite matter-of-factly yet without diminishing the real power of their God. It came to be the case that whoever went up into the mountain, apart from Moses and Aaron, would surely die. I think this is what Durkheim found remarkable about the natural means by which sacred objects move above and beyond—*really* above and *really* beyond—their natural ordinariness and about how the people who exert those natural means thereafter move in and out of awareness of how what was done was done. In other words, "Man makes God," as Marx wrote, but not in any way he pleases.

An object such as that mountain moves above and beyond its natural ordinariness in this way only within the ambit of a *conscience collective*—collective conscience normatively, in conduct, and collective consciousness cognitively, in thought. The two are not separate. *Conscience collective* is the achievement of mind that transfigures *the* real world and makes it *a* shared world that is in fact *the* real world as known and knowable by some group, some moral community. It would not be obvious to an ignorant foreign passerby how Mount Sinai was different from other mountains. He might well climb it with his shoes on, travel its slopes at will, and, caught in this profanation, might be "shot through." Readers may recognize this ignorant passerby as the sort favored by old-fashioned movies of colonization, in which the colonial officer in his pith helmet and shorts steps on the sacred spot or shoots the sacred animal for a drawing-room trophy, and to whom knowledge about the real power of the ordinary-seeming object arrives simultaneously with a real native rising, unwittingly detonated. The commonsense approach that would be satisfied with thinking about the power of the spot or the animal as merely imaginary, merely an amazing figment of superstition ablaze in each individual native mind but in no colonialist's, seems an unnecessarily roundabout route to grasping the *real* events that follow.[102]

Some years ago, as I was teaching *Formes* to an especially responsive group, my students demanded that we see as a class Stephen Spielberg's (and Harrison Ford's) first-rate adventure movie, *Raiders of the Lost Ark*. The story turns on ignorant passersby, good guys and bad guys, engaged in archaeological excavation in a race to acquire the power of the Ark as a kind of ultimate weapon. With a sophistication that thrilled their teacher, my students pronounced judgment on *Raiders*'s ark: The real Ark was a far more interesting object than the fantasy one because it had a complex human nature. The Ark's power inhered in its sacredness, and its sacredness was a feature of its collective life. But what is true of sacred objects is also true of the transcendent beings that communicate with humankind. Strip away the collectivity that makes sacredness real, and you are left with what individuals can manage, acting alone: Freud's patients with the oddball reverences for animals that occasioned their going to the doctor,[103] the bag lady out of whose mouth Jehovah God speaks incessantly in the unknown tongue, the innocuous bourgeois who secretes living and dead things in a hideous private shrine. Strip away sacredness as a feature of that maddening Durkheimian reality *pensée collective*, and you have not a collectively knowable world at all but a whole set of problems about how this or that person could leap to believing this or that strange thing. Your hands are tied to do anything other than suspend disbelief about the ontological claims for whatever it is, incant the formula about things believed in as real as real in their consequences, humor the believer, or just believe the claims.

The real Ark was what it was by virtue of what Durkheim calls "moral" or "ideal" forces, that is, collective human forces. Depending on its life within some given collectivity, anything can become the container of such forces, not just a wooden box made in a certain way. But like the fantasizers of the movie, some theorists have imagined the process to be otherwise, beginning somehow in the inherent grandeur of the object (the naturists' mistake) or in the inherent confusion of the believer's mind (the animists' mistake). Anyone who thinks either way will miss Durkheim's point that the same human capacities that make society possible make what Durkheim calls *la vie religieuse* inevitable. The truth of the mind is in the fictions[104] that, via *conscience collective*, construct the real. If there is ever to be a general theory of the mind that can be reduced to specific capacities of the brain, or an "artificial intelligence" whose discriminations and combinations have anything like the complexity of what we observe in even commonplace acts and facts of human life, then the theory of the brain's perceptual capacity must include things like the *collective* representation that makes it possible for a man, a mountain, a box of bones, or a louse to be perceived as themselves one moment and as themselves-plus, the next.

Religious Life in Seemingly Nonreligious Life

Durkheim sums up what makes *la vie religieuse* inevitable:

> [I]n all its aspects and at every moment of its history, social life is only possible thanks to a vast symbolism. The physical emblems and figurative representations with which I have been especially concerned in the present study are one form of it, but there are a good many others."[105]

With that summing up, he suggests that we could apply the same analysis in domains remote from anything we could call "religious"—politics certainly, from which Durkheim draws some of his own examples, and status orders of various kinds (think of the notion "blueblood," a racialized shorthand for the "set apart and forbidden" qualities of West European aristocrats, and white bones for those of Russia, as opposed to the black bones of Russian serfs).[106] All such phenomena seem the more outlandish, and the more distinct from reason, the further they seem to be from our own experience of the real. But the burden of Durkheim's argument is that they are not to be separated from human reason, in full operation—hence, from us. Toward the end of Chapter 7, he uncovers the roots of scientific abstraction in the same processes of abstraction that make collective identities possible. Therefore, it is no more remarkable that a man should in totemic observances manage to affirm his kinship with a white cockatoo (despite physical dissimilarities) than that he should manage to affirm his kinship with men and women of the White Cockatoo clan (for, again, it is physical dissimilarities that must be overcome). Both involve abstraction, by which invisible qualities are *added to* what is visible, for there is no other route to unifying the discrete individualities that our sensory experience gives us. That the manner in which this is done may be crude is beside the point:

> The great service that religions have rendered to thought is to have constructed a first representation of what the relations of kinship between things might be. Given the conditions in which it was tried, that enterprise could obviously lead only to makeshift results. But then, are the results of any such

enterprise ever definitive, and must it not be taken up again and again? Furthermore, it was less important to succeed than to dare. What was essential was not to let the mind be dominated by what appears to the senses, but instead to teach the mind to dominate it and to join together what the senses put asunder. As soon as man became aware that internal connections exist between things, science and philosophy became possible.[107]

That which makes *la vie religieuse* inevitable also links our ways of knowing community and identity with our ways of knowing the natural world. Soul was needed to account theoretically for aspects of our human experience, and empirical needs localized it in selected parts of natural bodies. The experience of force arose first in human relations, but it was found again in nature, in relations among things. By so doing, Durkheim says, humankind made room for nature in society, imagining it on the model provided by schemes for ordering collective life. But by the same stroke, the way nature's order was imagined in turn became consequential for human order. Like the Australians, all human beings acquire *a* world of nature, as if it was *the* world of nature, knowledge of which is mediated by relations with human contemporaries. Although that real world varies from place to place and from one historical epoch to another, the fact that it is consequential for the way humans live in common does not vary.

Thinking through what those connections still mean is one of the intellectual demands that Durkheim's expedition in *Formes* leads us to confront. It is not true that science is consequential only for those who do science. Early in this century, the Russian philosopher Lev Shestov contrasted the way a child learned that ghosts do not exist but at the same time was "given reliable information, the implausibility of which surpasses absolutely every fib ever told . . . that the earth is not motionless, as the evidence indicates, that the Sun does not revolve around the Earth, that the sky is not a solid, that the horizon is only an optical illusion and so on."[108] Once that child's view was *the* world of nature, as adult human beings knew it. That knowledge, in turn, was consequential for their relations to one another. For the kind of reason that *Formes* draws attention to, it was obvious straightaway that Copernicus's discovery affected not only ideas of the relationships heavenly bodies have to one another but ideas of relationships among earthly, human bodies, a connection that the Inquisition did not fail to notice. Cosmology was not imagined in isolation from morality. Not then, but also not now: Our own recent debates in America today over creation science and evolution turn on questions of how citizens should be taught morally (and legally) to regard and relate to one another. Creationism dresses itself in the forms of scientific discourse, if not their spirit; evolutionism sheds the open-endedness of scientific discourse and reclothes itself as hard nuggets of constitutionally correct scientific content for school-children's *unexperimental* consumption. The heat on both sides points to the dual aspect of *conscience collective*—normative and cognitive—to which Durk-heim's intellectually demanding expedition takes us.

That expedition is morally demanding as well, if we reflect on further implications of its discoveries. The passage I just quoted seems to ennoble religion as the source of quintessentially human achievements. But like every other human achievement, its mechanism can turn in more than one way. If Durkheim's analysis is right, it suggests that this century's monstrosities in collective life arise not from aberrations in human reason but from what is fundamental to it. That analysis also leads to a disturbing suggestion: that the ordinary human agents who serve as raw material for extraordinary abusers of human dignity are, in vast majority, the normal and the socially responsible—not deviants, sociopaths, or the crazy. It suggests, finally, that the human nature on which we depend, our social nature, is our uplift and our downfall. The only exit from this dilemma appears to be individualism. But the incompatibility of individualist assumptions with human nature *as it can be observed in the real world* was chief among Durkheim's discoveries in *Formes* and throughout his work. What we see, through his theoretical lens of *conscience collective*, is present in a social world of the real that cannot be arrived at with notions of individual *conscience,* alone. We see that Socrates' individualistic preference for the cup of hemlock over intellectual conformity has appealed down the ages precisely because, in that respect, he was not human in the sense we can observe day in and day out—in social life as empirically available to us. There, we see individual doubt, inherently present, and we see how doubt is overcome. Thus, in the end, there is a deep and tragic tension in Durkheim's discoveries.

FORMES IN FRENCH AND IN ENGLISH

A new translation need not be the occasion to deny the merit of an old one. Joseph Ward Swain gave *Formes* monumental life in English to generations of scholars, and that life in English has been richly productive. No one with a full understanding of what translating *Formes* demands even now should do anything but salute Dr. Swain's achievement. I re-do that work now with the benefit of the use I have made of the book, in English and in French. That use itself has benefited from almost ninety years of critique, the availability of specialized readings and field applications by some of the great anthropologists (Claude Lévi-Strauss, E. E. Evans-Pritchard, and Bronislaw Malinowski, to name only three), various English translations of Durkheim's other work, and good partial retranslations of *Formes* itself. These are aids that Swain did not have. Although my main purposes are both to re-present *Formes* in idiomatic English and correct Swain's inaccuracies, I differ with Swain without immodesty. The accuracy of many passages cannot be improved upon. Indeed, the very alienness of Swain's English, to our ears, is in a sense faithful to Durkheim, whose ideas are not idiomatic to English speakers—and ultimately, of course, there is no substitute for reading a work in its native language. Whatever its aims, translation requires scholarly, interpretive, and stylistic judgments at many levels.

Readable English has been my goal throughout. To this end, I have chosen resonant English equivalents whenever I could—for example, "outward and visible" for *externel et visible,* and "neighbor" for *semblable,* in cases where religious resonance seems important. (Compare "Thou shalt love thy neighbor as thyself.") To the same end, I have replaced French with English word order, dividing or moving Durkheim's frequent parenthetical insertions accordingly, and I have not hesitated to change the punctuation and division into paragraphs, if such changes seemed to me to improve the text's clarity in English or its accessibility to a well-educated reader. I have, in addition, repeated the subject in those new, shortened, sentences—grammatical gender and verb endings are not signposts in English for what goes with what. Furthermore, I have done whatever I had to in the service of good English style, avoiding double genitives and multiple uses of "it" with multiple antecedents (besetting sins in the older work).

In the service of future scholarly work, I have also checked, supplemented, and in some instances corrected as many of the original footnotes as I could, abbreviating the journal titles differently than Durkheim did and bracketing the new information in Durkheim's footnotes. In many cases, I did not change those very short paragraphs, sometimes only a sentence long, that Durkheim used more or less as section headings. Where I did make changes in structure, they are not marked, to avoid riddling the text. In any case, we still have Joseph Ward Swain's text, which makes few concessions to readable English and can serve as a rough-and-ready check for readers who do not wish to tackle the French. In their high-quality partial retranslation of *Formes,* Pickering and Redding deliberately keep the original structure.[109] I have decided differently. My own aim, besides accuracy, is removal of structural and stylistic impediments to encountering the book as the exciting read that I consider it to be.

A sample passage will illustrate my changes. In the Introduction, Durkheim draws an analogy to make his point about studying the simplest case available, in order to uncover the fundamental sources of religious life. His own enterprise is like that of a doctor seeking to uncover the cause of a delusion. The French passage seems reminiscent of Freud; Swain's English passage does not; mine recovers the resemblance to Freud. Here is Swain's passage:

> In order to understand a hallucination perfectly, and give it its most appropriate treatment, a physician must know its original point of departure. Now this event is proportionately easier to find if he can observe it near its beginnings. The longer the disease is allowed to develop, the more it evades observation [*au contraire, plus on laisse à la maladie le temps de se développer, plus il se dérobe à l'observation*]; that is because all sorts of interpretations have intervened as it advanced, which tend to force the original state into the background [*qui tendent a refouler dans l'inconscient l'état originel*], and across which it is sometimes difficult to find the initial one.[110]

Now consider the same passage as it appears in the new translation:

> To understand a delusion properly and to be able to apply the most appropriate treatment, the doctor needs to know what its point of departure was. That event is more easily detected the nearer to its beginning the delusion can be observed. Conversely, the longer the sickness is left to develop, the more that original point of departure slips out of view. This is so because all sorts of interpretations have intervened along the way, and the tendency of those interpretations is to repress the original state into the unconscious and to replace it with other states through which the original one is sometimes not easy to detect.

It is the point of departure of an illness (not the illness itself) that is screened from view. That, plus the terms "repress" and "unconscious," instead of "force" and "background," allow the new passage to sound reminiscent of Freud. I probably have not uncovered a missing link between Durkheim and Freud; Steven Lukes's exhaustive research turned up "no evidence" that Durkheim knew of Freud's work.[111] On the other hand, there is good reason to think Durkheim knew of the celebrated work being done in the 1880s at the Hôpital Salpêtrière in Paris by Jean-Martin Charcot, Freud's predecessor in the study of hysteria, and of the huge controversy about that work in the mid-1890s.[112] So for now, we can be tantalized. Present in the passage is the notion that today we term "screen memories," which is generally credited to Freud, not Charcot.[113] The plot thickens when we realize that Freud certainly knew of and cited Durkheim's work (including *Formes*) in his 1912 paper, "The Return of Totemism in Childhood."[114] In this way, correcting Swain's inaccuracies can add nuance to a scholarly question.

My goal, though, was not merely to correct Swain's work. I tackled the French originals[115] with an eye to the difficulties I have wrestled with and to the characteristic problems I have found in teaching this work to American students. For those reasons, I did not settle for merely literal renderings. If a literal translation conveyed nothing definite in English, I sought a clearer alternative. Of course, the search for expressive equivalents has its limits. Regarding the phrase *solution de continuité*, my colleague Andrée Douchin told me, "Let's face it. That phrase goes back to 1314."[116] She meant there are things about that phrase, literally "dissolution of continuity," that cannot be naturalized. Try naturalizing this illustration from the *Petit Robert*, quoting Victor Hugo, "Between present and future, there is *solution de continuité*." Hence, although the translator's responsibility is to move Durkheim's text linguistically toward the reader, part of the reader's own responsibility is to move intellectually toward Durkheim.[117] Still, it does not follow that the English itself must sound alien. Literal equivalents of the words and most of the syntax are to be found in Swain. But as I have just shown, literalness is no guarantee against all mistakes.

Moreover, to be literal is not necessarily to be faithful. Durkheim's language was precise and scholarly, to be sure, but his text reads well in French. As a rule, his sentences do not force a calisthenics of decipherment upon the reader. Nor do they assail the reader's ear with ugly rhythms, rhymes, and assonances or with images that clash. I have tried not to let *Formes* read less well in English than it does in French. I have also tried as much as possible to render a feature of Durkheim's personal style that can be lost in translation that is not literal enough: the metaphorical content in his word choices. Durkheim, the workmanlike scientist, deliberately avoided literary flights in scientific writing, but he sometimes thought in poetic ways. His word choices push a whole world of images into the text, and I have tried to keep that world in the new English *Formes*. Durkheim's images give us insight into his mode of thinking and thus into some of the intuitive leaps that mobilized his work. Still, the notes in the mind of the creative genius are not available to be played by his interpreter. Even when the translator's search for equivalents is well informed and resolute, the results stand at a distance from the original text.

Every translation is a reconstruction. Many words and turns of phrase have no exact equivalents between one language and another. Often the same is true even of words that move bodily. Consider the French words *opinion* and *attitude*. Durkheim's *opinion* could have been rendered as "public opinion," if that term had not come to mean discrete bits of mental material to be drawn from individual minds by pollsters and measured as to their frequency of occurrence. That meaning of "public opinion" carries us to the diametrical opposite of what Durkheim meant by *représentation collective*.[118] In a similar vein, it is now hard to extract "attitude" from the mind—the senses of "doing" or "conduct" are no longer on its surface. To dramatize the French term, as well as an older English sense, consider the *painted* attitudes of Jesus's disciples in *The Last Supper*. Now consider "virtue," which no longer has some of the meanings that are present in Durkheim's *vertu*. Just as, in the King James Bible, the salt can lose its savor, so a medicine or magical object could lose its virtue (or virtues), meaning its material potency, as well as the moral meaning evident in the phrase "a man of virtue," or the curiously different one if we shift gender. In the text, *vertu* goes with other words, *efficace* and *efficacité*, whose English equivalents are oldish but whose more modern-sounding equivalents seem out of place. Hence: The *potency* of the chemical called fluoxetine hydrochloride makes Prozac *effective*, but the *virtues* in blood sprinkled on the sacred rock make the *Intichiuma* rites *efficacious*.

In some instances, Durkheim's meaning and our own everyday one intersect but then diverge so far that our own familiar word becomes strange to us. One such word is "moral." In *Formes, moral* is often synonymous with "social," very nearly the inverse of what we usually mean by "moral."[119] Its most important antonym is not "immoral," as we might think, but "material," "tangible," and "physical." Consequently, "moral" is real but not material. "Good" is often not its synonym; together with "social," "spiritual" and "mental" often are. "Individual" stands with the antonyms of "moral," because Durkheim's "individual" denotes the body, its drives and appetites, its sensory apparatus—in short, our bodily being considered as distinct from our human being. The "social" is the source from which comes the humanizing discipline of the "individual" that creates the "person." Hence, the following distinction between "individual" and "person": "Our sensations are in their essence individual. But the more emancipated we are from the senses, and the more capable we are of thinking and acting conceptually, the more we are persons."[120]

Not only is "moral" not necessarily "good"; it is often not even on the same terrain as abstract judgments of "good" and "bad." For Durkheim, those judgments can be made only in particular social settings.[121] What is "moral" is "social"; both vary with time and place. Accordingly, the domain of the "moral" is not private, with its origin in some mysterious somewhere in the depths of the physical individual, as our commonsense usage suggests. Clearly, by that point, we are on ground quite alien to our own. On Durkheim's ground, there can be no full-fledged person standing apart from the "moral," as instituted in some historically given social setting. Thus, whereas in our own habitual way of thinking, that which is best in us stands apart from the social, in Durkheim's it is that, precisely, which is at war with our humanity.[122] For Durkheim, what stands apart is a being that is no more than the body, and all that the body tows along with it: The brain is there but not what we recognize as thinking; movement is there but not what we recognize as human doing. The mere co-presence of many such bodies is just that, a mere co-presence, as lacking in mutually recognizable identity as so many potatoes in a sack. With nothing but the merely physical and material collection of "individuals," there is neither reason nor identity nor community. There is no language and no kinship; there are age differences but no generations; there are sex differences but no genders.

Unlike *morale*, which can broaden along with its place in a distinctive system of thought, the term *culte* narrows in American English. Although "cult" once meant "a system of religious worship, especially with reference to its rites and ceremonies," it now has a pejorative connotation that gives an odd ring to such sentences as these of Durkheim: "But feasts and rites—in a word, *the cult*—are not the whole of religion."[123] Again: "Although in principle derived from the beliefs, the cult nevertheless reacts upon them, and the myth is often modeled on the rite so as to account for it. . . ."[124] "Cult" now connotes not just feasts and rites but excessive and perhaps obsessive ones, attached to beliefs assumed to be outlandish.[125] For that reason, used without warning today, it can plant in the American reader's mind a different attitude toward the totemic cults than Durkheim had. I decided nevertheless, to retain "cult" in most contexts, for this reason: If it is dropped in favor of terms like "worship" and "practice," which sometimes will do, Durkheim's own use of *le culte* decouples from the cognate term "culture." But that will not do at all. Durkheim's own formidable exploration of religious beliefs and rites—of *représentations collectives*, and *conscience collective*, that is, of shared ways of thinking and acting—was seminal to the vast twentieth-century exploration of "culture."

Different problems arise with the use of "essential," which is nearly, but not entirely, synonymous in English and French. In both, it means "fundamental" and "necessary"; but in America today, if I quote Durkheim as having called religion "an essential and permanent aspect of humanity," he may seem to be saying that religion is "indispensable" and, possibly, advocating it. Some readers might expect a case for prayer in schools to follow or other resuscitations of old-time religion in the public realm. But when Durkheim calls religion an "*essentiel et permanent*" aspect of humanity, he means no such thing. His use of a similar phrase, "integral and permanent," to describe society, brings out what he does mean: Society "arouses in us a whole world of ideas and feelings that express it but at the same time are an *integral and permanent* part of ourselves."[126] A third phrase, describing *conscience collective,* works similarly: "Being outside and above individual and local contingencies, collective consciousness sees things only in their permanent and fundamental aspect."[127] Therefore, noting Durkheim's own substitutions of "integral" and "fundamental" for "essential," treating the three synonymously, and taking into account subtle differences of shading in different contexts of use, I have sometimes rendered *essentiel* as "essential" but far more often as "fundamental" or "basic."[128] These are, unavoidably, choices. That virtually every one could have been made otherwise inserts the translator's own response to the text into what cannot help but appear to be what it cannot possibly be: the original text "itself," only put into English.

Now, finally, three smaller matters of choice need to be noted here; others will appear in footnotes, as they come up in the text. First, now that we have animated cartoons, the word "animate," as a verb, has a certain incongruous humor. But in *Formes,* "animate" goes with the quite serious ideas of "soul" and "spirit." For one reason or another, though, the alternatives are just as hard to naturalize—or they are humorous as well: "quicken" (as in "the quick and the dead"), "enliven," "vivify," "vitalize." Since we have Tylor and "animist" theory, I kept "animate." The next matter concerns *sentiment,* which in today's American English strongly connotes a feeling that is said (as on a Hallmark card) or at least formulated (sentiment against intervening militarily). In French, it often means direct "feeling," or "awareness" rather than their formulized versions. In English, we cannot say, "I have the sentiment that it will rain." I dropped Swain's "sentiment" almost everywhere. Finally, *se représenter* means to "present to the mind"—in other words, to "conceive" or "imagine." Translating literally, one can arrive at "represent to oneself," and that can mislead. In my first reading of Swain's, "Religion is, above all, a system of ideas by which men *represent to themselves* the society of which they are members," I pictured them creating emblems. Wrong.

But left untouched are certain famous set phrases that after eighty-plus years I feel cannot be extricated from Durkheim's life in English without doing violence to that life—for example, Swain's rendering of Durkheim's celebrated definition of religion and his marvelous phrase "thoroughgoing idiocy" for *illogique foncière,* a brilliantly nonliteral rendering that captures not only Durkheim's sense but also his attitude toward certain accounts of a supposed *mentalité primitive* to which logic is utterly alien.

Sometimes the problem of equivalents lies at a different level from terms and phrases or structure. There is no serviceable American equivalent for Durkheim's nineteenth-century French and academic mode of expression, even in most scholarly writing. Therefore, paradoxically, the search for equivalence led me to one change that may at first seem radical. What, for example, could be our idiomatic equivalent to Durkheim's editorial "we"? Michael Gane recounts a parody by Maurice Roche that brings out part of the problem.[129] In it, a hapless lecturer, sleepwalking annually through Durkheim's classic *The Rules of Sociological Method*, collides with a wide-awake undergraduate. The student refuses to grant anything, not least Durkheim's "we," the very first word in that text, as it is in *Formes*. The student brings the class to a halt by demanding to know who precisely "we" are. What is more, he refuses to cooperate when what he calls an authoritarian voice addresses him with the "we" that apparently means "you and I": It was unearned common ground.

I too stumble over the editorial "we" in the existing English translations. In Durkheim's day, it was the simply the modest, objective voice of academic or scientific writing (as it is still in the preferred rhetoric of some disciplines).[130] As such, that modest, objective "we" formally gestured toward a scientific collectivity standing behind every published work, despite solo authorship.[131] Nonetheless, it is merely a rhetorical device.[132] So to render the text in an English rhetoric that does not draw the wrong sort of attention to itself, we have substituted "I" for "we," except when "we" seems in context to mean "you and I," including the reader. We have, however, retained the first-person plural in the many statements Durkheim makes about the behavior of human beings generally, including both himself and the reader, or in reference to himself as a member of a group that excludes the reader. We have shifted to the editorial "we" to illustrate our point about how the text sounds without our effort, in retranslating, to reconstruct the plain-sounding neutrality of the original.

We have not changed the text in one respect that may disconcert some readers: *homme* is translated as "man" or "mankind." "Human being" renders *être humain;* and "person," *personne*. This translation does not try to reconstruct Durkheim's gender vocabulary or his outlook. Durkheim's *homme,* "man," includes "woman," at least some of the time; but nowadays we insist on saying "human being" or "person" all of the time. In *Formes,* however, "person" (as used in everyday speech) will not work. Why not? We quote Durkheim: "The two terms [person and individual] are by no means synonymous. In a sense, they oppose more than they imply one another."[133] Besides, while Durkheim is a theorist of social conduct, considered globally and embracing all human beings, it would be an abuse to mark this by inserting a modern terminology that achieves this embrace by means of linguistic affirmative action—in *our* own time, and for *us* (a pronoun which from now on does not designate an editorial "we," but is meant to include me and the reader). *Our* own usage implies the (ideally) inclusive gender conventions that belong to our own day; Durkheim's implies the quite different gender conventions of his own.

These conventions are implicit in all his writing, and sometimes they are explicit. Like many of his contemporaries, he believed woman's brain and mental capacity to be smaller than man's. Much to take issue with followed from that belief. Although the temptation arises to improve upon the elegant old furniture that is *Formes,* I have resisted it. To give in would amount to Durkheim's posthumous "reconstruction" by me, in a different and unacceptable sense. I cannot be in the business of rehabilitating Durkheim's unenlightened attitudes about women. If sufficient to sink him forever, they should be allowed to. Reconstruction on this account is doubly unacceptable, because it would profoundly alter Durkheim's meaning as that meaning can be objectively known from the passage just cited, and at the same time introduce a deep illogic into the book as a whole. The argument is constructed using evidence from rituals that Durkheim imagines as having had almost exclusively male participation. When Durkheim says "he," referring to an Australian or to a deity, that is most often what he literally means.[134]

Moreover, conducting repairs would displace certain possible critiques. For example, Nancy Jay, a feminist sociologist of religion, argued that insofar as exclusively male rituals provide the empirical foundation for Durkheim's social account of reason, it commits him to one of two anomalous conclusions: Women cannot reason, which is false, or women's ability to reason would require a separate theory.[135] Additionally, reconstructing Durkheim's gender outlook would conceal the sense in which his grand oppositions between sacred and profane, social and individual, mind and body, person and individual, moral and material, are latently an opposition between male and female.[136] Surely it must be the goal of translation to leave intact the internal tensions of the original text—in this case, the limits of the boldly universalistic argument, stunning for its time, that the book attempts. Reconstruction of elegant old furniture must not mean sanding away characteristic features of its original design.

Swain's own reconstruction of Durkheim's French title as "The Elementary Forms of the Religious Life" now carries the patina of respectable age. This title has become so much part of the book's life in English that, except in the deletion of one "the," I have not changed it. But I would have preferred the term "elemental," even though *élémentaire* expresses both. The question is not right or wrong translation but the scope each alternative leaves for right or wrong understanding. On the one hand, "elementary" will do in some respects; think of the concept "elementary particles," defined as being the smallest and most fundamental particles known. On the other hand, in day-to-day usage, "elementary" has a diminutive and vaguely dismissive connotation and sets up the same potential problem for some readers as "simple." Consider Sherlock Holmes's "Elementary, my dear Watson," or consider the charge, "You just don't seem to get the most elementary points," which means the easiest or simplest—addressed by a scold to a dimwit. Durkheim means "simplest" as well, but (in addition to the other considerations already referred to) he means it as particle physicists mean it, scientists who assuredly mean things that challenge the intellect. He seeks to explore building blocks of human social life, as physicists explore building blocks of matter. "Elementary" is suitable only if used in a restricted sense that is not altogether Sir Arthur Conan Doyle's and not at all the scold's. In a sense, Durkheim was attempting in his study what the Curies were attempting in their labs.

Durkheim's "simplest" forms are indispensably part of the most complex. Alternatively, they can be thought of as atoms and compared to the chemical substances that make up the periodic chart, the elements. The *formes* that he discovers in this particular study are the elements to be found in the makeup of the religions he thought of as more *complexes* or as "higher" in an evolutionary sense. Durkheim is interested in "a fundamental and permanent" aspect of humanity and in its "ever-present source," which can be discerned if studied in what he takes to be its *elemental* forms. Whatever those forms are (and I now paraphrase a physicist),[137] they have an underlying identity that persists despite unceasing change and limitless diversity. Moreover, as in the physicist's search for elementary particles, the question of chronological origins is related and yet separable. So if we understand the phrase *formes élémentaires* in that way, we need not get bogged down, as some have, in the notion that Durkheim made the error of thinking totemism brought him to origins in a chronological sense. Instead, we can take him at his word.

Whether he was right or wrong about thinking this or about thinking that the study of Australians could possibly yield up religion in *elemental* form are valid but separate questions. What is important is to grasp the scientific exploration that Durkheim attempted. The burden of the book as a whole is that an aspect of humanity's "fundamental and permanent" nature is to be found in humanity's social nature. And that human, social nature is nothing other than its *vie religieuse*. To show us what is included in this *vie religieuse* requires the full length of a long book. We can already say that this notion goes far beyond what people do specifically as churchmen or -women.

Accordingly, the new title rejects Swain's rendering "*the* religious life." If taken as an unfortunate artifact of literal translation, the phrase "*the* religious life" furnishes Durkheim with a voice in a heavily accented and game but clumsy use of English. It is as if he offered a Gallic shrug to an intellectually swamped American undergraduate and said to him, "As we tell in France, '*c'est la vie*'—that's the life'!" Well, *Non*. The definite article definitely does not belong there. But what about the English phrase "religious life," which suggests a life apart? From the argument of the preceding paragraph, it is obvious that the book is not about monasteries or religious virtuosi, or about beliefs and practices sealed off within a separate sphere of human life uniquely their own. In our own day, "religious life" connotes an exclusively inward and private sphere—but the seventeenth-century world that was hostile to Pilgrims and Puritans did not, and the world of *Formes* does not. Think back to the way Durkheim answered those who believe the function of religion is to offer a theory of the world: "Its true function is to make us act and to help us live."

Finally, I think Durkheim does mean "*the* elemental forms." He offers his study based on Australian ethnographies as a "single, well-conducted experiment." It is very clear, from the first page, that although based upon observations in Aboriginal Australian societies, he intends his findings to reveal the fundamental building blocks of all religion, its ever-present source and natural resource in the mentality, and in the reality, of humankind. Whatever is in theirs is in his and in ours.

Karen E. Fields
Rochester, New York
October 1994

NOTES

1. Emile Durkheim, "Contribution to discussion 'Religious Sentiment at the Present Time,'" reproduced in W. S. F. Pickering, *Durkheim on Religion: A Selection of Readings with Bibliographies,* London, Routledge, 1975, p. 184, which includes new translations by Pickering and Jacqueline Redding.
2. Introduction, p. 2.
3. A. A. Goldenweiser, "Emile Durkheim—*Les Formes élémentaires de la vie religieuse: Le Système totémique en Australie,* 1912," originally published in *American Anthropologist* 17, 1915, reproduced in Peter Hamilton, ed., *Emile Durkheim: Critical Assessments,* London and New York, Routledge, 1990, 3:240.
4. Durkheim published three other major books during his lifetime: *The Division of Labor in Society* (1893), *The Rules of Sociological Method* (1895), and *Sui-*

cide (1897). For a comprehensive bibliography of his work, see W. S. F. Pickering, *Durkheim's Sociology of Religion: Themes and Theories,* London, Routledge & Kegan Paul, 1984, pp. 535–543.

5. Introduction, pp. 2–3.

6. I refer to Paul Tillich's (1955) essay "Religion" in Mark Van Doren, ed., *Man's Right to Knowledge and the Free Use Thereof,* New York, Columbia, 1955, and to Rudolf Otto's (1917) book *Das Heilige,* translated in 1923 as *The Idea of the Holy: An Inquiry into the Non-rational Factor in the Idea of the Divine and Its Relation to the Rational,* John W. Harvey, trans., London, Oxford, 1923.

7. P. 426.

8. P. 9.

9. Goldenweiser, "Emile Durkheim," p. 218. My italics.

10. P. 349 and n. 55.

11. P. 437. One of the many delights of *Formes* is to encounter the nineteenth-century philologists, whose explorations of how language shapes reality (in the Vedas, twenty Sanskrit words for "sky") remain important even today. See p. 75.

12. P. 227.

13. Here I am talking about rhetorical features of the text. On its characteristic logical features, Steven Lukes has written a comprehensive analysis: *Emile Durkheim: His Life and Work, A Historical and Critical Study,* London, Penguin, 1973.

14. Durkheim used the word *paradoxale,* which literally means "against doctrine," but the everyday meaning of its English counterpart waters down into mere strangeness.

15. Gaston Richard, originally published in *Revue d'histoire et de philosophie religieuse* (1923), reproduced in Pickering, *Durkheim on Religion.* Pickering and Redding explain that they substituted "English" for Richard's own term "Anglican." I imagine he said what he meant.

16. Not being grounded in the real, magic did not survive, except as entertainment. Here, briefly, is the threefold analytical distinction that Durkheim makes: (1) religion is social, built on communities, whereas magical practices are individual, linking a practitioner and a client; (2) religion builds on altruism, and magic on individual utility; and (3) given the previous two points, religion works in the real, whereas magic does not, because religion works morally rather than materially, that is, on human minds operating collectively rather than on things. See pp. 41–42, pp. 360, 363. My own example: It has turned out that gold cannot be made from baser metals, but paper money can be made to be as good as gold.

17. Dominick LaCapra, *Emile Durkheim: Sociologist and Philosopher,* Chicago, University of Chicago Press, 1972.

18. Lukes, *Emile Durkheim,* p. 4.

19. Talcott Parsons, *The Structure of Social Action,* New York, Free Press, 1968 [1937], 1:421–429.

20. Raymond Aron, *Main Currents of Sociological Thought*, Middlesex, England, Penguin, 1967, 2:66–68.

21. I say this in full awareness of Mordecai Kaplan's embrace of *Formes* as an intellectual foundation for Reconstructionist Judaism and even though Kaplan's student, the well-known popularizer Harold Kushner, uses somewhat Durkheimian formulations. See *To Life! A Celebration of Jewish Being and Thinking*, Boston, Little, Brown, 1993, esp. chap. 3.

22. Parsons, *Structure of Social Action*, p. 421.

23. But see a splendid article by Patricia Cormack, "*The Rules of Sociological Method*: The Paradox of Durkheim's Manifesto," *Theory and Society*, forthcoming.

24. Judith Ryan provides an illuminating account of the links joining physics, psychology, philosophy, painting, and literature in *The Vanishing Subject: Early Psychology and Literary Modernism*, Chicago, University of Chicago Press, 1991.

25. According to Frank Pearce, *The Radical Durkheim*, London, Unwin, 1989, p. 3, Foucault did not usually acknowledge his debt to Durkheim. However, according to Stuart Hall, he did indeed. Discussion following a paper, "Constructing the Black Subject." Presented at the conference Race Matters: U.S. Terrain, Princeton University, April 29, 1994.

26. See Terry F. Godlove, *Religion, Interpretation, and Diversity of Belief: The Framework Model from Kant to Durkheim to Davidson*, Cambridge, Cambridge University Press, 1989.

27. In this context, "empirical science" will do, but I retain the French phrase, so that the dense tangle of meanings can be unraveled by the reader according to context. The following statement by Auguste Comte can serve as a guide: "Considered first in its oldest and commonest sense, the word 'positive' designates the real as opposed to the chimerical. In this respect, it well suits the new philosophical spirit, the mark of which is its constant dedication to research that is accessible to our intelligence, to the permanent exclusion of the impenetrable mysteries with which it was occupied in its infancy." See André Lalande, *Vocabulaire technique et critique de la philosophie*, Paris, F. Alcan, 1926, p. 597.

28. On this point, see the papers collected in Said A. Arjomand, ed., *The Political Dimensions of Religion*, Albany, State University of New York Press, 1993.

29. P. 419.

30. Durkheim titled his chapter on soul *La Notion d'âme*—"the idea of soul"— but he could have said *La Notion de l'âme*—"the idea of the soul."

31. P. 262.

32. An 1894 publication, a classic almost instantly, launched modern research on the early Greek idea of the soul: E. Rhode, *Seelencult und Unsterblichkeitsglaube der Griechen*, 2 vols., Freiburg, Leipzig, and Tübingen, which appeared in English as *Psyche: The Cult of Souls and Belief in Immortality among the Greeks*, W. B. Hillis, trans., London, 1925, cited by Jan Bremmer, *The Early Greek Concept of the Soul*, Princeton, NJ, Princeton University Press, 1983, p. 6.

33. Empedocles was one of the early Greek philosophers who thought (like the

Australians) that the soul resides in the blood. And consider this: In Homer, the soul leaves the body via wounds. See Bremmer, *Early Greek Concept,* pp. 3, 15, which also brings out the multifariousness of that concept. For helpful conversation and references, I am indebted to my colleagues Lewis W. Beck, Deborah Modrak, and George Dennis O'Brien.

34. P. 49.
35. P. 54.
36. Pp. 65, 66, 67.
37. P. 271.
38. This argument also lays the foundation for an argument (made in Bk. III, chap. 3, esp. p. 368) against the claim that the concept "cause" can be derived from the individual experience of willing.
39. P. 368.
40. To get a sense of what is involved, work through the intricate diagram in Craig Barclay, "Autobiographical Remembering: Creating Personal Culture," in M. A. Conway, D. C. Rubin, and W. Wagenaar, eds., *Theoretical Perspectives on Autobiographical Memory,* Netherlands, Kluwer Academic Publishers, 1992, esp. p. 2.
41. Michel Foucault, *Discipline and Punish: The Birth of the Prison,* Alan Sheridan, trans., New York, Vintage, 1979, pp. 23ff.
42. For conversation and references on this and many of the points that follow, I am indebted to my colleague Ayala Gabriel.
43. P. 265.
44. Adin Steinsaltz, *The Thirteen Petalled Rose: A Discourse on the Essence of Jewish Existence and Belief,* Yehuda Hanegbi, trans., New York, Basic Books, 1980, pp. 51–52.
45. Nor does the fact that a powerful abstract notion is to be found in religious tradition by any means make its use suggest residual believerhood.
46. P. 8.
47. P. 419.
48. P. 177. This chapter especially, including its footnotes, has many dry rejoinders.
49. Pickering, *Durkheim's Sociology of Religion,* p. xxiv; Lewis A. Coser, *Masters of Sociological Thought: Ideas in Historical and Social Context,* New York, Harcourt, 1971, pp. 162–163.
50. Quoted from Gouldner's *The Coming Crisis of Western Sociology* in a valuable discussion of Durkheim by Peter Ekeh: *Social Exchange Theory: The Two Traditions,* Cambridge, Harvard University Press, 1974, p. 12.
51. Aron, *Main Currents,* pp. 13–14.
52. Stjepan G. Meštrović formulated the question properly in his *Emile Durkheim and the Reformation of Sociology,* Totowa, NJ, Rowman & Littlefield, 1987, p. 19. There is also a speculative, Freudianized article by J. C. Filloux, "Il ne faut pas oublier que je suis fils de rabbin," *Revue française de sociologie* 17, no. 2, 1976, pp. 259–266.

53. For fascinating suggestions about the relationships between Comte's historical epistemology of science and modern writers, see Johan Heilbron, "Auguste Comte and Modern Epistemology," *Sociological Theory* 8, no. 2, Fall 1990, pp. 152–162. Full-scale analysis of Durkheim's work by professional philosophers has been relatively rare. But see, in addition to Godlove, *Religion, Interpretation, and Diversity,* Warren Schmaus, *Durkheim's Philosophy of Science and the Sociology of Knowledge: Creating an Intellectual Niche,* Chicago, University of Chicago Press, 1994.

54. Robert Bellah has disposed of the myths that Durkheim was antipsychological and that he thought a sociology wholly independent of psychology was possible. Robert N. Bellah, *Emile Durkheim on Morality and Society,* Chicago, University of Chicago Press, 1973, pp. xx–xxi. And see Ryan, *Vanishing Subject,* for an excellent introduction to early psychology and its entrance into the consciousness of educated turn-of-the-century West European and American audiences. Ryan, however, excludes psychoanalysis. See also John Kerr, *A Most Dangerous Method: The Story of Jung, Freud, and Sabina Spielrein,* New York, Vintage Books, 1993, pp. 27–29. Kerr's Introduction provides a sense of the milieu in which Durkheim discussed phenomena such as transmigration of souls and metempsychosis. For a time, investigations into spiritualism were not sharply distinguished from what would later be designated specifically as scientific work.

55. With his characteristic acuteness but without lasting effect on subsequent commentary, Talcott Parsons pointed out that the absence of a theory of social change does not render a theory ahistorical. *Structure of Social Action,* 1:450

56. But see Parsons's brilliant 1937 synthesis, which revealed how ambiguous the relationship of *Formes* is to functionalism (*Structure of Social Action,* esp. 1:441–450), and Pickering, *Durkheim's Sociology of Religion,* pp. 88–89, 300–317—both of which read *Formes* rather differently than I have done here.

57. P. 1.

58. Benedict Anderson, *Imagined Communities: Reflections on the Origin and Spread of Nationalism,* London, Verson, 1983.

59. For a crisply made case of why not, see Lukes, *Emile Durkheim,* pp. 477–479. For early ethnographers' criticisms of the work that emerged almost immediately, see A. A. Goldenweiser, "Review of *Les Formes élémentaires de la vie religieux: Le Système totémique en Australie*" (originally published in 1915), in Peter Hamilton, ed., *Emile Durkheim: Critical Assessments,* London and New York, Routledge, 1990, 3:238–252; and another review (published in 1913), reproduced in Pickering, *Durkheim on Religion,* pp. 205–208.

60. Lukes, *Emile Durkheim.*

61. Robert Nisbet, *The Sociology of Emile Durkheim,* New York, Oxford, 1974.

62. Pickering, *Durkheim's Sociology of Religion.*

63. Although many readers have arrived at this under their own steam, scholarly sources include Mary Douglas's view on "the Durkheimian premise that soci-

ety and God can be equated." Mary Douglas, *Natural Symbols: Explorations in Cosmology,* London, Barrie and Rockliff, 1970, quoted by Pickering, *Durkheim's Sociology of Religion* (whose discussion, pp. 227–241, provides a learned analysis and many useful references). See also Aron's very strong statement in *Main Currents:* "It seems to me absolutely inconceivable to define the essence of religion in terms of the worship which the individual pledges to the group, for in my eyes the essence of impiety is precisely the worship of the social order. To suggest that the object of the religious feelings is society transfigured is not to save but to degrade that human reality which sociology seeks to understand" (p. 68).

64. P. 44. *Le Petit Robert* quotes this definition to illustrate the term *système* in the sense of "a structured set of abstract things."

65. He is thought to have been influenced in this direction by his reading of Robertson Smith's *Lectures on the Religion of the Semites* (Pickering, *Durkheim's Sociology of Religion,* p. 63). But readers who hear echoes of historical materialism in this movement from deed to idea are referred to, pp. 385ff. There Durkheim talks about the elaboration of rites in a way that brings to mind the later Marxist use of "relative autonomy," to discuss the elaboration of beliefs.

66. A main argument of Bk. I, Chap. 4, esp. p. 93. It sometimes goes unnoticed that Durkheim points out precisely those traits of the clan that make its coherence improbable: no stable authority, not based on well-defined territory or common residence, not necessarily consanguineous, and virtually no utilitarian functions. Cf., p. 234.

67. This formulation is drawn from Nancy Jay, *Throughout Your Generations Forever: Sacrifice, Religion, and Paternity,* Chicago, University of Chicago Press, 1992, pp. 17–19.

68. P. 208. My italics. The French reads as follows: [*Le totem*] *exprime et symbolise deux sortes de choses différentes. D'une part, il est la forme extérieure et sensible de ce que nous avons appelé le principe ou le dieu totémique. Mais d'un autre côté, il est aussi le symbole de cette société déterminée qu'on appelle le clan. C'en est le drapeau; c'est le signe par lequel chaque clan se distingue des autres, la marque visible de sa personnalité, marque que porte tout ce qui fait partie du clan à un titre quelconque, hommes, bêtes et choses. Si donc il est, à la fois, le symbole du dieu et de la société, n'est-ce pas que le dieu et la société ne font qu'un? Comment l'emblème du groupe aurait-il pu devenir la figure de cette quasi divinité, si le groupe et la divinité étaient deux réalités distinctes? Le dieu du clan, le principe totémique, ne peut donc être autre chose que le clan lui-même, mais hypostasié et représenté aux imaginations sous les espèces sensibles du végétal ou de l'animal qui sert de totem.*

69. The controverted "reduction" of God to society can be taken in at least two senses: simplifying something complex to the point of distorting it, or restating something in different but equivalent terms (e.g., $2/6 = 1/3$). The fact that both in this context imply diminishment reveals the theological strata of the controversy. (A third sense, the theory of *explanation,* is not at issue.) If God is

in the definition of religion, keeping theological and nontheological things
aloft is like juggling rubber balls and wooden Indian clubs at the same time.

70.　The reader who is prepared to jump to conclusions about what the Durkheim
whom we saw addressing "free believers" was prepared to say about God
should turn now to p. 15, and reflect on the nicety of this statement about
man's social being, which "represents within us the highest reality in the intellectual and moral realm *that is knowable through observation:* I mean society."
My italics.

71.　In these terms, I miss the point of laboring to protect God's separateness, as in
the following passage of Pickering's (*Durkheim's Sociology of Religion,* p. 235):
"The danger is always to jump the parallel [society is to its members as God
is to the faithful] and make the two concepts or realities identical, or at least
to suggest that one *is* the other. Critics claim that Durkheim makes such a
step, but they disregard all caution. . . . Durkheim is much more careful, and
nowhere does he take the final and irrevocable step."

72.　For a carefully reasoned statement of this view, see Melford E. Spiro, "Religion: Problems of Definition and Explanation," in Michael Banton, ed., *Anthropological Approaches to the Study of Religion,* London, Tavistock, 1966.

73.　P. 172.

74.　See, for example, p. 77, on naturism: "It is not by praying to them, celebrating them in feasts and sacrifices, and imposing fasts and privations on himself
that he could have prevented them from harming him or obliged them to
serve his purposes. Such procedures could have succeeded only on very rare
occasions—miraculously, so to speak. If the point of religion was to give us a
representation of the world that would guide us in our dealings with it, then
religion was in no position to fulfill its function, and all peoples would not
have been slow to notice that fact: Failures, infinitely more common than
successes, would have notified them very quickly that they were on the
wrong path; and religion, constantly shaken by these constant disappointments, would have been unable to last."

75.　P. 239.

76.　Durkheim not only denies that reconciliation is possible but also dismisses
that argument along those lines as beside the point. Pp. 419–431ff. See La-
Capra, *Emile Durkheim,* p. 289.

77.　See Jay, *Throughout Your Generations,* pp. 30–40, where we encounter an instructive example of beliefs that could not exist if, to exist, they had to be
merely believable—for example, male priests disguised as pregnant women and
conducting blood sacrifices. Jay argues that unilineal descent through fathers is
publicly done through blood sacrificial rites, in rites that are often explicitly
formulated as transcending birth from mothers. It is precisely through participation in those rites that (a counterfactual) one-sided descent is collectively established as real.

78. To any reader who imagines doubt as the exclusive intellectual property of recent times or of cultures near our own, I recommend a spectacular article by Claude Lévi-Strauss, Durkheim's direct intellectual descendant: "The Sorcerer and His Magic," in *Structural Anthropology*, Garden City, NY, Doubleday, 1967 [1963].

79. P. 214. Durkheim does not make the assumption that the rational capacity of man differs from race to race or from time to time. For him, humanity is one. For a statement of the opposite assumption, see Lucien Lévy-Bruhl, *Les Fonctions mentales dans les sociétés inférieures*, Paris, Alcan, 1910, which Durkheim disputes throughout *Formes*.

80. This remark by Comte appears in the *Petit Robert*, to illustrate one sense of the word *simple*.

81. Cormack, "Rules of Sociological Method," has pointed out that this strategy is akin to that used by the ancient Greek rhetoricians, especially the sophists.

82. He repeats this point in criticizing concepts like "primitive" and "savage," and elsewhere. See his side criticism of Frazer, for example, p. 183, and the distinction between origins and elements that he takes for granted throughout, for example, p. 55.

83. See Durkheim's rationale for simplifying in order to reduce differences and variations to a minimum (pp. 5–7). Note also that he opens the first chapter of Book One with the observation that even the simplest religions known are of very great complexity (p. 45).

84. One sometimes hears the simplistic consideration that Durkheim might have found exotic cases expedient at a time in France when religion was a hot button issue, and the anti-Semitism exposed in the Dreyfus Affair might have made it still hotter for Durkheim. But then, what would we make of the fact that an international legion of scholars accorded totemism general theoretical interest? See Claude Lévi-Strauss, *Totemism*, Rodney Needham, trans., Boston, Beacon Press, 1963.

85. Peter Berger drew out some of these implications of *Formes* by devising the concept of "plausibility structures," communities whose everyday life takes for granted religious definitions of reality. See *The Sacred Canopy*, Garden City, NY, Doubleday, 1967, pp. 16, 46, 156.

86. P. 206.

87. Psychologist Craig Barclay tells me that the scheme Durkheim lays out is more or less the classical paradigm of conditioned response. Little has been written about how closely Durkheim followed developments in psychology. Lukes's footnotes indicate that Durkheim read Wilhelm Wundt through the 1880s and 1890s, and it is clear in *Formes* that he closely read the work of William James, whose *Principles of Psychology* appeared in French translation in 1910. Besides, James (according to Ryan, *Vanishing Subject*, pp. 12, 17) disseminated and received ideas, on and from both sides of the Atlantic, even as he developed his

own, and his earliest publications in France appeared in a journal edited by Durkheim's teacher, Charles Renouvier.

88. See Trudier Harris, *Exorcising Blackness: Historical and Literary Lynching and Burning Rituals,* Bloomington, Indiana University Press, 1984, on the passage of such *effervescences* into American literary art; Albert Speer, *Inside the Third Reich: Memoirs,* New York, Macmillan, 1970, the self-aware artist of buildings and Nazi *effervescences;* and Marcel Mauss, Durkheim's younger collaborator who lived to see the Nazis' *effervescences* and then saw how "many large modern societies" could be "hypnotized like Australians are by their dances, and set in motion like a children's roundabout." Quoted in Lukes, *Emile Durkheim,* p. 338n.

89. P. 213.

90. Ibid.

91. P. 211.

92. P. 223.

93. Cf. the classically instructive but (I believe) mistaken view of Parsons, *Structure of Social Action,* pp. 442ff. Parsons objected to Durkheim's *pensée* and *conscience collectives* as reified "group mind" concepts. But actually, I think, not only the mind but also the senses are not fully accounted for if conceived of in their individual aspects alone. Consider what the neurologist Oliver Sacks tells us about "Virgil," blind from early childhood, who through surgery forty-five years later regained the physical capacity to see. But, not having "spent a lifetime *learning* to see," he did not regain the seen world of his contemporaries—a condition for which neurologists have the interesting term "agnostic." See Oliver Sacks, *An Anthropologist on Mars: Seven Paradoxical Tales,* New York, Knopf, 1995, pp. 108–151, esp. pp. 114–115.

94. Approvingly quoted by Lukes, *Emile Durkheim,* p. 25.

95. See ibid., pp. 25–26.

96. P. 122.

97. Alan Unterman, *Dictionary of Jewish Lore and Legend,* London, Thames and Hudson, 1991, p. 25.

98. P. 226. Here is a glaring mistake by Joseph Ward Swain, who for *l'étendu* and *l'inétendu* wrote, respectively, "heard" and "not heard" (as if Durkheim had written *l'entendu* and *l'inentendu*), thereby making the connection to Descartes disappear and also the logic that joins this chapter with the one immediately following, on the idea of soul. The 1975 translation by Pickering and Redding (*Durkheim on Religion,* p. 134) renders *étendu* and *inétendu* as if the difference was a matter of size: "The impressions made on us by the physical world cannot, by definition, embody anything which transcends this world. The tangible can only be made into the tangible; the *vast* cannot be made into the *minute.*" My italics.

99. Lukes, *Emile Durkheim,* p. 26.

100. I have no access to the evolving *représentations*, but even at this distance, stand-
     ing only within the argument of *Formes*, I venture to predict that, by now, the
     bones were not preserved by human beings but preserved themselves, were
     not dusted off by human hands but resurrected themselves, that in so doing
     they towed upward with them on the rope of miracle the eternal Lithuanian
     nation-state, and that, for some among Lithuanians sons and daughters, they
     have acquired exceptional virtues.

101. After defining *sacré*, Durkheim sometimes uses the term *saint*, without saying
     how the two are related. I speculate that the shifting has to do, at least in part,
     with the problem sacred objects posed for Durkheim's written representation.
     If "holy" is used to render *saint*, there is a risk of sliding over into religious ac-
     tors' point of view, where religious objects are intrinsically holy. But at the
     same time, given in French was a fixed phrase incorporating the term *saint*:
     L'arche sainte specifically denotes the Holy Ark but is also equivalent to "sacred
     cow." The term *saint* is more frequent in Book III than elsewhere, four of
     whose five chapters are about ritual conduct regarding things that *have already
     been sanctified* (but are, from the actors' standpoint, intrinsically holy). As the
     context shifts, the same object comes into view as different at different mo-
     ments, one during the process of sanctification, the other after the process of
     sanctification is complete. To be represented was not only changing time, and
     not only changing viewpoints, but also the changing fundamental nature of
     the object itself. I speculate that, for Durkheim, the two terms were some-
     times synonymous and sometimes not.

102. A serviceable concept of "believing" need imply no more than this. In three
     studies about colonial settings, I have shown how British rulers came to ac-
     cept witchcraft and prophetic dreaming as real and how supernatural utter-
     ance by millenarian prophets forced real-world colonial police into action.
     See "Political Contingencies of Witchcraft in Colonial Central Africa: Cul-
     ture and the State in Marxist Theory," *Canadian Journal of African Studies* 16,
     no. 3, December 1982; *Revival and Rebellion in Colonial Central Africa*, Prince-
     ton, Princeton University Press, 1985; "I Had a Dream: Dreams and Visions
     upon the Political Landscape of Waking Life," *Etnofoor* 4, no. 2, 1991.

103. See the articles Freud published in 1913 as *Totem and Taboo*. Do not overlook
     his footnote references to Durkheim's work, including *Formes*.

104. In one place, Durkheim uses the term "fiction" but spins it: There is a reality
     that gains religious expression only through imaginative transfiguration (p. 385).

105. P. 223.

106. See Peter Kolchin, *Unfree Labor: American Slavery and Russian Serfdom*, Cam-
     bridge, Harvard University Press, 1987, pp. 170–191, quoted in Barbara
     Jeanne Fields, "Slavery, Race, and Ideology in the United States of America,"
     New Left Review, no. 181, May–June 1990, pp. 95–118, an exploration of rea-
     son, identity, and community deployed within the socially constructed frame-
     work of quasi-biological race.

107. P. 239.
108. Quoted by Czeslaw Milosz, *The Witness of Poetry*, Cambridge, Harvard University Press, 1983, p. 42.
109. Pickering, *Durkheim on Religion*, pp. ix, 102–166.
110. P. 19 in Swain translation; pp. 6–7 in present one.
111. Lukes, *Emile Durkheim*, p. 433n.
112. See Kerr, *A Most Dangerous Method*, pp. 27–29.
113. On this point I am indebted to my colleague William J. McGrath, author of *Freud's Discovery of Psychoanalysis: The Politics of Hysteria*, Ithaca, NY, Cornell University Press, 1986. Personal communication, February 20, 1994. McGrath confirms the absence of correspondence between the two men.
114. In *Totem and Taboo: Some Points of Agreement Between the Mental Lives of Savages and Neurotics*, New York, Norton, 1952, pp. 100–161. In addition, Meštrović, *Emile Durkheim*, p. 109, has pointed out a striking kinship of approach to magic as early as the 1907 paper, "Obsessive Acts and Religious Practices," in which Freud describes the obsessional neurosis as a "privatized religious system."
115. My heart nearly stopped when, two years into the project and working from the first edition, I found something in the Bibliothèque nationale called a second, "revised" edition of *Formes*, published in 1921. Why or under what inspiration (Durkheim having been dead since 1917) proved impossible to discover. Comparison showed that this "revision" contains many typographical errors not present in the first. The current Presses Universitaires de France paperback is based on that second edition.
116. Looking for something abstract, I queried various colleagues as to the possibility of its having a technical meaning in some body of philosophical work but turned up nothing. What I found in the *Petit Robert* was horrifyingly literal: fourteenth-century *surgeons* coined the term.
117. Robert Alun Jones and Douglas Kibbee have argued this point quite cogently in "Durkheim in Translation: Durkheim and Translation," a paper presented at the conference Humanistic Dilemmas: Translation in the Humanities and Social Sciences, State University of New York at Binghamton, September 27–28, 1991.
118. See his "Représentations individuelles et représentations collectives," *RMM*, 6, 1898.
119. On this point, see Nisbet, *Sociology of Emile Durkheim*, p. 187, and the clear discussion of Durkheim on morality that follows. Note as well Durkheim's contrast of "moral" and "physical" at p. 192.
120. P. 275.
121. On this point, see Durkheim's famous discussion of crime in *The Rules of Sociological Method*.
122. Meštrović, *Emile Durkheim*, makes a good case that this view is common in-

tellectual ground between Durkheim and Freud (in *Civilization and Its Discontents*). Durkheim's "individual" would parallel Freud's "*es*," which entered English as "id."

123. P. 430. My italics.

124. P. 99.

125. In fact, survey research has shown that the term "cult" in this pejorative sense has become sufficiently potent not only to color the response in America to those "new" religious movements that are called "cults," but indeed to influence legal proceedings—so much so that a strong case has been made for abandoning the term altogether in serious scholarship. See James T. Richardson, "Definitions of Cult: From Sociological-Technical to Popular-Negative," *Review of Religious Research* 34, no. 4, June 1993, who also surveys the evolution of the term's scholarly usages in the twentieth century. I am indebted to Dr. Richardson for sharing with me various references on this terrain of contested words.

126. P. 226. My italics.

127. P. 445.

128. Durkheim brings out this nuance on p. 5. "Everything is boiled down to what is absolutely indispensable, to that without which there would be no religion. But the indispensable is also the fundamental [*essentiel*], in other words, that which it is above all important for us to know."

129. Michael Gane, *On Durkheim's Rules of Sociological Method*, London, Routledge, 1989, p. 9.

130. However, Claude Lévi-Strauss has given unsettling philosophical reasons for referring to himself in the third person or as "we": "Throughout these pages, the 'we' the author has deliberately adhered to has not been meant simply as an expression of diffidence. . . . If there is one conviction that has been intimately borne upon the author of this work during twenty years devoted to the study of myths . . . it is that the solidity of the self, the major preoccupation of the whole of Western philosophy, does not withstand persistent application to the same object, which comes to pervade it through and through and to imbue it with an experiential awareness of its own unreality" (p. 625). I am indebted to the philosopher V. Y. Mudimbe for this reference and for instructive correspondence on several issues.

131. Durkheim's scientific collectivity included distinguished researchers in their own right, such as Marcel Mauss and Henri Hubert, whose works he continually cites.

132. See the discussion on this issue by John and Doreen Weightman, translators of Claude Lévi-Strauss's *The Naked Man: Introduction to a Science of Mythology*, vol. 4, New York, Harper & Row, 1981 [1971], p. 625.

133. P. 274–275.

134. Women come up explicitly, however, in various contexts—for example, male

initiation rites (in which they are designated as profane), observances regarding maternal totems, and, occasionally, female mythical messages.

135. Nancy Jay, "Gender and Dichotomy," *Feminist Studies* 7, no. 1, pp. 38–56.
136. Jay, *Throughout Your Generations,* p. 136.
137. Leon Lederman, *The God Particle: If the Universe Is the Answer, What Is the Question?,* Boston, Houghton Mifflin, 1993, p. 34.

The Elementary Forms of

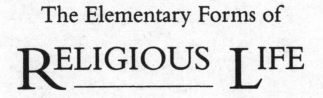

RELIGIOUS LIFE

INTRODUCTION

I

I propose in this book to study the simplest and most primitive religion that is known at present, to discover its principles and attempt an explanation of it. A religious system is said to be the most primitive that is available for observation when it meets the two following conditions: First, it must be found in societies the simplicity of whose organization is nowhere exceeded;[1] second, it must be explainable without the introduction of any element from a predecessor religion.

I will make every effort to describe the organization of this system with all the care and precision that an ethnographer or a historian would bring to the task. But my task will not stop at description. Sociology sets itself different problems from those of history or ethnography. It does not seek to become acquainted with bygone forms of civilization for the sole purpose of being acquainted with and reconstructing them. Instead, like any positive science,* its purpose above all is to explain a present reality that is near to us and thus capable of affecting our ideas and actions. That reality is man. More especially, it is present-day man, for there is none other that we have a greater interest in knowing well. Therefore, my study of a very archaic religion will not be for the sheer pleasure of recounting the bizarre and the eccentric. I have made a very archaic religion the subject of my research because it seems better suited than any other to help us comprehend the religious nature of man, that is, to reveal a fundamental and permanent aspect of humanity.

This proposition is bound to provoke strong objections. It may be thought strange that, to arrive at an understanding of present-day humanity, we should have to turn away from it so as to travel back to the beginning of history. In the matter at hand, that procedure seems especially unorthodox. Religions are held to be of unequal value and standing; it is commonly said that not all contain the same measure of truth. Thus it would seem that the higher forms of religious thought cannot be compared with the lower with-

---

*Here, knowledge (*science*) acquired by means of systematic observation. This use of the term *positive* is indebted to Auguste Comte (1798–1857) who postulated a human evolution from the theological to metaphysical to positive epochs. The complexities of the term *positive* in general, and in Comte's use of it, are examined by André Lalande, *Dictionnaire technique de la philosophie,* Paris, F. Alcan, 1923, pp. 595–600.

[1] I will call those societies and the men of those societies primitive in the same sense. This term certainly lacks precision, but it is hard to avoid; if care is taken to specify its meaning, however, it can safely be used.

1

out bringing the higher forms down to the lower level. To grant that the crude cults of Australian tribes might help us understand Christianity, for example, is to assume—is it not?—that Christianity proceeds from the same mentality, in other words, that it is made up of the same superstitions and rests on the same errors. The theoretical importance sometimes accorded to primitive religions could therefore be taken as evidence of a systematic irreligion that invalidated the results of research by prejudging them.

I need not go into the question here whether scholars can be found who were guilty of this and who have made history and the ethnography of religion a means of making war against religion. In any event, such could not possibly be a sociologist's point of view. Indeed, it is a fundamental postulate of sociology that a human institution cannot rest upon error and falsehood. If it did, it could not endure. If it had not been grounded in the nature of things, in those very things it would have met resistance that it could not have overcome. Therefore, when I approach the study of primitive religions, it is with the certainty that they are grounded in and express the real. In the course of the analyses and discussions that follow, we will see this principle coming up again and again. What I criticize in the schools I part company with is precisely that they have failed to recognize it. No doubt, when all we do is consider the formulas literally, these religious beliefs and practices appear disconcerting, and our inclination might be to write them off to some sort of inborn aberration. But we must know how to reach beneath the symbol to grasp the reality it represents and that gives the symbol its true meaning. The most bizarre or barbarous rites and the strangest myths translate some human need and some aspect of life, whether social or individual. The reasons the faithful settle for in justifying those rites and myths may be mistaken, and most often are; but the true reasons exist nonetheless, and it is the business of science to uncover them.

Fundamentally, then, there are no religions that are false. All are true after their own fashion: All fulfill given conditions of human existence, though in different ways. Granted, it is not impossible to rank them hierarchically. Some can be said to be superior to others, in the sense that they bring higher mental faculties into play, that they are richer in ideas and feelings, that they contain proportionately more concepts than sensations and images, and that they are more elaborately systematized. But the greater complexity and higher ideal content, however real, are not sufficient to place the corresponding religions into separate genera. All are equally religious, just as all living beings are equally living beings, from the humblest plastid to man. If I address myself to primitive religions, then, it is not with any ulterior motive of disparaging religion in general: These religions are to be respected no less than the others. They fulfill the same needs, play the same role, and proceed from the same causes; therefore, they can serve just as well to elucidate the nature of religious life and, it follows, to solve the problem I wish to treat.

Still, why give them a kind of priority? Why choose them in preference to others as the subject of my study? This choice is solely for reasons of method.

First of all, we cannot arrive at an understanding of the most modern religions without tracing historically the manner in which they have gradually taken shape. Indeed, history is the only method of explanatory analysis that can be applied to them. History alone enables us to break down an institution into its component parts, because it shows those parts to us as they are born in time, one after the other. Second, by situating each part of the institution within the totality of circumstances in which it was born, history puts into our hands the only tools we have for identifying the causes that have brought it into being. Thus, whenever we set out to explain something human at a specific moment in time—be it a religious belief, a moral rule, a legal principle, an aesthetic technique, or an economic system—we must begin by going back to its simplest and most primitive form. We must seek to account for the features that define it at that period of its existence and then show how it has gradually developed, gained in complexity, and become what it is at the moment under consideration.

It is easy to see how important the determination of the initial starting point is for this series of progressive explanations. A cartesian principle had it that the first link takes precedence in the chain of scientific truths. To be sure, it is out of the question to base the science of religions on a notion elaborated in the cartesian manner—that is, a logical concept, pure possibility constructed solely by force of intellect. What we must find is a concrete reality that historical and ethnographic observation alone can reveal to us. But if that primary conception must be arrived at by other methods, the fact remains that it is destined to have an important influence on all the subsequent propositions that science establishes. Biological evolution was conceived altogether differently from the moment the existence of unicellular organisms was discovered. Likewise, the particulars of religious facts are explained differently if naturism is placed at the beginning of religious evolution than if animism, or some other form, is placed there. Indeed, even the most specialized scholars must choose a hypothesis and take their inspiration from it if they want to try to account for the facts they analyze—unless they mean to confine themselves to a task of pure erudition. Willy-nilly, the questions they ask take the following form: What has caused naturism or animism to take on such and such a particular aspect here or there, and to be enriched or impoverished in such and such a way? Since taking a position on the initial problem is unavoidable, and since the solution given will affect the science as a whole, the problem is best confronted at the outset. This is what I propose to do.

Besides, apart from those indirect consequences, the study of primitive religions in itself has immediate interest of the first importance.

If it is useful to know what a given religion consists of, it is far more important to examine what religion is in general. This is a problem that has always intrigued philosophers, and not without reason: It is of interest to all humanity. Unfortunately, the method philosophers ordinarily use to solve it is purely one of dialectic: All they do is analyze the idea they have of religion, even if they have to illustrate the results of that mental analysis with examples borrowed from those religions that best suit their model. But while this method must be abandoned, the problem of definition remains; and philosophy's great service has been to prevent it from being settled once and for all* by the disdain of the savants. The problem can in fact be approached in another way. Since all religions may be compared, all being species within the same genus, some elements are of necessity common to them all. By that I mean not only the outward and visible features that they all equally exhibit and that make it possible to define religion in a provisional way at the beginning of research. The discovery of these apparent signs is relatively easy, for the observation required does not go beyond the surface of things. But these external resemblances presuppose deeper ones. At the foundation of all systems of belief and all cults, there must necessarily be a certain number of fundamental representations and modes of ritual conduct† that, despite the diversity of forms that the one and the other may have taken on, have the same objective meaning everywhere and everywhere fulfill the same functions. It is these enduring elements that constitute what is eternal and human in religion. They are the whole objective content of the idea that is expressed when *religion* in general is spoken of.

How, then, can those elements be uncovered?

Surely it is not by observing the complex religions that have arisen in the course of history. Each of those religions is formed from such a variety of elements that it is very hard to distinguish what is secondary to them from what is primary, and what is essential from what is accessory. Simply consider religions like those of Egypt, India, or classical antiquity! Each is a dense tangle of many cults that can vary according to localities, temples, generations, dynasties, invasions, and so on. Popular superstitions intermingle in them with the most sophisticated dogmas. Neither religious thinking nor religious

---

*Swain rendered Durkheim's *prescrit* as "suppressed," as if he had written *proscrit.*

†*Attitudes rituelles.* On this phrase, see below, p. 301n.

practice is shared equally among the mass of the faithful. The beliefs as well as the rites are taken in different ways, depending on men, milieux, and circumstances. Here it is priests, there monks, elsewhere the laity; here, mystics and rationalists, theologians and prophets, and so on. Under such conditions, it is difficult to perceive what might be common to all. It is indeed possible to find ways of studying some particular phenomenon fruitfully—such as prophetism, monasticism, or the mysteries—through one or another of those systems in which it is especially well developed. But how can one find the common basis of religious life under the luxuriant vegetation that grows over it? How can one find the fundamental states characteristic of the religious mentality in general through the clash of theologies, the variations of ritual, the multiplicity of groupings, and the diversity of individuals?

The case is altogether different in the lower societies. The lesser development of individuality, the smaller scale of the group, and the homogeneity of external circumstances all contribute to reducing the differences and variations to a minimum. The group regularly produces an intellectual and moral uniformity of which we find only rare examples in the more advanced societies. Everything is common to everyone. The movements are stereotyped; everyone executes the same ones in the same circumstances; and this conformity of conduct merely translates that of thought. Since all the consciousnesses are pulled along in the same current, the individual type virtually confounds itself with the generic type. At the same time that all is uniform, all is simple. What could be more basic than those myths composed of a single theme, repeated endlessly, or than those rites composed of a small number of movements, repeated until the participants can do no more. Neither the popular nor the priestly imagination has yet had the time or the means to refine and transform the basic material of ideas and religious practices; reduced to essentials, that material spontaneously presents itself to examination, and discovering it calls for only a minimal effort. Inessential, secondary, and luxurious developments have not yet come to hide what is primary.[2] Everything is boiled down to what is absolutely indispensable, to that without which there would be no religion. But the indispensable is also the fundamental, in other words, that which it is above all important for us to know.

Thus, primitive civilizations are prime cases because they are simple cases. This is why, among all the orders of facts, the observations of ethnog-

[2]This is not to say, of course, that primitive cults do not go beyond bare essentials. Quite the contrary, as we will see, religious beliefs and practices that do not have narrowly utilitarian aims are found in every religion (Bk.III, chap.4, §2). This nonutilitarian richness is indispensable to religious life, and of its very essence. But it is by far less well developed in the lower religions than in the others, and this fact will put us in a better position to determine its raison d'être.

raphers have often been veritable revelations that have breathed new life into the study of human institutions. Before the middle of the nineteenth century, for example, it was generally believed that the father was the essential element of the family; it was not even imaginable that there could be a family organization of which paternal power was not the keystone. Bachofen's discovery toppled that old notion. Until quite recent times, it was thought obvious that the moral and legal relations that constitute kinship were only another aspect of the physiological relations that result from shared descent. Bachofen and his successors, McLennan, Morgan, and many others, were still operating under the influence of that preconception. But, quite the contrary, we have known ever since we became acquainted with the nature of the primitive clan that kinship cannot be defined by common blood.* To return to religions: Exclusive consideration of the religious forms that are the most familiar to us long led us to believe that the idea of god was characteristic of all that is religious. The religion I will study below is largely a stranger to any notion of divinity. In it, the forces to which the rites are addressed differ greatly from those that are of paramount importance in our modern religions, and yet they will help us to understand our modern religions better. Nothing is more unjust, therefore, than the disdain with which too many historians still regard ethnographers' work. In point of fact, ethnography has often brought about the most fertile revolutions in the various branches of sociology. For the same reason, moreover, the discovery of unicellular creatures, which I noted earlier, transformed the idea of life that was widely held. Since life is down to its fundamental features among very simple beings, those features may be less easily misread.

But primitive religions do not merely allow us to isolate the constituent elements of religion; their great advantage is also that they aid in its explanation. Because the facts are simpler, the relations between them are more apparent. The reasons men invoke to explain their actions to themselves have not yet been refined and revamped by sophisticated thought: They are closer and more akin to the motives that caused those actions. To understand a delusion properly and to be able to apply the most appropriate treatment, the doctor needs to know what its point of departure was. That event is the more easily detected the nearer to its beginnings the delusion can be observed.

*Jacob Johann Bachofen (1815–1887) postulated the existence of matriliny (reckoning descent through the female line) and matriarchy or mother right, a stage he envisaged as standing between primitive promiscuity and patriarchy. Ethnographic study worldwide has borne out the first and discredited the second. Like Bachofen, John Ferguson McLennan (1827–1881) and Lewis Henry Morgan (1818–1881) were lawyers interested in the rules that govern family and property. Among other achievements, Morgan pioneered the study of kin statuses distinct from blood relationship; McLennan is credited with having drawn attention to totemism. See below, Bk.I. chap.4, p. 85.

Conversely, the longer a sickness is left to develop, the more that original point of departure slips out of view. This is so because all sorts of interpretations have intervened along the way, and the tendency of those interpretations is to repress the original state into the unconscious and to replace it with other states through which the original one is sometimes not easy to detect. The distance between a systematized delusion and the first impressions that gave birth to it is often considerable. The same applies to religious thought. As it progresses historically, the causes that called it into existence, though still at work, are seen no more except through a vast system of distorting interpretations. The popular mythologies and the subtle theologies have done their work: They have overlaid the original feelings with very different ones that, although stemming from primitive feelings of which they are the elaborated form, nevertheless allow their true nature to show only in part. The psychological distance between the cause and the effect, and between the apparent cause and the effective cause, has become wider and more difficult for the mind to overcome. The remainder of this work will be an illustration and a test of this methodological point. We will see how, in the primitive religions, the religious phenomenon still carries the visible imprint of its origins. It would have been much more difficult for us to infer those origins by considering more developed religions alone.

Thus, the study I undertake is a way of taking up again the old problem of the origin of religions *but under new conditions*. Granted, if by origin one means an absolute first beginning, there is nothing scientific about the question, and it must be resolutely set aside. There is no radical instant when religion began to exist, and the point is not to find a roundabout way of conveying ourselves there in thought. Like every other human institution, religion begins nowhere. So all speculations in this genre are rightly discredited; they can consist of only subjective and arbitrary constructions without checks of any sort. The problem I pose is altogether different. I would like to find a means of discerning the ever-present causes on which the most basic forms of religious thought and practice depend. For the reasons just set forth, the causes are more easily observable if the societies in which they are observed are less complex. That is why I seek to get closer to the origins.[3] The reason is not that I ascribe special virtues to the lower religions. Quite the contrary, they are crude and rudimentary; so there can be no question of making them out to be models of some sort, which the later religions would

[3]It will be seen that I give the word "origins," like the word "primitive," an entirely relative sense. I do not mean by it an absolute beginning but the simplest social state known at present—the state beyond which it is at present impossible for us to go. When I speak about origins and the beginnings of history or religious thought, this is the sense in which those phrases must be understood.

only have had to reproduce. But their very lack of elaboration makes them instructive, for in this way they become useful experiments in which the facts and the relations among facts are easier to detect. To uncover the laws of the phenomena he studies, the physicist seeks to simplify those phenomena and to rid them of their secondary characteristics. In the case of institutions, nature spontaneously makes simplifications of the same kind at the beginning of history. I wish only to put those simplifications to good use. Doubtless, I will be able to obtain only very elementary facts by this method. When I have accounted for them, to the extent this will be possible, the novelties of all kinds that have been produced in the course of evolution will still not be explained. But although I would not dream of denying the importance of the problems such novelties pose, I think those problems benefit by being treated at the proper time, and there is good reason not to tackle them until after those whose study I have undertaken.

II

My research is not solely of interest to the science of religions. There is an aspect of every religion that transcends the realm of specifically religious ideas. Through it, the study of religious phenomena provides a means of revisiting problems that until now have been debated only among philosophers.

It has long been known that the first systems of representations that man made of the world and himself were of religious origin. There is no religion that is not both a cosmology and a speculation about the divine. If philosophy and the sciences were born in religion, it is because religion itself began by serving as science and philosophy. Further, and less often noted, religion has not merely enriched a human intellect already formed but in fact has helped to form it. Men owe to religion not only the content of their knowledge, in significant part, but also the form in which that knowledge is elaborated.

At the root of our judgments, there are certain fundamental notions that dominate our entire intellectual life. It is these ideas that philosophers, beginning with Aristotle, have called the categories of understanding: notions of time, space,[4] number, cause, substance, personality.* They correspond to

---

*Usually referred to in Kantian circles as the "categories of understanding" or the "categories of the understanding," technically these are called "pure concepts of understanding"—that is, concepts, or rules for organizing the variety of sense perceptions, that lie ready in the mind and are brought into play by our efforts to make sense of our sensations. For clarifying correspondence on these points, I thank Professor Robert Paul Wolff.

[4]I call time and space categories because there is no difference between the role these notions play in intellectual life and that which falls to notions of kind and cause. (See on this point [Octave] Hamelin, *Essai sur les éléments principaux de la représentation*, Paris, Alcan [1907], pp. 63, 76.)

the most universal properties of things. They are like solid frames that confine thought. Thought does not seem to be able to break out of them without destroying itself, since it seems we cannot think of objects that are not in time or space, that cannot be counted, and so forth. The other ideas are contingent and changing, and we can conceive of a man, a society, or an epoch that lacks them; but these fundamental notions seem to us as almost inseparable from the normal functioning of the intellect. They are, as it were, the skeleton of thought. Now, when one analyzes primitive religious beliefs methodically, one naturally finds the principal categories among them. They are born in and from religion; they are a product of religious thought. This is a point that I will make again and again in the course of this book.

Even now that point has a certain interest of its own, but here is what gives it its true significance.

The general conclusion of the chapters to follow is that religion is an eminently social thing. Religious representations are collective representations that express collective realities; rites are ways of acting that are born only in the midst of assembled groups and whose purpose is to evoke, maintain, or recreate certain mental states of those groups. But if the categories are of religious origin, then they must participate in* what is common to all religion: They, too, must be social things, products of collective thought. At the very least—since with our present understanding of these matters, radical and exclusive theses are to be guarded against—it is legitimate to say that they are rich in social elements.

This, it must be added, is something one can begin to see even now for certain of the categories. For example, what if one tried to imagine what the notion of time would be in the absence of the methods we use to divide, measure, and express it with objective signs, a time that was not a succession of years, months, weeks, days, and hours? It would be nearly impossible to conceive of. We can conceive of time only if we differentiate between moments. Now, what is the origin of that differentiation? Undoubtedly, states of consciousness that we have already experienced can be reproduced in us in the same order in which they originally occurred; and, in this way, bits of our past become immediate again, even while spontaneously distinguishing themselves from the present. But however important this distinction might

---

*The phrase "participate in," which occurs frequently, has usually not been replaced with simpler possibilities such as "partakes of" or "shares in" because the notion of participation that can be seen in the sentence "Jesus participated in divine and human nature" must be borne in mind, together with an argument in which Durkheim was engaged. Lucien Lévy-Bruhl, whose book *Les Fonctions mentales dans les sociétés inférieures* Durkheim criticizes, considered "participations" to exemplify the inherent illogic of "primitive" thought. Durkheim held just the opposite.

be for our private experience, it is far from sufficient to constitute the notion or category of time. The category of time is not simply a partial or complete commemoration of our lived life. It is an abstract and impersonal framework that contains not only our individual existence but also that of humanity. It is like an endless canvas on which all duration is spread out before the mind's eye and on which all possible events are located in relation to points of reference that are fixed and specified. It is not *my time* that is organized in this way; it is time that is conceived of objectively by all men of the same civilization. This by itself is enough to make us begin to see that any such organization would have to be collective. And indeed, observation establishes that these indispensable points, in reference to which all things are arranged temporally, are taken from social life. The division into days, weeks, months, years, etc., corresponds to the recurrence of rites, festivals, and public ceremonies at regular intervals.[5] A calendar expresses the rhythm of collective activity while ensuring that regularity.[6]

The same applies to space. As Hamelin[7] has shown, space is not the vague and indeterminate medium that Kant imagined. If purely and absolutely homogeneous, it would be of no use and would offer nothing for thought to hold on to. Spatial representation essentially consists in a primary coordination of given sense experience. But this coordination would be impossible if the parts of space were qualitatively equivalent, if they really were mutually interchangeable. To have a spatial ordering of things is to be able to situate them differently: to place some on the right, others on the left, these above, those below, north or south, east or west, and so forth, just as, to arrange states of consciousness temporally, it must be possible to locate them at definite dates. That is, space would not be itself if, like time, it was not divided and differentiated. But where do these divisions that are essential to

---

[5]In support of this assertion, see Henri Hubert and Marcel Mauss, *Mélanges d'histoire des religions*, the chapter on "La Représentation du temps dans la religion," Paris, Alcan [1909].

[6]Through this we see how completely different are the complexus of sensations and images that serves to orient us in duration, and the category of time. The first are the summary of individual experiences, which hold only for the individual who has had them. By contrast, the category of time expresses a time common to the group—social time, so to speak. This category itself is a true social institution. Thus it is peculiar to man; animals have no representation of this kind.

This distinction between the category of time and the corresponding individual sensations could easily be made in regard to space and cause. This may perhaps help clear up certain confusions, which have fed controversies on these questions. I will return to this point at the Conclusion of the present work.

[7]Hamelin, *Essai sur les éléments principaux de la représentation*, pp. 75ff.

space come from? In itself it has no right, no left, no high or low, no north or south, etc. All these distinctions evidently arise from the fact that different affective colorings have been assigned to regions. And since all men of the same civilization conceive of space in the same manner, it is evidently necessary that these affective colorings and the distinctions that arise from them also be held in common—which implies almost necessarily that they are of social origin.[8]

Besides, in some instances this social character is made manifest. There are societies in Australia and North America in which space is conceived in the form of an immense circle, because the camp itself is circular;[9] and the spatial circle is divided in exactly the same way as the tribal circle and in its image. As many regions are distinguished as there are clans in the tribe, and it is the place the clans occupy in the encampment that determines the orientation of the regions. Each region is defined by the totem of the clan to which it is assigned. Among the Zuñi, for example, the pueblo is made up of seven sections; each of these sections is a group of clans that has acquired its own unity. In all likelihood, it was originally a single clan that later subdivided. Space similarly contains seven regions, and each of these seven sections of the world is in intimate relationship with a section of the pueblo, that is, with a group of clans.[10] "Thus," says Cushing, "one division is considered to be in relation with the north; another represents the west, another the south,[11] etc." Each section of the pueblo has its distinctive color, which symbolizes it; each region has its own color, which is that of the corresponding section. Over the course of history, the number of basic clans has varied, and the number of regions has varied in the same way. Thus, spatial organization was modeled on social organization and replicates it. Far from being built into human nature, no idea exists, up to and including the distinction be-

[8]Otherwise, in order to explain this agreement, one would have to accept the idea that all individuals, by virtue of their organico-psychic constitution, are affected in the same manner by the different parts of space—which is all the more improbable since the different regions have no affective coloring. Moreover, the divisions of space vary among societies—proof that they are not based exclusively on the inborn nature of man.

[9]See Emile Durkheim and Marcel Mauss, "De Quelques formes primitives de la classification," *AS*, vol. VI, 1903, pp. 47ff.

[10]Ibid., pp. 34ff.

[11][Frank Hamilton] Cushing, "Outlines of Zuñi Creation Myths," *Thirteenth Report*, BAE, Washington, DC, Government Printing Office, 1896, pp. 367ff. [Throughout, quoted material is translated into English from Durkheim's French renderings.]

tween right and left, that is not, in all probability, the product of religious, hence collective, representations.[12]

Analogous demonstrations concerning the notions of genus, force, personality, and efficacy will be found below. One might even ask whether the notion of contradiction does not also arise from social conditions. What tends to make this plausible is the fact that the hold the notion of contradiction has had over thought has varied with times and societies. Today the principle of identity governs scientific thought; but there are vast systems of representation that have played a major role in the history of ideas, in which it is commonly ignored: These systems are the mythologies, from the crudest to the most sophisticated.[13] Mythologies deal with beings that have the most contradictory attributes at the same time, that are one and many, material and spiritual, and capable of subdividing themselves indefinitely without losing that which makes them what they are. These historical variations of the rule that seems to govern our present logic show that, far from being encoded from eternity in the mental constitution of man, the rule depends at least in part upon historical, hence social, factors. We do not know exactly what these factors are, but we can presume that they exist.[14]

Once this hypothesis is accepted, the problem of knowledge can be framed in new terms.

Up to the present, only two doctrines have opposed one another. For some, the categories cannot be derived from experience. They are logically prior to experience and condition it. They are thought of as so many simple data that are irreducible and immanent in the human intellect by virtue of its natural makeup. They are thus called *a priori*. For others, by contrast, the categories are constructed, made out of bits and pieces, and it is the individual who is the artisan of that construction.[15]

[12]See Robert Hertz, "La Prééminence de la main droite: Etude de polarité religieuse," *RP,* December, 1909. On this question of the relations between the representation of space and the form of the group, see the chapter in [Friedrich] Ratzel, *Politische Geographie* [Leipzig, R. Oldenbourg, 1897], titled "Der Raum im Geiste der Völker" [pp. 261–262].

[13]I do not mean to say that it is unknown to mythological thinking but that mythological thinking departs from this principle more often and more overtly than scientific thought. Conversely, I will show that science cannot help but violate it, even while following it more scrupulously than religion does. In this respect and many others, there are only differences of degree between science and religion; but if these should not be overstated, it is important to notice them, for they are significant.

[14]This hypothesis has already been advanced by the founders of *Völkerpsychologie.* It is referred to, for example, in a short article by Wilhelm Windelband titled, "Die Erkenntnisslehre unter dem Völkerpsychologischen Geschichtspunkte," in *ZV* [Lichtenstein, Kraus Reprints, Ltd., 1968], VIII, pp. 166ff. Cf. a note by [Heymann] Steinthal on the same subject, ibid., pp. 178ff.

[15]Even in the theory of [Herbert] Spencer, the categories are constructed from experience. The only difference in this respect between ordinary and evolutionary empiricism is that, according to the latter,

Both solutions give rise to grave difficulties.

Is the empiricist thesis adopted? Then the categories must be stripped of their characteristic properties. In fact, they are distinguished from all other knowledge by their universality and their necessity. They are the most general concepts that exist, because they are applied to all that is real; and just as they are not attached to any particular object, they are independent of any individual subject. They are the common ground where all minds meet. What is more, minds meet there of necessity: Reason, which is none other than the fundamental categories taken together, is vested with an authority that we cannot escape at will. When we try to resist it, to free ourselves from some of these fundamental notions, we meet sharp resistance. Hence, far from merely depending upon us, they impose themselves upon us. But the characteristics of empirical data are diametrically opposite. A sensation or an image is always linked to a definite object or collection of definite objects, and it expresses the momentary state of a particular consciousness. It is fundamentally individual and subjective. Moreover, we can do as we wish with representations that are of this origin. Of course, when sensations are present to us, they impose themselves on us *in fact*. *By right,* however, we remain free to conceive them otherwise than they are and to picture them as occurring in an order different from the one in which they occurred. In regard to them, nothing is binding on us unless considerations of a different sort intervene. Here, then, are two sorts of knowledge that are like opposite poles of the intellect. Under these conditions, to reduce reason to experience is to make reason disappear—because it is to reduce the universality and necessity that characterize reason to mere appearances, illusions that might be practically convenient but that correspond to nothing in things. Consequently, it is to deny all objective reality to that logical life which the function of the categories is to regulate and organize. Classical empiricism leads to irrationalism; perhaps it should be called by that name.

Notwithstanding the sense we ordinarily attach to the labels, it is the apriorists who are more attentive to the facts. Since they do not take it as self-evident truth that the categories are made of the same elements as our sense representations, they are not committed to impoverishing the categories systematically, emptying them of all real content and reducing them to mere verbal artifices. Quite the contrary, apriorists leave the categories with all their distinctive characteristics. The apriorists are rationalists; they believe

---

the results of individual experience are consolidated by heredity. But that consolidation adds nothing essential; no element enters into their composition that does not originate in the experience of the individual. Also, according to that theory, the necessity with which the categories impose themselves upon us in the present is itself the product of an illusion, a superstitious prejudice that is deeply rooted in the organism but without foundation in the nature of things.

that the world has a logical aspect that reason eminently expresses. To do this, however, they have to ascribe to the intellect a certain power to transcend experience and add to what is immediately given. But for this singular power, they offer neither explanation nor warrant. Merely to say it is inherent in the nature of human intellect is not to explain that power. It would still be necessary to see where we acquire this astounding prerogative and how we are able to see relationships in things that mere spectating cannot reveal to us. To confine oneself to saying that experience itself is possible only on that condition is to shift the problem, perhaps, but not to solve it. The point is to know how it happens that experience is not enough, but presupposes conditions that are external and prior to experience, and how it happens that these conditions are met at the time and in the manner needed. To answer these questions, it has sometimes been imagined that, beyond the reason of individuals, there is a superior and perfect reason from which that of individuals emanated and, by a sort of mystic participation, presumably acquired its marvelous faculty: That superior and perfect reason is divine reason. But, at best, this hypothesis has the grave disadvantage of being shielded from all experimental control, so it does not meet the requirements of a scientific hypothesis. More than that, the categories of human thought are never fixed in a definite form; they are ceaselessly made, unmade, and remade; they vary according to time and place. By contrast, divine reason is immutable. How could this invariance account for such constant variability?

Such are the two conceptions that have competed for centuries. And if the debate has gone on and on, it is because the arguments back and forth are in fact more or less equivalent. If reason is but a form of individual experience, then reason is no more. On the other hand, if the capacities with which it is credited are recognized but left unaccounted for, then reason apparently is placed outside nature and science. Faced with these opposite objections, the intellect remains uncertain. But if the social origin of the categories is accepted, a new stance becomes possible, one that should enable us, I believe, to avoid these opposite difficulties.

The fundamental thesis of apriorism is that knowledge is formed from two sorts of elements that are irreducible one to the other—two distinct, superimposed layers, so to speak.[16] My hypothesis keeps this principle intact. The knowledge that people speak of as empirical—all that theorists of empiricism have ever used to construct reason—is the knowledge that the direct

---

[16]It is perhaps surprising that I should not define apriorism by the hypothesis of innateness. But that idea actually has only a secondary role in the doctrine. It is a simplistic way of portraying the irreducibility of rational cognition to empirical data. To call it innate is no more than a positive way of saying that it is not a product of experience as usually conceived.

action of objects calls forth in our minds. Thus they are individual states that are wholly[17] explained by the psychic nature of the individual. But if the categories are essentially collective representations, as I think they are, they translate states of the collectivity, first and foremost. They depend upon the way in which the collectivity is organized, upon its morphology, its religious, moral, and economic institutions, and so on. Between these two kinds of representations, then, is all the distance that separates the individual from the social; one can no more derive the second from the first than one can deduce the society from the individual, the whole from the part, or the complex from the simple.[18] Society is a reality *sui generis;* it has its own characteristics that are either not found in the rest of the universe or are not found there in the same form. The representations that express society therefore have an altogether different content from the purely individual representations, and one can be certain in advance that the former add something to the latter.

The manner in which both kinds of representations are formed brings about their differentiation. Collective representations are the product of an immense cooperation that extends not only through space but also through time; to make them, a multitude of different minds have associated, intermixed, and combined their ideas and feelings; long generations have accumulated their experience and knowledge. A very special intellectuality that is infinitely richer and more complex than that of the individual is distilled in them. That being the case, we understand how reason has gained the power to go beyond the range of empirical cognition. It owes this power not to some mysterious virtue but simply to the fact that, as the well-known formula has it, man is double. In him are two beings: an individual being that has its basis in the body and whose sphere of action is strictly limited by this fact, and a social being that represents within us the highest reality in the intellectual and moral* realm that is knowable through observation: I mean so-

---

*On Durkheim's characteristic uses of the term "moral," see above, p. lv–lvi.

[17]At least to the extent that there are individual, and thus fully empirical, representations. But in fact there probably is no case in which those two sorts of elements are not found closely bound up together.

[18]Furthermore, this irreducibility should not be understood in an absolute sense. I do not mean that there is nothing in the empirical representations that announces the rational ones, or that there is nothing in the individual that can be considered the harbinger of social life. If experience was completely foreign to all that is rational, reason would not be applicable to it. Likewise, if the psychic nature of the individual was absolutely resistant to social life, society would be impossible. Therefore a full analysis of the categories would look for the seeds of rationality in individual consciousness. I shall have occasion to return to this point in my Conclusion. All I wish to establish here is that there is a distance between the indistinct seeds of reason and reason properly so-called that is comparable to the distance between the properties of mineral elements, from which the living being is made, and the characteristic properties of life, once constituted.

ciety [*J'entends la société*]. In the realm of practice, the consequence of this duality in our nature is the irreducibility of the moral ideal to the utilitarian motive; in the realm of thought, it is the irreducibility of reason to individual experience. As part of society, the individual naturally transcends himself, both when he thinks and when he acts.

This same social characteristic enables us to understand where the necessity of the categories comes from. An idea is said to be necessary* when, due to some sort of internal property, it enjoys credence without the support of any proof. It thus contains in itself something that compels the intellect and wins over intellectual adherence without prior examination. Apriorism postulates that remarkable capacity without accounting for it. To say that the categories are necessary because they are indispensable to thought is simply to repeat that they are necessary. But if they have the origin that I am attributing to them, nothing about their ascendancy should surprise us any longer. They do indeed express the most general relationships that exist between things; having broader scope than all our ideas, they govern all the particulars of our intellectual life. If, at every moment, men did not agree on these fundamental ideas, if they did not have a homogeneous conception of time, space, cause, number, and so on. All consensus among minds, and thus all common life, would become impossible.

Hence society cannot leave the categories up to the free choice of individuals without abandoning itself. To live, it requires not only a minimum moral consensus but also a minimum logical consensus that it cannot do without either. Thus, in order to prevent dissidence, society weighs on its members with all its authority. Does a mind seek to free itself from these norms of all thought? Society no longer considers this a human mind in the full sense, and treats it accordingly. This is why it is that when we try, even deep down inside, to get away from these fundamental notions, we feel that we are not fully free; something resists us, from inside and outside ourselves. Outside us, it is opinion that judges us; more than that, because society is represented inside us as well, it resists these revolutionary impulses from within. We feel that we cannot abandon ourselves to them without our thought's ceasing to be truly human. Such appears to be the origin of the very special authority that is inherent in reason and that makes us trustingly accept its promptings. This is none other than the authority of society[19] passing into certain ways of thinking that are the indispensable conditions of all

---

*Note here that the sense of the word "necessary" is distinct from the everyday concept of need. See also the next paragraph.

[19]It has often been noticed that social disturbances multiply mental disturbances. This is further evidence that logical discipline is an aspect of social discipline. The former relaxes when the latter weakens.

common action. Thus the necessity with which the categories press themselves upon us is not merely the effect of habits whose yoke we could slip with little effort; nor is that necessity a habit or a physical or metaphysical need, since the categories change with place and time; it is a special sort of moral necessity that is to intellectual life what obligation is to the will.[20]

But if the categories at first do no more than translate social states, does it not follow that they can be applied to the rest of nature only as metaphors? If their purpose is merely to express social things, it would seem that they could be extended to other realms only by convention. Thus, insofar as they serve us in conceiving the physical or biological world, they can only have the value of artificial symbols—useful perhaps, but with no connection to reality. We would thus return to nominalism and empiricism by another route.

To interpret a sociological theory of knowledge in that way is to forget that even if society is a specific reality, it is not an empire within an empire: It is part of nature and nature's highest expression. The social realm is a natural realm that differs from others only in its greater complexity. It is impossible that nature, in that which is most fundamental in itself, should be radically different between one part and another of itself. It is impossible that the fundamental relations that exist between things—precisely those relations that the categories serve to express—should be fundamentally dissimilar in one realm and another. If, for reasons that we shall have to discover,[21] they stand out more clearly in the social world, it is impossible that they should not be found elsewhere, though in more shrouded forms. Society makes them more manifest but has no monopoly on them. This is why notions worked out on the model of social things can help us think about other sorts of things. At the very least, if, when they deviate from their initial meaning, those notions play in a sense the role of symbols, it is the role of well-founded symbols. If artifice enters in, through the very fact that these are constructed concepts, it is an artifice that closely follows nature and strives to come ever closer to nature.[22] The fact

---

[20]There is an analogy between this logical necessity and moral obligation but not identity—at least not at present. Today, society treats criminals differently from people who are mentally handicapped. This is evidence that, despite significant similarities, the authority attached to logical norms and that inherent in moral norms are not of the same nature. They are two different species of one genus. It would be interesting to research what that difference (probably not primitive) consists of and where it comes from, since for a long time public consciousness barely distinguished the delinquent from the mentally ill. From this example, we can see the numerous problems raised by the analysis of these notions, which are generally thought elementary and simple but actually are extremely complex.

[21]This question is treated in the Conclusion of this book.

[22]Hence the rationalism that is immanent in a sociological theory of knowledge stands between empiricism and classical apriorism. For the first, the categories are purely artificial constructs; for the second, on the other hand, they are naturally given; for us, they are works of art, in a sense, but an art that imitates nature ever more perfectly.

that the ideas of time, space, genus, cause, and personality are constructed from social elements should not lead us to conclude that they are stripped of all objective value. Quite the contrary, their social origin leads one indeed to suppose that they are not without foundation in the nature of things.[23]

In this fresh formulation, the theory of knowledge seems destined to join the opposite advantages of the two rival theories, without their disadvantages. It preserves all the essential principles of apriorism but at the same time takes inspiration from the positive turn of mind that empiricism sought to satisfy. It leaves reason with its specific power, but accounts for that power, and does so without leaving the observable world. It affirms as real the duality of our intellectual life, but explains that duality, and does so with natural causes. The categories cease to be regarded as primary and unanalyzable facts; and yet they remain of such complexity that analyses as simplistic as those with which empiricism contented itself cannot possibly be right. No longer do they appear as very simple notions that anyone can sift from his personal observations, and that popular imagination unfortunately complicated; quite the contrary, they appear as ingenious instruments of thought, which human groups have painstakingly forged over centuries, and in which they have amassed the best of their intellectual capital.[24] A whole aspect of human history is, in a way, summed up in them. This amounts to saying that to succeed in understanding and evaluating them, it is necessary to turn to new procedures. To know what the conceptions that we ourselves have not made are made of, it cannot be enough to consult our own consciousness. We must look outside ourselves, observe history, and institute a whole science, a complex one at that, which can advance only slowly and by collective labor. The present work is an attempt to make certain fragmentary contributions to that science. Without making these questions the direct subject of my study, I will take advantage of all the opportunities that present themselves to capture at birth at least some of those ideas that, while religious in origin, were bound nevertheless to remain at the basis of human mentality.

---

[23]For example, the category of time has its basis in the rhythm of social life; but if there is a rhythm of collective life, one can be certain that there is another in the life of the individual and, more generally, that of the universe. The first is only more marked and apparent than the others. Likewise, we will see that the notion of kind was formed from that of the human group. But if men form natural groups, one can suppose that there exist among things groups that are at once similar to them and different. These natural groups of things are genera and species.

[24]This is why it is legitimate to compare the categories with tools: Tools, for their part, are accumulated material capital. Moreover, there is close kinship between the three ideas of tool, category, and institution.

BOOK ONE

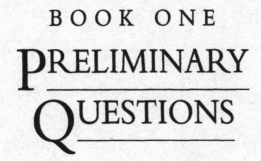

PRELIMINARY QUESTIONS

CHAPTER ONE

DEFINITION OF RELIGIOUS PHENOMENA AND OF RELIGION[1]

In order to identify the simplest and most primitive religion that observation can make known to us, we must first define what is properly understood as a religion. If we do not, we run the risk of either calling a system of ideas and practices religion that are in no way religious, or of passing by religious phenomena without detecting their true nature. A good indication that this danger is not imaginary, and the point by no means a concession to empty methodological formalism, is this: Having failed to take that precaution, M. Frazer,* a scholar to whom the comparative science of religions is nevertheless greatly indebted, failed to recognize the profoundly religious character of the beliefs and rites that will be studied below—beliefs and rites in which, I submit, the original seed of religious life in humanity is visible. In the matter of definition, then, there is a prejudicial question that must be treated before any other. It is not that I hope to arrive straightaway at the deep and truly explanatory features of religion, for these can be determined only at the end of the research. But what is both necessary and possible is to point out a certain number of readily visible outward features that allow us to recognize religious phenomena wherever they are encountered, and that prevent their being confused with others. I turn to this preliminary step.

If taking this step is to yield the results it should, we must begin by freeing our minds of all preconceived ideas. Well before the science of religions instituted its methodical comparisons, men had to create their own idea of what religion is. The necessities of existence require all of us, believers and unbelievers, to conceive in some fashion those things in the midst of which

*Sir James George Frazer (1854–1941).

[1] I have already tried to define the phenomenon of religion, in a work published by *AS,* vol. II [1899], pp. 1ff. ["De la Définition des phénomènes religieux"]. As will be seen, the definition given there differs from the one I now propose. At the end of this chapter (p. 44, n. 68), I will give the reasons for these modifications. They do not, however, involve any fundamental change in the conceptualization of the facts.

we live, about which we continually make judgments, and of which our conduct must take account. But since these notions are formed unmethodically, in the comings and goings of life, they cannot be relied on and must be rigorously kept to one side in the examination that follows. It is not our preconceptions, passions, or habits that must be consulted for the elements of the definition we need; definition is to be sought from reality itself.

Let us set ourselves before this reality. Putting aside all ideas about religion in general, let us consider religions in their concrete reality and try to see what features they may have in common: Religion can be defined only in terms of features that are found wherever religion is found. In this comparison, then, we will incorporate all the religious systems we can know, past as well as present, the most primitive and simple as well as the most modern and refined, for we have no right to exclude some so as to keep only certain others, and no logical method of doing so. To anyone who sees religion as nothing other than a natural manifestation of human activity, all religions are instructive, without exception of any kind: Each in its own way expresses man, and thus each can help us understand better that aspect of our nature. Besides, we have seen that the preference for studying religion among the most civilized peoples is far from being the best method.[2]

Before taking up the question and in order to help the mind free itself of commonsense notions whose influence can prevent us from seeing things as they are, it is advisable to examine how those prejudices have entered into some of the commonest definitions.

I

One notion that is generally taken to be characteristic of all that is religious is the notion of the supernatural. By that is meant any order of things that goes beyond our understanding; the supernatural is the world of mystery, the unknowable, or the incomprehensible. Religion would then be a kind of speculation upon all that escapes science, and clear thinking generally. According to Spencer, "Religions that are diametrically opposite in their dogmas agree in tacitly recognizing that the world, with all it contains and all that surrounds it, is a mystery seeking an explanation"; he makes them out basically to consist of "the belief in the omnipresence of something that goes

---

[2]See above, p. 3. I do not push the necessity of these definitions further or the method to be followed. The exposition is to be found in my *Règles de la méthode sociologique* [Paris, Alcan, 1895], pp. 43ff. Cf. *Le Suicide*; [*étude de sociologie*] (Paris, F. Alcan [1897]), pp. 1ff.

beyond the intellect."[3] Similarly, Max Müller saw all religion as "an effort to conceive the inconceivable and to express the inexpressible, an aspiration toward the infinite."[4]

Certainly the role played by the feeling of mystery has not been unimportant in certain religions, including Christianity. Even so, the importance of this role has shown marked variation at different moments of Christian history. There have been periods when the notion of mystery has become secondary and even faded altogether. To men of the seventeenth century, for example, dogma contained nothing that unsettled reason. Faith effortlessly reconciled itself with science and philosophy; and thinkers like Pascal, who felt strongly that there is something profoundly obscure in things, were so little in harmony with their epochs that it was their fate to be misunderstood by their contemporaries.[5] Therefore, it would seem rash to make an idea that has been subject to periodic eclipse the essential element even of Christianity.

What is certain, in any case, is that this idea appears very late in the history of religions. It is totally alien not only to the peoples called primitive but also to those who have not attained a certain level of intellectual culture. Of course, when we see men imputing extraordinary virtues to insignificant objects, or populating the universe with extraordinary principles made up of the most disparate elements and possessing a sort of ubiquity that is hard to conceptualize, it is easy for us to find an air of mystery in these ideas. It seems to us that these men have resigned themselves to ideas so problematic for our modern reason only because they have been unable to find more rational ones. In reality, however, the explanations that amaze us seem to the primitive the simplest in the world. He sees them not as a kind of *ultima ratio** to which the intellect resigns itself in despair but as the most direct way of conceiving and understanding what he observes around him. For him, there is nothing strange in being able, by voice or gesture, to command the elements, hold up or accelerate the course of the stars, make the rain fall or stop it, and so on. The rites he uses to ensure the fertility of the soil or of the animal species that nourish him are no more irrational in his eyes than are, in our

*Last resort.

[3][Herbert Spencer, *First Principles,* New York, D. Appleton, 1862, French translation based on the sixth English edition], Paris, F. Alcan [1902], pp. 38–39, [p. 37 in the English edition. Trans.].

[4]Max Müller, *Introduction to the Science of Religions* [London, Longmans, 1873], p. 18. Cf. [*Lectures on*] *the Origin and* [*Growth*] *of Religion* [*as Illustrated by the Religions of India,* London, Longmans, 1878], p. 23.

[5]The same turn of mind is also to be found in the period of scholasticism, as is shown in the formula according to which the philosophy of that period was defined, *Fides quaerens intellectum* [Faith in search of intellect. Trans.].

own eyes, the technical processes that our agronomists use for the same purpose. The forces he brings into play by these various means do not seem to him particularly mysterious. Certainly, these forces differ from those the modern scientist conceives of and teaches us to use; they behave differently and cannot be controlled in the same way; but to the one who believes in them, they are no more unintelligible than gravitation or electricity is to physicists today.

Furthermore, as we will see in the course of this work, the idea of natural forces is very likely derived from that of religious forces, so between the one and the other there cannot be the chasm that separates the rational from the irrational. Not even the fact that religious forces are often conceived of as spiritual entities and conscious wills is any proof of their irrationality. Reason does not resist *a priori* the idea that inanimate bodies might be moved by intelligences, as human bodies are, even though present-day science does not easily accommodate this hypothesis. When Leibniz proposed to conceive the external world as an immense society of intelligences, between which there were not and could not be any but spiritual relations, he meant to be working as a rationalist. He did not see this universal animism as anything that might offend the intellect.

Besides, the idea of the supernatural, as we understand it, is recent. It presupposes an idea that is its negation, and that is in no way primitive. To be able to call certain facts supernatural, one must already have an awareness that there is a *natural order of things,* in other words, that the phenomena of the universe are internally linked according to necessary relationships called laws. Once this principle is established, anything that departs from those laws necessarily appears as beyond nature and, thus, beyond reason: For what is in this sense natural is also rational, those relations expressing only the manner in which things are logically connected. Now, the idea of universal determinism is of recent origin; even the greatest thinkers of classical antiquity did not achieve full awareness of it. That idea is territory won by the empirical sciences; it is the postulate on which they rest and which their advancement has proved. So long as this postulate was lacking or not well established, there was nothing about the most extraordinary events that did not appear perfectly conceivable. So long as what is immovable and inflexible about the order of things was unknown, and so long as it was seen as the work of contingent wills, it was of course thought natural that these wills or others could modify the order of things arbitrarily. For this reason, the miraculous interventions that the ancients ascribed to their gods were not in their eyes miracles, in the modern sense of the word. To them, these interventions were beautiful, rare, or terrible spectacles, and objects of surprise and wonder (θαύματα, *mirabilia, miracula*); but they were not regarded as glimpses into a mysterious world where reason could not penetrate.

That mind-set is all the more readily understandable to us because it has not completely disappeared. Although the principle of determinism is firmly established in the physical and natural sciences, its introduction into the social sciences began only a century ago, and its authority there is still contested. The idea that societies are subject to necessary laws and constitute a realm of nature has deeply penetrated only a few minds. It follows that true miracles are thought possible in society. There is, for example, the accepted notion that a legislator can create an institution out of nothing and transform one social system into another, by fiat—just as the believers of so many religions accept that the divine will made the world out of nothing or can arbitrarily mutate some beings into others. As regards social things, we still have the mind-set of primitives. But if, in matters sociological, so many people today linger over this old-fashioned idea, it is not because social life seems obscure and mysterious to them. Quite the opposite: If they are so easily contented with such explanations, if they cling to these illusions that are repeatedly contradicted by experience, it is because social facts seem to them the most transparent things in the world. This is so because they have not yet appreciated the real obscurity, and because they have not yet grasped the need to turn to the painstaking methods of the natural sciences in order progressively to sweep away the darkness. The same cast of mind is to be found at the root of many religious beliefs that startle us in their oversimplification. Science, not religion, has taught men that things are complex and difficult to understand. But, Jevons replies,[6] the human mind has no need of properly scientific education to notice that there are definite sequences and a constant order of succession between phenomena or to notice that this order is often disturbed. At times the sun is suddenly eclipsed; the rain does not come in the season when it is expected; the moon is slow to reappear after its periodic disappearance, and the like. Because these occurrences are outside the ordinary course of events, people have imputed to them extraordinary, exceptional—in a word, extranatural—causes. It is in this form, Jevons claims, that the idea of the supernatural was born at the beginning of history; and it is in this way and at this moment that religion acquired its characteristic object.

The supernatural, however, is not reducible to the unforeseen. The new is just as much part of nature as the opposite. If we notice that, in general, phenomena occur one after the other in a definite order, we also notice that

[6][Frank Byron] Jevons, *Introduction to the History of Religions* [London, Methuen, 1896], p.15.

the order is never more than approximate, that it is not exactly the same at different times, and that it has all kinds of exceptions. With even very little experience, we become accustomed to having our expectations unmet; and these setbacks occur too often to seem extraordinary to us. Given a certain element of chance, as well as a certain uniformity in experience, we have no reason to attribute the one to causes and forces different from those to which the other is subject. To have the idea of the supernatural, then, it is not enough for us to witness unexpected events; these events must be conceived of as impossible besides—that is, impossible to reconcile with an order that rightly or wrongly seems to be a necessary part of the order of things. It is the positive sciences that have gradually constructed this notion of a necessary order. It follows that the contrary notion cannot have predated those sciences.

Furthermore, no matter how men have conceived their experience of novelties and chance occurrences, these conceptions can in no way be used to characterize religion. Religious conceptions aim above all to express and explain not what is exceptional and abnormal but what is constant and regular. As a general rule, the gods are used far less to account for monstrosity, oddity, and anomaly than for the normal march of the universe, the movement of the stars, the rhythm of the seasons, the annual growth of vegetation, the perpetuation of species, and so forth. Hence, any notion that equates religion with the unexpected is wide of the mark. Jevons's reply is that this way of conceiving religious forces is not primitive. According to him, people conceived of them first in order to account for disorder and accident, and only later used them to explain the uniformities of nature.[7] But it is unclear what could have made men impute such obviously contradictory functions to them, one after the other. Moreover, the supposition that sacred beings were at first confined to the negative role of disturbers is completely arbitrary. As indeed we will see, starting with the simplest religions we know, the fundamental task of sacred beings has been to maintain the normal course of life by positive action.[8]

Thus the idea of mystery is not at all original. It does not come to man as a given; man himself has forged this idea as well as its contrary. For this reason, it is only in a small number of advanced religions that the idea of mystery has any place at all. Therefore it cannot be made the defining characteristic of religious phenomena without excluding from the definition most of the facts to be defined.

[7]*Ibid.*, p. 23.

[8]See below Bk. III. chap. 2.

II

Another idea by which many have tried to define religion is that of divinity. According to M. Réville,[9] "Religion is the determination of human life by the sense of a bond joining the human mind with the mysterious mind whose domination of the world and of itself it recognizes, and with which it takes pleasure in feeling joined." It is a fact that if the word "divinity" is taken in a precise and narrow sense, this definition leaves aside a multitude of obviously religious facts. The souls of the dead and spirits of all kinds and ranks, with which the religious imaginations of so many diverse peoples have populated the world, are always the objects of rites and sometimes even of regular cults. Strictly speaking, however, they are not gods. Still, all that is necessary to make the definition include them is to replace the word "god" with the more inclusive term "spiritual being."

This is what Tylor has done. "In studying the religions of lower races," he says, "the first point is to define and specify what one means by religion. If one insists that the term means belief in a supreme being . . . , a certain number of tribes will be excluded from the world of religion. But that too-narrow definition has the flaw of identifying religion with certain of its particular developments. . . . It seems better to set 'spiritual beings' as a minimum definition."[10] "Spiritual beings" must be understood to mean conscious subjects that have capacities superior to those of ordinary men, which therefore rightly includes the souls of the dead, genies, and demons as well as deities, properly so-called. It is important to notice immediately the particular idea of religion that this definition entails. The only relations we can have with beings of this sort are determined by the nature ascribed to them. They are conscious beings, and we can only influence them as we influence consciousnesses generally, that is, by psychological means, by trying to convince or rouse them either with words (invocations and prayers) or with offerings and sacrifices. And since the object of religion would then be to order our relations with these special beings, there could be religion only where there are prayers, sacrifices, propitiatory rites, and the like. In this way, we would have a very simple criterion for distinguishing what is religious from what is not. Frazer[11] systematically applies this criterion, as do several ethnographers.[12]

[9][Albert Réville], *Prolégomènes de l'histoire des religions* [Paris, Fischbacher, 1881], p. 34.

[10]Edward Burnett Tylor, *Primitive Culture*, vol. I [London, John Murray, 1873, p. 491].

[11]Starting with the first edition of *The Golden Bough*, vol. I, pp. 30–32. [James Frazer, *The Golden Bough*, 2 vols., London and New York, Macmillan, 1890.]

[12]Including [Sir Baldwin] Spencer and [Francis James] Gillen and even [Konrad Theodor] Preuss, who calls all nonindividualized religious forces magic.

But however obvious this definition may seem, given habits of mind that we owe to our own religious upbringing, there are many facts to which it is not applicable but that nevertheless belong to the domain of religion.

In the first place, there are great religions from which the idea of gods and spirits is absent, or plays only a secondary and inconspicuous role. This is the case in Buddhism. Buddhism, says Burnouf, "takes its place in opposition to Brahmanism as a morality without god and an atheism without Nature."[13] "It recognizes no god on whom man depends," says M. Barth; "its doctrine is absolutely atheist."[14] And M. Oldenberg, for his part, calls it "a religion without god."[15] The entire essence of Buddhism is contained in four propositions that the faithful call the Four Noble Truths.[16] The first states that the existence of suffering is tied to the perpetual change of things; the second finds the cause of suffering in desire; the third makes the suppression of desire the only way to end suffering; the fourth lists the three stages that must be passed through to end suffering—uprightness, meditation, and finally wisdom, full knowledge of the doctrine. The end of the road—deliverance, salvation by Nirvana—is reached after these stages have been passed through.

In none of these principles is there any question of divinity. The Buddhist is not preoccupied with knowing where this world of becoming in which he lives and suffers came from; he accepts it as a fact,[17] and all his striving is to escape it. On the other hand, for this work of salvation he counts only on himself; he "has no god to thank, just as in his struggle he calls upon none to help."[18] Instead of praying—in the usual sense of the word, turning to a superior being to beg for help—he withdraws into himself and meditates. This is not to say "that he denies outright the existence of beings

---

[13][Eugène] Burnouf, *Introduction à l'histoire du bouddhisme indien*, 2d. ed. [Paris, Maisonneuve, 1876], p. 464. The last word of the text means that Buddhism does not even accept the existence of an eternal Nature.

[14]Auguste Barth, *The Religions of India* [translated from French by Rev. J. Wood, London, Houghton Mifflin, 1882], p. 110.

[15][Hermann] Oldenberg, *Le Bouddha* [*Sa vie, sa doctrine, sa communauté*, translated from the German by A. Foucher, Paris, F. Alcan, 1894, p. 51. I could not find an edition Durkheim lists as translated by "Hoey" and giving the page as 53. Trans.].

[16]Ibid. [pp. 214, 318]. Cf. Hendrick Kern, *Histoire du bouddhisme dans l'Inde*, vol. I [Paris, Ernest Leroux, 1901], pp. 389ff.

[17]Oldenberg, *Bouddha*, p. 259 [this passage actually examines the denial of the existence of the soul. Trans.]; Barth, *Religions of India*, p. 110.

[18]Oldenberg, *Bouddha*, p. 314.

named Indra, Agni, or Varuna;[19] but he feels that he owes them nothing and has nothing to do with them," because their power is effective only over the things of this world—and those things, for him, are without value. He is thus atheist in the sense that he is uninterested in whether gods exist. Moreover, even if they exist and no matter what power they may have, the saint, or he who is unfettered by the world, regards himself as superior to them. The stature of beings lies not in the extent of their power over things but in the extent of their progress along the way to salvation.[20]

It is true that, in at least some divisions of the Buddhist church,* the Buddha has come to be regarded as a kind of god. He has his temples and has become the object of a cult. But the cult is very simple, essentially limited to offerings of a few flowers and the veneration of relics or sacred images. It is little more than a commemorative cult. But further, assuming the term to be apposite, this *divinization* of the Buddha is peculiar to what has been called Northern Buddhism. "The Buddhists of the South," says Kern, "and the least advanced among the Buddhists of the North can be said, according to presently available evidence, to speak of the founder of their doctrine as if he were a man."[21] They probably do ascribe to the Buddha extraordinary powers, superior to those ordinary mortals possess; but it is a very old belief in India (and a belief widespread in many different religions) that a great saint is gifted with exceptional virtues.[22] Still, a saint is not a god, any more than a priest or a magician is, despite the superhuman faculties that are often ascribed to them. Besides, according to the best scholarly authority, this sort of theism and the complex mythology that ordinarily goes with it are no more than a derivative and deviant form of Buddhism. At first, the Buddha was not regarded as anything other than "the wisest of men."[23] "The conception of a Buddha who is other than a man who has reached the highest degree of holiness is," says Burnouf, "outside the circle of ideas that are the very founda-

---

*Here, as in the definition of religion (p. 44), Durkheim capitalizes the word "church."

[19]Barth [*Religions of India*], p. 109. "I am deeply convinced," says Burnouf as well, "that if Çâkya had not found around him a Pantheon full of the gods whose names I gave, he would have seen no need whatever to invent it" ([Eugene Bournouf], *Bouddhisme indien*, p. 119).

[20]Burnouf, *Bouddhisme indien*, p. 117.

[21]Kern, *Histoire du bouddhisme*, vol. I, p. 289.

[22]"The belief universally accepted in India that great holiness is necessarily accompanied by supernatural faculties, is the sole support that he (Çâkya) had to find in spirits" (Burnouf, *Bouddhisme indien*, p. 119).

[23]Ibid., p. 120.

tion of even the simple Sutras";[24] and as the same author adds elsewhere, "his humanity has remained a fact so uncontestably acknowledged by all that it did not occur to the myth makers, to whom miracles come very easily, to make a god out of him after his death."[25] Hence, one may ask whether he has ever reached the point of being completely stripped of human character and thus whether it would be proper to liken him to a god;[26] whatever the case is, it would be to a god of a very special nature, and whose role in no way resembles that of other divine personalities. A god is first of all a living being on whom man must count and on whom he can count; now, the Buddha has died, he has entered Nirvana, and he can do nothing more in the course of human events.[27]

Finally, and whatever else one may conclude about the divinity of the Buddha, the fact remains that this conception is wholly extraneous to what is truly fundamental in Buddhism. Buddhism consists first and foremost in the idea of salvation, and salvation only requires one to know and practice the right doctrine. Of course, that doctrine would not have been knowable if the Buddha had not come to reveal it; but once that revelation was made, the Buddha's work was done. From then on, he ceased to be a necessary factor in religious life. The practice of the Four Holy Truths would be possible even if the memory of the one who made them known was erased from memory.[28] Very different from this is Christianity, which is inconceivable without the idea of Christ ever present and his cult ever practiced; for it is through the ever-living Christ, daily sacrificed, that the community of the faithful goes on communicating with the supreme source of its spiritual life.[29]

[24]Ibid., p. 107.

[25]Ibid., p. 302.

[26]Kern makes this point in the following terms: "In certain respects, he is a man; in certain respects, he is not a man; in certain respects, he is neither one nor the other" (*Histoire du bouddhisme* vol. I, p. 290).

[27]"The idea that the divine head of the Community is not absent from among his people, but in reality remains among them as their master and king, in such a way that the cult is nothing other than the expression of the permanence of that common life—this idea is entirely foreign to Buddhists. Their own master is in Nirvana; if his faithful cried out to him he could not hear them" (Oldenberg, *Le Bouddha* [p. 368]).

[28]"In all its basic traits, the Buddhist doctrine could exist, just as it does in reality, even if the idea of Buddha remained wholly foreign to it" (Oldenberg, *Le Bouddha*, p. 322). And what is said of the historical Buddha also applies to all the mythological ones.

[29]See in this connection Max Müller, *Natural Religion* [London, Longmans, Green & Co., 1889], pp. 103ff., 190.

All the preceding applies equally to another great religion of India, Jainism. Additionally, the two doctrines hold practically the same conception of the world and of life. "Like the Buddhists," says M. Barth, "the Jainists are atheists. They reject the idea of a creator; for them, the world is eternal and they explicitly deny that there could exist a being perfect from all eternity." Like the Northern Buddhists, the Jainists, or at least certain of them, have nevertheless reverted to a sort of deism; in the inscriptions of the Deccan, one *Jinapati** is spoken of, a kind of supreme Jina who is called the first creator; but such language, says the same author, "conflicts with the most explicit statements of their most authoritative authors."[30]

Furthermore, this indifference to the divine is so developed in Buddhism and Jainism because the seed existed in the Brahmanism from which both religions derive. In at least certain of its forms, Brahmanic speculation led to "a frankly materialist and atheist explanation of the universe."[31] With the passage of time, the multiple deities that the peoples of India had learned to worship were more or less amalgamated into a kind of abstract and impersonal principal deity, the essence of all that exists. Man contains within himself this supreme reality, in which nothing of divine personhood remains; or rather, he is one with it, since nothing exists apart from it. Thus to find and unite with this reality, he does not have to search for support outside himself; all it takes is for him to focus on himself and meditate. Oldenburg says, "When Buddhism takes up the grand endeavor of imagining a world of salvation in which man saves himself, and of creating a religion without a god, Brahmanic speculation has already prepared the ground. The notion of divinity has gradually receded; the figures of the ancient gods dim, and slowly disappear. Far above the terrestrial world, Brahma sits enthroned in his eternal quiet, and only one person remains to take an active part in the great work of salvation: Man."[32] Note, then, that a considerable part of religious evolution has consisted of a gradual movement away from the ideas of spiritual being and divinity. Here are great religions in which invocations, propitiations, sacrifices, and prayers properly so-called are far from dominant, and therefore do not exhibit the distinguishing mark by which, it is claimed, specifically religious phenomena are to be recognized.

---

*This term means "conquering lord" and, according to current scholarship, refers to a spiritual ideal, not to a creator. I am indebted to my colleague Douglas Brooks on this point.

[30]Barth, *Religions of India*, p. 146.

[31]Barth, ["Religions de l'Inde"] in *Encyclopédie des sciences religieuses* [Paris, Sandoz et Fischbacher, 1877–1882], vol. VI, p. 548.

[32]Oldenberg, *Le Bouddha* [p. 51].

But many rites that are wholly independent of any idea of gods or spiritual beings are found even in deistic religions. First of all, there are a multitude of prohibitions. For example, the Bible commands the woman to live in isolation for a definite period each month,[33] imposes similar isolation at the time of childbirth,[34] and forbids hitching a donkey and a horse together or wearing a garment in which hemp is mixed with linen.[35] It is impossible to see what role belief in Yahweh could have played in these prohibitions, for he is absent from all the relations thus prohibited and could hardly be interested in them. The same can be said for most of the dietary restrictions. Such restrictions are not peculiar to the Hebrews; in various forms, they are found in innumerable religions.

It is true that these rites are purely negative, but they are nonetheless religious. Furthermore, there are other rites that impose active and positive obligations upon the faithful and yet are of the same nature. They act on their own, and their efficacy does not depend upon any divine power; they mechanically bring about the effects that are their reason for being. They consist neither of prayers nor of offerings to a being on whose goodwill the anticipated result depends; instead, the result is achieved through the automatic operation of the ritual. Such is the case, for example, of sacrifice in Vedic religion. "Sacrifice," says M. Bergaigne, "exerts direct influence upon celestial phenomena";[36] it is all powerful by itself and without any divine influence. For instance, it is sacrifice that broke the doors of the cave where the auroras were imprisoned, and thus did daylight erupt into the world.[37] Likewise, it was appropriate hymns that acted directly to make the waters of the sky flow on earth—and *this despite the gods*.[38] Certain ascetic practices are equally efficacious. Consider this: "Sacrifice is so much the principle, par ex-

---

[33]I Sam. 21, 6. [This is in fact about the sexual purity of men. Trans.]

[34]Lev. 12.

[35]Deut. 12, 10–11. [These verses are in fact about establishing a place for God's name to dwell in. They go on to discuss sacrifices. Trans.]

[36]Abel Bergaigne, *La Religion védique* [*d'après les hymnes du Rig Véda*, 4 vols. Paris, F. Vieweg, 1878–1897], vol. I, p. 22.

[37]Ibid., p. 133.

[38]M. Bergaigne writes, "No text better reveals the inner meaning of magical action by man upon the waters of the sky than Verse X, 32, 7, in which that belief is expressed in general terms as applicable to the man of today as to his real or mythological ancestors. The ignorant man queried the savant; taught by the savant, he acts, and therein lies the benefit of his teaching, he conquers the rush of the rapids." Ibid. (p. 137).

cellence, that not only the origin of men but even that of the gods has been ascribed to it. Such an idea may very well seem strange. It is explicable, however, as one ultimate consequence, among others, of the idea that sacrifice is all powerful."[39] Thus, the whole first part of M. Bergaigne's work deals only with those sacrifices in which the deities play no role.

This fact is not peculiar to Vedic religion; to the contrary, it is quite widespread. In any cult, there are practices that act by themselves, by a virtue that is their own, and without any god's stepping in between the individual who performs the rite and the object sought. When the Jew stirred the air at the Feast of the Tabernacles by shaking willow branches in a certain rhythm, it was to make the wind blow and the rain fall; the belief was that the rite produced the desired result automatically, provided it was correctly performed.[40] It is this, by the way, that explains the primary importance that nearly all cults give to the physical aspect of ceremonies. This religious formalism (probably the earliest form of legal formalism) arises from the fact that, having in and of themselves the source of their efficacy, the formulas to be pronounced and the movements to be executed would lose efficacy if they were not exactly the same as those that had already proved successful.

Thus there are rites without gods, and indeed rites from which gods derive. Not all religious virtues emanate from divine personalities, and there are cult ties other than those that unite man with a deity. Thus, religion is broader than the idea of gods or spirits and so cannot be defined exclusively in those terms.

III

With these definitions set aside, let us now see how we can approach the problem.

First, let us note that, in all these formulas, scholars have been trying to express the nature of religion as a whole. Although religion is a whole composed of parts—a more or less complex system of myths, dogmas, rites, and ceremonies—they operate as if it formed a kind of indivisible entity. Since a whole can be defined only in relationship to the parts that comprise it, a better method is to try to characterize the elementary phenomena from which any religion results, and then characterize the system produced by their

---

[39]Ibid., p. 139.

[40]Other examples are to be found in [Henri] Hubert, "Magia," in *Dictionnaire des antiquités*, vol. VI, p. 1509 [Paris, Hachette, 1877–1918].

union. This method is all the more indispensable in view of the fact that there are religious phenomena that do not fall under the jurisdiction of any particular religion. Those that form the subject matter of folklore do not. In general, these phenomena are jumbled survivals, the remnants of extinct religions; but there are some as well that are formed spontaneously under the influence of local causes. In Europe, Christianity undertook to absorb and assimilate them; it imprinted them with Christian coloration. Nonetheless, there are many that have persisted until recently or that still persist more or less autonomously—festivals of the maypole, the summer solstice, carnival, assorted beliefs about genies and local demons, and so on. Although the religious character of these phenomena is receding more and more, their religious importance is still such that they have permitted Mannhardt* and his school to rejuvenate the science of religions. A definition of religion that did not take them into account would not encompass all that is religious.

Religious phenomena fall into two basic categories: beliefs and rites. The first are states of opinion and consist of representations; the second are particular modes of action. Between these two categories of phenomena lies all that separates thinking from doing.

The rites can be distinguished from other human practices—for example, moral practices—only by the special nature of their object. Like a rite, a moral rule prescribes ways of behaving to us, but those ways of behaving address objects of a different kind. It is the object of the rite that must be characterized, in order to characterize the rite itself. The special nature of that object is expressed in the belief. Therefore, only after having defined the belief can we define the rite.

Whether simple or complex, all known religious beliefs display a common feature: They presuppose a classification of the real or ideal things that men conceive of into two classes—two opposite genera—that are widely designated by two distinct terms, which the words *profane* and *sacred* translate fairly well. The division of the world into two domains, one containing all that is sacred and the other all that is profane—such is the distinctive trait of religious thought. Beliefs, myths, dogmas, and legends are either representations or systems of representations that express the nature of sacred things, the virtues and powers attributed to them, their history, and their relationships with one another as well as with profane things. Sacred things are not

*Wilhelm Mannhardt (1831–1880). Influenced by Jakob Grimm and borrowing methods from the new disciplines of geology and archaeology, he pioneered the scientific study of oral tradition in Germany. James G. Frazer's *The Golden Bough* drew on Mannhardt's European material.

simply those personal beings that are called gods or spirits. A rock, a tree, a spring, a pebble, a piece of wood, a house, in a word anything, can be sacred. A rite can have sacredness; indeed there is no rite that does not have it to some degree. There are words, phrases, and formulas that can be said only by consecrated personages; there are gestures and movements that cannot be executed by just anyone. If Vedic sacrifice has had such great efficacy—if, indeed, sacrifice was far from being a method of gaining the gods' favor but, according to mythology, actually generated the gods—that is because the virtue it possessed was comparable to that of the most sacred beings. The circle of sacred objects cannot be fixed once and for all; its scope can vary infinitely from one religion to another. What makes Buddhism a religion is that, in the absence of gods, it accepts the existence of sacred things, namely, the Four Noble Truths and the practices that are derived from them.[41]

But I have confined myself thus far to enumerating various sacred things as examples: I must now indicate the general characteristics by which they are distinguished from profane things.

One might be tempted to define sacred things by the rank that is ordinarily assigned to them in the hierarchy of beings. They tend to be regarded as superior in dignity and power to profane things, and particularly to man, in no way sacred when he is only a man. Indeed, he is portrayed as occupying a rank inferior to and dependent upon them. While that portrayal is certainly not without truth, nothing about it is truly characteristic of the sacred. Subordination of one thing to another is not enough to make one sacred and the other not. Slaves are subordinate to their masters, subjects to their king, soldiers to their leaders, lower classes to ruling classes, the miser to his gold, and the power seeker to the power holders. If a man is sometimes said to have the religion of beings or things in which he recognizes an eminent value and a kind of superiority to him, it is obvious that, in all such cases, the word is taken in a metaphorical sense, and there is nothing in those relations that is religious in a strict sense.[42]

On the other hand, we should bear in mind that there are things with which man feels relatively at ease, even though they are sacred to the highest degree. An amulet has sacredness, and yet there is nothing extraordinary about the respect it inspires. Even face to face with his gods, man is not always in such a marked state of inferiority, for he very often uses physical coercion on them to get what he wants. He beats the fetish when he is

---

[41]Not to mention the sage or the saint who practices these truths, and who is for this reason sacred.

[42]This is not to say that the relations cannot take on a religious character, but that they do not necessarily.

displeased, only to be reconciled with it if, in the end, it becomes more amenable to the wishes of its worshipper.[43] To get rain, stones are thrown into the spring or the sacred lake where the god of the rain is presumed to reside; it is believed that he is forced by this means to come out and show himself.[44] Furthermore, while it is true that man is a dependent of his gods, this dependence is mutual. The gods also need man; without offerings and sacrifices, they would die. I will have occasion to show that this dependence of gods on their faithful is found even in the most idealistic* religions.

However, if the criterion of a purely hierarchical distinction is at once too general and too imprecise, nothing but their heterogeneity is left to define the relation between the sacred and the profane. But what makes this heterogeneity sufficient to characterize that classification of things and to distinguish it from any other is that it has a very particular feature: *It is absolute.* In the history of human thought, there is no other example of two categories of things as profoundly differentiated or as radically opposed to one another. The traditional opposition between good and evil is nothing beside this one: Good and evil are two opposed species of the same genus, namely morals, just as health and illness are nothing more than two different aspects of the same order of facts, life; by contrast, the sacred and the profane are always and everywhere conceived by the human intellect as separate genera, as two worlds with nothing in common. The energies at play in one are not merely those encountered in the other, but raised to a higher degree; they are different in kind. This opposition has been conceived differently in different religions. Here, localizing the two kinds of things in different regions of the physical universe has appeared sufficient to separate them; there, the sacred is thrown into an ideal and transcendent milieu, while the residuum is abandoned as the property of the material world. But while the forms of the contrast are variable,[45] the fact of it is universal.

This is not to say that a being can never pass from one of these worlds to the other. But when this passage occurs, the manner in which it occurs

---

*For the meaning of "idealistic," bear in mind Durkheim's contrast (above, p. 2) between religions that contain more concepts and fewer sensations and images.

[43][Fritz] Schultze, [Der] *Fetichismus* [*Ein Beitrag zur Anthropologie und Religionsgeschichte,* Leipzig, C. Wilfferodt, 1871], p. 129.

[44]Examples of these customs will be found in [James George] Frazer, *Golden Bough,* 2d ed., vol. I [New York, Macmillan, 1894], pp. 81ff.

[45]The conception according to which the profane is opposed to the sacred as the rational is to the irrational; the intelligible to the mysterious, is only one of the forms in which this opposition is expressed. Science, once constituted, has taken on a profane character, especially in the eyes of the Christian religions; in consequence, it has seemed that science could not be applied to sacred things.

demonstrates the fundamental duality of the two realms, for it implies a true metamorphosis. Rites of initiation, which are practiced by a great many peoples, demonstrate this especially well. Initiation is a long series of rites to introduce the young man into religious life. For the first time, he comes out of the purely profane world, where he has passed his childhood, and enters into the circle of sacred things. This change of status is conceived not as a mere development of preexisting seeds but as a transformation *totius substantiae.* * At that moment, the young man is said to die, and the existence of the particular person he was, to cease—instantaneously to be replaced by another. He is born again in a new form. Appropriate ceremonies are held to bring about the death and the rebirth, which are taken not merely in a symbolic sense but literally.[46] Is this not proof that there is a rupture between the profane being that he was and the religious being that he becomes?

Indeed, this heterogeneity is such that it degenerates into real antagonism. The two worlds are conceived of not only as separate but also as hostile and jealous rivals. Since the condition of belonging fully to one is fully to have left the other, man is exhorted to retire completely from the profane in order to live an exclusively religious life. From thence comes monasticism, which artificially organizes a milieu that is apart from, outside of, and closed to the natural milieu where ordinary men live a secular life, and that tends almost to be its antagonist. From thence as well comes mystic asceticism, which seeks to uproot all that may remain of man's attachment to the world. Finally, from thence come all forms of religious suicide, the crowning logical step of this asceticism, since the only means of escaping profane life fully and finally is escaping life altogether.

The opposition of these two genera is expressed outwardly by a visible sign that permits ready recognition of this very special classification, wherever it exists. The mind experiences deep repugnance about mingling, even simple contact, between the corresponding things, because the notion of the sacred is always and everywhere separate from the notion of the profane in man's mind, and because we imagine a kind of logical void between them. The state of dissociation in which the ideas are found in consciousness is too strongly contradicted by such mingling, or even by their being too close to

---

*Of the whole essence.

[46]See James George Frazer, "On Some Ceremonies of the Central Australian Tribes," in *AAAS* [Melbourne, Victoria, published by the association], 1901 [vols. VIII–IX], pp. 313ff. The concept is, moreover, very common. In India, mere participation in the sacrificial act has the same effects; the sacrificer, by the very fact of entering into the circle of sacred things, changes personality. (See Henri Hubert and Marcel Mauss, "Essai sur [la nature et fonction du] sacrifice," *AS*, vol. II [1897], p. 101.)

one another. The sacred thing is, par excellence, that which the profane must not and cannot touch with impunity. To be sure, this prohibition cannot go so far as to make all communication between the two worlds impossible, for if the profane could in no way enter into relations with the sacred, the sacred would be of no use. This placing in relationship in itself is always a delicate operation that requires precautions and a more or less complex initiation.[47] Yet such an operation is impossible if the profane does not lose its specific traits, and if it does not become sacred itself in some measure and to some degree. The two genera cannot, at the same time, both come close to one another and remain what they were.

Now we have a first criterion of religious beliefs. No doubt, within these two fundamental genera, there are secondary species that are themselves more or less incompatible with each other.[48] But characteristically, the religious phenomenon is such that it always assumes a bipartite division of the universe, known and knowable, into two genera that include all that exists but radically exclude one another. Sacred things are things protected and isolated by prohibitions; profane things are those things to which the prohibitions are applied and that must keep at a distance from what is sacred. Religious beliefs are those representations that express the nature of sacred things and the relations they have with other sacred things or with profane things. Finally, rites are rules of conduct that prescribe how man must conduct himself with sacred things.

When a certain number of sacred things have relations of coordination and subordination with one another, so as to form a system that has a certain coherence and does not belong to any other system of the same sort, then the beliefs and rites, taken together, constitute a religion. By this definition, a religion is not necessarily contained within a single idea and does not derive from a single principle that may vary with the circumstances it deals with, while remaining basically the same everywhere. Instead, it is a whole formed of separate and relatively distinct parts. Each homogeneous group of sacred things, or indeed each sacred thing of any importance, constitutes an organizational center around which gravitates a set of beliefs and rites, a cult of its own. There is no religion, however unified it may be, that does not acknowledge a plurality of sacred things. Even Christianity, at least in its Catholic form, accepts the Virgin, the angels, the saints, the souls of the dead, etc.—

---

[47]See what I say about initiation on p. 37, above.

[48]Later I will show how, for example, certain species of sacred things between which there is incompatibility exclude one another as the sacred excludes the profane (Bk.III, chap.5, §4).

above and beyond the divine personality (who, besides, is both three and one). As a rule, furthermore, religion is not merely a single cult either but is made up of a system of cults that possess a certain autonomy. This autonomy is also variable. Sometimes the cults are ranked and subordinated to some dominant cult into which they are eventually absorbed; but sometimes as well they simply exist side by side in confederation. The religion to be studied in this book will provide an example of this confederate organization.

At the same time, we can explain why groups of religious phenomena that belong to no constituted religion can exist: because they are not or are no longer integrated into a religious system. If, for specific reasons, one of those cults just mentioned should manage to survive while the whole to which it belonged has disappeared, it will survive only in fragments. This is what has happened to so many agrarian cults that live on in folklore. In certain cases, what persists in that form is not even a cult, but a mere ceremony or a particular rite.[49]

Although this definition is merely preliminary, it indicates the terms in which the problem that dominates the science of religions must be posed. If sacred beings are believed to be distinguished from the others solely by the greater intensity of the powers attributed to them, the question of how men could have imagined them is rather simple: Nothing more is needed than to identify those forces that, through their exceptional energy, have managed to impress the human mind forcefully enough to inspire religious feelings. But if, as I have tried to establish, sacred things are different in nature from profane things, if they are different in their essence, the problem is far more complex. In that case, one must ask what led man to see the world as two heterogeneous and incomparable worlds, even though nothing in sense experience seems likely to have suggested the idea of such a radical duality.

IV

Even so, this definition is not yet complete, for it fits equally well two orders of things that must be distinguished even though they are akin: magic and religion.

Magic, too, is made up of beliefs and rites. Like religion, it has its own myths and dogmas, but these are less well developed, probably because, given its pursuit of technical and utilitarian ends, magic does not waste time in pure speculation. Magic also has its ceremonies, sacrifices, purifications, prayers,

---

[49]This is the case, for example, of certain marriage and funeral rites.

songs, and dances. Those beings whom the magician invokes and the forces he puts to work are not only of the same nature as the forces addressed by religion but very often are the same forces. In the most primitive societies, the souls of the dead are in essence sacred things and objects of religious rites, but at the same time, they have played a major role in magic. In Australia[50] as well as in Melanesia,[51] in ancient Greece as well as among Christian peoples,[52] the souls, bones, and hair of the dead figure among the tools most often used by the magician. Demons are also a common instrument of magical influence. Now, demons are also surrounded by prohibitions; they too are separated and live in a world apart. Indeed, it is often difficult to distinguish them from gods proper.[53] Besides, even in Christianity, is not the devil a fallen god? And apart from his origins, does he not have a religious character, simply because the hell of which he is the keeper is an indispensable part in the machinery of the Christian religion? The magician can invoke regular and official deities. Sometimes these are gods of a foreign people: For example, the Greek magicians called upon Egyptian, Assyrian, or Jewish gods. Sometimes they are even national gods: Hecate and Diana were objects of a magic cult. The Virgin, the Christ, and the saints were used in the same manner by Christian magicians.[54]

Must we therefore say that magic cannot be rigorously differentiated from religion—that magic is full of religion and religion full of magic and, consequently, that it is impossible to separate them and define the one without the other? What makes that thesis hard to sustain is the marked repugnance of religion for magic and the hostility of magic to religion in return. Magic takes a kind of professional pleasure in profaning holy things,[55] inverting religious ceremonies in its rites.[56] On the other hand, while religion has not always condemned and prohibited magic rites, it has generally re-

[50]See [Sir Baldwin] Spencer and [Francis James] Gillen, *The Native Tribes of Central Australia* [London, Macmillan, 1889], pp. 534ff., and *Northern Tribes of Central Australia* [London, Macmillan, 1904], p. 463; [Alfred William] Howitt, *Native Tribes of South East Australia* [London, Macmillan, 1904], pp. 359–361.

[51]See [Robert Henry] Codrington, *The Melanesians* [*Studies in Their Anthropology and Folklore*, Oxford, Clarendon Press, 1891], chap. 12.

[52]See Hubert, "Magia," in *Dictionnaire des antiquités*.

[53]For example, in Melanesia the *tindalo* is a spirit that is sometimes religious and sometimes magical (Codrington, *The Melanesians*, pp. 125ff., 194ff.).

[54]See Hubert and Mauss, "Esquisse d'une théorie générale de la magie," *AS*, vol. VII [1904], pp. 83–84.

[55]For example, the Host is profaned in the Black Mass.

[56]See Hubert, "Magia," in *Dictionnaire des antiquités*.

garded them with disfavor. As messieurs Hubert and Mauss point out, there is something inherently antireligious about the maneuvers of the magician.[57] So it is difficult for these two institutions not to oppose one another at some point, whatever the relations between them. Since my intention is to limit my research to religion and stop where magic begins, discovering what distinguishes them is all the more important.

Here is how a line of demarcation can be drawn between these two domains.

Religious beliefs proper are always shared by a definite group that professes them and that practices the corresponding rites. Not only are they individually accepted by all members of that group, but they also belong to the group and unify it. The individuals who comprise the group feel joined to one another by the fact of common faith. A society whose members are united because they imagine the sacred world and its relations with the profane world in the same way, and because they translate this common representation into identical practices, is what is called a Church.* In history we do not find religion without Church. Sometimes the Church is narrowly national; sometimes it extends beyond frontiers; sometimes it encompasses an entire people (Rome, Athens, the Hebrews); sometimes it encompasses only a fraction (Christian denominations since the coming of Protestantism); sometimes it is led by a body of priests; sometimes it is more or less without any official directing body.[58] But wherever we observe religious life, it has a definite group as its basis. Even so-called private cults, like the domestic cult or a corporate cult, satisfy this condition: They are always celebrated by a group, the family or the corporation. And, furthermore, even these private religions often are merely special forms of a broader religion that embraces the totality of life.[59] These small Churches are in reality only chapels in a larger Church and, because of this very scope, deserve all the more to be called by that name.[60]

---

*Durkheim capitalizes this term.

[57]Hubert and Mauss, "Esquisse," p. 19.

[58]Certainly it is rare for each ceremony not to have its director at the moment it is conducted; even in the most crudely organized societies, there generally are men designated, due to the importance of their social role, to exercise a directive influence upon religious life (for example, the heads of local groups in certain Australian societies). But this attribution of functions is nevertheless very loose.

[59]In Athens, the gods addressed by the domestic cult are only specialized forms of the gods of the City (Ζεὺς κτήσιος, Ζεὺς ἑρκεῖος). [Zeus, protector of property, Zeus, the household god. Trans.] Similarly, in the Middle Ages, the patrons of brotherhoods are saints of the calendar.

[60]For the name of Church ordinarily applies only to a group whose common beliefs refer to a sphere of less specialized things.

Magic is an entirely different matter. Granted, magic beliefs are never without a certain currency. They are often widespread among broad strata of the population, and there are even peoples where they count no fewer active followers than religion proper. But they do not bind men who believe in them to one another and unite them into the same group, living the same life. *There is no Church of magic*. Between the magician and the individuals who consult him, there are no durable ties that make them members of a single moral body, comparable to the ties that join the faithful of the same god or the adherents of the same cult. The magician has a clientele, not a Church, and his clients may have no mutual relations, and may even be unknown to one another. Indeed, the relations they have with him are generally accidental and transient, analogous to those of a sick man with his doctor. The official and public character with which the magician is sometimes invested makes no difference. That he functions in broad daylight does not join him in a more regular and lasting manner with those who make use of his services.

It is true that, in certain cases, magicians form a society among themselves. They meet more or less periodically to celebrate certain rites in common in some instances; the place held by witches' meetings in European folklore is well known. But these associations are not at all indispensable for the functioning of magic. Indeed, they are rare and rather exceptional. To practice his art, the magician has no need whatever to congregate with his peers. He is more often a loner. In general, far from seeking company, he flees it. "He stands aloof, even from his colleagues."[61] By contrast, religion is inseparable from the idea of Church. In this first regard, there is already a fundamental difference between magic and religion. Furthermore, and above all, when magic societies of this sort are formed, they never encompass all the adherents of magic. Far from it. They encompass only the magicians. Excluded from them are the laity, as it were—that is, those for whose benefit the rites are conducted, which is to say those who are the adherents of regular cults. Now, the magician is to magic what the priest is to religion. But a college of priests is no more a religion than a religious congregation that worships a certain saint in the shadows of the cloister is a private cult. A Church is not simply a priestly brotherhood; it is a moral community* made up of all the faithful, both laity and priests. Magic ordinarily has no community of this sort.[62]

---

*Note the first use in this book of this fundamentally important Durkheimian concept which can also be thought of as "imagined community." See pp. xxii–xxxiii, xiv.

[61]Hubert and Mauss, "Esquisse," p. 18.

[62][William] Robertson Smith had already shown that magic is opposed to religion as the individual is to the social ([*Lectures on*] *the Religion of the Semites*, 2d ed. [London, A. & C. Black, 1894], pp. 264–265).

But if one includes the notion of Church in the definition of religion, does one not by the same stroke exclude the individual religions that the individual institutes for himself and celebrates for himself alone? There is scarcely any society in which this is not to be found. As will be seen below, every Ojibway has his personal *manitou* that he chooses himself and to which he bears specific religious obligations; the Melanesian of the Banks Islands has his *tamaniu*;[63] the Roman has his *genius*;[64] the Christian has his patron saint and his guardian angel, and so forth. All these cults seem, by definition, to be independent of the group. And not only are these individual religions very common throughout history, but some people today pose the question whether such religions are not destined to become the dominant form of religious life—whether a day will not come when the only cult will be the one that each person freely practices in his innermost self.[65]

But, let us put aside these speculations about the future for a moment. If we confine our discussion to religions as they are in the present and as they have been in the past, it becomes obvious that these individual cults are not distinct and autonomous religious systems but simply aspects of the religion common to the whole Church of which the individuals are part. The patron saint of the Christian is chosen from the official list of saints recognized by the Catholic Church, and there are canonical laws that prescribe how each believer must conduct this private cult. In the same way, the idea that every man necessarily has a protective genie is, in different forms, at the basis of a large number of American religions, as well as of Roman religion (to cite only these two examples). As will be seen below, that idea is tightly bound up with the idea of soul, and the idea of soul is not among those things that can be left entirely to individual choice. In a word, it is the Church of which he is a member that teaches the individual what these personal gods are, what their role is, how he must enter into relations with them, and how he must honor them. When one analyzes the doctrines of that Church systematically, sooner or later one comes across the doctrines that concern these special cults. Thus there are not two religions of different types, turned in opposite

---

Further, in thus differentiating magic from religion, I do not mean to set up a radical discontinuity between them. The frontiers between these two domains are often blurred.

[63][Robert Henry] Codrington, "Notes on the Customs of Mota, Bank Islands in *RSV,* vol. XVI [1880], p. 136.

[64][Augusto] Negrioli, *Dei Genii presso i Romani,* [Bologna, Ditto Nicola Zanichelli, 1900].

[65]This is the conclusion at which [Herbert] Spencer arrives in his *Ecclesiastical Institutions* [Part VI of *The Principles of Sociology,* New York, D. Appleton, 1886], chap. 16. It is also the conclusion of [Auguste] Sabatier, in his *Esquisse d'une philosophie de la religion d'après la Psychologie et l'Histoire,* [Paris, Fischbacher, 1897], and that of the entire school to which he belongs.

directions, but the same ideas and principles applied in both cases—here, to circumstances that concern the group as a whole, and there, to the life of the individual. Indeed, this unity is so close that, among certain peoples,[66] the ceremonies during which the believer first enters into communication with his protective genie are combined with rites whose public character is incontestable, namely, rites of initiation.[67]

What remains are the present-day aspirations toward a religion that would consist entirely of interior and subjective states and be freely constructed by each one of us. But no matter how real those aspirations, they cannot affect our definition: This definition can be applied only to real, accomplished facts, not to uncertain possibilities. Religions can be defined as they are now or as they have been, not as they may be tending more or less vaguely to become. It is possible that this religious individualism is destined to become fact; but to be able to say in what measure, we must first know what religion is, of what elements it is made, from what causes it results, and what function it performs—all questions whose answers cannot be preordained, for we have not crossed the threshold of research. Only at the end of this study will I try to look into the future.

We arrive thus at the following definition: *A religion is a unified system of beliefs and practices relative to sacred things, that is to say, things set apart and forbidden—beliefs and practices which unite into one single moral community called a Church, all those who adhere to them.* The second element thus holds a place in my definition that is no less essential than the first: In showing that the idea of religion is inseparable from the idea of a Church, it conveys the notion that religion must be an eminently collective thing.[68]

---

[66]Among numerous Indian peoples of North America, in particular.

[67]However, that factual point does not settle the question of whether external and public religion is anything other than the development of an interior and personal religion that would be the primitive phenomenon, or whether, on the other hand, the personal religion is the extension, inside individual consciousnesses, of the exterior one. The problem will be taken up directly below (Bk. II, chap. 5, §2. Cf. Bk. II, chap. 6 and Bk. II, chap. 7, §1). For now I merely note that the individual cult presents itself to the observer as an element and an appendage of the collective cult.

[68]It is there that my definition picks up the one I proposed some time ago in the *Année sociologique.* In that work, I defined religious beliefs exclusively by their obligatory character; but that obligation evidently arises, as I showed, from the fact that those beliefs belong to a group that imposes them on its members. Thus the two definitions partly overlap. If I have thought it necessary to propose a new one, it is because the first was too formal and went too far in downplaying the content of religious representations. In the discussions that follow, we will see the point of having placed in evidence immediately what is characteristic of this content. In addition, if the imperative character is indeed a distinctive feature of religious beliefs, it has infinite gradations; consequently, it is not easily perceptible in some cases. There arise difficulties and troublesome questions that are avoided if this criterion is replaced by the one I have used above.

CHAPTER TWO

THE LEADING CONCEPTIONS OF THE ELEMENTARY RELIGION

I. Animism

With this definition in hand, we can set out in search of the elementary religion, our intended goal.

Even the crudest religions that history and ethnography make known to us are already so complex that they do not fit the notion people sometimes have of primitive mentality. They display not only a luxuriant system of beliefs but such variety in principles and wealth in basic ideas that it has seemed impossible to regard them as anything but a late product of a rather long evolution. From this scholars have concluded that in order to uncover the truly original form of religious life, they had to delve beneath these observable religions, analyze them to identify the basic elements they share, and find out whether there is one such element from which the others are derived.

Set in those terms, the problem has received two contrary solutions.

It can be said that there is no religious system, old or new, in which we do not find what amounts to two religions existing side by side and in various forms. Although closely allied and even interpenetrating, yet they remain distinct. One is addressed to phenomena in nature—whether great cosmic forces, such as the winds, the rivers, the stars, the sky, etc., or the objects of all sorts that populate the earth's surface, such as plants, animals, rocks, etc. For this reason, it is given the name "naturism." The other is addressed to spiritual beings—spirits, souls, genies, demons, deities proper. These beings are animate and conscious agents, like man, but differ from man in the nature of the powers ascribed to them, in particular the special characteristic that they do not affect the senses in the same way; they are not usually perceptible to human eyes. This religion of spirits is called "animism." Two incompatible theories have been put forward to explain the more or less

universal coexistence of the two sorts of cult. Some hold animism to have
been the primary religion, and naturism only a derivative and secondary
form. Others hold that the cult of nature was the starting point of religious
evolution, and the cult of spirits only a special case of it.

Up to now, these two theories have been the only ones by which people
have tried to explain the origins of religious thought rationally.[1] Thus, the
chief problem that the science of religions most often sets itself comes down
to deciding which of these two solutions must be adopted, or whether it is
not better to combine them and, if so, what place should be assigned to each
of the two elements.[2] Even those scholars who accept neither hypothesis in
its entirety still retain some of the propositions on which they rest.[3] Thus we
have a certain number of ready-made ideas and seeming truisms that must be
subjected to critique before we take up the study of the facts on our own account. How indispensable it is to try a new approach will be clearer once the
inadequacy of these traditional notions is understood.

I

Tylor developed the animist theory in its essential features.[4] It is true that
Spencer, who thereafter took it up, did not merely copy it without modification.[5] But, on the whole, both Tylor and Spencer pose the questions in the
same terms, and, with one exception, the solutions adopted are identical. I

---

[1]Thus I leave aside here the theories that, wholly or in part, involve supraexperimental data. This is
true, for example, of the theory Andrew Lang set forth in his book *The Making of Religion* [London, Longmans, 1898], and that Wilhelm Schmidt took up again, with variations of detail, in a series of articles on
"L'Origine de l'idée de Dieu" (in *Anthropos* [vols. III, IV], 1908, 1909). Lang does not wholly reject either animism or naturism but accepts that, in the last analysis, there is a sense or a direct intuition of the
divine. Also, while I do not believe I must present and discuss that idea in this chapter, I do not intend to
pass over it in silence, but will return to it below, when I explain the facts to which it is applied (II.9,
p. 4).

[2]This is the case, for example, of Fustel de Coulanges, who accepts the two ideas concurrently (see
Bk. I and Bk. III, chap. 2 [of *La Cité antique*, Paris, Hachette, 1870] .

[3]In this way, Jevons, while criticizing animism as set forth by Tylor, accepts his theories on the genesis of the idea of soul and the anthropomorphic instinct of man. Inversely, while [Hermann Karl] Usener,
in his *Gotternämen* [*Versuch einer Lehre von der religiosen Degengriffebildung*, Bohn, F. Cohen, 1887], rejects
certain of hypotheses of Max Müller to be presented below, he accepts the chief postulates of naturism.

[4][Edward Burnett] Tylor, *Primitive Culture* [2 vols., London, J. Murray, 1871], chaps. 11, 18.

[5]See [Herbert Spencer], *Principles of Sociology*, 1st and 6th parts [New York, D. Appleton, 1886].

can therefore combine the two doctrines in the following exposition, noting the point at which they part company.

Three conditions must be met if animist beliefs and practices are legitimately to be seen as the original form of religious life: First, because on that hypothesis the idea of soul is the cardinal idea of religion, one must show how it was formed, without taking any of its elements from an earlier religion; second, it must be shown how souls became the object of a cult and turned into spirits; third, since the cult of spirits is not the whole of any religion, how the cult of nature was derived from that cult must also be explained.

According to animist theory, the idea of soul was suggested to man by the poorly understood spectacle of the double life that he normally leads, on the one hand while awake, on the other while asleep. The claim is that, for the savage,[6] the representations he has in his mind are of the same significance whether he is awake or dreaming. He objectifies both; that is, he sees them as the images of external objects, the entire appearance of which they reproduce more or less accurately. Thus, when he dreams of having visited a far-off country, he believes he really has gone there. But he can have gone there only if two beings exist in him: one, his body, which remained stretched out on the ground and which, when he awakens, he finds still in the same position; and another, which has moved through space during that same time. Likewise, if while he sleeps, he sees himself talking with one of his friends who he knows is far away, he concludes that this friend, too, is composed of two beings: one who is sleeping some distance away, and another who has manifested himself through the dream. From the repetition of such experiences, little by little the idea emerges that a double, another self, exists in each of us, and that in particular conditions it has the power to leave the body in which it lives and to travel far and wide.

Of course, this double replicates all the basic features of the visible being that serves as its external envelope. At the same time, however, it differs from the visible being in several respects. It is more mobile, since it can cover vast distances in an instant. It is more malleable and more plastic; for, to leave the body, it must be able to pass through the body's openings, especially the nose and mouth. It is conceived of as somehow made of matter, but of a much more subtle and ethereal matter than any we know empirically. This double

---

[6]This is the word Tylor [*Primitive Culture*, pp. 489ff.] uses. It has the drawback of seeming to imply that human beings, in the full sense of the term, exist before civilization exists. However, there is no suitable term to render the idea; the term "primitive," which I prefer to use for want of anything better, is, as I have said, far from satisfactory.

is the soul. And it is beyond doubt that, in many societies, the soul has been thought of as an image of the body. It is even thought to reproduce accidental deformities, such as those caused by wounds or mutilations. Certain Australians cut off their enemy's right thumb after killing him, so that his soul, having been relieved of its own thumb by the same stroke, cannot throw a spear and avenge itself. But at the same time, even though it resembles the body, there is something already semi-spiritual about it. People say that "it is the most insubstantial part of the body, as light as air," that "it has neither flesh, nor bones, nor nerves"; that it is "like a purified body."[7]

In addition, other facts of experience that turned minds onto the same path quite naturally tended to gather around this fundamental fact of the dream: fainting, apoplexy, catalepsy, ecstasy—every state of temporary unconsciousness. Actually, they are explained very well by the hypothesis that the principle of life and awareness can momentarily leave the body. Besides, it was natural that this principle should have been merged with the double, since each day the absence of the double during sleep suspends life and thought. Thus various observations seemed mutually to test and confirm the idea of the built-in duality of man.[8]

But the soul is not a spirit. It is attached to a body from which it exits quite rarely; and, so long as it is nothing more, it is the object of no cult. By contrast, although the spirit generally has a definite thing as its residence, it can move away at will, and man can enter into relations with it only by taking ritual precautions. The soul could become spirit, then, only if it transformed itself. This metamorphosis was quite easily arrived at, merely by the application of the foregoing ideas to the reality of death. To a rudimentary intellect, death is not much different from a long fainting spell or a prolonged sleep; it has all their traits. Thus, death also seems to consist in a separation of soul and body, analogous to the separation that occurs each night; but because they do not see the body to revive, they come to accept the idea of a separation that is not limited to a specified period. Indeed, once the body is destroyed—and the object of funeral is in part to hasten this destruction—the separation is of necessity considered final. Here, then, are spirits detached from any body and at liberty in space. In this way a population of souls is formed all around the living, their number growing over time. Because these souls of men have the needs and passions of men, they seek to involve them-

---

[7]Ibid., vol. I, pp. 455ff.

[8]See Spencer, *Principles of Sociology*, vol. I, pp. 143ff.; and Tylor, *Primitive Culture*, vol. I, pp. 434ff., 445ff.

selves in the lives of their former companions and to help the living or harm them, depending on the feelings they still have for them. Their nature makes them either very precious allies or very formidable enemies. Thanks to their extreme fluidity, they can go inside bodies and cause them disorders of all kinds, or they can increase the bodies' vitality. And so people take up the habit of ascribing to them all the events of life that are slightly unusual: There are hardly any they cannot account for. In this way they constitute a veritable arsenal of causes, always at hand, never leaving the mind that is in search of explanations unequipped. Does a man seem inspired; does he speak with eloquence; does he seem lifted above both himself and the ordinary level of men? It is because a benevolent spirit is in him, animating him. Is another man taken by a seizure or by madness? An evil spirit has entered his body, agitating him. There is no sickness that cannot be put down to some such influence. In this way, the power of souls increases from all that is attributed to them, so much so that, in the end, man finds himself a captive in this imaginary world, even though he is its creator and model. He becomes the vassal of those spiritual forces that he has made with his own hands and in his own image. For if these souls are so much in control of health and illness and of good and evil things, it is wise to seek their benevolence or to appease them when they are annoyed. From thence come offerings, sacrifices, prayers—in short, the whole apparatus of religious observances.[9]

Behold, then, the soul transformed. It has gone from being merely a life principle animating a human body, to being a spirit, a good or evil genie, and even a deity, depending on the scope of the effects imputed to it. But since it is death that is presumed to have brought about this apotheosis, in the end it is to the dead, to the souls of the ancestors, that the first cult that humanity has known was addressed. Thus: The first rites were mortuary rites; the first sacrifices, food offerings to satisfy the needs of the departed; and the first altars, tombs.[10]

But because these spirits were of human origin, they were interested only in the lives of men and were thought to act only upon human events. Yet to be explained is how other spirits were imagined in order to account for other phenomena of the universe, and how a cult of nature was then formed alongside the cult of the ancestors.

As Tylor has it, this extension of animism is due to the peculiar mentality of the primitive, who, like the child, does not distinguish the animate

---

[9]Tylor, *Primitive Culture*, vol. II [pp. 113ff.].

[10]Ibid., vol. I [pp. 113ff., 481ff.].

from the inanimate. Because the first beings of which the child begins to form any idea are humans—himself and his parents—he tends to imagine all things on the model of human nature. He sees the toys he uses, and the various objects that affect his senses, as living beings like himself. The primitive thinks like a child, so he too is inclined to endow things, even inanimate things, with a nature similar to his own. And thus, for the reasons already given, once he has arrived at the idea that man is a body that a spirit animates, then he must of necessity impute to natural bodies that same sort of duality, plus souls like his own. The sphere of influence could not be the same for both, however. The souls of men have direct influence only over the world of men. They have a sort of predilection for the human body, once death has given them their liberty. On the other hand, the souls of things reside above all in things and are viewed as the operative causes of all that happens to things. Health or illness, agility or clumsiness, and the rest, are accounted for by the souls of men; the phenomena of the physical world above all—the movement of the waters or of the stars, the germination of the plants, the abundant reproduction of the animals, and the rest—are accounted for by the souls of things. Thus, the finishing touch to that first philosophy of man, on which the cult of the ancestors is based, was a philosophy of the world.

Vis-à-vis those cosmic spirits, man found himself in an even more obvious state of dependence than vis-à-vis the wandering doubles of his ancestors. With the ancestors, he could only have ideal* and imaginary relations, but he really does depend upon things. Since he needs their cooperation in order to live, man came to believe that he also needed the spirits that were held to animate those things and control their various manifestations. He implored their help through offerings and prayers. Thus, the finishing touch to the religion of man was a religion of nature.

Herbert Spencer objects that this explanation rests on a hypothesis that is contradicted by the facts. It is held, he says, that there was a time when man did not grasp the differences between the animate and the inanimate. But as we ascend among the animals, we see an increasing capacity to make that distinction. The higher animals do not confuse an object that moves by itself, whose movements are directed toward goals, with objects that are moved mechanically from outside. "When a cat who is playing with a mouse he has caught sees that it stays still for a long while, he touches it with his claw to make it run. Obviously, the cat thinks that a living being that one bothers will try to escape."[11] Man, even primitive man, could not be less intelligent than

---

*Note Durkheim's use of this term in reference to things of the mind.

[11]Spencer, *Principles of Sociology*, vol. I [p.126].

animals lower than he on the scale of evolution. It was not through lack of discernment, then, that he moved from the cult of ancestors to the cult of things.

According to Spencer, who on this point (but on this point only) parts company with Tylor, this passage is indeed due to a confusion, but one of a different kind. He thinks it results, at least in the main, from the numberless ambiguities of language. In many lower societies, it is a very common custom to give each individual the name of an animal, plant, star, or some other natural object, either at birth or later. But, given the extreme imprecision of his language, it is very difficult for the primitive to distinguish a metaphor from reality. Thus he would quickly have lost sight of the fact that these names were only figures of speech and, by taking them literally, ended up believing that an ancestor called Tiger or Lion was actually a tiger or a lion. And so, the cult of which that ancestor had been the object theretofore, would have been transposed thereafter to the animal with which the ancestor had become one and the same. And, the same substitution being operative for the plants, stars, together with all the natural phenomena, the religion of nature took the place of the old religion of the dead. To be sure, Spencer points to other confusions besides this one, reinforcing its effect in this case or that. For example, as he proposes, the animals that frequent the environs of the tombs or houses of men were taken for reincarnated souls and revered as such;[12] or else, the mountain held by tradition to be the site where the race began was taken to be its actual founder; the ancestors being presumed to have come from it, and the men to be its descendants, the mountain itself was therefore treated as an ancestor.[13] But as Spencer admits, these additional causes could have had only a secondary influence. Principally, what led to the institution of naturism was "the literal interpretation of metaphorical names."[14]

For the sake of completeness in my own exposition of animism, I had to give an account of this theory, but it is too inadequate to the facts, and today too universally abandoned, to warrant being dwelled upon further. For a phenomenon as widespread as the religion of nature to be explainable by an illusion, the cause of the very illusion that is invoked would have to be equally widespread. Even when such errors as those of which Spencer reports a few isolated examples (where we find such examples) can indeed explain the transformation of the cult of ancestors into a cult of nature, it is not

[12]Ibid., pp. 322ff.

[13]Ibid., pp. 366–367.

[14]Ibid., p. 346. Cf. p. 384.

clear why they would be so widely produced. No psychic mechanism necessitates them. No doubt, through their own ambiguity, words could lead people to be mistaken; but, at the same time, all the personal memories that the ancestor left in men's memories must have worked against the confusion. Why would the tradition that portrayed the ancestor as he had been—that is, as a man who had lived a man's life—have given way everywhere to the magic of words. Besides, people must have had a certain difficulty accepting the idea that men could have been born from a mountain or a star, an animal or a plant; the idea of such an exception to the ordinary conditions of procreation was bound to raise strong resistance. In this way, far from finding the way made straight, this error would have been impeded by all sorts of reasons defending minds against it. Therefore how its victory could have been so general, despite so many obstacles, is not clear.

II

There remains the theory of Tylor, which still has great authority. Since his hypotheses on dreams and on how the ideas of soul and spirit originated are still authoritative, it is important to evaluate them.

To begin, it must be acknowledged that the theorists of animism have rendered an important service to the science of religions, and indeed to the general history of ideas, by applying historical analysis to the idea of soul. Instead of taking it to be a simple and immediate given of consciousness, as so many philosophers have, they saw it—far more correctly—as a complex whole and as a product of history and mythology. It is beyond doubt that, by its nature, origins, and functions, the idea of soul is fundamentally religious. Philosophers received it from religion; and the form it takes among the thinkers of antiquity cannot be understood unless the mythical elements that entered into it are taken into account.

But even though setting the problem is to Tylor's credit, his solution nonetheless raises serious difficulties.

First, there are reservations to be had about the very principle on which his theory is based. It grants as self-evident that the soul is altogether distinct from the body, that it is the body's double, and that, whether inside or outside the body, it ordinarily lives its own autonomous life. Now, we will see[15] that this conception is not that of the primitive or, at least, that it expresses

[15]See below, Bk. II, chap. 8.

only one aspect of the idea he has of the soul. To the primitive, although the soul is in certain respects independent of the body it animates, nevertheless it is partly merged with the body, so much so that it cannot be radically separated from the body: Certain organs are not only the special seat of the soul but also its outward form and physical manifestation. The notion is more complex than the doctrine assumes, then, and so it is doubtful that the experiences invoked are sufficient explanation. For even if those experiences enabled one to understand how man came to believe he was double, they could not explain why that duality not only does not exclude, but actually entails, a profound unity and an intimate interpenetration of the two beings thus differentiated.

However, let us grant that the idea of soul is reducible to the idea of double and see how, according to Tylor, that second idea was formed. Supposedly the experience of dreaming suggested it to man. To understand how, as his body remained lying on the ground, he could see more or less distant places as he slept, he is led to think of himself as being made of two beings: on the one hand, his body, and, on the other, a second self able to leave the body in which it lives and move about in space. But, on the face of it, to have been able to thrust itself upon men with a kind of necessity, this idea would have to have been the only possible hypothesis, or at least the simplest. Now, in fact, there are simpler hypotheses, ideas that, it seems, must have come to mind just as naturally. For example, why would the sleeper not have imagined that he was able to see at a distance as he slept? Imputing such a capacity to himself would have taxed his imagination less than constructing such a complicated idea as that of a double—made of an ethereal substance, half-invisible, and with no example from direct experience.

In any case, granting that certain dreams call forth the animist explanation rather naturally, many others certainly are absolutely resistant to it. Very often, our dreams refer to past events; we see again what we have seen or done while awake, yesterday, day before yesterday, during our youth, and so on; such dreams are common, having a rather large place in our nighttime life: But the idea of a double cannot account for them. Even if the double can transport itself from one point to another in space, it is not clear how the double could go back through the stream of time. How could a man, however primitive his intellect, believe when he awakes that he has just been present at, or actually taken part in, events that he knows happened at a different time? How could he imagine that he had lived a life while sleeping that he knew was long since past? It would have been much more natural for him to see those renewed images as what they really are: memories like those he has in daytime, but of special intensity.

Besides, in the scenes we take part in and witness while we sleep, some contemporary is constantly taking some role at the same time as we. We think we see and hear him in the same place as we. According to animism, the primitive will explain these facts by imagining that his own double has been visited or met by the doubles of certain of his friends. But all it will take for him to notice that their experience does not coincide with his is to question them when he awakens. They, too, have had dreams at the same time, but entirely different ones. They did not see themselves taking part in the same scene but believe they visited entirely different places. And since, in that case, contradictions must be the rule, how would those contradictions not lead men to think that there was apparently an error, that they imagined it, that they were taken in by some illusion? For there is a certain oversimplification in the blind credulity that is ascribed to the primitive. He is far from finding it necessary to objectify all his sensations. He is not incapable of noticing that his senses sometimes trick him, even when he is awake. Why would he believe them to be more infallible at night than in daytime? Hence, a good many reasons stand in the way of his taking dreams for realities too easily and interpreting them by a doubling of his being.

Furthermore, even if the hypothesis of the double could satisfactorily explain all dreaming, and all dreaming could be explained in no other way, one would still have to say why man tried to explain it at all. No doubt, the dream has the makings of a possible problem. But we continually bypass problems that we do not see as such, whose existence we do not even suspect so long as nothing has made us feel any need to see them as problems. Even when the taste for pure speculation is wide awake, it is far from true that reflection raises all the questions to which it could possibly apply itself; only those that are of particular interest attract it. Especially when the phenomena in question always recur in the same manner, habit easily puts curiosity to sleep and we no longer even imagine querying ourselves. To shake off that torpor, practical needs, or at least very pressing theoretical interest, must attract our attention and turn it in that direction. And so it happens that, at every moment of history, there are a great many things that we give up trying to understand, without even noticing that we are so doing. Until not very long ago, the sun was believed to be only several feet in diameter. There was something incomprehensible in the fact that a luminous disc of such small diameter could be adequate to light the Earth—and yet centuries went by before humanity thought of resolving that contradiction.

Heredity is a phenomenon that has been known for a long time, but only very recently has anyone tried to construct a theory of it. Indeed, the acceptance of certain beliefs made it completely unintelligible. Thus, in certain

Australian societies to be discussed, the child is not physiologically the product of its parents.[16] Inevitably, such intellectual laziness is greatest in the primitive. This frail being, who must struggle so hard for his life against the forces that assail it, lacks the wherewithal for the luxury of speculation. He probably does not reflect unless he has to. It is therefore not easy to see what could have led him to make dreaming the topic of his meditations. What is dreaming in our life? What a small place it has, especially since it leaves very vague impressions in memory and is quickly erased; and how surprising, then, that a man of such crude intellect should have put so much effort into trying to explain it! Of the two existences that he leads one after the other, daytime and nighttime, it is the first, his daytime existence, that should interest him more. Is it not strange that the nighttime existence should have so captivated his attention that he made it the basis of a whole system of complicated ideas destined to have such profound influence on his thought and conduct?

Everything tends to prove, therefore, that the animist theory of the soul must be reassessed, despite its continuing authority. Today, the primitive probably does attribute his dreams, or certain of them, to the movements of his double. But this is not the same as saying that dreams actually provided the raw material from which the idea of double or soul was made. Instead of being derived from the phenomena of dreams, ecstasy, and possession, it could have been applied to them after the fact. As often happens, once an idea is formed, it is used to organize or to shed light (with light that is sometimes more apparent than real) on facts with which the idea was unconnected at first, and that, in themselves, could not have suggested it. Today, God and the immortality of the soul are often proved with a showing that those beliefs are implied in the basic principles of morality. In reality, those beliefs are of a completely different origin. The history of religious thought could provide numerous examples of these retrospective justifications that can teach us nothing about either the manner in which those ideas took form or about the elements of which they are made.

It is likely, furthermore, that the primitive distinguishes among his dreams and does not explain them all in the same way. Here in Europe, there are still many people for whom the state of sleep is a sort of magico-religious state in which the mind, partially unburdened of the body, has an acuteness

---

[16]See [Sir Baldwin] Spencer and [Francis James] Gillen, *The Native Tribes of Central Australia* [London, Macmillan, 1889], pp. 123–127; [Carl] Strehlow, *Die Aranda- und Loritja-Stämme in Zentral-Australien* [2 vols., Frankfurt, J. Baer, 1907], pp. 52ff.

of vision that it does not enjoy in wakefulness. Still they do not go so far as to consider all their dreams to be so many mystic intuitions. Instead, like everyone else, they see the majority of their dreams only as profane states and empty plays of images, mere hallucinations. The primitive can be thought of as always having made similar distinctions. Codrington states emphatically that the Melanesians do not indiscriminately explain all their dreams as migrations of souls, but only those that strike their imagination vividly.[17] We should probably understand that to mean those dreams in which the sleeper believes he is in touch with religious beings, good or evil genies, souls of the dead, and so on. Likewise, the Dieri make a very clear distinction between ordinary dreams and those nighttime visions in which some deceased friend or relative appears to them. They give different names to those two sorts of state. They see the first as a mere flight of the imagination, but they ascribe the second to the work of an evil spirit.[18] All the facts Howitt offers as examples, showing that the Australian ascribes to the soul the power to leave the body, also have a mystical character: The sleeper believes himself transported into the land of the dead, or else that he is talking with a deceased friend.[19] These dreams are common among primitives.[20] It is probably in connection with such facts that the theory took form. To account for them, the notion that the souls of the dead come back to be with the living as they sleep is accepted. Acceptance of this explanation was all the easier because no fact of experience could disconfirm it. But such dreams were possible only where people already had the ideas of spirits, souls, and lands of the dead—that is, only where religious evolution was relatively advanced. Far from having been able to provide religion with the fundamental idea on which it rests, they presupposed and were the result of a religious system already constituted.[21]

---

[17][Robert Henry Codrington], *The Melanesians* [Oxford, Clarendon Press, 1891], pp. 249–250.

[18][Alfred William] Howitt, *The Native Tribes of South-East Australia* [London, Macmillan, 1904], p. 358 (following Gason).

[19]Ibid., pp. 434–442.

[20]The Negroes of southern Guinea, says Tylor, have "during their sleep almost as many relations with the dead as they have during the day with the living" (*Primitive Culture*, vol. I, p. 443). Of these peoples, the same author cites this remark by an observer: "They regard *all their dreams* as visits by spirits of their dead friends" (ibid., vol. I, p. 514). The statement is surely exaggerated, but it is further proof that mystical dreams are common among primitives. This tends as well to confirm the etymology Strehlow offers for the Arunta word *altjirerama*, which means "to dream." It is composed of *altjira*, which Strehlow translates as "god," and *rama*, which means "see." So the dream would be the moment when the man is in relation with the sacred beings (*Aranda*, vol. I, p. 2).

[21]Andrew Lang (who also refuses to concede that the idea of the soul was suggested to man by the experience of dreaming) believed he could derive it from other experiential data: the facts of spiritism (telepathy, seeing at a distance, etc.). I do not think it necessary to discuss his theory, as set forth in his

III

But let us come to the very heart of the doctrine.

Wherever the idea of a double may come from, that idea is not enough—on the animists' own admission—to explain how the ancestor cult was formed, the cult that is regarded as the original type of all religions. To have become the object of a cult, the double had to cease being a mere replica of the individual. It had to take on the characteristics required for placement on a par with the sacred beings. Death is said to bring about this transformation. But where would the special property that people impute to death come from? Even if the analogy between sleep and death might have been enough to make people believe that the soul survives the body (and on this point, there are reservations to be had), why would this soul completely change its nature simply as a result of being now detached from the body? If, while it lived, it was only a profane thing, a walking life-principle, how would it suddenly become a sacred thing and the object of religious feelings? Apart from greater freedom of movement, death adds nothing essential to it. Being attached to no regular residence from then on, it can do at any time the things it once did only at night; but the things it can do are still of the same nature. So why would the living have seen this uprooted and vagabond double of yesterday's friend as anything but a fellow human? It was a fellow human whose nearness might indeed have been inopportune, but it was not a deity.[22]

In fact, it seems that, far from tending to increase the vital energies, death should actually have sapped them. It is a widespread belief in the lower societies that the soul shares intimately in the body's life. If the body is injured, the soul itself is injured in the corresponding place. Hence, it should

---

book *The Making of Religion*. In fact, it rests on the hypothesis that spiritism is a constant fact of observation, that seeing at a distance is a real faculty of man or, at least, of certain men—and we know the extent to which this postulate is disputed. What is still more disputable is that the facts of spiritism should be sufficiently apparent and sufficiently common to have been able to serve as the basis of all the religious beliefs and practices that bear upon souls and spirits. Examination of these questions would take me too far away from the object of my study. Furthermore, since Lang's theory remains open to several of the objections that I will address to Tylor's, my engaging in such an examination is still less necessary.

[22][Frank Byron] Jevons makes a similar observation. Along with Tylor, he accepts that the idea of the soul comes from dreaming and that, once this idea was created, man projected it into things. But, he adds, the fact that nature has been conceived of as animate in the way man is does not explain why it should have become the object of a cult. "From the fact that man sees a tree that bends and a flame that comes and goes as a living being like himself, it does not at all follow that either is considered a supernatural being; on the contrary, to the extent that they resemble him, they can do nothing that in his eyes is supernatural" (*An Introduction to the History of Religion* [London, Methuen, 1896], p. 55).

age along with the body. In fact, there are peoples among whom funeral respects are not paid to men who have reached senility; they are treated as if their souls had become senile as well.[23] There are even cases in which certain privileged individuals are lawfully put to death before they arrive at old age—for example, kings or priests thought to be vessels of some powerful spirit whose protection society is anxious to keep. The object in this is to prevent the spirit from being stricken with the physical degeneration of those who are its temporary trustees. Thus, the spirit is removed before age weakens the body in which it is residing; since it has lost none of its strength, the spirit is transferred into a younger body in which it will be able to keep its vitality intact.[24] But in that case, when death results from sickness or old age, it would seem that the soul could retain only diminished power. And indeed, if the soul is only the double of the body, it is unclear how it could survive at all once the body has finally disintegrated. From this point of view, the idea of its survival becomes barely intelligible. Hence, here is a gap—a logical and psychological void—between the idea of a double at liberty and that of a spirit to which a cult is addressed.

That void seems all the greater when we realize how wide an abyss separates the sacred world from the profane one. It is obvious that a mere change of degree could not possibly be enough to make a thing pass from one category to the other. Sacred beings are not distinguished from profane ones merely by the strange or unsettling forms they take on or by the wider powers they enjoy. There is no common measure between them. Now, there is nothing in the idea of a double that could account for such a radical heterogeneity. It is said that, once freed from the body, the double can do either great good or great harm to the living, depending on the manner in which it regards them. But upsetting those around him is not enough to make a being appear to be of a different nature from those whose peace it threatens. To be sure, some fear and restraint always enter into the feelings the faithful have for the things they reverence; but it is a fear *sui generis,* made of respect more than fear, and made mainly of that very special emotion that *majesty* elicits in man. The idea of majesty is essentially religious. In a sense, therefore, we have explained nothing about religion so long as we have not discovered where that idea comes from, what it corresponds to, and what could have

[23]See [Sir Baldwin] Spencer and [Francis James] Gillen, *Northern Tribes [of Central Australia,* London, Macmillan, 1904], p. 506; and *Native Tribes,* p. 512. [Reference is to the relationship of soul and life; it is not about funeral practices. Therefore the footnote is probably to the sentence ". . . the soul participates actively in the life of the body." Trans.]

[24]This is the ritual and mythical theme that [Sir James George] Frazer studies in his *The Golden Bough [a Study in Magic and Religion,* London, Macmillan, 1890].

awakened it in consciousnesses. Mere human souls could not possibly be invested with this trait for the simple reason that they are disembodied.

An example from Melanesia brings this out. The Melanesians believe that man possesses a soul that leaves the body at death, when it changes names and becomes what they call a *tindalo,* a *natmat,* etc. At the same time, they also have a cult to the souls of the dead: These souls are prayed to and invoked. Offerings and sacrifices are made to them. But not every tindalo* is the object of those ritual practices. That honor goes only to those that emanate from men who, during their lifetimes, were credited by public opinion with the very special virtue that the Melanesians call *mana.* Later, I explain the idea that this word expresses. For the time being, suffice it to say that it is the distinguishing characteristic of any sacred being. Mana, says Codrington, "is that which permits the production of effects that are outside the ordinary power of men, and outside the ordinary processes of nature."[25] A priest, a sorcerer, or a ritual formula has mana, as does a sacred stone or a spirit. Thus, the only tindalos given religious honors are those that were already sacred beings while their owners were alive. As to other souls, those that come from ordinary men, from the common herd of the profane, they are "nothings after death, as before," according to the same author.[26] Since it consummates the separation from profane things more fully and finally, death may very well reinforce the sacredness of the soul, if the soul already has this quality, but death does not create it.

Furthermore if, as the animist hypothesis assumes, the first sacred beings truly had been the souls of the dead, and the first cult had been that of the ancestors, one should notice that the lower the type of society is, the more predominant this cult is in religious life. Instead, the truth is the other way around. The ancestral cult develops and appears in its characteristic form only in advanced societies such as China, Egypt, and the Greek and Roman cities; on the other hand, it is lacking in the Australian societies, which represent, as we will see, the lowest and simplest form of social organization we know. To be sure, funeral and mourning rites are to be found in those societies, but even though the name "cult" has sometimes been given to practices of this sort, they do not constitute a cult. In fact, a cult is not a mere collection of ritual precautions that man is responsible for taking in certain

*The French text sometimes takes these foreign terms out of italics once they have been explained. I have done this consistently throughout.

[25]Codrington, *The Melanesians,* p. 119.

[26]Ibid., p. 125. [Although the passage Durkheim cites is indeed a discussion of mana, the quotation does not appear there. Trans.]

circumstances. It is a system of rites, feasts, and various ceremonies *all having the characteristic that they recur periodically.* They meet the need that the faithful feel periodically to tighten and strengthen the bond between them and the sacred beings on which they depend.* This is why one speaks of nuptial rites and not of a nuptial cult, of birth rites but not a cult of the newborn: The events that occasion these rites imply no periodicity. In the same way, there is an ancestor cult only if sacrifices are made on the tombs from time to time, if libations are poured there more or less frequently, or if regular feasts are celebrated in honor of the dead person. But the Australian does not have any dealings of this sort with his dead. Certainly he must ritually bury their remains, mourn them for a period and in a manner prescribed and, if need be, avenge them.[27] But once he has carried out these pious duties, once the bones are dry and the mourning has ended, then all is said and done, and the survivors have no further obligations toward those of their relatives who are no more. True, there is indeed a form in which the dead continue to keep a certain place in the lives of their kin, even after the mourning is over. Their hair or certain of their bones[28] are sometimes kept because of special virtues attached to them. Still, they have ceased to be like persons, and have dropped to the rank of anonymous and impersonal amulets. In that state, they are the object of no cult, and the only purposes they still have are magical.

However, some Australian tribes periodically celebrate rites in honor of fabled ancestors that tradition places at the origin of time. Generally these ceremonies consist in a sort of dramatic performance, in which are mimed the deeds attributed in myth to those legendary heroes.[29] Still, the personages thus depicted are not men who, after having experienced the life of men, were transformed by death into something like gods. Instead they are thought to have enjoyed superhuman powers throughout their lives. Everything great that was done in the history of the tribe, and even in the history of the world, is attributed to them. In large part, it is they who have made the earth as it is and men as they are. Thus the aura that continues to surround them does not come merely from the fact that they are ancestors—

*In nearly all contexts, the word "depend" seems to mean both "counting upon" and "being subjects of."

[27]Apparently sometimes there are even funeral offerings (see [Walter E.] Roth, "Superstition, Magic and Medicine," in *North Queensland Ethnography,* Bulletin, no. 5, sec. 69 [Brisbane, G. A. Vaughn, 1903]; and "Burial [Ceremonies and the Disposal of the Dead"] in *North Queensland Ethnography,* Bulletin, no. 10, in *RAM,* vol. VI, part 1907, 5, p. 395). But these offerings are not periodic.

[28]See Spencer and Gillen, *Native Tribes,* pp. 538, 553; and *Northern Tribes,* pp. 463, 543, 547.

[29]See especially Spencer and Gillen, *Northern Tribes,* chaps. 6, 7, 9.

which is to say, in sum, from the fact that they are dead—but from the fact that a divine characteristic is attributed to them, and has been down the ages. To repeat the Melanesian expression, they are by nature endowed with mana. Consequently, nothing in any of this demonstrates that death should have the least power to deify. Indeed, one cannot say without impropriety that these rites constitute an ancestor cult, since they are not addressed to ancestors as such. For a true cult of the dead to be possible, the real ancestors—the relatives that men really lose each day—must become the object of a cult after they die. Once again, no traces of a cult of this type exist in Australia.

Thus the cult that should have been dominant in the lower societies, according to the hypothesis, is nonexistent in them, according to reality. In the final analysis, the Australian is concerned with his dead only at the very moment of death and immediately following. Nevertheless, as we will see, in regard to sacred beings of an altogether different nature, these same peoples practice a complex cult made up of multiple ceremonies that sometimes occupy weeks and even months. It is unthinkable that the few rites the Australian performs when he happens to lose one of his relatives should have been the origin of those permanent cults that return regularly every year and take up a significant part of his life. The contrast is so great, in fact, that one might well ask whether it is not the first that derives from the second—whether the souls of men, far from being the model on which the gods were imagined, were from the beginning conceived of as emanations of the deity.

IV

If the cult of the dead is not primitive, animism has no basis. It might therefore seem pointless to examine the third thesis of the system, concerning the transformation of the cult of the dead into a cult of nature. But its examination is necessary, since the postulate on which it rests is found even among historians of religion who do not accept animism properly so-called, such as Brinton,[30] Lang,[31] Réville,[32] and Robertson Smith himself.[33]

---

[30][Daniel Garrison Brinton], *The Religions of Primitive Peoples* [New York, G. P. Putnam's, 1897], pp. 47ff.

[31][Andrew Lang], *Mythes, cultes et religions* [Paris, F. Alcan, 1896], p. 50.

[32][Albert Réville], *Les Religions des peuples non civilisés*, vol. II [Paris, Fischbacher, 1883], Conclusion.

[33][William Robertson Smith, *Lectures on the Religions] of the Semites*, 2d ed. [London, A & C Black, 1894], pp. 126, 132.

This extension of the cult of the dead to the whole of nature is thought to arise from the fact that we tend instinctively to conceive all things in our own image, that is, as living and thinking beings. We saw that Spencer has already disputed the reality of this so-called instinct. Since an animal clearly distinguishes living bodies from natural objects, it seemed to him impossible that man, as heir of the animal, should not have had this same faculty of discrimination from the start. But as sure as may be the facts that Spencer cites, in this particular case they do not have the character of proof that he believes they have. Indeed, his argument assumes that all the faculties, instincts, and abilities of the animal have passed to man in their entirety. But a great many errors originate in this principle, which is wrongly taken as self-evident truth. For example, from the fact that sexual jealousy is generally very strong among the higher animals, it has been concluded that this same jealousy must be found in man, from the beginning of history and with the same intensity.[34] Today it cannot be doubted that man is able to practice a sexual communism that would be impossible if that jealousy could not weaken or even disappear when necessary.[35] This is so because man is not simply an animal, plus certain qualities: He is something different. Human nature is the product of a recasting, so to speak, of animal nature. There have been gains as well as losses in the course of the intricate operations of which this recasting is the result. How many instincts have we not lost! We have lost them because man is in relationship not only with a physical milieu, but also with a social milieu that is infinitely more extensive, stable, and powerful than those to whose influence animals are subject. In order to live, then, he must adapt to it. Now, to maintain itself, society often needs us to see things from a certain standpoint and feel them in a certain way. It therefore modifies the ideas we would be inclined to have about them, and the feelings to which we would be inclined if we obeyed only our animal nature—even to the extent of replacing them with quite opposite feelings. Does society not go so far as to make us see our own life as a thing of little value, while for animals life is property par excellence?[36] Thus to try to infer the mental makeup of the primitive man from that of the higher animals is a vain quest.

[34]Such, for example, is the reasoning of [Edward Alexander] Westermarck (*Origine du marriage dans l'espèce humaine* [Paris, Guillaumain, 1895], p.6).

[35]By sexual communism, I do not mean that state of promiscuity in which man supposedly recognized no matrimonial rules. I believe that such a state has never existed. But it has often happened that a group of men have regularly united with one or several women.

[36]See my [*Le*] *Suicide*, [Paris, F. Alcan, 1897], pp. 233ff.

But while the objection raised by Spencer does not have the force its author thought it did, neither can the animist postulate draw any authority from the confusions children seem to make. When we hear a child angrily abusing an object that has hit him, we conclude that he sees the object as a conscious being like himself; but this is a poor understanding of his speech and gestures. In reality, he is a stranger to the very complex reasoning that is imputed to him. He blames the table that has hurt him not because he supposes it to be animate and intelligent, but because it has hurt him. Once anger is aroused by the pain, it seeks something on which to discharge itself; the anger naturally goes to the very same thing that provoked it, even though that thing can do nothing. The behavior of the adult in a similar case is often just as unreasonable. When we are intensely angry, we feel the need to abuse and destroy, but without imputing any sort of conscious ill will to the objects on which we vent our anger. There is so little confusion that, when the emotion of the child has cooled, he knows very well how to distinguish a chair from a person: He does not treat both in the same way. His tendency to treat his toys as if they were human beings is explained similarly. His very intense need to play creates suitable material for itself, just as, in the preceding case, the strong feelings that pain had unleashed created their own, out of nothing. Thus, to be able to play conscientiously with his puppet, he imagines it as a living person. The illusion is the easier for him, moreover, because imagination is his sovereign mistress; he scarcely thinks in anything but images, and we know to what extent images are pliable things that bend in obedience to all that desire commands. But so little is he the dupe of his own fiction that if it suddenly became reality and his puppet bit him, he would be the first astonished.[37]

Let us therefore put aside these dubious analogies. To know if man was originally inclined toward the confusions that are ascribed to him, it is not the animal or the child of today that must be considered, but the primitive beliefs themselves. If the spirits and gods of nature really are constructed in the image of the human soul, they must bear the mark of their origin and the essential traits of their model. To be conceived of as the inward principle that animates the body is the trait par excellence of the soul. It is the soul that moves the body and makes it live, such that life ends or is suspended when the soul leaves. It is in the body that the soul has its natural residence—so long as the body exists, at least. Such is not the case for the spirits in charge of the various natural phenomena. The god of the sun is not necessarily in

---

[37]Spencer, *Principles of Sociology,* p. 188.

the sun, or the spirit of a certain rock in the rock that serves as its primary residence. A spirit undoubtedly has close relations with the body to which it is attached, but to call that spirit its soul is to use a very inaccurate phrase. "In Melanesia," says Codrington, "it does not seem that people believe in the existence of spirits that animate a natural object, such as a tree, a waterfall, a storm or a rock, in such a way as to be for that object what the soul is believed to be for the human body. It is true that Europeans talk about spirits of the sea, the storm, or the forest; but the idea of the natives that is translated in this way is altogether different. The natives think that the spirit frequents the forest or the sea and has the power to raise storms and make travelers sicken."[38] Whereas the soul is basically the inside of the body, the spirit pursues the greater part of its existence outside the object that serves as its base. Here, then, is a difference that does not seem to show that the idea of spirit came from the idea of soul.

From another point of view, if man really had been driven to project his image into things, the first sacred beings would have been conceived of in his image. Now, far from being primitive, anthropomorphism is the mark of a relatively advanced civilization. At the beginning, sacred beings are conceived of in the form of animals or plants, from which human form has slowly emerged. It will be seen below that in Australia, animals and plants are in the highest rank of sacred things. Even among the Indians of North America, the great cosmic deities that are beginning to be the object of a cult are very often conceived of in the form of animals.[39] "According to this turn of mind," says Réville, not without surprise, "no distinction is made between animal, man, and divine being," "and, most often, *one would say that the animal form is the fundamental form*."[40]

To find a god constructed entirely out of human elements, one must come almost to Christianity. In Christianity, the God is a man, not only in the physical aspect in which he temporarily manifested himself but also in the ideas and feelings he expresses. But even though the gods in Rome and Greece were generally represented with human traits, several mythical personages nonetheless carried the mark of an animal origin. There is Dionysus, whom one often meets in the form of a bull or at least with the horns of a bull; there is Demeter, represented with the mane of a horse; there are Pan,

---

[38]Codrington, *The Melanesians*, p. 123.

[39][James Owen] Dorsey, "A Study of Siouan Cults," in *XIth Annual Report of the Bureau of American Ethnology* [Washington, D.C., Government Printing Office, 1894], pp. 431ff.

[40]Réville, *La Religion des peuples non civilisés*, vol. I, p. 248.

Silenus, the Fauns, etc.[41] Thus, it is far from true that man was strongly inclined to impose his form upon things. What is more, he began to imagine himself as a close participant in animal nature. Indeed, there is a belief that is nearly universal in Australia, and also very widespread among the Indians of North America, that the ancestors of men were animals or plants, or at least that, wholly or in part, the first men had the distinguishing characteristics of certain animal or plant species. Thus, man did not see beings like himself everywhere—far from it. He started out thinking of himself in the image of beings from which he specifically differed.

V

Further, the animist theory implies a consequence that is perhaps its own best refutation.

If that theory was true, one would have to accept the notion that religious beliefs are so many hallucinatory representations, without any objective basis. The assumption is that all those beliefs are derived from the idea of soul, since spirits and gods are seen as nothing more than purified souls. But, according to Tylor and his followers, the very notion of soul itself is made of the vague and variable images that fill our minds during sleep—for the soul is the double, and the double is nothing but the man as he appears to himself when he is asleep. From this point of view, sacred beings would be mere imaginings that man created in a sort of delirium that seizes him regularly each day; and, from this point of view, it is impossible to see what useful ends they serve or to what they correspond in reality. If he prays, if he makes sacrifices and offerings, if he binds himself to the multiple privations that ritual prescribes to him, that is only because some kind of inborn aberration has made him take dreams for perceptions, death for a prolonged sleep, and inanimate objects for living, thinking beings. In this way (as many have been led to concede), not only does the form in which religious forces are or have been conceived of fail to express them accurately, and not only do the symbols with whose help they have been thought about partially mask their nature, but, more even than that, there would be nothing behind these images and forms but the nightmares of uncultivated minds. In the end, religion would be only a dream,

[41] [Marinus Willem] de Visser, *De Graecorum diis non referentibus speciem humanam*, Lugduni-Batavorum, apud G. Los, 1900; Cf. [Paul] Perdrizet, *Bulletin de correspondance hellénique* [Athens, Ecole française d'Athènes], 1889, p. 635.

systematized and lived, but without foundation in the real.[42] And this is why, when the theorists of animism seek the origins of religious thought, they do not overly exert themselves. When they think they have managed to explain what could have led to imagine beings of strange and vaporous form, such as those we see in dreams, the problem appears solved.

In reality, the problem has not even been touched. It is unthinkable that systems of ideas like religions, which have held such a large place in history—the well to which peoples in all the ages have come to draw the energy they had to have in order to live—could be mere fabrics of illusion. Today we agree to recognize that law, morals, and scientific thought itself were born in religion, were long confounded with it, and have remained imbued with its spirit. How could a hollow phantasmagoria have been able to mold human consciousnesses so powerfully and so lastingly? Surely, it ought to be a principle for the science of religions that religion expresses nothing that is not in nature: There is no science except science of natural phenomena. To which realm of nature these realities belong, and what has made men conceive of them in the singular form that is peculiar to religious thought, is the whole question. But to make the posing of that question even possible, we must first allow that real things are conceived of in that way. When the philosophers of the eighteenth century treated religion as a vast error invented by priests, they could at least explain its persistence by the interest of the priestly caste in duping the masses. But if the people themselves created those systems of mistaken ideas, and at the same time were duped by them, how could this amazing dupery have perpetuated itself through the whole course of history?

Indeed, whether the term "science of religions" can be used without impropriety in those circumstances, is questionable. A science is a discipline that, however conceived, always applies to a reality that is given. Physics and chemistry are sciences because physicochemical phenomena are real, and of a reality that is independent of the truths those sciences demonstrate. There

---

[42]According to Spencer, however, the belief in spirits has a grain of truth: the idea "that the power that is manifested in consciousness is another form of the power that is manifested outside of consciousness" ([Herbert Spencer], "Ecclesiastical Institutions" [part VI, sec. 659], in *Principles of Sociology*, vol. III, p.169]). By this, Spencer means that the notion of force in general is the feeling of the force that we have, spread to the entire universe. Animism implicitly concedes this when it populates nature with spirits analogous to our own. But even if this hypothesis was true—and it calls forth serious reservations that I will state (Bk. III, chap. 3, §3)—it is not in any way religious; and it calls for no cult. Thus it would still be the case that the system of religious symbols and rites, the classification of things as sacred and profane—all that is properly religious in religion—does not correspond to anything in reality. Moreover, this grain of truth is also, and even more, a grain of error: For if it is true that the forces of nature and those of consciousness are akin, they are also profoundly different, and to treat them as identical is to open oneself to strange errors.

is a psychological science because there really are consciousnesses, which do not acquire from the psychologist their right to exist. But religion could not possibly survive the animist theory if one day it was recognized as true by all men: Men could not fail to free themselves from errors whose nature and origin would thus stand revealed. What sort of science is it whose principal discovery is to make the very object it treats disappear?

CHAPTER THREE

THE LEADING CONCEPTIONS
OF THE ELEMENTARY
RELIGION (CONTINUATION)

II. Naturism

The outlook of the naturist school has an entirely different inspiration. It is also recruited from different milieux. The animists are ethnographers or anthropologists, for the most part. The religions they have studied are among the crudest that humanity has practiced. Hence the primary importance these theorists give to the souls of the dead, spirits, and demons, that is, to spiritual beings of the second order: Spiritual beings of a higher order are virtually unknown in those religions.[1] By contrast, the theories I will now present are the work of scholars who have been mainly concerned with the great civilizations of Europe and Asia.

As soon as researchers, following the brothers Grimm, saw the fruitfulness of comparing the different mythologies of the Indo-European peoples, they were struck by the remarkable similarities these mythologies displayed. Mythical personages were identified that, although having different names, symbolized the same ideas and had the same functions. The names themselves were compared, and researchers believed it could sometimes be shown that they were not unrelated. It appeared that such similarities could be explained only by common origin. So researchers were led to suppose that, different as these ideas were in appearance, they were in reality different forms

[1]This no doubt explains as well the sympathy that folklorists like [Wilhelm] Mannhardt [1831–1880] have felt for animist ideas. In popular religions, as in the lower religions, spiritual beings of the second order have prominence. [Friedrich L. W. Schwartz] Der Ursprung der Mythologie, Berlin [W. Herzt], 1860.

originating from a common source that might be discoverable. They postulated that, by using the comparative method, it should be possible to go back, beyond the great religions, to a far more ancient system of ideas, a truly primitive religion from which the others derived.

What contributed most to arousing these ambitions was the discovery of the Vedas, a written text whose antiquity may well have been exaggerated at the moment it was discovered, but that nevertheless is one of the most ancient we have in an Indo-European language. Thus, by using the ordinary methods of philology, they were in a position to study a literature as old as or older than that of Homer and a religion thought to be more primitive than that of the ancient Germans. Clearly, a document of such value was bound to shed new light on the religious beginnings of humanity, and the science of religions could not fail to be revolutionized by it.

So much was the conception thus born called for by the state of science and by the general current of ideas that it emerged at almost the same time in two different countries. In 1856, Max Müller set forth the principles in his *Oxford Essays*.[2] Clearly in the same spirit, Adalbert Kuhn's book, *Origine du feu et de la boisson divine*,[3] appeared three years later. Once advanced, the idea spread very rapidly in scientific circles. Kuhn's name is closely associated with that of his brother-in-law [Friedrich] Schwartz, whose book *L'Origine de la mythologie*[4] appeared shortly after Kuhn's. [Hymann] Steinthal and the whole German school of *Voelkerpsychologie*[*] belong to the same movement. The theory was imported into France in 1863 by M. Michel Bréal.[5] It met so little resistance that, according to [Otto] Gruppe,[6] "there came a time when, apart from a few classical philologists working outside Vedic studies, all the

---

[*] *Folk Psychology*, the title of a ten-volume work by Wilhelm Wundt (1832–1920). The founder of experimental psychology, Wundt envisaged a comparative social psychology to supplement individual experimental psychology with research into the data of anthropology, history, and linguistics.

[2] In an essay titled *Comparative Mythology* [New York, Arno Press, 1977], pp. 47ff. [The French translation was titled, *Essai de mythologie comparée*, Paris-London, 1859].

[3] [Adalbert, Kuhn], *Herabkunft des Feuers und Gottertranks*, Berlin [F. Dummler],1859 (a new edition of it was done by Ernst Kuhn in 1886). Cf. *Der Schuss des Wilden Jägers auf den Sonnenhirsch*, *ZDP*, vol. I (1869), pp. 89–169; *Entwickelungsstufen des Mythus*, Berlin Academy, 1873.

[4] [Schwartz], *Der Ursprung der Mythologie*, F.1.

[5] In his book *Hercule et Cacus, Etude de mythologie comparée* [Paris, A. Durand, 1863, p. 12]. *L'Essaie de mythologie comparée* by Max Müller is cited there as a work "that marks a new era in the history of Mythology" (p. 12).

[6] [Otto Gruppe], *Die griechischen Kulte und Mythen* [*Ihren Beziehungen zu der orientalischen Religionen*, Leipzig, B. G. Teubner, 1887].

mythologists took the principles of Max Müller or of Kuhn as the starting point of their explanations."[7] It is important, therefore, to examine what they are and what they are worth.

Since no one has presented those principles more systematically than Max Müller, I take from him the elements of the exposition to follow.[8]

I

We have seen that the underlying assumption of animism is that religion, at least at its origin, does not express any experiential reality. Max Müller sets out from the opposite principle. For him, it is axiomatic that religion rests on an experience from which it draws its entire authority. "To hold its proper place as a legitimate element of our consciousnesses," he says, "religion must begin, as does all our knowledge, with sense experience."[9] Taking up the old empiricist adage *Nihil est in intellectu quod non ante fuerit in sensu,* * he applies it to religion and asserts that there can be nothing in the faith that was not first in the senses. Here is a doctrine that seemingly ought to escape the serious objection I raised to animism. Indeed, it seems that religion must of necessity appear, from this point of view, not as a kind of vague and confused dreaming but as a system of ideas and practices well grounded in reality.

But what are the sense experiences that give rise to religious thought? This is the question the study of the Vedas should have helped to resolve.

The names of its gods are generally either common nouns still used as such or archaic common nouns whose original meaning can be recovered. Both designate the principal phenomena of nature. Thus at first *Agni,* the

---

*Nothing is in the mind that was not first in the senses.

[7][Ernest] Renan must be counted among the writers who adopted that conception. See his *Nouvelles études d'histoire religieuse* [Paris, Calman Lévy], 1884, p. 31.

[8]Apart from his *Comparative Mythology,* the works of Max Müller in which his general theories of religion are presented are the following: *The Hibbert Lectures* [*Lectures on the Origin and Growth of Religion as Illustrated by the Religions of India,* London, Longmans, Green & Co.] (1878), translated into French under the title *Origine et développement de la religion* [*étudiés à la lumière des religions de l'Inde,* Paris, C. Reinwald, 1879] ; *Natural Religion* [London, Longmans, 1889]; *Physical Religion* [London, Longmans, 1891]; *Anthropological Religion* [London, Longmans, 1892];*Theosophy or Psychological Religion* [London, Longmans, 1895]; *Contributions to the Science of Mythology* [London, Longmans, 1897]. Because of the relationships between the mythological theories of Max Müller and his linguistic philosophy, the foregoing works must be compared with those of his books that are devoted to language or to logic, in particular, *Lectures on the Science of Language* [London, Longmans, 1873], translated into French as *Nouvelles leçons sur la science du langage*], and *The Science of Thought* [London, Longmans, 1878].

[9]Müller, *Natural Religion,* p. 114.

name of one of India's principal deities, meant only the natural phenomenon of fire as the senses perceive it, without any mythological addition. In the Vedas themselves, it is still used in that meaning; in any case, the fact of its preservation in other Indo-European languages clearly shows that this meaning was primitive: The Latin *ignis*, the Lithuanian *ugnis*, and the ancient Slav *ogny* are close relatives of *Agni*. Similarly, the kinship of the Sanskrit *Dyaus*, the Greek *Zeus*, the Latin *Jovis*, and the High German *Zio* is undisputed today. That kinship proves that these different words denote one and the same deity, recognized as such by different Indo-European peoples before their separation. Now, *Dyaus* means "the bright sky." These facts and others like them tend to demonstrate that, among these peoples, the bodies and forces of nature were the first objects to which religious feeling became attached. They were the first things to be deified. Taking a further step along the road to generalization, Max Müller believed he had valid grounds for concluding that the religious evolution of humanity in general had the same starting point.

He justifies that inference almost exclusively with psychological considerations. To him, the varied spectacles that nature offers to man seem to meet all the necessary conditions for arousing the religious idea in the mind directly. In fact, he says, "at the first glance men cast upon the world, nothing appeared less natural to them than nature. Nature was for them the great surprise and the great fear; it was a permanent marvel and a permanent miracle. It was only later, when men discovered their constancy, their invariance, and their regular recurrence, that certain aspects of that miracle were called natural, in the sense that they were foreseen, ordinary, and intelligible. . . . It is this vast domain open to feelings of surprise and fear, this marvel, this miracle, this immense unknown opposed to what is known . . . that provided the first impulse to religious thought and religious language."[10] And, to illustrate his thought, he applies it to a natural force that has a large place in Vedic religion: fire. "Try," he says, "to transport yourself backward in thought to that stage in primitive life where, of necessity, one must place the origin and even the first phases of the religion of nature; you will find it easy to imagine what impression the first appearance of fire must have made on the human mind.

No matter how it first appeared—whether it came from lightning, whether it was obtained by rubbing tree branches against one another, or whether it sprang forth as sparks from rocks—it was something that moved, that progressed, from which one had to protect oneself, that carried destruction with it; but at the same time, it was something that made life possible in

[10]Müller, *Physical Religion*, pp. 119–120.

winter, gave protection at night, and served as both an offensive and a defensive weapon. Thanks to fire, man ceased to be a devourer of raw meat and became an eater of cooked foods. Later, it was also by means of fire that metals were worked, and tools and weapons made; it thus became an indispensable factor in all technical and artistic progress. Where would we be, even now, without fire?"[11]

Man cannot enter into relations with nature without gaining a sense of its infinity and its immensity, as the same author says in another work. It surpasses him in every direction. Beyond the spaces he sees, there are others that stretch out limitlessly; each moment of duration is preceded and followed by a time to which no limit can be set; the flowing river manifests an infinite force, since nothing exhausts it.[12] There is no aspect of nature that is not equipped to awaken in us the overwhelming sensation of an infinite that envelops and dominates us.[13] For Müller, it is from this sensation that religions are derived.[14]

However, only their seed was present in the sensation.[15] Religion is truly formed only when these natural forces are no longer conceived of abstractly. They must be transformed into personal agents, living and thinking beings, spiritual powers, gods; for the cult is usually addressed to beings of this sort. We have seen that animism, too, must pose this question, and how it answers: Man supposedly had some certain inborn inability to distinguish the animate from the inanimate, together with an irresistible urge to conceive of the inanimate in animate form. This solution, Max Müller rejects.[16] According to him, it is language that brought about the metamorphosis, through its influence over thought.

That metamorphosis is easily understood in the following way: Puzzled by these marvelous forces on which they felt dependent, men were roused to think about them; they asked themselves what those forces consisted of and tried to replace the vague awareness they originally had of them with a clearer idea, a better-defined concept. But as our author quite rightly says,[17]

[11]Ibid., p. 121; cf. p. 304.

[12]Müller, *Natural Religion*, pp. 121ff., 149–155.

[13]"The overwhelming pressure of the infinite" (ibid., p. 138).

[14]Ibid., pp. 195–196.

[15]Max Müller goes so far as to say that, when thought has not gone beyond that phase, it has only a very few of the features that we now impute to religion (*Physical Religion*, p. 120).

[16]Ibid., p. 128.

[17]See Müller, *The Science of Thought*, p. 30.

ideas and concepts are impossible without words. Language is not only the outward clothing of our thought; it is thought's internal skeleton. Language does not merely stand outside thought, translating something that is already formed, but in actuality serves to form thought. However, since language has its own nature, its laws are not the same as those of thought. Thus since language helps to fashion thought, it is bound to do a certain measure of violence to thought and to distort it. Distortion of this kind supposedly gave rise to the peculiarity of our religious representations.

To think is actually to order and thus to classify our ideas. To think of fire, for example, is to place it into such and such category of things, so as to be able to say it is this or that, this and not that. At the same time, to classify is to name, for a general idea has no existence and no reality except in and through the word that expresses it, and that alone makes it what it is. So the language of a people always influences the manner in which the new things that people come to know are classified in their minds—those things must fit into preexisting frameworks. For this reason, when men set out to make a comprehensive representation of the universe, the language they spoke indelibly marked the system of ideas that was then born.

We still know some part of that language—at least the Indo-European peoples do. Despite its remoteness, our languages still contain relics that enable us to imagine what it must have been. These relics are the roots. Max Müller considers these root words—these words from which the other words we use are derived and which are found as the basis of all the Indo-European idioms—as so many echoes of the language spoken by the ancient people before their separation: that is, as the moment when that religion of nature, the object of explanation, was being formed. Now, the roots display two remarkable characteristics that, although as yet well documented for this particular group of languages only, our author believes to be equally verifiable in the other linguistic families.[18]

First, the roots are typified. That is, they express not particular things or individuals but types—and indeed types having very wide application. They represent the most general themes of thought. The fundamental categories of the mind that govern the whole of mental life at each historical moment—and whose order philosophers have often tried to reconstruct—are found in them fixed and crystallized, as it were.[19]

[18]Müller, *Natural Religion*, pp. 393ff.

[19]Müller, *Physical Religion*, p. 133; *The Science of Thought*, p. 219, *Nouvelles leçons sur la science du langage*, vol. II, pp. 1ff.

Second, the types to which they correspond are types of action, not types of objects. What they express are the most general ways of acting that can be observed among living things, particularly among humans: the acts of striking, pushing, rubbing, tying, lifting, pressing, climbing, descending, walking, and so on. In other words, man generalized and named his principal modes of action before generalizing and naming the phenomena of nature.[20]

By virtue of their extreme generality, these words could easily be applied to all sorts of objects that they did not originally include. Moreover, this extreme suppleness enabled them to give birth to the many words that are derived from them. So when man, turning to things, set out to name them in order to be able to think about them, he applied those words to things even though they had not been meant for things. By virtue of their origin, they could designate the various forces of nature only by those manifestations that most resembled human actions: The thunderbolt was called *that thing* that digs up the ground when it descends or spreads fire, the wind *that thing* that moans or blows, the sun *that thing* that hurls golden arrows though space, the river *that thing* that runs, and so on. But because natural phenomena became assimilated to human actions in this way, this something to which they were joined was of necessity imagined in the form of personal agents more or less like man. This was only a metaphor, but one that was taken literally. The error was inevitable because the science that alone could have swept away the illusion did not yet exist. In sum, because it was made up of human elements that translated human states, language could not be applied to nature without transfiguring it.[21] Even today, remarks M. Bréal, it somehow slants the manner in which we imagine things. "We do not express an idea, even when it merely denotes a quality, without giving it a gender, that is to say, a sex. We cannot speak of an object, even if it is considered in a general way, without specifying it with an article. Every subject of a sentence is presented as an acting being, every idea as an action, and the duration of each action, passing or permanent, as delimited by the tense in which we put the verb."[22] Of course, our scientific culture makes it easy for us to correct the errors that language might thereby suggest to us, but the influence of words must have been all powerful when they had no counterweight. Thus, upon the physical world, as it is revealed to our senses, language superimposed a

[20]Müller, *The Science of Thought*, p. 272.

[21]Ibid., vol. I, p. 327; *Physical Religion*, pp. 125ff.

[22] [Michel Jules Alfred Bréal], *Mélanges de mythologie et de linguistique* [Paris, Hachette, 1877], p. 8.

new world, a world comprising only spiritual beings that it had created out of nothing and that were from then on regarded as the determining causes of physical phenomena.

Moreover, the workings of language did not stop there. Once words had been forged to designate these personalities, which popular imagination had put behind things, the personalities reacted upon the words themselves, thereby creating the riddles of all kinds that the myths were invented to solve. Sometimes a single object received several names corresponding to the several aspects in which it presented itself to experience. So it came about that there are more than twenty words in the Vedas to denote the sky. Being different, the words were believed to correspond to as many distinct personalities. But at the same time, these personalities were strongly felt to have an air of kinship. To account for that kinship, they were imagined as forming one family; genealogies, a marital status, and a history were invented for them. In other cases, different things were designated by a single term. To explain how different things came to have the same name, it was allowed that the corresponding things were really transformations of one another; and new fictions were forged to make these metamorphoses intelligible. Or again, a word that had ceased to be understood was the origin of fables intended to give it a meaning. Thus the creative work of language continued, in ever more complex constructions. And as mythology came to endow each god with an ever more extensive and complete biography, the divine personalities, at first undistinguished from things, now separated from things and stood on their own.

Thus, supposedly, the notion of the divine was formed. The religion of the ancestors? Only an echo of the earlier religion.[23] According to this theory, the idea of the soul was formed for reasons rather similar to those Tylor gave, except that, for Max Müller, the purpose of that idea was to account for death, not for dreams.[24] Then, under the influence of various (in part, accidental) circumstances,[25] the souls of men, once separated from the body, were drawn little by little into the circle of divine beings, and thus were ultimately deified as well. But this new cult was merely the product of a secondary formation. Further proof: Deified men have very often been

[23] Müller, *Anthropological Religion*, pp. 128–130.

[24] This explanation, however, is no better than [Edward Burnett] Tylor's. According to Max Müller, man was unable to accept that life ended with death. For that reason, he concluded that there are two beings in him, one of which survives the body. It is hard to see what could have made people believe that life continues, when the body is in full decomposition.

[25] See for details, Müller, *Anthropological Religion*, pp. 351ff.

imperfect gods, or demigods, which all peoples have always known how to distinguish from deities proper.[26]

II

This doctrine rests in part on various linguistic postulates that were then and still are very much in dispute. Scholars have questioned the reality of many concordances that Max Müller thought he saw among the names of gods in the various European languages. They have especially cast doubt on his interpretation of them: They have questioned whether, far from being the mark of a very primitive religion, the concordances might not be the late result of either direct borrowings or natural interchange among peoples.[27] Moreover, it is no longer accepted today that roots could have existed in isolation as autonomous realities—or, consequently, that they enable us even hypothetically to reconstruct the primitive language of the Indo-European peoples.[28] Finally, recent studies would tend to prove that not all the Vedic deities had the exclusively naturist quality that Max Müller and his school attributed to them.[29] But I will leave aside questions whose examination presupposes the linguist's very specialized competence, in order to take up the general principles of the system. Besides, the naturist idea should not be too closely mingled with the disputed postulates, for that idea is accepted by a number of scholars who do not ascribe to language the dominant role Max Müller did.

That man has an interest in knowing the world around him and that, consequently, his reflection was quickly applied to it, everyone will readily accept. The help of the things with which he was in immediate contact was so necessary that he inevitably tried to investigate their nature. But if, as na-

---

[26]Ibid., p. 130. This does not stop Max Müller from seeing Christianity as the high point of this entire development. The religion of the ancestors, he says, assumes there is something divine in man. Is that not the idea that is at the basis of the teaching of Christ (ibid., pp. 378ff)? There is no need to emphasize what is odd about a conception that makes Christianity the culmination of the cult of the dead.

[27]On this same point, see the critique to which Gruppe subjects the hypotheses of Max Müller in *Grieschischen Kulte und Mythen*, pp. 79–184.

[28]See [Antoine] Meillet, *Introduction à l'étude comparative des langues indo-européennes* [Paris, Hachette, 1903], p. 119.

[29][Herman] Oldenberg, *Die Religion des Veda* [Berlin, W. Hertz, 1844], pp. 59ff.; [Antoine] Meillet, "Le Dieu Iranien Mithra," *JA*, vol. X, no. 1 (July–August 1907), pp. 143ff.

turism contends, religious thought was born from these particular reflections, then it becomes inexplicable that religious thought should have survived the first tests made, and unintelligible that religious thought has been maintained. If, in fact, we have a need to know things, it is in order to act in a manner appropriate to them. But the representation of the universe that religion gives us, especially at the beginning, is too grossly incomplete to have been able to bring about practices that had secular utility. According to that representation of the universe, things are nothing less than living, thinking beings—consciousnesses and personalities like those the religious imagination has made into the agents of cosmic phenomena. So it is not by conceiving of them in that form and treating them according to that notion that man could have made them helpful to him. It is not by praying to them, celebrating them in feasts and sacrifices, and imposing fasts and privations on himself that he could have prevented them from harming him or obliged them to serve his purposes. Such procedures could have succeeded only on very rare occasions—miraculously, so to speak. If the point of religion was to give us a representation of the world that would guide us in our dealings with it, then religion was in no position to carry out its function, and humanity would not have been slow to notice that fact: Failures, infinitely more common than successes, would have notified them very quickly that they were on the wrong path; and religion, constantly shaken by these constant disappointments, would have been unable to last.

No doubt, sometimes an error does indeed perpetuate itself in history. But barring an altogether unusual conjunction of circumstances, it cannot maintain itself this way unless it proves to be *practically true*—that is to say, if, while not giving us a correct theoretical idea of the things to which it is related, it expresses correctly enough the manner in which those things affect us, for better or for worse. Under those conditions, behavior decided upon for the wrong reasons has every chance of being the right behavior, at least overall; and so why the error could have survived the test of experience becomes understandable.[30] On the other hand, an error, and especially an organized system of errors that leads and can only lead to practical setbacks, is not viable. What is there in common between the rites by which the faithful have tried to act on nature and the procedures that the sciences have taught us to use and that we now know to be the only effective ones? If that is what men asked of religion, we cannot understand why religion should have been able to survive, unless clever tricks prevented them from noticing that it did

---

[30]This is applicable to numerous maxims of popular wisdom.

not give them what they expected of it. It would therefore be just as well to go back once more to the simplistic explanations of the eighteenth century.[31]

Only in appearance, therefore, does naturism escape the objection I made against animism a short while ago. Since naturism reduces religion to nothing more than an immense metaphor without objective foundation,* it too makes religion out to be a system of hallucinatory images. It does, of course, assign religion a point of departure in reality—namely, the sensations that the phenomena of nature induce in us; but by the magical workings of language, this sensation is transformed into bizarre ideas. Religious thought comes into contact with reality only to shroud it straightaway with a thick veil that hides its true forms, this veil being the fabric of fabulous beliefs spun by mythology. Thus, like the delirious individual, the believer lives in a world populated with beings and things that have only a verbal existence. What is more, Max Müller himself recognizes this, since for him myths arise from a malady of thought. At first, he ascribed them to a malady of language, but since language and thought are inseparable to him, what is true of one is true of the other. "When I tried briefly to characterize the inner nature of mythology," he says, "I called it a malady of language more than a one of thought. But after all I had said in my book *The Science of Thought* about the inseparability of thought and language, and therefore about the absolute identity between a malady of language and one of thought, no further equivocation seemed possible. . . . Depicting the high God as guilty of every crime, tricked by men, out of sorts with his wife, and beating his children, is surely symptomatic of an abnormal condition or a malady of thought, or better, of madness outright."[32] This argument is valid not only against Max Müller and

---

* *Valeur objective.* Compare the similar passage on p. 80.

[31] It is true that this argument does not change the minds of those who see religion as a technique (especially a hygienic technique), the rules of which were well founded, even if sanctioned by imaginary beings. But I will not tarry here to criticize an idea that is so untenable and that, in fact, has never been argued systematically by minds that were even minimally well informed in the history of religions. It is difficult to show in what way the terrible practices of initiation sustain the health that they place in jeopardy; in what way the dietary prohibitions, which very commonly apply to perfectly wholesome animals, are hygienic; in what way sacrifices, which took place during the building of a house, made the house more solid, and so forth. No doubt, there are religious precepts that turn out to have technical utility at the same time, but they disappear in the mass of others. And indeed, very often the services that they do render have their opposites. If there is a religious prophylaxis, there is also a religious filth deriving from the same principles. The commandment to take the deceased person away from the camp because he is the seat of a dreaded spirit has practical utility. But the same belief has the relatives anointing themselves with the liquids that come from the body as it rots, because they are thought to have exceptional virtues. In matters technical, magic has served more often than religion.

[32] Müller, [*Etudes de mythologie comparée*, pp. 51–52].

his theory but against the very principle of naturism, however applied. Do what we may, if expressing the forces of nature is made out to be the principal object of religion, it is impossible to see religion as anything other than a system of deceiving fictions, the survival of which is incomprehensible.

True, Max Müller thought he escaped that objection, the seriousness of which he sensed, by radically distinguishing mythology from religion and excluding it from religion. He claims the right to reserve the name "religion" only for beliefs that conform to the prescriptions of wholesome morality and to the teachings of a rational theology. He considered myths, on the other hand, to have been parasitic developments that, under the influence of language, came to graft themselves onto the fundamental representations and pervert them. Thus, for him, the belief in Zeus was religious to the extent that the Greeks saw Zeus as a supreme God, father of humanity, protector of laws, avenger of crimes, and so forth. But everything about the biography of Zeus, his marriages and his adventures, was only mythology.[33]

But this distinction is arbitrary. While there is no doubt that mythology is important to aesthetics as well as to the science of religions, it is nonetheless one of the essential elements of religious life. If myth is withdrawn from religion, ritual must also be withdrawn: Rites are most commonly addressed to definite personalities that have a name, a character, definite attributes, and a history; and those vary according to the way in which the personalities are conceived. The cult one renders to the deity depends on the form ascribed to that deity. Indeed the rite is often nothing other than the myth in action. The Christian communion is inseparable from the paschal myth from which it takes its entire meaning. Thus if all mythology results from a sort of verbal delusion, the question I posed remains intact: The existence and, above all, the persistence of the cult become inexplicable. It does not make sense that men could go on doing things for centuries, pointlessly. Besides, it is not only the particular traits of divine figures that are specified by the myths. The very idea that there are gods, spiritual beings, and custodians assigned to various departments of nature is essentially mythical, no matter how those beings are depicted.[34] What remains if one takes away from the religions of the

---

[33]See Müller, *Science du langage* [vol. II, p. 147]; and *Physical Religion*, pp. 276ff. In the same vein is Bréal, *Mélanges de mythologie et de linguistique*, p. 6: "To bring to the question of the origin of mythology the necessary clarity, it is necessary to distinguish carefully the *gods*, who are a direct product of human intellect, from the *legends*, which are only its indirect and involuntary product."

[34]Max Müller recognizes this. See *Physical Religion*, p. 132, and *Mythologie Comparée*, p. 58. "The gods," he says, "are *nomina* [names] and not *numina* [shades], names without being and not beings without name."

past everything that rests on the notion of gods conceived as cosmic agents? The idea of divinity in itself, of a transcendent power to which man is subordinate and on which he leans? But that is a philosophical and abstract conception that has never been realized as such in any historical religion; it is without interest for the science of religions.[35] Let us therefore guard against differentiating among religious beliefs, keeping some because they seem just and wholesome, to us, and rejecting others as unworthy of being called religious because they offend and unsettle us. All myths, even those we find most unreasonable, have been objects of faith.[36] Man believed in them no less than in his own sensations; he regulated his conduct in accordance with them. Despite appearances, therefore, they cannot be without objective foundation [fondement objectif].

Nevertheless, it will be said, no matter how religions are explained, they have certainly erred about the true nature of things: The sciences have demonstrated that. So the modes of action they encouraged or imposed upon man could only rarely have had useful effects: It is not with purifications that sicknesses are cured, or with sacrifices or songs that the crop is made to grow. In this way, the objection that I have made against naturism seems applicable to all possible systems of explanation.

But there is one that escapes it. Let us suppose that religion answers a need quite different from adapting us to tangible things: There will be no risk of its being weakened solely because it satisfies this need poorly or not at all. If religious faith was not born to place man in harmony with the physical world, the errors it might have caused him to make in his struggle with the world would not harm it at its source, since it is fed from another. If it was not for such reasons that people were led to believe, they must have gone on believing even when those reasons were contradicted by the facts. One even imagines that faith could have been rather strong, strong enough not only to

---

[35]Granted, Max Müller holds that, for the Greeks, "Zeus was and remained the name of the supreme deity despite all the mythological obscurities" (Science du Langage [vol. II, p. 173]). I will not dispute that assertion, which in historical terms is quite disputable; but in any case, that conception of Zeus could never be other than a glimmering amid the totality of the Greeks' religious beliefs.

Moreover, in a later work, Max Müller goes as far as to make the very idea of god in general the product of a wholly verbal process and, in consequence, a mythological elaboration (Physical Religion, p. 138).

[36]Apart from myths proper, there certainly have always been fables that were not believed or, at least, were not believed to the same degree and in the same manner and that for this reason were not religious in character. The line of demarcation between fables and myths is certainly fluid and hard to determine. But this is no reason to make all the myths into fables, any more than we would dream of making all the fables into myths. There is at least one characteristic that is sufficient in many cases to differentiate the religious myth, and that is its relationship to the cult.

endure such contradictions but also to deny them and inhibit the believer from perceiving their import—thus making them harmless to religion. When a religious feeling is strong, it does not accept that religion could be guilty, and it readily prompts explanations that acquit religion: If the rite does not produce the expected results, the failure is imputed either to some flaw of execution or to the intervention of a contrary deity. But for that to occur, religious ideas must not draw their origin from a feeling that is disturbed by the setbacks of experience, for otherwise, where would their resilience come from?

III

What is more, even though man might have had reason to go on explaining the cosmic phenomena with religious symbols, despite every setback, still those symbols would have to have been the kind that suggest such interpretation. Where would they have acquired such a property? Here again, we come face to face with one of those postulates that seem obvious only because they have not been examined critically. It is set up as axiomatic that the natural play of physical forces has all it takes to arouse the idea of the sacred in us. But when the evidence (sketchy, by the way) that has been adduced to support this proposition is examined more closely, we notice that it boils down to a preconceived idea.

We talk about the amazement that men must have felt as they discovered the world. But it is a regularity shading off into monotony that above all characterizes the life of nature. Every morning, the sun climbs the horizon, and every evening it sets; every month, the moon completes the same cycle; the river flows uninterruptedly in its bed; the same seasons periodically bring back the same sensory experiences. Some unexpected event occurs here and there, no doubt: The sun is eclipsed, the moon disappears behind the clouds, the river floods. But these passing disturbances can never give birth to anything but equally passing impressions, the memory of which is erased after a time; so they could not possibly serve as the basis of those stable and permanent systems of ideas and practices that constitute religions. Ordinarily, the course of nature is uniform, and uniformity cannot produce strong emotions. To conceive the savage as being full of admiration before these marvels is to transfer to the origin of history feelings that are much more modern. He is too used to those marvels to be powerfully surprised. It takes intellectual cultivation and reflection to shake off this yoke of habit and discover all that is amazing even in that very regularity. Furthermore, as I observed earlier,[37]

---

[37]See above p. 25.

it is not enough that we admire an object for it to appear to us as sacred—that is, for it to be marked with the quality that makes all direct contact with it seem a profanation and a sacrilege. We misunderstand what is specific to religious feeling if we confuse it with every impression of admiring surprise.

But failing admiration, some say, there is one impression that man cannot help but feel in the presence of nature. He cannot enter into relations with nature without realizing that it goes as far as he can be, or see, and then beyond that. Its immensity overwhelms him. That sensation of an infinite space surrounding him, of an infinite time preceding and to follow the present moment, of forces infinitely superior to those at his disposal, cannot fail to arouse the idea inside him that there is an infinite power outside him to which he is subject. This idea then enters into our conception of the divine as an essential element.

But let us remember what is at issue. The question is how man could have arrived at thinking that there are, in reality, two categories of radically heterogeneous and incomparable things. How could the panorama of nature have given us the idea of that duality? Nature is always and everywhere identical to itself. It does not matter that nature extends to the infinite: Beyond the farthest limit of my gaze, it does not differ from what it is this side. The space that I conceive beyond the horizon is still space, identical to the space I see. The time that passes endlessly is made up of moments identical to those I have lived through. Space, like time, repeats itself indefinitely; if the portions of it that I reach have no sacredness in themselves, how could the others have any? The fact that I do not perceive them directly is not sufficient to transform them.[38] It makes no difference for a world of profane things to be limitless; it remains a profane world. Does one say that the physical forces with which we interact exceed our own? But the sacred forces are not distinguished from the profane merely by their greater intensity; they are different; they have special qualities that the profane have not. On the other hand, all those forces manifest in the universe—both those in us and those outside us—are of the same nature. Most of all, what could have enabled us to lend any sort of preeminence to some, as compared to others? Nothing. So if religion was really born out of the need to assign causes to physical phenom-

---

[38]Furthermore, there is actual twisting of words in Max Müller's language. Sense experience, he says, implies, at least in certain cases, "that beyond the known there is *something unknown, something that I ask permission to call infinite*" (*Natural Religion*, p. 195. Cf. p. 218). The unknown is no more necessarily the infinite than the infinite is necessarily the unknown—if it is totally identical to itself and, thus, to what we do know about it. It would have to be shown that what we perceive of the infinite is different in nature from what we do not.

ena, the forces imagined in this way would not be more sacred than those that the scientist of today conceives of in accounting for the same facts.[39] There would not have been sacred beings—or, consequently, religion.

Furthermore, even supposing that this sensation of "being overwhelmed" really could suggest the idea of religion, it would not have had that effect on the primitive—for that sensation he does not have. He has absolutely no awareness that cosmic forces are so far superior to his own. Because science has not yet come to teach him modesty, he ascribes to himself a dominion over things that he does not have, but the illusion of it is enough to prevent him from feeling dominated by them. As I have said, he believes he can tell the elements what to do: unchain the wind, force the rain to fall, stop the sun with a wave of the hand, etc.[40] Religion itself helps to give him that security, for it is believed to arm him with broad powers over nature. In part, the rites are meant to enable him to impose his wishes on the world. Thus, far from being inspired by a sense man has of his smallness before the universe, religions have the opposite inspiration. The effect of even the most elevated and idealistic is one of reassuring man in his struggle with things. It professes that faith, by itself, is able "to move mountains"—that is, to dominate the forces of nature. How could they provide this confidence if their origin really was a sensation of weakness and powerlessness?

Furthermore, if natural things truly had become sacred beings by virtue of their imposing forms or the force they display, we would observe that the sun, the moon, the sky, the mountains, the sea, the winds—in short, the great cosmic phenomena—were the first to be lifted to that status; none are better equipped to dazzle the senses and the imagination. But in fact, the great cosmic phenomena were not deified until fairly recent times. The first beings to which the cult was addressed—the proof of this will be given in the chapters to follow—are humble plants and animals in relation to which man found himself on an equal footing at the very least: the duck, the hare, the kangaroo, the emu, the lizard, the caterpillar, the frog, and so forth. Their objective qualities surely could not have been the origin of the religious feelings they inspired.

[39]This Max Müller unintentionally acknowledges in certain places. He admits seeing little difference between the notion of Agni, the god of fire, and the notion of ether by which the modern physicist explains light and heat (*Physical Religion*, pp. 126–127). Besides, he connects the idea of divinity to that of *agency* (p. 138), to an idea of causality that is in no way natural and profane. The fact that religion depicts the causes thus conceived in the form of personal agents is insufficient to explain why those causes should have sacredness. A personal agent can be profane, and, besides, many religious forces are essentially impersonal.

[40]When I come to speak about rites and about faith in their efficacy, we will see how these illusions can be understood (Bk. III, chap. 2).

CHAPTER FOUR

TOTEMISM AS ELEMENTARY RELIGION

Review of the Question—Method of Treating It

Although seemingly quite opposed in their conclusions, the two systems I have just examined are nonetheless in agreement on a fundamental point: They frame the problem in identical terms. Both set out to construct the notion of the divine out of the sensations that certain natural phenomena, either physical or biological, arouse in us. According to the animists, dreams were the starting point of religious evolution; according to the naturists, certain cosmic manifestations were. According to both, however, the seed of the great opposition between the sacred and the profane is to be found in nature.

But such an enterprise is impossible. It assumes a veritable creation out of nothing. No fact of ordinary experience can give us the idea of something whose defining trait is to be outside the world of ordinary experience. A man as he appears to himself in his dreams is only a man. The natural forces that our senses perceive are only natural forces, however intense they may be. Hence my criticism of both doctrines. To explain how these supposed data of religious thought could take on a sacredness that has no objective basis, they had to adopt the notion that a whole world* of hallucinatory representations superimposed themselves upon those data of experience, distorting them to the point of making them unrecognizable, and replacing reality with mere figments of the imagination. In one case, it is the illusions of dreaming that supposedly brought about such a transfiguration; in the other, it is the brilliant but vacant march of images evoked by words. But in either case, one arrived necessarily at religion as the product of delirious interpretation.

Thus one positive conclusion arises from this critical examination. Since, in themselves, neither man nor nature is inherently sacred, both acquire sa-

* The first edition says *monde*, or "world"; the second says *mode*.

credness elsewhere. Beyond the human individual and the natural world, then, there must be some other reality in relation to which this species of delirium that every religion is, in some sense, takes on meaning and objective significance. In other words, beyond what has been called naturism and animism, there must be another more fundamental and more primitive cult, of which animism and naturism are derivative forms or particular aspects.

That cult exists. It is the one to which the ethnographers have given the name "totemism."

I

The word "totem" appeared in the ethnographic literature only at the end of the eighteenth century. It crops up first in the book of an Indian interpreter, J. Long, which was published in London in 1791.[1] For nearly half a century, totemism was known exclusively as an American institution.[2] It was only in 1841 that Grey, in a passage that is still celebrated,[3] drew attention to the existence of similar practices in Australia. From then on, scholars began to realize that they were in the presence of a system that has a certain generality.

But they saw it as being essentially an archaic institution, an ethnographic curiosity without much interest for the historian. McLennan was the first to try to connect totemism with general human history. In a series of articles published in the *Fortnightly Review*,[4] he set out to show not only that totemism was a religion but also that a multiplicity of beliefs and practices that recur in much more advanced religious systems were derived from it. He even went so far as to make it the source of all the animal- and plant-worshipping cults that can be observed among ancient peoples. That extension of totemism was surely overstated. The cult of animals and plants has multiple causes that cannot be reduced to only one without very great oversimplification. Yet by its overstatements, this simplification had the advantage of drawing attention to the historical importance of totemism.

For their part, the Americanists had long since noticed that totemism was linked with a definite social organization, one based on the division of

---

[1][John Long], *Voyages and Travels of an Indian Interpreter and Trader,* [Cleveland, A. H. Clark, 1904].

[2]This idea was so widespread that M. [Albert] Réville still treated America as the classical locale of totemism ([*Les*] *Religions des peuples non civilisés,* vol. I [Paris, Fishbacher, 1883], p. 242).

[3][George Grey,] *Journals of Two Expeditions in North-West and Western Australia,* vol. II [London, T. & W. Boone, 1841], p. 228.

[4][James Ferguson McLennan] "The Worship of Animals and Plants" ["Totems and Totemism"—apparently Durkheim's expansion of the title. Trans.], [*FR,* vol. XII old series, vol. VI new series (1869), pp. 407–427, 562–582], [vol. XIII old series, vol. VII new series (1870), pp. 194–200].

society into clans.[5] In 1877, in his *Ancient Society*,[6] Lewis H. Morgan undertook the study of this social organization in order to determine its distinguishing features and, at the same time, to show its prevalence among the Indian tribes of North and Central America. At almost the same time, and moreover at Morgan's suggestion, Fison and Howitt[7] documented the existence of the same social system in Australia, as well as its relations with totemism.

Under the influence of these leading ideas, studies could be done more methodically. Research encouraged by the Bureau of American Ethnology contributed greatly to the progress of these studies.[8] By 1887, the documents were of sufficient number and significance for Frazer to have judged it opportune to collect and present them to us in a systematic overview. Such is the object of his small book titled *Totemism*,[9] in which totemism is studied as both religion and legal institution. But this study was purely descriptive, making no effort either to explain totemism[10] or to delve into its fundamental ideas.

Robertson Smith was the first to take up the task of elaboration. He realized more keenly than his predecessors how rich in seeds for the future this

[5]This idea is clearly expressed in a study by [Albert] Gallatin, "A Synopsis of the Indian Tribes" (*Archaeologia Americana* vol. II, pp. 109ff. [also New York, AMS Press, 1973.]), and in a circular letter of Morgan [an article under the name A. P. Morris. Trans.], reproduced in *CJ* (1860), p. 149.

[6][Lewis Henry Morgan, *Ancient Society or Researches in the Lines of Human Progress from Savagery, through Barbarism to Civilisation*, London, Macmillan, 1887.] This work had been prepared for and preceded by two others by the same author: [Lewis Henry Morgan, *The League of the [Hodenosaunee or] Iroquois*, New York, M. H. Newman, 1851; and *Systems of Consanguinity and Affinity of the Human Family*, Washington, D.C., Smithsonian Institution, 1870].

[7][Lorimer Fison and Alfred Howitt], *Kamilaroi and Kurnai [Group Marriage and Relationship, and Marriage by Element, Drawn Chiefly from the Usage of the Australian Aborigines*, Melbourne, G. Robertson, 1880].

[8]Beginning with the first volumes of the *Annual Report of the Bureau of American Ethnology* [First Annual Report, 1879–1881, Washington, DC, Government Printing Office, 1881. Trans.], we find the study of [John Wesley] Powell, "Wyandot Government" (vol. I, p. 59), those of [Frank Hamilton] Cushing, "Zuñi Fetishes" (vol. II, p. 9), [Erminnie Adele] Smith, "Myths of the Iroquois" (vol. II, p. 76), and the important work of [J. Owen] Dorsey "Omaha Sociology" (vol. III, p. 211), which are all contributions to the study of totemism.

[9]It [James George Frazer, "Totemism"] first appeared, abridged, in the *Encyclopedia Britannica* [9th ed., Edinburgh, Adam & Charles Black, 1887].

[10]In his *Primitive Culture* [New York, Henry Holt, 1871], Tylor [Edward Burnett] had already attempted an explanation of totemism, to which I will return later but do not recount here; by reducing totemism to no more than a special case of the ancestor cult, that explanation completely misunderstands the importance of totemism. I mention in this chapter only the observations or theories that have led to important advances in the study of totemism.

crude and confused religion was. To be sure, McLennan had already compared totemism with the great religions of antiquity, but that was only because he thought he had found a cult of animals and plants in both. But to reduce totemism to a kind of animal or plant worship was to see only what was most superficial and, even at that, to misunderstand its true nature. Smith set out to move beyond the letter of totemic beliefs in order to find the fundamental principles governing them. In his book *Kinship and Marriage in Early Arabia*,[11] he had already shown that totemism presupposes a consubstantiality of man and animal (or plant), whether natural or acquired. In his *Religion of the Semites*,[12] he made this same idea the origin of the whole sacrificial system. He contended that humanity owes the principle of alimentary communion to totemism. Certainly we may find Smith's theory one-sided, and it is no longer adequate to the facts we now have. Nonetheless, it contains an ingenious insight and it has had a fruitful influence on the science of religions. Frazer draws upon these same ideas in *The Golden Bough*.[13] In it he relates to European folklore the totemism that McLennan had related to the religions of classical antiquity and Smith to those of the Semitic peoples. McLennan's school and Morgan's thus came to join that of Mannhardt.[14]

During this time, the American tradition continued to develop, and with an independence, moreover, that it has kept until quite recently. Three groups of societies in particular were the object of research on totemism: the tribes of the Northwest—the Tlingit, the Haida, the Salish, and the Tshimshian; the great Sioux nation; and finally, in America's center, the Pueblo Indians. The first were studied principally by Dall, Krause, Boas, Swanton, and Hill Tout; the second by Dorsey; the last by Mindeleff, Mrs. Stevenson, and Cushing.[15] But however rich the harvest of facts collected, the available documents remained fragmentary. Although the American religions contain many traces of totemism, they have nevertheless gone beyond the totemic phase proper. On the other hand, documentation on Australia scarcely went beyond isolated

[11][William Robertson Smith], *Kinship and Marriage in Early Arabia*, Cambridge [Cambridge University Press], 1885.

[12][William Robertson Smith], *Lectures on the Religion of the Semites* [London, A & C Black, 1889]. This is the published version of a course taught at the University of Aberdeen in 1888. Cf. the article "Sacrifice" in the *Encyclopedia Britannica* [9th ed., Edinburgh, Adam & Charles Black, 1887].

[13][James George] Frazer, *The Golden Bough* [*A Study in Magic and Religion*], London [and New York, Macmillan], 1890. Since then, a three-volume second edition has appeared (1900), and the third of five volumes is in the process of publication. [This text was reissued by St. Martin's Press in 1990. Trans.]

[14]It is well to cite the interesting work of [Edwin] Sidney Hartland, *The Legend of Perseus*, 3 vols. [London, D. Nutt, 1894–1896] in this connection.

[15]Here I confine myself to giving the authors' names; the books will be indicated below, as I use them.

beliefs and rites, rites of initiation and prohibitions relative to the totem. Thus it is with facts taken from hither and yon that Frazer tried to sketch an overall picture of totemism. Whatever its obvious merit, a reconstruction undertaken in these conditions could only be incomplete and hypothetical. All things considered, a fully functioning totemic system had not yet been seen.

This gap has been filled only in recent years. Two remarkably astute observers, Messieurs Baldwin Spencer and F. J. Gillen, have discovered,[16] in the interior of the Australian continent, a rather large number of tribes in which they saw in operation a full religious system whose basis and coherence were provided by totemic beliefs. The results of their inquiry were set forth in two works that have given new life to the study of totemism. The first, The Native Tribes of Central Australia,[17] treats the most central of those tribes, the Arunta, the Luritcha,* and, a little farther south, on the western shore of Lake Eyre, the Urabunna. The second, titled The Northern Tribes of Central Australia,[18] treats the societies to the north of the Urabunna: They occupy the territory that extends from the Macdonnell Ranges to the Carpenter Gulf. To cite only the main groups, these are the Unmatjera, the Kaitish, the Warramunga, the Tjingilli, the Binbinga, the Walpari, the Gnanji and finally, on the very shores of the gulf, the Mara and the Anula.[19]

*The spelling "Loritja" is used elsewhere.

[16]Although Spencer and Gillen were the first to study these tribes thoroughly they were not the first to speak about them. Howitt had drawn attention to the social organization of the Wuaramongo (Warramunga of Spencer and Gillen) as long ago as 1888 in "Further Notes on the Australian Class [Systems]," JAI, [vol. XVIII (1889)], pp. 44–45. The Arunta had already been studied in summary fashion by [Reverend Louis] Schulze ("The Aborigines of the Upper and Middle Finke River" [RSSA, vol. XIV, pp. 210–246], 2d installment]; the organization of the Chingalee (the Tjingilli of Spencer and Gillen), the Wombya, etc., by [R. H.] Mathews, "Wombya Organization of the Australian Aborigines, " AA, vol. II new series [1900], p. 494; "Divisions of Some West Australian Tribes, ibid., p. 185; ["Divisions of Australian Tribes"], APS, vol. XXXVII [1898], pp. 151–152 and ["Australian Divisional Systems"], JRS, vol. XXXII, p. 71, vol. XXXIII, p. 111). In addition, he first cites results of the study conducted on the Arunta that had already been published in [Baldwin Spencer], Report on the Work of the Horn Scientific Expedition to Central Australia, part IV [London, Dulau], 1896. The first part of this Report is by [Edward] Stirling, the second is Gillen's; and the entire publication was directed by Baldwin Spencer.

[17][Sir Baldwin Spencer and Francis James Gillen], The Native Tribes of Central Australia [London, Macmillan, 1899], hereafter abbreviated, Native Tribes or Nat. Tr. [I have used Native Tribes. Trans.]

[18][Sir Baldwin Spencer and Francis James Gillen], The Northern Tribes of Central Australia [London, Macmillan,1904], hereafter Northern Tribes or North. Tr. [I have used Northern Tribes. Trans.]

[19]I write "the Arunta," "the Anula," "the Tjingilli," etc. without adding an "s" to these names to mark the plural. It seems illogical to incorporate into words that are not French a grammatical sign that has its meaning only in our language. I will make exception to this rule only when the tribal name has obviously been gallicized (les Hurons, for example). [I have followed Durkheim in not adding "s" to proper nouns, but to avoid the confusion that can arise because English articles do not indicate plurals, I have made common nouns plural by adding "s." Trans.]

More recently, Carl Strehlow, a German missionary who also spent many years in these same societies of central Australia,[20] has begun to publish his own studies on two of these tribes, the Aranda and the Loritja (Arunta and Luritcha of Spencer and Gillen).[21] Having mastered the language spoken by these peoples,[22] Strehlow was able to report many totemic myths and religious songs, most of which are given to us in their original texts. Notwithstanding variations of detail that are easily explained and whose importance has been greatly exaggerated,[23] we will see that Strehlow's observations, while complementing, specifying, and sometimes correcting those of Spencer and Gillen, on the whole confirm them.

These discoveries gave rise to an abundant literature, to which I will have occasion to return. The works of Spencer and Gillen especially have had great influence, not only because they were the oldest but because the data were presented in a systematic form that enabled them to guide later studies[24] and also to provoke speculation. The results were commented upon, debated, and interpreted in all kinds of ways. At the same time Howitt, whose fragmentary studies were scattered through many different publications,[25]

---

[20][Carl] Strehlow has been in Australia since 1892. He lived first among the Dieri and moved from there to live among the Arunta.

[21]Strehlow, *Die Aranda-und Loritja-Stämme in Zentral-Australien* [Frankfurt, Joseph Baer, 1907]. To date, four volumes have been published; the first appeared when this book had just been completed. I was unable to evaluate it. The first two volumes deal with myth and legend, the third with the cult. It is proper to add to Strehlow's name that of [Gustav] von Leonhardi, who played an important role in the publication. Not only was he responsible for editing Strehlow's manuscripts, but also, by judicious questions on more than one point, he led Strehlow to specify some of his observations. By the way, an article that Leonhardi gave to *Globus* [Hildbringhausen, Brunswick, 1861–1910] may profitably be consulted; and one will find many extracts from his correspondence with Strehlow ("Ueber einige religiöse und totemistische Vorstellungen der Aranda und Loritja in Zentral-Australien," *Globus* vol. XCI, p. 285). Cf. on the same subject an article of Northcote W. Thomas ["Religious Ideas of the Arunta"], *Folklore* vol. XVI [1905], pp. 428ff.

[22]While not ignorant of the language, Spencer and Gillen know it far less well than Strehlow.

[23]Notably by [Hermann] Klaatsch, "Schlussbericht über meine Reise nach Australien in den jahren 1904-1907," *ZE*, vol. XXIX [1907], pp. 635ff.

[24]The book of K. Langloh Parker [Catherine Somerville Parker], *The Euahlayi Tribe* [London, A. Constable, 1905]; that of [Erhard] Eylmann, *Die Eingeborenen der Kolonie Südaustralien* [Berlin, D. Reimer, 1908]; that of John Mathew, *Two Representative Tribes of Queensland* [London, T. F. Urwin, 1910]; and certain recent articles by Mathew show the influence of Spencer and Gillen.

[25]The list of these publications is to be found in the preface of [Alfred William] Howitt [*Native Tribes of South-East Australia*, New York, Macmillan, 1904], pp. 8–9.

undertook to do for the southern tribes what Spencer and Gillen had done for those of the center. In his *Native Tribes of South-East Australia*,[26] he gives us an overview of social organization among the peoples who occupy southern Australia, New South Wales, and a large part of Queensland. The advances thus achieved prompted Frazer to supplement his *Totemism* with a sort of compendium[27] that brings together all the important documents that concern either totemic religion or the kinship and marriage organization that is thought, rightly or wrongly, to be connected with it. The aim of this work is not to give us a general and systematic view of totemism but rather to make available to researchers the materials necessary for constructing one.[28] In it the facts are arranged in a strictly ethnographic and geographical order: Each continent and, within each continent, each tribe or ethnic group is studied separately. A study as broad as this, passing so many different peoples in review one after the other, certainly could not be equally detailed throughout; but it is still a useful reference that can facilitate research.

II

It emerges from this brief account that Australia is the most favorable terrain for the study of totemism. For this reason, I will make it the principal area of my observation.

In *Totemism*, Frazer was interested primarily in collecting every trace of totemism that can be found in history and ethnography. This led him to include in his study societies whose kind and degree of cultural development are quite disparate: Ancient Egypt,[29] Arabia, Greece,[30] and the southern

---

[26]Ibid. From now on, I will cite this book with the abbreviation *Nat. Tr.* [*Native Tribes.* Trans.], but always preceded by the name "Howitt" to distinguish it from the first book of Spencer and Gillen, whose title I abridge in the same way. [To avoid the confusion that can arise from these abbreviations, I precede every short citation by the author's surname. Trans.]

[27][James George Frazer], *Totemism and Exogamy*, 4 vols., London [Macmillan], 1910. This work begins with a republication of the little book *Totemism*, reproduced without fundamental changes. [This republication is found in vol. I. Trans.]

[28]It is true that, at the beginning and end, we find general theories of totemism that will be set forth and discussed further on. But these theories are relatively independent of the collected facts accompanying them, for they had already been published in various review articles well before this work appeared. Those articles were reproduced in the first volume (pp. 89–172).

[29]Ibid., p. 12.

[30]Ibid., p. 15.

Slavs[31] figure alongside the tribes of Australia and America. This procedure was unsurprising in a disciple of the anthropological school. The aim of that school is not to situate religions in the social milieux of which they are part[32] and to differentiate among them on that basis. Instead, as the name indicates, the aim is to go beyond national and historical differences in order to arrive at the universal and truly human basis of religious life. They assume that man possesses a religious nature in and of himself, by virtue of his own constitution and independent of all social conditions, and they propose to determine* what that nature is.[33] In research of this sort, all peoples can be drawn upon. No doubt, it would be preferable to inquire most of the most primitive, because among primitives that original nature is more likely to be in the open; but since it can also be found among the more civilized, they too are naturally called upon to testify. Even more will all those thought to be not very distant from the origins (all those assembled haphazardly under the imprecise rubric of *savages*) be put on the same plane and consulted interchangeably. Moreover, since from this point of view the facts are of interest only in proportion to their degree of universality, researchers feel obliged to amass the largest possible number of them. It is not thought possible to make the scope of comparison too broad.

Such cannot be my method, and for several reasons.

First, for the sociologist as for the historian, social facts exist in relationship with the social system to which they belong†; hence they cannot be understood apart from it. This is why two facts belonging to two different societies cannot be fruitfully compared simply because they resemble one another. Those societies must also resemble one another—which is to say that the societies themselves must be varieties of the same species. The comparative method would be impossible if social types did not exist, and it cannot

*The typo-ridden French second edition says *terminer* ("to finish" or "finish off"), instead of *déterminer.*

†The term "function," in one of the senses associated with functionalism, appears in the French text: *Les faits sociaux sont fonction du système social dont ils font partie.*

[31]Ibid., p. 32. [Frazer's actual reference is to Transylvania, not to the southern Slavs. Trans.]

[32]In this regard, it should be noted that the more recent work, *Totemism and Exogamy*, marks an important advance in Frazer's thought and method. Whenever he describes the religious or household institutions of a tribe, he makes an effort to determine the geographical and social conditions in which that tribe is found. As sketchy as these analyses may be, they still suggest a break with the old methods of the anthropological school.

[33]Of course, I, too, consider that the principal object of the science of religions is to arrive at an understanding of the religious nature of man. But since I see it not as an innate given but a product of social causes, there can be no question of determining it wholly apart from the social milieu.

be usefully applied except within the same type. What mistakes have been left unmade through failure to understand this rule! So it is that scholars have improperly compared facts that, despite external resemblances, had neither the same meaning nor the same import: primitive democracy and that of today, the collectivism of lower societies and the socialist tendencies of today, the monogamy that is prevalent among the Australian tribes and that sanctioned by our codes, etc. Confusions of this sort are found even in Frazer's book. He often jumbles together mere animal-worship and practices that are specifically totemic, even though the sometimes enormous distance between the corresponding social milieux precludes any notion of assimilating the two. Thus, if we do not wish to fall into the same mistakes, we must concentrate our research on a clearly defined type of society rather than extend our research over all possible societies.

Indeed, it is important to focus as narrowly as possible. We can usefully compare only facts that we know well. When we undertake to encompass all sorts of societies and civilizations, we cannot know any with the requisite competence; when we put together facts from everywhere to compare them, we are forced to take them indiscriminately, having neither the means nor, for that matter, the time to treat them critically. These chaotic and sketchy comparisons have discredited the comparative method among a certain number of good minds. That method can yield serious results only if it is applied to a rather limited number of societies, so that each of them can be studied with adequate precision. The key is to choose those in which the investigation has the greatest chance of being fruitful.

In any event, the quality of the facts is much more important than their number. Quite secondary, in my view,[34] is the question whether totemism was more widespread or less so. If totemism interests me, that is mainly because, through studying it, I hope to discover relationships that will help us understand what religion is. To establish relationships, it is neither necessary nor always useful to stack experiments one upon the other. It is far more important to have well-done experiments that are truly significant. A solitary fact can shed light on a law, while a multitude of vague and imprecise observations can lead only to confusion. In every kind of science, the scientist would be submerged by the facts that present themselves if he did not make a choice among them. He must perceive which ones promise to be the most instructive and turn his attention to those, while turning aside from the others temporarily.

[34]Hence the importance I ascribe to totemism is entirely independent of the question whether it was universal, a point that cannot be repeated too many times.

This is why, with one exception that will be indicated later, I propose to limit my research to the Australian societies. They fulfill all the conditions that have just been listed. They are completely homogeneous; and while one can discern varieties among them, they belong to the same type. Indeed, their homogeneity is so great that the framework of social organization is not only the same but designated by names that are either identical or equivalent in many tribes that are sometimes very far from one another.[35] In addition, the most thorough documentation we have concerns Australian totemism. Finally, what I propose above all to study in this work is the most primitive and the simplest religion that can be found. To discover that religion, therefore, it is natural for me to address myself to societies that stand as close as possible to the origins of evolution. It is obviously there that I have the greatest chance of discovering that religion and studying it properly. Now, there are no societies that exhibit this characteristic more fully than do the Australian tribes. Not only is their technology quite rudimentary—the house and even the hut are still unknown among them—but their organization is the most primitive and the simplest known. It is the organization that I have called elsewhere[36] "organization based upon clans." Beginning in the next chapter, I will set out its basic traits.

Still, while making Australia the main object of my research, I think it useful not to disregard completely the societies in which totemism was first discovered: the Indian tribes of North America.

There is nothing ill founded about expanding the field of comparison in this way. Granted, the American peoples are more advanced than those of Australia. The technology has become more developed, the people live in houses or tents, and there are even fortified villages. The social density is greater, and centralization, which is altogether absent in Australia, begins to appear: There are vast confederations under a central authority, such as that of the Iroquois. Sometimes there is a complex system of differentiated and hierarchically ordered classes. Nonetheless, the basic lines of societal structure remain what they are in Australia; it is still organization based on clans. Thus we do not have two different types but two varieties of the same type, which are rather close

---

[35]This is the case of the phratries and the marriage classes; on this point, see Spencer and Gillen, *Northern Tribes*, chap. III; Howitt, *Native Tribes*, pp. 109, 137–142; [Northcote Whitridge] Thomas, *Kinship [Organizations] and [Group] Marriage in Australia* [Cambridge, Cambridge University Press, 1906], chaps. VI, VII.

[36] Emile Durkheim, *Division du travail social*, 3d ed. [Paris, F. Alcan, (1893) 1902], p. 150. [Also in *Emile Durkheim on the Division of Labor in Society*, New York, Macmillan, 1933, p. 175. Trans.].

to one another. They are two successive moments in a single evolution; in consequence, they are similar enough to make comparisons possible.

Besides, such comparisons can have their uses. Precisely because the technology of the Indians is much more advanced than that of the Australians, certain aspects of the social organization common to both are more easily studied among the Indians. As long as men are still making their first steps in the art of expressing their thought, it is not easy for the observer to perceive what moves them; for nothing translates in an obvious way what happens in these obscure minds that have only a confused and fleeting self-awareness. For example, religious symbols are at that point only formless combinations of lines and colors, the meaning of which is not easy to guess, as we will see. There are indeed many actions and movements by which inward states are expressed; but since those states are by nature fleeting, they quickly disappear from view. The reason totemism was noticed earlier in North America than in Australia is this: it was more readily seen—even though in America it had a relatively smaller place in the totality of religious life. Besides, where the beliefs and institutions are not captured in a rather definite material form, they are more likely to change under the influence of the slightest circumstance, or to be erased from memory altogether. Thus, there is something changeable and protean about the Australian clans, whereas the corresponding organization in America most often has greater stability and more clearly defined contours. Thus, although American totemism is further from the origins than Australia's, there are important features whose remnants it has better preserved for us.

In the second place, to understand an institution properly, it is often well to follow it into advanced phases of its evolution,[37] for sometimes it is only when the institution is fully developed that its true meaning appears with greatest clarity. On those grounds as well, since American totemism has a longer history, it can help clarify certain aspects of Australian totemism.[38] At the same time, it will put us in a better position to see how totemism is connected with the religious forms that have come later and to place it within the context of historical development.

[37]Of course, things do not always work in this fashion. As I have said, the simplest forms frequently help us better understand the more complex. On this point, no rule of method is automatically applicable to all possible cases.

[38]It is in this way that individual totemism in America will help us understand its role and importance in Australia. Since individual totemism is very rudimentary in Australia, it probably would have passed unnoticed.

In the analyses to follow, I will not bar myself from using certain data drawn from the Indian societies of North America. I use it not because there could be any question of studying American totemism here.[39] Such a study must be done directly, in and of itself, and not buried in the study I will undertake: It would pose different problems and would involve a whole set of specific investigations. I use American data only as a supplement and only when it appears well suited to helping us understand the Australian data better. The latter are the real and immediate object of my research.[40]

[39]Moreover, in America there is not one type of totemism but different types that would have to be distinguished.

[40]I will depart from that circle of facts quite rarely, when a particularly instructive comparison seems essential.

BOOK TWO
THE ELEMENTARY
BELIEFS

CHAPTER ONE

THE PRINCIPAL TOTEMIC BELIEFS

The Totem as Name and as Emblem

Owing to its nature, my study will be in two parts. Since every religion is made up of intellectual conceptions and ritual practices, I must treat in succession the beliefs and rites that make up totemic religion. Nevertheless, these two elements of religious life are too closely allied for any radical separation to be possible. Although in principle derived from the beliefs, the cult nevertheless reacts upon them, and the myth is often modeled on the rite so as to account for it, especially when the meaning of the rite is not, or is no longer, apparent. Conversely, there are beliefs that do not clearly manifest themselves except through rites that translate them. Thus, the two parts of the analysis cannot fail to interpenetrate. Still, they are of such a different order that separate study of them is indispensable. And since it is impossible to understand anything about a religion without knowing the ideas on which it rests, we must first become acquainted with those ideas.

My intention is not to retrace here all the speculative byways of religious thought, even among the Australians. I wish to get down to the elementary ideas at the basis of religion, but the point is not to follow speculative thought through all the sometimes quite luxuriant detail that the mythological imagination has given them in these societies. When myths can aid in understanding the fundamental notions better, I will certainly use those, but without making mythology itself the object of study. Besides, insofar as mythology is a work of art, it does not belong solely to the science of religions. In addition, the mental processes of which it is the outcome are far too complex to allow them to be studied indirectly and obliquely. Mythology is a difficult problem in its own right, one that must be treated in and of itself and according to its own specialized method.

Among the beliefs on which totemic religion rests, the most important are those that concern the totem, and so we must begin with those beliefs.

I

At the basis of most Australian tribes, we find a group that has a dominant place in collective life: That group is the clan. Two essential traits characterize it.

First, the individuals who comprise it consider themselves joined by a bond of kinship but a bond of a particular sort. This kinship does not arise from the fact that they have well-defined relations of common blood; they are kin solely because they bear the same name. They are not fathers, mothers, sons or daughters, uncles or nephews of one another in the sense we now give those terms; nevertheless they regard themselves as forming a single family, which is broad or narrow depending on the size of the clan, solely because they are collectively designated by the same word. And if we say they regard one another as being of the same family, it is because they acknowledge reciprocal obligations identical to those that have been incumbent on kin in all ages: obligations of help, vengeance, not marrying one another, and so forth.

In this first characteristic, the clan is not different from the Roman *gens* and the Greek γένος, for kinship among the *gentiles* arose exclusively from the fact that all the members of the *gens* carried the same name,[1] the *nomen gentilicium*. And of course the *gens* is in sense a clan, but it is a variety of the genus that must not be confused with the Australian clan.[2] What distinguishes the Australian clan is that the name it bears is also that of a definite species of material things with which it thinks it has special relations whose nature I will address below, in particular, relations of kinship. The species of things that serves to designate the clan collectively is called its *totem*. The clan's totem is also that of each clan member.

Every clan has a totem that belongs to it alone; two different clans of the same tribe cannot have the same one. Indeed, one is part of a clan only by virtue of having a certain name. So all who bear this name are members of it in the same right; however scattered across the tribal territory they may be, they all have the same kin relations with one another.[3] In consequence, two

---

[1] Here is the definition Cicero gave to gentility. *Gentiles sunt qui inter se eodem nomine sunt* (Top. 6). [Members of a *gens* are those who have the same family name. Trans.]

[2] In general, a clan is a family group in which kinship results only from having the same name. It is in this sense that the *gens* is a clan. The totemic clan is a particular species within the genus thus constituted.

[3] To a certain extent, the ties of solidarity extend even beyond the limits of the tribe. When individuals of different tribes have the same totem, they have special duties toward one another. This fact is explicitly stated for certain tribes of North America. (See [James George] Frazer, *Totemism and Exogamy,* vol.

groups that have the same totem can only be two sections of the same clan. It is common for a clan not to reside in the same place, but to have members in different places. Even so, the clan's unity is felt, though it has no geographical basis.

Regarding the word "totem": The Ojibway, an Algonquin tribe, use this word to denote the species of things whose name a clan bears.[4] Although the term is not Australian,[5] and in fact is found in only one society of America, ethnographers have adopted it and use it generally to denote the institution I am describing. Schoolcraft, the first to extend the meaning in this sense, spoke of a "totemic system."[6] This extension, of which there are numerous examples in ethnography, does have drawbacks. It is not quite right for an institution of such importance to bear a name that is given haphazardly, taken from a strictly local dialect, and in no way reflecting the distinctive traits of the thing it expresses. But today this usage of the word is so universally accepted that it would be an excess of purism to rebel against it.[7]

In the great majority of cases, the objects that serve as totems* belong to

---

III [4 vols., London, Macmillan, 1910], pp. 57, 81, 299, 356–357. The texts on Australia are less explicit. Still, the prohibition of marriage between members of the same totem is probably international.

*In this chapter, Durkheim applies the adjective "totemic" (*totémique*) to "system," "group," "belief," "mark," "representation," "significance," "coat of arms," "symbol," and "decoration"—indeed, to everything except the animal or plant that serves as the totem of some group. I believe he intends to keep reminding the reader that while an animal or plant is the totem of some group, in itself it is not the totem; hence his careful locution, "the animal that serves as totem," which weighs down English sentences. Having stated this reminder, I simplify with "totemic animal" from now on.

[4][Lewis Henry] Morgan, *Ancient Society [or Researches in the Lines of Human Progress from Savagery through Barbarism to Civilization*, London, Macmillan, 1877], p. 165.

[5]In Australia, the words used vary by tribe. In the regions observed by Grey, people said *Kobong*; the Dieri say *Murdu* ([Alfred William] Howitt, *The Native Tribes of South-East Australia* [New York, Macmillan, 1904], p. 91), the Narrinyeri, *Ngaitye* ([Rev. George] Taplin, in [Edward] Micklethwaite Curr, [*The Australian Race; Its Origin, Languages, Customs, Place of Landing in Australia, and the Routes by Which It Spread Itself over That Continent*], vol. II ([Melbourne, J. Ferres, 1886–87], p. 244), the Warramunga, *Mungái* or *Mungáii* [Sir Baldwin Spencer and Francis James Gillen] *Northern Tribes [of Central Australia*, London, Macmillan, 1904], p. 754), etc.

[6][Henry Rowe] Schoolcraft, [*Historical and Statistical Information Respecting the History, Condition, and Prospects of the] Indian Tribes of the United States*, IV [Philadelphia, Lippincott Grambo, 1851–1857], p. 86. [The phrase "totemic element" appears on this page, but the passage is not about a "totemic system." Trans.]

[7]And yet the fate of this word is all the more regrettable, since we do not even know exactly how it is spelled. Some spell it *totam*, others *toodaim* or *dodaim* or *ododam*. See Frazer, *Totemism and Exogamy*, vol. I, p. 1. Even the meaning of the word is not exactly defined. If we rely on the first observer of the Ojibway, J. Long, the word *totem* designates the protective genie, the individual totem (to be discussed later, Bk. II, chap. 4), and not the totem of the clan. But the reports of other explorers say exactly the opposite (see on this point Frazer, *Totemism and Exogamy*, vol. III, pp. 49–52).

either the plant or animal kingdom but mainly to the latter. Inanimate things are used much more rarely. Of more than 500 totemic names listed by Howitt from among the tribes of the Australian Southwest, barely forty are not names of either plants or animals: They are clouds, rain, hail, frost, moon, sun, wind, autumn, summer, winter, certain stars, thunder, fire, smoke, water, red ochre, and sea. To be noted is the very limited place given to heavenly bodies and, more generally, to the great cosmic phenomena that nonetheless were to have a great future in the course of religious development. Among all the clans of which Howitt speaks, there are only two with the moon as totem,[8] two with the sun,[9] three with a star,[10] three with the thunder,[11] and two with lightning.[12] Only the rain is an exception; unlike the others, rain is very common.[13]

Such are the totems that may be called normal, but totemism has its abnormalities as well. Sometimes the totem is not a whole object but part of one. This seems to be rather uncommon in Australia;[14] Howitt cites only a single example.[15] However, it might well turn out to be a rather frequent occurrence in tribes in which the totemic groups have been excessively subdivided, in which one could say that the totems themselves must have been broken in order to provide names for the many divisions. This seems to have happened among the Arunta and the Loritja. In those two societies, Strehlow lists as many as 442 totems, several of which designate not an animal species but a particular part of such animals—for example, the tail or the stomach of the opossum, or the fat of the kangaroo.[16]

[8]The Wotjobaluk (p. 121) and the Buandik (p. 123).

[9]Ibid.

[10]The Wolgal (p. 102), the Wotjobaluk, and the Buandik.

[11]The Muruburra (p. 117), the Wotjobaluk, and the Buandik.

[12]The Buandik and the Kaiabara (p. 116). Note that all these examples are taken from only five tribes.

[13]Similarly, of 204 kinds of totems collected by Spencer and Gillen in a large number of tribes, 188 are animals or plants. Inanimate objects are the boomerang, cold water, darkness, fire, lightning, the moon, red ochre, resin, salt water, the evening star, a stone, the sun, water, the whirlwind, the wind, and hailstones (Spencer and Gillen, *Northern Tribes*, p. 773. Cf. Frazer, *Totemism and Exogamy*, vol. I, pp. 253–254).

[14]Frazer (*Totemism and Exogamy*, pp. 10, 13) cites numerous cases and even makes them a genus apart, which he calls *split-totems*. But these examples are taken from tribes in which totemism is profoundly altered, as in Samoa and in the tribes of Bengal.

[15]Howitt, *Native Tribes*, p. 107.

[16]See the tables compiled by [Carl] Strehlow, *Die Aranda- und Loritja-Stämme in Zentral-Australien*, Frankfurt, J. Baer, 1907, vol. II, pp. 61–72 (cf. III, xiii–xvii). It is worth noting that these fragmentary totems are exclusively animal totems.

The totem is ordinarily not an individual but a species or a variety: It is not such and such kangaroo or crow but the kangaroo or the crow in general. Nonetheless, it is sometimes a particular object. This is unavoidably the case when a thing that is unique of its kind serves as totem: the sun, the moon, such and such constellation, and so forth. But sometimes, as well, clans draw their names from this fold, that geologically caused depression in the terrain, that anthill, and so forth. While it is true that we have only a small number of examples in Australia, Strehlow mentions some.[17] But the very causes that have given rise to these abnormal totems show that they are of relatively recent origin. What actually has caused the erection of certain sites into totems is that a mythical being is thought to have stopped there and to have done some deed of his legendary life.[18] These ancestors are at the same time presented to us in the myths as themselves belonging to clans that once had perfectly normal totems, that is, taken from animal or plant species. So the totemic names that commemorate the exploits of these heroes cannot be primitive, but instead are linked with a form of totemism that is already derivative and altered. The question arises whether the meteorological totems are not of the same origin, since the sun, moon, and stars are often identified with ancestors of the mythical age.[19]

Sometimes—though rarely—a group of ancestors or a single ancestor is used as a totem. The totem in this case is not named after a real thing or a species of real things but after a purely mythical being. Spencer and Gillen long ago noted two or three totems of this sort. Among the Warramunga and among the Tjingilli is a clan that bears the name of an ancestor called Thaballa, who seems to incarnate gaiety.[20] Another Warramunga clan bears the name of a fabulous giant snake named Wollunqua, from whom the clan is held to be descended.[21] We are indebted to Strehlow for several examples of

[17]Ibid., pp. 52, 72.

[18]For example, one of those totems is a depression in which an ancestor of the wildcat totem rested; another is an underground gallery dug by an ancestor of the Mouse clan (ibid., p. 72).

[19][Sir Baldwin Spencer and Francis James Gillen], *Native Tribes [of Central Australia*, London, Macmillan, 1899], pp. 561ff. Strehlow [*Aranda*], vol. II, p. 71 n. 2. [Alfred William] Howitt, *Native Tribes*, pp. 426ff.; "On Australian Medicine Men," *JAI*, vol. XVI (1887), p. 53; "Further Notes on the Australian Class Systems," *JAI*, vol. XVIII [1899], pp. 63ff.

[20]According to the translation of Spencer and Gillen, "Thaballa" means "the boy who laughs." The members of the clan that bears his name believe they hear him laugh in the rocks that serve as his residence (Spencer and Gillen, *Northern Tribes*, pp. 207, 215 [227 n.]). According to the myth reported on p. 422, there was an initial group of mythical Thaballas (cf. p. 208). The clan of the Kati, fully developed men ("full-grown men" as Spencer and Gillen say) seems to be of the same sort (p. 207).

[21]Ibid., pp. 226ff.

this sort.[22] In all these cases, it is rather easy to see what must have happened. Under the influence of various causes, and through the development of mythological thought itself, the collective and impersonal totem gave way to certain mythical personages who moved to the first rank and became totems themselves.

Thus, as interesting as these various irregularities may be, nothing about them should require us to modify our definition of the totem. They do not, as was once believed,[23] constitute so many kinds of totems more or less irreducible to one another and to the normal totem, as I have defined it. They are only secondary and sometimes mutant forms of one and the same notion that is by far the most common and that there is every reason to regard also as the most primitive.

How the totemic name is acquired bears more on the recruitment and organization of the clan than on religion; it thus belongs more to the sociology of the family than to religious sociology.[24] Therefore, I will not go beyond a summary sketch of the most basic governing principles.

Depending on the tribe, three different rules are in use.

In many societies, in fact in most, the child has the totem of its mother, by birth: This is the case among the Dieri and the Urabunna of south-central Australia; the Wotjobaluk and the Gournditch-Mara of Victoria; the Kamilaroi, the Wiradjuri, the Wonghibon, and the Euahlayi of New South Wales; the Wakelbura, the Pitta-Pitta, and the Kurnandaburi of Queensland, to cite only the most important names. Since in this case the mother must be of a different totem from her husband, given the rule of exogamy, and yet lives at her husband's place of origin, the members of a single totem are of necessity dispersed among different places, depending on marriages. As a result, the totemic group has no territorial base.

Elsewhere, the totem is transmitted in the paternal line. In that case, the child remains near its father, and the local group is essentially made up of people who belong to the same totem, with only the married women in them

[22]Strehlow [*Aranda*], vol. II, pp. 71–72. Strehlow reports from among the Loritja and the Arunta the totem of a mythical water snake, which is very like that of the serpent Wollunqua.

[23]This is true of Klaatsch, in his article previously cited (see [Hermann Klaatsch, "Schlussbericht über meine Reise nach Australien in den Jahren 1904–1907"], *ZE*, vol. XXXIX ([1907], above, p. 89, n. 23).

[24]As I indicated in the preceding chapter, totemism concerns both religion and the family. In lower societies, these problems are closely interrelated, but both are so complex that they must be dealt with separately. Moreover, familial organization cannot be understood in advance of knowing primitive religious ideas, for those ideas serve as principles of the family. This is why it was necessary to study totemism as religion before studying the totemic clan as family grouping.

representing foreign totems. In other words, each locality has its own totem. In Australia until recent times, this mode of organization had only been met with in some tribes where totemism is in decay—for example, among the Narrinyeri, where the totem has virtually no religious character anymore.[25] Thus there was good reason to believe that a close connection existed between the totemic system and descent in the maternal line. But Spencer and Gillen have observed, in the northern part of central Australia, a whole group of tribes in which the totemic religion is still practiced and yet the transmission of the totem moves through the paternal line: These are the Warramunga, the Gnanji, the Umbaia, the Binbinga, the Mara, and the Anula.[26]

Finally, a third combination is observed among the Arunta and the Loritja. Here the totem of the child is not necessarily that of either its mother or its father but that of the mythical ancestor who mystically impregnated the mother at the time of conception, by procedures that the observers report in different ways.[27] A definite technique permits recognition of which ancestor it is and to which totemic group he belongs.[28] But because chance places one ancestor and not another close to the mother, the totem of the child turns out to be subject to fortuitous circumstances.[29]

Above and beyond the totems of clans are the totems of phratries. Although not different in nature from clan totems, they must nevertheless be distinguished.

A group of clans united by particular bonds of fraternity is called a phratry. Normally, an Australian tribe is divided into two phratries, with the various clans divided between them. Although there are societies from

[25]See Taplin, "The Narrinyeri Tribe," in Curr, *The Australian Race,* vol. II, pp. 244–245; Howitt, *Native Tribes,* p. 131.

[26]Spencer and Gillen, *Northern Tribes,* pp. 163, 169, 170, 172. Still, it should be noted that in all these tribes except the Mara and the Anula, the transmission of the totem in the paternal line is apparently the most widespread rule, but there are exceptions.

[27]According to Spencer and Gillen (*Native Tribes,* pp. 123ff.), the ancestor's soul is incarnated in the body of the mother and then becomes the soul of the child. According to Strehlow (*Aranda,* vol. II, pp. 51ff.), although conception is the work of the ancestor, it does not involve a reincarnation. But in both interpretations, the totem specific to the child does not necessarily depend on that of its parents.

[28]Spencer and Gillen, *Native Tribes,* p. 133; Strehlow, *Aranda,* vol. II, p. 53.

[29]For the most part, it is the locality where the mother thinks she conceived that determines the totem of the child. As we will see, each totem has its center, and the ancestors prefer to frequent the places that serve as the centers of their respective totems. The totem of the child is thus that of the locality where the mother thinks she conceived. Further, as the mother must be most often in the environs of the place that is the totemic center of her husband, the child usually has the same totem as the father. This doubtless explains why most of the inhabitants in each locality belong to the same totem ([Spencer and Gillen] *Native Tribes,* p. 9).

which that organization has disappeared, there is every reason to believe that it was once widespread. In Australia, at any rate, no tribe has more than two phratries.

In almost all cases in which the phratries have a name whose meaning could be determined, the name turned out to be that of an animal; it therefore seems to be a totem. A. Lang has shown this clearly in a recent book.[30] Accordingly, among the Gournditch-Mara (Victoria), one of the phratries is called Krokitch and the other Kaputch; the first of these means "white cockatoo" and the second "black cockatoo."[31] The same terms are found, wholly or in part, among the Buandik and the Wotjobaluk.[32] Among the Warramunga, the names used, Bunjil and Waangqui, mean eaglehawk and crow.[33] The words "Mukwara" and "Kilpara" are used for the same objects in a large number of tribes in New South Wales;[34] they designate the same animals.[35] The eaglehawk and the crow have also given their names to the two phratries of the Ngarigo and the Wolgal.[36] Among the Kuinmurbura, it is the white cockatoo and the crow.[37] Other examples could be cited. Thus we come to see the phratry as an ancient clan that was broken up, the present clans as the result of this dismemberment, and the solidarity that joins them as a relic of their original unity.[38] It is true that the phratries in certain tribes seem no longer to have definite names; in others, where names exist, the meaning is no longer known even to the natives. This is in no way surprising. The phratries are doubtless a primitive institution, since they are receding everywhere;

[30][Andrew Lang], *The Secret of the Totem* [London, Longmans, 1905], pp. 159ff. Cf. [Lorimer] Fison and [Alfred William] Howitt, *Kamilaroi and Kurnai* [*Group Marriage by Elopement Drawn Chiefly from the Usage of Australian Aborigines; also The Kurnai Tribe, Their Customs in Peace and War*, Melbourne, G. Robertson, 1880], pp. 40–41; John Mathew, *Eaglehawk and Crow* [London, D. Nutt, 1899]; [Northcote Whitridge] Thomas, *Kinship [Organization] and [Group] Marriage in Australia* [Cambridge, Cambridge University Press, 1906], pp. 52ff.

[31]Howitt, *Native Tribes*, p. 124.

[32]Ibid., pp. 121, 123, 124; Curr [*The Australian Race*], vol. III, p. 461.

[33]Howitt, *Native Tribes*, p. 126.

[34]Ibid., pp. 98ff.

[35]Curr [*The Australian Race*], vol. II, p. 165; [Robert] Brough Smyth, [*The Aborigines of Victoria*, vol. I, Melbourne, J. Ferres, Government Printer, 1878], p. 423; Howitt, *Native Tribes*, p. 429.

[36]Howitt, *Native Tribes*, pp. 101–102.

[37][John] Mathew, *Two Representative Tribes of Queensland* [London, T. F. Unwin, 1910], p. 139.

[38]Other support for this hypothesis could be adduced, but that would make it necessary to bring in considerations relative to familial organization, and I am trying to keep the two matters separate. Moreover, that question is of only secondary relevance to my subject.

it is the clans, their offspring, that have come to the fore. So it is natural that the names the phratries bore should gradually have been erased from memory or that people should have ceased to understand them, for they must have belonged to a very archaic language that is no longer used. As proof of this, in several cases in which we know what animal's name it bears, the word that designates that animal in everyday language is entirely different from the one that designates the phratry.[39]

There is a kind of subordination between the phratry totem and the clan totems. Each clan in principle belongs to one and only one phratry. It is very unusual for a clan to have members in the other phratry, a case that is almost never seen outside certain tribes of the center, especially the Arunta.[40] Still, even where disruptive influences have produced overlappings of that kind, the majority of clan members are entirely contained in one of the tribe's two halves; only a minority are found on the other side.[41] Hence, the two phratries do not as a rule interpenetrate; hence, the possible totems an individual can have are determined by the phratry to which he belongs. In other words, the phratry totem is like a genus of which the clan totems are species. We will see that this comparison is not purely metaphorical.

In addition to the phratries and clans, we often find in Australian societies a secondary group that is not without a certain distinctiveness: the marriage class.

Subdivisions of the phratry, whose number may vary from tribe to tribe, are called marriage classes; sometimes we find two per phratry and sometimes four.[42] Their recruitment and functioning are regulated by two principles. First, in each phratry, each generation belongs to a different class from the generation directly preceding it, so when there are two classes per phratry, they necessarily alternate in each generation. The children belong to the

[39]For example, *Mukwara*, which designates a phratry among the Barkinji, the Paruinji, and the Milpulko, means "eaglehawk," according to Brough Smyth; among the clans included in that phratry, there is one that has the eaglehawk as its totem, but here that animal is designated by the word *Bilyara*. The reader will find several cases of this sort cited by Lang, *Secret of the Totem*, p. 162.

[40]Spencer and Gillen, *Native Tribes*, p. 115. According to Howitt (*Native Tribes* pp. 121, 454), among the Wotjobaluk, the Pelican clan is also represented in both phratries. This seems to me doubtful. Possibly the two clans had two different species of pelicans as their totems. This is what seems to emerge from the information given by [R. H.] Mathews on the same tribe ("[Ethnological Notes on the] Aboriginal Tribes of New South Wales and Victoria," in *RSNSW* [vol. XXXVIII], 1904, pp. 287–288).

[41]On this question, see my article [with Marcel Mauss] "[Sur] le Totémisme," in *AS*, vol. V [1902], pp. 82ff.

[42]On the question of Australian classes in general, see my article "La Prohibition de l'inceste," in *AS*, vol. I [1898], pp. 9ff., and specifically on the tribes having eight classes, "L'Organisation matrimoniale des sociétés australiennes," in *AS*, vol. VIII [1905], pp. 118–147.

class to which their parents do not belong, and the grandchildren are of the same class as their grandparents. Thus, among the Kamilaroi, the Kupathin phratry comprises two classes, Ippai and Kumbo; the Dilbi phratry comprises two others, called Murri and Kubbi. Since filiation goes in the maternal line, the child is of its mother's phratry; if the mother is Kupathin, the child will also be a Kupathin. But if she is of the Ippai class, he will be a Kumbo; then, if female, that child's children will again count within the Ippai class. Likewise, the children of women of the Murri class will be of the Kubbi class, and the children of the Kubbi women will again be Murri.* When there are four classes per phratry instead of two, the system is more complex, but the principle is the same. The four classes basically form two pairs of two classes each, and these two classes alternate in each generation in the manner just indicated. Second, in principle, the members of a class can contract marriage in only one class of the other phratry.[43] The Ippai must marry in the Kubbi class; the Murri, in the Kumbo class. Because this organization profoundly affects marriage relations, these groupings have been given the name "marriage classes."

Scholars have asked whether these classes sometimes had totems, as the phratries and the clans do. This question arose because, in certain Queensland tribes, each marriage class is subject to dietary restrictions peculiar to it. The individuals who comprise it must abstain from the flesh of certain animals that the other classes may freely eat.[44] Would these animals not be totems?

The dietary restriction, however, is not the characteristic mark of totemism. The totem is, first and foremost, a name and, as we will see, an emblem.† In the societies just examined, no marriage class bears the name of an animal or plant or has an emblem.[45] It is possible, of course, that these re-

*The children of the Kubbi men will take their class from their mother. Trans.

†That is, a stylized representation of the group designated—flags, coats of arms, and distinctive painting on people and things are examples.

[43]This principle is not upheld everywhere with equal rigor. In the tribes of the center that have eight classes, in particular, beyond the class with which marriage is regularly permitted, there is another with which people have a kind of secondary *connubium* (Spencer and Gillen, *Northern Tribes*, p. 126). The same is true of certain tribes with four classes. Each class has the choice between two classes of the other phratry. This is true of the Kabi (see Mathew, in Curr, vol. III, p. 162 [This reference remains obscure. Trans.]).

[44]See [Walter Edmund] Roth, *Ethnological Studies among the North-West-Central Queensland Aborigines* (Brisbane, E. Gregory, Government Printer, 1897), pp. 56ff.; [Edward] Palmer, "Notes on Some Australian Tribes," *JAI*, vol. XIII (1894), [pp. 302ff.].

[45]Still, a few tribes are cited in which marriage classes have the names of animals or plants. This is the case of the Kabi (Mathew, *Two Representative Tribes*, p. 150), tribes observed by Mrs. [Daisy M.] Bates ("The Marriage Laws and Customs of the W. Australian Aborigines," in *VGJ*, vols. XXIII–XXIV, p. 47) and perhaps of two tribes observed by Palmer. But these phenomena are very rare and their significance

strictions derive from totemism indirectly. Conceivably the animals protected by them originally served as totems for clans that have since disappeared, while the marriage classes have remained. Sometimes indeed they do have a staying power that clans do not have. As a result, the restrictions now adrift from their original supports may have spread throughout each class, since there were no longer any other groupings to which they could become attached. But even if that rule was born of totemism, clearly it no longer represents anything more than a weakened and diluted form of totemism.[46]

All that has just been said of the totem in the Australian societies is applicable to the Indian tribes of North America. The only difference is that totemic organization among the Indians has a boundedness and a stability that it lacks in Australia. The Australian clans are not simply very numerous but of almost unlimited number in a single tribe. The observers cite some of them by way of example but never succeed in giving us a full list. The reason is that the list is never definitively closed. The same process of segmentation that originally dismembered the phratry and gave rise to clans proper goes on endlessly within the clans; as a consequence of that progressive crumbling, a clan often has only a very small membership.[47] In America, by contrast, the form of the totemic system is better defined. In America the

poorly established. Moreover, it is not surprising that the classes, as well as the sexual groups, have sometimes adopted the names of animals. This unusual extension of totemic names in no way modifies my conception of totemism. [The ethnographer Durkheim identified simply as "Mrs. Bates" is the subject of a full-scale biography: Julia Blackburn, *Daisy Bates in the Desert*, New York, Pantheon, 1994. Trans.]

[46]The same explanation perhaps applies to certain other tribes of the Southeast and East in which, if Howitt's informants are to be believed, one would find totems specifically assigned to each marriage class as well. This presumably would be the case among the Wiradjuri, the Wakelbura, and the Bunta-Murra of the River Bulloo (Howitt, *Native Tribes* pp. 210, 221, 226). However, by his own admission, the testimonies he gathered are suspect. In fact, it emerges from the lists he compiled that several totems are found in both classes of the same phratry.

The explanation I propose, after Frazer (*Totemism and Exogamy*, pp. 531ff.), raises another difficulty. In principle, each clan, hence each totem, is represented indiscriminately in both classes of a single phratry, since one of those classes is that of children and the other that of the parents from whom the children get their totems. Thus, when the clans disappeared, the totemic prohibitions that survived must have remained common to the two marriage classes, since, in the cases cited, each class has its own. Whence that differentiation? The example of the Kaiabara (a tribe of the south of Queensland) enables us, perhaps, to visualize how this differentiation occurred. In that tribe, the children have their mother's totem, but it is individualized by a distinctive mark. If the mother has the black eaglehawk totem, the child's is the white eaglehawk (Howitt, *Native Tribes*, p. 229). Here, apparently, are beginnings of a tendency for totems to differentiate according to marriage class.

[47]A tribe of a few hundred people sometimes has as many as fifty or sixty clans and even many more. See on this point Durkheim and Mauss, "De Quelques formes primitives de classification," in *AS*, vol. VI (1903), p. 28, n.1.

tribes are, on the average, markedly bigger than in Australia but there are fewer clans. Since a single tribe rarely has more than about ten,[48] and often fewer, each clan is a much larger group. Most of all, their number is better defined: People know how many there are and tell us.[49]

This difference is due to their more advanced social organization. From the first time those tribes were observed, the social groups were deeply rooted in the soil and consequently better able to withstand the forces toward dispersion that assailed them. At the same time, the society already had too strong a sense of its unity to remain unconscious of itself and the parts comprising it. Thus, the American example gives us a better grasp of organization based on clans. To judge that organization by the way it now appears in Australia would be misleading. There, in fact, it is in a state of disorder and dissolution that is by no means normal; it ought to be seen instead as the product of a decay that is attributable as much to the natural wear and tear of time as to the disorganizing influence of the whites. To be sure, it is unlikely that the Australian clans were ever as large or as structurally durable as the American clans. Still, there must have been a time when the distance between the two was not so great as it is today. The societies of America would never have managed to equip themselves with the substantial skeleton they did if the clan had always been so fluid and insubstantial.

Indeed, that greater stability has enabled the archaic system of phratries to persist in America with a clarity and relief that it no longer has in Australia. In Australia, the phratry is everywhere in decline; it is often nothing more than a group without a name. When it does have a name, that name is taken from a foreign language or from one that is no longer spoken and is no longer understood or no longer means much to the native. We have been able to infer the existence of phratry totems from a few survivals* that are, for the most part, so inconspicuous that they have escaped a number of observers. By contrast, in certain parts of America, this system of phratries has remained at the fore. The tribes of the northwest coast, in particular the Tlingit and the Haida, have attained a relatively advanced level of civilization, and yet they

---

*Rendered here as "survivals," which is seldom used today, Durkheim's term *survivances* belongs to evolutionary theories of the late nineteenth and early twentieth centuries. It refers to traits thought of as vestiges from an earlier stage and, consequently without present meaning or function.

[48]Except among the Pueblo Indians of the Southwest, where they are more numerous. See [Frederick Webb] Hodge, "Pueblo Indian Clans," in *AA*, 1st ser., vol. IX (October 1895), pp. 345ff. Even so, we can ask whether the groups having those totems are clans or subclans.

[49]See the tables compiled by Morgan in *Ancient Society*, pp. 153–185.

are divided into two phratries that are subdivided into a number of clans: phratries of the Crow and the Wolf among the Tlingit,[50] and of the Eagle and the Crow among the Haida.[51] That division is not merely nominal; it corresponds to existing custom and profoundly marks life. Compared to the distance between the phratries, the moral distance between clans is small.[52] The name each of them bears is not a mere word whose meaning has been forgotten or is known but vaguely. It is a totem in the full sense of the word, and it has all the essential attributes of the totem, such as they will be described below.[53] So on this point as well, there was good reason not to disregard the tribes of America, because there we can directly observe examples of phratry totems, whereas Australia only offers us a few dim vestiges of them.

II

The totem is not simply a name; it is an emblem, a true coat of arms, and its resemblance to the heraldic coat of arms has often been commented upon. "Every family," says Grey of the Australians, "adopts an animal or a plant as their crest and sign"[54]—and what Grey calls a family is indisputably a clan. As Fison and Howitt also say, "The Australian organization shows that the totem is, first of all, the badge of a group."[55] Schoolcraft speaks in the same terms about the totems of North America: "The totem is in fact a design that corresponds to the heraldic emblems of the civilized nations, and each person is authorized to wear it as proof of the identity of the family to which he belongs. This is shown by the real etymology of the word from which *dodaim*

---

[50][Avrel] Krause, *Die Tlinkit-Indianer* [Jena, H. Constenoble, 1885], p. 112; [John Reed] Swanton, "Social Condition, Beliefs and Linguistic Relationship of the Tlingit Indians," BAE, *XXVIth Report* [1908], p. 398.

[51][John Reed] Swanton, *Contributions to the Ethnology of the Haida* [Leiden, E. J. Brill, 1905], p. 62.

[52]"The distinction between the two clans is absolute in every respect," says Swanton, p. 68; he calls "clans" what I call "phratries." The two phratries, he says elsewhere, are like two peoples foreign to one another.

[53]Among the Haida at least, the totem of the clans proper is even more altered than the totem of the phratries. The custom that permits a clan to give or to sell the right to wear its totem arises from the fact that each clan has a number of totems, some of them shared with other clans (see Swanton, pp. 107, 268). Because Swanton calls clans phratries, he is obliged to give the name "family" to clans proper, and the name "household" to real families. But the actual meaning of the terminology he adopts is not in doubt.

[54][George Grey], *Journals of Two Expeditions in Northwestern and Western Australia*, II [London, T. and W. Boone, 1841], p. 228.

[55][Fison and Howitt], *Kamilaroi and Kurnai*, p. 165.

is derived, which means village or residence of a family group."[56] Therefore, when the Indians entered into relations with the Europeans and made contracts with them, each clan sealed the treaties thus concluded with its totem.[57]

The nobles of the feudal age sculpted, engraved, and in every way displayed their coats of arms on the walls of their castles, on their weapons, and on all kinds of other objects belonging to them. The blacks of Australia and the Indians of North America do the same with their totems. The Indians who accompanied Samuel Hearne painted their totems on their shields before going into battle.[58] In time of war, according to Charlevoix, certain Indian tribes had banners, made of bits of bark attached to the end of a pole on which the totems were represented.[59] Among the Tlingit, when a conflict breaks out between two clans, the champions of the two enemy groups wear helmets on which their respective totems are painted.[60] Among the Iroquois, the skin of the totemic animal was placed on each wigwam, as a mark of the clan.[61] According to another observer, the animal was stuffed with straw and placed in front of the door.[62] Among the Wyandot, each clan has its own ornaments and distinctive painting.[63] Among the Omaha, and among the Sioux more generally, the totem is painted on the tent.[64]

Wherever the society has become sedentary, where the house has replaced the tent and the plastic arts are more developed, the totem is carved

[56][Schoolcraft], *Indian Tribes*, vol. I, p. 420. [The quoted material is not on this page, nor is the discussion relevant. Trans.] Cf. vol. I, p. 52. This etymology is, by the way, very disputable. Cf. [Frederick Webb Hodge], *Handbook of American Indians North of Mexico* (Smithsonian Institution, Bureau of Ethnology, IId part [Washington, Government Printing Office, 1907–1910], p. 787.

[57][Schoolcraft] *Indian Tribes*, vol. III, p. 184. Garrick Mallery, *Picture-Writing of the American Indians*, BAE, *Xth Report*, 1893, p. 377.

[58][Samuel] Hearne, [A] *Journey [from Prince of Wale's Fort in Hudson's Bay] to the Northern Ocean* [Dublin, Printed for P. Byrne and J. Rice, 1796], p. 148 (cited in [James George] Frazer, "Totemism" ([*Encyclopedia Britannica*, 9th ed. (Edinburgh, Adam and Charles Black, 1887)], p. 30).

[59][Pierre François Xavier de] Charlevoix, *Histoire et description de la Nouvelle France*, vol. V [Paris, Chez la Veuve Ganeau, 1744], p. 329.

[60]Krause, *Tlinkit-Indianer*, p. 248.

[61]Erminnie A. Smith, "Myths of the Iroquois," BAE *Second [Annual] Report* [Washington, Government Printing Office, 1883], p. 78.

[62][Richard Irving] Dodge, *Our Wild Indians* [Hartford, A. D. Washington and Co., 1882], p. 225.

[63][John Wesley] Powell, "Wyandot Government," *First Annual Report*, BAE, Washington, Government Printing Office, 1881), p. 64.

[64][James Owen] Dorsey, "Omaha Sociology," *Third [Annual] Report*, [BAE, Washington, Government Printing Office, 1884], pp. 229, 240, 248.

on the wood and on the walls. This occurs, for example, among the Haida, the Tshimshian, the Salish, and the Tlingit. Krause says, "The totemic arms are a very special house decoration among the Tlingit." These are animal forms combined in certain cases with human forms and sculpted on poles that rise beside the door as high as fifteen meters; they are usually painted in very flashy colors.[65] Yet totemic representations are not very numerous in a Tlingit village; there are only a few, and those are found in front of the houses of chiefs and the rich. They are much more common, often several per house, in the neighboring tribe of the Haida.[66] With its many sculpted poles standing on all sides and sometimes very tall, a Haida village gives the impression of a holy city bristling with tiny bell towers and minarets.[67] Among the Salish, the totem is often drawn on the interior walls of the house.[68] Elsewhere it is found on canoes, utensils of all kinds, and funeral monuments.[69]

The preceding examples are taken exclusively from among the Indians of North America because such sculptures, engravings, and permanent representations are possible only where the technology of the arts already has a degree of refinement that the Australian tribes have not yet attained. In consequence, the totemic representations of the kind just mentioned are rarer and less apparent in Australia than in America. Nonetheless, there are some examples. Among the Warramunga, at the end of the funeral ceremonies, the bones of the deceased are buried after having been dried and reduced to powder; a figure representing the totem is traced on the ground beside the place where they are deposited.[70] Among the Mara and the Anula, the body is placed in a piece of hollowed-out wood that is also decorated with the identifying designs of the totem.[71] In New South Wales, Oxley

[65]Krause, *Tlinkit-Indianer*, pp. 130–131.

[66]Ibid., p. 308.

[67]See the photograph of a Haida village in Swanton, *Haida*, Pl. IX. Cf. [Edward] Tylor, "Totem Post of the Haida Village of Masset," *JAI*, New Series, vol. I [1907], p. 133.

[68]Charles Hill Tout, "Report on the Ethnology of the Statlumh of British Columbia," *JAI*, vol. XXXV, 1905, p. 155.

[69]Krause, *Tlinkit-Indianer*, p. 230; Swanton, *Haida*, pp. 129, 135ff.; Schoolcraft, *Indian Tribes*, vol. I, pp. 52–53, 337, 356. In this last case, the totem is represented upside down as a sign of mourning. Similar customs are found among the Creek (C. Swan, in Schoolcraft, *Indian Tribes of the United States*, vol. V, p. 265), among the Delaware ([John Gottlieb Ernestus] Heckwelder, *An Account of the History, Manners, and Customs of the Indian Nations Who Once Inhabited Pennsylvania* [Philadelphia, A. Small, 1818], pp. 246–247).

[70]Spencer and Gillen, *Northern Tribes*, pp. 168, 537, 540.

[71]Ibid., p. 174.

found carvings on trees near the tomb where a native was buried, to which Brough Smyth ascribes totemic significance.[72] The natives of Upper Darling engrave their shields with totemic images.[73] According to Collins, almost all the utensils are covered with ornaments that probably have the same meaning; figures of this sort are also found on rocks.[74] Since, for reasons to be set forth below, it is not always easy to interpret these totemic designs, they may well be more common than they seem.

These varied facts provide a sense of the large place held by the totem in the social life of primitives. Thus far, however, it has appeared to us more or less as apart from man himself; we have seen it represented only on things. But totemic images are not only reproduced on the outsides of houses and canoes, on weapons, instruments, and tombs; they recur on men's bodies. Men do not simply place their emblem on the objects they possess but also wear it on their persons; they imprint it in their flesh, and it becomes part of them. This mode of representation is in fact, and by far, the most important one.

Indeed, generally the members of each clan seek to give themselves the outward appearance of their totem. At certain religious festivals among the Tlingit, the person who conducts the ceremony wears a costume that wholly or in part represents the body of the animal whose name the clan bears.[75] Special masks are used for this purpose. The same practices crop up again throughout the American Northwest.[76] They are also found among the Minnitaree when they go into battle[77] and among the Pueblo Indians.[78] Elsewhere, when the totem is a bird, the individuals wear its feathers on their heads.[79] Among the Iowa, each clan has a special way of cutting the hair. In the Eagle clan, two large tufts are arranged at the front of the head, while an-

---

[72]Brough Smyth, *Aborigines of Victoria*, vol. I, p. 99n.

[73]Ibid., p. 284. Strehlow cites an example of the same sort among the Arunta, *Aranda*, vol. III, p. 68.

[74][David Collins], *An Account of the English Colony in New South Wales*, vol. II [London, Printed for T. Cadell and W. Davies, 1804], p. 381.

[75]Krause, *Tlinkit-Indianer*, p. 327.

[76]Swanton, "Social Conditions," pp. 435ff.; [Franz] Boas, "The Social Organization and the Secret Societies of the Kwakiutl Indians," in *Report of the United States National Museum for 1895*, Washington, Government Printing Office, 1897, p. 358.

[77]Frazer, *Totemism and Exogamy*, vol. I, p. 26.

[78][John Gregory] Bourke, *The Snake Dance of the Moquis of Arizona* [Chicago, Rio Grande Press, 1962], p. 229; J. W. Fewkes, "The Group of Tusayan Ceremonials Called Katcinas," in *XVth Report* [*BAE*, Washington, Government Printing Office], 1897, pp. 251–263.

[79][Johann Georg] Müller, *Geschichte der amerikanischen Urreligionen* [Basel, Schewighauser, 1855], p. 327.

other hangs behind; in the Buffalo clan, the hair is arranged in the shape of horns.[80] Similar arrangements are found among the Omaha: Each clan has its own hairstyle. In the Tortoise clan, for example, the head is shaved, leaving six curls—two on each side, one in front and one behind—so as to imitate the feet, head, and tail of the animal.[81]

But it is most often on the body itself that the totemic mark is imprinted, for this is a mode of representation that is within the reach of less advanced societies. It has sometimes been asked whether the common rite of extracting a young man's two upper incisors when he reaches puberty might not have the purpose of imitating the form of the totem. This has not been established as fact, but it is worth noting that the natives themselves sometimes explain the custom in that way. For example, among the Arunta, the extraction of teeth is practiced only in the clan of rain and water. According to tradition, that operation is performed to make them resemble certain black clouds with light edges that are held to announce the speedy coming of rain—the clouds being considered as things of the same family.[82] This is evidence that the native himself realizes that the purpose of these deformations is to give him the appearance of his totem, at least conventionally. Also among the Arunta, during the rites of subincision,* specific kinds of gashes are made on the sisters and the future wife of the novice; the form of the resulting scars appears as well on a sacred object called the *churinga,*† of which I will presently speak. The lines drawn on the churinga are emblematic of the totem.[83] Among the Kaitish, the euro is considered to be closely akin to the rain;[84] the people of the rain clan wear small earrings made of euro teeth.[85] Among the Yerkla, a certain number of gashes that leave scars are inflicted on the young man during initiation; the number and form of these

---

*A form of genital mutilation that involves a cut made along the underside of the penis, and that in some traditions is accompanied by circumcision as well.

†Durkheim's convention of not pluralizing words that are not pluralized in their original languages by the addition of "s" (like "churinga," "waninga," and "nurtunja") can lead to confusion in English, in which articles do not have plurals. For that reason where he says *les churinga,* I say "the churingas." Also, I have followed his tendency to remove Australian terms from italics, once they have been explained.

[80]Schoolcraft, *Indian Tribes,* vol. III, p. 269.

[81]Dorsey, "Omaha Sociology," pp. 229, 238, 240, 245.

[82]Spencer and Gillen, *Native Tribes,* p. 451.

[83]Spencer and Gillen, *Native Tribes,* p. 257.

[84]What these relations of kinship signify will be seen below (Bk. II, chap. 4).

[85]Spencer and Gillen, *Northern Tribes,* p. 296.

scars vary according to totem.[86] One of Fison's informants notes the same sort of thing in the tribes he studied.[87] According to Howitt, the same sort of relationship between certain scarifications and the water totem exists among the Dieri.[88] Finally, among the Indians of the Northwest, the custom of tattooing the totem on the body is very widespread.[89]

The tattoos made by mutilation or scarification do not always have totemic significance;[90] but the case is otherwise for simple designs painted on the body: Those usually represent the totem. True, the native does not wear them every day. When he engages in purely economic occupations, as when the small family groups disperse for hunting and fishing, they do not encumber themselves with this paraphernalia, which can be quite elaborate. But when the clans come together to share a common life and devote themselves to religious ceremonies, wearing it is obligatory. As we will see, each of those ceremonies is the affair of a specific totem, and, in principle, the rites that are addressed to a totem can be performed only by the people of that totem. Those who conduct them,[91] playing the role of celebrants—and sometimes even those who are present as spectators—always wear designs on their bodies that represent the totem.[92] One of the principal rites of initiation, the one that initiates the young man into the religious life of the tribe, is the painting of the totemic symbol upon his body.[93] It is true that, among

[86]Howitt, *Native Tribes*, pp. 744–746; cf. p. 129.

[87]*Kamilaroi and Kurnai*, p. 66 n. It is true that this is disputed by other informants.

[88]Howitt, *Native Tribes*, p. 744.

[89]Swanton, *Haida*, pp. 41ff. See plates XX and XXI; Boas, *The Social Organization of the Kwakiutl*, p. 318; Swanton, *Tlinkit*, Plates xviff. In one case outside the two ethnographic regions we are specifically studying, such tattoos are placed on the animals that belong to the clan. The Bechuana of southern Africa are divided into a certain number of clans: the people of the crocodile, the buffalo, the monkey, etc. The people of the crocodile, for example, make an incision on the ears of their beasts, the shape of which resembles the face of the animal ([Eugene Arnaud] Casalis, *Les Bassoutos* [English trans., *The Basutos*, Capetown, C. Struik, 1965], p. 221). According to [William] Robertson Smith, the same custom existed among the ancient Arabs (*Kinship and Marriage in Early Arabia* [Cambridge, Cambridge University Press, 1885], pp. 212–214).

[90]According to Spencer and Gillen, there are some that have no religious meaning (see *Native Tribes*, pp. 41–42; *Northern Tribes*, pp. 45, 54–56).

[91]Among the Arunta, this rule has exceptions that will be explained below.

[92]Spencer and Gillen, *Native Tribes*, p. 162; *Northern Tribes*, pp. 179, 259, 292, 295–296; Schulze, [Reverend Louis, "Aborigines of the Upper and Middle Finke River," *RSSA*, vol. XIV, 1891], p. 221. What is represented in this way is not always the totem itself but one of those objects that, being associated with the totem, are regarded as things of the same family. [The reference states that bodies are painted; it does not mention painting as a religious rite. Trans.]

[93]This is the case, for example, among the Warramunga, the Walpari, the Wulmala, the Tjingilli, the Umbaia, and the Unmatjera (Spencer and Gillen, *Northern Tribes*, pp. 339, 348). Among the Warramunga,

the Arunta, the design thus made does not always and necessarily represent the totem of the novice;[94] but this is an exception, no doubt a result of the disturbed state into which the totemic organization of that tribe has fallen.[95] What is more, even among the Arunta, at the most solemn moment of the initiation (its high point and consecration being the moment when the novice is admitted to the sanctuary where the sacred objects of the clan are kept), an emblematic painting is drawn on him. This time it is indeed the totem of the young man that is represented.[96] The ties that bind the individual to his totem are so close that, in the tribes of the North American northwest coast, the emblem of the clan is painted not only on the living but even on the dead: A totemic mark is placed on the corpse before burial.[97]

---

at the moment the design is made, the officiants say the following words to the novice: "This mark belongs to your place: Do not turn your eyes to another place." According to Spencer and Gillen, "This language means that the young man must not involve himself in any ceremonies but those that concern his totem; they also testify to the close association that is held to exist between a man, his totem, and the place especially consecrated to that totem." (*Northern Tribes,* p. 584.) Among the Warramunga, the totem is transmitted from father to children; consequently each locality has its own.

[94]Spencer and Gillen, *Native Tribes,* pp. 215, 241, 376.

[95]It will be recalled (see p. 105 above) that in this tribe, the child can have a different totem from his father or his mother and, more generally, of his kin. The relatives of both sides are the designated celebrants of the initiation ceremonies. As a result, since a man in principle is qualified as operator or celebrant only for ceremonies of his own totem, it follows that in certain cases, the rites at which the child is initiated necessarily concern a totem other than his own. This is how it comes about that the paintings made on the body of the novice do not necessarily represent his totem. Cases of this kind are to be found in Spencer and Gillen, *Native Tribes,* p. 229. This shows, moreover, that if there is an anomaly, it is because the ceremonies of circumcision nevertheless belong essentially to the totem that would be the totem of the novice himself if the totemic organization was not disturbed—if the totemic organization was among the Arunta what it is among the Warramunga (ibid., p. 219).

The same disruption has had another consequence. Its effect everywhere has been to loosen somewhat the bonds that unite each totem with a definite group, since the same totem can include members in all the possible local groups, and even in the two phratries indiscriminately. The idea that ceremonies of a totem could be conducted by an individual of a different totem—an idea that is contrary to the very principles of totemism, as we will see better below—has thus been able to establish itself without excessive resistance. It is conceded that a man to whom a spirit has revealed the formula of a ceremony is qualified to preside in it, even though he was not of the totem concerned (ibid., p. 519). Proof that this is an exception to the rule, and the result of a kind of toleration, is that the beneficiary of the formula thus revealed cannot do with it as he pleases. If he transmits the formula, and such transmissions are common, it can only be to a member of the totem to which the rite refers (ibid.).

[96]Ibid., p. 140. In this case, the novice keeps the decoration in which he was dressed until it goes away by itself with the passage of time.

[97]Franz Boas, "First General Report on the Indians of British Columbia," in *BAAS, Fifth Report of the Committee on the North-Western Tribes of the Dominion of Canada* [London, Offices of the Association, 1890], p. 41.

III

These totemic decorations suggest that the totem is not merely a name and an emblem. They are used during religious ceremonies and are part of the liturgy: Thus, while the totem is a collective label, it also has a religious character. In fact, things are classified as sacred and profane by reference to the totem. It is the very archetype of sacred things.

The tribes of central Australia, principally the Arunta, the Loritja, the Kaitish, the Unmatjera, and the Ilpirra,[98] use certain instruments in their rites that, among the Arunta, are called churingas, according to Spencer and Gillen and, according to Strehlow, *Tjurunga*.[99] They are pieces of wood or bits of polished stone of various shapes but generally oval or oblong.[100] Each totemic group has a more or less sizable collection of them. *Upon each of them is engraved a design representing the totem of this group.*[101] Some churingas are pierced at one end, with a string made from human hair or opossum fur passed through the hole. Those that are made of wood and pierced in this way serve the same purpose as those cult instruments* to which the English ethnographers have given the name "bull roarers." Held by the string from which they are suspended, they are rapidly whirled in the air so as to produce the same sort of humming that is made by the "devils" that our children use as toys today; this deafening noise has ritual meaning and accompanies all religious ceremonies of any importance. Thus, churingas of this kind are actually bull roarers. Others, which are not wooden or are not pierced, cannot be used in this manner. Nevertheless, they evoke the same feelings of religious respect.

Indeed every churinga, however used, counts among the most preeminently sacred things. Nothing has surpassed it in religious dignity. The word that designates it makes this immediately clear. At the same time that "churinga" is a noun, it is also an adjective—meaning "sacred." Thus, among

---

*This term applies to special containers, knives, coverings, bells, and other objects used in the course of religious rites.

[98]There are some among the Warramunga as well, but fewer than among the Arunta, and although they have a certain place in the myths, they do not figure in the totemic ceremonies (Spencer and Gillen, *Northern Tribes*, p. 163).

[99]Other names are used in other tribes. I give the Arunta term a generic sense, because it is in that tribe that the churingas have greatest importance and are the best studied.

[100]Strehlow, *Aranda*, vol. II, p. 81.

[101]There are some, but not many, that do not bear any obvious design (see Spencer and Gillen, *Native Tribes*, p. 144).

the names that each Arunta has, there is one so sacred that it must not be revealed to a stranger; it is pronounced but rarely and in a low voice, a sort of mysterious murmur. That name is called *aritna churinga* (*aritna* means "name").[102] More generally, the word "churinga" designates all ritual acts; for example, *ilia churinga* means the cult of the Emu.[103] Thus, churinga, period, used as a noun, is the thing whose quintessential feature is to be sacred. The profane, therefore—women and young men not yet initiated into religious life—may not touch or see the churingas; they are only permitted to look from afar and even then rarely.[104]

The churingas are piously kept in a special place the Arunta call the *ertnatulunga*—a sort of small cave hidden in a deserted place.[105] The entrance is carefully closed with rocks placed so skillfully that a passing stranger never suspects that the religious treasury of the clan is nearby. Such is the churingas' sacredness that it is passed on to the place where they are deposited; women and the uninitiated may not come near it. Young men may do so only when their initiation is completely over, and even then, some are judged to merit that privilege only after several years of trial.[106] The religiousness of the place radiates beyond and is transfused into all that surrounds it: Everything participates in the same quality and is for that reason insulated from profane contact. Is a man chased by another? He is safe if he reaches the ertnatulunga; he cannot be captured there.[107] Even a wounded animal that takes refuge there

---

[102]Ibid., pp. 139, 648; Strehlow, *Aranda*, vol. II, p. 75.

[103]Strehlow, who spells it *Tjurunga*, translates the word a little differently. "This word," he says, "means all that is secret and personal" (*der eigene geheime*). *Tju* is an old word that means hidden, secret, and *runga* means that which is personal to me." But Kempe, who has more authority than Strehlow in the matter, translates *tju* as "great," "powerful," or "sacred" ([Reverend H.] Kempe, "Vocabulary of the Tribes Inhabiting the Macdonnell Ranges," in *RSSA*, vol. XIV (1890–1891, 1898), pp. 1–54], under "*Tju.*" Moreover, Strehlow's translation is basically not so far from the preceding as one might think at first glance, for what is secret is that which is taken away from the knowledge of the profane, in other words, that which is sacred. As concerns the meaning of the word *runga*, that seems very doubtful. The ceremonies of the emu belong to all the members of the Emu clan; all can participate in them; they are not the personal property of any member.

[104]Spencer and Gillen, *Native Tribes*, pp. 130–132; Strehlow, *Aranda*, vol. II, p. 78. A woman who has seen the churinga and the man who has shown it to her are both put to death.

[105]Strehlow calls that place, defined exactly in the same terms Spencer and Gillen use, *arknanuaua* instead of *ertnatulunga* (Aranda, vol. II, p. 78).

[106][Spencer and Gillen], *Northern Tribes*, p. 270, and *Native Tribes*, p. 140.

[107]Ibid., p. 135.

must be respected.[108] Quarrels are prohibited. It is a place of peace, as is said in the Germanic societies; it is the sanctuary of the totemic group; it is a true asylum.

The churinga's virtues are manifested not only by the way it keeps the profane at a distance. It is isolated in this way because it is a thing of great religious value, and its loss would tragically injure the group and the individuals. The churinga has all sorts of miraculous qualities. By its touch, wounds are healed, especially those resulting from circumcision;[109] it is similarly effective against illness;[110] it makes the beard grow;[111] it conveys important powers over the totemic species, whose normal reproduction it ensures;[112] it gives men strength, courage, and perseverance, while depressing and weakening their enemies. Indeed, this last belief is so deep-rooted that when two fighters are battling, if one happens to glimpse that his opponent is wearing churingas, he instantly loses confidence and his defeat is certain.[113] Thus, no ritual instruments have a more important place in religious ceremonies.[114] Their powers are passed on to the celebrants or to the congregation by a kind of anointing; the faithful are smeared with fat and then the churingas are rubbed against their arms, legs, and stomach.[115] Or the churingas are covered with down that flies away in all directions when they are whirled, this being one way to spread the virtues they contain.[116]

Churingas are not merely useful to individuals; the collective fate of the entire clan is bound up with theirs. Losing them is a disaster, the greatest misfortune that can befall the group.[117] Sometimes churingas leave the ertnatu-

---

[108]Strehlow, *Aranda*, vol. II, p. 78. However, Strehlow says that a murderer who takes refuge near an ertnatulunga is mercilessly pursued there and put to death. I have some difficulty reconciling that fact with the privilege the animal enjoys and wonder if the greater rigor with which the criminal is treated is not recent and if it should not be ascribed to a weakening of the taboo that originally protected the ertnatulunga.

[109][Spencer and Gillen], *Native Tribes*, p. 248.

[110]Ibid., pp. 545–546; Strehlow, *Aranda*, vol. II, p. 79. For example, the dust scraped from a stone churinga and dissolved in water makes a potion that heals the sick.

[111]Spencer and Gillen, *Native Tribes*, pp. 545–546; Strehlow, *Aranda* vol. II, p. 79 disputes that.

[112]For example, a churinga of the Yam totem that is placed in the ground makes yams grow at that spot (Spencer and Gillen, *Northern Tribes*, p. 275). It has the same power over the animals (Strehlow, *Aranda*, vol. II, pp. 76, 78; vol. III, pp. 3, 7).

[113][Spencer and Gillen], *Native Tribes*, p. 135; Strehlow, *Aranda*, vol. II, p. 79.

[114][Spencer and Gillen], *Northern Tribes* p. 278.

[115]Ibid., p. 180.

[116]Ibid., pp. 272–273.

[117] Spencer and Gillen, *Native Tribes*, p. 135.

lunga—for example, when they are lent to some foreign group.[118] There is real public mourning when this happens. For two weeks, the people of the totem cry and lament, covering their bodies with white clay as they do when they have lost one of their kin.[119] The churingas are not left for individuals to do with as they please; the ertnatulunga where they are kept is under the control of the group's chief. To be sure, each individual has special rights over certain of them;[120] but even if he is to some extent their owner, he can use them only with the consent of the chief and under the chief's guidance. It is a collective treasury, the Holy Ark* of the clan.[121] The devotion they receive further illustrates the great value that is attached to them. They are handled with a respect that is displayed by the solemnity of the movements.[122] They are cared for, oiled, rubbed, and polished; when they are carried from one place to another, it is in the midst of ceremonies, proof that this travel is considered an act of the very highest importance.[123]

In themselves, the churingas are merely objects of wood and stone like so many others; they are distinguished from profane things of the same kind by only one particularity: The totemic mark is drawn or engraved upon them. That mark, and only that mark, confers sacredness on them. To be sure, Spencer and Gillen believe that the churinga serves as the residence of an ancestral soul and that the authority of that soul gives the object its properties.[124] Strehlow views that interpretation as incorrect but the one he pro-

---

*Here, Durkheim shifts from the term *sacré* to the term *sainte*, using the expression *l'arche sainte*, which is a fixed phrase meaning "something that may not be touched"—quite like the English "sacred cow," which in turn derives from ritual practice in India. I have used the term "holy" not only because "Holy Ark" is the standard expression in American English, but also to let the reader note the shift and reflect on its possible implications (see p. lxix).

[118]A group lends its churinga to another with the idea that those latter will pass on to it some of the virtues they have and that their presence will rejuvenate individuals and the collectivity (ibid., pp. 158ff.).

[119]Ibid., p. 136.

[120]Each individual has a personal bond first of all to one special churinga that serves as a security for his life and then to those he has inherited from his relatives.

[121]Spencer and Gillen, *Native Tribes*, p. 154; *Northern Tribes*, p. 193. The churingas are so marked with collective significance that they replace the "message sticks" that envoys carry when they go to summon foreign groups to a ceremony (*Native Tribes*, pp. 141–142).

[122]Spencer and Gillen, *Native Tribes*, p. 326. [Neither "solemnity" nor other words describing movements appear at this place. Trans.] It should be noted that the bull roarers are treated in the same way (Mathews, "Aboriginal Tribes" pp. 307–308).

[123]Spencer and Gillen, *Native Tribes*, pp. 161, 250ff.

[124]Ibid., p. 138.

poses does not markedly differ from it: He is of the opinion that the churinga is regarded as an image of the ancestor's body or as the body itself.[125] Thus, again, it is feelings inspired by the ancestor and projected onto the material object that make it into a kind of fetish. Yet both conceptions—which barely differ except in the literal detail of the myth—were obviously forged after the fact to make the sacredness imputed to churingas intelligible. There is nothing in the makeup of those pieces of wood and stone, and in their appearance, that predestines them to being regarded as the seat of an ancestral soul or the image of the ancestor's body. So that respect was not caused by the myth; far from it. If men conceived this myth, it was to account for the religious respect that those things elicited. Like so many other mythical explanations, this one resolves the question only by repeating it in slightly different terms, for to say that the churinga is sacred, and that it has such and such relationship with a sacred being, is not to account for the fact but to state one fact in two different ways. Second, as Spencer and Gillen admit, even among the Arunta, there are churingas that are made by the elders of the group, with the full knowledge of and in full view of everyone;[126] those obviously do not come from the great ancestors. Still, despite a few differences, they have the same power as the others and are kept in the same way. Finally, there are whole tribes in which a churinga is not at all thought of as being associated with a spirit.[127] Its religious nature comes to it from another source; and what would be the source if not the totemic imprint it bears? Thus, the outward displays of the rite are addressed to that image, and that image sanctifies* the object on which it is engraved.

Among the Arunta and in the neighboring tribes, there exist two other liturgical instruments that are clearly attached to the totem and to the

---

*To express the idea "to make something sacred," Durkheim uses the word *sanctifier.* That idea should be kept distinct from other meanings of the verb "to sanctify."

[125]Strehlow, *Aranda,* vol. II, pp. 76, 77, 82. For the Arunta, it is the actual body of the ancestor; for the Loritja, it is only the body's image.

[126]Just after the birth of a child, the mother shows the father where she believes the soul of the ancestor entered her. Accompanied by several relatives, the father goes to that place, and they look for the churinga that they believe the ancestor dropped at the moment of reincarnating himself. If one is found, it is probably because some elder of the totemic group put it there (the hypothesis of Spencer and Gillen). If they do not find it, they make a new churinga according to a prescribed technique (Spencer and Gillen, *Native Tribes,* p. 132; cf. Strehlow, *Aranda,* vol. II, p. 80).

[127]This is true of the Warramunga, the Urabunna, the Worgaia, the Umbaia, the Tjingilli, and the Gnanji (Spencer and Gillen, *Northern Tribes,* pp. 258, 275–276). Then, say Spencer and Gillen, "they were regarded as having especial value because of their association with a totem" (ibid., p. 276). There are examples of the same sort among the Arunta (*Native Tribes,* p. 156).

churinga itself, which ordinarily enters into their making: the *nurtunja* and the *waninga*.

The *nurtunja*,[128] which is found among the Arunta of the north and their immediate neighbors,[129] is a vertical support consisting of either a lance, several lances tied together in a bundle, or simply a pole.[130] Bunches of plants are fastened all around it with belts or bands made of hair. Down, arranged either in circles or in parallel lines running from top to bottom of the support, is attached to the upper end. The top is decorated with feathers of the eaglehawk. (This is the commonest and most typical form; there are many variations in particular cases.)[131]

The *waninga*, which is found only among the southern Arunta, the Urabunna, and the Loritja, has no one model either. Reduced to its most basic components, it also has a vertical support made with a stick about a foot long or with a lance several meters high that is cross-cut, sometimes by one or sometimes by two pieces.[132] In the first case, it resembles a cross. Diagonally crossing the space between the arms of the cross and the ends of the central axis are ties made with either human hair or the fur of an opossum or a bandicoot; they are pressed tightly together, forming a diamond-shaped web. When there are two cross-bars, the belts go from one to the other, and from there to the top and bottom of the support. They are sometimes covered with a coat of down thick enough to hide them from view. The waninga thus looks quite like a flag.[133]

Having their own role in many rites, nurtunjas and waningas are objects of religious respect entirely like the respect evoked by the churingas. Making and erecting them is carried out with the greatest solemnity. Whether fixed

[128]Strehlow says *Tnatanja* (*Aranda*, vol. I, pp. 4–5).

[129]The Kaitish, the Ilpirra, and the Unmatjera, but it is rare among the last group.

[130]Sometimes the pole is replaced with very long churingas placed end to end.

[131]Sometimes a smaller nurtunja is suspended at the top of the main one. In other cases, the nurtunja is given the form of a cross or a *T*. More rarely, the central support is absent (Spencer and Gillen, *Native Tribes*, pp. 298–300, 360–364, 627).

[132]Sometimes there are three such transverse bars.

[133]Spencer and Gillen, *Native Tribes*, pp. 231–234, 306–310, 627. In addition to the nurtunja and the waninga, Spencer and Gillen distinguish a third sort of sacred pole or flag, the *kauaua* (*Native Tribes*, pp. 364, 370, 629), whose functions they admit not having been able to determine exactly. They note only that the kauaua "is regarded as something common to the members of all the totems." But according to Strehlow (*Aranda*, vol. III, p. 23, n.2), the kauaua of which Spencer and Gillen speak is merely the nurtunja of the Wild Cat totem. Since that animal is the object of a tribal cult, it is understandable that the veneration its nurtunja receives should be common to all the clans.

on the ground or carried by a celebrant, they mark the central point of the ceremony; the dances take place and the rites unfold around them. During initiation, the novice is led to the foot of a nurtunja that has been erected for the occasion. "Here," he is told, "is the nurtunja of your father; it has already served to make many young men." After this, the neophyte must kiss the nurtunja.[134] With this kiss, he enters into relations with the religious principle that is held to reside in it; it is a genuine communion that is to give the young man the strength he must have to endure the terrible operation of subincision.[135] In addition, the nurtunja plays an important role in the mythology of these societies. The myths report that, in the mythical age of the great ancestors, the territory of the tribe was crisscrossed in all directions by companies made up exclusively of individuals having the same totem.[136] Each of those bands carried a nurtunja. When a company stopped to make camp and before they dispersed to hunt, the people set their nurtunja into the ground and suspended the churingas from the top.[137] In other words, they entrusted it with their most valuable possessions. At the same time, it was a sort of flag that served as the rallying point of the group. One cannot fail to be struck by the similarities of the nurtunja to the sacred poles of the Omaha.[138]

This sacredness stems from one cause: It is a material representation of the clan. In fact, the vertical lines or rings of down that cover it, or indeed the belts that join the arms of the waninga to the central axis (of different colors, as well), are not arranged arbitrarily, at the whim of those officiating. They must affect a form that is strictly imposed by tradition and that, in the minds of the natives, represents the totem.[139] Here we need wonder no longer, as in the case of the churingas, if the veneration this cult instrument receives merely reflects that inspired by the ancestors: It is a rule that each nurtunja or waninga lasts only during the ceremony in which it is used. An entirely new one is made each time one is needed; when the rite is finished, it is stripped of its ornaments, and the elements from which it is made are scattered.[140]

[134]Spencer and Gillen, *Northern Tribes*, p. 342; *Native Tribes*, p. 309.

[135]Spencer and Gillen, *Native Tribes*, p. 255.

[136]Ibid., chaps. 10 and 11.

[137]Ibid., pp. 138–144.

[138]See [James Owen] Dorsey, "[A Study of] Siouan Cults," *BAE, Eleventh Report* [Washington, Government Printing Office, 1894], p. 413, and "Omaha Sociology," p. 234. While it is true that there is only one sacred pole for the tribe, and yet one nurtunja for each clan, the principle is the same.

[139]Spencer and Gillen, *Native Tribes*, pp. 232, 308, 313, 334, etc.; *Northern Tribes*, pp. 182, 186, etc.

[140]Spencer and Gillen, *Native Tribes*, p. 346. They do say, it is true, that the nurtunja represents the lance of the ancestor who, in Alcheringa times, was the head of each clan. But it is only a symbolic rep-

Thus it is no more than an image of the totem—indeed a temporary image—and therefore plays its religious role in this right and in this right only.

The churinga, the nurtunja, and the waninga owe their religious nature solely to the fact that they bear the totemic emblem. What is sacred is the emblem. It retains this sacredness whatever the object on which it is represented. It is sometimes painted on rocks—these paintings being called *churinga ilkinia,* sacred designs.[141] The decorations in which the celebrants and the congregation adorn themselves during religious ceremonies have the same name, and it is forbidden for children and women to see them.[142] In certain rites, the totem is sometimes drawn on the ground. The very technique of doing so testifies to the feelings that the design elicits and to the high value that is imputed to it. The drawing is done on ground that has been sprinkled and saturated beforehand with human blood;[143] we will see below that the blood itself is a sacred liquid that is reserved exclusively for pious use. Once the image has been made, the faithful remain seated on the ground in front of it, in an attitude of pure devotion.[144] Provided we assign a sense appropriate to the mentality of the primitive, one can say that they worship and glorify it.* This enables us to understand why the totemic emblem has remained a very precious thing to the Indians of North America: It is always surrounded by a sort of religious aura.

It is not without interest to know what totemic representations are made of, in addition to understanding how it happens that they are so sacred.

Among the Indians of North America, totemic representations are painted, engraved, or sculpted images that attempt to reproduce the outward appearance of the totemic animal as faithfully as possible. The techniques are those that we use today in similar cases, except that in general they are cruder than our own. But it is not the same in Australia, and of course it is in the Australian societies that we must seek the origin of these representations. Although the Australian may show himself to be fairly capable of imitating the

---

resentation of that; it is not a sort of relic, like the churinga, which is thought to emanate from the ancestor himself. Here the secondary character of the interpretation is especially apparent.

A condition de donner au mot un sense approprié à la mentalité du primitif, on peut dire qu'ils l'adorent. What it is about the verb *adorer* that must be specially understood is not made explicit.

[141]Ibid., pp. 614ff., esp. p. 617; *Northern Tribes,* p. 749.

[142]*Native Tribes,* p. 624.

[143]Ibid., p. 179.

[144]Ibid., p. 181. [The reference does not describe their demeanor; it says that they chant. Trans.]

forms of things, at least in a rudimentary way,[145] the sacred decorations seem to exhibit no preoccupations of this kind: They consist chiefly of geometric designs made on the churingas or on men's bodies. They are straight or curved lines painted in various ways,[146] together having and only capable of having a conventional meaning. The relation between the drawing and the thing drawn is so remote and indirect that the uninformed cannot see it. Only clan members can say what meaning they attach to this or that combination of lines.[147] In general, men and women are represented by semicircles; animals, by complete circles or by spirals;[148] the tracks of a man or an animal, by lines of points. The meanings of the drawings thus produced are indeed so arbitrary that the same drawing can have two different meanings for the people of two totems—representing a certain animal in one place and another animal or a plant elsewhere. This is perhaps even more apparent in the case of the nurtunjas and waningas; each of which represents a different totem. But the few very simple elements that enter into their composition cannot lend themselves to very diverse combinations. As a result, two nurtunjas can look exactly the same and yet convey two things as different as a gum tree and an emu.[149] When the nurtunja is made, it is given a meaning that it retains during the whole ceremony, but a meaning that ultimately is set by convention.

As these facts prove, while the Australian has quite a strong inclination to represent his totem, he does not do so in order to have a portrait before his eyes that perpetually renews the sensation of it; he does so simply because he feels the need to represent the idea he has by means of an outward and physical sign, no matter what that sign may be. We cannot go further toward understanding what made the primitive write the idea he had of his totem on his person and on various objects, but it has been important to note straightaway the nature of the need that has given birth to these numerous representations.[150]

---

[145]See some examples in Spencer and Gillen, Native Tribes, fig. 131. Among the designs there, several are obviously intended to represent animals, plants, the heads of men, etc.—very schematically, of course.

[146]Spencer and Gillen, Native Tribes, p. 617; Northern Tribes, pp. 716ff.

[147][Spencer and Gillen], Native Tribes, p. 145; Strehlow, Aranda, vol. II, p. 80.

[148][Spencer and Gillen], Native Tribes, p. 151.

[149]Ibid., p. 346.

[150]Moreover, these designs and paintings undoubtedly have an aesthetic quality as well; they are an early form of art. Since they are also, and even most of all, a written language, it follows that the origins of drawing and those of writing merge into one another. Indeed, it seems that man must have begun to draw less to fix onto wood or stone beautiful forms that charmed the senses than to express his thought materially (cf. Schoolcraft, Indian Tribes, vol. I, p. 405; Dorsey, Siouan Cults, pp. 394ff.).

CHAPTER TWO

THE PRINCIPAL TOTEMIC BELIEFS (CONTINUED)

The Totemic Animal and Man

But totemic images are not the only sacred things. There are real beings that are also the object of rites, because of their relationship with the totem. They are, first and foremost, the creatures of the totemic species and the members of the clan.

I

Since the designs that represent the totem stir religious feelings, it is natural that the things represented should have the same property to some degree.

The things represented are mainly animals and plants. Since the profane role of plants and certainly that of animals ordinarily is to serve as food, the sacredness of the totemic animal or plant is signified by the prohibition against eating it. Of course, because they are holy things,* they can enter into the composition of certain mystic meals, and we will see in fact that they sometimes serve as true sacraments; in general, however, they cannot be used for ordinary eating. Anyone who violates that prohibition exposes himself to extremely grave danger. This is not to say that the group always intervenes to punish every such infraction artificially; the sacrilege is thought to bring about death automatically. A dreaded principle that cannot enter into a profane body without disrupting or destroying it is thought to reside within the

---

*Choses saintes. I indicate Durkheim's alternation between *sacré* and *saint*. On these terms, see above p. lxix, n. 101, and p. 121n.

totemic plant or animal.[1] In certain tribes at least, old men are exempted from that prohibition;[2] later, we will see why.

But although the prohibition is absolute in a great many tribes[3] (with exceptions that will be pointed out), unquestionably it tends to weaken as the old totemic organization breaks down. But the very restrictions that persist even then show that these attenuations have not been easily accepted. For example, where eating the totemic animal or plant is permitted, the eating is still not entirely free but is limited to small amounts at a time. To exceed this limit is a ritual offense and has grave consequences.[4] Elsewhere, the restriction remains intact for the parts that are considered the most precious, that is, the most sacred—for example, the eggs or the fat.[5] In yet other places, unrestricted eating is tolerated only if the animal eaten has not yet reached full maturity.[6] In this case, the animal's sacredness is probably assumed to be as yet incomplete. Thus, the barrier that isolates and protects the totemic being gives way but slowly, and not without strong resistance—which is evidence of what it must originally have been.

It is true that Spencer and Gillen do not believe such restrictions are survivals of a once-rigorous prohibition that is gradually weakening, but instead that they are the prelude to one just beginning to establish itself. Once upon

---

[1]See the example in [Rev. George] Taplin, "The Narrinyeri Tribe" [in James Dominick Woods, *The Native Tribes of South Australia,* Adelaide, E. S. Wigg & Son, 1879], p. 63; [Alfred William] Howitt, *Native Tribes [of South-East Australia,* London, Macmillan, 1904], pp. 146, 769; [Lorimer] Fison and [Alfred William] Howitt, *Kamilaroi and Kurnai* [Melbourne, G. Robertson, 1880], p. 169; [Walter Edmund] Roth, *Superstition, Magic and Medicine* [in *North Queensland Ethnography,* Bulletin, no. 5, Brisbane, G. A. Vaughn, 1903], §150; [W.] Wyatt, "Adelaide and Encounter Bay Tribes" [in Woods, *The Native Tribes of South Australia*], p. 168 [H. E. A.] Meyer, "Manners and Customs of the Aborigines of Encounter Bay," [in Woods, *The Native Tribes of South Australia*], p. 186.

[2]This is the case among the Warramunga. [Sir Baldwin Spencer and Francis James Gillen, *Northern Tribes of Central Australia,* London, Macmillan, 1904], p. 168. [That discussion does not concern dietary practices. Trans.]

[3]For example, among the Warramunga, the Urabunna, the Wonghibon, the Yuin, the Wotjobaluk, the Buandik, the Ngeumba, and others.

[4]Among the Kaitish, if a member of the clan eats too much of his totem, the members of the other phratry have recourse to a magical procedure that is thought to kill (ibid., p. 294; cf. [Sir Baldwin Spencer and Francis James Gillen], *Northern Tribes,* p. 294, and *Native Tribes [of Central Australia,* London, Macmillan, 1899], p. 204 [The discussion does not concern dietary practices. Trans.]; Langloh Parker [Catherine Sommerville Field Parker], *The Euahlayi Tribe,* [London, A. Constable, 1905], p. 20).

[5]Spencer and Gillen, *Native Tribes,* p. 202n.; [Carl] Strehlow, *Die Aranda- und Loritja-Stämme in Zentral-Australien,* vol. II [Frankfurt, J. Baer, 1907], p. 58.

[6][Spencer and Gillen], *Northern Tribes,* p. 173.

a time, according to these writers,[7] there was total freedom of consumption, and the restrictions applied today are fairly recent. They believe they have found proof of their thesis in the two following facts. First, there are solemn occasions when the men of the clan or their chief not only may but must eat the totemic animal and plant, as I have just noted. Second, the myths report that the great founding ancestors of the clans regularly ate their totem. These stories cannot be understood, say they, except as the echo of a time when restrictions did not exist.

The fact that it is ritually obligatory to partake of the totem during certain religious ceremonies (moderately, at that) in no way implies that it ever served as ordinary food. Quite the contrary, the food eaten during mystical meals is sacred in its essence and hence forbidden to the profane. As to the myths, to impute to them the value of historical documents so easily is to follow a rather slipshod critical method. As a rule, the object of myths is to interpret the existing rites rather than to commemorate past events; they are more an explanation of the present than they are a history. In this case, those traditions in which the legendary ancestors ate their totem are in perfect accord with beliefs and rites that are still in force. The old men, and others who have attained high religious status, are not bound by the prohibitions as are ordinary men.[8] They may eat of the holy thing* because they are holy themselves; moreover, this rule is not peculiar to totemism alone but is found in the most disparate religions. Since the ancestral heroes were virtually gods, it must have seemed all the more natural that they should have been able to eat the sacred† food,[9] but that is no reason for the same privilege to have been conferred upon mere profane beings.[10]

---

* *Chose sainte.*

† *Aliment sacré.*

[7] Ibid., pp. 207ff.

[8] See above p. 128.

[9] It should also be borne in mind that in the myths, the ancestors are never represented as feeding on their totem *routinely.* Quite the contrary; this sort of consumption is the exception. According to Strehlow, their everyday fare was the same as that of the corresponding animal (Strehlow, *Aranda*, vol. I, p. 4).

[10] Furthermore, this whole theory rests on a completely arbitrary hypothesis: Spencer and Gillen, like [James George] Frazer, concede that the tribes of Central Australia, including the Arunta, represent the most archaic and, consequently, the purest form of totemism. I will say below why this conjecture seems to me to be contrary to all likelihood. It is in fact probable that these authors would not so easily have accepted the thesis they defend if they had not refused to see totemism as a religion and thus had not failed to recognize the sacredness of the totem.

However, it is neither certain nor even likely that the prohibition was ever absolute. It seems always to have been superseded by necessity—for example, when the native is starving and has nothing else to eat.[11] All the more is this the case when the totem is a kind of food that man cannot do without. For example, many tribes have a water totem—a case in point in which strict prohibition clearly is impossible. But even in this case, the concession is subject to restrictions, which goes to show that the concession deviates from an accepted principle. Among the Kaitish and the Warramunga, a man of this totem cannot drink water freely, is prohibited from drawing it himself, and can receive it only from the hands of a third person, who must belong to the phratry of which he is not a member.[12] The complexity and inconvenience of this procedure are yet other ways of recognizing that access to the sacred thing is not free. In certain tribes of the center, the same rule applies whenever the totem is eaten, whether out of necessity or for any other reason. It should be reiterated that when this formality itself cannot be executed—that is, when an individual is by himself or is surrounded by members of his own phratry—he may do without any intermediary if there is urgent need. It is clear that the prohibition can be mitigated in various ways.

Still, the prohibition rests on ideas that are so deeply rooted in the mind that it often outlives its original reasons for being. We have seen that, in all probability, the various clans of a phratry are subdivisions of an original clan that broke up. Thus there was a time when all the clans were but one and had the same totem; therefore, whenever the memory of that common origin is not completely erased, each clan continues to feel solidarity with the others and to consider their totems as not foreign to it. For this reason, an individual is not entirely free to eat the totems assigned to the various clans of the phratry to which he belongs; he may touch the forbidden plant or animal only if it has been presented to him by a member of the other phratry.[13]

[11]Taplin, 'The Narrinyeri," p. 64; Howitt, Native Tribes, pp. 145, 147; Spencer and Gillen, Native Tribes, p. 202; [George] Grey, Journals of Two Expeditions in North-West and Western Australia, vol. II, London, T. and W. Boone, 1841; Curr, The Australian Race, vol. III, p. 462.

[12][Spencer and Gillen], Northern Tribes, pp. 160, 167. It is not enough for the intermediary to be of another totem. As we will see, to some extent, any totem of a phratry is forbidden to other members of that phratry who are of different totems.

[13]Ibid., p. 167. We can better understand now how it happens that, when the prohibition is not observed, it is the other phratry that carries out punishment for the sacrilege (see p. 128, n. 4 above). It is because that phratry has the greatest interest in seeing that the rule is respected. It is believed likely, in fact, that when the rule is violated, the totemic species will not reproduce abundantly. Since the members of the other phratry are the ones who regularly eat it, they are the ones affected. This is why they avenge themselves.

Another survival of the same kind relates to the maternal totem. There are good reasons for believing that totems were at first transmitted through the maternal line. And so, wherever descent through the paternal line has become the custom, this most likely has occurred only after a long period during which the opposite principle was in use; hence the child had the totem of its mother and was subject to all the prohibitions attached thereto. Now although in certain tribes today, the child inherits the totem of its father, something remains of the prohibitions that originally protected the mother's totem: It cannot be partaken of freely.[14] Yet nothing else in the present state of things corresponds to that prohibition.

A prohibition against killing the totem (or picking it, if it is a plant) is often added to the prohibition against eating.[15] But, here again, there are many exceptions and mitigations. For instance, there is the case of necessity—when, for example, the totem is a dangerous animal[16] or when one has nothing to eat. There are even tribes that prohibit hunting the animal whose name one bears for oneself, but nevertheless permit its killing for someone else.[17] In general, though, the manner in which the act is carried out clearly indicates that there is something illicit about it. One says "excuse me" as if for an offense, displays sadness and repugnance,[18] and

[14]This is the case among the Loritja (Strehlow, *Aranda*, vol. II, pp. 60, 61), the Worgaia, the Warramunga, the Walpari, the Mara, the Anula, the Binbinga (Spencer and Gillen, *Northern Tribes*, pp. 166, 171, 173). Among the Warramunga and the Walpari, it may be eaten but only if it is offered by a member of the other phratry. Spencer and Gillen point out (p. 167 n.) that, in this respect, the paternal and maternal totems are apparently subject to different rules. It is true that, in either case, the offer must come from the other phratry. But when the totem in question is that of the father, the totem proper, that other phratry is the one to which the totem does not belong; the inverse applies when it is the totem of the mother. This is the case, most likely, because the principle was at first established for the father's, then extended automatically to the mother's, even though the situation was different. Once it was instituted, the rule that one could avoid the restriction protecting the totem only when the offer was made by someone of the other phratry was applied without modification to the mother's totem.

[15]For example, among the Warramunga (Spencer and Gillen, *Northern Tribes*, p. 166), the Wotjobaluk, the Buandik, and the Kurnai (Howitt, *Native Tribes*, pp. 146–147), and the Narrinyeri (Taplin, "The Narrinyeri," p. 63).

[16]And still not in all cases. The Arunta of the Mosquito totem must not kill that insect, even when it is inconvenient not to, but must settle for flicking it away (Strehlow, *Aranda*, vol. II, p. 58. Cf. [Rev. George] Taplin, "The Narrinyeri," p. 63). [It is possible that, in certain of his footnotes, Durkheim conflated two articles by Taplin, one in Curr and the other in Woods. Trans.]

[17]Among the Kaitish and the Unmatjera (Spencer and Gillen, *Northern Tribes*, p. 160). Indeed sometimes an elder gives one of his churingas to a young man of a different totem, to enable the young man to hunt the giver's totemic animal more easily (ibid., p. 272).

[18]Howitt, *Native Tribes*, p. 146; Grey, *Journals of Two Expeditions*, vol. II, p. 228. [Rev. Eugene Arnaud] Casalis, *The Bassutos* [Capetown, C. Struik, 1965], p. 211. Among these latter, "one must be purified after committing such a sacrilege."

takes the necessary to ensure that the animal suffers as little as possible.[19]

In addition to the basic prohibitions, there are examples of a prohibition against contact between a man and his totem. Thus, among the Omaha, no one of the Elk clan may touch any part of the male elk; and in a subclan of the Buffalo, no one may touch this animal's head.[20] Among the Bechuana, no one would dare to wear the skin of the animal that is his totem.[21] But these cases are rare; and it is natural that they should be, since, normally a man must wear the image of his totem or something reminiscent of it. Tattooing and totemic costumes would be impractical if contact was prohibited altogether. It should be noticed, furthermore, that this prohibition is followed not in Australia but only in societies where totemism is already far from its original form; apparently, then, it is of recent origin and due perhaps to the influence of ideas that are not specifically totemic at all.[22]

If we now compare these various prohibitions with those applied to the totemic emblem, it seems—contrary to what might be predicted—that those applied to the totemic emblem are the more numerous, strict, and rigorously imperative. All kinds of figures representing the totem are surrounded with a markedly greater respect than the being itself, whose form the figures imitate. Churingas, nurtunjas, and waningas must never be handled by women or uninitiated men, who are not permitted even to glimpse them except from a respectful distance and, at that, only on rare occasions. On the other hand, the plant or animal whose name the clan bears may be seen and

[19]Strehlow, *Aranda*, vol. II, pp. 58, 59, 61.

[20][James Owen] Dorsey, "Omaha Sociology," in *Third Annual Report, BAE* [Washington, Government Printing Office, 1881–1882], pp. 225, 231.

[21]Casalis [*The Bassutos,* p. 211].

[22]Even among the Omaha, it is not certain that the prohibitions against contact, some examples of which I have just reported, are specifically totemic in nature. Several of them have no direct relations with the animal that serves as the clan's totem. Thus, in a subclan of the Eagle, the characteristic prohibition is that against touching the head of a buffalo (Dorsey, "Omaha Sociology," p. 239); in another subclan of the same totem, verdigris, charcoal, or something else must not be touched (p. 245).

I do not mention other prohibitions noted by Frazer, such as naming or looking at an animal or plant, for those are even less clearly of totemic origin, except perhaps in the case of certain instances observed among the Bechuana ([James George] Frazer, *Totemism and Exogamy,* [London, Macmillan, 1910], pp. 12–13). Frazer once accepted too easily (and on this point he has had imitators) that every prohibition against eating or touching an animal necessarily arises from totemic beliefs. However, there is one case in Australia in which the sight of the totem appears to be forbidden. According to Strehlow (*Aranda,* vol. II, p. 59), among the Arunta and the Loritja, a man whose totem is the moon must not look at it very long; to do so would be to expose himself to death at the hands of an enemy. I believe this is a unique case. Moreover we should bear in mind that the astronomical totems are probably not primitive in Australia, so this prohibition might be the outcome of a complex elaboration. This hypothesis is supported by the fact that, among the Euahlayi, the prohibition against looking at the moon applies to all mothers and children, whatever their totems (Parker, *Euahlayi,* p. 53).

touched by everyone. Churingas are kept in a sort of temple, at the threshold of which the din of profane life settles into silence; it is the domain of sacred things.

Unlike the churingas, totemic animals and plants live on profane ground and are part and parcel of everyday life. And since the number and importance of the restrictions that isolate a sacred thing, withdrawing it from circulation, correspond to the degree of sacredness with which it is invested, we arrive at the remarkable result that *the images of the totemic being are more sacred than the totemic being itself.* Moreover, it is the churunga and the nurtunja that hold the highest rank in the ceremonies of the cult; only on extremely rare occasions does the animal appear in them. In one rite, of which I will have occasion to speak,[23] it is the basis of a religious meal but has no active role. The Arunta dance around the nurtunja, gathering before the image of their totem and worshiping it; never is there a similar display before the totemic being itself. If this being was the holy thing* par excellence, then that being, the sacred plant or animal, would be the one the young novice must commune with when brought into the sphere of religious life; we have seen instead that the moment when the novice enters the sanctuary of the churingas is the most solemn of the initiation. It is with them and with the nurtunja that he communes. So the representations of the totem are more efficacious than the totem itself.

II

We must now determine the place of man in the system of religious things.

A whole set of received notions and the power of language itself incline us to think of ordinary men, the ordinary faithful, as essentially profane beings. This conception may well not be literally true of any religion;[24] it certainly does not apply to totemism. Each member of the clan is invested with a sacredness that is not significantly less than the sacredness we just recognized in the animal. The reason for this personal sacredness is that the man believes he is both a man in the usual sense of the word and an animal or plant of the totemic species.

* *Chose sainte.*

[23]See Bk. III, chap. 2, §2.

[24]There is perhaps no religion that regards man as an exclusively profane being. For the Christian, there is something sacred about the soul that each of us carries within, and that constitutes the very essence of our personality. As we will see, this idea of the soul is as old as religious thinking. But man's own place in the hierarchy of sacred things is rather high.

In fact, he bears its name. At that stage, identity in name is presumed to entail an identity in nature. Having the same name is not thought of merely as an outward sign of having the same nature but as logically presupposing it. For the primitive, the name is not simply a word, a mere combination of sounds; it is part of the being and, indeed, an essential part. When a member of the Kangaroo clan calls himself a kangaroo, he is in a sense an animal of that species. "A man," say Spencer and Gillen, "regards the being that is his totem as the same thing as himself. A native with whom we were discussing the matter responded by showing us a photograph we had just taken of him: 'Look who is exactly the same thing as I. Well! It is the same with the kangaroo.' The kangaroo was his totem."[25] Thus, each individual has a dual nature: Two beings coexist in him, a man and an animal.

To give a semblance of intelligibility to this duality, which to us is so strange, the primitive has conceived myths that of course explain nothing and only displace the difficulty, but that, in displacing it, seem at least to diminish the logical shock. With variations of detail, they are all constructed on the same plan. Their object is to establish genealogical relations between the man and the totemic animal that make the man the animal's kin. By that shared (and variously imagined) origin, people believe they are accounting for their shared nature. The Narrinyeri, for example, have conceived the idea that certain of the first men had the power to transform themselves into animals.[26] Other Australian societies place strange animals at the beginning of humanity, animals from which men descended in some way or other,[27] or they place mixed beings intermediate between the two realms there,[28] or else formless, barely representable creatures without defined organs or appendages, and whose various body parts are barely drawn.[29] Mythical powers, sometimes conceived in the form of animals, intervened at that point, trans-

---

[25]Spencer and Gillen, *Native Tribes*, p. 202.

[26]Taplin, "The Narrinyeri," pp. 59–61.

[27]Among certain Warramunga clans, for example (Spencer and Gillen, *Northern Tribes*, p. 162).

[28]Among the Urabunna (ibid., p. 147). Even when we are told that those first beings were men, in reality they are only semihumans and participate in an animal nature at the same time. This is the case of certain Unmatjera (ibid., pp. 153–154). Here are ways of thinking whose blurred distinctions [*confusions*] unsettle us, but that must be accepted as they are. [Here and elsewhere in this text, the noun *confusion* and the corresponding verb, *confondre*, convey blending. They express a form of conceptual practice, not a state of mental disorder. See below, p. 241. Trans.] If we tried to introduce a tidiness that is alien to them, we would distort them (cf. Spencer and Gillen, *Native Tribes*, p. 119).

[29]Among certain Arunta (Spencer and Gillen, *Native Tribes*, pp. 388ff.); and among certain Unmatjera (Spencer and Gillen, *Northern Tribes*, p. 153).

forming into men these ambiguous and unnameable beings that represent, as Spencer and Gillen say, "a transitional phase between man and animal."[30] These transformations are presented to us as the outcome of violent and quasi-surgical operations. It is with blows of an axe or, when the operator is a bird, with pecks of the beak that the human is thought to have been sculpted in that amorphous mass, the arms and legs separated from one another, the mouth and nostrils opened.[31] Similar legends crop up in America, but because of the more developed mentality of those peoples, the representations they use are not confused and confusing in the same way. Here, it is a legendary personage who, acting on his own, metamorphosed the clan's eponymous animal into man.[32] There, the myth tries to explain how, by a series of more or less natural events and a sort of spontaneous evolution, the animal transformed itself little by little, finally taking on human form.[33]

True, there are societies (Haida, Tlingit, Tshimshian) in which the idea that man was born of an animal or plant is no longer accepted. Yet, the idea of an affinity between the animals of the totemic species and the members of the clan has survived, and it is explained in myths that differ from the preceding but are basically reminiscent of them. Here, then, is one of their fundamental themes. The eponymous ancestor is represented as a human being but one who, following various ups and downs, was induced to live for a more or less long time among legendary animals of the same species that gave

---

[30]Spencer and Gillen, *Native Tribes*, p. 389. Cf. Strehlow, *Aranda*, vol. I, pp. 2–7.

[31]Spencer and Gillen, *Native Tribes*, p. 389. Strehlow, *Aranda*, vol. I, pp. 2ff. This mythical theme is undoubtedly an echo of the initiation rites. The purpose of the initiation is to make of the young man a complete man, and it also implies surgical operations (circumcision, subincision, extraction of teeth, etc.). It must have been natural for them to conceive the processes used to make the first men according to the same model.

[32]This is true for the nine clans of the Moqui ([Henry Rowe] Schoolcraft, [*Historical and Statistical Information Respecting the History, Condition, and Prospects of the*] *Indian Tribes* [*of the United States*, vol. IV, Philadelphia, Lippincott, Grambo, 1851–1857], p. 86), the Crane clan of the Ojibway ([Lewis Henry] Morgan, *Ancient Society* [London, Macmillan, 1877], p. 180), and the clans of the Nootka ([Franz] Boas, "Second General Report on the Indians of British Columbia," in, BAAS, *VIth Rep. on the North-Western Tribes of Canada* [London, Offices of the Association, 1891], p. 43), etc.

[33]Thus did the Turtle clan of the Iroquois take form. A group of tortoises had to leave the lake where they lived and find another habitat. The heat made it difficult for one of them, who was larger than the others, to endure the exercise. It struggled so violently that it came out of its shell. Once begun, the process of transformation continued by itself, and the turtle became a man who was the ancestor of the clan (Erminnie A. Smith, "The Myths of the Iroquois," in *Second Annual Report* [*BAE*, Washington, Government Printing Office, 1883], p. 77). The Crawfish [Ecrevisse] clan of the Choctaw is said to have been formed in a similar way. Some men surprised a certain number of crawfish that lived in their vicinity, took the crawfish home with them, taught them to speak and walk, and finally adopted them into their society ([George] Catlin, [*Letters and Notes on the Manners, Customs and Condition of the*] *North American Indians*, vol. II [London, Tosswil and Myers, 1841], p. 128.

the clan its name. As a result of these intimate and prolonged dealings, he became so like his new companions that when he returned to the community of men, they no longer recognized him. He was therefore given the name of the animal he resembled. From his sojourn in the mythical land, he brought back the totemic emblem, together with the powers and virtues thought to be attached to it.[34] In this case as in the preceding, then, the man is thought to participate in the nature of the animal, even though that participation is imagined somewhat differently.[35]

Thus he too has something sacred about him. Diffused throughout the body, this quality is especially evident at certain sites. Some organs and tissues are especially identified with it: most of all, the blood and the hair.

To begin with, human blood is such a holy* thing that, among the tribes of central Australia, it is very often used to consecrate the most respected instruments of the cult. In some cases, for example, the nurtunja is religiously anointed from top to bottom with human blood.[36] Among the Arunta, the men of the Emu draw the sacred emblem on ground that is thoroughly soaked with blood.[37] We will see further on how streams of blood are poured

* Chose sainte.

[34]Here, for example, is a legend of the Tsimshian. During a hunt, an Indian met a black bear who took him home and taught him to catch salmon and build canoes. The man stayed with the bear for two years, after which he returned to his native village. But because he was just like a bear, the people were afraid of him. He could not talk and could eat only raw foods. Then he was rubbed with magical herbs, after which he gradually regained his original form. Later, when he was in need, he called his friends the bears, who came to his aid. He built a house and painted a bear on its facade. His sister made a blanket for the dance, on which a bear was drawn. This is why the descendants of that sister had the bear as their emblem ([Franz] Boas, ["The Social Organization and Secret Societies of the] Kwakiutl [Indians," in RNM for 1895, Washington, Government Printing Office, 1897], p. 323. Cf. Boas, "First General Report on the Indians of British Columbia," in BAAS [Fifth] Report [of the Committee] on the North Western Tribes of [the Dominion of] Canada [London, Offices of the Association, 1890], pp. 23, 29ff.; [Charles] Hill Tout, "Report on the Ethnology of the Statlumh of British Columbia," in JAI, vol. XXXV (1905), p. 150.

From this, we see the drawback of making mystic kinship between man and animal the distinguishing feature of totemism, as M. Van Gennep proposes ([A. Van Gennep], "Totémisme et méthode comparative," RHR, vol. LVIII [juillet 1908], p. 55). Since this kinship is a mythical expression of facts that are deeply rooted for other reasons, the essential traits of totemism do not disappear in its absence. Doubtless, there are always close ties between the people of the clan and the totemic animal, but they are not necessarily ties of blood, although they most commonly are conceived as such.

[35]In some Tlingit myths, moreover, the relationship of descent between the man and the animal is affirmed more specifically. The clan is said to be the offspring of a mixed marriage, if such terms can be used—that is, one in which either the man or the woman was an animal of the species whose name the clan bears ([John Reed] Swanton, "Social Condition, Beliefs, [and Linguistic Relationship] of the Tlingit Indians," Twenty-Sixth Annual Report, BAE, Washington, Government Printing Office, 1908], pp. 415–418.

[36]Spencer and Gillen, Native Tribes, p. 284.

[37]Ibid., p. 179.

on the rocks that represent the totemic plants or animals.[38] There is no religious ceremony in which blood does not have some role to play.[39] Sometimes in the course of initiation, adults open their veins and sprinkle the novice with their blood, this blood being such a sacred* thing that women are forbidden to be present while it is flowing. Like the sight of a churinga,[40] the sight of this blood is forbidden to them. The blood that the young neophyte loses during the violent operations he has to undergo has altogether exceptional properties: It is used in various communions.[41] Among the Arunta, the blood that flows during subincision is piously collected and buried in a place on which a piece of wood is set to indicate to passersby the sacredness of the spot; no woman must approach it.[42] In the second place, the religious nature of blood also explains why red ochre has a religious role and is frequently used in ceremonies. The churingas are rubbed with it, and it is used in ritual decorations.[43] This is because ochre is regarded as a substance akin to blood, by virtue of its color. Indeed, several deposits of ochre that are found at different sites on the territory of the Arunta are thought to be coagulated blood that certain heroines of the mythical epoch allowed to flow onto the ground.[44]

Hair has similar properties. The natives of central Australia wear sashes made of human hair. The religious function of those narrow bands, as already noted, is to wrap certain cult objects.[45] Has a man lent one of his churingas to another? As a show of gratitude, the borrower makes a present of hair to the lender; the two sorts of things are considered to be of the same order and of equivalent value.[46] Accordingly, the operation of hair cutting is a ritual act

---

* *Chose sacrée.*

[38]See Bk. III, chap. 2. Cf. Spencer and Gillen, *Native Tribes*, pp. 184, 201.

[39]Ibid., pp. 204, 262, 284.

[40]Among the Dieri and the Parnkalla. See Howitt, *Native Tribes*, pp. 658, 661, 668, 669–671.

[41]Among the Warramunga, the blood of circumcision is drunk by the mother (Spencer and Gillen, *Northern Tribes*, p. 352). Among the Binbinga, the blood that soils the knife used in the subincision must be licked by the initiate (p. 368). In general, the blood that comes from the genitals is deemed to be exceptionally sacred (Spencer and Gillen, *Native Tribes*, p. 464; *Northern Tribes*, p. 598).

[42]Spencer and Gillen, *Native Tribes*, p. 268.

[43]Ibid., pp. 144, 568.

[44]Spencer and Gillen, *Native Tribes*, pp. 442, 464. And this myth is common in Australia.

[45]Ibid., p. 627.

[46]Ibid., p. 466.

that is accompanied by special ceremonies. The individual having his hair cut must crouch on the ground with his face turned in the direction of the place where mythical ancestors from his mother's side are thought to have camped.[47]

For the same reason, as soon as a man dies, his hair is cut and put in a secluded place, for neither women nor uninitiated men should see it; and it is there, far from profane eyes, that the sashes are made.[48]

One could point out other organic tissues that, to varying degrees, display similar properties—the sideburns, the foreskin, the fat of the liver, and others.[49] But there is no point in piling up examples. The foregoing are sufficient to prove the existence in man of something that keeps the profane at a distance and has religious efficacy. In other words, the human body conceals in its depths a sacred principle that erupts onto the surface in particular circumstances. This principle is not different in kind from the one that gives the totem its religious character. We have just seen, in fact, that the various substances in which it is incarnated to the highest degree enter into the ritual composition of the instruments of the cult (nurtunjas, totemic designs), or are used in anointings for the purpose of increasing the virtues of either the churingas or the sacred rocks. These are things of the same kind.

The religious dignity that, in this sense, is inherent in each member of the clan is not equal in all. Men possess it to a higher degree than women, who are like profane beings in comparison to men.[50] Thus, whenever there is an assembly of either the totemic group or the tribe, the men form a camp distinct from the women's camp and closed to them: The men are set apart.[51]

---

[47]Ibid. It is believed that if all these formalities are not strictly observed, grave calamities for the individual will result.

[48]Ibid., p. 538; *Northern Tribes,* p. 604.

[49]Once detached by circumcision, the foreskin is sometimes hidden from sight, like the blood, and it has special virtues—for example, ensuring the fertility of certain plant and animal species (*Northern Tribes,* pp. 353–354). The sideburns are assimilated to the hair and treated like it (pp. 544, 604). Moreover, they play a role in the myths (p. 158). The sacred character of fat arises from the use made of it in certain funeral rites.

[50]This is not to say that the woman is absolutely profane. In the myths, at least among the Arunta, she plays a far more important religious role than is hers in reality (Spencer and Gillen, *Native Tribes* [pp. 195–196]). Even now, she takes part in certain initiation rites. Finally, her blood has religious virtues (see *Native Tribes,* p. 464; cf. [Emile Durkheim], "La Prohibition de l'inceste et ses origines," *AS,* vol. I [1898], pp. 51ff.).

The exogamic prohibitions derive from this complex situation of the woman. I will not speak of those here, because they are more directly relevant to the subject of family organization and marriage.

[51]Spencer and Gillen, *Native Tribes,* p. 460.

But men differ too in the way the religious quality stands out. Since young, uninitiated men are totally without it, they are not admitted to the ceremonies. It reaches maximum intensity among old men. Old men are so sacred that they are permitted certain things that are forbidden to ordinary men: They can eat the totemic animal more freely, and, as we have seen, there are even tribes in which they are exempt from all dietary restrictions.

Therefore we must be careful not to see totemism as a kind of zoolatry. Since man belongs to the sacred world, his attitude toward the animals or plants whose name he bears is by no means the attitude a believer has toward his god. Rather, their relations are those of two beings who are basically at the same level and of equal value. The most one can say, at least in some cases, is that the animal seems to occupy a slightly higher rank among sacred things. Thus, the totem is sometimes called the father or grandfather of the men of the clan, which seems to indicate that they feel they are in a state of moral dependency upon it.[52] Yet as often happens—and perhaps most often of all—the phrases used denote a feeling of equality instead. The totemic animal is called the friend or the elder brother of its human kin.[53] To sum up, the ties between them and him far more closely resemble those that bind members of the same family: Animals and men are made of the same flesh, as the Buandik say.[54] By reason of that kinship, man sees the animals of the totemic species as kindly associates, whose help he believes he can count on. He calls them to his aid,[55] and they come to guide his hand in the hunt and to avert dangers that he may encounter.[56] In exchange, he treats them considerately and does not brutalize them,[57] but the care with which he treats them in no way resembles a cult.

[52]Among the Wakelbura, according to Howitt, *Native Tribes*, pp. [147–148]; among the Bechuana, according to Casalis, *The Basutos*, p. [211].

[53]Among the Buandik and the Kurnai, Howitt, ibid., pp. 147–148; among the Arunta, Strehlow, *Aranda*, vol. II, p. 58.

[54]Howitt, *Native Tribes*, pp. [147–148].

[55]On the Tully River, according to [Walter Edmund] Roth (*Superstition, Magic and Medicine* [Brisbane, G. A. Vaughn, Government Printer, 1903], *North Queensland Ethnography* [Bulletin] no. 5, §74), when a native goes to bed or rises in the morning, he pronounces the name of the animal after whom he himself is named in a rather soft voice. The aim of this practice is to make the man skillful or lucky in the hunt or to avoid the dangers associated with that animal. For example, a man who has a species of snake as his totem is protected from bites if this invocation has been consistently done.

[56]Taplin, "The Narrinyeri," p. 64; Howitt, *Native Tribes*, p. 147; Roth, "Superstition, Magic and Medicine," no. 5, §74.

[57]Strehlow, *Aranda*, vol. II, p. 58.

Sometimes man even appears to have a sort of mystical property right over his totem. The prohibition against killing and eating it of necessity applies only to the members of the clan; it cannot extend to outsiders without making life impossible as a practical matter. In a tribe such as the Arunta, where there are a great many different totems, if it was forbidden to eat not only the animal or plant whose name one bears, but also all the animals and all the plants that serve other clans as totems, the food resources would be reduced to none. Still, there are tribes in which unrestricted eating of the totemic animal or plant is not allowed, even by outsiders. Among the Wakelbura, this eating should not occur in the presence of people belonging to the totem.[58] Elsewhere, their permission is required. For example, among the Kaitish and the Unmatjera, when a man of the Emu clan, finding himself in a locality occupied by a grass-seed clan, gathers some of these seeds, he must go find the chief before eating any, and say to him: "I have gathered these seeds in your land." To which the chief replies: "It is good; you may eat them." But if the Emu man ate before asking permission, it is believed that he would fall ill and possibly even die.[59] In some cases, the chief of the group must take a small part of the food and eat it himself: It is a kind of tax that must be paid.[60] For the same reason, the churinga confers upon the hunter a certain power over the corresponding animal. By rubbing his body with a euro churinga, for example, he has a better chance of bagging euros.[61] This proves that participating in the nature of a totemic being confers a sort of eminent domain over it. Finally, there is a tribe in North Queensland, the Karingbool, in which the people of the totem have the exclusive right to kill the totemic animal or, if the totem is a tree, to strip its bark. Their cooperation is indispensable to any outsider who wants to use the flesh of that animal or the wood of that tree for personal ends.[62] Thus, they play the role of owners, though, as is obvious, the property is of a very particular sort, which we have difficulty imagining.

[58]Howitt, *Native Tribes*, p. 148.

[59][Spencer and Gillen], *Northern Tribes*, pp. 159–160.

[60]Ibid.

[61]Ibid., p. 255, and *Native Tribes*, pp. 202–203.

[62]A. L. P. Cameron, "On Two Queensland Tribes," in *Science of Man, Australasian Anthropological Journal*, vol. VII, 1904, p. 28, col. 1.

CHAPTER THREE

THE PRINCIPAL TOTEMIC BELIEFS (CONTINUED)

*The Cosmological System of Totemism and the Notion of Kind**

We are beginning to see that totemism is a far more complex religion than it appeared at first glance to be. We have already distinguished three categories of things that it recognizes as sacred in varying degrees: the totemic emblem, the plant or animal whose appearance that emblem imitates, and the members of the clan. But this list is not yet complete. A religion is not merely a collection of disconnected beliefs about very special objects such as those just mentioned. To a greater or lesser degree, all known religions have been systems of ideas that tend to embrace the universality of things and to give us a representation of the world as a whole. If totemism is to be open to consideration as a religion comparable to others, it too must offer a conception of the universe. It meets this criterion.

I

The reason this aspect of totemism has been widely neglected is that the clan has been too narrowly conceived. In general, the clan has been viewed as merely a group of human beings, merely a subdivision of the tribe. As such, it seems, the clan could only be made up of men. But when we reason this way, we substitute our European ideas for those the primitive has about the world and society. For the Australian, things themselves—all of the things that make up the universe—are part of the tribe. Since they are constituents of it and, in a sense, full-fledged members, they have a definite place in the scheme of society, just as men do. "The savage of South Australia," M. Fison

---

* *Genre* is here rendered as "kind" or "genus," according to context, but usually not as "class," so as to avoid confusion with other uses of that term, in biology and sociology.

says, "considers the universe as a large tribe to one of whose divisions he belongs; and all things that are classified in the same group as he, both animate and inanimate, are parts of the body of which he himself is a part."[1] By virtue of this principle, when the tribe is divided into two phratries, all known beings are divided between them. "All of nature," says Palmer of the tribes of the Bellinger River, "is divided according to the names of phratries. . . . The sun, the moon and the stars . . . belong to this or that phratry just as the Blacks themselves do."[2] The Port MacKay tribe in Queensland is made up of two phratries that carry the names Yungaroo and Wootaroo, and it is the same in the neighboring tribes. According to Bridgmann, "All animate and inanimate things are divided by these tribes into two classes called Yungaroo and Wootaroo."[3] But the classification does not stop there. The men of each phratry are divided among a certain number of clans; similarly, the things assigned to each phratry are divided in turn among the clans that comprise it. Such and such tree, for example, will be ascribed to the Kangaroo clan and to it alone, and thus, like the human members of that clan, will have the Kangaroo totem; such and such other will belong to the Snake clan; the clouds will be classified in a particular totem, the sun in another, and so on. Thus, the known beings will be found to have their places on a kind of table, a systematic classification that includes the whole of nature.

I have reproduced a certain number of these classification systems elsewhere;[4] here I will repeat only some of those examples. One of the best known is the system that has been studied in the Mount Gambier tribe. This tribe has two phratries, one called Kumite and the other Kroki, each divided into five clans. Now, "Everything in nature belongs to one or the other of those ten clans."[5] Fison and Howitt say that all those things are "included" in one. In fact, they are classified under ten totems, like species of the respec-

---

[1][Lorimer Fison and Alfred William Howitt], *Kamilaroi and Kurnai: [Group Marriage and Relationship, and Marriage by Elopement; Drawn Chiefly from the Usage of the Australian Aborigines; also The Kurnai Tribe; Their Customs in Peace and War*, Melbourne, G. Robertson, 1880], p. 170.

[2][Edward Palmer], "Notes on Some Australian Tribes" [*JAI*], vol. XIII [1884], p. 300.

[3][Edward Micklethwaite] Curr, *The Australian Race: [Its Origin, Languages, Customs, Place of Landing in Australia and the Routes by Which It Spread Itself over That Continent*, vol. III, Melbourne, J. Ferres, 1886–1887], p. 45; [Robert] Brough Smyth, *The Aborigines of Victoria*, vol. I [Melbourne, J. Ferres, 1878], p. 91 [The quoted material is not verbatim. The text reads this way: "Blacks seem to have an idea that these classes are universal laws of nature, so they divide everything among them." Trans.]; Fison and Howitt, *Kamilaroi and Kurnai*, p. 168.

[4][Emile] Durkheim and [Marcel] Mauss, "De Quelques formes primitives de classification. [Contribution à l'étude des représentations collectives]" in *AS*, vol. VI [1903], pp. 1ff.

[5]Curr, *The Australian Race*, vol. III, p. 461.

PHRATRIES	CLANS	THINGS CLASSIFIED IN EACH CLAN
Kumite	Fish-hawk – – – – – – – – –	Smoke, honeysuckle, certain trees, etc.
	Pelican – – – – – – – – – –	Blackwood trees, dogs, fire, frost, etc.
	Crow – – – – – – – – – – –	Rain, thunder, lightning, clouds, hail, winter, etc.
	Black cockatoo – – – – – –	Stars, moon, etc.
	A nonvenomous snake – – –	Fish, seal, conger eel, stringy-bark tree, etc.
Kroki	Tea tree – – – – – – – – – –	Duck, crawfish, owl, etc.
	An edible root – – – – – – –	Bustard, quail, a sort of kangaroo, etc.
	A crestless white cockatoo–	Kangaroo, summer, sun, wind, autumn, etc.
	There are no details about the fourth and fifth Kroki clans.	

tive genera. This is shown by the above chart, constructed from data collected by Curr, and by Fison and Howitt.[6]

The list of things attached to each clan is, quite incomplete; Curr himself warns us that he has confined himself to enumerating only some of them.
Today, however, thanks to the work of Mathews and Howitt,[7] we have more
extensive information on the classification adopted by the Wotjobaluk tribe,
and that information enables us to understand better how a system of this
kind can embrace the whole universe known to the natives. The Wotjobaluk
themselves are divided into two phratries, called Gurogity and Gumaty
(Krokitch and Gamutch, according to Howitt).[8] To avoid an overly long list,
I will enumerate (after Mathews) only the things classified in each clan of the
Gurogity phratry.

[6]Curr and Fison got their information from the same person, D. S. Stewart.

[7][Robert Hamilton] Mathews, ["Ethnological Notes on the] Aboriginal Tribes of New South Wales
and Victoria," in *RSNSW,* vol. XXXVIII (1904) [pp. 287–288]. [Alfred William] Howitt, *The Native
Tribes* [*of South-East Australia,* New York, Macmillan, 1904], p. 121.

[8]The feminine form of nouns given by Mathews is Gurogigurk and Gamatykurk. These are the forms
that Howitt has rendered with a slightly different spelling. Also, these names are equivalent to those in use
in the Mount Gambier tribe (Kumite and Kroki).

Classified in the Yam clan are the plains turkey, the native cat, the *mopoke*, the *dyim-dyim* owl, the *mallee* chicken, the rosella parrot, and the *pee-wee*. In the Mussel[9] clan: the gray emu, the porcupine, the curlew, the white cockatoo, the wood duck, the *mallee* lizard, the stinking turtle, the flying squirrel, the ring-tailed opossum, the bronze-wing pigeon, and the *wijuggla*. In the Sun clan: the bandicoot, the moon, the rat kangaroo, the black and white magpies, the *ngùrt* hawk, the gum tree grub, the *u mimoisa* (wattle tree) grub, and the planet Venus. In the Warm Wind clan:[10] the gray-headed ea-glehawk, the carpet snake, the smoker parrot, the shell parakeet, the *murrakan* hawk, the *dikkomur* snake, the ring-neck parrot, the *mirudai* snake, the shingle-back lizard.

If we imagine that there are many other clans (Howitt names a dozen of them, while Mathews names fourteen and warns that his list is very incomplete),[11] we will see how all the things that interest the native as a matter of course find a place in these classifications.

Similar arrangements have been observed in the most dissimilar parts of the Australian continent: in southern Australia, in the state of Victoria, and in New South Wales (among the Euahlayi);[12] very obvious traces of them are found among the tribes of the center.[13] In Queensland, where the clans seem to have disappeared and where the marriage classes are the only subdivisions of the phratry, things are distributed between the classes. Hence, the Wakel-bura are divided into two phratries, Mallera and Wutaru. The classes of the first are called Kurgilla and Banbe; those of the second, Wungo and Obu. To the Banbe belong the opossum, the kangaroo, the dog, the honey of the small bee, etc. To the Wungo are ascribed the emu, the bandicoot, the black duck, the black snake, the brown snake; to the Obu, the carpet snake, the

[9]The indigenous name of this clan is Dyàlup, which Mathews does not translate. This word seems to be identical to "Jallup," by which Howitt designates a subclan of that same tribe and which he translates as "mussel." For this reason, I think I can chance this translation.

[10]This is Howitt's translation; Mathews translates this word (*Wartwurt*) as "heat of the midday sun."

[11]Mathews's table and Howitt's disagree on more than one important point. It even appears that the clans ascribed by Howitt to the Kroki phratry are counted by Mathews in the Gamutch phratry, and vice versa. This is evidence of the very great difficulties that such studies present. However these discrepancies have no import for the question being treated.

[12]Mrs. Langloh Parker [Catherine Sommerville Field Parker], *The Euahlayi Tribe* [London, A. Constable, 1905], pp. 12ff.

[13]These facts are to be found below.

honey of stinging bees, etc.; to the Kurgilla, the porcupine, the plains turkey, water, rain, fire, thunder, etc.[14]

The same organization is found among the Indians of North America. The Zuñi have a system of classification whose basic outline is comparable in every respect to those just described. That of the Omaha rests on the same principles as that of the Wotjobaluk.[15] Echoes of the same ideas persist even in the more advanced societies. Among the Haida, all the gods and mythical beings that govern the various phenomena of nature are also classified in one of the tribe's two phratries, just as men are. Some are Eagles and the others, Crows.[16] The gods that govern things are but another aspect of the things they govern.[17] This mythological classification, then, is but a different form of the preceding ones. Hence, we can be confident that this way of conceiving the world is quite independent of ethnic or geographical particularity. At the same time, however, it emerges quite clearly that this way of conceiving the world is tightly bound up with the whole system of totemic beliefs.

II

In the work to which I have already alluded several times, I showed how these facts illuminate the manner in which the idea of genus or class took form among humans. These classifications are indeed the first that we meet in history. We just saw that they are modeled on social organization, or rather that they have taken the actual framework of society as their own. It was the phratries that served as genera and the clans as species. It is because men formed groups that they were able to group things: All they did was make room for things in the groups they themselves already formed. And if these various classes of things were not simply juxtaposed to one another, but arranged instead according to a unified plan, that is because the same social groups to which they are assimilated are themselves unified and, through that

[14]Curr [*Australian Race*], vol. III, p. 27. Howitt, *Native Tribes*, p. 112. I confine myself to citing the most characteristic facts. The paper already mentioned, "Classification primitive," can be referred to for details.

[15]Durkheim and Mauss, "Classification primitive," pp. 34ff.

[16][John Reed] Swanton, [*Contributions to the Ethnology of*] *the Haida* [Leiden, E. J. Brill, 1905], pp. 13–14, 17, 22. [Actually, this English text says "raven." Since all ravens are crows but not all crows are ravens, I have rendered Durkheim's *corbeau* as "crow" throughout. Trans.]

[17]This is particularly evident among the Haida. According to Swanton, every animal has two aspects. From one point of view, it is an ordinary creature that can be hunted and eaten, but at the same time, it is a supernatural being with the outward form of an animal, and to which man is subject. The mythical beings that correspond to various cosmic phenomena have the same ambiguity (ibid., pp. 14, 16, 25).

union, form an organic whole: the tribe. The unity of these first logical systems merely reproduces that of society. Thus we have our first opportunity to test the proposition put forward at the beginning of this work and to assure ourselves that the fundamental notions of the intellect, the basic categories of thought, can be the product of social factors. The preceding shows that this is indeed the case for the notion of category itself.

I do not mean to deny that the individual consciousness, even on its own, has the capacity to perceive resemblances between the particular things it conceives of. To the contrary, it is clear that even the most primitive and simple classifications already presuppose that faculty. The Australian does not place things at random in the same or different clans. In him as in us, similar images attract and opposite ones repel one another, and he classifies the corresponding things in one or the other according to his sense of these affinities.

Moreover, we can see in some cases the reasoning that inspires them. It is quite probable that the initial, and fundamental, frameworks for these classification systems were constituted by the two phratries and that consequently they began as dichotomous. When a classification has only two genera, they are almost necessarily conceived as antithetical. They are used first as a means of clearly separating those things between which the contrast is most pronounced. Some are placed to the right, the others to the left. The Australian classifications are of this kind. If the white cockatoo is classified in one phratry, the black cockatoo is in the other; if the sun is to one side, the moon and stars are on the opposite side.[18] Very often, the beings that serve the two phratries as totems have opposite colors.[19] Some of these oppositions are found even outside Australia. Where one of the phratries is in charge of peace, the other is in charge of war;[20] if one has water as its totem, the other has land.[21] This is probably why the two phratries have often been considered naturally antagonistic. It is accepted that a rivalry, even an innate hostil-

[18]See p. 142 above. This is the case among the Gournditch-mara (Howitt, *Native Tribes*, p. 124), among the tribes observed by Cameron near Mortlake, and among the Wotjobaluk (Howitt, *Native Tribes*, pp. 125, 250).

[19]J[ohn] Mathew, *Two Representative Tribes [of Queensland]*, London, T. F. Unwin, 1910, p. 139; [Northcote Whitridge] Thomas, *Kinship [Organizations] and [Group] Marriage in [Australia]*, Cambridge, Cambridge University Press, 1906, pp. 53–54.

[20]For example, among the Osage, see [James Owens] Dorsey, "Siouan Sociology," in *XVth Annual Rep.* [BAE, Washington, Government Printing Office, 1897], pp. 233ff.

[21]At Mabuiag, an island in the Torres Strait ([Alfred C.] Haddon, *Head Hunters [Black, White, and Brown*, London, Methuen, 1901], p. 132). The same opposition is also to be found between the two phratries of the Arunta: One comprises people of water, the other people of land ([Carl] Strehlow, [*Die Aranda- und Loritja-Stämme in Zentral-Australien*], vol. 1 [Frankfurt, J. Baer, 1907], p. 6).

ity, exists between them.[22] Once the logical contrast has replicated itself as a kind of social conflict,[23] the opposition of things is extended to persons.

Inside each phratry, on the other hand, the things that seem to have the greatest affinity with the thing serving as the totem have been classified with it in the same clan. For example, the moon has been placed with the black cockatoo; the sun, by contrast, with the white cockatoo, along with the atmosphere and the wind. Here is another example: The totemic animal is grouped with everything that serves as its food,[24] plus the animals with which it is most closely associated.[25] Of course, we cannot always understand the obscure psychology that has presided over many of these joinings and separations. But the preceding examples are sufficient to show that a certain intuition of the similarities and differences presented by things has played a role in creating these classifications.

But a feeling of similarity is one thing; the notion of kind is another. Kind is the external framework whose content is formed, in part, by objects perceived to be like one another. The content cannot itself provide the framework in which it is placed. The content is made up of *vague and fluctuating images* caused by the superimposition and partial fusion of *a definite number of individual images* that are found to have elements in common. By

[22]Among the Iroquois, the two phratries hold tournaments of a sort ([Lewis Henry] Morgan, *Ancient Society* [London, Macmillan, 1877], p. 94). Among the Haida, Swanton says, the members of the two phratries of the Eagle and the Crow "are often regarded as avowed enemies. Husbands and wives (who must be of different phratries) do not hesitate to betray one another" (Swanton, *The Haida*, p. 62). In Australia, this hostility is expressed in the myths. The two animals that serve as the totems of the two phratries are often represented as being perpetually at war with one another (see J[ohn] Mathew, *Eaglehawk and Crow: [A Study of Australian Aborigines*, London, D. Nutt. 1899], pp. 14ff.). In games, each phratry is the natural competitor of the other (Howitt, *Native Tribes*, p. 770).

[23]Thus, Mr. Thomas mistakenly criticized my theory on the origin of phratries as unable to explain their opposition (*Kinship and Marriage in Australia*, p. 69). Still, I do not think it necessary to relate that opposition to the opposition between the profane and the sacred (see [Robert] Hertz, "La Prééminence de la main droite," in *RP,* vol. LXVIII (December 1909), p. 559). The things that belong to one phratry are not profane for the other; both are part of the same religious system (see p. 156 below).

[24]For example, the Tea Tree clan includes the vegetation and consequently herbivorous animals (see Fison and Howitt, *Kamilaroi and Kurnai*, p. 169). Such, probably, is the explanation of a particularity that Boas notes in the totemic emblems of North America. "Among the Tlinkit," he says, "and in all the other tribes of the coast, the emblem of a group includes the animals that are food for the one whose name the group bears." ([Franz] Boas, ["First General Report on the Indians of British Columbia," in *BAAS*], *Fifth Report of the Committee [on the North-Western Tribes of the Dominion of Canada*, London, Offices of the Association, 1890], p. 25).

[25]Thus, among the Arunta, the frogs are associated with the Gum Tree totem, because they are often found in the cavities of that tree; the water is connected with the water fowl; the kangaroo with a sort of parakeet that is commonly seen flying around it ([Sir Baldwin] Spencer and [Francis James] Gillen, *The Native Tribes [of Central Australia*, London, Macmillan, 1899], pp. 146–147, 448).

contrast, the framework is a definite form having fixed contours, but can be applied to an indefinite number of things, whether perceived or not and whether existing or possible. Indeed, the potential scope of every genus is infinitely greater than the circle of objects whose resemblance we have become aware of through direct experience. This is why a whole school of thinkers refuse to identify the idea of kind with that of generic image, and not without reason. A generic image is only the residual representation that similar representations leave in us when they present themselves in consciousness at the same time, and its boundaries are indeterminate; but a genus is a logical symbol by means of which we think clearly about these similarities and others like them. Besides, our best evidence of the gulf between those notions is that the animal is capable of forming generic images, whereas it does not know the art of thinking in terms of genera and species.

The idea of genus is a tool of thought that obviously was constructed by men. But to construct it, we had to have at least a model, for how could that idea have been born if there had been nothing within us or outside us that could have suggested it? To answer that it is given to us a priori is not to answer; as has been said, that lazy solution is the death of analysis. It is not clear where we would have found that indispensable model if not in the panorama of collective life. A genus is in fact an ideal, yet clearly defined, grouping of things with internal bonds among them that are analogous to the bonds of kinship. The only groupings of that kind with which experience acquaints us are those that men form by coming together. Material things can form collections, heaps, or mechanical assemblages without internal unity, but not groups in the sense I have just given the word. A heap of sand or a pile of stones is in no way comparable to the sort of well-defined and organized society that is a genus. In all probability, then, we would never have thought of gathering the beings of the universe into homogeneous groups, called genera, if we had not had the example of human societies before our eyes—if, indeed, we had not at first gone so far in making things members of the society of men, that human and logical groupings were not at first distinguished.[26]

[26]One sign of that original distinction is the fact that, like the social divisions with which they were originally merged, genera sometimes have a territorial base assigned to them. Thus, among the Wotjobaluk in Australia, and among the Zuñi in America, things are thought of as being distributed among the different regions of space, as are the clans. The regional division of things and that of clans coincide (see Durkheim and Mauss, "Classification primitive," pp. 34ff.). Even up to and including relatively advanced peoples, for example in China, the classifications retain something of this spatial character (pp. 55ff.).

From another standpoint, a classification is also a system whose parts are arranged in a hierarchical order. Some are dominant features, and others are subordinated to those. The species and their distinctive properties are subsumed under genera having their own distinctive properties; and the different species of the same genus are conceived as being on a par with one another. Is the standpoint of comprehensiveness the preferred one? In that case, things are represented in an inverse order, the most particular species and the richest in reality being placed at the top, and at the bottom the most general ones and the poorest in detail. But conceiving of them hierarchically is unavoidable either way. And we must guard against thinking that the word has only metaphorical meaning here. The purpose of a classification is to establish relations of subordination and coordination, and man would not even have thought of ordering his knowledge in that way if he had not already known what a hierarchy is. Neither the panorama of physical nature nor the mechanisms of mental association could possibly give us the idea of it. Hierarchy is exclusively a social thing. Only in society do superiors, subordinates, and equals exist. Therefore, even if the facts were not sufficiently conclusive, the analysis of those notions would be sufficient in itself to reveal their origin. We have taken them from society and projected them into our representation of the world. Society furnished the canvas on which logical thought has worked.

III

The relevance of these primitive classifications to the origin of religious thought is no less direct. They in fact imply that all the things thereby classified in the same clan or the same phratry are closely akin to one another and to that which serves as the totem of the clan or of the phratry. When the Australian of the Port MacKay tribe says that the sun, snakes, etc. are of the Yungaroo phratry, he does not simply mean to apply to all those disparate beings a common, but purely conventional, label; the word has an objective meaning for him. He believes that, really, "the alligators are Yungaroo, the moon Wootaroo and so on for the constellations, the trees, the plants, and so forth.[27] An internal tie binds them to the group in which they are classified, and they are regular members of it. They are said to belong to that group,[28]

---

[27][George] Bridgmann, in Brough Smyth, *The Aborigines of Victoria,* vol. I, p. 91.

[28]Fison and Howitt, *Kamilaroi and Kurnai,* p. 168; Howitt, "Further Notes on the Australian Class Systems," *JAI,* vol. XVIII (1889), p. 60.

just as do the human individuals who are part of it, and so a relationship of the same kind joins the human individuals. Man sees the things of his clan as relatives and associates; he calls them friends and considers them to be made of the same flesh as he.[29] Hence, there are elective affinities and quite special relations of compatibility between them and him. Things and men attract one another, in some sense understand one another, and are naturally attuned. For example, when a Wakelbura of the Mallera phratry is buried, the scaffold on which the body is exposed "must be made from the wood of any tree belonging to the Mallera phratry."[30] The same applies to the branches that cover the corpse. If the deceased is of the Banbe class, a Banbe tree must be used. In the same tribe, a magician can use in his art only things that belong to his phratry.[31] Because the others are foreign to him, he cannot make them obey. In this way, a bond of mystical sympathy joins each individual to other beings that are associated with him, living or not. From this arises the belief that he can infer what he will do or is doing from what they do. Among this same group, the Wakelbura, when an individual dreams that he has killed an animal belonging to such and such a social division, he expects to meet a man of that same division the next day.[32] Conversely, the things assigned to a clan or a phratry cannot be used against members of that clan or phratry. Among the Wotjobaluk, each phratry has its own trees. To hunt an animal of the Gurogity, they can only use weapons made of wood taken from trees of the other phratry, and vice versa; otherwise the hunter is sure to miss his mark.[33] The native is convinced that the arrow would turn away from the target by itself and, in a manner of speaking, refuse to touch an animal who is a relative and a friend.

By their joining, then, the people of the clan and the things classified in it form a unified system, with all its parts allied and vibrating sympathetically. This organization, which might at first have seemed to us purely logical, is moral at the same time. The same principle both animates it and makes it cohere: That principle is the totem. Just as a man who belongs to the Crow clan has something of that animal in him, so too the rain. Since rain is of the same clan and belongs to the same totem, it is also and necessarily considered as "being the same thing as a crow." For the same reason, the moon is a black

[29]Curr, *Australian Race*, vol. III, p. 461, concerning the Mount Gambier tribe.

[30][Alfred William] Howitt, "On Some Australian Beliefs," *JAI*, vol. XIII [1884], p. 191 n. 1.

[31][Alfred William] Howitt, "Notes on Australian Message-Sticks and Messengers," *JAI*, vol. XVIII (1889), p. 326; "Further Notes," p. 61 n. 3.

[32]Curr, *Australian Race*, vol. III, p. 28.

[33]Mathews, "Aboriginal Tribes," p. 294.

cockatoo, the sun a white cockatoo, and every blackwood tree a pelican, and so forth. Thus, all the beings classified in a single clan—men, animals, plants, inanimate objects—are only modalities of the totemic being. This is the meaning of the formula I have already reported. What makes them genuine kin is this: All really are of the same flesh, in the sense that they all participate in the nature of the totemic animal. Moreover, the adjectives applied to them are the same as those applied to the totem.[34] The Wotjobaluk call both the totem and the things subsumed under it by the same name, *Mir*.[35] Among the Arunta, where, as we will see, there are still traces of classification, it is true that different words designate the totem and the beings attached to it; however, the name given to these latter bespeaks the close relations that join them to the totemic animal. They are said to be its *intimates*, its *associates*, and its *friends*; they are thought to be inseparable from it.[36] These things are felt to be closely akin.

At the same time, we know that the totemic animal is a sacred being. Therefore, because they are in a sense animals of the same species, just as man is, so all the things that are classified in the clan of which it is the emblem are of the same character. They themselves are also sacred, and the classifications that situate them in relation to the other things of the universe at the same time assign them a place within the religious system as a whole. This is why the animals or plants among them cannot be freely eaten by the human members of the clan. Thus, in the Mount Gambier tribe, the people whose totem is the nonvenomous snake must abstain not only from the flesh of that snake; the meat of seals, conger eels, etc. is also prohibited to them.[37] If, driven by necessity, they permit themselves to partake of those things, they must at least diminish the sacrilege by expiatory rites, just as if those things were the totem, proper.[38] Among the Euahlayi,[39] where use but not abuse of the totem is permitted, the same rule applies to the other things of the clan. Among the Arunta, the prohibition that protects the totemic animal extends to other animals associated with it;[40] and in any case, the latter

[34]Cf. Curr, *Australian Race*, vol. III, p. 461, and Howitt, *Native Tribes*, p. 146. The terms *Tooman* and *Wingo* are applicable to both.

[35]Howitt, *Native Tribes*, p. 123.

[36]Spencer and Gillen, *Native Tribes*, pp. 447ff.; cf. Strehlow, *Aranda*, vol. III, p. xiiff.

[37]Fison and Howitt, *Kamilaroi and Kurnai*, p. 169.

[38]Curr, *Australian Race*, vol. III, p. 462.

[39]Parker, *Euahlayi*, p. 20.

[40][Sir Baldwin] Spencer and [Francis James] Gillen, *Northern Tribes [of Central Australia*, London, Macmillan, 1904], p.151; *Native Tribes*, p. 447; Strehlow, *Aranda*, vol. III, p. xii.

are owed special consideration.[41] The feelings inspired by both are identical.[42]

But the fact that on occasion they play the same role is even better evidence that all the things we see attached to a totem are not fundamentally different from it and, in consequence, have a religious nature. These are accessory and secondary totems, or subtotems, to use a word that today is consecrated by usage.[43] Within a clan, smaller groups constantly form under the influence of friendships and personal affinities. With their more limited membership, these smaller groups tend to live in relative autonomy and to form what amounts to a new subdivision or subclan within the clan. To distinguish and individualize itself, this subclan has need of its own totem—voilà, the subtotem.[44] The totems of these secondary groups are chosen from among those various things that are classified under the principal totem, so they are virtual totems—literally, for the least circumstance is all it takes to make them become actual ones. They have a latent totemic nature that becomes manifest as soon as circumstances permit or require it. In this way, one individual sometimes has two totems: a principal totem that is shared by the whole clan and a subtotem that is specific to the subclan of which he is part. These are somewhat analogous to the *nomen* and the *cognomen* of the Romans.[45]

---

[41]Spencer and Gillen, *Native Tribes*, p. 449.

[42]However, there are certain tribes of Queensland in which the things thus assigned to a social group are not forbidden to the members of that group. Such, for example, is the case of the Wakelbura. It should be borne in mind that the marriage classes serve in this society as frameworks for classification (see p. 144 above). Not only can the people of a class eat the animals ascribed to that class, but *they cannot eat others.* All other food is forbidden to them (Howitt, *Native Tribes*, p. 113; Curr, *Australian Race*, vol. III, p. 27).

Nonetheless, we must take care not to conclude that these animals are considered profane. To be noted is that the individual not only may but must eat them, since he is forbidden to eat anything else. This imperativeness of the prescription is a sure sign that we are in the presence of things that are religious in nature. But the religiousness that marks them has given birth to a positive obligation rather than to that negative obligation which is the prohibition. Perhaps, indeed, it is not impossible to see how that deviation could have happened. We have seen above (see p. 140) that every individual is thought to have a sort of property right over his totem and, in consequence, over the things that come under it. If special circumstances influenced the development of that aspect of the totemic relation, then people would come naturally to believe that only the members of a clan could use their totem and all that is assimilated to it; that the others, by contrast, did not have the right to touch it. Under these circumstances, a clan could feed itself only with things ascribed to the clan.

[43]Mrs. Parker uses the expression "multiplex totems."

[44]As examples, see the Euahlayi tribe in the book of Mrs. Parker (pp. 15ff.) and the Wotjobaluk (Howitt, *Native Tribes*, pp. 121ff.); cf. the previously cited article of Mathews.

[45]See examples in Howitt, *Native Tribes*, p. 122.

Sometimes, indeed, we see that a subclan emancipates itself completely and becomes an autonomous group, an independent clan. The subtotem then becomes a totem in the full sense. One tribe in which this process of segmentation has been taken virtually to its outermost limit is the Arunta tribe. The information contained in the first book of Spencer and Gillen indicated back then that there were some 60 totems among the Arunta,[46] but the more recent research of Strehlow has established that the number is much larger. He counts not less than 442 totems.[47] Spencer and Gillen were in no way exaggerating when they said that "in the land occupied by the natives, there is no object, animate or inanimate, that does not give its name to some totemic group of individuals."[48] That multitude of totems, which is prodigious when compared with the size of the population, comes of the fact that, under the influence of particular circumstances, the original clans have divided and subdivided infinitely; as a result, almost all the subtotems have gained the status of totems.

Strehlow's studies have definitively shown this. Spencer and Gillen cited only a few isolated cases of allied totems.[49] Strehlow established that this was actually a universal form of organization. He drew up a table on which almost all the totems of the Arunta are classified according to this principle. All are attached to some sixty principal totems as either allies or auxiliaries.[50] The allied totems are held to be at the service of the principal one.[51] This state of relative subordination is probably the echo of a time when today's "allies" were only subtotems, and therefore a time when the tribe had only a

[46]See Durkheim and Mauss, "Classification primitive," p. 28 n. 2.

[47]Strehlow, *Aranda*, vol. II, pp. 61–72.

[48]Spencer and Gillen, *Native Tribes*, p. 112.

[49]See especially ibid., p. 447, and *Northern Tribes*, p. 151.

[50]Strehlow, *Aranda*, vol. III, pp. xiii–[xvii]. Sometimes the same secondary totems are attached to two or three principal totems at once. This is probably because Strehlow could not establish with certainty which of those totems was truly the main one.

Two interesting facts, which emerge from this table, confirm certain propositions I have already set forth. First, with very few exceptions, almost all the principal totems are animals. Next, the stars are never anything but secondary or allied totems. This is further evidence that originally the preference was to choose totems from the animal kingdom, and that the allied totems were not promoted to the status of totems until later.

[51]According to myth, in legendary times the allied totems served as food for the people of the principal totem and, if they were trees, provided shelter (Strehlow, *Aranda*, vol. III, p. xii; Spencer and Gillen, *Native Tribes*, p. 403). However, the fact that the allied totem is thought to have been eaten does not imply that it is considered profane. It is believed that, in mythical times, the principal totem was eaten by the ancestors who founded the clan.

small number of clans subdivided into subclans. Numerous survivals confirm
that hypothesis. The two groups that are allied in this way often have the
same totemic emblem. The oneness of that emblem is inexplicable unless the
two groups were originally one.[52] Elsewhere, the kinship of the two clans is
shown by the role and interest that each of them takes in the rites of the
other. The two cults are still not completely separate, most likely because initially they were completely merged.[53] Tradition explains the tie that binds
them by imagining how, long ago, the two clans lived very near each other.[54]
In other cases, myth even states explicitly that the one was derived from the
other. They say that the allied animal once upon a time belonged to the
species that is still the principal totem and was not differentiated until a later
epoch. In this way, the chantunga birds, which now are associated with the
witchetty grub, were witchetty grubs in legendary times and later transformed themselves into birds. Two species that are now attached to the totem
of the honey ant were honey ants in the past, and so forth.[55] Further, that
transformation of a subtotem into a totem happens imperceptibly, with the
result that the status is ill defined in some cases, and it is not easy to say
whether one is dealing with a principal or a secondary totem.[56] As Howitt
says regarding the Wotjobaluk, there are subtotems that are totems in the
process of formation.[57] In this way, the various things classified in a totem are
like many nuclei around which new totemic cults can form. This is the best
evidence of the religious feelings they inspire. If they did not have this sacredness, they could not so easily be promoted to the same status as those sacred things par excellence, the totems proper.

Thus, the circle of religious things extends well beyond what at first
seemed to be its boundaries. Not only are the totemic animals and the members of the clan enclosed within that circle; but since there is nothing known
that is not classified within a clan and under a totem, there is also nothing
that does not receive a reflection of that religiousness, to some degree. When

[52]Thus, in the Wild Cat clan, the designs carved on the churinga represent the flowering tree called
hakea, which today is a distinct totem (Spencer and Gillen, Native Tribes [pp. 147–148]). Strehlow (Aranda,
vol. III, p. xii n. 4) says that this is common.

[53]Spencer and Gillen, Northern Tribes, p. 182; Native Tribes, pp. 151, 297.

[54]Native Tribes, pp. 151, 158.

[55]Ibid., pp. 447–449.

[56]It is in this way that Spencer and Gillen speak to us of the pigeon called Inturita sometimes as a principal totem (Native Tribes [p. 410]), and sometimes as an allied totem (p. 448).

[57]Howitt, "Further Notes," pp. 63–64.

actual gods appear in the religions that form later, each of them will be set over a particular category of natural phenomena—this one the sea, that one the air, another the fruit harvest, and so on, and each of those provinces of nature will be thought of as drawing the life that is within it from the god to which it is subject. Such a distribution of nature among various deities is precisely what constitutes the representation of the universe that religions give us. So long as humanity has not moved beyond the phase of totemism, the role the various totems of the tribe play is precisely the one that will later belong to divine personalities. In the Mount Gambier tribe, which I have taken as the main example, there are ten clans, and so the whole world is divided into ten classes, or rather into ten families, each originating in a special totem. The things classified in a clan take their reality from that origin, for they are conceived of as various modes of the totemic being—according to our example, rain, thunder, lightning, clouds, hail, and winter are regarded as various kinds of crow. Taken together, these ten families of things constitute a systematic and complete representation of the world, and that representation is religious, since religious notions furnish the principle of it. Far from being restricted to one or two categories of beings, then, the domain of totemic religion extends to the farthest limits of the known universe. Like the religion of Greece, it places the divine everywhere. The well-known formula Πάντα πλήρη θεῶν* can serve as its motto as well.

To be in a position to conceive totemism in this way, we must modify the longstanding notion of it on one fundamental point. Until the discoveries of recent years, totemism was defined as the religion of the clan and was thought to consist entirely in the cult of a particular totem. From this point of view, it seemed that there were as many independent totemic religions as there were different clans. Moreover, that notion was in harmony with the commonly held notion of the clan: It is seen as an autonomous society,[58] more or less closed to similar societies or having only external and superficial relations with them. But the reality is more complex. Certainly the cult of each totem has its home in the corresponding clan; it is celebrated there and only there; the members of the clan are responsible for it; it is transmitted by them from one generation to another, along with the beliefs on which it is based.

On the other hand, the various totemic cults that are practiced within a single tribe do not develop in parallel and in ignorance of one another, as

---

*Everything is full of gods. Trans.

[58]Thus it happens that the clan has often been confounded with the tribe. Curr especially has been guilty of this confusion, which often imports problems into ethnographers' descriptions ([*The Australian Race*], vol. I, pp. 61ff.).

though each was a complete religion and sufficient unto itself. Instead, they imply one another. Each is only one part of the same whole, an element of the same religion. The men of a clan in no way regard the beliefs of the neighboring clans with the indifference, skepticism, or hostility that is ordinarily inspired by a religion to which one is a stranger; they themselves share the beliefs. The Crow people are also convinced that the Snake people have a mythical snake as their ancestor and owe special qualities and capacities to that origin. Have we not seen that, under certain conditions at least, a man eats a totem that is not his own only after having observed ritual formalities? For example, he requests permission from the individuals of that totem, if there are any present. This is so because that food is not merely profane for him either. He, too, accepts that there are affinities between the members of a clan he is not part of and the animal whose name they bear. Moreover, that commonality of belief is sometimes manifested in the cult. Although, in principle, the rites that concern a totem can be performed only by people of that totem, it is nonetheless very common for representatives of different clans to be present. Indeed, sometimes their role is not one of mere spectating. Although of course they are not the celebrants, they decorate those who are, and they prepare the service. They, too, have an interest in the rite's being conducted; hence, in certain tribes it is they who invite the proper clan to conduct the ceremony.[59] Indeed, there is a whole cycle of rites that must take place in the presence of the assembled tribe: the totemic ceremonies of initiation.[60]

In sum, totemic organization as just described clearly must result from a sort of consensus among all the members of the tribe, without distinction. Each clan cannot possibly have developed its beliefs in an absolutely independent manner; the cults of the various totems complement one another exactly, and so they must necessarily have been in some sense adjusted to one another. In fact, as we have seen, a single totem did not ordinarily repeat itself in the same tribe, and the whole universe was divided among the totems thus constituted in such a way that the same object should not be found in two different clans. So systematic a division would have been impossible to achieve without a tacit or concerted agreement in which the whole tribe would have had to participate. The whole set of beliefs that was born in this way is in part (but only in part) an affair of the tribe.[61]

[59]This is the case, for example, of the Warramunga (Spencer and Gillen, *Northern Tribes*, p. 298).

[60]See, for example, Spencer and Gillen, *Native Tribes*, pp. 380 et passim.

[61]One could even ask whether tribal totems do not sometimes exist. Thus, among the Arunta, the wild cat is the totem of a particular clan and yet is forbidden to the whole tribe; even the people of other

To summarize: In developing an adequate conception of totemism, we must not enclose ourselves within the boundaries of the clan but consider the tribe as a whole. Each clan's own cult enjoys great autonomy. Indeed, we can anticipate even now that the active ferment of religious life will be found in the clan. On the other hand, all these cults are unified, and totemic religion is the complex system formed by that union, just as Greek polytheism was formed by the union of all the cults that were addressed to the various deities. I have shown that when totemism is understood in this way, it too has a cosmology.

---

clans may eat it only in moderation (Spencer and Gillen, *Native Tribes*, p. 168). But I believe it would be an exaggeration to speak of a tribal totem in that instance, for it does not follow from the prohibition against eating it freely that the animal is a totem. A prohibition may have other causes. Undoubtedly, the religious unity of the tribe is real, but that unity is affirmed with the aid of other symbols. Further on, I will show what those symbols are (Bk. II, chap. 9).

CHAPTER FOUR

THE PRINCIPAL TOTEMIC BELIEFS (END)

The Individual Totem and the Sexual Totem

Thus far, I have examined totemism solely as a public institution. The only totems discussed have been those shared by a clan, a phratry, or, in a sense, the tribe.[1] The individual had a part in them only as a member of the group. But we understand that there is no religion without an individual aspect. This general observation applies to totemism. Apart from the impersonal and collective totems that are foremost, there are others that belong to each individual, that express his personality, and whose cult he celebrates privately.

I

In some Australian tribes and in most of the Indian societies of North America,[2] each individual maintains a personal relationship with a particular object, which is comparable to the relationship that each clan maintains with its totem. That object is sometimes an inanimate being or something manmade, but it is often an animal. In some cases, only a particular part of the body, such as the head, the feet, or the liver, has the same function.[3]

The name of the thing also serves as the name of the individual. It is his personal name, a first name that is added to his collective totem, just as the

---

[1] The totems are the tribe's property in the sense that the tribe as a whole has an interest in the cult each clan owes to its totem.

[2] Frazer has made a full compilation of the texts about individual totemism in North America ([James George Frazer], *Totemism and Exogamy*, vol. III [London, Macmillan, 1910], pp. 370–456).

[3] For example, among the Hurons, the Iroquois, and the Algonquins ([Pierre François Xavier de] Charlevoix, *Histoire [et description générale de la Nouvelle France]*, vol. VI [Paris, Chez la Veuve Ganeau, 1744], pp. 67–70; [Gabriel] Sagard, *Le Grand voyage au pays des Hurons* [Paris, Tross, 1865], p. 160), and among the Thompson Indians ([James Alexander] Teit, "The Thompson Indians of British Columbia," *AMNH*, vol. II (1900), p. 355).

praenomen of the Romans is added to the *nomen gentilicium*. It is true that this is documented for only a certain number of societies,[4] but it is probably widespread. Indeed, I will presently show that the thing and the individual are of the same kind. Identity of kind entails identity of name. Being given in the course of especially important religious ceremonies, this forename has a quality of sacredness. It is not pronounced in the ordinary circumstances of profane life. Sometimes, indeed, the word used in everyday language to designate the thing is somewhat modified for that special use[5]—this, because the words of everyday language are excluded from religious life.

In the American tribes, at least, an emblem is added to this name, which belongs to each individual and in various ways represents the thing designated by the name. For example, each Mandan wears the skin of the animal whose namesake he is.[6] If it is a bird, he adorns himself with the bird's feathers.[7] The Hurons and the Algonquins tattoo its image on their bodies.[8] It is represented on his weapons.[9] Among the tribes of the Northwest, the individual emblem is carved or sculpted on utensils, houses, and so forth, as is the collective emblem of the clan.[10] The individual emblem serves as a mark of personal property.[11] Often the two coats of arms are combined, which partly explains why the totemic escutcheons show such variety among these peoples.[12]

There are the closest of bonds between the individual and the animal

[4]This is the case for the Yuin ([Alfred William] Howitt, *The Native Tribes [of South-East Australia*, New York, Macmillan, 1904], p. 133); the Kurnai (*Native Tribes*, p. 135); several tribes of Queensland ([Walter Edmund] Roth, *Superstition, Magic and Medicine, North Queensland Ethnography*, Bulletin no. 5 [Brisbane, G. A. Vaughn, 1903], p. 19; [Alfred C.] Haddon, *Head-Hunters, [Black, White, and Brown*, London, Methuen, 1901], p. 193); among the Delaware ([John Gottlieb Ernestus] Heckewelder, "An Account of the History [Manners and Customs] of the Indian Nations [Who Once Inhabited Pennsylvania"], *HLCAPS*, vol. I [1819], p. 238); among the Thompson Indians (Teit, "Thompson Indians," p. 355); and among the Salish Statlumh ([Charles] Hill Tout, "Report on the Ethnology of the Statlumh of British Columbia," *JAI*, vol. XXXV [1905], pp. 147ff.).

[5]Hill Tout, "Ethnology of the Statlumh," p. 154.

[6][George] Catlin, *Illustration of the Manners, Customs [and Condition of the North American Indians*, 2 vols.], London [H. G. Bohn], 1876, vol. I, p. 36.

[7][George] Catlin, [*Nouvelles des missions d'Amérique, extraits des] lettres édifiantes et curieuses*, 6th ed. [Paris, Martial, 1883], pp. 172ff.

[8]Charlevoix, *Histoire de la nouvelle France*, vol. VI, p. 69.

[9][James Owen] Dorsey, "A Study of Siouan Cults," in *XIth Annual Report [BAE*, Washington, Government Printing Office, 1894], p. 443.

[10][Franz] Boas, ["The Social Organization and Secret Societies of the] Kwakiutl [Indians," in *RNM for 1895*, Washington, Government Printing Office, 1897], p. 323.

[11]Hill Tout, "Ethnology of the Statlumh," p. 154.

[12]Boas, "Kwakiutl," p. 323.

whose name he bears. The nature of the animal is part and parcel of the man, who has its qualities as well as its faults. For example, it is thought that a man with the eagle as his individual emblem possesses the gift of seeing the future; if he carries the name of the bear, it is said that he is likely to be wounded in fights, the bear being slow, heavy, and easily trapped;[13] if the animal is despised, the man is the object of the same contempt.[14] Indeed, the kinship between the two is so great that in certain circumstances, especially danger, the man is thought capable of assuming the animal's form.[15] Inversely, the animal is regarded as the man's double, his alter ego.[16] The association between the two is so close that their destinies are often considered to be interdependent: Nothing can happen to one without repercussions felt by the other.[17] If the animal dies, the life of the man is threatened. Hence a very common rule is that one must neither kill the animal nor, especially, eat its flesh. When applied to the clan, this prohibition carries with it all sorts of allowances and compromises, but in this case it is far more categorical and absolute.[18]

For its part, the animal protects the man and is a kind of patron. It alerts him to possible dangers and to means of escaping them;[19] it is said to be the man's friend.[20] In fact, since it is often presumed to have miraculous powers,

[13]Miss [Alice C.] Fletcher, "The Import of the Totem, A Study from the Omaha Tribe, *RSI* [Washington, Government Printing Office], 1897, p. 583. Similar facts will be found in Teit, "Thompson Indians," pp. 354, 356; Peter Jones, *History of the Ojibway Indians: [With Especial Reference to Their Conversion to Christianity,* London, A. W. Bennet, 1869], p. 87.

[14]This is, for example, the case of the dog among the Salish Statlumh because of the servile state in which he lives (Hill Tout, "Ethnology of the Statlumh," p. 153).

[15]Langloh Parker [Catherine Sommerville Field Parker], [*The*] *Euahlayi* [*Tribe*] [London, A. Constable, 1905], p. 21.

[16]"The spirit of a man," says Mrs. Parker (ibid.), "is in his Yunbeai (individual totem) and his Yunbeai is in him."

[17]Parker, *Euahlayi*, p. 20. It is the same among certain Salish ([Charles] Hill Tout, "Ethnological Report on the Stseelis and Skaulits Tribes [of the Halokmelem Division of the Salish of British Columbia]," *JAI*, vol. XXXIV [1904], p. 324). This is common among the Indians of Central America ([Daniel G.] Brinton, "Nagualism: A Study in Native American Folk-lore and History," *APS*, vol. XXXIII [1894], p. 32).

[18]Parker, *Euahlayi*, p. 20; Howitt, *Native Tribes*, p. 147; Dorsey, "Siouan Cults," p. 443. Incidentally, Frazer has surveyed the American cases and has established the universality of this prohibition (*Totemism and Exogamy*, vol. III, p. 450). True, we have seen that in America the individual had to begin by killing the animal whose skin was used to make what the ethnographers call his "medicine bag." But this custom has been found only in five tribes; it is probably a late and altered form of the institution.

[19]Howitt, *Native Tribes*, pp. 135, 147, 387, and "On Australian Medicine Men," *JAI*, vol. XVI (1887), p. 34; [James Alexander] Teit, "The Shuswap" [*AMNH*, Leiden, E. J. Brill, 1908], p. 607.

[20][Rev. A.] Meyer, "Manners and Customs of the Aborigines of the Encounter Bay Tribe," in [James Dominick] Woods [*The Native Tribes of South Australia*, Adelaide, E. S. Wigg. 1879], p. 197.

it passes those on to its human partner, who believes them to be proof against bullets, arrows, and every sort of blow.[21] The individual has such confidence in the efficacy of his protector that he braves the greatest dangers and performs the most breathtaking feats of prowess with serene fearlessness. Faith gives him the necessary courage and strength.[22] Nevertheless, the man's ties with his patron are not ones of dependency, pure and simple. The man, for his part, can act upon the animal. He gives it orders and has power over it. A Kurnai whose friend and ally is the shark believes that, with an incantation, he can disperse sharks that threaten a boat.[23] In other cases, the tie contracted in this way is thought to bestow upon the man a special capacity for success in hunting the animal.[24]

By their very nature, these relations seem strongly to imply that the being with which each individual is thus associated can itself be only an individual, not a species. No one has a species as alter ego. In some cases, in fact it quite clearly is such and such a definite tree, rock, or stone that plays this role.[25] Whenever it is an animal, or whenever the lives of the animal and the man are considered to be bound up together, such is necessarily the case. It is not possible to be joined with a whole species in an interdependence of this kind, because there is no day, or for that matter no instant, in which the species does not lose one of its members. Still, the primitive has a certain inability to conceive of the individual apart from the species. The bond that unites him with the one extends altogether naturally to the other; he has the same feeling for both. Thus it comes about that the whole species is sacred to him.[26]

[21][Franz] Boas, "Second General Report on the Indians of British Columbia," in [*BAAS*], *VIth Report on the North-Western Tribes of Canada* [London, Offices of the Association, 1891], p. 93; Teit, "Thompson Indians," p. 336; Boas, "Kwakiutl," p. 394.

[22]Corroborating evidence is to be found in Hill Tout, "Ethnology of the Statlumh," pp. 144–145. Cf. Parker, *Euahlayi*, p. 29.

[23]According to information given Frazer by Howitt in a personal letter (*Totemism and Exogamy*, vol. I, p. 495, n.2).

[24]Hill Tout, "Stseelis and Skaulits Tribes," p. 324.

[25]Howitt, "Australian Medicine Men," *JAI*, vol. XVI, p. 34; [Joseph François] Lafitau, *Moeurs des sauvages américains*, vol. I [Paris, Saugrain l'ainé, 1724], p. 370; Charlevoix, *Histoire de la Nouvelle France*, vol. VI, p. 68. The same is true of the *atai* and the *tamaniu* at Mota ([Robert Henry] Codrington, *The Melanesians*, [Oxford, Clarendon Press, 1891], pp. 250–251).

[26]Consequently, the line of demarcation that Frazer thought he could establish between these animal protectors and the fetishes does not exist. He thought fetishism would begin where the protector being is an individual object and not a class (Frazer, *Totemism and Exogamy*, p. 56); as we know from as early as the tribes of Australia, however, a specific animal sometimes plays this role (see Howitt, "[On] Australian Medicine Men; [or Doctors and Wizards of Some Australian Tribes], *JAI*, vol. XVI, [1887], p. 34). The truth is that the notions of fetish and fetishism do not correspond to anything definite.

This protector being is called by different names in different societies: *nagual* among the Indians of Mexico,[27] *manitou* among the Algonquins, *okki* among the Hurons,[28] *snam* among certain Salish[29] and *sulia* among others,[30] *budjan* among the Yuin,[31] *yunbeai* among the Euahlayi,[32] and so on. Because of the importance these beliefs and practices have among the Indians of North America, some have proposed to create the word *nagualism* or *manitouism* to designate them.[33] But by giving them a special and distinctive name, we may well misconstrue their relationship with totemism. In fact, the same principles are applied, in one case to the clan, in the other to the individual. In both, the belief is the same: There are living ties between things and men, and the things are endowed with special powers from which the human allies benefit. The custom is also the same: Giving the man the name of the thing with which he is associated, and adding an emblem to this name. The totem is the patron of the clan, just as the patron of the individual is a personal totem. So there is good reason for the terminology to make this kinship between the two systems visible. This is why, with Frazer, I will call the cult that each individual renders to his patron *individual totemism*. Use of this terminology is further justified by the fact that in some cases the primitive himself uses the same word to designate the totem of the clan and the animal protector of the individual.[34] Tylor and Powell have rejected it and called for different terms for the two sorts of religious institutions because, in their view, the collective totem is only a name, a shared label without re-

---

[27] Brinton, "Nagualism," *APS*, vol. XXXIII [1894], p. 32.

[28] Charlevoix, *Histoire de la Nouvelle France*, p. 67.

[29] Hill Tout, "Ethnology of the Statlumh," p. 142.

[30] Hill Tout, "Stseelis and Skaulits Tribes," pp. 311ff.

[31] Howitt, *Native Tribes*, p. 133.

[32] Parker, *Euahlayi*, p. 20.

[33] [Edwin Sidney Hartland], "An American View of Totemism, [A Note on Major Powell's Article] in *Man*, vol. II (1902), 84, pp. 113–115 [This does not mention "nagualism," and says "manitu," not "manituism." Trans.]; [Edward Burnett] Tylor, "Note on the Haida Totem-Post Lately Erected in the Pitt River Museum at Oxford," *Man*, vol. II, (1902), pp. 1–3, [Again, there is no mention of "nagualism." Trans.]; [Andrew] Lang expressed similar ideas in *Social Origins* [London, Longmans, 1903], pp. 133–135. Finally, in a revision of his earlier view, Frazer himself now believes that it is best to designate collective totems and guardian spirits by different names until the relationship that exists between them is better known (*Totemism and Exogamy*, vol. III, p. 456).

[34] This is the case in Australia among the Yuin (Howitt, *Native Tribes*, p. 81) and among the Narrinyeri (Meyer, "The Encounter Bay Tribe," in Woods, *Native Tribes of South Australia*, pp. 197ff.).

ligious characteristics.[35] But to the contrary, we know that it is a sacred thing to an even greater degree than the animal protector. As this study develops, the extent to which the two sorts of totemism are inseparable will be shown.[36]

Nonetheless, however great the kinship between these two institutions, there are important differences between them. Whereas the clan considers itself to be the offspring of the totemic animal or plant, the individual does not believe he has any relation of descent with his personal totem. It is a friend, a partner, and a protector, but it is not a relative. The individual makes use of the virtues it is held to possess, but he is not of the same blood. Second, the members of a clan permit neighboring clans to eat the animal whose name they collectively bear, provided that the necessary formalities are observed. By contrast, the individual not only respects the species to which his personal totem belongs but also does his utmost to defend it against strangers, at least wherever the destinies of the man and the animal are thought to be bound up together.

These two kinds of totems differ most in the manner by which they are acquired.

The collective totem belongs to the legal status of every individual. Generally speaking, it is hereditary; at any rate, it is birth that designates it and men's will has no role. The child sometimes has the totem of its mother (Kamilaroi, Dieri, Urabunna, etc.), sometimes that of its father (Narrinyeri, Warramunga, etc.), and sometimes the totem that is most important at the place where his mother conceived (Arunta, Loritja). But the individual totem is acquired by a deliberate act:[37] Determining it requires a series of rites. The method most widely used among the Indians of America is the following: Toward puberty, as the time of initiation approaches, the young

---

[35]"The totem no more resembles the patron of the individual," says Tylor, "than an escutcheon resembles an image of a saint." ("The Haida Totem-Post," p. 2.) Likewise, today Frazer rallies to Tylor's opinion, because he now denies that the totem of the clan is in any way religious (*Totemism and Exogamy*, vol. III, p. 452).

[36]See below, Bk. 2, chap. 9.

[37]However, according to a passage in Mathews, the individual totem is hereditary among the Wotjobaluk. "Each individual," he says, "lays claim to an animal, a plant, or an inanimate object as its special and personal totem, which he inherits from his mother" ([Robert Hamilton] Mathews, ["Ethnological Notes on the Aboriginal Tribes of New South Wales and Victoria"], *RSNSW*, vol. XXXVIII (1904), p. 291). But it is obvious that if all the children of the same family had the totem of their mother as their personal totem, neither they nor their mother would have personal totems. Mathews probably means that each individual chooses his individual totem from among a group of things attributed to the mother's clan. We will see, in fact, that each clan has its own individual totems that are its exclusive property and that the members of other clans cannot use them. In this sense, birth in some measure (but in that measure only) defines the personal totem.

man withdraws to a place apart—a forest, for example. There, during a period that varies from a few days to several years, he submits to all kinds of exercises that are exhausting and contrary to his nature. He fasts, mortifies
himself, and mutilates himself. Sometimes he wanders, uttering terrible
screams and howls; sometimes he stays still, stretched out on the ground,
groaning. He dances sometimes, prays sometimes, and sometimes calls out to
his ordinary deities. Proceeding in this way, he finally works himself into a
state of intense super-excitement that is very close to delirium. When he has
reached this paroxysm, his mental representations easily take on a hallucinatory character. "When," says Heckewelder, "a boy is on the eve of being initiated, he is subjected to an alternating regime of fasting and medical
treatment; he abstains from all food, he swallows the most powerful and repulsive drugs; on occasion, he drinks intoxicating concoctions until his mind
is genuinely in a state of confusion. At that moment, he has or believes he has
visions, extraordinary dreams to which the entire exercise has naturally predisposed him. He imagines himself flying through the air, moving under the
ground, jumping over valleys from one summit to the other, fighting and de-
feating giants and monsters."[38] Under these conditions, if while dreaming or
awake he sees (or thinks he sees, which amounts to the same thing) an animal appearing to him that seems to show friendly intentions, he will imagine he has discovered the patron that he has been waiting for.[39]

This process is rarely used in Australia.[40] There, the personal totem seems
instead to be imposed by a third person, either at birth[41] or at initiation.[42] It is
usually a relative who plays this role, or it can be a person with special powers,
such as an old man or a magician. Divination is sometimes used for this purpose. At Charlotte Bay, at Cape Bedford, or on the Proserpine River, for
example, the grandmother or another old woman takes a small part of the

[38]Heckewelder, "Manners and Customs of the Indian Nations," *HLCAPS*, vol. I, p. 238.

[39]See Dorsey, "Siouan Cults," p. 507; Catlin, *North American Indians*, vol. I, p. 37; Fletcher, "The Import of the Totem," in *Smithsonian Rep. for 1897*, p. 580; Teit, "Thompson Indians," pp. 317–320; Hill
Tout, "Ethnology of the Statlumh," p. 144.

[40]Still, one finds examples. The Kurnai magicians see their personal totems revealed in dreams
(Howitt, *Native Tribes*, p. 387, and "Australian Medicine Men," p. 34). The men of Cape Bedford believe
that when an old man dreams of something during the night, that thing is the personal totem of the first
person he will meet the next day (Roth, *Superstition, Magic, and Medicine*, p. 19). But it is probable that only
complementary and accessory personal totems are acquired by this method; for, as I say in the text, within
that same tribe, a different process is used at initiation.

[41]In certain tribes about which Roth speaks (*Superstition, Magic and Medicine*); and in certain tribes in
the vicinity of Maryborough (Howitt, *Native Tribes*, p. 147).

[42]Among the Wiradjuri (Howitt, *Native Tribes*, p. 406, and "Australian Medicine Men," p. 50).

umbilical cord attached to the placenta and whirls it quite forcefully. During this time, other old women seated in a circle propose different names, one after the other. The name that is pronounced just at the moment the cord breaks is adopted.[43] Among the Yaraikanna of Cape York, the young novice is given a little water to rinse his mouth after his tooth has been pulled, and he is asked to spit into a bucket filled with water. The old men carefully examine the kind of clot that is formed by the blood and saliva he has spat out, and the natural object of which its shape reminds them becomes the personal totem of the young man.[44] In other cases, the totem is transmitted directly from one individual to another, for example, from father to son or uncle to nephew.[45] This method is also used in America. In an example that Hill Tout reports, the operator was a shaman[46] who wanted to transmit his totem to his nephew:

> The uncle took the symbolic emblem of his *snam* (personal totem), which in this case was the dried skin of a bird. He asked his nephew to blow on it, then he himself did likewise and pronounced some secret words. It then seemed to Paul (which was the nephew's name) that the skin became a living bird that began to fly around them for several moments before disappearing. Paul received instructions to procure the skin of a bird of the same species that very day, and to wear it; this he did. The following night, he had a dream in which the *snam* appeared to him in the form of a human being who revealed to him the secret name by which it might be summoned, and who promised him its protection.[47]

Not only is the individual totem acquired, not given, but more than that, the acquisition of one is not obligatory everywhere. There are many Australian tribes in which that custom seems to be completely unknown.[48] And

---

[43]Ibid.

[44]Haddon, *Head Hunters,* pp. 193ff.

[45]Among the Wiradjuri, [Howitt, *Native Tribes,* p. 406, and "On Australian Medicine Men," in *JAI,* vol. XVI, p. 50].

[46]In general, it seems clear that these transmissions from father to son occur only when the father is a shaman or a magician. This is also the case among the Thompson Indians (Teit, "The Thompson Indians," p. 320) and among the Wiradjuri, to whom reference has been made.

[47]Hill Tout ("Ethnology of the Statlumh," pp. 146–147). The basic rite is the one that consists of blowing on the skin. If it had not been done correctly, the transmission would not have occurred because the breath is the soul. When both blow on the skin of the animal, the magician and the recipient exhale parts of their souls, and these parts interpenetrate one another while communing with the nature of the animal, which is also (in the form of its symbol) a participant in the ceremony.

[48][Northcote Whitridge] Thomas, "Further Remarks on Mr. Hill Tout's Views on Totemism," in *Man,* vol. IV (1904), 53, p. 85.

even where it does exist, it is often optional. Among the Euahlayi, all the magicians have individual totems from which they get their powers, but a great many laymen have none at all. It is a favor the magician can dispense but one he reserves for his friends and favorites and for those who aspire to become his colleagues.[49] Likewise, among certain Salish, only individuals who want to excel in war or hunting, or who aspire to become shamans, equip themselves with protectors of this sort.[50] Thus, at least among certain peoples, the individual totem seems to be regarded more as an advantage or a convenience than as a necessity. It is good to obtain one, but there is no obligation to do so. On the other hand, there is no obligation to settle for only one. If one wants to be better protected, nothing stands in the way of trying to obtain several;[51] and inversely, if the protector one has played its role poorly, it can be replaced.[52]

But while there is something more optional and free about individual totemism, it has staying power that the totemism of the clan cannot match. One of Hill Tout's main informants was a baptized Salish. Although he had sincerely abandoned all the beliefs of his ancestors and had become a model catechist, his faith in the efficacy of personal totems remained unshakable.[53] Similarly, although no visible traces of collective totemism are left in the civilized countries, a notion of solidarity between each individual and an animal, plant, or some other external object is the basis of customs that can still be observed in several European countries.[54]

II

Between individual and collective totemism, there is an intermediate form that has something of both: sexual totemism. Found only in Australia and in a small number of tribes, it has been reported mainly in Victoria and in New

[49]Langloh Parker, *Euahlayi*, pp. 20, 29.

[50]Hill Tout, "Ethnology of the Statlumh," pp. 143, 146; "Stseelis and Skaulits Tribes," p. 324.

[51]Parker, *Euahlayi*, p. 30; Teit, "The Thompson Indians," p. 320; Hill Tout, "Ethnology of the Statlumh," p. 144.

[52]Charlevoix, *Histoire de la Nouvelle France*, vol. VI, p. 69.

[53]Hill Tout, "Ethnology of the Statlumh," p. 145.

[54]Thus, at the birth of a child, people plant a tree on which they lavish pious care, for they believe that its fate and the infant's are conjoined. In his *Golden Bough*, Frazer reported numerous customs or beliefs that express the same idea in various ways (Cf. [Edwin Sidney] Hartland, *Legend of Perseus*, vol. II [London, D. Nutt, 1894–1896], pp. 1–55).

South Wales.[55] True, Mathews claims to have observed it in every part of Australia he visited but without providing specifics to support his claim.[56]

Among these different peoples, all the men of the tribe, on the one hand, and, on the other, all the women form what amounts to two distinct and even antagonistic societies, no matter what clan they belong to. Each of these two sexual corporations believes itself to be joined by mystical ties to a specific animal. Among the Kurnai, all the men consider themselves as brothers of the emu-wren (Yeerùng), all the women as sisters of the linnet (Djeetgùn); all the men are Yeerùng and all the women Djeetgùn. Among the Wotjobaluk and the Wiradjuri, respectively, this role is played by the bat and the nightjar (a sort of screech owl). In other tribes, the woodpecker replaces the nightjar. Each sex sees the animal to which it is kin as a protector that must be treated with great respect. To kill or eat it is therefore forbidden.[57]

This animal protector plays the same role with respect to each sexual society that the totem of the clan plays with respect to the clan. Hence the phrase "sexual totemism," which I take from Frazer,[58] is warranted. In particular, this new sort of totem resembles that of the clan as well, in the sense that it too is collective. It belongs without distinction to all individuals of the same sex. It resembles the clan totem also in that it implies a relationship of descent and common blood between the animal patron and the corresponding sex. Among the Kurnai, all the men are said to be descended from Yeerùng and all the women from Djeetgùn.[59] The first observer to have described that curious institution, as early as 1834, used the following terms: "Tilmun, a small bird the size of a thrush (a sort of woodpecker), is considered by the women as having been the first to make women. These birds are

---

[55]Howitt, *Native Tribes*, pp. 148ff. [Lorimer] Fison and [Alfred William] Howitt, *Kamilaroi and Kurnai* [Melbourne, G. Robertson, 1880], pp. 194, 201ff. [James] Dawson, *Australian Aborigines* [Melbourne, G. Robertson, 1881], p. 52. Petrie reports it also in Queensland ([Constance Campbell Petrie], *Tom Petrie's Reminiscences of Early Queensland* [Ferguson, Watson, 1904], pp. 62, 118).

[56]Mathews, "Aboriginal Tribes," p. 339. Should one see a trace of sexual totemism in the following custom of the Warramunga? Before a dead person is buried, a bone from the arm is kept. If it is a woman's, feathers of the emu are added to the bark in which it is shrouded; if a man's, the feathers of an owl ([Sir Baldwin Spencer and F. James Gillen, *Northern Tribes of Central Australia*, London, Macmillan, 1904], p. 169).

[57]There is even a case cited in which each sexual group has two sexual totems; in this way would the Wiradjuri have joined the sexual totems of the Kurnai (emu-wren and linnet) with those of the Wotjobaluk (bat and nightjar wood owl). See Howitt, *Native Tribes*, p. 150.

[58]Frazer, *Totemism and Exogamy*, p. 51.

[59]Fison and Howitt, *Kamilaroi and Kurnai*, p. 215.

held in veneration by women only."[60] Thus it was a great ancestor. Seen from another point of view, this totem resembles the individual totem, in that each member of the sexual group is believed to be personally allied with a definite individual of the corresponding animal species. The two lives are so closely linked that the death of the animal brings about that of the human. "The life of a bat," say the Wotjobaluk, "is the life of a man."[61] This is why each sex not only honors its totem but also forces the members of the other sex to do so as well. Any violation of this prohibition gives rise to real and bloody battles between men and women.[62]

In sum, what is truly unique about these totems is that, in a sense, they amount to tribal totems. Indeed, they arise from the fact that people conceive of the whole tribe as being the offspring of a legendary couple. Such a belief seems to imply that the sense of tribe has become strong enough to overcome the particularism of the clans to some extent. As to the reasons that separate origins are assigned to men and women, one must probably look to the fact that the sexes live apart.[63]

It would be interesting to know how, in the mind of an Australian, sexual totems are related to clan totems—what relations there are between the two ancestors that are placed at the origin of the tribe and those from which each particular clan is thought to descend. But the ethnographic data we have at present do not permit us to resolve that question. Furthermore, the natives may never have asked that question of themselves, however natural and even necessary it may seem to us, for they do not feel the need to coordinate and systematize their beliefs to the same extent we do.[64]

---

[60]Threlkeld, cited by Mathews, "The Aboriginal Tribes," p. 339.

[61]Howitt, *Native Tribes,* pp. 148, 151.

[62]Fison and Howitt, *Kamilaroi and Kurnai,* pp. 200–203; Howitt, *Native Tribes,* p. 149; Petrie, *Reminiscences,* p. 62. Among the Kurnai, these bloody struggles often end in marriages, to which they are a kind of ritual prologue. Sometimes the battles become mere games (*Tom Petrie's Reminiscences*).

[63]On this point, see my study [Emile Durkheim] "La Prohibition de l'inceste et ses origines," in *AS,* vol. I (1898), pp. 44ff.

[64]However we will see below (Chap. 9) that there is a relationship between sexual totems and the high gods.

CHAPTER FIVE

ORIGINS OF THESE BELIEFS

Critical Examination of the Theories

The beliefs I have just reviewed are clearly religious in nature, for they involve a classification of things as sacred and profane. Spiritual beings are doubtless not at issue. In the course of my exposition, I have had no need even to say the words "spirits," "genies," or "divine personages." However, if, for this reason, some writers (about whom I shall have more to say) have refused to see totemism as a religion, it is because they have been operating with a mistaken idea of the religious phenomenon.

At the same time, religion is guaranteed to be the most primitive that can be observed now and in all probability the most primitive that has ever existed, for it is inseparable from social organization based upon clans. I have shown that totemism can only be defined in terms of that social organization and, furthermore, that clans, in the form they take in a great many Australian societies, could not have come into being without the totem. The members of a single clan are joined to one another by neither common residence nor common blood, since they are not necessarily consanguineous and are often scattered throughout the tribal territory. Their unity arises solely from having the same name and the same emblem, from believing they have the same relations with the same categories of things, and from practicing the same rites—in other words, from the fact that they commune in the same totemic cult. Thus, at least insofar as the clan is not identical with the local group, totemism and the clan imply one another. Organization based on clans is the simplest we know, for it exists in all its essentials the moment a society has two primary clans. It follows that there cannot be a simpler society, so long as none with only a single clan has yet been found—and I believe no trace of that has been up to now. A religion so closely allied with the social system that is simpler than all others can be regarded as the most elementary we can know. If we can find out the origin of the beliefs just analyzed, we may well discover by the same stroke what kindled religious feeling in humanity.

It is useful, before addressing this problem, to examine the most authoritative solutions that have been offered.

I

We start with a group of scholars who believe they can explain totemism by deriving it from an earlier religion. For Tylor[1] and for Wilken,[2] totemism is a special form of the ancestor cult. For them, transmigration of souls—widespread, to be sure—is the doctrine that served as a transition between these two religious systems. A great many peoples believe that the soul does not remain eternally disembodied after death but comes again to animate some living body. Besides, "as the psychology of the inferior races establishes no clear-cut line of demarcation between the souls of men and those of animals, it has no trouble accepting the transmigration of human souls into the bodies of animals."[3] Tylor cites a number of such cases.[4] Under these circumstances, the religious respect inspired by the ancestor is quite naturally transferred to the animal with which it is thenceforth assimilated. The animal thus serving all that ancestor's descendants as the vessel of a revered being becomes a sacred thing and the object of a cult—in short, a totem for the clan that is the ancestor's issue.

Facts reported by Wilken about the societies of the Malay Archipelago would tend to prove that this is indeed the way in which totemic beliefs developed there. In Java and Sumatra, crocodiles are especially honored; people view them as benevolent protectors and make offerings to them. The cult that is also rendered to them stems from the belief that they incarnate the souls of ancestors. The Malays of the Philippines consider the crocodile to be their grandfather. The tiger is treated in the same way, for the same reasons. Similar beliefs have been found among the Bantu peoples.[5] In Melanesia, an

---

[1][Edward Burnett Tylor], *Primitive Culture*, vol. I [New York, Henry Holt, 1874], [vol. I,] p. 402, vol. II, p. 237, and "Remarks on Totemism, with Special Reference to Some Modern Theories [Respecting] It," in *JAI*, vol. XXVIII [1899, pp. 133–148], and vol. I, new series, p. 138.

[2][Albertus Christian Kruijt Wilken], *Het Animisme bij den Volken van den indischen Archipel* ['s Gravenhage, M. Nijhoff, 1906], pp. 69–75.

[3]Tylor, *Primitive Culture* [vol. II, p. 6].

[4]Ibid. [vol. II, pp. 6–18].

[5]G. McCall Theal, *Records of South-Eastern Africa*, vol. VII. I know this work only through an article by [James George] Frazer, "South African Totemism," which appeared in *Man* [vol. I], 1901, no. 111 [pp. 135–136].

influential man who is at the point of death sometimes announces his desire to be reincarnated in such and such an animal or plant. It is easy to see that some particular object chosen for his posthumous residence thereafter becomes sacred for his whole family.[6] Far indeed from being a primitive fact, then, totemism would then be merely the product of a more complex predecessor religion.[7]

The societies from which these examples are drawn have already attained a relatively high level of culture; at any rate, they have gone beyond the phase of pure totemism. In those societies, there are families, not totemic clans.[8] Indeed, the majority of the animals that are given religious honors are venerated not by specific family groups but by entire tribes. Thus, even if these beliefs and practices may be related to the ancient totemic cults, they are hardly well suited to revealing the origins of those cults to us,[9] since now they represent those cults only in altered forms. It is not by considering an institution when it is in full decline that we can gain an understanding of how it was formed. If we wish to know how totemism was born, it must be observed neither in Java nor in Sumatra nor in Melanesia, but in Australia. Here we find neither the cult of the dead[10] nor the doctrine of transmigration. Of course, the mythical heroes who founded the clan are believed to be regularly reincarnated—*but in human bodies only.* As we will see, each birth is the result of such a reincarnation. Thus, if the animals of the totemic species are the objects of rites, it is not because ancestral spirits are held to reside in them. While it is true that these first ancestors are often depicted in animal form (and this representation, which is very common, is an important fact that will have to be explained), belief in metempsychosis could not have given rise to it in the societies of Australia, since that belief is unknown there.

Moreover, far from being able to explain totemism, the belief itself presupposes one of the fundamental principles on which totemism rests; that is,

---

[6][Robert Henry] Codrington, *The Melanesians* [Oxford, Clarendon Press, 1891], pp. 32–[33], and a personal letter of the same author cited by Tylor in "Remarks on Totemism," p. 147.

[7]Such also, with minor differences, is the solution adopted by [Wilhelm] Wundt (*Mythus und Religion* [3 vols., as vol. II, parts 1–3 of *Völkerpsychologie, Eine Untersuchung der Entwicklungsgesetze von Sprache, Mythus und Sitte*, Leipzig, W. Englemann, 1900–1909], vol. II, p. 269).

[8]It is true that, for Tylor, the clan is but an enlarged family, so in his way of thinking, what can be said of the one group applies to the other ("Remarks on Totemism," p. 157). But this idea is highly questionable. Only the clan presupposes the totem, which has its full meaning only in and through the clan.

[9]In the same vein, [Andrew] Lang, *Social Origins* [London, Longmans, 1903], p. 150.

[10]See above, p. 59.

it assumes the very thing that must be explained. In fact, it implies, just as totemism implies, a concept of men as being closely akin to animals. If these two realms were clearly distinguished in people's minds, the soul would not be thought capable of passing so easily from one into the other. Indeed, the body of the animal would have to be considered its true homeland, because the human soul is presumed to go there the moment it regains its freedom. The doctrine of transmigration indeed postulates this singular affinity but by no means explains it. The only explanation Tylor offers is that on occasion certain traits of the man's anatomy and psychology remind people of the animal. "The savage," he says, "observes the half-human traits, actions, and characteristics of animals with sympathetic wonderment. Is the animal not the very incarnation, we might say, of qualities that are familiar to man; and when we apply epithets like lion, bear, fox, owl, parrot, viper, and worm to certain men, are we not epitomizing in a word certain traits characteristic of a human life?"[11] But if one does come upon any of these resemblances, they are ambiguous and rare. Man looks like his relatives and his friends most of all, not like plants or animals. Such rare and dubious similarities could not defeat such consistent and obvious ones, nor could they encourage man to imagine himself and his ancestors in forms that fly in the face of all his everyday experience. So the question remains, and since it is not solved, totemism cannot be said to have been explained.[12]

Finally, this whole theory rests on a fundamental misunderstanding. For Tylor as for Wundt, totemism is nothing more than a special case of animal

[11]Tylor, *Primitive Culture*, vol. II, p. 17. [Cf. Tylor's English text: "The half-human features and actions and characters of animals are watched with wondering sympathy by the savage, as by the child. The beast is the very incarnation of familiar qualities of man: and such names as lion, bear, fox, owl, parrot, viper, worm, when we apply them as epithets to men, condense into a word some leading features of a human life." Trans.]

[12][Wilhelm] Wundt, who took up Tylor's theory in its basic outlines, tried to explain this mysterious relation of man and animal otherwise—with sight of the decomposing corpse supposedly suggesting the idea of it. Having seen the worms that come out of the body, they believed that the soul was incarnated in them and departed with them. So the worms and by extension the reptiles (snakes, lizards, etc.) would be the first animals to have served as vessels for the souls of the dead; consequently, they would also have been the first to be venerated and to play the role of totems. Only later would other animals, and even plants and inanimate objects, have been elevated to the same rank. But this hypothesis does not rest on even the beginnings of a proof. Wundt claims (*Mythus und Religion*, vol. II, p. 269) that the reptiles are much more common totems than the other animals, from which he concludes that they are the most primitive. But it is impossible for me to see what can justify that assertion, in support of which the author does not adduce a single fact. It in no way emerges from the lists of totems collected, whether in Australia or in America, that any animal species, anywhere, has had a preponderant role. Totems vary from one region to another with the state of the flora and fauna. Moreover, if the original set of totems had been so narrowly restricted, it is not clear how totemism would have been able to satisfy the fundamental principle that two clans or subclans of a single tribe must have different totems.

worship.[13] We know, quite to the contrary, that it must be seen as something entirely different from a sort of zoolatry.[14] The animal is not worshipped. And far from being subordinated to it as a believer is to his god, the man is almost its equal and sometimes even treats it as his property. If the animals of the totemic species really were thought of as incarnating the ancestors, members of other clans would not be allowed to eat their flesh freely. In reality, the cult is not addressed to the animal itself but to the emblem, that is, to the image of the totem. In fact, there is no connection between this religion of the emblem and the cult of the ancestors.

Whereas Tylor reduces totemism to the cult of the ancestors, Jevons ties it to the cult of nature.[15] This is how he does so.

In the grip of confusion brought upon him by irregularities in the course of natural phenomena, man supposedly populated the world with supernatural beings.[16] Having done this, he felt the need to come to terms with the awesome forces with which he had surrounded himself. He understood that the best way to avoid being crushed by them was to ally himself with certain of them, thereby garnering their help. At that moment in history, he knew no other form of alliance and association than that created by kinship. All the members of the same clan help one another because they are kin or (what amounts to the same thing) because they consider one another as kin; on the other hand, different clans treat one another as enemies because they are of different blood. So the only way to arrange the support of supernatural beings was to adopt them and to have oneself adopted by them as kin. The well-known procedures of blood covenant enabled man to obtain this result easily. But since, at that moment, the individual did not yet have his own personality, because he was viewed only as a certain part of his group—that is, his clan—it was not the individual but the clan as a unit that contracted the kinship jointly. For the same reason, the individual did not contract it with a particular object but with the natural group, that is, with the species to which the object belonged. Man thinks of the world as he thinks of himself and, just as he does not think of himself as being separate from his clan, so he cannot

[13]"Certain animals are sometimes worshipped," says Tylor, "because they are regarded as the incarnation of the divine soul of the ancestors; this belief constitutes a sort of common denominator between the cult rendered to the shades and the cult rendered to the animals" (*Primitive Culture*, vol. II, p. 305; cf. 309 *in fine*). Similarly, Wundt presents totemism as a branch of animalism (*Mythus und Religion*, vol. II, p. 234).

[14]See above, p. 139.

[15][Frank Byron] Jevons, *Introduction to the History of Religion* [London, Methuen, 1902, pp. 96ff.].

[16]See above, p. 25.

think of a thing as being separate from the species to which it belongs. According to Jevons, a species of things that is united with a clan by ties of kinship is a totem.

It is certain that totemism involves a close association between a clan and a definite category of objects. But the notion Jevons puts forward—that such an association was contracted deliberately, in full awareness of the goal sought—seems in little accord with what history teaches us. Religions are complex things, and the needs they satisfy are so numerous and so obscure that they cannot possibly have originated in a well-considered act of will. Moreover, this hypothesis both sins by oversimplification and abounds in unlikelihoods. Man is said to have tried to garner the help of the supernatural beings to which things are subordinate. But in that case, he ought to have addressed himself to the most powerful among them, to those whose protection was likely to produce the maximum result.[17] Instead, the beings with which he has cemented this mystical kinship most often include the humblest that exist. Furthermore, if it truly was only a matter of creating allies and defenders, man would have tried to have as many as possible; there is no such thing as being too well protected. Yet each clan routinely contents itself with a single totem—that is, with a single protector—leaving the other clans to enjoy their own in perfect freedom. Each group strictly encloses itself within its own religious domain, never trying to encroach upon that of its neighbors. Within the terms of the hypothesis we are examining, such discretion and restraint are unintelligible.

II

Further, all of these theories wrongly omit a question that is central to the subject as a whole. We have seen that there are two sorts of totemism: that of the individual and that of the clan. The close links between them are too obvious for them to be unrelated. So, it is appropriate to ask whether the one is not derived from the other and, if the answer is yes, to ask which is the more primitive. According to the solution adopted, the problem of how totemism originated will be framed in different terms. This question is all the more pressing since it is of very general interest. Individual totemism is the individual aspect of the totemic cult. Thus, if it came first, we must say that religion

---

[17]Jevons himself recognizes this. "There is good reason to presume," he says, "that in the choice of an ally, man would have preferred . . . the species that possessed the greatest power" (*History of Religions*, p. 101).

was born in the individual consciousness, that it responds above all to individual aspirations, and that it has taken a collective form only secondarily.

The simplistic reasoning that still too often guides ethnographers and sociologists, in this case as in others, was bound to lead a number of scholars to explain the complex by the simple and the totem of the group by that of the individual. And indeed, the theory argued by Frazer in his *Golden Bough*,[18] by Hill Tout,[19] Miss Fletcher,[20] Boas,[21] and Swanton,[22] is of this kind. Moreover, since religion is widely viewed as an altogether private and personal thing, this theory has the advantage of being in accord with the idea many people have of religion. Within this perspective, the totem of the clan can only be an individual totem that has spread. A prominent man who has experienced the value of a totem he freely chose for himself transmits it to his descendants. Multiplying as time goes on, these descendants eventually form the extended family that is the clan; thus does the totem become collective.

Hill Tout thought he found support for that theory in the way totemism is understood in certain societies of the American Northwest, notably by the Salish and the Thompson River Indians. Both individual totemism and the totemism of the clan are found among these peoples, but they either do not coexist in the same tribe or are unequally developed when they do. They vary in inverse proportion with one another. Where the clan totem tends to be the general rule, individual totem tends to disappear, and vice versa. Is this not to say that the first is a more recent form of the second, which replaces and thus excludes it?[23] Mythology appears to confirm this interpretation. In the same societies, it turns out, the ancestor of the clan is not a totemic animal, but the founder of the group is usually depicted as a human being who

---

[18][James George Frazer, *The Golden Bough: A Study in Magic and Religion*, 2d ed., vol. III, New York, Macmillan, 1894], pp. 416ff.; see esp. p. 419 n. 5. In more recent articles, to be analyzed below, Frazer has put forward a different theory that nevertheless does not completely exclude from his thinking the one presented in the *Golden Bough*.

[19][Charles Hill Tout], "The Origin of the Totemism of the Aborigines of British Columbia," *RSC*, vol. VII, §2 (2d series), (1901) pp. 3ff. Similarly, "Report on the Ethnology of the Statlumh," *JAI*, vol. XXXV (1905), p. 141. Hill Tout has answered various objections that have been made against his theory in volume IX of the *RSC*, pp. 61–99.

[20]Alice C. Fletcher, "The Import of the Totem: [A Study from the Omaha Tribe]," *RSI for 1897* (Washington, Government Printing Office, 1898), pp. 577–586.

[21]Franz Boas, "The Social Organization and Secret Societies of the Kwakiutl Indians" [in *RNM for 1895*, Washington, Government Printing Office, 1897], pp. 323ff., 336–338, 393.

[22][John Reed Swanton], "The Development of the Clan System [and of Secret Societies among the North-Western Tribes]," in *AA*, vol. VI (new ser., 1904), pp. 477–864.

[23]Hill Tout, "Ethnology of the Statlumh," p. 142.

at some point entered into relations and close dealings with a mythical animal, from which he is held to have acquired his totemic emblem. This emblem, with the special powers that are attached to it, is then passed by inheritance to the descendants of the mythical hero. Hence these peoples themselves appear to see the collective totem as an individual one that was passed on in a single family.[24] Furthermore, even today a father sometimes transmits his own totem to his children. So to imagine that the collective totem has had this same origin universally is no more than to state that something still observable in the present was the same in the past.[25]

Still to be explained is the origin of individual totemism. The response to this question varies among authors.

Hill Tout views it as a special case of fetishism. For him, it is the individual who, feeling himself surrounded by dreaded spirits, feels the same emotion that Jevons attributed to the clan: To sustain himself, he seeks some powerful protector in the hidden world. Thus is the custom of the personal totem established.[26] For Frazer, this same institution is a subterfuge, a military ruse men invent to escape certain dangers. We know that, according to a very common belief in a great many lower societies, the human soul can temporarily leave the body in which it lives, without ill effects; no matter how far away from the body it may go, it goes on animating that body by a kind of action at a distance. But at certain critical moments when life is thought to be particularly threatened, there may be something to gain by withdrawing the soul from the body and depositing it in a place or thing where it would be safer. There are, in fact, various methods of extracting the soul, thereby removing it from some real or imaginary danger.

For example, when people are on the point of entering a newly built house, a magician extracts their souls and places them in a bag, for return to the owners once the threshold has been crossed. This is done because the moment of entering a new house is exceptionally critical. There is a risk of disturbing and thus offending the spirits that live in the ground, especially under the door sill, and if a man did not take precautions, they could make him pay dearly for his boldness. Once the danger is past, once he has been able to prevent their anger, and even garner their support by conducting cer-

---

[24]Ibid., p. 150. Cf. [Franz Boas, "First General Report on the Indians of British Columbia," in *BAAS, Fifth Report of the Committee on the North-Western Tribes of the Dominion of Canada* (London, Offices of the Association, 1890),] p. 24. I have reported a myth of this sort above.

[25]Hill Tout, "Ethnology of the Statlumh," p. 147.

[26]Hill Tout, "Totemism of the Aborigines," p. 12.

tain rites, the souls can safely return to their usual place.[27] This same belief, Hill Tout thinks, gave rise to the individual totem. To protect themselves from magical charms, men thought it prudent to hide their souls in the anonymous crowd of an animal or plant species. But having set up such dealings, each individual found himself closely joined with the animal or plant in which his life-principle presumably resided. Two beings so closely joined ended up by being considered more or less indistinguishable: They were thought to participate in one another's nature. Once accepted, this belief eased and activated the transformation of the personal totem into a hereditary totem and, thereafter, into a collective one, for it seemed altogether obvious that this kinship of nature must be transmitted by heredity from father to children.

I will not tarry long in discussing these two explanations of the individual totem. They are ingenious intellectual constructions, but they are totally without empirical support. For totemism to be reducible to fetishism, it would have to be established that fetishism preceded totemism. Not only is no evidence given to prove this hypothesis, but it is also contradicted by all we know. The ill-defined collection of rites that are given the name fetishism seems to appear only among peoples who have already arrived at a certain level of civilization; it is a kind of cult that is unknown in Australia. The churinga has been called a fetish,[28] true enough, but even if that characterization was warranted, it could not demonstrate the priority that is assumed. Quite to the contrary, the churinga presupposes totemism, since in its very essence it is an instrument of the totemic cult and since it owes the virtues ascribed to it to totemic beliefs alone.

Turning now to Frazer's theory, this author assumes a kind of thoroughgoing idiocy on the part of the primitive that the facts do not allow us to ascribe to him. He does have a logic, strange though it may sometimes seem to us. Short of being utterly without logic, he could not be guilty of the reasoning that is imputed to him. Nothing was more natural than for him to have believed that he could ensure the survival of his soul by hiding it in a secret and inaccessible place, as so many heroes of myths and legends are said to have done. But how could he have judged his soul to be safer in an animal's body than in his own? Of course, the chances are that it could more

---

[27]Frazer, *The Golden Bough* vol. III, pp. 351ff. Wilken had already noted similar facts in "De Simonsage," in *De Gids, 1890*; "De Betrekking tusschen Menschen-Dieren en Plantenleve," in *Indische Gids*, 1884, 1888; *Ueber das Haaropfer*, in *Revue coloniale internationale*, pp. 1886–1887.

[28]For example, [Erhard] Eylmann in *Die Eingeborenen der Kolonie Südaustralien* [Berlin, D. Reimer, 1908], p. 199.

easily have escaped the spells of the magician by being lost in the species, but it thereby found itself at the same time a sitting duck for hunters. Hiding it in a physical form that exposed it to danger at all times was an odd way to shelter it.[29] Most of all, it is inconceivable that whole peoples should have been able to give themselves over to such an eccentricity.[30] Finally, in a great many cases, the function of the individual totem is manifestly very different from the function Frazer ascribes to it. First and foremost, it is a means of conferring unusual powers upon magicians, hunters, and warriors.[31] So far as the solidarity of the man with the thing is concerned (given all the drawbacks of solidarity), it is accepted as an unavoidable consequence of the rite, but is not desired in and of itself.

Another reason not to tarry over this controversy is that it is beside the point. What is important to know, above all, is whether the individual totem really is the primitive fact from which the collective totem derives. Depending upon our answer, we will have to look in two opposite directions for the seat of religious life.

There is such a confluence of decisive facts against the hypothesis of Hill Tout, Miss Fletcher, Boas, and Frazer that one wonders how it could have been accepted so easily and so widely.

First, we know that man often has a pressing interest not only in respecting the animals of the species that serves as his personal totem but also in having it respected by his fellow men: His own life is at stake. Thus, even

---

[29]Mrs. Parker says of the Euahlayi that if the Yunbeai "confers exceptional power, it also exposes one to exceptional dangers, for all that injures the animal injures the man" ([Catherine Somerville Field Parker, *The Euahlayi Tribe*, London, A. Constable, 1905], p. 29).

[30]In an earlier work ("The Origin of Totemism," in *FR* (May, 1899), pp. 844–845), Frazer raises the objection himself. He says, "If I left my soul in the body of a rabbit, and if my brother John (member of a different clan) kills, roasts, and eats that rabbit, what happens to my soul? To prevent this danger, my brother John has to know this situation of my soul, and in consequence, when he kills a rabbit, he must be careful to take that soul out of it and give it back to me before cooking the animal and making it his dinner." Frazer believes he finds this practice customary in the tribes of central Australia. Each year, during a rite that I will describe below, when the animals of the new generation reach maturity, the first game killed is presented to the men of the totem, who eat a little; and it is only afterward that the men of the other clans may eat it freely. This, says Frazer, is a means of returning to the men of the totem the soul that they may have entrusted to those animals. But apart from the fact that this interpretation of the rite is completely arbitrary, it is difficult not to find this method of protection extraordinary. The ceremony is annual, allowing many days to pass after the moment the animal was killed. During this time, what has become of the soul it guarded and of the individual whose life-principle of life that soul is? But it is pointless to emphasize all that is unlikely about that explanation.

[31]Parker, *Euahlayi*, p. 20; [Alfred William] Howitt, "Australian Medicine Men," in *JAI*, vol. XVI (1887), 34, [49–50]; Hill Tout, "Ethnology of the Statlumh," p. 146.

if collective totemism was not the generalized form of the individual totem, it should rest on the same principle. Not only should the people of a clan abstain from killing and eating their totemic animal themselves, but they should also do everything in their power to impose this same restriction upon others. As it turns out, far from imposing any such privation on the whole tribe, each clan (by means of the rites that I will later describe) takes steps to ensure that the plant or animal whose name it bears increases and prospers, so as to provide abundant food to the other clans. Thus it should at least be granted that individual totemism profoundly transformed itself in becoming collective and that this transformation must be explained.

Second, how can this hypothesis explain why, except where totemism is in decline, two clans of the same tribe always have different totems? Nothing would seem to prevent two or several members of a single tribe from choosing personal totems from the same animal species, despite their having no tie of kinship, and then passing it on to their descendants. Does it not happen today that two distinct families bear the same name? The strictly regulated manner in which totems and subtotems are distributed between the two phratries first, and then among the various clans of each phratry, obviously presupposes a societal consensus and a collective organization. In other words, totemism is something other than an individual practice that has spontaneously generalized itself.

Furthermore, collective totemism can be reduced to individual totemism only if the differences between them are misconstrued. The one is assigned to the child by birth and is an element of his civil status. The other is acquired in the course of life and presupposes the performance of a specific rite as well as a change of state. Some think they are lessening this distance by inserting between them, as a kind of middle term, the right that anyone who has a totem supposedly has to transmit it to whomever he pleases. But wherever one observes them, such transfers are rare and relatively exceptional; they can be done only by magicians or other persons gifted with special powers,[32] and, in any event, they can take place only by means of ritual ceremonies that effect the change. So it would then be necessary to explain how something that was the prerogative of certain people later became the right of all; how something that implied a profound change in the religious and moral constitution of the individual could have become an element of that

---

[32]According to Hill Tout himself, "The gift or transmission (of a personal totem) can only be effectuated by certain persons like shamans or men who possess great mystical power" ("Ethnology of the Statlumh," p. 146). Cf. Parker, *Euahlayi*, pp. 29–30.

constitution; and, finally, how a transmission that at first was the outcome of a rite, was considered thereafter to produce itself, inescapably and without the intervention of any human will.

In support of his interpretation, Hill Tout alleges that certain myths impute an individual origin to the totem of the clan. They tell how the totemic emblem was acquired by a particular individual who then transmitted it to his descendants. These myths, however, are taken from Indian tribes in North America, that is, from societies that have attained a rather high level of culture. How could a mythology so far removed from its origins enable us to reconstruct the original form of an institution with any confidence? The likelihood is that intervening causes greatly distorted the memory that these men could have kept. More than that, it is very easy to set against these myths other myths that seem more primitive and whose meaning is entirely different. In the myths, the totem is represented as the very being from which the clan is descended. Hence it constitutes the substance of the clan; individuals carry it from birth, and, far from having come to them from outside themselves, it is part of their flesh and blood.[33] Furthermore, the very myths on which Hill Tout relies themselves echo that ancient idea. The eponymous founder of the clan does indeed have the form of a man, but it is a man thought to have ended up resembling a definite species of animals after having lived among them. This probably happened because there came a time when minds became too sophisticated to go on accepting, as they had in the past, that men could be an animal's offspring. They therefore substituted a human being for the animal ancestor, the idea of which had become untenable; but they imagined the man as having acquired certain animal features by imitation or by other means. Thus, even this recent mythology bears the mark of a more distant epoch when the totem of the clan was not at all conceived of as a sort of individual creation.

But this hypothesis does not merely raise serious logical difficulties; it is also directly contradicted by the facts that follow.

If individual totemism was the primitive fact, then the more primitive the societies, the more developed and more apparent it should be; and inversely, we would expect to see it lose ground to the collective totem among the more advanced peoples and then disappear. The opposite is true. The Australian tribes are far more backward than those of North America, but Australia is the classic locale of collective totemism. *In the great majority of*

---

[33]Cf. [Edwin Sidney] Hartland, "Totemism and Some Recent Discoveries," *Folklore*, vol. XI [1900], pp. 59ff.

tribes, it reigns alone, whereas there is none, to my knowledge, in which individual totemism is practiced alone.[34] Individual totemism in its characteristic form is found in an infinitesimal number of tribes.[35] And where it is found, it is most often in only a rudimentary state, consisting of individual and optional practices without wider scope. Only magicians know the art of creating mystical relationships with the animal species to which they are not naturally related. Ordinary folk do not enjoy this privilege.[36] In America, on the other hand, the collective totem is in full decline, and in the societies of the Northwest particularly, it no longer has anything more than a rather unobtrusive religious character. Inversely, the individual totem plays a large role among these same peoples, where it is credited with great efficacy and has become an authentically public institution. This is so because it is characteristic of a more advanced civilization. This, no doubt, is how the inversion between these two forms of totemism that Hill Tout thought he saw is to be understood. If individual totemism is almost entirely absent where collective totemism is fully developed, it is not because the second gave way to the first but the other way around: because not all the conditions necessary to its existence have been met.

Still more conclusive is the fact that individual totemism, far from having given rise to the totemism of the clan, presupposes the clan. Individual totemism was born in and moves within the framework of collective totemism, forming an integral part of it. In fact, in the very societies where it is preponderant, the novices may not take just any animal as their personal totem; they are not permitted to make their choices outside a certain number of particular species assigned to each clan. On the other hand, the species that belong to each clan thus become its exclusive property; the members of a foreign clan may not usurp them.[37] Those species are thought of as having close ties of dependence with the one that serves as the totem of the entire clan. Indeed, in some cases, these relationships are detectable, such as those

[34]Except perhaps among the Kurnai, but in that tribe, there are sexual as well as personal totems.

[35]Among the Wotjobaluk, the Buandik, the Wiradjuri, the Yuin and the tribes neighboring Maryborough (Queensland). See [Alfred William] Howitt, *Native Tribes [of South-East Australia*, New York, Macmillan, 1904], pp. 114–147; [Robert Hamilton] Mathews, "Ethnological Notes on the Aboriginal Tribes of New South Wales and Victoria", *RSNSW,* vol. XXXVIII (1904), p. 291. Cf. [Northcote Whitridge] Thomas, "Further Notes on Mr. Hill Tout's *Views of Totemism,*" in *Man* [vol. IV], 1904, 53, p. 85.

[36]This is true for the Euahlayi and for phenomena of personal totemism noted by Howitt in "Australian Medicine Men," pp. 34, 45, 49–50.

[37]Fletcher, "The Import of the Totem," p. 586; Boas, "The Kwakiutl Indians," p. 322. Similarly, Boas, "First Report on the Indians of British Columbia," p. 25; Hill Tout, "Ethnology of the Statlumh," p. 148.

in which the individual totem represents a part or a particular aspect of the collective totem.[38] Among the Wotjobaluk, each member of the clan considers the personal totems of his fellows as being somewhat his own;[39] hence these are most probably subtotems. Just as the species presupposes the genus, so the subtotem presupposes the totem. Therefore, the first form of individual religion that we meet in history appears to us not as the active principle of the public religion but as merely an aspect of it. Far from being the seed of the collective cult, the cult that the individual organizes for himself, and within his inner self, is in a sense the collective cult adapted to the needs of the individual.

III

In a more recent book,[40] which was suggested to him by the books of Spencer and Gillen, Frazer tried to replace the explanation of totemism that he originally proposed (and that I have just discussed) with a new one. This new explanation rests on the postulate that the totemism of the Arunta is the

[38]The proper names of different *gentes*, says Boas of the Tlinkit, are derived from their respective totems, each *gens* having its special names. The connection between the name and the totem (collective) is sometimes not very apparent, but it always exists (Boas, "First Report on the Indians of British Columbia," p. 25). The phenomenon of individual names' being the property of the clan, and distinctive to it as surely as its totem, is also observed among the Iroquois ([Lewis Henry] Morgan, *Ancient Society: [Or Researches in the Lines of Human Progress from Savagery through Barbarism to Civilization*, London, Macmillan, 1877], p. 78); among the Wyandot ([John Wesley] Powell, "Wyandot Government," *First Annual Report*, [1879–1880], *BAE*, Washington, Government Printing Office, 1881], p. 59); among the Shawnee, the Sauk, the Fox (Morgan, *Ancient Society*, pp. 72, 76–77); among the Omaha ([James Owen] Dorsey, "Omaha Sociology," in *Third Annual Report* [(1881–1882)] [*BAE*, Washington, Government Printing Office, 1884], pp. 227ff.). We know what relation exists between given names and personal totems (see above, p. 159.)

[39]"For example," says Mathews, "if you ask a Wartwurt man what his totem is, he will first tell you his personal totem, but, most likely, he will then enumerate the other personal totems of his clan" ("The Aboriginal Tribes," p. 291).

[40][James George] Frazer, "The Beginnings of Religion and Totemism among the Australian Aborigines," in *FR* [vol. LXXXIV, old series, vol. LXVIII, new series] (July 1905), pp. 162ff., and (September 1905), p. 452. Cf. Frazer "The Origin of Totemism," *FR*, vol. LXXI, old series, vol. LXV, new series (April 1899), pp. 648ff. and (May 1899), pp. 835ff. These latter articles, which are a little older, differ from the more recent on one point, but the core is not fundamentally different. Both are reproduced in *Totemism and Exogamy*, vol. I [London, Macmillan, 1910], pp. 89–172. See, in the same vein, [Sir Baldwin] Spencer and [Francis James] Gillen, "Some Remarks on Totemism as Applied to Australian Tribes," *JAI*, vol. XXVIII (1899), pp. 275–280, and the comments of Frazer on the same subject, *Totemism and Exogamy*, London, Macmillan, 1910, pp. 281–286.

most primitive we know. Frazer even goes so far as to say that it barely differs from the truly and absolutely original type.[41]

What is noteworthy about this explanation is that the totems are attached neither to persons nor to definite groups of persons but to places. Each totem does indeed have its center in a particular place. It is there that the souls of the first ancestors who formed the totemic group at the beginning of time are thought to have their preferred residence. There is the sanctuary where the churingas are kept; there, the cult is celebrated. This geographic distribution of totems also determines the manner in which the clans recruit their members. The child's totem is thus neither its father's nor its mother's but the one whose center is at the place where its mother believes she felt the first symptoms of her coming motherhood. The Arunta does not know the precise relations that connect the fact of begetting to the sexual act,[42] it is said, but attributes every conception to a kind of mystic impregnation. According to him, conception implies that an ancestral soul has gone into the body of a woman, there to become the principle of a new life. Thus, when the woman feels the first stirrings of the infant, she imagines that she has just been entered by one of the souls whose primary residence is at the place where she finds herself. And since the child born thereafter is none other than that ancestor reincarnate, it necessarily has the same totem, which is to say that its clan is determined by the locality where he is held to have been mystically conceived.

This local totemism would then be the original form of totemism, or at most but a very short step away from it. Frazer explains its origin thus.

At the precise instant when the woman feels she is pregnant, she must be thinking that the spirit with which she believes herself possessed has come to her from the objects surrounding her, and in particular from one that was attracting her attention at that instant. If she has been busy collecting some plant or looking after an animal, she will believe that the soul of this animal or that plant has passed into her. First among the things to which she would be especially inclined to attribute her pregnancy are the foods she has just eaten. If she has recently had emu or yam, she will be in no doubt that an emu or a yam has been born and is developing in her. That being the case,

---

[41]"Perhaps we may . . . say that it is but one remove from the original pattern, the absolutely primitive type of totemism" (Frazer, "The Beginnings," p. 455).

[42]On this point, the testimony of [Carl] Strehlow confirms that of Spencer and Gillen ([*Die Aranda- und Loritja-Stämme in Zentral-Australien*], vol. II [New York, Dover, 1968], p. 52). In the opposite vein, see [Andrew] Lang, *The Secret of the Totem* [London, Longmans, 1905], p. 190.

one understands why, in turn, the baby should be considered a kind of yam or emu, why he should regard himself as a kinsman of animals or plants of the same species, why he should show them friendship and consideration, why he should bar himself from eating them, and so forth.[43] From then on, totemism exists in its fundamental features. Since, supposedly, the native's idea of conception gave birth to totemism, Frazer calls this primeval totemism "conceptional."

All the other forms of totemism would then derive from this first type. "If several women, one after another, perceive the first signs of maternity in the same place and the same circumstances, that place will be regarded as being haunted by spirits of a particular sort; and so, in time, the region will be endowed with totemic centers and divided into totemic districts."[44] This is how, on Frazer's account, the local totemism of the Arunta was born. For the totems to become detached from their territorial base, all it will take is to imagine that instead of remaining immutably fixed in one place, the ancestral souls can move freely over the whole territory and follow the travels of the men and women who are of the same totem as they. In that fashion, it will be possible for a woman to be impregnated by a spirit of her own totem or her husband's, even though she is living in a different totemic district. Depending on whether it is the husband's totem or the wife's that is imagined to be trailing the young couple, on the lookout for opportunities to reincarnate itself, the child's totem will be that of its father or mother. In fact, the Gnanji and the Umbaia, on the one hand, and the Urabunna, on the other, do indeed explain their systems of descent in this way.

But like Tylor's, this theory begs the question. If it is to be imaginable that human souls are the souls of animals or plants, it must already be believed that man takes what is most fundamental to him from either the animal or plant world. This belief is precisely one of those on which totemism is based, so to put it forward as self-evident is to assume what must be explained.

Moreover, the religious character of the totem is wholly unexplainable in terms of this view, for the vague belief in an obscure kinship of man and animal is not enough to found a cult. This merging of distinct realms cannot lead to dividing the world between the sacred and the profane. It is true that

---

[43]A closely related idea had already been expressed by [Alfred C.] Haddon in his "Address to the Anthropological Section" (*BAAS*, 1902, 8ff.). He assumes that each local group originally had a food that was especially its own. The plant or animal that thus served as the principal item of consumption would have become the totem of the group. All these explanations imply that the prohibitions against eating the totemic animal were not original and were even preceded by the opposite prescription.

[44]Frazer, "The Beginnings," p. 458.

Frazer is self-consistent and refuses to see totemism as a religion—on the grounds that there are neither spiritual beings nor prayers nor invocations nor offerings, and so on. According to him, it is only a system of magic, by which he means a crude and erroneous sort of science, a first try at discovering the laws of things.[45] But we know what is wrong with this idea of religion and magic. There is religion as soon as the sacred is distinguished from the profane, and we have seen that totemism is a vast system of sacred things. So to explain it is to show how those things came to acquire that trait.[46] Tylor does not even set this problem.

What brings about the downfall of this system is that the postulate on which it rests is untenable. All of Frazer's argumentation assumes that the local totemism of the Arunta is the most primitive known, and in particular that it is distinctly prior to hereditary totemism, whether matrilineal or patrilineal. By following only the facts available in the first work of Spencer and Gillen, I have been able to conjecture that there must have been a moment in the history of the Arunta people when the totems were transmitted by inheritance from the mother to the children instead of being attached to localities.[47] This conjecture is definitively proved by the new facts that Strehlow[48] discovered and that confirm previous observations by Schulze.[49] In fact, these two authors inform us that, even now, in addition to his local totem, each Arunta has another that is independent of any geographic condition and belongs to him by birth: that of his mother. Like the first, this second totem is considered by the natives as a friendly and protective power that provides for their food, warns them of possible dangers, and so forth. They are permitted to take part in its cult. When they are buried, the body is so arranged that the

---

[45]Frazer, "The Origin of Totemism," p. 835, and "The Beginnings," pp. 162ff.

[46]All the while seeing totemism as nothing but a system of magic, Frazer recognizes that one sometimes finds in magic the first seeds of religion properly so called ("The Beginnings," p. 163). On the way in which he thinks religion developed out of magic, see *Golden Bough*, 2d ed., vol. I, pp. 75–78 n. 2.

[47][Emile Durkheim], "Sur le totémisme," *AS*, vol. V (1902), pp. 82–121. Cf. on this same question, [Edwin Sidney] Hartland, "Presidential Address [Totemism and Some Recent Discoveries,]" *Folklore*, vol. XI [(1900)] p. 75; [Andrew] Lang, "A Theory of Arunta Totemism," *Man* [vol. IV] (1904), no. 44, [pp. 67–69]; Lang, "Conceptional Totemism and Exogamy," *Man*, vol. VII, 1907, 55, pp. 88–90; Lang, *The Secret of the Totem*, ch. IV; [Northcote W.] Thomas, "Arunta Totemism [a Note on Mr. Lang's Theory]," *Man*, vol. IV, (1904), 68, pp. 99–101; P. W. Schmidt, "Die Stellung der Aranda unter den australischen Stämmen, in *ZE*, vol. XL (1908), pp. 866ff.

[48]Strehlow, *Aranda*, vol. II, pp. 57–58.

[49][Rev. Louis] Schulze, "Aborigines of the Upper and Middle Finke River," *RSSA*, vol. XVI, 1891, pp. 238–239.

face is turned toward the region where the mother's totemic center is this, because the center is also in some respect that of the deceased. And thus, it is given the name *tmara altjira,* which means, "camp of the totem that is associated with me." Hence it is certain that, among the Arunta, hereditary totemism in the maternal line did not come later than local totemism but, quite the contrary, must have preceded it. Today the maternal totem has no more than an accessory and complementary role; it is a second totem, and this explains why it could have escaped such careful and well-informed observers as Spencer and Gillen. But for that totem to have been able to maintain itself in this second rank, used side by side with the local totem, there must have been a time when it occupied the first rank in religious life. It is in part a totem that has lapsed, but one that harks back to an era when the totemic organization of the Arunta was very different from today's. Thus is Frazer's entire construction undermined at its foundation.[50]

IV

Although Andrew Lang has vigorously attacked Frazer's theory, his own, as proposed in recent works,[51] is close to it on more than one point. Indeed, like Frazer, he takes the whole of totemism to consist of belief in a sort of consubstantiality between man and animal, but he explains it differently.

He derives it entirely from the fact that the totem is a name. According to him, from the moment organized human groups come into existence,[52] each feels the need to distinguish itself from the neighboring groups with which it is in contact and, to this end, gives them different names. Names taken from the environing flora and fauna are preferred, because animals and plants can easily be designated by means of gestures or represented by draw-

---

[50]It is true that Frazer says, in the conclusion of *Totemism and Exogamy* (vol. IV, pp. 58–59), that there exists a still more ancient totemism than that of the Arunta. It is that which [W. H. R.] Rivers observed on the Banks Islands ("Totemism in Polynesia and Melanesia," *JAI* vol. XXXIX [1909], p. 172. Among the Arunta, it is an ancestor spirit that is held to impregnate the mother; on the Banks Islands, it is an animal or plant spirit, as the theory supposes. But as the ancestral spirits of the Arunta have an animal or plant form, the difference is upheld. Hence, I have not treated it in my exposition.

[51]Lang, *Social Origins,* esp. chap. 8, "The Origin of Totem Names and Beliefs"; and *The Secret of the Totem.*

[52]Especially in his *Social Origins,* Lang uses conjecture to try to reconstruct the form these original groups must have had. It seems unnecessary to restate those hypotheses, which do not affect his theory of totemism.

ings.[53] The more or less exact resemblances that men can have with one or another of those objects defines the manner in which these collective namings are distributed among the groups.[54]

It is well known that "for primitive minds, names and the things designated by those names are joined in a mystic and transcendental relationship."[55] For example, the name an individual bears is not regarded simply as a word or a conventional sign but as an essential part of the individual himself. Thus, when it is the name of an animal, the man who bears it must necessarily believe that he possesses the most characteristic traits of that animal. This idea gained credence the more easily as the historical origins of these namings receded into the past and gradually disappeared from people's memories. Myths formed to make this strange ambiguity of human nature easier to envisage. To explain it, people thought of the animal as the man's ancestor or of both as descendants of a common ancestor. Thus were conceived the bonds of kinship that are said to join each clan with the species whose name it bears. Once the origins of that mythical kinship are explained, it seems to our author that the mystery of totemism is gone.

But, then, from what does the religious character of totemic beliefs and practices arise? Man's belief that he is an animal of some species does not explain why he imputes amazing virtues to that species or, most of all, why he renders a genuine cult to the images that symbolize it. To this question Lang offers the same response as Frazer: He denies that totemism is a religion. "I find in Australia," he says, "no example of religious practices such as praying to, feeding, or burying the totem."[56] Only in a later age and after it was already organized was totemism, so to speak, attracted to and absorbed into a system of properly religious ideas. According to an observation by Howitt,[57] when the natives set out to explain the totemic institutions, they attribute them neither to the totems themselves, nor to a man, but to some supernatural being such as Bunjil or Baiame. "If," says Lang, "we accept this testimony, one source of the religious character of totemism stands revealed to us.

---

[53]On this point, Lang is close to the theory of Julius Pikler (see [Julius] Pikler and [Felix] Szomlo, *Der Ursprung des Totemismus. Ein Beitrag zur materialistischen Geschichtstheorie* [Berlin, K. Hoffmann, 1900], p. 36). The difference between the two hypotheses is that Pikler ascribes greater importance to the pictographic representation of the name than to the name itself.

[54]Lang, *Social Origins*, p. 166.

[55]Lang, *The Secret of the Totem*, pp. 116–117, 121.

[56]Ibid., p. 136.

[57]Howitt, "Further Notes on the Australian Class Systems," *JAI* [vol. XVIII, 1889], pp. 53–54; cf. *Native Tribes*, pp. 89, 488, 498.

Totemism obeys the decrees of Bunjil, as the Cretans obeyed the decrees of Zeus at Minos." According to Lang, the notion of high gods was formed outside the totemic system. Therefore this system is not in itself a religion; it became colored with religiousness only through contact with a religion, properly so called.

But those very myths are in conflict with Lang's idea of totemism. If the Australians had seen the totem as nothing more than a human and profane thing, they would not have imagined making a divine institution out of it. If, on the other hand, they felt the need to relate the totem to a deity, they did so because they acknowledged its sacredness. These mythological interpretations thus display, but do not explain, the religious nature of totemism.

Besides, Lang himself realizes that this solution cannot possibly do. He admits that totemic things are treated with religious respect[58] and that, in particular, the blood of the animal (like that of the man, incidentally) is the object of multiple prohibitions or of taboos, as he says, that this more or less late mythology cannot explain.[59] Where, then, do they come from? Lang answers the question in these terms: "As soon as the groups with names of animals had developed universally held beliefs about wakan and mana, or about the mystical and sacred quality of the blood, the various totemic taboos must also have made their appearance."[60] As we will see in the next chapter, the words *wakan* and *mana* imply the idea of *sacred* itself (the first is taken from the language of the Sioux, the second from that of the Melanesian peoples). To explain this sacredness of totemic things by postulating it is to answer the question with the question. What should be shown is where this notion of wakan comes from, and how it is applied to the totem and to all that derives from the totem. So long as these two problems go unsolved, nothing is explained.

V

I have reviewed these principal explanations of totemic beliefs,[61] trying to do justice to each one individually. Now that this examination is completed, I can note that all are subject to the same criticism.

---

[58]"With reverence," as Lang says (*The Secret of the Totem*, p. 111).

[59]To these taboos, Lang adds those that are at the basis of the practices of exogamy.

[60]Lang, ibid., pp. 136–137.

[61]I have not spoken about Spencer's theory. This is because it is only a special case of the general theory by which he explains the transformation of the cult of the dead into a cult of nature. Having already set it forth, I would be repeating myself here.

If we restrict our inquiry to what these formulas literally say, they seem to fall into two categories. Some (Frazer's and Lang's) deny the religious character of totemism, but that amounts to denying the facts. Others acknowledge this religious character but believe they can explain it by deriving it from an earlier religion, treating totemism as its offspring. In reality, this distinction is more apparent than real, the first category being contained within the second. Neither Frazer nor Lang has been able to hold on to his principle entirely and explain totemism as if it was not a religion. The nature of the facts forced them to slide notions of a religious nature into their explanations. We have just seen how Lang had to bring in the idea of the sacred, the bedrock idea of any religion. For his part, Frazer overtly calls on the ideas of soul and spirit in the two theories he proposed, one after the other. In his view, totemism arises either from the fact that men believed they could safely place their souls in external objects or from the fact that they attributed conception to a kind of disembodied impregnation, the agent of which is a spirit. Since the soul and, even more, the spirit are sacred things and objects of rites, the ideas that express them are fundamentally religious. In consequence, it is in vain that Frazer makes totemism out to be merely a system of magic, for he too manages to explain it only in terms of another religion.

But I have shown the inadequacies of naturism and animism. One cannot use them, as Tylor and Jevons did, without exposing oneself to the same objections. And yet neither Frazer nor Lang seems even to glimpse the possibility of another hypothesis.[62] From another standpoint, we see that totemism is closely allied with the most primitive social organization that is known and even, in all probability, that is conceivable. Therefore, to assume it to have been preceded by another religion different from it only in degree is to leave behind the data of observation and enter the domain of arbitrary and unverifiable conjectures. If we wish to stay in accord with the results previously obtained, we must, while affirming the religious nature of totemism, refrain from reducing it to a religion different from it. This is not because there could be any question of designating nonreligious ideas as its causes. But among the representations that are part of its origin, and of which it is the result, there may be some that by themselves invoke its religious character, and invoke it directly. These are the ones we must look for.

---

[62]Except that Lang derives the idea of high gods from another source. It is supposedly due, as I have said, to a sort of primitive revelation. But Lang does not include this idea in his explanation of totemism.

CHAPTER SIX

ORIGINS OF THESE BELIEFS (CONTINUED)

The Notion of Totemic Principle, or Mana, and the Idea of Force*

S ince individual totemism comes after that of the clan and in fact seems to be derived from it, clan totemism must be taken up first. Before going further, however, since my analysis thus far has broken it down into a multiplicity of beliefs that may appear disparate, I must try to visualize its internal coherence.

I

We have seen that totemism places figurative representations of the totem in the first rank of the things it considers sacred; then come the animals or plants whose name the clan bears, and finally the members of the clan. Since all these things are sacred in the same right, albeit unequally so, their religiousness cannot arise from any of the particular traits that distinguish them from one another. If a given animal or plant is the object of reverent fear, that reverence is not evoked by its particular traits. The members of the clan have the same status, albeit to a slightly lesser degree, and the mere image of this same plant or animal evokes even more marked respect. Obviously the similar feelings that these dissimilar kinds of things evoke in the consciousness of the faithful, and that constitute their sacredness, can derive only from a principle that is shared by all alike—totemic emblems, people of the clan, and individuals of the totemic species. This is the common principle to which the

---

*It may be that, here, the shift from *notion* to *idée* connotes a difference in clarity and distinctness. It may also be that Durkheim's shifts among those terms, plus *conception* and *concept*, sometimes amount to no more than stylistic variation. I have left the question open in this chapter by rendering each with its English counterpart.

cult is in reality addressed. In other words, totemism is not the religion of certain animals, certain men, or certain images; it is the religion of a kind of anonymous and impersonal force that is identifiable in each of these beings but identical to none of them. None possesses it entirely, and all participate in it. Such is its independence from the particular subjects in which it is incarnated that it both precedes and outlives them. The individuals die; the generations pass on and are replaced by others; but this force remains always present, alive, and the same. It animates the generations of today as it animated those of yesterday and will animate those of tomorrow. Taking the word "god" in a very broad sense, one could say that it is the god that each totemic cult worships. But it is an impersonal god, without name, without history, immanent in the world, diffused in a numberless multitude of things.

And yet we still have only an incomplete idea of the true ubiquity that quasi-divine entity has. It does not merely pervade the whole totemic species, the whole clan, and all the objects that symbolize the totem; the scope of its influence is wider still. We have seen that, above and beyond those eminently sacred things, all the things that are ascribed to the clan as dependents of the principal totem have some measure of the same sacredness. Because certain of them are protected by restrictions and others have definite functions in the cult ceremonies, they too are to some degree religious. This quality of religiousness does not differ in kind from that of the totem under which they are classified; it necessarily derives from the same principle. This is so because—to repeat the metaphorical expression I just used—the totemic god is in them, just as it is in the totemic species and in the people of the clan. That it is the soul of so many different beings shows how different it is from the beings in which it resides.

But the Australian does not conceive of this impersonal force abstractly. Influences that we will have to seek out led him to conceive of it in the form of an animal or plant, that is, in the form of a material thing. Here, in reality, is what the totem amounts to: It is the tangible form in which that intangible substance is represented in the imagination; diffused through all sorts of disparate beings, that energy alone is the real object of the cult. We are now in a better position to comprehend what the native means when he affirms, for example, that the people of the Crow phratry are crows. He does not exactly mean that they are crows in the everyday empirical sense of the word, but that the same principle is found in all of them. That principle constitutes what they all most fundamentally are, is shared between people and animals of the same name, and is conceptualized as having the outward form of the crow. In this way the universe, as totemism conceives it, is pervaded and enlivened by a number of forces that the imagination represents in forms that, with only a few exceptions, are borrowed from either the animal or the plant kingdom. There are as many of these forces as there are clans in the tribe, and each of them pervades certain categories of things of which it is the essence and the life-principle.

When I speak of these principles as forces, I do not use the word in a metaphorical sense; they behave like real forces. In a sense, they are even physical forces that bring about physical effects mechanically. Does an individual come into contact with them without having taken proper precautions? He receives a shock that has been compared with the effect of an electrical charge. They sometimes appear to be conceived of more or less as fluids that escape via the extremities.[1] When they enter into a body that is not meant to receive them, they cause sickness and death by a wholly mechanical reaction.[2] Outside man, they play the role of life-principle; as we will see,[3] by acting upon them, the reproduction of species is ensured. All life is based on them.

And in addition to their physical nature, they have a moral nature. When a native is asked why he follows his rites, he replies that ancestors have always done so and that he must follow their example.[4] If he conducts himself with totemic beings in this or that way, it is not only because the forces that reside in them are inaccessible and forbidding in a physical sense, but also because he feels morally obligated so to conduct himself; he feels he is obeying a sort of imperative, fulfilling a duty. He not only fears but also respects the sacred beings. Moreover, the totem is a source of the clan's moral life. All the beings that participate in the same totemic principle consider themselves, by that very fact, to be morally bound to one another; they have definite obligations of assistance, vengeance, and so on, toward each other, and it is these that constitute kinship. Thus, the totemic principle is at once a physical force and a moral power, and we will see that it is easily transformed into divinity proper.

This is by no means specific to totemism. Even in the most advanced religions, there is perhaps no god that has failed to retain some of this ambiguity and that does not perform both cosmic and moral functions. At the same time as it is a spiritual discipline, every religion is a sort of technique that

[1] In a Kwakiutl myth, for example, an ancestor hero pierces the head of an enemy by stretching forth his fingers ([Franz] Boas, ["First General Report on the Indians of British Columbia,"] in *BAAS, Vth Report of the Committee on the Northern Tribes of the Dominion of Canada* [London, Offices of the Association, 1890], p. 30).

[2] References in support of this assertion will be found on p. 128, n. 1, and p. 325, n. 98.

[3] See Bk III, chap. 2.

[4] See, for example, [Alfred William] Howitt, *Native Tribes, [of South-East Australia,* New York, Macmillan, 1904], p. 482; [C. W.] Schürmann, "The Aboriginal Tribes of Port Lincoln," in [James Dominick] Woods, [*The*] *Native Tribes of S. Australia* [Adelaide, E. S. Wigg, 1879], p. 231.

helps man to confront the world more confidently. Even for the Christian, is God the Father not the guardian of physical order, as well as the legislator and judge of human conduct?

II

Perhaps some will ask whether, by interpreting totemism in this way, I am not imputing ideas to the primitive that are beyond his intellect. In truth, I am not in a position to state positively that he imagines these forces with the relative clarity that I have had to give them in my analysis. I can show quite clearly that this idea is implicit in the beliefs taken as a whole and that it is central to them, but I cannot say to what extent it is explicitly conscious or, on the other hand, only implicit and vaguely felt. There is no way to specify the degree of clarity that an idea such as this one can have in consciousnesses obscure* to us. At any rate, what shows quite well that the idea is in no way beyond the primitive, and even confirms the result I have just arrived at, is this: Whether in societies akin to the Australian tribes or in those very tribes, we find—and in explicit form—conceptions that differ only in degree and nuance from the foregoing.

The native religions of Samoa have certainly passed the totemic phase. They have genuine gods with names of their own and, to some degree, distinctive personal traits. Yet the relics of totemism are hard to dispute. In fact, each god is attached to a territorial or familial group, just as the totem has its clan.[5] Each of these gods is conceived of as immanent in a definite animal species. It certainly does not reside in any particular subject. It is in all at the same time, pervasive throughout the species. When an animal dies, the people of the group that venerate it mourn and render it their pious respects because a god inhabits it, but the god has not died. Like the species, it is eternal. Nor, indeed, is the god confused with the preceding generation, for it was already the soul of the one that preceded, just as as it will be the soul of the one to follow.[6] Thus, it has all the characteristics of the totemic principle but

---

Consciences obscures. Whether the obscurity is in the mind of the observed or the observer is ambiguous. Swain, who says "obscure minds" (p. 219), seems to have opted for the mind of the observed. I opted for the observer's, in light of the next sentence and the general context provided by the chapter.

[5][James George] Frazer even takes up from Samoa many facts that he presents as characteristically totemic (see *Totemism [and Exogamy*, London, Macmillan, 1910], pp. 6, 12–15, 24, etc.). True enough, I have said that Frazer was not always sufficiently critical in his choice of examples. But obviously such numerous borrowings would have been impossible if in Samoa there really had not been important survivals from totemism.

[6]See [George] Turner, *Samoa* [London, Macmillan, 1884], p. 21, and chaps. IV and V.

a totemic principle that the imagination has developed in somewhat personal forms. Even so, this personal quality should not be overblown, as it is hardly compatible with the qualities of pervasiveness and ubiquity. If the contours of the totemic principle were clearly defined, it would not be able to spread as it does and infuse a multitude of things.

In this case, the notion of impersonal religious force is unquestionably beginning to change. In other cases, however, it is maintained in its abstract purity and even achieves distinctly greater generality than in Australia. Although the totemic principles to which the various clans of the same tribe address themselves are distinct from one another, they remain fundamentally comparable to one another, for they all play the same role in their respective domains. There are societies that attained the sense of this shared nature and then advanced to the idea of a single religious force that unifies the universe, all that is; all the other sacred principles are but modalities of that force. And since those societies are still thoroughly imbued with totemism and bound to a social organization identical to that of the Australian peoples, totemism may be said to have carried that idea in its womb.

This can be observed in many American tribes, especially in those belonging to the great family of the Sioux: Omaha, Ponka, Kansas, Osage, Assiniboin, Dakota, Iowa, Winnebago, Mandan, Hidatsa, and the others. Several of these societies, such as the Omaha[7] and the Iowa,[8] are still organized in clans; others were not long ago and, Dorsey says, "all the foundations of the totemic system, just as in other societies of the Sioux,"[9] are still identifiable in them. Among these peoples, there is a preeminent power above all the particular gods men worship, which they call wakan[10]—all the rest being, in a sense, derivations of it. Because of the preeminent status assigned to this principle in the Sioux pantheon, it has sometimes been seen as a kind of sovereign god, a Jupiter or a Yahweh, and travelers have often translated wakan as "great spirit." This was a profound misunderstanding of its true nature.

Wakan is not in any way a personal being; the natives do not imagine it in definite forms. "They say," reports an observer cited by Dorsey, "that they

[7]Alice [C.] Fletcher, "A Study of the Omaha Tribe: [The Import of the Totem"], in RSI for 1897 [Washington, Government Printing Office, 1898], pp. [582–583].

[8][James Owen] Dorsey, "Siouan Sociology," in Fifteenth Annual Report, BAE [Washington, Government Printing Office, 1897], p. 238.

[9]Ibid., p. 221.

[10]Riggs and [James Owen] Dorsey, Dakota English Dictionary, in CNAE, vol. VII [Washington, Government Printing Office, 1890], p. 508. Several observers cited by Dorsey identify the word wakan with the words wakanda and wakanta, which are derived from it but have a more precise meaning.

have never seen wakanda, so they cannot pretend to personify it."[11] It cannot even be defined by specific attributes and qualities. "No term," says Riggs, "can express the meaning of the word among the Dakota. It embraces all mystery, all secret power, all divinity."[12] All the beings that the Dakota revere, "the earth, the four winds, the sun, the moon, the stars, are manifestations of that mysterious life and power" that circulates through all things. It is imagined as the wind, as a breath that has its seat at the four cardinal points and moves everything.[13] It is the voice that is heard when the thunder resounds;[14] the sun, moon, and stars are wakan.[15] But enumeration cannot exhaust this infinitely complex notion. It is not a defined or definable power, the power to do this or that; it is Power in the absolute, without qualification or limitation of any kind. The various divine powers are only particular manifestations and personifications; each of them is this power seen in one of its many aspects.[16] This led one observer to say that "it is basically a protean god, changing its attributes and functions according to circumstance."[17] And the gods are not the only beings it animates. It is the principle of all that lives, all that acts, all that moves. "All life is wakan. And so it is for all that manifests any power—whether it be positive action, like the winds and the clouds gathering in the sky, or passive resistance, like the rock at the side of the path."[18]

The same idea is found among the Iroquois, whose social organization is still more markedly totemic. The word *orenda* that is used to express it is exactly equivalent to the wakan of the Sioux. "It is a mystic power," says Hewitt, "that the savage conceives of as inherent in all the objects that make up the environment in which he lives . . . , in rocks, streams, plants and trees,

---

[11][James Owen] Dorsey, "A Study of Siouan Cults," in *Eleventh Annual Report*, [vol. XI], §21, *BAE* [Washington, Government Printing Office, 1893], p. 372. Miss Fletcher, while no less clearly recognizing the impersonal character of wakanda, adds that a certain anthropomorphism has slowly become grafted on to this idea. But this anthropomorphism concerns the various manifestations of wakanda. The rock or tree where they think they feel the presence of wakanda are addressed as if they were personal beings, but the wakanda itself is not personified (*RSI for 1897*, p. 579).

[12][Stephen Return] Riggs, *Tah-Koo Wah-Kon* [*or the Gospel among the Dakotas*, Boston, Congregational Publishing Society, 1869], pp. 56–57, cited after Dorsey "Siouan Cults," §95, p. 433.

[13]Dorsey, "Siouan Cults," §33, p. 380.

[14]Ibid., §35 [p. 381].

[15]Ibid., §28, p. 376; §30, p. 378; cf. §138, p. 449.

[16]Ibid., §95, p. 432.

[17]Ibid., §92, p. 431.

[18]Ibid., §95, p. 433.

animals and man, winds and storms, clouds, thunder, flashes of lightning, etc."[19] This power is "regarded by the undeveloped intellect of man as the efficient cause of all the phenomena and of all the activities that are occurring around him."[20] A sorcerer or a shaman has orenda, as does a man who is successful in his affairs. Basically nothing in the world is without its own share of orenda, but the shares are unequal. Some beings—men or things—are favored, and others are relatively disadvantaged; all of life is made up of struggles among these orenda of unequal intensity. The most intense subjugate the weakest. Does a man win out over his competitors in the hunt or in war? It is because he has more orenda. If an animal escapes the hunter who chases him, it is because the animal's orenda was greater than the hunter's.

The same idea is found among the Shoshone, with the name *pokunt*; among the Algonquins, *manitou*;[21] *mauala* among the Kwakiutl;[22] *yek* among the Tlingit;[23] and *sgâna* among the Haida.[24] But it is not peculiar to the Indians of America; it was first studied in Melanesia. On certain Melanesian islands, it is true, the social organization is no longer based on totemism, but totemism is still visible on all of them[25]—notwithstanding what Codrington has said on the subject. We find among these peoples, under the name "mana," a notion that is exactly equivalent to the wakan of the Sioux and the orenda of the Iroquois. Here is Codrington's definition of it:

> The Melanesians believe in the existence of a force absolutely distinct from any physical force, that works in all kinds of ways, for good or evil, and that it is in man's best interest to take in hand and control: That force is mana. I

[19][J. N. B. Hewitt], "Orenda and a Definition of Religion," in *AA*, vol. IV (1903), p. 33.

[20]Ibid., p. 36.

[21]Tesa, *Studi del Thavenet*, p. 17.

[22][Franz] Boas, ["The Social Organization and Secret Societies of the] Kwakiutl [Indians," in *RNM for 1895*, Washington, Government Printing Office, 1897], p. 695.

[23][John Reed] Swanton, "Social Condition, Beliefs [and Linguistic Relationship] of the Tlingit Indians," *Twenty-Sixth Report BAE* [Washington, Government Printing Office, 1905], p. 451 n. 3.

[24][John Reed] Swanton, *Contributions to the Ethnology of the Haida* [Leiden, E. J. Brill, 1905], p. 14. Cf. *Tlingit Indians*, p. 479.

[25]In certain Melanesian societies (Banks Islands, northern New Hebrides), the two exogamic phratries that characterize Australian organization crop up again ([R. H. Codrington, *The Melanesians* [Oxford, Clarendon Press, 1891], pp. 23ff.). In Florida, there are true totems, called *butos* (p. 31). An interesting discussion on this point is to be found in A. Lang, *Social Origins* [London, Longmans, 1903], pp. 176ff. Cf. on the same subject, and in the same vein, W. H. R. Rivers, "Totemism in Polynesia and Melanesia," in *JAI*, vol. XXXIX [1909], pp. 156ff.

believe I understand the meaning this term has for the natives. . . . It is a force, a nonmaterial and, in a sense, supernatural influence; but it reveals itself by physical force, or else by any kind of power and superiority that man possesses. Mana is by no means fixed on a definite object; it can be carried by any sort of thing. . . . The whole religion of the Melanesian consists in procuring mana for himself, for his own benefit or someone else's.[26]

Is this not the same notion of a diffuse and anonymous force whose seed in Australian totemism we were uncovering a moment ago? The impersonality is the same. As Codrington says, we must avoid seeing it as a kind of supreme being; such an idea "is absolutely alien" to Melanesian thought. The ubiquity is the same. Mana has no definite location and is everywhere. All forms of life, and all the active potencies of men, living things, or mere minerals are ascribed to its influence.[27]

Therefore, it is by no means reckless to impute to the Australian societies an idea such as the one I have drawn from my analysis of totemic beliefs: The same idea is to be found, though at a higher level of generalization and abstraction, in religions whose roots go back to Australian thought and that visibly bear its mark. The two conceptions are obviously akin, differing only in scale. Whereas mana is diffused throughout the whole universe, what I have called the god (or more accurately, the totemic principle) is localized in a broad but nonetheless more limited circle of creatures and things of various species. It is mana, but a rather more specialized mana—even though, in the end, this specialization may only be quite relative.

There are cases, moreover, in which this kin relation becomes especially apparent. Among the Omaha, all kinds of individual and collective totems exist;[28] both are forms of wakan. "The Indian's faith in the efficacy of the totem," says Miss Fletcher, "was based on his conception of nature and life. That conception was complex and involved two key ideas. First, all things, animate and inanimate, are imbued with a common life-principle; and second, this life is continuous."[29] This common life-principle is wakan. The totem is the means by which the individual is put in touch with that source of energy. If the totem has powers, it has them because it incarnates wakan.

---

[26]Codrington, *The Melanesians*, p. 118 n. 1; [Richard Heinrich Robert] Parkinson, *Dreissig Jahre in der Südsee* [Stuttgart, Strecker und Schroeder, 1907], pp. 178, 392, 394, etc.

[27]An analysis of this idea is to be found in [Henri] Hubert and [Marcel] Mauss, ["Esquisse d'une] théorie générale de la magie," *AS*, vol. VII [1904], p. 108.

[28]There are totems not only of clans but also of brotherhoods (Fletcher, "Import of the Totem," pp. 581ff.).

[29]Ibid. [pp. 578–579].

If the man who has violated the prohibitions that protect his totem is stricken by illness or death, it is because the mysterious force that he ran afoul of, wakan, reacted against him with an intensity proportionate to the shock it suffered.[30] Inversely, just as the totem is wakan, so the manner in which wakan is conceived sometimes recalls its totemic origins. As Say tells us, among the Dakota, the *wahconda* is manifested sometimes in the form of a gray bear, sometimes a bison, a beaver, or other animal.[31] This formulation cannot, of course, be unreservedly accepted. Since wakan resists all personification, it is unlikely to have been conceived of in its abstract generality by means of precise symbols. However, Say's observation probably is applicable to the particular forms it takes as it becomes specialized amid the concrete reality of life. If there truly was a time when those specializations of wakan evidenced such a marked affinity with animal form, that would be further proof of the close ties between that notion and totemic beliefs.[32]

Besides, one can explain why the idea of mana could not attain the degree of abstraction and generalization in Australia that it did in more advanced societies. The reason is not merely some insufficient capacity of the Australian to think abstractly and generalize; it is above all the nature of the social milieu that imposed this particularism. As long as totemism remains the basis of cult organization, the clan maintains an autonomy within the religious society that, although not absolute, nonetheless remains very pronounced. Undoubtedly, one can say in a sense that each totemic group is only a chapel of the tribal Church,* but a chapel that enjoys broad independence. Although the cult that is celebrated within the clan does not form a whole sufficient unto itself, the relations it has with the others are merely external. The cults are juxtaposed but not interpenetrating. The totem of a clan is fully sacred only for that clan. As a result, the group of things assigned to each clan, and that are part of the clan in the same right as the men, has the same individuality and the same autonomy. Each of them is imagined as being irreducible to similar groups that are radically discontinuous with it and as constituting what amounts to a distinct realm. Under these conditions, it would occur to no one that these heterogeneous worlds were only different

---

*Here again, Durkheim capitalizes.

[30]Ibid., p. 583. Among the Dakota, the totem is called wakan. See Riggs and Dorsey, *Dakota Texts and Grammar*, in *CNAE* [vol. IX, Washington, Government Printing Office, 1893], p. 219.

[31]"James's Account of Long's Expedition in the Rocky Mountains," vol. I, p. 268 (cited by Dorsey in "Siouan Cults," §92, p. 431).

[32]I do not mean to argue that in principle every theriomorphic representation of religious forces is the mark of a preexisting totemism. But in terms of societies where totemism is still apparent, as in the case of the Dakota, it is natural to think that these conceptions are not unknown to it.

manifestations of one and the same fundamental force. It must have been assumed instead that a specifically different mana corresponded to each of them, the power of which could not extend beyond the clan and the things assigned to it. The notion of one universal mana could be born only when a religion of the tribe developed above the clan cults and absorbed them more or less completely. It is only with the sense of tribal unity that a sense of the world's unity arose. I will show later on[33] that the societies of Australia were already acquainted with a cult shared by the entire tribe. But although that cult represents the highest form of the Australian religions, it did not succeed in rupturing the principles on which they rest and transforming them. Totemism is basically a federative religion that cannot go beyond a certain level of centralization without ceasing to be itself.

One characteristic fact illuminates the profound reason why the notion of mana has been kept so specialized in Australia. The religious forces proper—those thought of as totems—are not the only ones the Australian believes he must reckon with. There are also the forces that the magician especially has at his disposal. Whereas the religious forces are considered to be salutary and beneficent in principle, the function of magic forces is above all to cause death and illness. They differ both in the nature of their effects and in the relations they have with social organization. A totem always belongs to a clan; magic, on the other hand, is a tribal and even an intertribal institution. Magical forces do not particularly belong to any definite group of the tribe. To use those forces, it is enough to have the efficacious recipes. Similarly, everyone is vulnerable to their effects and so must try to guard against them. These are nebulous forces that are not attached to any definite social division and can even extend their influence beyond the tribe. It is noteworthy that, among the Arunta and the Loritja, they are conceived of simply as aspects and particular forms of one and the same force, called in Arunta *Arungquiltha* or *Arúnkulta*.[34] "It is," say Spencer and Gillen, "a term of rather vague meaning; but, basically, one always finds the idea of a supernatural power endowed with an evil nature. . . . This word is applied indiscriminately either to the evil influence that comes from an object or to the very object in which it temporarily or permanently resides."[35] "By Arúnkulta," says Strehlow, "the

[33]See Bk. II, chap. 9 §4, pp. 288–298.

[34]The first spelling is that of [Sir Baldwin] Spencer and [Francis James] Gillen; the second, [Carl] Strehlow's.

[35]Spencer and Gillen, *Native Tribes [of Central Australia,* London, Macmillan, 1899], p. 548, n. 1. Granted, Spencer and Gillen add, "The best way of rendering the idea would be to say that the arungquiltha object is possessed by an evil spirit." But that free translation is an unwarranted interpretation by them. The notion of arungquiltha in no way implies the existence of spiritual beings. This point emerges from Strehlow's context and definition.

native means a force that suddenly suspends life and brings death to whomever it enters."[36] This term is applied to bones, to the pieces of wood that give off evil spells, and to animal or plant poisons. It is very definitely a harmful mana. Grey mentions a completely identical notion in the tribes he has observed.[37] Among these dissimilar peoples, then, the properly religious forces do not manage to break free of a certain heterogeneity, but the magical forces are conceived of as being all of the same nature; they are conceived of generically. The reason is this: Since the magical forces hover above the divisions and subdivisions of the social organization, they move in a homogeneous and continuous space where they do not encounter anything to differentiate them. On the other hand, since religious forces are localized within definite and distinct social settings, they become differentiated and specialized according to the setting in which they happen to be.

From this we see to what extent the notion of impersonal religious force is in the letter and spirit of Australian totemism, for it constitutes itself distinctly as soon as no contrary cause opposes it. Granted, the arungquiltha is a purely magical force. But magic forces and religious forces are not different in their essence.[38] Indeed, they are sometimes designated by the same word. In Melanesia, the magician and his charms have mana just as do the agents and rites of the regular cult.[39] Among the Iroquois,[40] the word "orenda" is used in the same way. Therefore, we can legitimately infer the nature of each from that of the other.[41]

[36]Strehlow, *Die Aranda- [und Loritja-Stämme in Zentral-Australien]*, vol. II [Frankfurt, J. Baer, 1907], p. 76n.

[37]With the name Boyl-ya ([George] Grey, *Journals of Two Expeditions [in North-West and Western Australia]*, vol. II [London, T. W. Boone, 1841], pp. 337–338).

[38]See above, p. 400. Moreover, Spencer and Gillen implicitly recognize this when they say that the arungquiltha is "a supernatural force." Cf. Hubert and Mauss, "Théorie générale," p. 119.

[39]Codrington, *The Melanesians*, pp. 191ff.

[40]Hewitt, "Orenda," p. 38.

[41]One may even ask whether a concept analogous to wakan or mana is altogether lacking in Australia. As it happens, the word "churinga" (or *Tjurunga*, in Strehlow's spelling) has closely related meaning among the Arunta. Spencer and Gillen say that this term designates "all that is secret or sacred. It is applied as much to an object as to the quality it possesses" (*Native Tribes*, p. 648). This is almost the definition of mana. Sometimes, indeed, Spencer and Gillen use that word to designate religious power or force in general. In describing a ceremony among the Kaitish, they say that the celebrant is "full of churinga," that is, they continue, full of "the magical power that emanates from the objects called churingas." However, it does not seem that the notion of churinga is constituted in Australia with the clarity and precision that the notion of mana has in Melanesia or that wakan has among the Sioux.

III

The result to which the preceding analysis has led us is relevant not only to the history of totemism but also to the formation of religious thought generally.

On the grounds that man is at first ruled mainly by his senses and by sensuous representations, it has often been argued that he began by imagining the divine in the concrete form of definite and personal beings. The facts do not confirm that presumption. I have just described a logically unified set of religious beliefs that I have good reason to consider very primitive, and yet I have not encountered personalities of this kind. The totemic cult proper is addressed neither to such and such definite animals nor to such and such definite plants but to a sort of diffuse power that permeates things.[42] Even in the advanced religions that have arisen out of totemism, like those we see appearing among the Indians of North America, that idea, far from being effaced, becomes more conscious of itself, expressing itself with a clarity it did not previously have, and at the same time taking on greater generality. That idea dominates the whole religious system.

Such is the basic material from which were made the various beings that religions of all times have worshipped and sanctified. The spirits, demons, genies, and gods of every degree are only the concrete forms taken by this energy (this "potentiality," as Hewitt calls it[43]) as it became individualized and fixed upon some definite object or point in space, and condensed around some being that is ideal or legendary, yet conceived of as real in popular imagination. A Dakota interviewed by Miss Fletcher described this essential consubstantiality in language full of bold images:

> All that moves stops at one place or another, at one moment or another.
> The bird that flies stops somewhere to make its nest, somewhere else to rest
> from flight. The man who walks stops when he pleases. The same is true
> for the deity. The sun, so bright and magnificent, is one place where the
> deity has stopped. The trees and the animals are others. The Indian thinks
> of these places and sends his prayers there, that they may reach the place
> where god has stopped and thus obtain succor and benediction.[44]

In other words, wakan (for that is what he was talking about) goes and comes through the world, and the sacred things are the places where it has alighted.

[42]Certainly, we will see below (Bk. II, chaps. 8 and 9) that the idea of mythic personality is not altogether foreign to totemism. But I will show that these conceptions result from secondary formations. Far from being the basis of the beliefs just analyzed, they derive from those beliefs.

[43]Hewitt, "Orenda," p. 38.

[44]"Report of the Peabody Museum," vol. III, p. 276n. (cited by Dorsey, "Siouan Cults," p. 435).

Here we find ourselves far from naturism and animism alike. If the sun, moon, and stars have been worshipped, they have not owed this honor to their inherent nature or distinctive properties but to the fact that they were conceived of as participating in that force which alone gives things their sacredness and is found in many other beings, even the very smallest. The souls of the dead have been objects of rites not because they are considered to be made of some fluid and ethereal substance and not because they resemble the shadow of a body or its reflection on the face of the deep. Lightness and fluidity are not enough to confer sacredness on them; they have been invested with that honor only insofar as they possessed some of that very force, the fount of all that is religious.

Why we could not define religion by the idea of mythical personalities, gods, or spirits now becomes clearer. That way of imagining religious things is by no means inherent in their nature. At the origin and basis of religious thought, we find not definite and distinct objects or beings that in themselves possess sacredness but indefinite powers and anonymous forces. They are more or less numerous in different societies (sometimes, indeed, they are only one force), and their impersonality is exactly comparable to that of the physical forces whose manifestations are studied by the sciences of nature. Turning to particular sacred things, those are but individualized forms of this basic principle. Thus, it is not surprising that even in religions in which gods indisputably exist, there are rites that are efficacious by themselves, independent of divine action. This is so because that force can attach to words spoken and gestures made, as well as to material substances. Voice and movement can serve as its vehicle, and it can produce its effects through them without help from any god or spirit. Indeed, let that force become primarily concentrated in a rite, and through it that rite will become the creator of deities.[45] This is also why there is perhaps no divine personality without an impersonal element. Even those who most clearly imagine divine personality in a concrete and tangible form imagine it at the same time as an abstract power that can be defined only by the nature of its effects, as a force that deploys itself in space and that is in each of its effects, at least in part. It is the power to produce the rain or the wind, the harvest or the light of day; Zeus is in each drop of rain that falls, just as Ceres is in each sheaf of the harvest.[46] Indeed, more often than not, this efficacy is so incompletely defined that the believer can

[45]See above, p. 33.

[46]Expressions such as Ζεὺς ὕει, or Ceres succiditur, show that this conception lived on in Greece and in Rome. Moreover [Hermann] Usener, in his Götternamen: [Versuch einer Lehre von der religiosen Debriffebildung, Bonn, F. Cohen, 1896], has clearly shown that the gods of Greece, as of Rome, were originally impersonal forces that were only thought of in terms of their attributes.

have only a very vague notion of it. Moreover, this vagueness has made possible the unions and divisions in the course of which the gods were fragmented, dismembered, and combined in all sorts of ways. There is perhaps not a single religion in which the original mana, whether unitary or compound, has fully evolved into a well-defined number of discrete beings that are sealed off from one another. Each of those beings retains a nebulous sort of impersonality that enables it to enter into new combinations—it has that capacity not simply because it remains as a relic but because it is in the nature of religious forces to be incapable of full individualization.

This conception, which the study of totemism alone suggested to me, is further recommended by the fact that, of late, several scholars have been led to it independently, in the course of quite different research. There is an emerging tendency toward spontaneous agreement on this point, which is worth noting for it creates a presumption of objectivity.

As early as 1899, I was arguing the necessity of not putting any notion of mythical personality into the definition of religion.[47] In 1900, Marrett called attention to the existence of a phase in religion that he called preanimist, in which the rites were addressed to impersonal forces, such as Melanesian mana or the wakan of the Omaha and the Dakota.[48] Nevertheless, Marrett did not go so far as to hold that, always and in all cases, the notion of spirit logically or chronologically comes after that of mana or is derived from it. Indeed, he seemed disposed to allow that it is sometimes formed independently, and hence that religious thought flows from a double source.[49] On the other hand, he conceived mana as a property inherent in things, as an element of their specific character. According to him, mana is simply the trait we impute to anything that departs from the ordinary, to everything that makes us feel admiration or fear.[50] This was tantamount to rehabilitating the naturist theory.[51]

A short time later, Hubert and Mauss, setting out to devise a general the-

---

[47][Emile Durkheim, "De la] Définition des phénomènes religieux," *AS,* vol. II [1897–1898], pp. 14–16.

[48][R. R. Marrett], "Preanimistic Religion," in *Folk-lore,* vol. XI (1900), pp. 162–182.

[49]Ibid., p. 179. In a more recent work, "The Conception of Mana" (in *TICHR,* vol. II [Oxford, Clarendon Press, 1908], pp. 54ff.), Marrett tends even more to subordinate the animist conception to the notion of mana. However, his thought remains hesitant and reserved on this point.

[50]Ibid., p. 168.

[51]This return of preanimism to naturism is still more marked in a communication by Clodd at the Third Congress on the History of Religions ("Preanimistic Stages in Religion," in *TICHR,* vol. I, pp. 33).

ory of magic, established that magic as a whole is based on the notion of mana.[52] Given the close kinship of magical rites with religious ones, we might expect the same theory to be applicable to religion. Preuss argued this in a series of articles that appeared in *Globus*[53] the same year. Relying on facts he had drawn mainly from American civilizations, Preuss set out to show that the ideas of soul and spirit were formed only after those of impersonal power and force, that soul and spirit are only transformations of impersonal power and force, and that until fairly recent times, those latter retained the mark of their original impersonality. He did indeed show that, even in the advanced religions, spirit and soul are conceived of in the form of vague discharges spontaneously emitted from the things in which the mana resides, and sometimes tending to escape using all available routes: mouth, nose, and every other body opening, breath, gaze, speech, and so on. At the same time, Preuss showed their protean quality, the extreme plasticity that enables them to serve the most varied uses, in succession and almost simultaneously.[54] True enough, if that author's terminology was taken literally, one might think those forces are, for him, of a magical and not a religious nature. He calls them charms (*Zauber, Zauberkräfte*). But since he shows them to be active in rites that are fundamentally religious, for example, the great Mexican ceremonies[55], it is evident that, by using such terms, he does not mean to place those forces outside religion. If he uses them, it is probably for want of others that better indicate their impersonality and the sort of mechanism by which they operate.

Thus, the same idea is tending to appear from all quarters.[56] The impression increasingly is that the mythological constructions, even the most elementary ones, are secondary[57] products overgrowing a substratum of beliefs—simpler and more obscure, vaguer and more fundamental—that con-

[52]Hubert and Mauss, "Théorie générale de la magie," pp. 108ff.

[53][Konrad Theodor] Preuss, "Der Ursprung der Religion und Kunst," in *Globus,* vol. LXXXVI (1904), pp. 321, 355, 376, 389; vol. LXXXVII, pp. 333, 347, 380, 394, [419].

[54]Ibid., vol. LXXXVII, p. 381.

[55]He clearly opposes them to all influences that are profane in nature (ibid., vol. LXXXVI, p. 379a).

[56]They are found even in the recent theories of Frazer. If this scholar refuses to ascribe a religious character to totemism so as to make it a kind of magic, he does so precisely because the forces that the totemic cult puts into operation are impersonal, like those the magician manipulates. Frazer recognizes the fundamental fact I have just established, but he draws a different conclusion from it than I do, because, according to him, there is religion only if there are mythical personalities.

[57]However, I do not take this word in the same sense as Preuss and Marrett. According to them, there was a definite moment in religious evolution when men knew neither souls nor spirits, a *preanimist* phase. This hypothesis is highly questionable. I will offer further explanation on this point below (Bk. II, chaps. 8 and 9).

stitute the firm foundations on which the religious systems were built. This is the primitive stratum that the analysis of totemism has enabled us to reach. The various writers whose research I have just mentioned arrived at that conception using facts taken from quite disparate religions, some of which correspond to an already well-advanced civilization—the religions of Mexico, for example, which Preuss used a great deal. It might then be asked whether the theory was applicable to the simplest religions as well. But since one can descend no further than totemism, we run no risk of error. At the same time, we may possibly have found the original notion from which the ideas of wakan and mana are derived: the notion of the totemic principle.[58]

IV

The role that notion has played in the development of religious ideas is not the only reason for its primary importance. It has a secular aspect that gives it relevance for the history of scientific thought as well. It is the notion of force in its earliest form.

In the world as the Sioux conceive it, wakan plays the same role as the forces by which science explains the varied phenomena of nature. This is not to say that it is thought of in the form of an exclusively physical energy; we will see in the next chapter that, instead, the elements used to form an idea of it are taken from the most disparate realms. But precisely that composite nature enables it to be used as a principle of universal explanation. The whole of life comes from it;[59] "all life is wakan"; and by the word "life" must be understood all that acts and reacts and all that moves and is moved, as much in the mineral kingdom as in the biological one. Wakan is the cause of all the movement that takes place in the universe. We have also seen that the orenda of the Iroquois is "the efficient cause of all the phenomena, and all the activities, that manifest themselves around man." It is a power "inherent in all bodies and all things."[60] It is orenda that makes the wind blow, the sun shine and warm the earth, the plants grow, the animals multiply, and that makes

---

[58]On this same question, see the article of Alessandro Bruno, "Sui fenomeni magico-religiosi delle comunità primitive," in *Rivista italiana di Sociologia*, vol. XII, fasc. IV–V, pp. 568ff., and an unpublished paper by W. Bogoras at the XIVth Congress of Americanists, held at Stuttgart in 1904. This paper is analyzed by Preuss in *Globus*, vol. LXXXVI, p. 201.

[59]"All things," says Miss Fletcher, "are pervaded by a common principle of life." "Import of the Totem," p. 579.

[60]Hewitt, "Orenda," p. 36.

man strong, skillful, and intelligent. When the Iroquois says that the life of all nature is the product of conflicts between the unequally intense orenda of different beings, he is expressing in his language the modern idea that the world is a system of forces that limit, contain, and equilibrate one another.

The Melanesian imputes the same sort of efficacy to mana. It is thanks to his mana that a man succeeds in hunting or in war, that his gardens produce a good yield, that his herds prosper. Because it is full of mana, the arrow reaches its mark, a net takes many fish, a canoe holds the sea well,[61] and so on. It is true that if certain of Codrington's phrases were taken literally, mana would be the cause to which people specifically ascribe "all that exceeds the power of man, all that is outside the ordinary course of nature."[62] But it emerges from the very examples he cites that the sphere of mana is a good deal broader than that. In reality, it serves to explain usual and everyday phenomena. There is nothing superhuman or supernatural in the fact that a boat sails or a hunter takes game. Among those events of everyday life, there are some so insignificant and so familiar that they go by unperceived: No one takes note of them, and, consequently, no one feels a need to explain them. The concept of mana is applied only to those that are important enough to provoke reflection, to awaken a modicum of interest and curiosity. For all that, however, they are not miraculous. And what is true of mana as well as orenda or wakan is equally true of the totemic principle. By that principle are maintained the lives of the clan's people, the lives of the animals or plants of the totemic species, the lives of all things that are classified under the totem and participate in its nature.

Thus the idea of force is of religious origin. From religion, philosophy first and later the sciences borrowed it. Such is the intuition Comte already had when he called metaphysics the heir of "theology." But his conclusion was that, because of its metaphysical origins, the idea of force was fated to disappear from science, and he denied it any objective meaning. I will show, to the contrary, that religious forces are real, no matter how imperfect the symbols with whose help they were conceived of. From this it will follow that the same is true for the concept of force in general.

[61]Codrington, *The Melanesians*, pp. 118–120.

[62]Ibid., p. 119.

CHAPTER SEVEN

ORIGINS OF THESE BELIEFS (CONCLUSION)

Origin of the Notion of Totemic Principle, or Mana

T he proposition established in the preceding chapter defines the terms in which the problem of how totemism originated must be posed. The central notion of totemism is that of a quasi-divine principle that is immanent in certain categories of men and things and thought of in the form of an animal or plant. In essence, therefore, to explain this religion is to explain this belief—that is, to discover what could have led men to construct it and with what building blocks.

I

It is manifestly not with the feelings the things that serve as totems are capable of arousing in men's minds. I have shown that these are often insignificant. In the sort of impression lizards, caterpillars, rats, ants, frogs, turkeys, breams, plum trees, cockatoos, and so forth make upon man (to cite only the names that come up frequently on lists of Australian totems), there is nothing that in any way resembles grand and powerful religious emotions or could stamp upon them a quality of sacredness. The same cannot be said of stars and great atmospheric phenomena, which do have all that is required to seize men's imaginations. As it happens, however, these serve very rarely as totems; indeed, their use for this purpose was probably a late development.[1] Thus it was not the intrinsic nature of the thing whose name the clan bore that set it apart as the object of worship. Furthermore, if the emotion elicited by the thing itself really was the determining cause of totemic rites and beliefs, then this thing would also be the sacred being par excellence, and the

[1] See above, p. 102.

207

animals and plants used as totems would play the leading role in religious life. But we know that the focus of the cult is elsewhere. It is symbolic representations of this or that plant or animal. It is totemic emblems and symbols of all kinds that possess the greatest sanctity. And so it is in totemic emblems and symbols that the religious source is to be found, while the real objects represented by those emblems receive only a reflection.

The totem is above all a symbol, a tangible expression of something else.[2] But of what?

It follows from the same analysis that the totem expresses and symbolizes two different kinds of things. From one point of view, it is the outward and visible form of what I have called the totemic principle or god; and from another, it is also the symbol of a particular society that is called the clan. It is the flag of the clan, the sign by which each clan is distinguished from the others, the visible mark of its distinctiveness, and a mark that is borne by everything that in any way belongs to the clan: men, animals, and things. Thus, if the totem is the symbol of both the god and the society, is this not because the god and the society are one and the same? How could the emblem of the group have taken the form of that quasi-divinity if the group and the divinity were two distinct realities? Thus the god of the clan, the totemic principle, can be none other than the clan itself, but the clan transfigured and imagined in the physical form of the plant or animal that serves as totem.

How could that apotheosis have come about, and why should it have come about in that fashion?

II

Society in general, simply by its effect on men's minds, undoubtedly has all that is required to arouse the sensation of the divine. A society is to its members what a god is to its faithful.* A god is first of all a being that man conceives of as superior to himself in some respects and one on whom he believes he depends. Whether that being is a conscious personality, like Zeus or Yahweh, or a play of abstract forces as in totemism, the faithful believe

---

*Le fidèle. To avoid translating this term, which connotes loyal adherence, as "the believer," thereby leaving no room for a contrast with le croyant, which connotes belief, I have usually rendered it as "the faithful." Durkheim analyzes the stance of what one might call the "unbelieving faithful." See Bk. III, chap. 3, §2.

[2]In the small book cited above, [Julius] Pikler, [Der Ursprung der Totemismus. Ein Beitrag zur materialischen Geschichtheorie, Berlin, K. Hoffmann, 1900] has already expressed, in a somewhat dialectical fashion, the belief that this fundamentally is what the totem is.

they are bound to certain ways of acting that the nature of the sacred principle they are dealing with has imposed upon them. Society also fosters in us the sense of perpetual dependence. Precisely because society has its own specific nature that is different from our nature as individuals, it pursues ends that are also specifically its own; but because it can achieve those ends only by working through us, it categorically demands our cooperation. Society requires us to make ourselves its servants, forgetful of our own interests. And it subjects us to all sorts of restraints, privations, and sacrifices without which social life would be impossible. And so, at every instant, we must submit to rules of action and thought that we have neither made nor wanted and that sometimes are contrary to our inclinations and to our most basic instincts.

If society could exact those concessions and sacrifices only by physical constraint, it could arouse in us only the sense of a physical force to which we have no choice but to yield, and not that of a moral power such as religions venerate. In reality, however, the hold society has over consciousness owes far less to the prerogative its physical superiority gives it than to the moral authority with which it is invested. We defer to society's orders not simply because it is equipped to overcome our resistance but, first and foremost, because it is the object of genuine respect.

An individual or collective subject is said to inspire respect when the representation that expresses it in consciousness has such power that it calls forth or inhibits conduct automatically, *irrespective of any utilitarian calculation of helpful or harmful results.* When we obey someone out of respect for the moral authority that we have accorded to him, we do not follow his instructions because they seem wise but because a certain psychic energy intrinsic to the idea we have of that person bends our will and turns it in the direction indicated. When that inward and wholly mental pressure moves within us, respect is the emotion we feel. We are then moved not by the advantages or disadvantages of the conduct that is recommended to us or demanded of us but by the way we conceive of the one who recommends or demands that conduct. This is why a command generally takes on short, sharp forms of address that leave no room for hesitation. It is also why, to the extent that command is command and works by its own strength, it precludes any idea of deliberation or calculation, but instead is made effective by the very intensity of the mental state in which it is given. That intensity is what we call moral influence.

The ways of acting to which society is strongly enough attached to impose them on its members are for that reason marked with a distinguishing sign that calls forth respect. Because these ways of acting have been worked out in common, the intensity with which they are thought in each individual mind finds resonance in all the others, and vice versa. The representations that translate them within each of us thereby gain an intensity that mere private states of consciousness can in no way match. Those ways of acting gather strength from the countless individual representations that have served to form each of them. It is society that speaks through the mouths of those who affirm them in our presence; it is society that we hear when we hear them; and the voice of all itself has a tone that an individual voice cannot have.[3] The very forcefulness with which society acts against dissidence, whether by moral censure or physical repression, helps to strengthen this dominance,[4] and at the same time forcefully proclaims the ardor of the shared conviction. In short, when something is the object of a state of opinion, the representation of the thing that each individual has draws such power from its origins, from the conditions in which it originated, that it is felt even by those who do not yield to it.* The mental representation of a thing that is the object of a state of opinion has a tendency to repress and hold at bay those representations that contradict it; it commands instead those actions that fulfill it. It accomplishes this not by the reality or threat of physical coercion but by the radiation of the mental energy it contains. The hallmark of moral authority is that its psychic properties alone give it power. Opinion, eminently a social thing, is one source of authority. Indeed, the question arises whether authority is not the daughter of opinion.[5] Some will object that science is often the antagonist of opinion, the errors of which it combats and corrects. But science can succeed in this task only if it has sufficient authority, and it can gain such authority only from opinion itself. All the scientific demonstrations in the world would have no influence if a people had no faith in science. Even today, if it should happen that science resisted a very powerful current of public opinion, it would run the risk of seeing its credibility eroded.[6]

*For example, the thief acknowledges a "state of opinion" by taking precautions not to be discovered. As this example suggests, once upon a time Durkheim's term *opinion* could have been translated as "public opinion" without confusion, but not in America today. Our present usage connotes the discrete bits of "opinion" that pollsters elicit through replies to questionnaires. Trans.

[3]See my [*De la*] *Division du travail social: Etude sur l'organisation de sociétés supérieures,* 3d ed. [Paris, F. Alcan, 1902], pp. 64ff.

[4]Ibid., p. 76.

[5]This is the case at least for all moral authority that is recognized as such by a group.

[6]I hope this analysis and those that follow will put an end to an erroneous interpretation of my ideas, which has more than once led to misunderstanding. Because I have made constraint the *external feature* by which social facts can be most easily recognized and distinguished from individual psychological ones, some have believed that I consider physical constraint to be the entire essence of social life. In reality, I have never regarded constraint as anything more than the visible, tangible expression of an underlying, inner fact that is wholly ideal: *moral authority.* The question for sociology—if there can be said to be *one* so-

Because social pressure makes itself felt through mental channels, it was bound to give man the idea that outside him there are one or several powers, moral yet mighty, to which he is subject. Since they speak to him in a tone of command, and sometimes even tell him to violate his most natural inclinations, man was bound to imagine them as being external to him. The mythological interpretations would doubtless not have been born if man could easily see that those influences upon him come from society. But the ordinary observer cannot see where the influence of society comes from. It moves along channels that are too obscure and circuitous, and uses psychic mechanisms that are too complex, to be easily traced to the source. So long as scientific analysis has not yet taught him, man is well aware that he is acted upon but not by whom. Thus he had to build out of nothing the idea of those powers with which he feels connected. From this we can begin to perceive how he was led to imagine those powers in forms that are not their own and to transfigure them in thought.

A god is not only an authority to which we are subject but also a force that buttresses our own. The man who has obeyed his god, and who for this reason thinks he has his god with him, approaches the world with confidence and a sense of heightened energy. In the same way, society's workings do not stop at demanding sacrifices, privations, and efforts from us. The force of the collectivity is not wholly external; it does not move us entirely from outside. Indeed, because society can exist only in and by means of individual minds,[7] it must enter into us and become organized within us. That force thus becomes an integral part of our being and, by the same stroke, uplifts it and brings it to maturity.*

This stimulating and invigorating effect of society is particularly apparent in certain circumstances. In the midst of an assembly that becomes worked

---

ciological question—is to seek, throughout the various forms of external constraint, the correspondingly various kinds of moral authority and to discover what causes have given rise to the latter. Specifically, the main object of the question treated in the present work is to discover in what form the particular kind of moral authority that is inherent in all that is religious was born, and what it is made of. Further, it will be seen below that in making social pressure one of the distinguishing features of sociological phenomena, I do not mean to say that this is the only one. I will exhibit another aspect of collective life, virtually the opposite of this one, but no less real. (See p. 213.)

* *L'élève et le grandit.* This phrase can also mean "uplifts and enlarges" it. Swain chose the verbs "elevate" and "magnify." Durkheim may have intended both the physical and the moral meanings: "to lift" as well as "to bring up" or "rear"; to "enlarge" as well as to "raise in stature" or "bring to maturity."

[7]Which does not mean, of course, that collective consciousness does not have specific traits (Durkheim, "Représentations individuelles et représentations collectives," *RMM*, vol. VI ([1898]), pp. 273ff.).

up, we become capable of feelings and conduct of which we are incapable when left to our individual resources. When it is dissolved and we are again on our own, we fall back to our ordinary level and can then take the full measure of how far above ourselves we were. History abounds with examples. Suffice it to think about the night of August 4*, when an assembly was suddenly carried away in an act of sacrifice and abnegation that each of its members had refused to make the night before and by which all were surprised the morning after.[8] For this reason all parties—be they political, economic, or denominational—see to it that periodic conventions are held, at which their followers can renew their common faith by making a public demonstration of it together. To strengthen emotions that would dissipate if left alone, the one thing needful is to bring all those who share them into more intimate and more dynamic relationship.

In the same way, we can also explain the curious posture that is so characteristic of a man who is speaking to a crowd—if he has achieved communion with it. His language becomes high-flown in a way that would be ridiculous in ordinary circumstances; his gestures take on an overbearing quality; his very thought becomes impatient of limits and slips easily into every kind of extreme. This is because he feels filled to overflowing, as though with a phenomenal oversupply of forces that spill over and tend to spread around him. Sometimes he even feels possessed by a moral force greater than he, of which he is only the interpreter. This is the hallmark of what has often been called the demon of oratorical inspiration. This extraordinary surplus of forces is quite real and comes to him from the very group he is addressing. The feelings he arouses as he speaks return to him enlarged and amplified, reinforcing his own to the same degree. The passionate energies that he arouses reecho in turn within him, and they increase his dynamism. It is then no longer a mere individual who speaks but a group incarnated and personified.

Apart from these passing or intermittent states, there are more lasting ones in which the fortifying action of society makes itself felt with longer-term consequences and often with more striking effect. Under the influence

---

*Durkheim is probably alluding to the night of 4 August 1789, when France's new National Assembly ratified the total destruction of the feudal regime.

[8]The proof of this is the length and passion of the debates at which legal form was given to the resolutions in principle that were taken in a moment of collective enthusiasm. More than one, among clergy and nobility alike, called that famous night "dupes' night," or, with Rivarol, the "Saint Bartholomew's of the landed estates." [This apparently alludes to two events. The *Journée des Dupes* was the day, not the night, of 30 November 1630, when Cardinal Richelieu's enemies came to believe the cardinal had lost the king's ear for good and had fallen in disgrace; they were proved wrong. *La St. Barthélemy* was a massacre of Protestants 23–24 August 1527, which led to civil war. Trans.] See [Otto] Stoll, *Suggestion und Hypnotismus in der Völkerpsychologie*, 2d ed. [Leipzig, Veit, 1904], p. 618 n. 2.

of some great collective shock in certain historical periods, social interactions become much more frequent and active. Individuals seek one another out and come together more. The result is the general effervescence that is characteristic of revolutionary or creative epochs. The result of that heightened activity is a general stimulation of individual energies. People live differently and more intensely than in normal times.* The changes are not simply of nuance and degree; man himself becomes something other than what he was. He is stirred by passions so intense that they can be satisfied only by violent and extreme acts: by acts of superhuman heroism or bloody barbarism. This explains the Crusades,[9] for example, as well as so many sublime or savage moments in the French Revolution.[10] We see the most mediocre or harmless bourgeois transformed by the general exaltation into a hero or an executioner.[11] And the mental processes are so clearly the same as those at the root of religion that the individuals themselves conceived the pressure they yielded to in explicitly religious terms. The Crusaders believed they felt God present among them, calling on them to go forth and conquer the Holy Land, and Joan of Arc believed she was obeying celestial voices.[12]

This stimulating action of society is not felt in exceptional circumstances alone. There is virtually no instant of our lives in which a certain rush of energy fails to come to us from outside ourselves. In all kinds of acts that express the understanding, esteem, and affection of his neighbor, there is a lift that the man who does his duty feels, usually without being aware of it. But that lift sustains him; the feeling society has for him uplifts the feeling he has for himself. Because he is in moral harmony with his neighbor, he gains new confidence, courage, and boldness in action—quite like the man of faith who believes he feels the eyes of his god turned benevolently toward him. Thus is produced what amounts to a perpetual uplift of our moral being. Since it varies according to a multitude of external conditions—whether our relations with the social groups that surround us are more or less active and what those groups are—we cannot help but feel that this moral toning up has an external cause, though we do not see where that cause is or what it is. So we readily conceive of it in the form of a moral power that, while immanent in us, also represents something in us that is other than ourselves. This is

---

* *On vit plus et autrement qu'en temps normal.*

[9]Ibid., pp. 353ff.

[10]Ibid., pp. 619, 635.

[11]Ibid., pp. 622ff.

[12]Feelings of fear or sadness can also develop and intensify under the same influences. As we will see, those feelings correspond to a whole aspect of religious life (Bk. III, chap. 5).

man's moral consciousness and his conscience.* And it is only with the aid of religious symbols that most have ever managed to conceive of it with any clarity at all.

In addition to those free forces that continuously renew our own, there are other forces congealed in the techniques we use and in traditions of all kinds. We speak a language we did not create; we use instruments we did not invent; we claim rights we did not establish; each generation inherits a treasury of knowledge that it did not itself amass; and so on. We owe these varied benefits of civilization to society, and although in general we do not see where they come from, we know at least that they are not of our own making. It is these things that give man his distinctiveness among all creatures, for man is man only because he is civilized. Thus he could not escape the sense of mighty causes existing outside him, which are the source of his characteristic nature and which, like benevolent forces, help and protect him and guarantee him a privileged fate. He naturally accorded to those powers a respect commensurate with the great value of the benefits that he attributed to them.[13]

Thus the environment in which we live seems populated with forces at once demanding and helpful, majestic and kind, and with which we are in touch. Because we feel the weight of them, we have no choice but to locate them outside ourselves, as we do for the objective causes of our sensations. But from another point of view, the feelings they provoke in us are qualitatively different from those we have for merely physical things. So long as these perceptions are no more than the empirical characteristics that ordinary experience makes manifest, and so long as the religious imagination has not yet transfigured them, we feel nothing like respect for them, and they have nothing of what it takes to lift us above ourselves. Therefore the representations that express them seem to us very different from those that collective influences awaken in us. The two sorts of representation form two kinds of mental state, and they are as separate and distinct as the two forms of life to which they correspond. As a result, we feel as though we are in touch with two distinct sorts of reality with a clear line of demarcation between them: the world of profane things on one side, the world of sacred things on the other.

*Conscience. To bring out that the French conscience refers simultaneously to intellectual cognition and moral obligation, I have used both "conscience" and "consciousness."

[13]Such is the other aspect of society, which seems to us demanding as well as good and kindly. It dominates us; it helps us. If I have defined social fact more by the first characteristic than by the second, it is because the dominance is more easily observable and because it is expressed by external and visible signs; but I am far from ever having intended to deny the reality of the second. ([Emile Durkheim,] Les Règles de la méthode sociologique, 2d ed. [Paris, Alcan, 1901], preface, p. xx n.1).

Furthermore, now as in the past, we see that society never stops creating new sacred things. If society should happen to become infatuated with a man, believing it has found in him its deepest aspirations as well as the means of fulfilling them, then that man will be put in a class by himself and virtually deified. Opinion will confer on him a grandeur that is similar in every way to the grandeur that protects the gods. This has happened to many sovereigns in whom their epochs had faith and who, if not deified outright, were looked upon as direct representatives of the godhead. A clear indication that this apotheosis is the work of society alone is that society has often consecrated men whose personal worth did not warrant it. Moreover, the routine deference that men invested with high social positions receive is not qualitatively different from religious respect. The same movements express it: standing at a distance from a high personage; taking special precautions in approaching him; using a different language to speak with him and gestures other than those that will do for ordinary mortals. One's feeling in these circumstances is so closely akin to religious feeling that many do not distinguish between them. Sacredness is ascribed to princes, nobles, and political leaders in order to account for the special regard they enjoy. In Melanesia and Polynesia, for example, people say that a man of influence possesses mana and impute his influence to this mana.[14] It is clear, nonetheless, that his position comes to him only from the importance that opinion gives him. Thus, both the moral power conferred by opinion and the moral power with which sacred beings are invested are of fundamentally the same origin and composed of the same elements. For this reason, one word can be used to designate both.

Just as society consecrates men, so it also consecrates things, including ideas. When a belief is shared unanimously by a people, to touch it—that is, to deny or question it—is forbidden, for the reasons already stated. The prohibition against critique is a prohibition like any other and proves that one is face to face with a sacred thing. Even today, great though the freedom we allow one another may be, it would be tantamount to sacrilege for a man wholly to deny progress or to reject the human ideal to which modern societies are attached. Even the peoples most enamored of free thinking tend to place one principle above discussion and regard it as untouchable, in other words, sacred: the principle of free discussion itself.

Nowhere has society's ability to make itself a god or to create gods been more in evidence than during the first years of the Revolution. In the general enthusiasm of that time, things that were by nature purely secular were

[14][Robert Henry] Codrington, *The Melanesians* [Oxford, Clarendon Press, 1891], pp. 50, 103, 120. Moreover, it is generally believed that in the Polynesian languages, the word *mana* originally meant "authority." (See [Edward] Tregear, *Maori Polynesian Comparative Dictionary*, s.v. [Wellington, Lyon and Blair, 1891].)

transformed by public opinion into sacred things: Fatherland, Liberty, Reason.[15] A religion tended to establish itself spontaneously, with its own dogma,[16] symbols,[17] altars,[18] and feast days.[19] It was to these spontaneous hopes that the Cult of Reason and the Supreme Being tried to give a kind of authoritative fulfillment. Granted, this religious novelty did not last. The patriotic enthusiasm that originally stirred the masses died away,[20] and the cause having departed, the effect could not hold. But brief though it was, this experiment loses none of its sociological interest. In a specific case, we saw society and its fundamental ideas becoming the object of a genuine cult directly—and without transfiguration of any kind.

All these facts enable us to grasp how it is possible for the clan to awaken in its members the idea of forces existing outside them, both dominating and supporting them—in sum, religious forces. There is no other social group to which the primitive is more directly or tightly bound. The ties that bind him to the tribe are looser and less strongly felt. Although the tribe is certainly not foreign to him, it is with the people of his clan that he has most in common, and it is the influence of this group that he feels most immediately, and so it is also this influence, more than any other, that was bound to find expression in religious symbols.

This first explanation is too general, though, since it can be applied indiscriminately to any kind of society and hence to any kind of religion. Let us try to specify what particular form collective action takes in the clan and how in the clan it brings about the sense of the sacred, for collective action is nowhere more easily observable or more obvious than in its results.

III

Life in Australian societies alternates between two different phases.[21] In one phase, the population is scattered in small groups that attend to their occupa-

[15]See Albert Mathiez, *Les Origines des cultes révolutionnaires 1789–1792* [Paris, G. Bellais, 1904].

[16]Ibid., p. 24.

[17]Ibid., pp. 29, 32.

[18]Ibid., p. 30.

[19]Ibid, p. 46.

[20]See [Albert] Mathiez, *La Théophilanthropie et le culte décadaire* [Paris, F. Alcan, 1903], p. 36.

[21]See [Sir Baldwin] Spencer and [Francis James] Gillen, *Northern Tribes [of Central Australia*, London, Macmillan, 1904], p. 33.

tions independently. Each family lives to itself, hunting, fishing—in short, striving by all possible means to get the food it requires. In the other phase, by contrast, the population comes together, concentrating itself at specified places for a period that varies from several days to several months. This concentration takes place when a clan or a portion of the tribe[22] is summoned to come together and on that occasion either conducts a religious ceremony or holds what in the usual ethnographic terminology is called a *corroboree*.[23]

These two phases stand in the sharpest possible contrast. The first phase, in which economic activity predominates, is generally of rather low intensity. Gathering seeds or plants necessary for food, hunting, and fishing are not occupations that can stir truly strong passions.[24] The dispersed state in which the society finds itself makes life monotonous, slack, and humdrum.[25] Everything changes when a corroboree takes place. Since the emotional and passionate faculties of the primitive are not fully subordinated to his reason and will, he easily loses his self-control. An event of any importance immediately puts him outside himself. Does he receive happy news? There are transports of enthusiasm. If the opposite happens, he is seen running hither and yon like a madman, giving way to all sorts of chaotic movements: shouting, screaming, gathering dust and throwing it in all directions, biting himself, brandishing his weapons furiously, and so on.[26] The very act of congregating is an exceptionally powerful stimulant. Once the individuals are gathered together, a sort of electricity is generated from their closeness and quickly launches them to an extraordinary height of exaltation. Every emotion expressed resonates without interference in consciousnesses that are wide open

[22]Indeed there are ceremonies, notably those that take place for initiation, to which members of foreign tribes are summoned. A system of messages and messengers is organized for the purpose of giving the notice that is indispensable for the grand ceremonies. (See [Alfred William] Howitt, "Notes on Australian Message-Sticks and Messengers," *JAI*, vol. XVIII (1889) [pp. 314–334]; Howitt, *Native Tribes* [of *South-East Australia*, New York, Macmillan, 1904], pp. 83, 678–691; Spencer and Gillen, *Native Tribes* [of *Central Australia*, London, Macmillan, 1899], p. 159; Spencer and Gillen, *Northern Tribes*, p. 551.

[23]The corroboree is distinguished from a religious rite proper in that it is accessible to women and the uninitiated. But although these two sorts of collective celebrations must be distinguished, they are closely related. I will return to and explain this relationship.

[24]Except in the case of the large bush-beating hunts.

[25]"The peaceful monotony of this part of his life," say Spencer and Gillen (*Northern Tribes*, p. 33).

[26]Howitt, *Native Tribes*, p. 683. Here it is the demonstrations that take place when an embassy sent to a foreign group returns to camp with news of a favorable result. [Durkheim will not be the one to report that the embassy in question had been entrusted to women. Howitt does not say what the women's mission was about. Trans.] Cf. [Robert] Brough Smyth, [*The Aborigines of Victoria*], vol. 1 [Melbourne, J. Ferres, 1878], p. 138; [Reverend Louis] Schulze, "Aborigines of the Upper and Middle Finke River," *RSSA*, vol. XVI [1891], p. 222.

to external impressions, each one echoing the others. The initial impulse is thereby amplified each time it is echoed, like an avalanche that grows as it goes along. And since passions so heated and so free from all control cannot help but spill over, from every side there are nothing but wild movements, shouts, downright howls, and deafening noises of all kinds that further intensify the state they are expressing. Probably because a collective emotion cannot be expressed collectively without some order that permits harmony and unison of movement, these gestures and cries tend to fall into rhythm and regularity, and from there into songs and dances. But in taking on a more regular form, they lose none of their natural fury. A regulated commotion is still a commotion. The human voice is inadequate to the task and is given artificial reinforcement: Boomerangs are knocked against one another; bull roarers are whirled. The original function of these instruments, used widely in the religious ceremonies of Australia, probably was to give more satisfying expression to the excitement felt. And by expressing this excitement, they also reinforce it. The effervescence often becomes so intense that it leads to outlandish behavior; the passions unleashed are so torrential that nothing can hold them. People are so far outside the ordinary conditions of life, and so conscious of the fact, that they feel a certain need to set themselves above and beyond ordinary morality. The sexes come together in violation of the rules governing sexual relations. Men exchange wives. Indeed, sometimes incestuous unions, in normal times judged loathsome and harshly condemned, are contracted in the open and with impunity.[27] If it is added that the ceremonies are generally held at night, in the midst of shadows pierced here and there by firelight, we can easily imagine the effect that scenes like these are bound to have on the minds of all those who take part. They bring about such an intense hyperexcitement of physical and mental life as a whole that they cannot be borne for very long. The celebrant who takes the leading role eventually falls exhausted to the ground.[28]

To illustrate and flesh out this unavoidably sketchy tableau, here is an account of scenes taken from Spencer and Gillen.

One of the most important religious celebrations among the Warra-

---

[27]See Spencer and Gillen, *Native Tribes,* pp. 96–97, *Northern Tribes,* p. 137; Brough Smyth, *Aborigines of Victoria,* vol. II, p. 319. This ritual promiscuity is practiced especially during initiation ceremonies (Spencer and Gillen, *Native Tribes,* pp. 267, 381; Howitt, *Native Tribes,* p. 657) and in totemic ceremonies (Spencer and Gillen, *Northern Tribes,* pp. 214, 237, 298). The ordinary rules of exogamy are violated during totemic ceremonies. Nevertheless, among the Arunta, unions between father and daughter, son and mother, brothers and sisters (all cases of blood kinship) remain forbidden (Spencer and Gillen, *Native Tribes* [pp. 96–97]).

[28]Howitt, *Native Tribes,* pp. 535, 545. This is extremely common.

munga concerns the snake Wollunqua. It is a series of rites that unfold over several days. What I will describe takes place on the fourth day.

According to the protocol in use among the Warramunga, representatives of the two phratries take part, some as celebrants and others as organizers and participants. Although only the people of the Uluuru phratry are authorized to conduct the ceremony, the members of the Kingilli phratry must decorate the participants, prepare the site and the instruments, and serve as the audience. In this capacity, they are responsible for mounding damp sand ahead of time, on which they use red down to make a drawing that represents the snake Wollunqua. The ceremony proper, which Spencer and Gillen attended, did not begin until nightfall. Around ten or eleven o'-clock, Uluuru and Kingilli arrived on the scene, sat on the mound, and began to sing. All were in a state of obvious excitement (*"every one was evidently very excited"*). A short time later in the evening, the Uluuru brought their wives and handed them over to the Kingilli,[29] who had sexual relations with them. The recently initiated young men were brought in, and the ceremony was explained to them, after which there was uninterrupted singing until three in the morning. Then came a scene of truly wild frenzy (*"a scene of the wildest excitement"*). With fires flickering on all sides, bringing out starkly the whiteness of the gum trees against the surrounding night, the Uluuru knelt in single file beside the mound, then moved around it, rising in unison with both hands on their thighs, kneeling again a little farther along, and so on. At the same time, they moved their bodies left and then right, at each movement letting out an echoing scream—actually a howl—at the top of their voices, *Yrrsh! Yrrsh! Yrrsh!* Meanwhile the Kingilli, in a high state of excitement, sounded their boomerangs, their chief appearing to be even more excited than his companions. When the procession of the Uluuru had circled the mound twice, they rose from their kneeling position, seated themselves, and took to singing again. From time to time, the singing would flag and almost die, then break out suddenly again. At the first sign of day, everyone jumped to their feet; the fires that had gone out were relit; urged on by the Kingilli, the Uluuru furiously attacked the mound with boomerangs, lances, and sticks, and in a few minutes it was in pieces. The fires died and there was profound silence.[30]

The same observers were present at a yet wilder scene among the Warramunga during the fire rituals. All sorts of processions, dances, and songs had been underway by torchlight since nightfall, and the general efferves-

---

[29]Since the women were also Kingilli, these unions violated the rule of exogamy.

[30]Spencer and Gillen, *Northern Tribes*, p. 237. [This account begins at p. 231. Trans.]

cence was increasingly intense. At a certain moment, twelve of those present each took in hand a large lighted torch; and, holding his own torch like a bayonette, one of them charged a group of natives. The blows were parried with staves and lances. A general melée followed. Men jumped, kicked, reared, and let out wild screams. The torches blazed and crackled as they hit heads and bodies, showering sparks in all directions. "The smoke, the flaming torches, the rain of sparks, the mass of men dancing and screaming—all that, say Spencer and Gillen, created a scene whose wildness cannot be conveyed in words."[31]

It is not difficult to imagine that a man in such a state of exaltation should no longer know himself. Feeling possessed and led on by some sort of external power that makes him think and act differently than he normally does, he naturally feels he is no longer himself. It seems to him that he has become a new being. The decorations with which he is decked out, and the masklike decorations that cover his face, represent this inward transformation even more than they help bring it about. And because his companions feel transformed in the same way at the same moment, and express this feeling by their shouts, movements, and bearing, it is as if he was in reality transported into a special world entirely different from the one in which he ordinarily lives, a special world inhabited by exceptionally intense forces that invade and transform him. Especially when repeated for weeks, day after day, how would experiences like these not leave him with the conviction that two heterogeneous and incommensurable worlds exist in fact? In one world he languidly carries on his daily life; the other is one that he cannot enter without abruptly entering into relations with extraordinary powers that excite him to the point of frenzy. The first is the profane world and the second, the world of sacred things.

It is in these effervescent social milieux, and indeed from that very effervescence, that the religious idea seems to have been born. That such is indeed the origin tends to be confirmed by the fact that what is properly called religious activity in Australia is almost entirely contained within the periods when these gatherings are held. To be sure, there is no people among whom the great cult ceremonies are not more or less periodical, but in the more advanced societies, there is virtually no day on which some prayer or offering is not offered to the gods or on which some ritual obligation is not fulfilled. In Australia, by contrast, the time apart from the feasts of the clan and the

---

[31]Ibid., p. 391. Other examples of collective effervescence during religious ceremonies are found in Spencer and Gillen, *Native Tribes*, pp. 244–246, 356–366, 374, 509–510. (The last occurs during a funeral rite.) Cf. Spencer and Gillen, *Northern Tribes*, pp. 213, 351.

tribe is taken up almost entirely with secular and profane activities. Granted, even during the periods of secular activity, there are prohibitions that must be and are observed. Freely killing or eating the totemic animal is never permitted, at least where the prohibition has kept its original strictness, but hardly any positive rite or ceremony of any importance is conducted. The positive rites and ceremonies take place only among assembled groups. Thus, the pious life of the Australian moves between successive phases—one of utter colorlessness, one of hyperexcitement—and social life oscillates to the same rhythm. This brings out the link between the two phases. Among the peoples called civilized, on the other hand, the relative continuity between them partially masks their interrelations. Indeed, we may well ask whether this starkness of contrast may have been necessary to release the experience of the sacred in its first form. By compressing itself almost entirely into circumscribed periods, collective life could attain its maximum intensity and power, thereby giving man a more vivid sense of the twofold existence he leads and the twofold nature in which he participates.

But this explanation is still incomplete. I have shown how the clan awakens in its members the idea of external forces that dominate and exalt it by the way in which it acts upon its members. But I still must ask how it happens that those forces were conceived of in the form of the totem, that is, in the form of an animal or plant.

The reason is that some animal or plant has given its name to the clan and serves as the clan's emblem. It is, in fact, a well-known law that the feelings a thing arouses in us are spontaneously transmitted to the symbol that represents it. Black is for us a sign of mourning; therefore it evokes sad thoughts and impressions. This transfer of feelings takes place because the idea of the thing and the idea of its symbol are closely connected in our minds. As a result, the feelings evoked by one spread contagiously to the other. This contagion, which occurs in all cases to some extent, is much more complete and more pronounced whenever the symbol is something simple, well defined, and easily imagined. But the thing itself is difficult for the mind to comprehend—given its dimensions, the number of its parts, and the complexity of their organization. We cannot detect the source of the strong feelings we have in an abstract entity that we can imagine only with difficulty and in a jumbled way. We can comprehend those feelings only in connection with a concrete object whose reality we feel intensely. Thus if the thing itself does not meet this requirement, it cannot serve as a mooring for the impressions felt, even for those impressions it has itself aroused. The symbol thus takes the place of the thing, and the emotions aroused are transferred to the symbol. It is the symbol that is loved, feared, and respected. It is to the symbol that one is grateful. And it is to the symbol that one sacrifices oneself. The soldier who dies for his flag dies for his country, but the idea of the flag is actually in the foreground of his consciousness. Indeed, the flag sometimes causes action directly. Although the country will not be lost if a solitary flag remains in the hands of the enemy or won if it is regained, the soldier is killed retaking it. He forgets that the flag is only a symbol that has no value in itself but only brings to mind the reality it represents. The flag itself is treated as if it was that reality.

The totem is the flag of the clan, so it is natural that the impressions the clan arouses in individual consciousness—impressions of dependence and of heightened energy—should become more closely attached to the idea of the totem than to that of the clan. The clan is too complex a reality for such unformed minds to be able to bring its concrete unity into clear focus. Besides, the primitive does not see that these impressions come to him from the group. He does not even see that the coming together of a certain number of men participating in the same life releases new energies that transform each one of them. All he feels is that he is lifted above himself and that he is participating in a life different from the one he lives ordinarily. He must still connect those experiences to some external object in a causal relation. Now what does he see around him? What is available to his senses, and what attracts his attention, is the multitude of totemic images surrounding him. He sees the waninga and the nurtunja, symbols of the sacred being. He sees the bull roarers and the churingas, on which combinations of lines that have the same meaning are usually engraved. The decorations on various parts of his body are so many totemic marks. Repeated everywhere and in every form, how could that image not fail to stand out in the mind with exceptionally sharp relief? Thus placed at center stage, it becomes representative. To that image the felt emotions attach themselves, for it is the only concrete object to which they can attach themselves.

The image goes on calling forth and recalling those emotions even after the assembly is over. Engraved on the cult implements, on the sides of rocks, on shields, and so forth, it lives beyond the gathering. By means of it, the emotions felt are kept perpetually alive and fresh. It is as though the image provoked them directly. Imputing the emotions to the image is all the more natural because, being common to the group, they can only be related to a thing that is equally common to all. Only the totemic emblem meets this condition. By definition, it is common to all. During the ceremony, all eyes are upon it. Although the generations change, the image remains the same. It is the abiding element of social life. So the mysterious forces with which men feel in touch seem to emanate from it, and thus we understand how men were led to conceive them in the form of the animate or inanimate being that gives the clan its name.

Having laid this foundation, we are in a position to grasp the essence of totemic beliefs. Because religious force is none other than the collective and anonymous force of the clan and because that force can only be conceived of in the form of the totem, the totemic emblem is, so to speak, the visible body of the god. From the totem, therefore, the beneficial or fearsome actions that the cult is intended to provoke or prevent will seem to emanate. So it is to the totem that the rites are specifically addressed. This is why the totem stands foremost in the ranks of sacred things.

Like any other society, the clan can only live in and by means of the individual consciousnesses of which it is made. Thus, insofar as religious force is conceived of as embodied in the totemic emblem, it seems to be external to individuals and endowed with a kind of transcendence; and yet, from another standpoint, and like the clan it symbolizes, it can be made real only within and by them. So in this sense, it is immanent in individual members and they of necessity imagine it to be. They feel within themselves the active presence of the religious force, because it is this force that lifts them up to a higher life. This is how man came to believe that he had within him a principle comparable to the one residing in the totem, and thus how he came to impute sacredness to himself—albeit a sacredness less pronounced than that of the emblem. This happens because the emblem is the preeminent source of religious life. Man participates in it only indirectly, and he is aware of that; he realizes that the force carrying him into the realm of sacred things is not inherent in himself but comes to him from outside.

For another reason, the animals or plants of the totemic species had to have the same quality to an even greater degree. For if the totemic principle is none other than the clan, it is the clan thought of in the physical form depicted by the emblem. Now, this is also the form of the real beings whose name the clan bears. Because of this resemblance, they could not fail to arouse feelings similar to those aroused by the emblem itself. Because this emblem is the object of religious respect, they too should inspire respect of the same kind and appear as sacred. Given forms so perfectly identical, the faithful were bound to impute forces of the same kind to both. This is why it is forbidden to kill or eat the totemic animal and why the flesh is deemed to have positive virtues that the rites put to use. The animal looks like the emblem of the clan—like its own image, in other words. And since it looks more like the emblem than the man does, its place in the hierarchy of sacred things is superior to man's. Clearly there is a close kinship between these two beings; both share the same essence, and both incarnate something of the totemic principle. But because the principle itself is conceived of in animal form, the animal seems to incarnate it more conspicuously than the man does. This is why, if the man respects the animal and treats it as a brother, he gives it at least the respect due an older brother.[32]

But although the totemic principle has its chief residence in a specific animal or plant species, it cannot possibly remain localized there. Sacredness is highly contagious,[33] and it spreads from the totemic being to everything that directly or remotely has to do with it. The religious feelings inspired by the animal passed into the substances it ate, thereby making or remaking its flesh and blood; those feelings passed into the things that resemble it and into the various creatures with which it is in constant contact. Thus, little by little, subtotems attached themselves to totems, and the cosmological systems expressed by the primitive classifications came into being. In the end, the whole world was divided up among the totemic principles of the same tribe.

We now understand the source of the ambiguity that religious forces display when they appear in history—how they come to be natural as well as human and material as well as moral. They are moral powers, since they are made entirely from the impressions that moral collectivity as a moral being makes on other moral beings, the individuals. Such moral powers do not express the manner in which natural things affect our senses but the manner in which the collective consciousness affects individual consciousnesses. Their authority is but one aspect of the moral influence that society exerts on its members. From another standpoint, they are bound to be regarded as closely akin to material things[34] because they are conceived of in tangible forms. Thus they bestride the two worlds. They reside in men but are at the same time the life-principles of things. It is they that enliven and discipline consciences; it is also they that make the plants grow and the animals multiply. Because of its double nature, religion was able to be the womb in which the

---

[32]It can be seen that this brotherhood, far from being the premise of totemism, is its logical consequence. Men did not come to believe they had duties toward the animals of the totemic species because they believed them to be kin; instead, they imagined that kinship in order to explain the nature of the beliefs and rites of which the animals were the object. The animal was considered man's relative because it was a sacred being like man; it was not treated like a sacred being because people saw him as a relative.

[33]See below, Bk. III, chap. 1, §3.

[34]Furthermore, at the basis of this idea is a well-founded and lasting awareness. Modern science also tends more and more to allow that the duality of man and nature does not preclude their unity, and that, while distinct, physical forces and moral ones are closely akin. We certainly have a different idea of this unity and kinship than the primitive's, but beneath the different symbols, the fact affirmed is the same for both.

principal seeds of human civilization have developed. Because religion has borne reality as a whole within itself, the material world as well as the moral world, the forces that move both bodies and minds have been conceived of in religious form. Thus it is that the most disparate techniques and practices—those that ensure the continuity of moral life (law, morals, fine arts) and those that are useful to material life (natural sciences, industrial techniques)—sprang from religion, directly or indirectly.[35]

IV

The first religious ideas have often been attributed to feelings of weakness and subjection or fear and misgiving, which supposedly gripped man when he came into contact with the world. The victim of a sort of nightmare fabricated by none other than himself, man imagines himself surrounded by those same hostile and fearsome powers, and appeasing them is the point of the rites. I have just shown that the first religions have an altogether different origin. The famous formula *Primus in orbe deos fecit timor** is in no way warranted by the facts. The primitive did not see his gods as strangers, enemies, or beings who were fundamentally or necessarily evil-minded or whose favor he had to win at all costs. Quite the contrary, to him the gods are friends, relatives, and natural protectors. Are these not the names he gives to the beings of the totemic species? As he imagines it, the power to which the cult is addressed does not loom far above, crushing him with its superiority; instead, it is very near and bestows upon him useful abilities that he is not born with. Never, perhaps, has divinity been closer to man than at this moment in history, when it is present in the things that inhabit his immediate surroundings and, in part, is immanent in man himself. In sum, joyful confidence, rather than terror or constraint, is at the root of totemism.

If we set aside funeral rites, the melancholy aspect of any religion, the totemic cult is celebrated with songs, dances, and dramatic performances. Cruel expiations are relatively rare in it, as we will see; even the painful and obligatory maimings that attend initiation are not of this character. The jealous and terrible gods do not make their appearance until later in religious

---

*First in the world, fear created the gods.

[35]I say that this derivation is sometimes indirect, because of techniques that, in the great majority of cases, seem to be derived from religion only via magic (see [Henri] Hubert and [Marcel] Mauss, [*Esquisse d'une*] *Théorie générale de la magie, AS*, vol. VII [1904], pp. 144ff; magic forces are, I think, only a special form of religious forces. I will have occasion to return more than once to this point.

evolution. This is so because primitive societies are not Leviathans that over-whelm man with the enormity of their power and subject him to harsh dis-cipline;[36] he surrenders to them spontaneously and without resistance. Since the social soul is at that time made up of only a small number of ideas and feelings, the whole of it is incarnated without difficulty in each individual's consciousness. Each individual carries the whole in himself. It is part of him, so when he yields to its promptings, he does not think he is yielding to co-ercion but instead doing what his own nature tells him to do.[37]

This way of understanding the origin of religious thought escapes the objections that the most respected classical theories are open to.

We have seen that the naturists and the animists purported to construct the notion of sacred beings from the sensations that various physical or bio-logical phenomena evoke in us. I have shown what was impossible and even contradictory about this enterprise. Nothing comes out of nothing. The sen-sations that the physical world evokes in us cannot, by definition, contain anything that goes beyond that world. From something tangible one can only make something tangible; from extended substance one cannot make unextended substance.* So to be in a position to explain how, under those conditions, the notion of the sacred could have been formed, most theorists were forced to assume that man has superimposed an unreal world upon re-ality as reality is available to observation. And this unreal world is constructed entirely with the phantasms that agitate his spirit during dreams, or with the often monstrous derangements that, supposedly, the mythological imagina-tion spawned under the deceptive, if seductive, influence of language. But it then became impossible to understand why humanity should have persisted for centuries in errors that experience would very quickly have exposed as such.

From my standpoint, these difficulties disappear. Religion ceases to be an inexplicable hallucination of some sort and gains a foothold in reality. In-deed, we can say that the faithful are not mistaken when they believe in the existence of a moral power to which they are subject and from which they

---

* *L'étendu* and *l'inétendu*. Literally, "something extended" and "something unextended," which corre-spond to Descartes' opposition between *res extensa* and *res inextensa*, classically the opposition between mind (or soul) and body.

[36]In any case, once he is adult and fully initiated. The rites of initiation, which introduce the young man into social life, in themselves constitute a harsh discipline.

[37]Concerning the specific nature of primitive societies, see [Durkheim,] *Division du travail social*, pp. 123, 149, 173ff.

receive what is best in themselves. That power exists, and it is society. When the Australian is carried above himself, feeling inside a life overflowing with an intensity that surprises him, he is not the dupe of an illusion. That exaltation is real and really is the product of forces outside of and superior to the individual. Of course, he is mistaken to believe that a power in the form of an animal or plant has brought about this increase in vital energy. But his mistake lies in taking literally the symbol that represents this being in the mind, or the outward appearance in which the imagination has dressed it up, not in the fact of its very existence. Behind these forms, be they cruder or more refined, there is a concrete and living reality.

In this way, religion acquires a sense and a reasonableness that the most militant rationalist cannot fail to recognize. The main object of religion is not to give man a representation of the natural universe, for if that had been its essential task, how it could have held on would be incomprehensible. In this respect, it is barely more than a fabric of errors. But religion is first and foremost a system of ideas by means of which individuals imagine the society of which they are members and the obscure yet intimate relations they have with it. Such is its paramount role. And although this representation is symbolic and metaphorical, it is not unfaithful. It fully translates the essence of the relations to be accounted for. It is true with a truth that is eternal that there exists outside us something greater than we and with which we commune.

That is why we can be certain that acts of worship, whatever they may be, are something other than paralyzed force, gesture without motion. By the very act of serving the manifest purpose of strengthening the ties between the faithful and their god—the god being only a figurative representation of the society—they at the same time strengthen the ties between the individual and the society of which he is a member. We can even understand how the fundamental truth that religion thus contained might have been enough to offset the secondary errors that it almost necessarily entailed and therefore how, despite the unpleasant surprises those errors caused, the faithful were prevented from setting religion aside. More often than not, the prescriptions it counseled for man's use upon things must surely have proved ineffective. But these setbacks could not have profound influence, because they did not strike at what is fundamental to religion.[38]

Nonetheless, it will be objected that even in terms of this hypothesis, religion is still the product of a certain delusion. By what other name can one

---

[38]Since I will return to this idea and will argue the case more explicitly in treating the rites (Bk. III), for now I confine myself to this general indication.

call the state in which men find themselves when, as a result of collective effervescence, they believe they have been swept up into a world entirely different from the one they have before their eyes?

It is quite true that religious life cannot attain any degree of intensity and
not carry with it a psychic exaltation that is connected to delirium. It is for
this reason that men of extraordinarily sensitive religious consciousness—
prophets, founders of religions, great saints—often show symptoms of an ex-
citability that is extreme and even pathological: These physiological defects
predisposed them to great religious roles. The ritual use of intoxicating
liquors is to be understood in the same way.[39] The reason is certainly not that
ardent faith is necessarily the fruit of drunkenness and mental disorders.
However, since experience quickly taught people the resemblances between
the mentalities of the delusive and of the seer, they sought to open a path to
the second by producing the first artificially. If, for this reason, it can be said
that religion does not do without a certain delirium, it must be added that a
delirium with the causes I have attributed to it *is well founded*. The images of
which it is made are not pure illusions, and unlike those the naturists and the
animists put at the basis of religion, they correspond to something real.
Doubtless, it is the nature of moral forces expressed merely by images that
they cannot affect the human mind with any forcefulness without putting it
outside itself, and plunging it into a state describable as "ecstatic" (so long as
the word is taken in its etymological sense [ἔκστασις, "stand" plus "out
of"]). But it by no means follows that these forces are imaginary. Quite the
contrary, the mental excitement they bring about attests to their reality. It
provides further evidence that a very intense social life always does a sort of
violence to the individual's body and mind and disrupts their normal functioning. This is why it can last for only a limited time.[40]

What is more, if the name "delirium" is given to any state in which the
mind adds to whatever is immediately given through the senses, projecting its
own impressions onto it, there is perhaps no collective representation that is
not in a sense delusive; religious beliefs are only a special case of a very general law. The whole social world seems populated with forces that in reality
exist only in our minds. We know what the flag is for the soldier, but in itself it is only a bit of cloth. Human blood is only an organic liquid, yet even

[39]On this point see [Thomas] Achelis, *Die Ekstase [in ihrer kulturellen Bedeutung*, Berlin, J. Rade, 1902],
esp. chap. 1.

[40]Cf. [Marcel] Mauss, "Essai sur les variations saisonnières des sociétés eskimos," in *AS*, vol. IX,
[1906], p. 127.

today we cannot see it flow without experiencing an acute emotion that its physicochemical properties cannot explain. From a physical point of view, man is nothing but a system of cells, and from the mental point of view, a system of representations. From both points of view, he differs from the animal only in degree. And yet society conceives him and requires that we conceive him as being endowed with a *sui generis* character that insulates and shields him from all reckless infringement—in other words, that imposes respect. This status, which puts him in a class by himself, seems to us to be one of his distinctive attributes, even though no basis for it can be found in the empirical nature of man. A cancelled postage stamp may be worth a fortune, but obviously that value is in no way entailed by its natural properties. There is a sense, of course, in which our representation of the external world is itself nothing but a fabric of hallucinations. The odors, tastes, and colors that we place in bodies are not there, or at least are not there in the way we perceive them. Nevertheless, our sensations of smell, taste, and sight do correspond to certain objective states of the things represented. After a fashion, they do express the properties of particular materials or movements of the ether that really do have their origin in the bodies we perceive as being fragrant, tasty, or colorful. But collective representations often impute to the things to which they refer properties that do not exist in them in any form or to any degree whatsoever. From the most commonplace object, they can make a sacred and very powerful being.

However, even though purely ideal, the powers thereby conferred on that object behave as if they were real. They determine man's conduct with the same necessity as physical forces. The Arunta who has properly rubbed himself with his churinga feels stronger; he is stronger. If he has eaten the flesh of an animal that is prohibited, even through it is perfectly wholesome, he will feel ill from it and may die. The soldier who falls defending his flag certainly does not believe he has sacrificed himself to a piece of cloth. Such things happen because social thought, with its imperative authority, has a power that individual thought cannot possibly have. By acting on our minds, it can make us see things in the light that suits it; according to circumstances, it adds to or takes away from the real. Hence, there is a realm of nature in which the formula of idealism is almost literally applicable; that is the social realm. There, far more than anywhere else, the idea creates the reality. Even in this case, idealism is probably not true without qualification. We can never escape the duality of our nature and wholly emancipate ourselves from physical necessities. As I will show, to express our own ideas even to ourselves, we need to attach those ideas to material things that symbolize them. But, here, the role of matter is at a minimum. The object that serves as a prop for the idea does not amount to much as compared to the ideal superstructure under which it disappears, and, furthermore, it has nothing to do with that superstructure. From all that has been said, we see what the pseudo-delirium met with at the basis of so many collective representations consists of: It is only a form of this fundamental idealism.[41] So it is not properly called a delusion. The ideas thus objectified are well founded—not, to be sure, in the nature of the tangible things onto which they are grafted but in the nature of society.

We can understand now how it happens that the totemic principle and, more generally, how any religious force comes to be external to the things in which it resides:[42] because the idea of it is not at all constructed from the impressions the thing makes directly on our senses and minds. Religious force is none other than the feeling that the collectivity inspires in its members, but projected outside the minds that experience them, and objectified. To become objectified, it fixes on a thing that thereby becomes sacred; any object can play this role. In principle, none is by nature predestined to it, to the exclusion of others, any more than others are necessarily precluded from it.[43] Where religious force becomes objectified depends entirely upon what circumstances cause the feeling that generates religious ideas to settle here or there, in one place rather than another. The sacredness exhibited by the thing is not implicated in the intrinsic properties of the thing: *It is added to them*. The world of the religious is not a special aspect of empirical nature: *It is superimposed upon nature.*

Finally, this idea of the religious enables us to explain an important principle found at the root of many myths: When a sacred being is subdivided, it remains wholly equal to itself in each of its parts. In other words, from the standpoint of religious thought, the part equals the whole; the part has the same powers and the same efficacy. A fragment of a relic has the same virtues

---

[41]One can see all that is wrong in theories like the geographic materialism of [Friedrich] Ratzel (see especially his "Der Raum im Geist der Völker" in *Politische Geographie*, [Leipzig, R. Oldenbourg, 1897]), which aim to derive all of social life from its material substrate (either economic or territorial). Their mistake is comparable to Maudsley's in individual psychology. Just as Maudsley reduced the psychic life of the individual to a mere epiphenomenon of its physiological base, they want to reduce all of the psychic life of the collectivity to its physical base. This is to forget that ideas are realities—forces—and that collective representations are forces even more dynamic and powerful than individual representations. On this point, see [Durkheim], "Représentations," *RMM*, 1898.

[42]See pp. 191, 196–197.

[43]Even excrement has a religious quality. See [Konrad Theodor] Preuss, "Der Ursprung der Religion und Kunst," esp. chap. 2, "Der Zauber der Defäkation, *Globus*, vol. LXXXVI [1904], pp. 325ff.

as the whole relic. The smallest drop of blood contains the same active principle as all the blood. As we will see, the soul can be broken up into almost as many parts as there are organs or tissues in the body; each of these partial souls is equivalent to the entire soul. This conception would be inexplicable if sacredness depended on the constitutive properties of the thing serving as its substrate, for sacredness would have to change with that thing, increasing and decreasing with it. But if the virtues the thing is deemed to have are not intrinsic to it, if they come to it from certain feelings that it calls to mind and symbolizes (even though such feelings originate outside it), it can play an evocative role whether it is whole or not, since in that role it does not need specific dimensions. Since the part evokes the whole, it also evokes the same feelings as the whole. A mere scrap of the flag represents the country as much as the flag itself; moreover, it is sacred in the same right and to the same degree.[44]

V

This theory of totemism has enabled us to explain the most characteristic beliefs of the religion, but it rests on a fact that is not yet explained. Given the idea of the totem, the emblem of the clan, all the rest follows, but we must still find out how that idea was formed. The question is twofold and can be broken down in this way: (1) What caused the clan to choose an emblem? (2) Why were those emblems taken from the world of animals and plants, but especially from the world of animals?

That an emblem can be useful as a rallying point for any sort of group requires no argument. By expressing the social unit tangibly, it makes the unit itself more tangible to all. And for that reason, the use of emblematic symbols must have spread quickly, as soon as the idea was born. Furthermore, this idea must have arisen spontaneously from the conditions of life in common, for the emblem is not only a convenient method of clarifying the awareness the society has of itself: It serves to create—and is a constitutive element of—that awareness.

By themselves, individual consciousnesses are actually closed to one another, and they can communicate only by means of signs in which their inner states come to express themselves. For the communication that is opening up between them to end in a communion—that is, in a fusion of all

---

[44]This principle has passed from religion into magic. It is the alchemists' *Totum ex parte* [the whole from the part. Trans.].

the individual feelings into a common one—the signs that express those feelings must come together in one single resultant.* The appearance of this resultant notifies individuals that they are in unison and brings home to them their moral unity. It is by shouting the same cry, saying the same words, and performing the same action in regard to the same object that they arrive at and experience agreement. Granted, individual representations also bring about repercussions in the body that are not unimportant; still, these effects can be treated as analytically distinct from physical repercussions that come with or after them but that are not their basis.

Collective representations are quite another matter. They presuppose that consciousnesses are acting and reacting on each other; they result from actions and reactions that are possible only with the help of tangible intermediaries. Thus the function of the intermediaries is not merely to reveal the mental state associated with them; they also contribute to its making. The individual minds can meet and commune only if they come outside themselves, but they do this only by means of movement. It is the homogeneity of these movements that makes the group aware of itself and that, in consequence, makes it be. Once this homogeneity has been established and these movements have taken a definite form and been stereotyped, they serve to symbolize the corresponding representations. But these movements symbolize those representations only because they have helped to form them.

Without symbols, moreover, social feelings could have only an unstable existence. Those feelings are very strong so long as men are assembled, mutually influencing one another, but when the gathering is over, they survive only in the form of memories that gradually dim and fade away if left to themselves. Since the group is no longer present and active, the individual temperaments quickly take over again. Wild passions that could unleash themselves in the midst of a crowd cool and die down once the crowd has dispersed, and individuals wonder with amazement how they could let themselves be carried so far out of character. But if the movements by which these feelings have been expressed eventually become inscribed on things that are durable, then they too become durable. These things keep bringing the feelings to individual minds and keep them perpetually aroused, just as

---

*Since Durkheim said "resultant" (*résultante*) and not "result" (*résultat*), he may have had in mind the mathematical notion of a vector sum of forces. A resultant may be defined as the single force, measured as velocity or acceleration, to which several forces taken together are equivalent. The term also has an analogous literary sense.

would happen if the cause that first called them forth was still acting. Thus, while emblematizing is necessary if society is to become conscious of itself, so is it no less indispensable in perpetuating that consciousness.

Hence, we must guard against seeing those symbols as mere artifices—a variety of labels placed on ready-made representations to make them easier to handle. They are integral to those representations. The fact that collective feelings find themselves joined in this way to things that are alien to them is not purely conventional. It tangibly portrays a real feature of social phenomena: their transcendence of individual consciousnesses. We know, in fact, that social phenomena are born not in the individual but in the group. No matter what part we may play in their genesis, each of us receives them from without.[45] Thus, when we imagine them as emanating from a material object, we are not entirely wrong about their nature. Although they certainly do not come from the specific thing to which we attribute them, still it is true that they originate outside us. And although the moral force that sustains the worshipper does not come from the idol he worships or the emblem he venerates, still it is external to him; and he feels this. The objectivity of the symbol is but an expression of that externality.

Thus, in all its aspects and at every moment of its history, social life is only possible thanks to a vast symbolism. The physical emblems and figurative representations with which I have been especially concerned in the present study are one form of it, but there are a good many others. Collective feelings can just as well be incarnated in persons as in formulas. Some formulas are flags; some real or mythic personages are symbols. But there is one sort of emblem that must have appeared very quickly, quite apart from any reflection or calculation, and it is this one that we have seen playing a considerable role in totemism: tattooing. Well-known facts demonstrate, in fact, that under certain conditions, it is produced by a sort of automatic action. When men of an inferior culture share in a common life, they are often led, almost instinctively, to paint themselves or to imprint images on their bodies that remind them of their common life. According to a text by Procope, the first Christians had the name of Christ or the sign of the cross imprinted on their skin.[46] For a long time, groups of pilgrims who went to Palestine also had themselves tattooed on their arms or wrists with designs representing the

---

[45]On this point, see [Durkheim], *Règles de la méthode sociologique*, pp. 5ff.

[46]Procopius of Gaza, *Commentarii in Isaiam*, p. 496. [It may be that Durkheim drew this fifth-century reference from *Procopii Gazaei . . . Opera omnia in unum corpus adunata*, Petit Montrouge, J. P. Migne, 1861. Trans.]

cross or the monogram of Christ.[47] The same custom is reported for pilgrimages to certain holy places in Italy.[48] Lombroso reported a curious example of spontaneous tattooing. When twenty young men from an Italian high school were about to separate, they had themselves decorated with tattoos that in various ways recorded the years they had just spent together.[49] The same practice has often been observed among soldiers of the same camp, sailors on the same ship, and prisoners in the same house of detention.[50] In fact, it is understandable, especially where technology is still undeveloped, that tattooing is the most direct and expressive means by which the communion of minds can be affirmed. The best way of testifying to oneself and others that one is part of the same group is to place the same distinctive mark on the body. Proof that such is indeed the *raison d'être* of the totemic image is that, as I have shown, it does not try to copy the appearance of the thing it is considered to represent. It is made of lines and points that are given an entirely conventional meaning.[51] The purpose of the image is not to represent or evoke a particular object but to testify that a certain number of individuals share the same moral life.

The clan is a society that is less able than any other to do without an emblem and a symbol, for there are few societies so lacking in cohesion. The clan cannot be defined by its leader, for although not absent altogether, central authority in it is at best shifting and unstable.[52] Nor can it be any better defined by the territory it occupies for, being nomadic,[53] the clan's population is not closely tied to any definite locality. Furthermore, given the rule of exogamy, the husband and wife must be of different totems. Thus, where the totem is transmitted in the maternal line—and today this descent system is

---

[47]See Thévenot, [*Suite de*] *voyage* [*de M. de Thévenot*] *au Levant*, Paris, 1689, p. 638. This phenomenon was observed again in 1862: cf. Berchon, "Histoire médicale du tatouage," *Archives de Médicine Navale*, vol. XI (1869), p. 377 n.

[48][Alexandre] Lacassagne, *Les Tatouages: [Étude anthropologique et médico légale*, Paris, Baillière, 1881], p. 10.

[49][Césare] Lombroso, *L'Homme criminel*, vol. I [Paris, Alcan, 1885], p. 292.

[50]Ibid., vol. I, pp. 268, 285, 291–292; Lacassagne, *Tatouages*, p. 97.

[51]See above, p. 126.

[52]On the authority of the chiefs, see Spencer and Gillen, *Native Tribes*, p. 10; Spencer and Gillen, *Northern Tribes*, p. 25; Howitt, *Native Tribes*, pp. 295ff.

[53]At least in Australia. In America, the population is most often sedentary, but the clan in America is a relatively advanced form of organization.

still the most widespread[54]—the children are of a different clan from their father, even when living with him. For all these reasons, we find all sorts of different clans represented within the same family and even within the same locality. The unity of the group can be felt only because of the collective name borne by all the members and because of the equally collective emblem representing the thing designated by that name. A clan is essentially a company of individuals who have the same name and rally around the same symbol. Take away the name and the symbol that gives it tangible form, and the clan can no longer even be imagined. Since the clan was possible only on condition of being imaginable, both the institution of the emblem and its place in the group's life are thus explained.

Still, we must find out why these names and emblems were taken almost exclusively from the animal and plant kingdoms, though mainly from the first.

It seems plausible that the emblem has played a more important role than the name. In any event, today the written sign still holds a more central place in the life of the clan than the spoken one. Now, the emblematic image called for a subject representable by a design. And besides, the things had to be from among those with which the men of the clan were most closely and habitually in contact. Animals met this condition best. For these hunting and fishing populations, animals were in fact the essential element of the economic environment. In this respect, plants took second place, for they are of only secondary importance as food so long as they are not cultivated. Besides, animals have a closer relationship to man's life than do plants, if only because of the kindred nature that joins these two creatures to one another. By contrast, the sun, moon, and stars were too far away and seemed to belong to a different world.[55] Further, since the constellations were not differentiated and classified, the starry sky did not present objects different enough from one another to be serviceable in designating all the clans and subclans of a tribe. On the other hand, the variety of the flora, and especially the fauna,

[54]To be convinced of this, it is enough to look at the map prepared by [Northcote Whitridge] Thomas in *Kinship* [*Organization and Group*] *Marriage in Australia* [Cambridge, Cambridge University Press, 1906], p. 40. To evaluate this map properly, we must take into account the fact that, for reasons unknown, the author has extended the system of totemic descent through the paternal line as far as the west coast of Australia, even though we have virtually no information about the tribes of this region (and which, besides, is mainly desert).

[55]As I will show in the next chapter, the stars are often considered, even by the Australians, as countries of souls or mythic personages—that is, they seem to constitute a world very different from that of the living.

was almost inexhaustible. For these reasons, the heavenly bodies were unsuited to the role of totems, notwithstanding their brilliance and the powerful impression they make upon the senses. Animals and plants were perfect for it.

An observation by Strehlow permits us to specify the manner in which these emblems were probably chosen. He reports having noticed that the totemic centers are most often situated near a mountain, spring, or gorge where the animals that serve as the group's totem are found in abundance, and he cites various examples.[56] These totemic centers are certainly the consecrated places where the clan held its meetings. It therefore seems likely that each group took as its emblem the animal or plant that was the most plentiful in the neighborhood of the place where it usually assembled.[57]

VI

This theory of totemism will provide us the key to a curious trait of the human mind that, although more pronounced long ago than now, has not disappeared and in any case has played a significant role in the history of thought. This will be yet another opportunity to observe that logical evolution is closely interconnected with religious evolution and, like religious evolution, depends upon social conditions.[58]

If there is a truth that today seems to us completely self-evident, it is this: Beings that differ not only in outward appearance but also in their most fundamental properties—such as minerals, plants, animals, and men—cannot be regarded as equivalent and interchangeable. Long-established practice, which scientific culture has rooted even more deeply in our minds, taught us to set up barriers between realms of nature, barriers whose existence even trans-

---

[56][Carl Strehlow, *Die Aranda- und Loritja-Stämme in Zentral Australien*], vol. 1 [Frankfurt, J. Baer, 1907], p. 4. Cf. along the same lines Schulze, "Aborigines of the . . . Finke River," p. 243.

[57]Of course, as I have already had occasion to show (see p. 156, above), this choice is not made without a more or less well-thought-out agreement among the different groups, since each of them had to adopt a different emblem from that of its neighbors.

[58]The turn of mind treated in this paragraph is identical to the one that [Lucien] Lévy-Bruhl calls the law of participation (*Les Fonctions mentales dans les sociétés inférieures* [Paris, Alcan, 1910], pp. 76ff.). These pages were already written when that work appeared; I publish them in their original form without any change but confine myself to adding certain explanations that indicate where I differ with Lévy-Bruhl in the evaluation of the evidence.

formism* does not deny. For although transformism grants that life could have been born from nonliving matter, and men from animals, it recognizes nonetheless that, once formed, living beings are different from minerals, and men from animals. Within each realm, the same barriers separate different classes. We cannot imagine how one mineral could have the distinctive characteristics of another mineral—or one animal species, those of another species. But these distinctions, which seem to us so natural, are not at all primitive. Originally, all the realms are merged. The rocks have a sex; they have the ability to procreate; the sun, moon, and stars are men and women, who feel and express human feelings, while humans are pictured as animals or plants. This merging is found again and again at the basis of all mythologies. From it arises the ambiguous nature of the beings that figure in myths. Those beings cannot be placed in any definite genus because they simultaneously participate in the most dissimilar ones. Moreover, it is conceded without difficulty that they can move from one into another, and it is through transmutations of this kind that men long believed they could explain the origins of things.

That the anthropomorphic instinct, with which the animists have endowed the primitive, cannot account for this turn of mind is shown by the nature of the errors that are typical of it. These errors arise not from man's having wildly expanded the human realm to the point of encompassing all the others but from his having merged the most disparate realms with one another. He has no more imagined the world in his own image than he has imagined himself in the image of the world. He has done both at once. In the way he thought about things, he of course included human elements, but in the way he thought about himself, he included elements that came to him from things.

However there was nothing in experience that could have suggested these mergers and mixtures to him. From the standpoint of observation

---

*The 1992 *Petit Robert* dictionary indicates a "scientific" term, *transformisme*, and a "philosophical" term, *evolutionnisme*, dating them, respectively, from 1867 and 1878. Both terms come after Charles Darwin's *The Origin of Species* (1859). According to André Lalande (*Vocabulaire technique et critique de la philosophie*, Paris, Alcan, 1902, p. 909), the difference between the two terms is as follows. In one sense, *transformisme* is a more general term in biology than *évolutionnisme*, because it also includes such notions as Lamarck's inheritance of acquired characteristics. In another sense, it is more specific than evolutionism because it is limited to biology, whereas evolutionism became a far more general philosophical notion considered to be applicable to all phenomena. It is clear from the context of the book as a whole that, in these terms, Durkheim had *évolutionnisme* in mind. But I have preserved his "transformism" so as not to obliterate the memory of two overlapping terms that had somewhat different, and no doubt contested, meaning in his day.

through the senses, everything is disparate and discontinuous. Nowhere in reality do we observe beings that merge their natures and change into one another. An exceptionally powerful cause would have had to intervene and so transfigure the real as to make it appear in a form not its own.

It is religion that carried out this transformation; it is religious beliefs that replaced the world as the senses perceive it with a different one. This, the case of totemism shows very well. What is fundamental to totemism is that the people of the clan, and the various beings whose form the totemic emblem represents, are held to be made of the same essence. Once that belief was accepted, the disparate realms were bridged. Man was conceived of as a kind of animal or plant, and the plants and animals as man's kin—or, rather, all these beings, so different according to the senses, were conceived of as participating in the same nature. Hence, the origin of that remarkable capacity to confound what seems to us so obviously distinct: The first forces with which the human intellect populated the universe were elaborated through religion. Since these forces were made of elements taken from different kingdoms, they became the principle common to the most disparate things, which were thereby endowed with one and the same essence.

We know furthermore that these religious ideas are the outcome of definite social causes. Because the clan cannot exist without a name and an emblem, and because that emblem is everywhere before the eyes of individuals, the feelings that society arouses in its members are directed toward the emblem and toward the objects whose image it is. In this way, men had no choice but to conceive the collective force, whose workings they felt, in the form of the thing that served as the flag of the group. Therefore, the most disparate realms found themselves merged in the idea of this force. In one sense, the force was fundamentally human, since it was made of human ideas and feelings; at the same time, it could not but appear as closely akin to the animate or inanimate being that gave it outward form. The cause we are capturing at work is not exclusive to totemism; there is no society in which it is not at work. Nowhere can a collective feeling become consciousness of itself without fixing upon a tangible object;[59] but by that very fact, it participates in the nature of that object, and vice versa. Thus, it is social requirements that have fused together ideas that at first glance seem distinct, and through the great mental effervescence that it brings about, social life has promoted that fusion.[60] This is further evidence that logical understanding is a function of

---

[59]See above, p. 231.

[60]Another cause accounts for a large part of this fusion: the extreme contagiousness of religious forces. They invade every object in their reach, whatever it may be. Hence the same religious force can animate

society, since logical understanding adopts the conventions and viewpoints that society imprints upon it.

This logic is unsettling, to be sure. Still, we must be careful not to depreciate it: However crude it may seem to us, it was a momentous contribution to the intellectual development of humanity. For through that logic, a first explanation of the world became possible. Of course, the mental habits it implies prevented man from seeing reality as his senses show it to him; but as the senses show it to him, reality has the grave disadvantage of being resistant to all explanation. For to explain is to connect things to other things; it is to establish relationships between things that make them appear to us as functions of one another and as vibrating sympathetically in accordance with an internal law that is rooted in their nature. Sense perception, which sees only from the outside, could not possibly cause us to discover such relationships and internal ties; only the intellect can create the notion of them. When I learn that A regularly precedes B, my knowledge is enriched with a new piece of knowledge, but my intelligence is in no way satisfied by an observation that does not carry a reason with it. I begin to *understand* only if it is possible for me to conceive of B in some way that makes it appear to me as not foreign to A but as united with A in some relation of kinship. The great service that religions have rendered to thought is to have constructed a first representation of what the relations of kinship between things might be. Given the conditions in which it was tried, that enterprise could obviously lead only to makeshift results. But, then, are the results of any such enterprise ever definitive, and must it not be taken up again and again? Furthermore, it was less important to succeed than to dare. What was essential was not to let the mind be dominated by what appears to the senses, but instead to teach the mind to dominate it and to join together what the senses put asunder. As soon as man became aware that internal connections exist between things, science and philosophy became possible. Religion made a way for them. It is because religion is a social thing that it could play this role. To make men take control of sense impressions and replace them with a new way of imagining the real, a new kind of thought had to be created: collective thought. If collective thought alone had the power to achieve this, here is the reason: Creating a whole world of ideals, through which the world of sensed realities seemed transfigured, would require a hyperexcitation of intellectual forces that is possible only in and through society.

---

the most dissimilar things, which by that very fact find themselves closely connected and classified in the same genus. I will return to this contagion below, while showing that it is related to the social origins of the idea of the sacred (Bk. III, chap. 1, end).

Hence, that mentality is far from being unrelated to our own. Our own logic was born in that logic. The explanations of contemporary science are more certain of being objective, because they are more systematic and based on more rigorously controlled observations, but they are not different in nature from those that satisfy primitive thought. Today as in the past, to explain is to show how a thing participates in one or several other things. It has been said that the participations whose existence mythologies presuppose violate the principle of contradiction and, on those grounds, are antithetical to the participations that scientific explanations involve.[61] Is not postulating that a man is a kangaroo and the sun a bird identifying one thing with another? We do not think any differently when we say of heat that it is a movement, and of light that it is a vibration of the ether, and so on. Every time we join heterogeneous terms by an internal tie, we of necessity identify contraries. The terms we join in this way are not, of course, the ones the Australian joins. We choose them according to different criteria and for different reasons, but the procedure by which the mind places them into relationship is not essentially different.

Granted, if primitive thought had the sort of universal and abiding indifference to contradiction that has been ascribed to it,[62] on this point it would contrast—and contrast very markedly—with modern thought, which is always careful to remain internally consistent. But I do not believe it possible to characterize the mentality of the lower societies by a sort of one-sided and exclusive inclination not to make distinctions. If the primitive puts together things that we keep separate, inversely, he separates other things that we put together, and he actually conceives of those distinctions as abrupt and pronounced oppositions. Between two beings that are classified in two different phratries, there is not only separation but also antagonism.[63] For this reason, the same Australian who puts the sun and the white cockatoo together opposes the black cockatoo to the white as to its opposite. The two seem to him to belong to two separate genera with nothing in common. There is an even more pronounced opposition between sacred and profane things. They repel and contradict one another so forcefully that the mind refuses to think of them at the same time. They expel one another from consciousness.

Hence, there is no gulf between the logic of religious thought and the logic of scientific thought. Both are made up of the same essential elements,

---

[61]Lévy-Bruhl, *Les Fonctions mentales,* pp. 77ff.

[62]Ibid., p. 79.

[63]See above, p. 146.

although these elements are unequally and differently developed. What appears above all to typify the logic of religious thought is a natural taste as much for unrestrained assimilations as for clashing contrasts. It is given to excess in both directions. When it brings things together, it mixes them together; when it distinguishes between things, it makes them opposites. It knows neither moderation nor nuance but seeks the extremes. As a result, it employs logical mechanisms with a certain gaucheness, but none of them are unknown to it.

CHAPTER EIGHT

THE NOTION OF SOUL*

I n the preceding chapters, we have studied the fundamental principles of totemic religion. We have found that the notions of soul, spirit, and mythic personage are absent from it. Yet although the notion of spiritual beings is not fundamental to totemism or, consequently, to religion in general, there is no religion from which it is absent—hence the importance of trying to discover how it came to be formed. To be sure that notion is in fact the result of a secondary formation, I must show how it is derived from the more fundamental ideas I have previously set forth and explained.

Of all the spirit beings, there is one that must claim our attention first and foremost, since it is the prototype from which the others have been built, and that is the soul.

I

Just as there is no known society without religion, there is no religion, however crudely organized, in which we do not find a system of collective representations dealing with soul—its origin and its destiny. So far as can be judged from the ethnographic data, the idea of soul seems to be contemporaneous with humanity. Indeed, it seems to have had all its basic features from the beginning, and to such an extent that the work of the more advanced religions and philosophy has only been to refine it rather than to add anything truly fundamental. All the Australian societies allow that every human body harbors an interior being, a life-principle that animates it; and that principle is the soul. True, women are sometimes the exception to that general rule:

---

*The French reads *la notion d'âme* but could have read *"la notion de l'âme."* Durkheim treats "soul" as both a thing and a generic substance that becomes thinglike when it becomes part of an individual. Cf. in this chapter, "the idea of mana" and "the idea of personality."

There are tribes in which they are considered to have no such thing as a soul.[1] If Dawson is to be believed on this subject, the same is true of young children in the tribes he observed.[2] But such cases are unusual, and probably late developments.[3] In fact, the latter case seems suspect and could well be the result of a misinterpretation of the facts.[4]

To determine what idea the Australian has of the soul is not easy, since his idea is vague and variable. But this should by no means surprise us. If we asked our own contemporaries how they imagine the soul, even those who believe the most firmly in its existence, the responses we would get would not have much greater coherence and precision. This is because the idea in question is very complex, containing a multitude of poorly analyzed impressions elaborated over centuries without men's having been fully conscious of that elaboration. Here, nonetheless, are the most basic, if often contradictory, features by which it is defined.

In some cases, we are told that the soul has the external appearance of the body.[5] In others, it is imagined as being the size of a grain of sand, so small that it can pass through the narrowest crevices and the tiniest cracks.[6] We will see that it is also thought of in the form of animals. In other words, its form

---

[1] This is the case of the Gnanji; see [Sir Baldwin] Spencer and [Francis James] Gillen, *Northern Tribes [of Central Australia*, London, Macmillan, 1904], pp. 170, 546; cf. a similar case, in [Robert] Brough Smyth [*The Aborigines of Victoria*, Melbourne, J. Ferres, 1878], vol. II, p. 269.

[2] [James] Dawson, *Australian Aborigines* [Melbourne, G. Robertson, 1881], p. 51.

[3] Among the Gnanji, there surely was a time when women had souls, for today a large number of women's souls still exist, but they never reincarnate themselves; and since, among this people, the soul that animates a newborn is an old one incarnated, it follows from the fact that the souls of women are not reincarnated that women cannot have souls. Incidentally, we can explain that absence of reincarnation. Descent among the Gnanji, which was once matrilineal, now follows the paternal line. The mother does not transmit her totem to her child. Thus the woman never has descendants who perpetuate her; she is *finis familiae suae* [the end of her family. Trans]. To explain that situation, there are only two possible hypotheses: either women do not have souls, or the souls of women are destroyed after death. The Gnanji have adopted the first of those two explanations. Certain peoples of Queensland have preferred the second (see [Walter Edmund] Roth, [*Superstition*] *Magic and Medicine* in *North Queensland Ethnography*, Bulletin no. 5, §68 [Brisbane, G. A. Vaughn, 1903]).

[4] "Children below four or five years of age have neither soul nor future life," says Dawson. But what Dawson translates in this way is simply the absence of funeral rites for very young children. We will see the true meaning of this later on.

[5] [James] Dawson, "Australian Aborigines," p. 51; [Langloh] Parker, [Catherine Sommerville Field Parker], *The Euahlayi* [*Tribe*] [London, A. Constable, 1905], p. 35; [Richard] Eylmann, [*Die*] *Eingeborenen* [*der Kolonie Sud Australien*, Berlin, D. Reumer, 1908], p. 188.

[6] [Spencer and Gillen], *Northern Tribes,* p. 542; Schürmann, "The Aboriginal Tribes of Port Lincoln," in [James Dominick] Woods [*The Native Tribes of South Australia* Adelaide, E. S. Wigg, 1879], p. 235.

is essentially unstable and indefinite;[7] it changes from moment to moment to suit circumstances and according to the demands of myth and rite. The substance of which it is made is no less undefinable. Since it has form, however vague, it is not immaterial. And in fact, during this life, it even has physical needs: It eats and, inversely, can be eaten. Sometimes it leaves the body and feeds on foreign souls during its travels.[8] Once it has become completely emancipated from the body, it is presumed to lead a life wholly similar to the one it led on this earth: It drinks, eats, hunts, and so forth.[9] When it flits about in tree branches, it makes rustlings and cracklings that even profane ears can hear.[10] At the same time, it is held to be invisible to the ordinary person.[11] To be sure, magicians or old men possess the faculty of seeing souls, but this is because they see things that escape our senses, by virtue of special powers they owe to either age or special knowledge. When it comes to ordinary individuals, however, that privilege is enjoyed at only one time in their lives: when they are on the eve of premature death. That near-miraculous vision is therefore regarded as a sinister portent. Now, invisibility is widely regarded as one among the signs of spiritualness.* Thus, the soul is conceived of as being immaterial, to a certain extent, since it does not affect the senses in the way bodies do; it has no bones, say the tribes of the Tully River.[12] To reconcile all these contradictory traits, it is imagined as being made of an infinitely more rarified and subtle material, as something ethereal,[13] comparable to shadow or wind.[14]

---

*Durkheim says *de la spiritualité*, but the English "spirituality" would mislead.

[7]This is the phrase Dawson uses.

[8]Strehlow [*Die Aranda- und Loritja-Stämme in Zentral-Australien*], vol. I [Frankfurt, J. Baer, 1907], p. 15 n. 1; [Reverend Louis] Schulze, "Aborigines of the Upper Middle Finke River," *RSSA*, vol. XVI [1891], p. 246. This is the theme of the vampire myth.

[9][Strehlow], *Aranda*, vol. I, p. 15; Schulze, "Aborigines," p. 244; Dawson, "Australian Aborigines," p. 51. True, souls are sometimes said to have nothing corporeal about them. According to certain accounts collected by Eylmann (p. 188), they are said to be *ohne Fleisch und Blut* [without flesh and blood. Trans.]. But these radical negatives leave me skeptical. The fact that offerings are not made to the souls of the dead in no way implies, as Roth thinks (*Superstition, Magic, etc.*, §65), that they do not eat.

[10]Roth, *Superstition, Magic*, §65; *Northern Tribes*, p. 500. Hence the soul sometimes emits odors (Roth, §68).

[11]Roth, *Superstition, Magic*, §67; Dawson, p. 51.

[12]Roth, *Superstition, Magic*, §65.

[13]Schürmann, "Aborigines," p. 235.

[14]Parker, *The Euahlayi*, pp. 29, 35; Roth, *Superstition, Magic*, §65, 67, 68.

The soul is distinct from and independent of the body because from the beginning of life, it can leave the body for short periods. It leaves the body during sleep, during a faint, and so forth.[15] Indeed, it can remain absent for a time without death's resulting. Even so, life is lessened during those absences, and in fact ends if the soul does not return home.[16] But it is above all at death that this distinctness and independence are most manifest. Whereas the body is no more, with no visible traces remaining, the soul continues to live, having an autonomous existence in a world apart.

But as real as this duality may be, it is in no way absolute. It would be a misunderstanding to conceive the body as a kind of lodging in which the soul resides but with which it has only external relations. Quite the contrary, it is bound to the body with the closest of ties; indeed, it can be separated from the body only with difficulty, and incompletely. We have already seen that it can take at least its external appearance from the body. Therefore, whatever harms the one harms the other; every wound of the body is propagated all the way to the soul.[17] The soul is so intimately connected with the life of the body that it matures and perishes with it. This is why the man who has reached a certain age enjoys privileges denied to young men. As he has advanced in years, the religious principle that is in him has gained capacity and power. But when there is actual senility, when the old man has become unable to play a useful role in the great religious ceremonies or in the vital interests of the tribe that are at stake, he is no longer shown respect. The feebleness of his body is considered to have spread to the soul. No longer having the same powers, the subject is no longer entitled to the same status.[18]

There is not only close interdependence between the soul and the body but also partial assimilation. Just as there is something of the body in the soul, since it sometimes reproduces the body's form, so there is something of the soul in the body. Certain regions and products of the body are thought to have a special affinity with the soul: the heart, the breath, the placenta,[19] the

---

[15]Roth, *Superstition, Magic*, §65; Strehlow, *Aranda*, vol. I, p. 15.

[16]Strehlow, *Aranda*, vol. I, p. 14 n. 1.

[17][James George] Frazer, "On Certain Burial Customs, as Illustrative of the Primitive Theory of the Soul," in *JAI*, vol. XV [1886], p. 66.

[18]This is the case among the Kaitish and the Unmatjera. See Spencer and Gillen, *Northern Tribes*, p. 506, and *Native Tribes*, p. 512.

[19]Roth, *Superstition, Magic*, §65–68.

blood,[20] the shadow,[21] the liver, the fat of the liver, and the kidneys,[22] and so forth. These various physical substrates are not mere lodgings for the soul; they are the soul itself viewed from outside. When the blood flows, the soul escapes with it. The soul is not in the breath; it is the breath. It is inseparable from the body part in which it resides—hence the idea that man has multiple souls. Diffused throughout the body, the soul became differentiated and fragmented. In a sense, each organ has individualized the bit of soul it contains, and each bit of soul has thereby become a distinct entity. That of the heart could not be identical with that of the breath, the shadow, or the placenta. All are related, yet they must be distinguished—and they have different names.[23]

Moreover, while the soul is most likely to be localized in certain parts of the body, it is not absent from the others. To varying degrees, it is diffused throughout the whole body. Funeral rites show this quite well. Once the last breath has been exhaled and the soul presumed to have departed, it would seem that the soul should make immediate use of the freedom it has just regained to move at will and return as quickly as possible to its true homeland, which is elsewhere. And yet it stays near the corpse, its bond with the corpse having stretched but not broken. A whole set of rites is necessary to make it go away once and for all. By gestures and expressive movements, it is invited to depart.[24] A way is opened for it, and exits are prepared so that it can fly away the more easily.[25] This is done because it has not come out of the body in one piece; it pervaded the body too completely to be able to leave it all at once. Here originates the common rite of funeral anthropophagy: The flesh of the deceased is eaten because a sacred principle is held to reside in it, that

---

[20]Ibid., §68. This passage says that when there is fainting from loss of blood, it is because the soul has left. Cf. Parker, *The Euahlayi Tribe,* p. 38.

[21]Parker, *The Euahlayi Tribe,* pp. 29, 35; Roth, *Superstition, Magic,* §65.

[22]Strehlow, *Aranda,* vol. I, pp. 12, 14. These several passages speak of evil spirits that kill small children and eat their souls, livers, and liver fat, or else their souls, livers, and kidneys. The fact that the soul is thereby placed on the same footing as various tissues and viscera, constituting a food of the same sort, clearly shows its close relationship with them. Cf. Schulze, p. 246.

[23]For example, among the people of the Pennefather River (Roth, *Superstition, Magic,* §68), there is one name for the soul that resides in the heart *(ngai)*, another for the one that resides in the placenta *(choi)*, a third for the one that mingles with the breath *(wanji)*. Among the Euahlayi, there are three or even four souls (Parker, *The Euahlayi Tribe,* p. 35).

[24]See the description of the Urpmilchima rite, among the Arunta (Spencer and Gillen, *Native Tribes,* pp. 503ff.).

[25]Ibid., pp. 497, 508.

sacred principle being none other than the soul.[26] The flesh is melted in order to uproot the soul for good, by subjecting it to heat, either of the sun[27] or of man-made fire.[28] The soul flows out with the liquids that result. But since the dried bones retain some part of it still, they are used as sacred objects or as instruments of magic.[29] If the principle they enclose is to be freed completely, the bones are broken.[30]

A moment comes when the irrevocable separation has been made, and the freed soul takes flight. The soul is by nature so intimately connected with the body that this tearing away does not happen without a profound transformation of its condition. Consequently, it then takes another name.[31] Although it retains all the distinctive traits of the individual it animated—his humor, his good and bad qualities[32]—still it has become a new being. From that moment, its new existence begins.

The soul goes to the land of souls. This land is conceived differently from tribe to tribe, and sometimes different ideas are found coexisting in the same society. For some, that land is underground, each totem having its own. It is the place where the first ancestors, the founders of the clan, at a certain moment vanished deep into the earth and where they went to live after death. Thus, in the subterranean world, there is a geographic distribution of the dead corresponding to that of the living. There shines a perpetual sun; there flow rivers that never run dry. Such is the conception that Spencer and Gillen attribute to the tribes of the center, Arunta,[33] Warramunga,[34] and others. It is shared by the Wotjobaluk.[35] Elsewhere, all the dead, whatever their totems, are thought to live together in the same place, which is rather

[26]Spencer and Gillen, *Northern Tribes,* pp. 547, 548.

[27]Ibid., pp. 506, 527ff.

[28]Meyer, "The Encounter Bay Tribe," in Woods, p. 198.

[29]Spencer and Gillen, *Northern Tribes,* pp. 551, 463; *Native Tribes,* p. 553.

[30]Spencer and Gillen, *Northern Tribes,* p. 540.

[31]For example, among the Arunta and the Loritja (Strehlow, *Aranda,* vol. I, p. 15 n. 2; vol. II, p. 77). During life, the soul is called *guruna* and after death *ltana.* The *Itana* of Strehlow is identical to the *ulthana* of Spencer and Gillen (*Native Tribes,* pp. 514ff.). The same is true among the Bloomfield River people (Roth, *Superstition, Magic,* §66).

[32]Eylmann, "Die Eingeborenen," p. 188.

[33]Spencer and Gillen, *Native Tribes,* pp. 524, 491, 496.

[34]Spencer and Gillen, *Northern Tribes,* pp. 542, 508.

[35][Robert Hamilton] Mathews, "Ethnological Notes on the Aboriginal Tribes of N.S. Wales and Victoria," in *RSNSW,* vol. XXXVIII, 1904, p. 287.

vaguely localized: beyond the sea, on an island,[36] or on the shores of a lake.[37] Finally, the dead are sometimes thought to go into the sky, beyond the clouds. "There," says Dawson, "is found a magnificent country, abounding in kangaroos and in game of every kind, and where a joyful life is led. The souls meet there and recognize one another."[38] Certain features included in this tableau were probably taken from the paradise of Christian missionaries.[39] However the idea that the souls, or at least certain souls, go to the sky after death would seem to be indigenous, for it recurs in other parts of the continent.[40]

In general, all the souls have the same fate and lead the same life. However, sometimes a different treatment is applied to them according to their conduct on earth, and one can see making its appearance something that approximates a first sketch of those distinct and even opposite compartments between which the world of the beyond will later be divided. The souls of those who excelled in life as hunters, fighters, dancers, and so forth do not melt into the crowd of the others. A special place is assigned to them,[41] sometimes the sky.[42] Indeed, Strehlow reports that, according to one myth, the souls of the mean are devoured by dreadful spirits and annihilated.[43] Nonetheless, these conceptions are still quite vague in Australia;[44] they begin to acquire a modicum of definition and clarity only in more advanced societies, such as those of America.[45]

---

[36]Strehlow, vol. I, pp. 15ff. Thus, according to Strehlow, among the Arunta the dead live on an island—but, according to Spencer and Gillen, in an underground place. It is probable that the two myths coexist and are not the only ones. We will see that there is even a third. On that conception of the island of the dead, cf. Howitt, *Native Tribes,* p. 498; C. W. Schürmann, "Aboriginal Tribes of Port Lincoln," in Woods, p. 235; Eylmann, p. 189.

[37]Schultze, "Aborigines of . . . Finke River," p. 244.

[38]Dawson [*The Australian Aborigines*], p. 51.

[39]Among these same tribes, there are obvious traces of a more ancient myth, according to which the souls lived in an underground place (ibid.).

[40]Taplin, "The Narrinyeri" [in James Dominick Woods, *The Native Tribes of South Australia,* Adelaide, E. S. Wigg, 1879], pp. 18–19, Howitt, *Native Tribes,* p. 473; Strehlow, *Aranda,* vol. I, p. 16.

[41]Howitt, *Native Tribes,* p. 498.

[42]Strehlow, *Aranda,* vol. I, p. 16; Eylmann, "Die Eingeborenen," p. 189; Howitt, *Native Tribes,* p. 473.

[43]These are the spirits of the ancestors of a special clan, the Venom Pouch clan (*Giftdrüsenmänner*).

[44]Sometimes the missionaries' influence is obvious. Dawson tells us of an authentic hell opposed to the paradise. He himself tends to regard this idea as a European import.

[45]See Dorsey, "Siouan Cults," in *XIth Rep.,* pp. 419–420, 422, 485; cf. Marillier, *La Survivance de l'âme et l'idée de justice chez les peuples non civilisés, Rapport de l'Ecole des Hautes Etudes,* 1893.

II

Such, in their most elementary form and stripped down to their most basic traits, are the beliefs relative to the nature of the soul and its destiny. We must now try to account for them. What is it that could have led man to think that there were two beings in him, one having characteristics as special as those just enumerated? To answer this question, let us begin by trying to find out what origin the primitive ascribes to the spirit principle that he thinks he feels within himself. If properly analyzed, his own idea will set us on the road to the answer.

Following the method I set out to use, I will study the ideas in question in a group of societies where they have been observed with exceptional precision: the tribes of central Australia. Therefore, although it is broad, the area of our observation will be limited. Still, there is reason to believe that the same ideas in various forms are or have been widespread, even outside Australia. Furthermore, and above all, the idea of soul is not distinctly different in these central tribes than in the other Australian societies, but has the same basic features everywhere. Since the same effect always has the same cause, there are grounds for thinking that this idea, which is the same everywhere, does not have different causes in different places. So the origin that the study of the tribes specifically in question will lead us to attribute to it should be regarded as true of the others as well. These tribes will provide the occasion to make a sort of experiment, the results of which, like those of any well-made experiment, will be generalizable. The homogeneity of Australian civilization would suffice in itself to warrant this generalization, but I will take the precaution of testing it against facts taken from among other peoples, in both Australia and America.

Since the ideas that are to provide the basis of our demonstration have been reported differently by Spencer and Gillen than by Strehlow, I will set forth these two versions, one after the other. Proper interpretation will show that they differ more in form than in substance and in the end have the same sociological import.

According to Spencer and Gillen, the souls that come in each generation to animate the bodies of the newborn do not result from special and original creations. All these tribes would agree that there is a finite stock of souls that are reincarnated periodically, the number of which cannot be increased by even a single one.[46] When an individual dies, his soul leaves the body in

---

[46]They can temporarily duplicate themselves, as we will see in the next chapter, but these doubles do not add even one to the number of souls capable of being reincarnated.

which it resided and, once the mourning is over, goes to the land of souls. After a certain period, the soul comes back to reincarnate itself, and it is these reincarnations that bring about conceptions and births. These fundamental souls are the ones that animated the founding ancestors of the clan at the very beginning of things. In a certain epoch beyond which the imagination does not go, and which is considered the very beginning of time, beings existed that were descended from none. For this reason, the Arunta calls these the *Altjirangamitjina*,[47] the uncreated ones—the ones that, from all eternity, are. According to Spencer and Gillen, the Arunta gives the name *Alcheringa*[48] to the period in which these mythic beings are thought to have lived. Organized in totemic clans like the men of today, they spent their time traveling, in the course of which they performed all kinds of prodigious deeds, which are recollected in myths. But a time came when that terrestrial life ended. Separately or in groups, they vanished into the ground. Their bodies changed into trees or rocks, still seen in the places where they are thought to have disappeared.* But their souls endure; they are immortal. They even continue to frequent the same places where the existence of their first hosts came to an end. Because of the memories attached to them, these places too have a quality of sacredness; to be found there are the *oknanikilla*, those sanctuaries in which the churingas of the clan are kept and which are like centers for the various totemic cults. When one of the souls that wander about one of these sanctuaries enters the body of a woman, conception results and later a birth.[49] Thus each individual is considered a new avatar of a definite ancestor. The individual is this very ancestor, reborn in a new body and with new features. But who were those ancestors?

First, they were endowed with infinitely greater capacities than those possessed by the men of today, including the most respected old men and the most renowned magicians. Virtues that may be called miraculous are attributed to them: "They could travel on the ground, under the ground, and in the air; by opening a vein, each of them could flood whole regions or, in-

---

*This sentence is absent from Swain's translation.

[47]Strehlow, *Aranda*, vol. I, p. 2.

[48]*Native Tribes*, p. 73 n. 1.

[49]On that body of ideas, see Spencer and Gillen, *Native Tribes*, pp. 119, 123–127, 387ff.; *Northern Tribes*, pp. 145–174. Among the Gnanji, conception does not necessarily occur near the *oknanikilla*. But they believe that each couple is accompanied on its peregrinations about the continent by a swarm of souls from the husband's totem. When the occasion comes, one of these souls goes into the body of the woman and impregnates her, wherever she may be (*Northern Tribes*, p. 169).

versely, cause new lands to emerge; in a wall of rocks, they would cause a lake to appear, or open a gorge as a passage-way; where they planted their nurtunja, rocks or trees came out of the ground."[50] It is they who gave the land its present form and who created all sorts of beings, men and animals. They are almost gods. Hence their souls also have a godlike quality. And since the souls of men are these ancestral souls reincarnated in human bodies, the souls themselves are sacred beings.

Second, these ancestors were not men in the true sense of the word, but animals or plants, or else mixed beings in which the animal or plant element predominated. "The ancestors who lived in those legendary times," say Spencer and Gillen, "were, in the opinion of the natives, so closely allied with the animals and plants whose names they bore that an Alcheringa personage who belongs to the Kangaroo totem, for example, is often portrayed in the myths as a man-kangaroo or a kangaroo-man. Its human personality is often absorbed by that of the plant or animal from which it is thought to be descended."[51] Their souls, which still endure, are necessarily of the same nature. The human and animal elements are joined inside them, with the animal having a certain tendency to predominate. So they are made of the same substance as the totemic principle, for we know that the defining characteristic of the totemic principle is that it possesses this dual aspect, synthesizing and amalgamating these two kingdoms within itself.

Since no other souls but these exist, we arrive at the conclusion that, in general terms, the soul is none other than the totemic principle incarnated in each individual. Nothing about this derivation should surprise us. We already know that this principle is immanent in each member of the clan, and that by permeating individuals, it inevitably becomes individualized. Since consciousnesses (of which it thereby becomes an integral element) differ from one another, the principle becomes differentiated in their image. Since each consciousness has its own form, the soul in each takes a distinct form. In itself, it undoubtedly remains a force external to and foreign to the man, but the portion of it that each is thought to possess cannot help but develop close affinities with the individual subject in which it resides. The soul participates in the nature of that subject, becoming in some measure the subject's own property. In this way, it comes to have two contradictory features, but their coexistence is among the distinguishing traits of the idea of soul. Today, as at other times, the soul is that which is best and most profound in

---

[50][Spencer and Gillen], *Native Tribes*, pp. 512–513; cf. chaps. X and XI.

[51]Ibid., p. 119.

us, on the one hand, and the eminent part of our being; on the other, it is a temporary guest that has come to us from outside, that lives a life inside us that is distinct from the body's, and that must one day regain its complete independence. In short, just as society exists only through individuals, the totemic principle lives only in and through the individual consciousnesses whose coming together forms the clan. If they did not feel the totemic principle within them, it would not be; it is they who put it into things. And so it must subdivide and fragment among individuals. Each of these fragments is a soul.

A myth that is found in a rather large number of societies of the center (and that, by the way, is but a special form of the preceding) shows even better that the raw material from which the idea of soul is made is of this kind. In these tribes, tradition places at the origin of each clan not several ancestors but only two,[52] or even only one.[53] So long as it remained alone, this single being contained within itself the whole totemic principle, for at that moment there was as yet nothing to which that principle could have been passed on. According to the same tradition, all the human souls that exist, both those now animating the bodies of men and those now unused but in reserve for the future, issued from that one personage and are made from the same substance. In moving on the surface of the earth, in stirring and shaking itself, it brought them out of its body and sowed them in the various places it is said to have traversed. Is this not to say, symbolically, that these are portions of the totemic deity?

Such a conclusion, however, presupposes that the tribes discussed accept the doctrine of reincarnation. Yet, according to Strehlow, that doctrine is unknown among the Arunta—that is, the society that Spencer and Gillen studied longest and best. If in this case these two observers were so mistaken, the whole of their study would have to be considered suspect, so it is important to determine the real scope of this divergence.

Once the rites of mourning free it from the body for good, the soul is not reincarnated, according to Strehlow. It goes to the island of the dead, where it spends its days sleeping and its nights dancing, until it rains on earth. It returns at that moment to the milieu of the living and plays the role of protective genie for young sons or, in the absence of the sons, among the grandsons left behind; it enters their bodies and assists their growth. So it remains

---

[52]Among the Kalish (*Northern Tribes*, pp. 154), and among the Urabunna (*Northern Tribes*, p. 146).

[53]This is the case among the Warramunga and related tribes, Walpari, Wulmala, Worgaia, Tjingilli (*Northern Tribes*, p. 161), and also among the Umbaia and the Gnanji (*Northern Tribes*, p. 170).

in the midst of its former family for a year or two, then returns to the land of souls. After a certain period, it leaves yet again to make a new sojourn on earth—moreover, its last. The time comes when it must again travel the road to the island of the dead, this time irrevocably; and there, after various incidents that need not be reported in detail, a storm occurs during which it is struck by lightning. Its career is finally over.[54]

Thus, it cannot reincarnate itself, and thus, conceptions and births are not due to the reincarnation of souls that periodically begin new existences in new bodies. To be sure, Strehlow, like Spencer and Gillen, declares that, for the Arunta, sexual intercourse is by no means the sufficient condition of procreation,[55] which instead is the outcome of mystic operations—different operations, however, from those Spencer and Gillen made known to us. It comes about in one of the two following ways.

Everywhere the Alcheringa ancestor[56] is thought to have sunk into the ground, there is a rock or a tree representing the body. According to Spencer and Gillen,[57] the tree or rock that has this mystic relation with the departed heroes is called *nanja* and, according to Strehlow, *ngarra*.[58] Sometimes it is a water hole that is said to have been formed in this way. On each of these trees and rocks, and in each of these water holes, live the embryos of babies, called *ratapa*,[59] which belong to the very same totem as the corresponding ancestor. For example, on a gum tree that represents an ancestor of the Kangaroo clan, there are ratapas that are all of the Kangaroo totem. If a woman belonging to the marriage class to which mothers of these ratapas must ordinarily belong

---

[54]Strehlow, *Aranda*, vol. I, pp. 15–16. For the Loritja, see Strehlow, [*Aranda*], vol. II, p. 7.

[55]Strehlow goes so far as to say that sexual relations are not even considered a necessary condition, a sort of preparation for conception (vol. II, p. 52 n. 7). It is true that he adds, a few lines further on, that the old men know perfectly well the relationship between physical intercourse and procreation—and that, so far as animals are concerned, even children know. This is bound to dilute somewhat the import of the first statement.

[56]I generally use the terminology of Spencer and Gillen, rather than that of Strehlow, because it has been sanctioned by long usage.

[57]*Native Tribes*, pp. 124, 513.

[58][Strehlow, *Aranda*], vol. I, p. 5. According to Strehlow, *ngarra* means "eternal." Among the Loritja, only rocks have this function.

[59]Strehlow translates it as *Kinderkeime* ("seeds of children"). However, Spencer and Gillen are far from having ignored the myth of the ratapa and the customs connected to them. They speak of it explicitly in *Native Tribes*, pp. 366ff. and 552. They note the existence of rocks called *Erathipa* in various parts of the Arunta territory, from which emanate "spirit children," souls of children, that enter into the bodies of women and impregnate them. According to Spencer and Gillen, *Erathipa* means "child," although they go on to say that this word is rarely used in this sense in everyday conversation (ibid., p. 338).

should happen to pass by,[60] one of them will be able to enter her through the hip. The woman learns of this possession through the characteristic pains that are the first signs of pregnancy. The child conceived in this way will naturally be from the same ancestor on whose mystical body it resided before incarnating itself.[61]

In other cases, the procedure used is slightly different, with the ancestor acting in person. At a given moment, the ancestor leaves its underground retreat and throws at the woman a small churinga of a special shape, called a *namatuna*.[62] The churinga enters the body of the woman and there takes human form, while the ancestor disappears again into the earth.[63]

These two modes of conception are held to be equally common. The shape of the child's face reveals the manner in which it was conceived. According to the width or narrowness of the face, conception is said to be due to the incarnation of a ratapa or a namatuna. Strehlow also notes a third method of impregnation, in addition to these two, but one that is said to be much rarer. After its namatuna has entered the body of the woman, the ancestor itself enters and voluntarily submits to a new birth. In this case, conception would result from a true reincarnation of the ancestor. But this case is highly unusual, and furthermore, when the man so conceived dies, the ancestral soul that animated him departs, as do ordinary souls, for the island of the dead, where it is finally destroyed after the usual period. It does not undergo new reincarnations.[64]

Such is Strehlow's version.[65] In his view, it is radically opposed to that of Spencer and Gillen. In reality, however, it differs only in the literal detail of the formulas and symbols, and, variations of form aside, the mythical theme is the same in both cases.

In the first place, all these observers agree in viewing every conception as the result of an incarnation. According to Strehlow, what is incarnated is not a

---

[60]The Arunta are divided sometimes into four, sometimes into eight marriage classes. The class of a child is determined by that of its father; inversely, the father's can be deduced from the child's. (See Spencer and Gillen, *Native Tribes*, pp. 70ff.; Strehlow [*Aranda*], vol. I, pp. 6ff.) We must still find out how the ratapa acquires a definite class; I will return to this point.

[61]Strehlow [*Aranda*], vol. II, p. 52. Sometimes, albeit seldom, conflicts do arise over which is the child's totem. Strehlow cites a case (p. 53).

[62]This is the same word as *namatwinna*, which is found in Spencer and Gillen (*Native Tribes*, p. 541).

[63]Strehlow [*Aranda*], vol. II, p. 53.

[64]Ibid., vol. II, p. 56.

[65]Mathews ascribes a similar theory of conception to the Tjingilli (also known as Chingalee). [Possibly, *Proceedings and Transactions of the Queensland Branch of the Royal Geographic Society of Australasia*, Brisbane], vol. XXII (1907), pp. 75–76. [This source remains obscure to me. Trans.]

soul but a ratapa or a namatuna. What, then, is a ratapa? It is, says Strehlow, a complete embryo, made of both a soul and a body, but the soul is always conceived of in physical forms. Since it sleeps, dances, hunts, eats, and so forth, it has a corporeal element as well. Inversely, the ratapa is invisible to ordinary men; no one sees it entering the woman's body;[66] it is made of material quite comparable to that of the soul. In this respect, therefore, it does not seem possible to differentiate clearly between the two. These are, in sum, mythical beings that are conceived more or less on the same model. Schulze calls them child-souls.[67] Moreover, like the soul, the ratapa has the closest relations with the ancestor of which the sacred tree or rock is a materialized form. It is of the same totem, the same phratry, and the same marriage class as that ancestor.[68] Its place in the social organization of the tribe is exactly the one the ancestor is said to have held once upon a time. It has the same name.[69] This is proof that these two personalities are very closely related to one another.

There is more: This kinship goes as far as complete identification. It is actually on the mystical body of the ancestor that the ratapa took form; it comes from this body and is like a bit that detached itself. In sum, therefore, what enters the womb of the mother and becomes the child is part of the ancestor. And by this route, we come back to the idea of Spencer and Gillen: Birth is due to the incarnation of an ancestral personage. Of course, what is incarnated is not the whole personage but only an emanation of it. However, this difference is of entirely secondary interest, for this reason: When a sacred being divides and replicates itself, it is found again, and with all its fundamental traits, in each of the fragments into which it has been divided. Basically, then, the Alcheringa ancestor is wholly within the element of itself that becomes a ratapa.[70]

[66]Sometimes the ancestor who is thought to have thrown the namatuna shows itself to the woman in the form of an animal or a man. This is further proof of the affinity the ancestral soul has for physical form.

[67]Schulze, "Aborigines of . . . Finke River," p. 237.

[68]This arises from the fact that the ratapa can only incarnate itself in the body of a woman who belongs to the same marriage class as the mother of the mythical ancestor. Thus I do not understand how Strehlow could say (*Aranda*, vol. I, p. 42, *Anmerkung*) that, except in this case, the myths do not assign the Alcheringa ancestors to definite marriage classes. His own theory of conception presupposes just the opposite (cf. II, pp. 53ff.).

[69]Strehlow, *Aranda*, vol. II, p. 58.

[70]The difference between the two versions narrows even more and diminishes almost to nothing if we notice that when Spencer and Gillen tell us that the ancestral soul is incarnated in the body of the woman, their mode of expression must not be taken literally. It is not the whole soul that comes to impregnate the mother but only an emanation of that soul. Indeed, on their own avowal, a soul equal and even superior in power to the one that is incarnated continues to reside in the nanja tree or rock (see *Native Tribes*, p. 514). I will have occasion to return to this point (cf. below, p. 277).

The second mode of conception that Strehlow distinguishes has the same meaning. In fact, the churinga, and especially the particular churinga that is called the namatuna, is considered an avatar of the ancestor: It is the ancestor's body, according to Strehlow,[71] just as the nanja tree is. In other words, the personality of the ancestor, its churinga, and its nanja tree are sacred things, which elicit the same feelings, and to which the same religious value is ascribed. Therefore, they change into one another: A sacred tree or rock came out of the ground in the place where the ancestor lost a churinga, just as in the places where he himself sank into the ground.[72] There is a mythical equivalence between an Alcheringa personage and his churinga, then; so when the personage throws a namatuna into a woman's body, it is as if that very personage entered her. In fact, we have seen that it sometimes enters in person, following the namatuna; and, according to other accounts, the personage enters before the namatuna, as if opening a way for it.[73] The fact that these themes coexist in the same myth shows definitively that the one is only a duplicate of the other.

Furthermore, no matter how conception occurs, there is no doubt that each individual is bound to a definite Alcheringa ancestor by extremely close ties. First, each man has his recognized ancestor; two persons cannot simultaneously have the same one. In other words, an Alcheringa being never has more than one representative among the living.[74] What is more, the one is only an aspect of the other. In fact, as we already know, the churinga left by the ancestor expresses his personality. If we adopt the interpretation that Strehlow reports, which is perhaps the more satisfactory, we will say that it is the ancestor's body. But this same churinga is related in the same way to the individual who is thought to have been conceived under the influence of the ancestor, that is, the one who is the fruit of his mystical labors. When the young neophyte is brought into the sanctuary of the clan, he is shown the churinga of his ancestor with the words: "You are this body; you are the

[71]Strehlow, *Aranda*, vol. II, pp. 76, 81. According to Spencer and Gillen, the churinga is not the body of the ancestor but the object in which the ancestor's soul resides. These two mythical interpretations are basically identical, and it is easy to see how one was able to pass over into the other: The body is the place where the soul resides.

[72]Ibid., vol. I, p. 4.

[73]Ibid., vol. I, pp. 53–54. In these accounts, the ancestor begins by entering the womb of the woman, bringing on the characteristic discomforts of pregnancy. Then he exits and only afterward leaves the namatuna.

[74]Ibid., vol. II, p. 76.

same thing as this."[75] Thus, in Strehlow's phrase, the churinga is "the common body of the individual and his ancestor."[76] From one point of view, at least, their two personalities have to be merged in order for them to have the same body. Strehlow explicitly recognizes this. He says: "By the Tjurunga (churinga), the individual is joined with his personal ancestor."[77]

To summarize, for Strehlow as well as for Spencer and Gillen, there is a religious and mystical principle in each newborn that emanates from an Alcheringa ancestor. It is this principle that forms the essence of each individual. So this principle is the individual's soul; or, in any case, the soul is made of the same matter and substance. I have relied on this fundamental fact only to determine the nature and origin of the idea of soul. The different metaphors by means of which this could have been expressed are of entirely secondary interest to me.[78]

Far from contradicting the data on which my thesis rests, the recent observations of Strehlow bring us new evidence that confirms it. My reasoning consisted of inferring the totemic nature of the human soul from the totemic nature of the ancestral soul, of which the human one is an emanation and a kind of replica. Certain of the new facts that we owe to Strehlow demonstrate this characteristic of both, even more unequivocally than those relied upon until now. First, like Spencer and Gillen, Strehlow insists on "the intimate relations that join each ancestor to an animal, a plant or another natural object." Certain of these Altjirangamitjina (these are the Alcheringa of Spencer and Gillen), he says, "must be directly manifested in the form of animals; others take animal form temporarily."[79] Even now, they are continually transforming themselves into animals.[80] In any case, and whatever their

---

[75]Ibid., p. 81. Here is the word-for-word translation of the terms used, as Strehlow gives them to us: *Dies du Körper bist; dies du der ähnliche.* In one myth, a civilizing hero, Mangarkunjerkunja, presents to each man the churinga of his ancestor, telling him, "You were born from this churinga" (ibid., p. 76).

[76]Ibid.

[77]Ibid.

[78]Basically, the only real divergence between Strehlow, on the one hand, and Spencer and Gillen, on the other, is the following. For Spencer and Gillen, after death the soul of the individual returns to the nanja tree where it is again assimilated into the soul of the ancestor (*Native Tribes*, p. 513); for Strehlow, it leaves for the island of the dead, where it is eventually destroyed. In neither myth does it survive individually. I make no attempt to determine the cause of this divergence. Possibly Spencer and Gillen, who do not speak of the island of the dead, made an error of observation. Possibly also, the myth is not the same among the eastern Arunta, which Spencer and Gillen mainly observed, and in the other parts of the tribe.

[79]Strehlow [*Aranda*], vol. II, p. 51.

[80]Ibid., vol. II, p. 56.

outward appearance, "in each of them, the special and distinctive qualities of the animal are quite evident." For example, the ancestors of the Kangaroo clan eat grass and flee the hunter, like real kangaroos; those of the Emu clan feed and flee like emus,[81] and so on. And consider this: Those of the ancestors who had a plant totem became the same plant at death.[82] Furthermore, this close kinship of the ancestor and the totemic being is so strongly felt by the native that it affects terminology. Among the Arunta, the child calls *altjira* the totem of its mother, which serves as its secondary totem.[83] Since descent was at first reckoned in the maternal line, there was a time when each individual had no totem other than its mother's; thus, quite probably, the term "altjira" designated the totem, period. Now it obviously enters into the composition of the word that means "great ancestor," altjirangamitjina.[84]

The ideas of totem and ancestor are so close, indeed, that they apparently are sometimes interchangeable. In this way, after having told us about the mother's totem or altjira, Strehlow adds: "This altjira appears to the blacks in dreams and utters warnings, just as it takes news of them to their sleeping friends."[85] This altjira that speaks, that is personally attached to each individual, is obviously an ancestor, and yet it is also an incarnation of the totem. A text by Roth that discusses invocations addressed to the totem must no doubt be interpreted in this way.[86] It seems, then, that the totem is sometimes imagined as a collection of ideal beings, mythic personages that are more or less distinct from the ancestors. In other words, the ancestors are the totem divided into parts.[87]

But if the ancestor is merged with the totemic being to this extent, it cannot be otherwise for the individual soul that is so closely related to the ancestral soul. Moreover, this also emerges from the close bonds that join each man to his churinga. We know that the churinga expresses the personality of the individual who is thought to have been born of it;[88] but it also expresses

---

[81]Ibid., vol. I, pp. 3–4.

[82]Ibid., vol. II, p. 61.

[83]See above, p. 185.

[84]Strehlow [*Aranda*], vol. II, p. 57, and vol. I, p. 2.

[85]Ibid., vol. II, p. 57.

[86]Roth, *Superstition, Magic*, §74.

[87]In other words, the totemic species is constituted more by the group of ancestors and by the mythic species than by the animal or plant species themselves.

[88]See above, p. 256.

the totemic animal. When the civilizing hero Mangakunjerkunja gave a personal churinga to each member of the Kangaroo clan, he spoke these words: "Here is the body of a kangaroo."[89] In this way, the churinga is the body of the ancestor, the actual individual, and the totemic animal, all at once: The three beings form, in the strong and apt phrase of Strehlow, "an indissoluble unity."[90] These terms are partially equivalent and interchangeable. That is, they are conceived of as different aspects of one and the same reality, which is also defined by the distinctive attributes of the totem. Their shared essence is the totemic principle. Language itself expresses this identification. The words *ratapa* and, in the language of the Loritja, *aratapi* designate the mythical embryo that detaches itself from the ancestor and becomes the child. But the same words also designate the totem of this same child, as determined by the place where the mother thinks she conceived.[91]

III

In the preceding, the doctrine of reincarnation was studied only in the tribes of central Australia; the bases on which my inference rests might therefore be judged too narrow. But in the first place, for the reasons already given, the scope of the experiment extends beyond the societies we have studied directly. Furthermore, abundant facts establish that the same or similar ideas are to be found in the most disparate parts of Australia or, at least, have left visible traces there. They are also to be found in America.

In southern Australia, Howitt reports them among the Dieri.[92] The word *Mura-mura*, which Gason translated as Good-Spirit (and in which he thought he saw belief in a creator god expressed[93]), is in reality a collective name that denotes the multitude of ancestors placed at the origin of the tribe. They continue to exist today, as in the past. "It is believed that they inhabit trees, which are sacred for this reason." Certain features of the ground, rocks,

---

[89]Strehlow [*Aranda*], vol. II, p. 76.

[90]Ibid.

[91]Ibid., pp. 57, 60, 61. Strehlow calls the list of the totems the list of the ratapas.

[92]Howitt, *Native Tribes*, pp. 475ff.

[93][Gason], "The Manners and Customs of the Dieyerie Tribe of Australian Aborigines," in [Edward M.] Curr [*The Australian Race, Its Origin, Languages, Customs, Place of Landing in Australia, and the Routes by Which It Spread Itself over That Continent*, Melbourne, J. Ferres, 1886–1887], vol. II, p. 47.

and springs are identified with these Mura-mura,[94] which, consequently, are remarkably like the Altjirangamitjina of the Arunta. Even though only vestiges of totemism still exist among them, the Kurnai of Gippsland also believe in the existence of ancestors called *Muk-Kurnai*, conceived of as beings midway between men and animals.[95] Among the Nimbaldi, Taplin has found a theory of conception like the one Strehlow ascribes to the Arunta.[96] In the state of Victoria, among the Wotjobaluk, we find in full the belief in reincarnation. According to Mathews: "The spirits of the dead gather in the *miyur*[97] of their respective clans; they come out in order to be born again in human form, when a favorable opportunity presents itself."[98] Mathews even states that "the belief in reincarnation or in the transmigration of souls is deeply rooted in all the Australian tribes."[99]

If we move on to the northern regions, we find in the northwest, among the Niol-Niol, the pure doctrine of the Arunta: Every birth is attributed to the incarnation of a preexisting soul that is introduced into the body of the woman.[100] In North Queensland, myths that differ from the preceding only in form translate exactly the same ideas. In the tribes of the Pennefather River, each man is believed to have two souls: one, called *ngai*, resides in the heart; the other, *choi*, remains in the placenta. Right after birth, the placenta is buried in a consecrated place. A personal genie named Anje-a, which is in charge of the phenomenon of procreation, comes to collect this choi, and to keep it until, having reached adulthood, the child marries. When the time has come to give him a son, Anje-a gathers a bit of that man's choi and inserts it into the embryo, which Anje-a makes and puts in the womb of the mother. Thus the child is made with the soul of its father. It is true that the child does not receive its full paternal soul right away, for the ngai remains in the father's heart for as long as he lives. But when he dies, the freed ngai also

[94]Howitt, *Native Tribes*, p. 482.

[95]Ibid., p. 487.

[96][George] Taplin, *Folklore, Customs, Manners, etc. [Customs and Languages] of South Australian Aborigines*, Adelaide, E. Spiller, 1879], p. 88.

[97]Each clan of ancestors has its special camp under the ground; the *miyur* is this camp.

[98]Mathews, "Aboriginal Tribes" in *RSNSW,* vol. XXXVIII, p. 293. Mathews reports the same belief in other tribes of Victoria (ibid., p. 197).

[99]Ibid., p. 349.

[100][P. Jos.] Bischofs, "Die Niol-Niol, [ein Eingeborenenstamm in Nordwest Australien"] in *Anthropos*, vol. III [1908], p. 35.

goes to incarnate itself in the bodies of children; if there are several, it divides itself equally among them. So there is perfect spiritual continuity between the generations: The same soul is transmitted from father to children and from them to their children; and this single soul, always identical to itself despite its successive divisions and subdivisions, is the one that animated the first ancestor, at the beginning of things.[101] There is only one difference of any importance between this theory and that of the central tribes: that reincarnation is not the work of the ancestors themselves but of a special genie, professionally assigned to that function. But it seems, actually, that this genie is the product of a syncretism that caused the multiple figures of the first ancestors to merge into one and the same figure. The fact that the words "Anje-a" and "Anjir" are apparently related quite closely makes this hypothesis at least plausible; now, "Anjir" designates the first man, the original ancestor from whom all men are descended.[102]

The same ideas recur among the Indian tribes of America. According to Krause, it is believed among the Tlingit that the souls of the departed return to earth to enter the bodies of the pregnant women who belong to their families. "So, when a woman dreams of such and such a deceased relative, during pregnancy, she believes that relative's soul has entered her." If the newborn displays some characteristic mark that the deceased had, it is thought to be the deceased himself, returned to earth, and is given the deceased's name.[103] This belief is also common among the Haida. It is the shaman who reveals which relative has reincarnated himself in the child and, consequently, what name the child should have.[104] It is believed among the Kwakiutl that the last to die returns to life in the person of the first child born in the family.[105] The same is true among the Huron, the Iroquois, the Tinneh, and many other tribes of the United States.[106]

---

[101]Roth, *Superstition, Magic*, §68; cf. §69a, the similar case of the natives of the Proserpine River. To simplify the exposition, I have left aside the complication that arises from sex difference. Girls' souls are made with the choi of their mothers, whereas they share with their brothers the ngai of their father. However this peculiarity, which perhaps arises from the fact that the two systems of descent have been in use one after the other, does not affect the principle of the soul's perpetuity.

[102]Ibid., p. 16.

[103][Aurel Krause], *Die Tlinkit-Indianer* [Jena, H. Constable, 1885], p. 282.

[104][John] Swanton, *Contributions to the Ethnology of the Haida* [Leiden, E. J. Brill, 1905], pp. 117ff.

[105]Boas, *Sixth Report of the Committee on the North-Western Tribes of Canada*, p. 59.

[106][Joseph François] Lafitau, *Moeurs des sauvages américains [comparées aux moeurs des premiers temps]*, vol. II [Paris, Saugrain l'aîné; Charles Estienne Hochereau, 1724], p. 434; [Emile Fortune Stanislas Joseph] Petitot, *Monographie des Dénè-Dindjié* [Paris, E. Leroux, 1876], p. 59.

The scope of these ideas extends naturally to the conclusion I have deduced from it: my proposed explanation for the idea of soul. Its general applicability is additionally confirmed by the following facts.

We know[107] that each individual harbors within himself something of the anonymous force that pervades the entire sacred species, for he himself is a member of that species—not, however, insofar as he is an empirical and visible being. In spite of the designs and symbolic signs with which he decorates his body, nothing about him brings to mind the form of an animal or plant. Hence, there is another being in him; and while not ceasing to recognize himself in that being, he imagines it in the form of an animal or plant. Is it not obvious that this double can only be the soul, since the soul, on its own, is already a double of the subject it animates? As final proof of this identification, the organs that most preeminently incarnate the totemic principle in each individual are the same as those in which the soul resides. This is true of the blood. The blood contains some part of the totemic essence, as is demonstrated by the role blood plays in totemic ceremonies.[108] But at the same time, the blood is one of the soul's residences; or, rather, it is the soul itself seen from outside. When it flows, life slips away, and the soul escapes then and there. Hence, it is identified with the sacred principle that is immanent in the blood.

To turn the matter around: If in fact my explanation is well founded, the totemic principle that enters (as I assume) into the individual must retain a certain autonomy there, for it is specifically distinct from the subject in which it is incarnated. Now, this is precisely what Howitt says he observed among the Yuin. He says, "The fact that the totem is conceived among these tribes as being in some way part of the man is clearly proved by the case of one Umbara, already mentioned. Umbara told the story of how, a few years ago, an individual of the Lace-Lizard clan sent him his totem as Umbara himself slept. It went down the throat of the sleeper and nearly ate his totem, which resided in his chest, and this nearly caused death."[109] So it is quite true that the totem divides as it becomes individualized and that each of the pieces that is thereby detached plays the role of a spirit, of a soul that resides in the body.[110]

[107]See above, pp. 133ff.

[108]See above, p. 136.

[109]Howitt, Native Tribes, p. 147. Cf. ibid., p. 769.

[110]Strehlow [Aranda] (vol. I, p. 15 n. 2), Schulze ("Aborigines of . . . Finke River," p. 246) portray the soul to us, as Howitt here portrays the totem, as coming out of the body to go and eat another being. Similarly, we earlier saw the altjira or maternal totem manifest itself in a dream, just as a soul or a spirit does.

Here are more directly telling facts. If the soul is but the totemic principle individualized, then in certain cases, at least, it must maintain more or less close relations with the animal or plant species whose form the totem reproduces. And, in fact, "The Gewwe-Gal (a tribe of New South Wales) believe that each person has within himself an affinity for the spirit of some bird, beast, or reptile. It is not that the individual is thought to be descended from that animal, but that a kinship is thought to exist between the spirit that animates the man and the spirit of the animal."[111]

Indeed, there are cases in which the soul is thought to emanate directly from the totemic plant or animal. Among the Arunta, according to Strehlow, it is believed that when a woman has eaten abundantly of a fruit, she will bear a child whose totem is that fruit. If she was looking at a kangaroo when she felt the first movements of the child, a kangaroo ratapa is believed to have entered her body and impregnated her.[112] H. Basedow has reported the same belief among the Wogait.[113] We know, on the other hand, that the ratapa and the soul are nearly indistinguishable. Now, it would not have been possible to ascribe such an origin to the soul if it was not thought to be made of the same substance as the animals and plants of the totemic species.

Thus the soul is often depicted as an animal. In the lower societies, as is well known, death is never considered a natural event, with purely physical causes, but is widely imputed to the machinations of some sorcerer. In many Australian tribes, to determine who is responsible for a murder, people start from the principle that, giving in to a sort of compulsion, the soul of the murderer inevitably comes to visit his victim. For this reason, the body is placed on a scaffold, and the ground under and all around the corpse is carefully smoothed, so that the slightest mark on it is easily seen. The people return the next day. If an animal has passed that way in the meantime, its tracks are easily recognized. Their shape reveals the species to which he belongs,

---

[111][Lorimer] Fison and [Alfred William] Howitt, *Kamilaroi and Kurnai: [Group Marriage and Relationship by Elopement, Drawn Chiefly from the Usage of the Australian Aborigines. Also the Kurnai Tribe, Their Customs in Peace and War*, Melbourne, G. Robertson, 1880], p. 280.

[112]*Globus*, vol. CXI, p. 289. Despite the objections of Leonhardi, Strehlow has stood behind his statements on this point. Leonhardi deems that there is a certain contradiction between this assertion and the theory that the ratapas emanate from trees, rocks, and churingas. But since the totemic animal incarnates the totem, just as does the nanja tree or rock, it can play the same role. These different things are mythologically equivalent.

[113][H. Basedow], "Notes on the West Coastal Tribes of the Northern Territory of S. Australia," in *RSSA*, vol. XXXI (1907), p. 4. Cf. regarding the tribes of the Cairns district (North Queensland), *Man* [vol. IX] (1909), p. 86.

and in that way, the social group to which the murder belongs is inferred. He is said to be a man of such and such class or clan,[114] if the animal is a totem of this or that class or clan. This is because the soul is thought to have come in the form of the totemic animal.

In other societies, where totemism has weakened or disappeared, the soul still continues to be thought of in animal form. The natives of Cape Bedford (North Queensland) believe that at the moment the child enters the body of its mother, it is a curlew if a girl and a snake if a boy. Only later does it take a human form.[115] According to the Prince of Wied, many Indians of North America say they have an animal in their body.[116] The Bororo of Brazil draw their souls in the form of a bird and for that reason believe they are birds of the same kind.[117] Elsewhere the soul is conceived of as a snake, a lizard, a fly, a bee, and so on.[118]

But it is above all after death that the animal nature of the soul manifests itself. During life, this feature is partially veiled, so to speak, by the very form of the human body. Once death has set the soul free, it becomes itself again. Among the Omaha, in at least two of the buffalo clans, the souls of the dead are believed to rejoin the buffalo, their ancestors.[119] The Hopi are divided into a certain number of clans, whose ancestors were animals or beings in animal form. As Schoolcraft reports, they say that at death they regain their original form. Each of them becomes a bear again, or a hart, according to the clan to which he belongs.[120] Often the soul is thought to reincarnate itself in

---

[114]Among the Wakelbura where, according to Curr and Howitt, each marriage class has its own totems, the animal determines the class (see Curr, vol. III, p. 28); among the Buandik, it determines the clan (Mrs. James S. Smith, *The Booandik Tribes of S. Australian Aborigines* [Adelaide, E. Spiller,1880], p.128). Cf. [Alfred William] Howitt, "On Some Australian Beliefs," in *JAI*, vol. XIII [1884], p. 191; XIV (1884), p. 362; [Northcote Whitridge] Thomas, "An American View of Totemism," in *Man* [vol. II] (1902), 85; [R. H.] Mathews, *RSNSW,* vol. XXXVIII, pp. 347–348; [Robert] Brough Smyth [*The Aborigines of Victoria,* Melbourne, J. Ferres, 1878], vol. I, p. 110; Spencer and Gillen, *Northern Tribes,* p. 513.

[115]Roth, *Superstition, Magic,* §83. This is probably a form of sexual totemism.

[116]Prinz [von Maximillian] Wied, *Reise in das innere Nord-Amerika in der Jahren 1832 bis 1834,* II [Koblenz, 1839], p. 190.

[117]K. von den Steinen, *Unter den Naturvölkern Zentral-Brasiliens* [Berlin, D. Reimer, 1894], pp. 511, 512.

[118]See Frazer, *Golden Bough,* 2d. ed., vol. 1, London, Macmillan, 1894, pp. 250, 253, 256, 257, 258.

[119][James Owen Dorsey, "Omaha Sociology,"] *Third [Annual] Report,* [*BAE,* Washington, Government Printing Office, 1884], pp. 229, 233.

[120][Schoolcraft], *Indian Tribes,* vol. IV, p. 86.

the body of an animal.[121] This, quite probably, is the source of the doctrine of metempsychosis, which is so widely held. We have seen how much trouble Tylor has accounting for it.[122] If the soul is fundamentally a human principle, what could be stranger than the marked predilection for animal form that it manifests in so many societies? On the other hand, all is explained if, in its very constitution, the soul is closely akin to the animal, for then, by returning after life to the animal world, it is only returning to its true nature. Thus, the quasi-universality of belief in metempsychosis is additional proof that the constitutive elements in the idea of the soul have been taken chiefly from the animal realm, as is presupposed by the theory just set forth.

IV

The idea of the soul is a particular application of the beliefs relative to sacred things. In this way may be explained the religious character this idea has displayed ever since it appeared in history and that it still has today. The soul has always been considered a sacred thing; in this respect it is opposed to the body, which in itself is profane. The soul is not merely distinct from its physical envelope, as the inside is from the outside, and it is not merely imagined as being made of a more subtle and fluid material than the body; more than that, it elicits in some degree those feelings that are everywhere reserved for that which is divine. If it is not made into a god, it is seen at least as a spark of the divinity. This fundamental characteristic would be inexplicable if the idea of the soul was no more than a prescientific solution to the problem of dreams. Since there is nothing in dreaming that can awaken religious emotion, the same must be true of the cause that accounts for dreaming. However, if the soul is a bit of divine substance, it represents something within

---

[121]For example, among the Batta of Sumatra (See *Golden Bough*, 2d. ed., vol. III, p. 420), in Melanesia (Codrington, *The Melanesians*, p. 178), in the Malay Archipelago (Tylor, "Remarks on Totemism," in *JAI*, new series, vol. I [1907], p. 147). It will be noticed that the cases in which the soul clearly presents itself after death as an animal are taken from societies in which totemism has been more or less breached. This is so because, where totemic beliefs are relatively pure, the idea of soul is necessarily ambiguous, for totemism implies that the soul participates in both realms at once. It cannot direct itself in either direction exclusively but sometimes takes one aspect and sometimes the other, depending on the circumstances. The more totemism recedes, the less necessary this ambiguity becomes, while, at the same time, the spirits feel a stronger need for differentiation. Then the quite marked affinities of the soul for the animal realm make themselves felt, especially so after it is liberated from the human body.

[122]See above, p. 172. On the universality of belief in metempsychosis, see Tylor, vol. II, pp. 8ff.

us that is other than ourselves, and if it is made of the same mental material as the sacred beings, it would naturally be the object of the same feelings.

Nor is the character man thus ascribes to himself the result of mere illusion. Like the ideas of religious force and divinity, the idea of the soul is not without reality. It is quite true that we are made of two distinct parts that are opposed to one another as the sacred is to the profane, and we can say that in a sense there is divinity in us. For society, that unique source of all that is sacred, is not satisfied to move us from outside and to affect us transitorily; it organizes itself lastingly within us. It arouses in us a whole world of ideas and feelings that express it but at the same time are an integral and permanent part of ourselves. When the Australian comes away from a religious ceremony, the representations that common life has awakened or reawakened in him do not instantly dissolve. The grand ancestral figures, the heroic exploits that the rites commemorate, the great things of all kinds that worship has made him participate in—in sum, the various ideals that he has elaborated with others—all these go on living in his consciousness. And by the emotions that are attached to them in his consciousness, by the very special influence they have, they clearly distinguish themselves from the ordinary impressions that his daily dealings with external things make upon him.

Moral ideas are of the same nature. It is society that has engraved them upon us, and since the respect society inspires is naturally passed on to all that comes from it, the imperative norms of conduct, because of their origin, become invested with an authority and a stature that our other inward states do not have. Therefore, we assign them a special place within the totality of our psychic life. Although our moral conscience is part of our consciousness, we do not feel on an equal footing with it. We cannot recognize our own voice in that voice that makes itself heard only to order us to do some things and not to do others. The very tone in which it speaks announces that it is expressing something in us that is other than us. This is what is objective about the idea of the soul. The representations that are the warp and woof of our inner life are of two different species, irreducible to one another. Some relate to the outward and physical world, some to an ideal world that we consider to be morally above the physical one. Thus, we are really made of two beings that are oriented in two divergent and virtually opposite directions, one of which exercises supremacy over the other. Such is the profound meaning of the antithesis that all peoples have more or less clearly conceived: between the body and the soul, between the physical being and the spiritual being that coexist in us. Moralists and preachers have often held that we cannot deny the reality and sacredness of duty without falling into materialism. And indeed, if we did not have the idea of moral and religious imperatives,[123] our psychic life would be flattened out, all our states of consciousness would be on the same plane, and all sense of duality would disappear. To make this duality intelligible, it is by no means necessary to imagine a mysterious and unrepresentable substance opposed to the body, under the name "soul." But in this case, too, as in that of the sacred, the error is in the literal character of the symbol used, not in the reality of the fact symbolized. It is true that our nature is double; there truly is a parcel of divinity in us, because there is in us a parcel of the grand ideals that are the soul of collectivity.

The individual soul is thus only a portion of the group's collective soul. It is the anonymous force on which the cult is based but incarnated in an individual whose personality it cleaves to: It is mana individualized. Dreaming may well have had a role in producing certain secondary characteristics of the idea. Perhaps the fluidity and instability of the images that occupy our minds during sleep, and their remarkable capacity to be transformed into one another, furnished the model of that subtle, diaphanous, and protean material of which the soul is thought to be made. Moreover, the phenomena of fainting, catalepsy, and so forth may have suggested the idea that the soul was mobile and, beginning in this life, temporarily left the body; this, in turn, has been used to explain certain dreams. But all these experiences and observations could only have had incidental, complementary influence, and indeed the existence of that influence is hard to establish. What is truly fundamental to the idea comes from elsewhere.

Does not this origin of the idea of soul misconceive its fundamental nature? If soul is but a special form of the impersonal principle that pervades the group, the totemic species, and all kinds of things that are attached to them, then it too is at bottom impersonal. And so, with only a few differences, it must therefore have the same properties as the force of which it is only a specialized form—in particular, the same diffuseness, the same capacity to spread contagiously, and the same ubiquity. Now, quite the contrary, it is easily imagined as a definite, concrete being, wholly self-contained and incommunicable to others; it is made the basis of our personality.

[123]If the religious and moral representations constitute the essential elements in the idea of soul, as I believe they do, I nonetheless do not mean to say that these are the only ones. Other states of conscience having this same quality, though to a lesser degree, come to group themselves around this central nucleus. This is true of all the higher forms of intellectual life, by reason of the quite special value and status that society attributes to them. When we live the life of science or art, we feel we are in contact with a circle of things above sensation (this, by the way, I will have occasion to show with greater precision in the Conclusion). This is why the higher functions of the intellect have always been regarded as specific manifestations of the soul's activity. But they probably could not have been enough to form the idea of soul.

But this way of thinking about soul is the product of recent and philosophical development. The popular conception, such as it has emerged
spontaneously from ordinary experience, is very different, especially at the
beginning. For the Australian, the soul is a very vague entity, indeterminate and fluid in form, pervading the entire body. Although it is especially
manifest in certain parts, there are probably none from which it is absent
altogether, so it has a diffuseness, a contagiousness, and an omnipresence
comparable to that of mana. Like mana, it can subdivide and replicate itself
infinitely, all the while remaining whole in each of those parts (the plurality
of souls resulting from those replications and divisions). In addition, the doctrine of reincarnation, whose widespread acceptance we have established,
shows what impersonal elements there are in the idea of soul and how fundamental they are. For the same soul to be able to take on a new personality
in each generation, the individual forms in which it is successively clothed
must also be external to it and unattached to its true nature. This is a kind of
generic substance that becomes individualized only secondarily and superficially. Moreover, this idea of soul is far from having totally disappeared. The
cult of relics shows that, for ordinary believers even today, the soul of a saint
continues to adhere to his various bones, and with all its essential powers—
which implies that it is imagined to be capable of diffusing and subdividing,
and of incorporating itself into all sorts of different things at the same time.

Just as we find in soul the characteristic attributes of mana, so too do secondary and superficial changes suffice for mana to become individualized as
soul. One moves on from the first idea to the second without any radical
jump. Every religious force that is regularly attached to a definite being participates in the characteristics of that being, takes its form, and becomes its
spirit duplicate. Tregear, in his Maori-Polynesian dictionary, believed he
could connect the word *mana* to a whole group of other words, like *manawa*,
manamana, and others, which seem to be of the same family and mean
"heart," "life," "consciousness." Is this not to say that some kinship between
the corresponding ideas must also exist, that is, between the ideas of impersonal power and those of inward life and mental force—in a word, of soul?[124]
This is why the question whether the churinga is sacred because it serves as
residence for a soul, as Spencer and Gillen believe, or because it has impersonal virtues, as Strehlow believes, is of little interest to me and with no sociological import. Whether the efficacy of a sacred object is imagined in
abstract form or ascribed to some personal agent is not the heart of the question. The psychological roots of both beliefs are identical. A thing is sacred

---

[124]F. Tregear, *The Maori-Polynesian Comparative Dictionary*, pp. 203–205.

because, in some way, it inspires a collective feeling of respect that removes it from profane contact. To understand this feeling, men sometimes relate it to a vague and imprecise cause and sometimes to a definite spiritual being with a name and a history. But these varying interpretations are added to a fundamental process that is the same in both cases.

This is what explains those extraordinary mixtures, examples of which we have encountered along the way. I said that the individual, the soul of the ancestor he reincarnates or of whom his own soul is an emanation, his churinga, and the animals of the totemic species are partially equivalent and interchangeable things. This is because, in certain respects, they all act upon the collective consciousness in the same way. If the churinga is sacred, it is sacred because the totemic emblem engraved on its surface provokes collective feelings of respect. The same feeling is attached to the animals or plants whose outward form the totem copies, to the soul of the individual (since it is itself thought of in the form of the totemic being), and finally to the ancestral soul of which the preceding is only a particular aspect. In this way, all these disparate objects, whether real or ideal, have a common element by which they arouse the same affective state in consciousness and consequently merge. To the extent that they are expressed by one and the same representation, they are indistinguishable. This is why the Arunta could be led to see the churinga as the body common to the individual, the ancestor, and even the totemic being. It is a way of saying to himself that the feelings of which those different things are the object are identical.

However, from the fact that the idea of soul derives from the idea of mana, it in no way follows either that the idea of soul was a relatively late development or that there was a historical time in which men knew the religious forces only in their impersonal forms. If by the word "preanimism" we mean to designate a historical period during which animism is thought to have been unknown, we set up an arbitrary hypothesis,[125] for there is no people among whom the idea of soul and the idea of mana do not coexist. We thus have no basis for supposing that they were formed in two distinct periods; all the evidence suggests instead that they are more or less contemporaneous. Just as there is no society without individuals, so the impersonal forces that arise from collectivity cannot take form without incarnating themselves in individual consciousnesses, in which they become individualized. These are not two different processes but two different aspects

[125]This is the thesis of [Konrad Theodor] Preuss in the *Globus* articles I have cited several times. Mr. Lévy-Bruhl also seems inclined toward the same idea (See *Fonctions mentales, etc.*, pp. 92–93).

of one and the same process. True, they are not of equal importance, since one is more fundamental than the other. If mana is to be able to individualize and fragment into particular souls, it must first exist, and what it is in itself does not depend on the forms it takes as it individualizes. Hence the idea of mana does not presuppose that of soul. Quite the contrary, the idea of soul cannot be understood except in relation to the idea of mana. In this regard, one can indeed say that it is due to a "secondary" formation—but a secondary formation in the logical, not the chronological, sense of the word.

V

But how did men come to believe that the soul survives the body and can even survive it indefinitely?

What emerges from the analysis I have conducted is that belief in immortality was not at all formed under the influence of ideas about morality. Man did not imagine extending his existence beyond the tomb so that a just retribution of moral acts could be provided in another life, if not in this one. We have seen that all considerations of this sort were foreign to the primitive idea of the beyond.

Nor are we any better off accepting the hypothesis that the other life was invented as a means of escape from the anguishing prospect of annihilation. First of all, the need for personal survival is far from having been very strong at the beginning. The primitive generally accepts the idea of death with a sort of indifference. Brought up to take little account of his individuality and accustomed to endangering his life continually, he easily lets go of it.[126] Second, the immortality that is promised to him by the religions he practices is not at all personal. In many cases, the soul does not continue the personality of the deceased, or does not continue it for long, since, forgetting its previous existence, it goes forth after a certain time to animate other bodies and becomes thereby the life-giving principle of new personalities. Even among more advanced peoples, it was not the colorless and sad existence led by the shades in Sheol or Erebus that could ease the sorrow left by the memory of the life lost.

The notion that connects the idea of a posthumous life to dream experiences is a more satisfactory explanation. Our dead relatives and friends

---

[126]On this point, see my [Le] Suicide [étude de sociologie, Paris, F. Alcan, 1897], pp. 233ff.

reappear to us in dreams. We see them acting and hear them speaking; it is natural to draw the conclusion that they still exist. But if those observations could have served as confirmation of the idea, once born, they do not seem capable of having called it forth from nothing. The dreams in which we see deceased persons alive again are too rare and too short, and the memories they leave are in themselves too vague, for dreams alone to have suggested such an important system of beliefs to men. There is a marked disproportion between the effect and the cause to which it is ascribed.

What makes the question troublesome is that, by itself, the idea of the soul did not entail the idea of survival but seemed to preclude it. Indeed, we have seen that the soul, while distinct from the body, is nevertheless thought to be closely linked with it. Since the soul grows old with the body and reacts to all the body's illnesses, it must have seemed natural for the soul to die with the body. The belief must at least have been that it ceased to exist the moment it irrevocably lost its original form, when nothing of what it had been remained. Yet it is at just this moment that a new life opens out before it.

The myths I have previously reported furnish us with the only possible explanation of that belief. We have seen that the souls of newborns were either emanations of ancestral souls or those same souls reincarnated. But to have been able either to reincarnate themselves or to give off new emanations periodically, they had to have outlived their first possessors, so it seems that the idea of the survival of the dead was accepted in order to make the birth of the living explicable. The primitive does not have the idea of an all-powerful god that pulls souls out of nothingness. It seems to him that one can only make souls with other souls. Those that are born in this way can only be new forms of those that existed in the past. Consequently, they must go on existing so that others can be formed. In sum, belief in the immortality of souls is the only way man is able to comprehend a fact that cannot fail to attract his attention: the perpetuity of the group's life. The individuals die, but the clan survives, so the forces that constitute his life must have the same perpetuity. These forces are the souls that animate the individual bodies, because it is in and by them that the group realizes itself. For that reason, they must endure. Indeed, while enduring, they also must remain the same. Since the clan always keeps its characteristic form, the spiritual substance of which it is made must be conceived of as qualitatively invariable. Since it is always the same clan with the same totemic principle, it must also be the same souls, the souls being nothing other than the totemic principle fragmented and particularized. Thus, there is a mystical sort of germinative plasma that is transmitted from generation to generation and that creates, or at least is held to create, the spiritual unity of the clan over time. And despite its symbolic nature, this belief is not without objective truth, for although the group is not immortal in the absolute sense of the word, yet it is true that the group lasts above and beyond the individuals and that it is reborn and reincarnated in each new generation.

One fact confirms this interpretation. We have seen that, according to Strehlow's account, the Arunta distinguish two sorts of souls: those of the Alcheringa ancestors and those of the individuals who at any moment in history constitute the body of the tribe. The souls of individuals outlive the body for only a rather short time and are soon nullified completely. Only those of the Alcheringa ancestors are immortal: Just as they are uncreated, so they do not perish. Now, it is to be noticed that these are also the only ones whose immortality is needed in order to explain the permanence of the group, for the function of ensuring the perpetuity of the clan falls to them and them alone: Every conception is their doing. In this regard, the others have no role to play. Thus the souls are said to be immortal only to the extent that this immortality is useful in making the continuity of collective life intelligible.

The causes of the first beliefs about another life were thus unrelated to the functions that institutions beyond the grave would later have to fulfill. But, once born, they were soon put to use for ends different from those that were their initial *raison d'être*. From the Australian societies on, we see those causes beginning to organize themselves to this end. To do so, furthermore, they had no need to undergo fundamental transformations. How true it is that the same social institution can fulfill different functions successively, without changing its nature!

VI

The idea of soul long was and in part still is the most widely held form of the idea of personality.[127] By examining how the idea of soul originated, therefore, we should come to understand how the idea of personality was formed.

---

[127]It might be objected that unity is the characteristic of personalities, while the soul has always been conceived as multiple and as capable of dividing and subdividing almost infinitely. But we know today that the unity of the person is also made up of parts, that it is itself also capable of dividing and subdividing itself. Still, the idea of personality does not disappear merely because we have ceased to think of it as an indivisible, metaphysical atom. The same is true of those commonsense ideas of personality that have found expression in the idea of soul. They show that all peoples have always felt that the human person did not have the absolute unity certain metaphysicians have imputed to it.

It is a consequence of the preceding that two sorts of elements produced the idea of person. One is essentially impersonal: It is the spiritual principle that serves as the soul of the collectivity. That principle is the very substance of which individual souls are made. It is not the property of anyone in particular but part of the collective patrimony; in and through that principle, all the consciousnesses commune. From a different point of view, if there are to be separate personalities, some factor must intervene to fragment and differentiate this principle; in other words, an element of individuation is necessary. The body plays this role. Since bodies are distinct from one another, since they occupy different positions in time and space, each is a special milieu in which the collective representations are gradually refracted and colored differently. Hence, even if all the consciousnesses situated in those bodies view the same world—namely, the world of ideas and feelings that morally unify the group—they do not all view it from the same viewpoint; each expresses it in his own fashion.

Of those two equally indispensable factors, the impersonal element is certainly not the less important, since it is the one that furnishes the raw material for the idea of soul. It will be surprising, perhaps, to see such an important role attributed to the impersonal element in the origin of the idea of personality. But the philosophical analysis of that idea, which stole a march on sociological analysis, and by a lot, arrived at similar results on this point. Of all the philosophers, Leibniz is one of those who had the most vivid sense of what the personality is, for the monad is, first of all, a personal and autonomous being. And yet, for Leibniz, the content of all the monads is identical. All in fact are consciousnesses that express one and the same object: the world. And since the world itself is but a system of representations, each individual consciousness is in the end only a reflection of the universal consciousness. However, each expresses it from its own point of view and in its own manner. We know how this difference of perspectives arises from the fact that the monads are differently placed with respect to one another and with respect to the whole system they comprise.

Kant expresses this same awareness differently. For him, the cornerstone of personality is will. Will is the capacity to act in accordance with reason, and reason is that which is most impersonal in us. Reason is not my reason; it is human reason in general. It is the power of the mind to rise above the particular, the contingent, and the individual and to think in universal terms. From this point of view, one can say that what makes a man a person is that by which he is indistinguishable from other men; it is that which makes him man, rather than such and such a man. The senses, the body, in short everything that individualizes, is, to the contrary, regarded by Kant as antagonistic to personhood.

This is because individuation is not the essential characteristic of the person. A person is not only a singular subject that is distinguished from all the others. It is, in addition and most of all, a being to which a relative autonomy is imputed in relation to the milieu with which it interacts most directly. A person is conceived of as being capable, in a certain measure, of moving on its own. This is what Leibniz expressed in an extreme fashion, saying that the monad is entirely closed to the outside. My analysis enables us to imagine how this conception was formed and to what it corresponds.

The nature of the soul, which is in fact a symbolic expression of the personality, is the same. Although in close union with the body, it is presumed to be profoundly distinct from and broadly independent of the body. During life, it can leave the body temporarily, and at death it retires therefrom for good. Far from being subordinated to the body, it dominates the body given its higher status. It may very well borrow from the body the outward form in which it becomes individualized, but it owes the body nothing essential. This autonomy that all peoples have ascribed to the soul is not mere illusion, and we now know its objective basis. Granted, the elements that constitute the idea of the soul, and those that enter into the idea [représentation] of the body, come from two sources different from and independent of one another. The first are made of impressions and images that come from every part of the body; the others consist of ideas and feelings that come from the society and express it. Hence, the first are not derived from the second.

In this way, there really is a part of us that is not directly subordinate to the organic factor: That part is everything that represents society in us. The general ideas that religion or science impresses upon our minds, the mental operations that these ideas presuppose, the beliefs and feelings on which our moral life is based—all the higher forms of psychic activity that society stimulates and develops in us—are not, like our sensations and bodily states, towed along by the body. This is so because, as I have shown, the world of representations in which social life unfolds is added to its material substrate, far indeed from originating there. The determinism that reigns in that world of representations is thus far more supple than the determinism that is rooted in our flesh-and-blood constitution, and it leaves the agent with a justified impression of greater liberty. The milieu in which we move in this way is somehow less opaque and resistant. In it we feel, and are, more at ease. In other words, the only means we have of liberating ourselves from physical forces is to oppose them with collective forces.

What we have from society we have in common with our fellow men, so it is far from true that the more individualized we are, the more personal we are. The two terms are by no means synonymous. In a sense, they oppose more than they imply one another. Passion individualizes and yet enslaves. Our sensations are in their essence individual. But the more emancipated we are from the senses, and the more capable we are of thinking and acting conceptually, the more we are persons. Those who emphasize all that is social in the individual do not mean by that to deny or denigrate personhood. They simply refuse to confound it with the fact of individuation.[128]

---

[128]For all that, I do not deny the importance of the individual factor, which is explained from my standpoint just as easily as its contrary. Even if the essential element of personality is that which is social in us, from another standpoint, there can be no social life unless distinct individuals are associated within it; and the more numerous and different from one another they are, the richer it is. Thus the individual factor is a condition of the personal factor. The reciprocal is no less true, for society itself is an important source of individual differentiation (See *De la Division du travail social*, 3d ed. [Paris, F. Alcan (1893), 1902], pp. 627ff.).

CHAPTER NINE

THE NOTION OF SPIRITS
AND GODS

With the notion of soul, we left the domain of impersonal forces. But even the Australian religions recognize higher-order mythical entities, above and beyond the soul: spirits, civilizing heroes, and even gods, properly so-called. Without entering into the mythologies in detail, we must try to discover what form these three categories of spiritual beings take in Australia and how they fit into the religious system as a whole.

I

A soul is not a spirit. A soul is shut up in a definite body, and although it can come out at certain times, normally it is the body's prisoner. It escapes for good only at death, and even so we have seen with what difficulty that separation is made final. On the other hand, although a spirit is often closely tied to a particular object as its preferred residence—a spring, a rock, a tree, a star, and so forth—it can leave at will to lead an independent life in space. As a result, its influence has a wider radius. It can act upon all individuals who approach it or are approached by it. By contrast, the soul has almost no influence over anything other than the body it animates; only in very rare instances during its earthly life does it affect anything else.

But if the soul lacks those features that define the spirit, it acquires them through death, at least in part. Once disincarnated, and so long as it has not come down again into a body, it has the same freedom of movement as a spirit. To be sure, it is thought to leave for the land of souls when the rites of mourning are completed, but before that, it remains in the vicinity of the tomb for a rather long time. Furthermore, even when it has left there for good, it is thought to continue prowling around the camp.[1] It is generally

---

[1] [Walter Edmund] Roth, *Superstition, Magic, etc.* [and Medicine, in *North Queensland Ethnography*, Bulletin no. 5, Brisbane, G. A. Vaughn, 1903], §65, 68; [Sir Baldwin] Spencer and [Francis James] Gillen [*The Native Tribes of Central Australia*, London, Macmillan, 1899], pp. 514, 516.

imagined as rather a kindly being, especially by the surviving members of its family. We have seen, in fact, that the soul of the father comes to nurture the growth of his children and grandchildren. Sometimes, however, depending entirely on its mood and its treatment by the living, it displays true cruelty.[2] Thus, especially for women and children, it is advisable not to venture outside the camp at night, so as to avoid the risk of dangerous encounters.[3]

A ghost, however, is not a true spirit. First, its power is usually limited; second, it does not have definite functions. It is a vagabond being with no clear-cut responsibility, since the effect of death was to set it outside all the regular structures. In relation to the living, it is demoted, as it were. On the other hand, a spirit always has some sort of power, and indeed it is defined by that power. It has authority over some range of cosmic or social phenomena; it has a more or less precise function to perform in the world scheme.

But some souls meet this dual condition and thus are spirits proper. These are the souls of mythical personages that are placed by popular imagination at the beginning of time: the Alcheringa or Altjirangamitjina people of the Arunta, the Mura-muras of the Lake Eyre tribes, the Muk-Kurnais of the Kurnai, and others. In a sense, these actually are still souls, since they are thought to have animated bodies in the past but to have separated from them at some point. However, as we have seen, even while they were living earthly lives, they already had exceptional powers. They had mana superior to that of ordinary men, and they kept it thereafter. Besides, they have definite functions.

To begin with, whether we accept Spencer and Gillen's account or Strehlow's, the responsibility for ensuring the periodic recruitment of the clan falls squarely on their shoulders. Matters of conception are their domain.

Once conception has taken place, the ancestor's task is not finished. It is up to him to watch over the newborn. Later, when the child has become a man, the ancestor accompanies him on the hunt and drives game toward him, warns him in dreams of dangers he may encounter, protects him from his enemies, and so forth. On this point, Strehlow is in entire agreement with Spencer and Gillen.[4] Granted, one may wonder how, on their account, the ancestor can perform this function. It would seem that because he reincarnates himself at the moment of conception, he would have to be assimi-

---

[2]Spencer and Gillen, *Native Tribes*, pp. 515, 521; [James] Dawson [*Australian Aborigines: The Languages, and Customs of Several Tribes of Aborigines in the Western District of Victoria, Australia*, Melbourne, G. Robertson, 1881], p. 58; Roth, *Superstition, Magic*, §67.

[3]Spencer and Gillen, *Native Tribes*, p. 517.

[4][Carl] Strehlow [*Die Aranda- und Loritja-Stämme in Zentral Australien*, Frankfurt, J. Baer, 1907], vol. II, p. 76 and n. 1; Spencer and Gillen, *Native Tribes*, pp. 514, 516.

lated with the child's soul and thus could not possibly protect it from outside. But he can because he does not reincarnate himself whole, but instead produces his double. One part enters the body of the woman and impregnates her; another continues to exist outside and, with the special name of Arumburinga, performs the function of tutelary genie.[5]

We can see how closely akin that ancestral spirit is to the *genius* of the Latins and the δαίμων of the Greeks.[6] Their functions are completely identical. Indeed the *genius* is, above all, the one who engenders—*qui gignit*. The *genius* expresses and personifies the generative force.[7] At the same time, it is the protector and guide of the particular individual to whose person it is attached.[8] Finally, it merges with that individual's very personality, representing the set of characteristic inclinations and tendencies that give him distinctiveness among other men.[9] Hence the well-known saying *indulgere genio, defraudare genium,** in the sense of "follow one's natural temperament." Fundamentally, the *genius* is another form of, and a double of, the individual's soul itself. The partial synonymy of *genius* and *manes* proves this.[10] The *manes* are the *genius* after death, but they are also the part of the deceased that survives—in other words, the soul of the deceased. In the same way, the Arunta's soul and the ancestral spirit that serve as his *genius* are but two different aspects of the same being.

The ancestor has a defined position, however, not only in relation to persons but also in relation to things. Though his true residence is presumed to be underground, the ancestor is thought to keep haunting the site of his nanja tree or rock, or of the water hole that was spontaneously formed at the exact moment he disappeared into the ground, after ending his first existence. Since that tree or rock is thought to represent the body of the hero, his soul itself is imagined to return there continually and to reside there more or less permanently. The presence of that soul accounts for the religious respect

---

*To indulge one's genius is to cheat one's genius. That is, to cater to one's genius, rather than letting it assert itself, is to frustrate it. Trans.

[5][Spencer and Gillen, *Native Tribes*], p. 513.

[6]See [Augusto] Negrioli on this question, *Dei Genii presso i Romani*, [Bologna, Ditta Nicola Zanichelli, 1900]; the articles "Daimon" and "Genius" in *Dictionnaire des antiquités* [*Grècques et Romaines*, Paris, Hachette, 1877–1919]; [Ludwig] Preller, *Roemische Mythologie* [Berlin, Weidmann, 1858], vol. II, pp. 195ff.

[7]Negrioli, *Dei Genii presso i Romani*, p. 4.

[8]Ibid., p. 8.

[9]Ibid., p. 7.

[10]Ibid., p. 11. Cf. Samter, "Der Ursprung des Larencultus," in *Archiv für Religionswissenschaft*, 1907, pp. 368–393.

evoked by those places. No one may snap a branch of the nanja tree without risk of falling ill.[11] "At one time, the act of felling or damaging it was punished with death. Killing an animal or bird that takes refuge there is forbidden. Even the surrounding bush has to be respected—the grass must not be burned. The rocks, too, must be treated with respect. To move or break them is forbidden."[12] Since this quality of sacredness is ascribed to the ancestor, he seems to be the spirit of that tree, rock, water hole, or spring[13]—let the spring be considered as having to do with the rain,[14] and he becomes a spirit of the rain. Thus, these same souls that, in one of their aspects, serve men as protective genies also perform cosmic functions. One of Roth's texts is probably to be understood in this way: In North Queensland, the nature spirits are said to be souls of the dead that have chosen to reside in the forests or in caves.[15]

Now we have spirit beings that are something other than wandering souls without specific powers. Strehlow calls them gods,[16] but this term is inappropriate, at least in the vast majority of cases. And in a society such as that of the Arunta, where each individual has a protecting ancestor, there would be as many gods as individuals, or more. To apply the noun "god" to a sacred being that has only one adherent would promote terminological confusion. It is true that an ancestor figure can sometimes become enlarged to the point that it resembles a deity proper. Among the Warramunga, as I have pointed out,[17] the entire clan is thought to be descended from a single ancestor. How, under certain conditions, this collective ancestor could have become the object of collective devotion is easily comprehended. This happened to the

---

[11][Rev. Louis] Schulze, "Aborigines of the Upper and Middle Finke River," *RSSA*, vol. XIV [1891], p. 237.

[12]Strehlow, *Aranda*, vol. I, p. 5. Cf. Spencer and Gillen, *Native Tribes*, p. 133; S. Gason, in [Edward Micklethwaite] Curr, [*The Australian Race: Its Origin, Languages, Customs, Place of Landing in Australia and the Routes by Which It Spread Itself over That Continent*, Melbourne, J. Ferres, 1886–1887], vol. II, p. 69.

[13]See, in [Alfred William] Howitt [*The Native Tribes of South East Australia*, London, Macmillan, 1904], p. 482), the case of a Mura-mura who is regarded as the spirit of certain hot springs.

[14][Baldwin Spencer and Francis James Gillen], *Northern Tribes* [*of Central Australia* London, Macmillan, 1904], pp. 313–314; [Robert Hamilton] Mathews, "[Ethnological Notes on the] Aboriginal Tribes of New South Wales and Victoria," *RSNSW,* vol. XXXVIII [1904], p. 351. Similarly, among the Dieri, there is a Mura-mura whose function is to produce rain (Howitt, *Native Tribes*, pp. 798–799).

[15]Roth, *Superstition, Magic*, §67. Cf. Dawson, *Australian Aborigines*, p. 58.

[16]Strehlow, *Aranda*, vol. I, pp. 2ff.

[17]See above, p. 252, n. 53.

snake Wollunqua, to take one example.[18] According to belief, this mythical animal (from which the clan of the same name is thought to originate) continues to live in a water hole that is held in religious veneration. Moreover, it is the object of a cult that the clan celebrates collectively. They try to please it and gain its favor by means of particular rites, making prayers of a sort to it, and so forth. Thus, one can say this mythical animal is like the god of the clan. But this is a very unusual case even, according to Spencer and Gillen, a unique one. Normally, "spirit" is the only word that is suitable for designating these ancestral personages.

As to the manner in which that idea was formed, we may say that it is obvious from all that has been said up to now.

As I have shown, once the existence of souls was accepted, it could not be comprehended without imagining, at the beginning of things, an original fund of fundamental souls from which all the others derived. These archetypical souls must necessarily have been imagined as containing in themselves the source of all religious efficacy, for, since the imagination goes back no further, all the sacred things are held to come from them: the instruments of the cult, the members of the clan, the animals of the totemic species. They incarnate all the religiousness that is diffused throughout the tribe and the world. This is why powers are attributed to them that are markedly superior to those enjoyed by the mere souls of men. Moreover, time itself increases and reinforces the sacredness of the things. A very old churinga elicits far greater respect than a modern one and is thought to have more virtues.[19] It is as though the feelings of veneration it has received through successive generations' handling are accumulated in it. For the same reason, the personages that have been the subjects of myths transmitted respectfully for centuries from mouth to mouth, and that are periodically enacted by rites, were bound to take an altogether special place in popular imagination.

But how does it happen that instead of remaining outside the framework of society, they have become regular members of it? The reason is that each individual is the double of an ancestor. Now, when two beings are so closely akin, they are naturally thought of as unified; since they share the same nature, what affects one seems necessarily to affect the other. In this way, the troop of the mythical ancestors became attached to the society of the living by a moral bond; the same interests and passions were imputed to both; and

[18]Spencer and Gillen, *Northern Tribes,* chap. VII.

[19]Ibid., p. 277.

they were seen as associates. But since the ancestors had higher status than the living, this association entered the public mind as a relationship between superiors and subordinates, patrons and clients, helpers and helped. Thus was born the curious notion of the tutelary genie attached to each individual.

How the ancestor was placed in contact not only with men but also with things might appear a more troublesome question. At first glance, it is not obvious what relationship could exist between a personage of this kind and a tree or rock. But a piece of information that we owe to Strehlow provides us with at least a plausible solution to this problem.

Those trees and rocks are not situated just anywhere in the tribal territory but are massed for the most part around certain sanctuaries (called ert-natulunga by Spencer and Gillen and arknanaua by Strehlow), where the churingas of the clan are kept.[20] How deeply these places are respected we know from the very fact that the most precious cult instruments are kept there. In addition, each of them radiates sanctity. This is why the nearby trees and rocks seem sacred, why it is forbidden to destroy or damage them, and why any violence against them is sacrilege. This sacredness stems from the phenomenon of psychic contagion. To account for it, the native is obliged to grant that these different objects are in relations with the beings that he sees as the source of all religious power—that is, with the Alcheringa ancestors. Therein originates the system of myths I have recounted. Each ertnatulunga was imagined to mark the place where a group of ancestors were swallowed up by the earth. The mounds and trees that then covered the ground were thought to represent their bodies. But because the soul generally retains a certain affinity for the body in which it once lived, people naturally came to believe that these ancestral souls preferred to keep frequenting the places where their physical envelope remained. Hence they were localized in trees, rocks, and water holes. In this way, each of them, while remaining attached to the guardianship of a definite individual, found itself transformed into a sort of *genius loci** and performed the function of one.[21]

---

* A spirit attached to a place. Standard Roman belief was that every place had one.

[20]Strehlow, *Aranda*, vol. I, p. 5.

[21]It is true that some nanja trees and rocks are not situated around the ertnatulunga but are scattered across various parts of the territory. They are said to correspond to places where a lone ancestor disappeared into the ground, lost an appendage, spilled some blood, or forgot a churinga that was transformed into either a tree or a rock. But these totemic sites have only secondary importance; Strehlow calls them *kleinere Totemplätze* (*Aranda*, vol. I, pp. 4–5). So we can imagine that they took on this character only by analogy with the principal totemic centers. The trees and rocks that in some way resembled those found in the neighborhood of the ertnatulunga stirred similar feelings, so as a result the myth that formed à propos of the place extended to the things.

Thus elucidated, these ideas put us in a position to understand a form of totemism that until now had to be left unexplained: individual totemism.

An individual totem is defined by essentially the two following characteristics: (1) it is a being in the form of an animal or plant whose function is to protect an individual; (2) the fate of the individual and that of its patron are closely interdependent. Everything that affects the patron is passed on sympathetically to the individual. The ancestral spirits just discussed fit the same definition. They also belong, at least in part, to the realm of animals or of plants. They too are tutelary genies. Finally, a sympathetic bond attaches each individual to his protecting ancestor. The nanja tree, the mystical body of that ancestor, cannot be destroyed without the man's feeling threatened. True, this belief is losing some of its force now, but Spencer and Gillen found it still in existence, and they judge it to have been widespread in the past.[22]

That these two ideas are identical can be seen even in the details. The ancestral souls live in trees or rocks that are considered sacred. Similarly, among the Euahlayi, the spirit of the animal that serves as an individual totem is held to live in a tree or stone.[23] This tree or stone is sacred: No one may touch it, except the one whose totem it is; and, when it is a stone or a rock, the prohibition is absolute.[24] The result is that these are true places of refuge.

Finally, we have seen that the individual soul is but a different aspect of the ancestral spirit; in a way, this spirit serves, to use Strehlow's phrase, as a second self.[25] Similarly, to use Mrs. Parker's phrase, the individual totem of the Euahlayi, called Yunbeai, is an alter ego of the individual: "The soul of the man is in his Yunbeai, and the soul of his Yunbeai is in him."[26] In essence, then, it is one soul in two bodies. The kinship of these two ideas is so great that they are sometimes expressed with one and the same word. This is true in Melanesia and Polynesia: *atai* on the island of Mota, *tamaniu* on the island of Aurora, and *talegia* at Motlaw designate both the soul of an individual and his personal totem.[27] The same is true of *aitu* in Samoa.[28] This is because the

[22][Spencer and Gillen], *Native Tribes*, p. 139.

[23][K. Langloh] Parker, [Catherine Sommerville Field Parker], *The Euahlayi* [*Tribe*, London, A. Constable, 1905], p. 21. The tree that serves this purpose is generally one of those that figure among the individual's subtotems. The reason given for this choice is that, being of the same family, they are probably more inclined to help him.

[24]Ibid., p. 36.

[25]Strehlow, *Aranda*, vol. II, p. 81.

[26]Parker, *Euahlayi Tribe* , p. 21.

[27][Robert Henry] Codrington, *The Melanesians* [Oxford, Clarendon Press, 1891], pp. 249–253.

[28][George] Turner, *Samoa*, London, Macmillan, 1884, p. 17.

individual totem is the outward and visible form of the self, the personality, and the soul is its inward and invisible form.[29]

Thus, the individual totem has all the essential characteristics of the protecting ancestor and plays the same role. All this is so because its origin is the same, and it arises from the same idea.

In fact, both involve a duplication of the soul. Like the ancestor, the totem is the individual's soul, but the soul externalized and invested with greater powers than those it is believed to have while inside the body. This duplication arises from a psychological need, for all it does is explain the nature of the soul which, as we have seen, is double. It is ours in a sense, it expresses our personality. But it is outside us at the same time, since it is the extension inside us of a religious force that is outside us. We cannot become fully merged with it because we ascribe to it a stature and a respect that lift it above us and our empirical individuality. There is a part of us, then, that we tend to project outside ourselves. This way of conceiving ourselves is so well established in our nature that even when we try to conceive of ourselves without using any religious symbol, we cannot escape it. Our moral consciousness is like the nucleus around which the idea of soul took form, and yet when it speaks to us, it seems to be a power outside of and greater than us, laying down the law to and judging us, but also helping and supporting us. When we have it on our side, we feel stronger amid the trials of life and more certain of overcoming, just as the Australian who has confidence in his ancestor or his personal totem feels more valiant against his enemies.[30] Thus there is something objective at the basis of these different ideas—be they the Roman *genius,* the individual totem, or the Alcheringa ancestor—and that is the reason they have survived in various forms until today. Everything works out as if we really did have two souls: one that is in us—or, rather, is us; another that is above us, and whose function is to oversee and assist the first. Frazer had an inkling that there was an external soul in the individual totem,

[29]These are the very words used by Codrington, *The Melanesians* (p. 251).

[30]This close relationship among the soul, the protective genie, and the moral consciousness of the individual is especially apparent among certain peoples of Indonesia: "One of the seven souls of the Toba-batak is buried with the placenta; while it prefers to reside there, it can leave to give warnings to the individual or to show approval when he conducts himself well. Thus, in a certain sense, it plays the role of moral conscience. However, its warnings do not extend only to the domain of moral affairs. It is called the younger brother of the soul, just as the placenta is called the younger brother of the child. . . . In war, it inspires the man with the courage to march against the enemy" ([Johannes Gustav] Warneck, *Der bataksche Ahnen und Geisterkult,* in *Allgemeine Missionszeitschrift,* Berlin, 1904, p. 10. Cf. [Albertus Christiaan] Kruijt, *Het Animisme in den indischen Archipel* ['s Gravenhage, M. Nijhoff, 1906], p. 25).

but he believed that externality was the result of an artifice or a magician's trick. In reality, it is implicit in the very constitution of the idea of soul.[31]

II

In the main, the spirits just discussed are kind. No doubt, they sometimes punish the man who does not treat them properly,[32] but doing harm is not their function.

In itself, however, the spirit can be used for evil as well as for good. This is why a class of clever genies naturally came into being opposite the auxiliary and tutelary spirits, which allowed men to explain the enduring evils they had to suffer—nightmares,[33] illnesses,[34] tornadoes, storms,[35] and so forth. Doubtless, this is not because all human miseries appeared to be too abnormal to be explained otherwise than by supernatural forces, but because, back then, all those forces were thought of in religious form. A religious principle is regarded as the source of life; hence it was logical for all the events that disturb or destroy life to be brought back to a principle of the same kind.

These harmful spirits seem to have been conceived according to the same model as the beneficent genies just discussed. They are conceived in the

[31]Still to be discovered is how it happens that, from some point in evolution on, this doubling of the soul was done in the form of the individual totem rather than that of the protecting ancestor. The question has perhaps more ethnographic than sociological interest. Still, here is how the origin of this substitution might be imagined.

The individual totem must have played a purely complementary role at first. The individuals who wished to acquire powers above the ordinary were not content, and could not be content, with only the protection of the ancestor. Hence they sought to fit themselves out with another auxiliary of the same kind. And so it is that, among the Euahlayi, the magicians are the only ones who have, or could have, procured individual totems. Since each of them also has a collective totem, they end up with several souls. There is nothing surprising about that multiplicity of souls; It is the condition of superior efficacy.

Once collective totemism lost ground and, in consequence, the notion of the protecting ancestor began to efface that of spirits, it became necessary to imagine the nature of the soul, which was still felt, differently. The idea remained that outside each individual soul there was another, responsible for watching over the first. In order to uncover that protective power, since it was not designated by the fact of birth itself, it seemed natural to use means similar to those magicians use to enter into dealings with the forces whose help those means ensure.

[32]See, for example, Strehlow, *Aranda*, vol. II, p. 82.

[33][J. P.] Wyatt, "Adelaide and Encounter Bay Tribes," in [James Dominick] Woods, [*The Native Tribes of South Australia*, Adelaide, E. S. Wigg, 1879], p. 168.

[34][Rev. George] Taplin, "The Narrinyeri" [in Woods, *The Native Tribes of South Australia*], pp. 62–63; Roth, *Superstition, Magic*, §116; Howitt, *Native Tribes*, pp. 356, 358; Strehlow, *Aranda*, vol. I, pp. 11–12.

[35]Strehlow, *Aranda*, vol. I, pp. 13–14; Dawson, *Australian Aborigines*, p. 49.

form of an animal, or as part animal and part human,[36] but people tend naturally to ascribe enormous dimensions and repulsive appearance to them.[37] Like the souls of ancestors, they are thought to live in trees, rocks, water holes, and underground caverns.[38] Many are presented to us as the souls of persons who have lived earthly lives.[39] Spencer and Gillen say explicitly, so far as the Arunta in particular are concerned, that these bad genies, known by the name Oruncha, are Alcheringa beings.[40] Among the personages of mythical times, there were different temperaments. Certain of them had and still have cruel and mean instincts,[41] while others were of innately poor constitution—thin and haggard. Therefore, when they went down into the ground, the nanja rocks to which they gave birth were considered to be centers of dangerous influences.[42]

Certain characteristics distinguish them from their brethren, the Alcheringa heroes. They do not reincarnate themselves; they are never represented among the living; and they are without human progeny.[43] So when, according to certain signs, a child is believed to be the product of their labors, it is put to death as soon as it is born.[44] In addition, these harmful spirits do not belong to any definite totemic center and are outside the social organization.[45] Through all these traits, we see that such powers are far more magic

---

[36]Strehlow, *Aranda*, vol. I, pp. 11–14; [Richard] Eylmann [*Die Eingeborenen der Kolonie Sud Australien, Berlin, D. Reumer*], pp. 182, 185, Spencer and Gillen, *Northern Tribes*, p. 211; [Rev. C. W.] Schürmann, *The Aboriginal Tribes of Port Lincoln*, in Woods [*The Native Tribes of South Australia*], p. 239.

[37]Eylmann, *Eingeborenen*, p. 182.

[38]Mathews, "Aboriginal Tribes," p. 345; [Lorimer] Fison and [Alfred William] Howitt, *Kamilaroi and Kurnai* [Melbourne, G. Robertson, 1880], p. 467; Strehlow, *Aranda*, vol. I, p. 11.

[39]Roth, *Superstition, Magic*, §115; Eylmann, *Eingeborenen*, p. 190.

[40]Spencer and Gillen, *Native Tribes*, pp. 390–391. Strehlow calls the bad spirits *Erintja*, but this word and *Oruncha* are obviously equivalents. Yet they are presented in different ways. The Oruncha, according to Spencer and Gillen, are more malicious than evil; indeed, according to these observers (p. 328), totally evil beings are unknown to the Arunta. By contrast, Strehlow's Erintja have the routine function of doing evil. Furthermore, according to certain myths that Spencer and Gillen themselves report (*Native Tribes*, p. 390), it seems that they have embellished the Oruncha figures somewhat. Originally, they were more like ogres (ibid., p. 331).

[41]Spencer and Gillen, *Native Tribes*, pp. 390–391.

[42]Ibid., p. 551.

[43]Ibid., pp. 326–327.

[44]Strehlow, *Aranda*, vol. I, p. 14. When there are twins, the firstborn is thought to have been conceived in that way.

[45]Spencer and Gillen, *Native Tribes*, p. 327.

than they are religious. And indeed, they are above all in contact with the magician, who often obtains his powers from them.[46] I thus arrive at the point where the world of religion ends and that of magic begins; and since magic is beyond the scope of my research, I need push that study no further.[47]

III

The appearance of the idea of spirit marks an important advance in the individuation of religious forces. Nevertheless, the spirit beings discussed up to now continue to be only secondary personages. Either they are evil genies that belong more to magic than to religion, or else, attached to a definite individual and place, they can make their influence felt only within a very limited radius. Therefore they can be the objects of only private and local rites. But once the idea of spirit took form, it naturally extended into the higher spheres of religious life. And in this way, higher-order mythical personalities were born.

Although the ceremonies proper to each clan differ from one another, they belong to the same religion nonetheless, and so there are basic similarities. Since every clan is but a part of one and the same tribe, the unity of the tribe cannot fail to show through the diversity of particular cults. And as it turns out, there is indeed no totemic group that does not have churingas and bull roarers, which are used everywhere in a similar way. The organization of the tribe into phratries, marriage classes, and clans, and the exogamic prohibitions attached thereto, are also genuinely tribal institutions. All the festivals of initiation involve certain basic practices—tooth extraction, circumcision, subincision, and others—that do not vary by totem within a single tribe. Uniformity in this matter is the more easily established since initiation always takes place in the presence of the tribe, or at least before an assembly to which different clans have been summoned. The reason is that the aim of initiation is to introduce the novice into the religious life of the tribe as a whole, not merely that of the clan into which he was born. Therefore the varied aspects of the tribal religion must be enacted before him and, in a sense, pass before his eyes. This is the occasion on which the moral and religious unity of the tribe is best demonstrated.

[46]Howitt, *Native Tribes*, pp. 358, 381, 385; Spencer and Gillen, *Native Tribes*, p. 334; *Northern Tribes*, p. 327.

[47]Nevertheless, the spirit beings discussed up to now continue to be spirits whose only function is to do ill; the others' role is to prevent or neutralize the evil influence of the first. Cases of this kind are to be found in *Northern Tribes*, pp. 501–502. What brings out clearly that both are magical is that, among the Arunta, both have the same name. Hence, these are different aspects of the same magical power.

Hence there are in each society a certain number of rites that are distinguished from all the others by their homogeneity and their universality. Because such a remarkable concordance did not seem explainable except by common origin, it was imagined that each group of similar rites had been instituted by one and the same ancestor, who had come to reveal them to the tribe as a whole. Thus, among the Arunta, an ancestor of the Wildcat clan, named Putiaputia,[48] is held to have taught men how to make churingas and use them ritually; among the Warramunga, it is Murtu-murtu;[49] among the Urabunna, it is Witurna;[50] Atnatu among the Kaitish[51] and Tundun among the Kurnai.[52] Similarly, the practices of circumcision are ascribed by the eastern Dieri and several other tribes[53] to two specific Mura-muras, and by the Arunta to an Alcheringa hero of the Lizard totem, named Mangarkunjerkunja.[54] To the same personage are ascribed the institution of marriage prohibitions and the social organization they entail, the discovery of fire, the invention of the spear, the shield, the boomerang, and so forth. Incidentally, the inventor of the bull roarer is often considered to be the founder of initiation rites, as well.[55]

These special ancestors could not be placed on a par with the others. For one thing, the feelings of veneration they inspired were not limited to one clan but were common to the whole tribe. For another, all that was valued most in the tribal civilization was attributed to them. For this twofold reason, they became the object of special veneration. For example, it is said that

---

[48]Strehlow, *Aranda*, vol. I, p. 9. Moreover, Putiaputia is not the only personage of this kind that is mentioned in the Arunta myths. Certain parts of the tribe give a different name to the hero to whom they attribute the same invention. It should be borne in mind that the breadth of the territory occupied by the Arunta does not permit the mythology to be perfectly homogeneous.

[49]Spencer and Gillen, *Northern Tribes*, p. 493.

[50]Ibid., p. 498.

[51]Ibid., pp. 498–499.

[52]Howitt, *Native Tribes*, p. 135.

[53]Ibid., pp. 476ff.

[54]Strehlow, *Aranda*, vol. I, pp. 6–8. Later, the work of Mangarkunjerkunja had to be taken in hand again by other heroes; according to a belief that is not peculiar to the Arunta, a moment came when men forgot the teachings of their first initiators and compromised themselves. [Here, Durkheim may well have been thinking of the biblical prophets. Notice that this point is unrelated to the one made in the text. Trans.]

[55]This is the case, for example, of Atnatu (Spencer and Gillen, *Northern Tribes*, p. 153), and of Witurna (ibid., p. 498). If Tundun did not initiate the rites, it is he who is charged with directing their celebration (Howitt, *Native Tribes*, p. 670).

Atnatu was born in the sky, even before Alcheringa times, and that he made and named himself. The stars are his wives or his daughters. Beyond the sky where he lives, there is another with another sun.* His name is sacred and must never be said before women or the uninitiated.[56]

Still, no matter how great the stature of these personages, there was never any reason to establish special rites in their honor, for they are themselves no more than the rite personified. The only reason they exist is to explain the practices that exist. They are but a different aspect of those practices. The churinga is inseparable from the ancestor who invented it; they sometimes have the same name.[57] When the bull roarer is sounded, the voice of the ancestor is said to be making itself heard.[58] But because each of these heroes is merged with the cult he is said to have instituted, he is thought to oversee the manner in which it is celebrated. Not satisfied unless the faithful perform their duties exactly, he punishes those who are neglectful.[59] Thus he is considered the guardian of the rite as well as its founder, and for that reason he becomes invested with an authentically moral role.[60]

IV

Yet even this mythological formation is not the most advanced that is to be found among the Australians. Several tribes have achieved the conception of a god who, if not the only one, is at the least the supreme one, and one to whom a preeminent position among all the other religious entities is ascribed.

The existence of that belief was long ago reported by various observers,[61] but Howitt has contributed most to establishing that it is relatively wide-

---

*In the first edition, "sun" and "moon" are not capitalized, but in the second they are. The rationale for capitalizing them probably was that they sometimes serve as proper names. In both editions, "Kangaroo," "Emu," and other nouns are capitalized when they refer to clans. Trans.

[56][Spencer and Gillen], *Northern Tribes*, p. 499.

[57]Howitt, *Native Tribes*, p. 493; [Fison and Howitt], *Kamilaroi and Kurnai*, pp. 197, 267; Spencer and Gillen, *Northern Tribes*, p. 492.

[58]See, for example, *Northern Tribes*, p. 499.

[59]Ibid., pp. 338, 347, 499.

[60]Spencer and Gillen contend that these mythical beings play no moral role (*Northern Tribes*, p. 493), true enough; but this is because they give the word too narrow a sense. Religious duties are duties; hence the fact of watching over the manner in which they are performed concerns morality—all the more because, at that moment, all morality is religious in character.

[61]This fact had been documented as far back as 1845 by [Edward John] Eyre, *Journals [of Expeditions of Discovery into Central Australia*, London, T. and W. Boone, 1845], vol. II, p. 362, and before Eyre, by Henderson, in his *Observations on the Colonies of New South Wales and Van Diemen's Land* [Calcutta, Baptist Mission Press, 1832], p. 147.

spread. Indeed, he has documented it for a very wide geographic area comprising Victoria State and New South Wales, and extending as far as Queensland.[62] Throughout that entire region, a large number of tribes believe in the existence of a genuinely tribal deity that has different names in different regions. The most frequently employed are Bunjil or Punjil,[63] Daramulun,[64] and Baiame.[65] But we also find the names Nuralie or Nurelle,[66] Kohin,[67] and Mungan-ngaua.[68] The same idea is found farther west, among the Narrinyeri, where the high god is called Nurunderi or Ngurrunderi.[69] Among the Dieri, it is quite probable that, above the Mura-muras or ordinary ancestors, there is one that enjoys a kind of supremacy.[70] Finally, in contrast to Spencer and Gillen, who claim not to have observed any belief in a god proper among the Arunta,[71] Strehlow assures us this people, as well as the Loritja, recognize a true "good god," with the name Altjira.[72]

The characteristics of this personage are fundamentally the same everywhere. It is an immortal and indeed an eternal being, since it is derived from

---

[62][Howitt], *Native Tribes*, pp. 488–508.

[63]Among the Kulin, the Wotjobaluk, and the Woëworung (Victoria).

[64]Among the Yuin, the Ngarrigo, and the Wolgal (New South Wales).

[65]Among the Kamilaroi and the Euahlayi (the northern part of New South Wales); and more toward the center of the same province, among the Wonghibon and the Wiradjuri.

[66]Among the Wiimbaio and the tribes of Lower Murry, [William] Ridley, *Kamilaroi*, [*and Other Australian Languages*, Sydney, T. Richards, 1875], p. 137; [Robert] Brough Smyth, [*The Aborigines of Victoria*, Melbourne, J. Ferres, 1878], vol. I, p. 423 n. 431).

[67]Among the tribes of the Herbert River (Howitt, *Native Tribes*, p. 498).

[68]Among the Kurnai.

[69]Taplin, "Narrinyeri," p. 55; Eylmann, *Eingeborenen*, p. 182.

[70]It is probably to this supreme Mura-mura that Gason alludes in the passage already cited ([Edward M.] Curr, [*The Australian Race*], vol. II, p. 55).

[71][Spencer and Gillen], *Native Tribes*, p. 246.

[72]The difference between Baiame, Bunjil, and Daramulun, on the one hand, and Altjira, on the other, would be that the last named is totally indifferent to everything that concerns humanity. It is not he who made men, and he does not concern himself with what they do. The Arunta neither love nor fear him. But even if that idea was accurately observed and analyzed, it is quite difficult to accept as original, for if Altjira plays no role, explains nothing, and serves no purpose, what would have made the Arunta imagine him? Perhaps he must be seen as a sort of Baiame who lost his former prestige, a former god whose memory gradually faded. Perhaps, as well, Strehlow wrongly interpreted the accounts he collected. According to Eylmann (who, granted, is neither a competent nor a very reliable observer), Altjira made men (*Eingeborenen*, p. 184). In addition, among the Loritja, the personage that, with the name Tukura, corresponds to the Altjira of the Arunta is believed to conduct the ceremonies of initiation himself.

no other. After having lived on earth for a time, he lifted himself, or was carried, to the sky.[73] He continues to live there surrounded by his family—one or several wives being widely attributed to him, as well as children and brothers[74] who sometimes assist him in his functions. Because of a stay in the sky (together with the family attributed to him), he is often identified with particular stars.[75] Moreover, he is said to have power over the stars. It is he who set up the movement of the sun and the moon;[76] he orders them about.[77] It is he who causes lightning to leap forth from the clouds and who hurls the thunder.[78] Because he is the thunder, he is associated with the rain as well,[79] and it is he who must be addressed when there is want of water or too much.[80]

He is spoken of as a sort of creator. He is called the father of men and is said to have made them. According to a legend once current near Melbourne, Bunjil is said to have made the first man in the following manner: He made a statuette out of clay;* then he danced all around it several times, breathed into its nostrils, and the statuette came alive and began to walk.[81] According to another myth, he lit the sun, whereupon the earth warmed up and men came out of it.[82] At the same time as he made men,[83] this divine

*Curiously, despite the Australian context, Swain (p. 324) wrote *"white* clay," although Durkheim merely said *argile.*

[73]For Bunjil, see Brough Smyth [*Aborigines of Victoria*], vol. I, p. 417; for Baiame, Ridley, *Kamilaroi*, p. 136; for Daramulun, Howitt, *Native Tribes*, p. 495.

[74]On the composition of Bunjil's family, for example, see Howitt, *Native Tribes*, pp. 128, 129, 489, 491; Brough Smyth [*Aborigines of Victoria*], vol. I, pp. 417, 423; for that of Baiame, Parker, *The Euahlayi*, pp. 7, 66, 103; Howitt, *Native Tribes*, pp. 407, 502, 585; for that of Nurunderi, Taplin, "The Narrinyeri" [in Woods, *The Native Tribes of South Australia*] pp. 57–58. Besides, the manner in which the families of the high gods are conceived has all sorts of variations. Such and such a personage is here the brother and elsewhere called the son. The number of wives and their names vary according to region.

[75]Howitt, *Native Tribes*, p. 128.

[76]Brough Smyth [*Aborigines of Victoria*], vol. I, pp. 430, 431.

[77]Ibid., vol. I, p. 432 n.

[78]Howitt, *Native Tribes*, pp. 498, 538; Mathews, "Aboriginal Tribes," *RSNSW,* vol. XXXVIII, p. 343; Ridley, *Kamilorai* p. 136.

[79]Howitt, *Native Tribes*, p. 538; Taplin, *The Narrinyeri*, pp. 57–58.

[80]Parker, *The Euahlayi*, p. 8

[81]Brough Smyth [*Aborigines of Victoria*], vol. I, p. 424.

[82]Howitt, *Native Tribes*, p. 492.

[83]According to certain myths, he made men and not women; this is what is said of Bunjil. But the origin of women is attributed to his son-brother, Pallyan (Brough Smyth [*Aborigines of Victoria*], vol. I, pp. 417, 423).

personage made the animals and the trees,[84] and all the arts of life—weapons, language, tribal rites[85]—are thanks to him. He is the benefactor of humanity. Even today, he plays the role of a kind of Providence for humanity. It is he who provides his own with all that is needful in their existence.[86] He communicates with them directly or through intermediaries.[87] And being at the same time the guardian of tribal morality, he punishes when that morality is violated.[88] Furthermore, if we can rely on the word of certain observers, he performs the function of judge after death, distinguishing between the good and the bad and not treating both the same.[89] In any event, he is often presented as gatekeeper for the land of the dead,[90] welcoming the souls when they arrive in the beyond.[91]

Since initiation is the principal form of the tribal cult, the rites of initiation are associated especially with him, and he is central to them. He is often represented in those rites by an image carved in tree bark or modeled out of earth. People dance around it, sing in its honor, and indeed actually pray to it.[92] They explain to the young men who the personage is that the image represents, telling them the secret name that women and the uninitiated must not know, recounting to them his history and his role in the life of the tribe according to tradition. At other moments, they raise their hands toward the sky, where he is thought to reside, or point the weapons or the ritual instruments they have in hand in the same direction[93]—means of entering into communication with him. They feel his presence everywhere. He watches over the novice while he is secluded in the forest.[94] He is vigilant about the manner in which the rites are conducted. Since initiation is his cult, he

[84]Howitt, *Native Tribes*, pp. 489, 492; Mathews, "Aboriginal Tribes," p. 340.

[85]Parker, *The Euahlayi*, p. 7; Howitt, *Native Tribes*, p. 630.

[86]Ridley, *Kamilaroi*, p. 136; L. Parker, *The Euahlayi*, p. 114.

[87][K. Langloh], Parker, *More Australian Legendary Tales* [London, D. Nutt, 1898], pp. 84–99, 90–91.

[88]Howitt, *Native Tribes*, pp. 495, 498, 543, 563, 564; Brough Smyth [*Aborigines of Victoria*], vol. I, p. 429; L. Parker, *The Euahlayi*, p. 79.

[89]Ridley, *Kamilaroi*, p. 137.

[90]Parker, *The Euahlayi*, pp. 90–91.

[91]Howitt, *Native Tribes*, p. 495; Taplin, "The Narrinyeri," in Woods, *The Native Tribes of South Australia*, p. 58.

[92]Howitt, *Native Tribes*, pp. 538, 543, 553, 555, 556; Mathews, "Aboriginal Tribes," p. 318; Parker, *The Euahlayi*, pp. 6, 79, 80.

[93]Howitt, *Native Tribes*, pp. 498, 528.

[94]Ibid., p. 493; Parker, *The Euahlayi*, p. 76.

makes sure that these rites, in particular, are correctly observed. When there are mistakes or negligence, he punishes those in a terrible way.[95]

The authority each of these high gods has is not restricted to a single tribe but is recognized as well by a number of neighboring tribes. Bunjil is worshipped in nearly the whole state of Victoria, Baiame in a sizable part of New South Wales, and so forth—facts that explain why there are so few gods for a relatively large geographic area. The cults of which they are objects therefore have an international character. Sometimes, in fact, the diverse mythologies blend into, combine with, and borrow from one another. Thus, the majority of the tribes that believe in Baiame also accept the existence of Daramulun, although they accord him lower standing. They take him to be a son or a brother of Baiame, and subordinate to him.[96] Thus in various forms, faith in Daramulun is general throughout New South Wales. Hence religious internationalism is far from being the exclusive province of the most modern and advanced regions. From the beginning of history, religious beliefs show a tendency not to confine themselves within a narrowly delimited political society. They naturally go beyond boundaries, spreading and becoming international. There certainly have been peoples and times in which that spontaneous aptitude was held in check by various social necessities. Nevertheless, it is real and, as we see, very primitive.

To Tylor this idea seemed to be of such advanced theology that he refused to see it as anything but a European importation, a somewhat distorted Christian idea.[97] By contrast, A. Lang[98] considers it to be indigenous. But at the same time he accepts the notion that it is in contrast with Australian beliefs as a whole and rests upon wholly different principles. And he concludes that the religions of Australia are made up of two heterogeneous systems, one superimposed on the other, and thus have a double origin. First come the ideas relative to totems and spirits, suggested to men by the spectacle of certain natural phenomena. At the same time, however, by a sort of intuition (the nature of which he refuses to explain[99]), the human intellect suddenly

---

[95]Parker, *The Euahlayi*, p. 76; Howitt, *Native Tribes*, pp. 493, 612.

[96]Ridley, *Kamilaroi*, p. 153; Parker, *The Euahlayi*, p. 67; Howitt, *Native Tribes*, p. 585; Mathews, "Aboriginal Tribes," p. 343. Daramulun is sometimes presented in opposition to Baiame as an inherently evil spirit (L. Parker, *The Euahlayi*; [William] Ridley, in Brough Smyth [*Aborigines of Victoria*], vol. II, p. 285).

[97][Edward Burnett Tylor, "On the Limits of Savage Religion,"] *JAI*, vol. XXI [1892], pp. 292ff.

[98][Andrew] Lang, *The Making of Religion* [London, Longmans, 1898], pp. 187–293.

[99]Ibid., p. 331. Mr. Lang says only that the hypothesis of St. Paul seems to him least defective ([not] the most unsatisfactory). [The reference is probably to St. Paul on the road to Damascus, when he "saw a great light," after which "the scales fell" from his eyes and he became a believer in Jesus Christ. Trans.]

manages to conceive of one god, creator of the world, legislator of the moral order. Lang even judges that at the beginning, in Australia especially, this idea is purer of all foreign elements than in the civilizations immediately following. Over time, it supposedly is little by little overgrown and obscured by the constantly growing mass of animist and totemist superstitions. In this way, it undergoes a sort of progressive degeneration until the day when, under the influence of a privileged culture, it manages to recover and reaffirm itself, with a brilliance and clarity that it did not originally have.[100]

But the facts do not support either the skeptical hypothesis of Tylor or the theological interpretation of Lang. In the first place, we know today for certain that the ideas relative to the tribal high god are indigenous. They were reported when the influence of the missionaries had not yet had time to make itself felt.[101] But that they must be attributed to a mysterious revelation does not follow. It is far from true that they originated elsewhere. Quite the contrary, they flow logically from the sources of totemism and are its most advanced form.

We have seen that the very principles on which totemism rests imply the idea of mythical ancestors, since each of those ancestors is a totemic being. Although the high gods are surely superior to them, the differences are only of degree; one passes from the first to the second without a radical break. In fact, a high god is himself an ancestor of special importance. He is spoken of as a man, one gifted with more than human powers, of course, but one who

[100]Father [Wilhelm] Schmidt has taken up the thesis of A. Lang in *Anthropos* ["L'Origine de l'idée de dieu," vol. III (1908), pp. 125–162, 336–368, 559–611, 801–836, vol. IV (1909), pp. 207–250, 505–524, 1075–1091]. Against Sidney Hartland, who had criticized Lang's theory in an article of *Folk-Lore* (vol. IX [1898], pp. 290ff., pp. 290ff.), titled "The 'High Gods' of Australia," Father Schmidt set out to demonstrate that Baiame, Bunjil, and the others are eternal gods, creators, omnipotent and omniscient, and guardians of the moral order. I will not enter into that discussion, which seems to me without interest and import. If those different adjectives are understood in a relative sense, in harmony with the Australian turn of mind, I am quite prepared to take them up on my own account and have even used them. From this point of view, "all-powerful" means one who has more power than the other sacred beings; "omniscient," one who sees things that escape the ordinary person and even the greatest magicians; and "guardian of the moral order," one who sees to it that the rules of Australian morality are respected, however different that morality may be from our own. But if one wants to give those words a meaning that only a Christian spiritualist can give them, it seems to me pointless to discuss an opinion so at odds with the principles of historical method.

[101]On that question, see N[orthcote] W[hitridge] Thomas, "Baiame and Bell-bird: A Note on Australian Religion," in *Man*, vol. V (1905), 28. Cf. Lang, *Magic and Religion*, p. 25. [Theodor] Waitz had already argued for the original character of this idea in *Anthropologie der Naturvölker* [Leipzig, F. Fleischer, 1877], pp. 796–798.

has lived a fully human life on earth.[102] He is depicted as a great hunter,[103] a powerful magician,[104] and the founder of the tribe.[105] He is the first of men.[106] He is even presented in one legend as a tired old man who can barely move.[107] If, among the Dieri, there was a high god called Mura-mura, that word is significant, since it is used to designate ancestors as a class. In the same way, Nuralie, the name of the high god among the tribes of the Murray River, is sometimes used as a collective phrase, collectively applied to the group of mythical beings that tradition places at the beginning of things.[108] They are entirely comparable to the Alcheringa personages.[109] We have already encountered in Queensland a god Anje-a or Anjir, who makes men and yet who seems only to be the first of them.[110]

What has helped the thought of the Australians to advance from the plurality of ancestral genies to the idea of the tribal god is that a middle term found its place between the two extremes and served as a transition: the civilizing heroes. The mythical beings called by this name are actually mere ancestors to whom mythology has ascribed a preeminent role in the history of the tribe and has therefore placed above the others. We have even seen that they were normally part of the totemic organization: Mangarkunjerkunja is of the Lizard totem and Putiaputia, of the Wildcat totem. But from another point of view, the functions they are said to perform, or to have performed, resemble those assigned to the high god very closely. He too is believed to have initiated men into the arts of civilization, to have been the founder of the principal social institutions, and to be the one who revealed the great religious ceremonies, which are still under his control. If he is the father of men, it is for having made rather than engendered them; but Mangarkun-

---

[102]Dawson, *Australian Aborigines*, p. 49; [Rev. A.] Meyer, "Encounter Bay Tribe," in Woods [*The Native Tribes of South Australia*], pp. 205, 206; Howitt, *Native Tribes*, pp. 481, 491, 492, 494; Ridley, *Kamilaroi*, p. 136.

[103]Taplin, "The Narrinyeri," in Woods, pp. 55–56.

[104]L. Parker, *More Australian Legendary Tales*, p. 94.

[105]Taplin, "The Narrinyeri," in Woods, p. 61.

[106]Brough Smyth [*Aborigines of Victoria*], vol. I, pp. 425–427.

[107]Taplin, "The Narrinyeri," in Woods, p. 60.

[108]"The world was created by beings called the Nuralie; some of these beings, which have existed for a long time, had the form of the crow and others, that of the eaglehawk" (Brough Smyth [*Aborigines of Victoria*], vol. I, pp. 423–424).

[109]"Byamee," says Mrs. L. Parker, "is for the Euahlayi what the Alcheringa is for the Arunta" (*The Euahlayi*, p. 6).

[110]See above, p. 261.

jerkunja did as much. Before him, there were no men, but only masses of formless flesh in which the different body parts and even the different individuals were not separated from one another. It is he who sculpted this raw material and who drew properly human beings out of it.[111] There are only slight shadings of difference between this method of fabrication and the one ascribed to Bunjil by the myth I cited. Moreover, the fact that a kin relation is sometimes set up between these two kinds of figure brings out the connection between them. Among the Kurnai and the Tundun, the hero of the bull roarer is the son of the high god Munganngaua.[112] Among the Euahlayi, in a similar way, Daramulun, the son or brother of Baiame, is identical to Gayandi, who is the equivalent of Tundun among the Kurnai.[113]

We certainly must not conclude from all these facts that the high god is no more than a civilizing hero. There are cases in which these two personages are clearly differentiated. But while they cannot be assimilated, they are at least akin. Sometimes, therefore, it is rather hard to differentiate between them, and some of them can be classified equally well in either category. Thus, we have spoken of Atnatu as a civilizing hero, but he is very close to being a high god.

Indeed, the notion of high god is so closely dependent upon the ensemble of totemic beliefs that it still bears their mark. Tundun is a divine hero who is very close to the tribal deity, as we have just seen. Now, among the Kurnai, the same word means "totem."[114] Similarly, "Altjira" is the name of the high god among the Arunta and also the name of the maternal totem.[115] Additionally, a number of high gods have an obviously totemic form. Daramulun is an eaglehawk;[116] his mother is an emu.[117] Baiame himself is portrayed with the characteristics of an emu.[118] The Altjira of the Arunta has the legs of an

---

[111]In another myth reported by Spencer and Gillen, an entirely similar role is performed by two personages who live in the sky and are called Ungambikula (*Native Tribes*, pp. 388ff.).

[112]Howitt, *Native Tribes*, p. 493.

[113]L. Parker, *The Euahlayi*, pp. 67, 62–66. Because the high god is in close relationship with the bull roarer, it is identified with the thunder, the rumbling that ritual instrument makes being assimilated to that of thunder.

[114]Howitt, *Native Tribes*, p. 135. The word that means "totem" is spelled by Howitt as *thundung*.

[115]Strehlow, *Aranda*, vol. I, pp. 1–2, and vol. II, p. 59. It will be recalled that, quite probably, among the Arunta the maternal totem was originally the totem, period.

[116]Howitt, *Native Tribes*, p. 555.

[117]Ibid., pp. 546, 560.

[118]Ridley, *Kamilaroi*, pp. 136, 156. He is depicted in that form during the initiation rites of the Kamilaroi. According to another legend, he is a black swan (Parker, *More Australian Legendary Tales*, p. 94).

emu.[119] As we saw, before being the name of a high god, Nuralie referred to the founding ancestors of the tribe; some of those ancestors were crows and others, hawks.[120] According to Howitt,[121] Bunjil is always represented in human form; however, the same word is used to denote the totem of a phratry, the eaglehawk. At least one son of his is one of the totems that comprise the phratry to which he gave or lent his name.[122] His brother is Pallyan, the bat; the bat serves as a men's sexual totem in many tribes of Victoria.[123]

We can go even further and specify the relationship that the high gods have with the totemic system. Daramulun, like Bunjil, is an eaglehawk, and we know that this animal is a phratry totem in many of the southeastern tribes.[124] As I have said, Nuralie seems to have been at first a collective term that designated the eaglehawks or the crows, interchangeably. In the tribes where this myth has been found, the crow serves as the totem of one of the two phratries, the eaglehawk of the other.[125] In addition, the legendary history of the high gods closely resembles that of the phratry totems. The myths, and sometimes the rites, commemorate the battles that each of these deities had to wage against a carnivorous bird that they did not easily defeat. Bunjil, or the first man, having made Karween, the second man, came into conflict with him and, in a kind of duel, gravely wounded him and changed him into a crow.[126] The two forms of Nuralie are depicted as two enemy groups that, at the beginning, were constantly at war.[127] For his part, Baiame fought against Mullian, the cannibal eaglehawk (who, moreover, is identical to Daramulun).[128] Now, as we have seen, there is also a sort of innate hostility between the phratry totems. This parallelism fully demonstrates that the mythology of the high gods and that of the totems are closely related. This

---

[119]Strehlow, *Aranda*, vol. I, p. 1.

[120]Brough Smyth [*Aborigines of Victoria*], vol. I, pp. 423–424.

[121]Howitt, *Native Tribes*, p. 492.

[122]Ibid., p. 128.

[123]Brough Smyth [*Aborigines of Victoria*], vol. I, pp. 417–423.

[124]See above, p. 106.

[125]These are the tribes whose phratries bear the names Kilpara (crow) and Mukwara. This explains even the myth reported by Brough Smyth ([*Aborigines of Victoria*], vol. I, pp. 423–424).

[126]Brough Smyth [*Aborigines of Australia*], vol. I, pp. 425–427; cf. Howitt, *Native Tribes*, p. 486; in this latter case, Karween is identified with the blue heron.

[127]Brough Smyth [*Aborigines of Victoria*], vol. I, p. 423.

[128]Ridley, *Kamilaroi*, p. 136; Howitt, *Native Tribes*, p. 585; Mathews, "Aboriginal Tribes," p. 111.

kinship will stand out even more clearly if we notice that the rival of the god is usually either the crow or the eaglehawk and that these are very common phratry totems.[129]

So Baiame, Daramulun, Nuralie, and Bunjil seem to be phratry totems that have been deified—and here is how we can envision this apotheosis as having come about. Clearly, it is in the assemblies held for initiation that this idea was developed; for, being strangers to the other religious ceremonies, only in these rites do the high gods play a role of any importance. Moreover, since initiation is the principal form of the tribal cult, a tribal mythology could have been born only on this occasion. We have already seen that the rituals of circumcision and subincision tended toward spontaneous personification as civilizing heroes. But these heroes had no supremacy; they were on the same footing as the other legendary benefactors of the society. On the other hand, where the tribe took on a more vivid awareness of itself, this awareness was embodied quite naturally in a personage that became its symbol. To comprehend the ties that bound them to one another, no matter what clan they belonged to, men imagined that they were of the same stock, that they were children of the same father, to whom they owed their existence even though he owed his own existence to no one. The god of initiation was perfectly suited for this role. According to a phrase that often recurs on the lips of the natives, the specific purpose of initiation is to make, to fabricate, men. Thus, a creative power was imputed to this god, and for all these reasons, he came to be endowed with a prestige that set him well above the other heroes of mythology. The others became his subordinates and helpers; they were made into his sons or his younger brothers, like Tundun, Gayandi, Karween, Pallyan, and so on. But there already were other sacred beings that held an equally prominent place in the religious system of the tribe; these were the phratry totems. Wherever these have endured, they are thought to have dominion over the clan totems. In this way, they had all they needed to become tribal divinities themselves. Naturally, these two sorts of mythical figures partially merged, and so it was that one of the two basic totems of the tribe lent his traits to the high god. But since it was necessary to explain why only one of them was called to this status, and the other excluded, the latter was presumed to have lost out during a fight against his rival, the exclusion being the consequence of his defeat. This idea was the more easily accepted because it accorded with the mythology as a whole, in which the phratry totems are generally viewed as enemies of one another.

---

[129]See above, p. 146; cf. P. Schmidt, "L'Origine de l'idée de Dieu," in *Anthropos*, 1909.

A myth among the Euahlayi studied by Mrs. Parker[130] can serve to corroborate this explanation, for it translates that explanation figuratively. As the story goes, the totems in this tribe were at first only the names given to different parts of Baiame's body. In that sense, the clans are like fragments of the divine body. Is this not another way of saying that the high god is the synthesis of all the totems and hence the personification of the tribe as a whole?

At the same time, however, Baiame took on an international character. In fact, the members of the tribe to which the young initiates belong are not the only ones who attend the initiation ceremonies. Representatives of the neighboring tribes are specifically invited to these festivals, which are rather like international fairs and are both religious and secular.[131] Beliefs that are fashioned in such social milieux cannot remain the exclusive patrimony of any one nationality. The foreigner to whom they have been revealed takes them back into his native tribe. And since, sooner or later, he must in turn invite his hosts of yesterday, continual exchanges of ideas between one society and another are created. In this way, an international mythology was formed. Since the mythology had its origin in the rites of initiation, which the god serves to personify, the high god was quite naturally the basic element in it. His name thus passed from one language to another, along with the symbols attached to it. The fact that the names of the phratries are usually common to very different tribes could only facilitate that diffusion. The internationalism of the phratry totems blazed a trail for the internationalism of the high god.

V

Thus we arrive at the most advanced idea that totemism achieved. This is the point at which it resembles and prepares the way for the religions that are to follow and helps us to understand them. At the same time, we can see that this culminating idea is continuous with the more rudimentary beliefs that we analyzed at the outset.

---

[130]Parker, *The Euahlayi Tribe*, p. 7. Among the same people, the principal wife of Baiame is also depicted as the mother of all the totems, without belonging to any totem herself (ibid., pp. 7, 78).

[131]See Howitt, *Native Tribes*, pp. 511–512, 513, 602ff.; Mathews, "Aboriginal Tribes," *RSNSW*, vol. XXXVIII (1904), p. 270. Invited to the feasts of initiation are not only the tribes with which a regular *connubium* is established but also those with which there are quarrels to settle. Vendettas that are half-ceremonial and half-serious take place on these occasions.

The tribal high god is actually none other than an ancestral spirit that eventually won a prominent place. The ancestral spirits are none other than entities forged in the image of the individual souls, the origin of which they are meant to account for. The souls, in turn, are none other than the form taken by the impersonal forces that we found at the basis of totemism, as these become individualized in particular bodies. The unity of the system is as great as its complexity.

The idea of soul has undoubtedly played an important part in this work of elaboration. Through it, the idea of personality was introduced into the domain of religion. But what the theorists of animism claim is far from true—that it contains the seed of the whole religion. For one thing, this idea presupposes that of mana or of totemic principle, of which it is only a particular form. For another, if the spirits and gods could not be conceived of before the soul was, still they are something other than mere human souls freed by death. Otherwise, where would they get their superhuman powers? The idea of soul has served only to orient the mythological imagination in a new direction and to suggest to it constructions of a new sort. The basic material for those constructions was not taken from the idea of soul but was instead drawn from that reservoir of anonymous and diffuse forces which is the original fount of religions. The creation of mythical personalities was only another way of conceiving these fundamental forces.

Turning to the high god, that notion is wholly attributable to an awareness whose influence we have already observed in the origin of the more specifically totemic beliefs: the awareness of tribe. We have seen that totemism was not the isolated work of the clans but that it was always elaborated in the midst of a tribe that was to some extent conscious of its unity. It is for this reason that the various cults peculiar to each clan come together and complement one another in such a way as to form a unified whole.[132] It is this same feeling of tribal unity that is expressed in the idea of a high god common to the whole tribe. From the bottom to the top of this religious system, then, the same causes are at work.

Up to now, we have considered these religious representations as if they were sufficient unto themselves and could be explained only in terms of themselves. In fact, they are inseparable from the rites, not only because the representations appear in the rites but also because the rites influence them. The cult not only rests on but also reacts on the beliefs. To understand those better, it is important to understand the cult better. The time has come to take up that study.

[132]See above, pp. 155–156.

BOOK THREE
THE PRINCIPAL MODES OF RITUAL CONDUCT*

---

* *Les Principales attitudes rituelles.* The contrast between *croyances* and *attitudes* in the titles of Books Two and Three, respectively, is that between thought and action.

CHAPTER ONE

THE NEGATIVE CULT
AND ITS FUNCTIONS

The Ascetic Rites

In what follows, I will not undertake a full description of the primitive cult. Since my main goal is to arrive at what is most elemental and fundamental in religious life, I will make no attempt at a detailed reproduction of all ritual acts in their often chaotic multiplicity. But in order to test and, if need be, fine-tune the results to which my analysis of the beliefs has led,[1] I will try to choose from the extremely diverse practices the most characteristic that the primitive follows in the celebration of his cult, to classify the most central forms of his rites, and to determine their origins and significance.

Every cult has two aspects: one negative, the other positive. Actually the two sorts of rites are intertwined; as we will see, they presuppose one another. But since they are different, we must distinguish between them, if only to understand their relationships.

I

By definition, sacred beings are beings set apart. What distinguishes them is a discontinuity between them and profane beings. Normally, the two sorts of beings are separate from one another. A whole complex of rites seeks to bring about that separation, which is essential. These rites prevent unsanctioned mixture and contact, and prevent either domain from encroaching on the other. Hence they can only prescribe abstinences, that is, negative acts. For this reason, I propose to use the term "negative cult" for the system

[1] I will completely leave aside one form of ritual: oral ritual, which is to be studied in a special volume of the *Collection of the année sociologique*.

formed by these particular rites. They do not mandate obligations to be carried out by the faithful but instead prohibit certain ways of acting. Accordingly, all take the form of prohibitions, or, to follow common usage in ethnography, the form of *taboo*. *Taboo* is the term used in the Polynesian languages to denote the institution in accordance with which certain things are withdrawn from ordinary use;[2] it is also an adjective that expresses the distinctive characteristic of those sorts of things. I have already had occasion to show how problematic it is to transform a local and dialectal term into a generic one. Since there is no religion in which prohibitions do not exist and play an important part, it is regrettable that this accepted terminology should seem to make such a widespread institution a peculiarity specific to Polynesia.[3] The terms "interdictions" or "prohibitions"[*] seem to me preferable by far. Still, like the word "totem," the word "taboo" is so widely used that to avoid it altogether would be an excess of purism. Besides, its liabilities diminish if its meaning and scope are carefully specified.

But prohibitions are of different kinds, and it is important to distinguish them. We need not treat every sort of prohibition in this chapter.

To begin, aside from those that belong to religion, there are others that belong to magic. What both have in common is that they define certain things as incompatible and prescribe the separation of the things so defined. But there are also profound differences. First, the punishments are not the same in the two cases. Certainly, as will be pointed out below, the violation of religious prohibitions is often thought automatically to cause physical disorders from which the guilty person is thought to suffer and which are considered punishment for his action. But even when that really does occur, this spontaneous and automatic sanction does not stand alone. It is always supplemented by another that requires human intervention. Either a punishment properly so-called is added (if it does not actually precede the automatic sanction), and that punishment is purposely inflicted by human beings; or, at the very least, there is blame and public disapproval. Even when

---

[*]Between these two terms there is a fine grading of abstractness, *interdiction* being more mundane or applied, and *interdit* more abstract; but Durkheim uses the two interchangeably, although *interdit* is more frequent. Both "interdict" and "interdiction" are good English words, but I have preferred their commoner synonyms: "prohibition," "restriction," "ban," and the like. Trans.

[2]See the article "Taboo" in the *Encyclopedia Britannica*, the author of which is [James George] Frazer [Edinburgh, Adam & Charles Black, 1887].

[3]The facts prove this to be a real liability. There is no dearth of writers who, taking the word literally, have believed that the institution designated by it was peculiar to primitive societies in general or even to the Polynesian peoples only (see [Albert] Réville, *Religion des peuples non civilisés*, Paris, Fischbacher, 1883, vol. II, p. 55; [Gaston] Richard, *La Femme dans l'histoire* [*étude sur l'évolution de la condition sociale de la femme*, Paris, O. Doin et Fils, 1909], p. 435).

sacrilege has already been punished by the sickness or natural death of its perpetrator, it is also denounced. It offends opinion, which reacts against it, and it places the culprit in a state of sin. By contrast, a magical prohibition is sanctioned only by the tangible consequences that the forbidden act is held to produce with a kind of physical necessity. By disobeying, one takes risks like those a sick person takes by not following the advice of his doctor; but in this case disobedience does not constitute sin and does not produce indignation. In magic, there is no such thing as sin.

In addition, the fact that the sanctions are not the same is part and parcel of a profound difference in the nature of the prohibitions. A religious prohibition necessarily involves the idea of the sacred. It arises from the respect evoked by the sacred object, and its purpose is to prevent any disrespect. By contrast, magic prohibitions presuppose an entirely secular idea of property—nothing more. The things that the magician recommends keeping separated are things that, because of their characteristic properties, cannot be mixed or brought near one another without danger. Although he may ask his clients to keep their distance from certain sacred things, he does not do so out of respect for those things or out of fear that they may be profaned (since, as we know, magic thrives on profanations).[4] He does so only for reasons of secular utility. In short, religious prohibitions are categorical imperatives and magic ones are utilitarian maxims, the earliest form of hygienic and medical prohibitions. Two orders of facts that are so different cannot be studied at the same time, and under the same rubric, without confusion. Here we need concern ourselves only with religious prohibitions.[5]

But a further distinction among these prohibitions themselves is necessary: There are religious prohibitions whose purpose is to separate different kinds of sacred things from one another. We recall, for example, that among the Wakelbura, the scaffold on which a dead person is laid out must be built exclusively with materials belonging to the phratry of the deceased. All contact is forbidden between the corpse, which is sacred, and things of the other phratry, which are sacred too, but in a different right. Elsewhere, the weapons used to hunt an animal must not be made of a wood that is classified in the same social group as the animal itself.[6] The most important of

[4]See p. 40, above.

[5]This is not to say that there is a radical discontinuity between religious and magic prohibitions. To the contrary, there are some whose true nature is ambiguous. In folklore, there are prohibitions that often cannot be easily said to be either religious or magic. Even so, the distinction is necessary, for magic prohibitions can be understood, I believe, only in relation to religious ones.

[6]See above, p. 150.

these prohibitions are examined in a later chapter: those aimed at preventing all contact between the sacred pure and the sacred impure, as well as between things that are sacred and auspicious and those that are sacred and disastrous. All of these prohibitions have a common trait: They do not arise from the fact that some things are sacred and others not but from the fact that there are relations of disparity and incompatibility among sacred things. Hence, they are not based upon what is fundamental to the idea of the sacred. Consequently, the observance of these prohibitions can give rise only to isolated, particular, and rather exceptional rites, but they cannot make up a cult, proper, for a cult is above all made up of regular relations between the profane and the sacred as such.

There is another much more extensive and important system of religious prohibitions—not the system that separates different species of sacred things but the one that separates all that is sacred from all that is profane. This system of religious prohibitions derives directly from the notion of sacredness, which it expresses and implements. This system furnishes the raw material for a genuine cult and, indeed, a cult that forms the basis of all the rest; for in their dealings with sacred things, the faithful must never depart from the conduct it prescribes. This is what I call the negative cult. These prohibitions can be said to be religious prohibitions par excellence.[7] They alone will be the subject of the following pages.

They take many forms. Here are the principal types found in Australia.

First and foremost come the prohibitions of contact. These are the primary taboos, and the others are little more than particular varieties of them. They rest on the principle that the profane must not touch the sacred. We

[7]Many of the prohibitions between sacred things are reducible, I think, to the prohibition between sacred and profane. This is true for prohibitions of age or grade. In Australia, for example, there are sacred foodstuffs that are reserved exclusively for the initiated. But those foodstuffs are not all equally sacred; there is a hierarchy among them. Nor are all the initiated equal. They do not enjoy the plenitude of their religious rights immediately, but rather enter into the domain of sacred things gradually. They must pass through a series of grades that are conferred upon them, one after the other, following ordeals and special ceremonies; it takes them months, sometimes even years, to reach the highest. Definite foods are assigned to each of these grades. Men of the lower grades must not touch foods that belong, as a matter of right, to men of the higher grades (see [Robert Hamilton] Mathews, "Ethnological Notes on the [Aboriginal Tribes of New South Wales and Victoria," *RSNSW,* vol. XXXVIII (1904)], pp. 262ff.; Mrs. [Langloh] Parker [Catherine Sommerville Field Parker], *The Euahlayi Tribe* [London, A. Constable, 1905], p. 23; [Sir Baldwin] Spencer and [Francis James] Gillen, *Northern Tribes [of Central Australia,* London, Macmillan, 1904], pp. 611ff.; [Sir Baldwin] Spencer and [F. James] Gillen, *Native Tribes [of Central Australia,* London, Macmillan, 1899], pp. 470ff.). The more sacred repels the less sacred, but this is because, compared to the first, the second is profane. In sum, all the religious prohibitions fall into two classes: the prohibitions between the sacred and the profane and those between the sacred pure and the sacred impure.

have already seen that the churingas or the bull roarers must under no circumstances be handled by the uninitiated. If adults have free use of those objects, that is only because initiation has conferred upon them a quality of sacredness. Blood (more specifically, the blood that flows during initiation) has a religious virtue[8] and is subject to the same prohibition.[9] The same is true of hair.[10] A dead person is a sacred being because the soul that animated the body adheres to the corpse. For this reason, it is sometimes forbidden to carry the bones of the corpse in any way other than wrapped in a sheet of bark.[11] The very place where the death occurred must be avoided, for the soul of the deceased is thought to remain there still. This is why the people break camp and move some distance away.[12] Sometimes they destroy the camp and all it contains,[13] and a period of time passes before they may return to the same place.[14] Sometimes the person who is dying creates a vacuum around himself, the others deserting him after having settled him as comfortably as possible.[15]

The consumption of food brings about an especially intimate form of contact. Thence arises the prohibition against eating sacred animals or plants, especially those serving as totems.[16] Such an act appears so sacrilegious that the prohibition covers even adults, or at least most adults, and only old men attain sufficient religious status to be not always subject to it. This prohibition has sometimes been explained in terms of the mythical kinship that

[8]See above, p. 136.

[9]Spencer and Gillen, *Native Tribes,* p. 463.

[10]Ibid., p. 538; Spencer and Gillen, *Northern Tribes,* p. 604.

[11]Spencer and Gillen, *Northern Tribes,* p. 531.

[12]Ibid., pp. 518–519; [Alfred William] Howitt, *Native Tribes [of South-East Australia,* London, Macmillan, 1904], p. 449.

[13]Spencer and Gillen, *Native Tribes,* p. 498; [Rev. Louis] Schulze, "Aboriginal Tribes of Upper and Middle Finke River," *RSSA,* vol. XIV [1891], p. 231.

[14]Spencer and Gillen, *Native Tribes,* p. 499.

[15]Howitt, *Native Tribes,* p. 451. [The point made is not at this place in Howitt. Trans.]

[16]The alimentary restrictions applied to the totemic plant or animal are the most important, but they are far from being the only ones. We have seen that there are foods that, because they are considered sacred, are forbidden to the uninitiated. Very different causes can make those foods sacred. For example, as we will see below, the animals that climb to the tops of trees are reputed to be sacred because they are neighbors of the high god that lives in the heavens. It is also possible that, for different reasons, the flesh of certain animals was reserved especially for old men and that, as a result, it seemed to participate in the sacredness that old men are acknowledged to have.

unites man with the animals whose name he bears—the animals being protected, presumably, by the sympathy they inspire, as kin.[17] That the origin of this prohibition is not simply revulsion caused by the sense of familial solidarity is brought out by the following: Consumption of the forbidden flesh is presumed to cause sickness and death automatically. Thus, forces of a different sort have come into play—forces analogous to those forces in all religions that are presumed to react against sacrilege.

Further, while certain foods, because sacred, are forbidden to the profane, other foods, because profane, are forbidden to persons endowed with special sacredness. Thus, certain animals are often specifically designated as food for women. For this reason, they are believed to participate in femaleness and hence are profane. On the other hand, the young initiate undergoes an especially harsh set of rites. An exceptionally powerful beam of religious forces is focused upon him, so as to make it possible to transmit to him the virtues that will enable him to enter the world of sacred things, from which he had previously been excluded. Since he is then in a state of sanctity that repels all that is profane, he is not allowed to eat game that is considered to be women's.[18]

Contact can be established by means other than touching. One is in contact with a thing simply by looking at it; the gaze is a means of establishing contact. This is why, in certain cases, the sight of sacred things is forbidden to the profane. A woman must never see the cult instruments and at most is allowed to glimpse them from afar.[19] The same applies to totemic painting done on the bodies of celebrants for especially important ceremonies.[20] In certain tribes, the exceptional solemnity of initiation rites makes it impossible for women even to see the place where they have been celebrated[21] or the novice himself.[22] The sacredness that is immanent in the entire ceremony is

---

[17]See [James George] Frazer, *Totemism [and Exogamy* London, Macmillan, 1910] p. 7.

[18]Howitt, *Native Tribes*, p. 674. I do not address one prohibition of contact because its precise nature is not easy to determine: sexual contact. There are religious periods in which men must not have contact with women (Spencer and Gillen, *Northern Tribes*, pp. 293, 295; Howitt, *Native Tribes*, p. 387). Is it because the woman is profane or because the sexual act is a dreaded act? This question cannot be settled in passing. I postpone it along with everything related to conjugal and sexual rites. They are too closely bound up with the problem of marriage and the family to be separated from it.

[19]Spencer and Gillen, *Native Tribes*, p. 134; Howitt, *Native Tribes*, p. 354.

[20]Spencer and Gillen, *Native Tribes*, p. 624.

[21]Howitt, *Native Tribes*, p. 572.

[22]Ibid., p. 661.

found as well in the persons of those who direct it or who take any part in it—with the result that the novice must not raise his eyes to them, a prohibition that continues even after the rite has been completed.[23] A corpse, too, is sometimes taken out of sight, the face being covered in such a way that it cannot be seen.[24]

Speech is another means of coming into contact with persons or things. The exhaled breath establishes contact, since it is a part of ourselves that spreads outside us. Thus the profane are barred from speaking to sacred beings or even speaking in their presence. Just as the neophyte must look at neither those presiding nor those in attendance, so he is also barred from talking to them in any way other than with signs. This prohibition continues until it is lifted by means of a special rite.[25] Among all the Arunta, there are moments in the grand ceremonies when silence is obligatory.[26] As soon as the churingas are displayed, talking stops; or, if there is talking, it is in a low voice and with the lips only.[27]

In addition to the things that are sacred, there are words and sounds that have the same quality; they must not be found on the lips of the profane or reach their ears. There are ritual songs that women must not hear, on pain of death.[28] They may hear the noise of the bull roarers, but only from a distance. Every personal name is considered an essential element of the person who carries it. Since it is closely associated with the idea of that person, the name participates in the feelings that person arouses. If the person is sacred, so is the name; hence it may not be pronounced in the course of profane life. Among the Warramunga is a totem that receives special veneration, the mythical serpent named Wollunqua; that name is taboo.[29] The same holds true for Baiame, Daramulun, and Bunjil; the esoteric forms of their names must not be revealed to the uninitiated.[30] During the period of mourning, the name of the dead person must be mentioned, at least by his relatives, only in cases of

---

[23]Spencer and Gillen, *Native Tribes*, p. 386; Howitt, *Native Tribes*, pp. 655, 665.

[24]Among the Wiimbaio, Howitt, *Native Tribes*, p. 451.

[25]Ibid., pp. 624, 661, 663, 667; Spencer and Gillen, *Native Tribes*, pp. 221, 382ff.; Spencer and Gillen, *Northern Tribes*, pp. 335, 344, 353, 369.

[26]Spencer and Gillen, *Native Tribes*, pp. 221, 262, 288, 303, 367, 378, 380.

[27]Ibid., p. 302.

[28]Howitt, *Native Tribes*, p. 581.

[29]Spencer and Gillen, *Northern Tribes*, p. 227.

[30]See above, p. 291.

absolute necessity, and even then they must only whisper it.[31] This restriction is often permanent for the widow and certain family members.[32] Among certain peoples, it extends even beyond the family, everyone who has the same name as the deceased being required to change it temporarily.[33] Furthermore, relatives and close friends ban certain words from everyday language, probably because they were used by the deceased. The gaps are filled with circumlocutions or with borrowings from some foreign dialect.[34] In addition to their ordinary, public name, men have another that is kept secret. Women and children do not know it, and it is never used in ordinary life because it has a religious quality.[35] Indeed, there are ceremonies during which the participants are required to speak in a special language whose use is forbidden in profane dealings. Here is a beginning of sacred language.[36]

Not only are sacred beings separated from profane ones, but in addition, nothing that directly or indirectly concerns profane life must be mingled with religious life. Total nakedness is often required of the native as the precondition of his being allowed to take part in a rite.[37] He must take off all his usual ornaments, even those he values most and from which he separates himself the less willingly because he imputes to them protective virtues.[38] If he must decorate himself for his ritual role, that decoration must be made especially for the occasion; it is a ceremonial costume, a feast-day vestment.[39] Since these ornaments are sacred by virtue of the use made of them, their use in profane activities is forbidden. Once the ceremony is over, they are buried or burned;[40] and indeed the men must wash themselves, so as not to take away with them any trace of the decorations that adorned them.[41]

[31]Spencer and Gillen, *Native Tribes*, p. 498; Spencer and Gillen, *Northern Tribes*, p. 526; [George] Taplin "The Narrinyeri" [in James Dominick Woods, *The Native Tribes of South Australia*, Adelaide, E. S. Wigg, 1879], p. 19.

[32]Howitt, *Native Tribes*, pp. 466, 469ff.

[33][J. P.] Wyatt, "Adelaide and Encounter Bay Tribes," in Woods, [*The Native Tribes of South Australia*], p. 165.

[34]Howitt, *Native Tribes*, p. 470. [It is actually at p. 466. Trans.]

[35]Ibid., p. 657; Spencer and Gillen, *Native Tribes*, p. 139; Spencer and Gillen, *Northern Tribes*, pp. 580ff.

[36]Howitt, *Native Tribes*, p. 537.

[37]Ibid., pp. 544, 597, 614, 620.

[38]For example, the hair belt that he usually wears (Spencer and Gillen, *Native Tribes*, p. 171).

[39]Ibid., pp. 624ff.

[40]Howitt, *Native Tribes*, p. 556.

[41]Ibid., p. 587.

More generally, the typical actions of ordinary life are forbidden so long as those of religious life are in progress. The act of eating is profane in itself. A daily occurrence, it satisfies basically utilitarian and physical needs and is part of our ordinary existence.[42] This is why eating is prohibited during religious periods. Thus, when a totemic group has lent its churinga to a foreign clan, the moment when they are brought back and returned to the ertnatulunga is one of great solemnity. All those who take part in the ceremony must abstain from eating as long as it lasts, and it lasts a long time.[43] The same rule is followed during the celebration of the rites[44] to be treated in the next chapter, as well as at certain times during initiation.[45]

For the same reason, all secular occupations are suspended when the great religious ceremonies take place. According to an observation by Spencer and Gillen,[46] cited previously, the life of the Australian has two quite distinct parts: One is taken up with hunting, fishing, and war; the other is dedicated to the cult. These two forms of activity are mutually exclusive and repel one another. The universal institution of religious days of rest is based on this principle. In all known religions, the distinguishing feature of feast days is the cessation of work and, beyond that, the suspension of public and private life, insofar as it has no religious object. This pause is not merely a kind of temporary relaxation that men take, so as to abandon themselves more freely to the feelings of elation that holidays generally arouse, since it is no less obligatory during those sad holidays that are devoted to mourning and penance. The reason for the pause is that work is the preeminent form of profane activity. It has no apparent aim other than meeting the secular needs of life, and it puts us in contact only with ordinary things. During holy days, on the other hand, religious life attains unusual intensity. Because the contrast between these two sorts of existence is particularly marked at that

[42]Granted, this act takes on a religious character when the food eaten is sacred. But the act in itself is profane, to such an extent that the consumption of a sacred food always constitutes a profanation. The profanation can be permitted or even prescribed but, as we will see below, only if rites to attenuate or expiate the profanation precede or accompany it. The existence of these rites clearly shows that the sacred thing itself resists being consumed.

[43]Spencer and Gillen, *Northern Tribes*, p. 263.

[44]Spencer and Gillen, *Native Tribes*, p. 171.

[45]Howitt, *Native Tribes*, p. 674. It may be that the prohibition against speaking during the great religious ceremonies derives in part from the same cause. In ordinary life, people speak, and in particular people speak loudly; therefore, in religious life, they must keep silent or speak in a low voice. The same consideration is germane to the dietary restrictions. (See above, p. 127).

[46]Spencer and Gillen, *Northern Tribes*, p. 33.

time, they cannot abut one another. Man cannot approach his god intimately while still bearing the marks of his profane life; inversely, he cannot return to his ordinary occupations when the rite has just sanctified him. Ritual cessation of work is thus no more than a special case of the general incompatibility that divides the sacred and the profane, and it is the result of a prohibition.

There is no way to enumerate every kind of prohibition that is observed, even in the Australian religions alone. Like the notion of the sacred on which it rests, the system of prohibitions extends into the most varied relations. It is even used intentionally for utilitarian purposes.[47] But however complex this system may be, in the end it comes down to two fundamental prohibitions that epitomize and govern it.

First, religious and profane life cannot coexist in the same space. If religious life is to develop, a special place must be prepared for it, one from which profane life is excluded. The institution of temples and sanctuaries arises from this. These are spaces assigned to sacred things and beings, serving as their residence, for they cannot establish themselves on the ground except by fully appropriating a part of it for themselves. Arrangements of this kind are so indispensable to all religious life that even the simplest religious cannot do without them. The ertnatulunga, the place where the churingas are stored, is a true sanctuary. The uninitiated are banned from approaching it, and indulging in any kind of profane occupation is forbidden there. We will see that there are other sanctified places where important ceremonies are conducted.[48]

[47]Since, from the beginning, there is a sacred principle within each man, the soul, the individual has been surrounded by prohibitions, the first form of the moral prohibitions that today insulate and protect the human person. It is in this way that the body of the victim is considered dangerous by the murderer (Spencer and Gillen, Native Tribes, p. 492) and is forbidden to him. Prohibitions that have this origin are often used by individuals as a means of withdrawing certain things from common use and establishing a right of property over them. "Does a man depart from camp, leaving weapons, food, etc. there?" asks [Walter Edmund] Roth with regard to the Palmer River tribes (North Queensland). "If he urinates near objects that he has thus left behind, they become tami (equivalent of the word "taboo"), and he can be assured of finding them intact upon his return" [possibly, "Marriage Ceremonies and Infant Life," North Queensland Ethnography, Bull. 10] in RAM, [Sydney, 1908], vol. VII, part 2, p. 75). This is because the urine, like the blood, is held to contain a part of the sacred force that is personal to the individual. Thus it keeps strangers at a distance. For the same reasons, speech also can serve as a vehicle for these same influences. This is why it is possible to ban access to an object simply by verbal declaration. Further, this power of creating prohibitions is variable according to individuals—the greater their sacredness, the greater this power. Men have the privilege of this power to the virtual exclusion of women (Roth cites a single example of a taboo imposed by women). It is at its maximum among chiefs and elders, who use it to monopolize the things they choose ([Walter Edmund] Roth, Superstition, Magic and Medicine [Brisbane, G. A. Vaughn, 1903], in North Queensland Ethnography, Bulletin No. 5, p. 77). In this way, religious prohibition becomes property right and administrative regulation.

[48]Bk. 3, chap. 2.

Likewise, religious and profane life cannot coexist at the same time. In consequence, religious life must have specified days or periods assigned to it from which all profane occupations are withdrawn. Thus were holy days born. There is no religion, and hence no society, that has not known and practiced this division of time into two distinct parts that alternate with one another according to a principle that varies with peoples and civilizations. In fact, probably the necessity of that alternation led men to insert distinctions and differentiations into the homogeneity and continuity of duration that it does not naturally have.[49] Of course, it is virtually impossible for religion ever to reach the point of being concentrated hermetically in the spatial and temporal milieux that are assigned to it; a little of it inevitably filters out. There are always sacred things outside the sanctuaries and rites that can be celebrated during workdays, but those are sacred things of the second rank and rites of lesser importance. Concentration is still the predominant characteristic of this structure; and indeed, concentration is generally total with respect to the public cult, which must be celebrated collectively. The private, individual cult is the only one that mingles more or less closely with secular life. Therefore, because the individual cult is at its least developed in the lower societies, such as the Australian tribes, the contrast between these two successive phases of human life is at its most extreme there.[50]

II

Thus far we have seen the negative cult only as a system of abstinences. It appears capable only of inhibiting activity, not stimulating and invigorating it. Nevertheless, through an unexpected reaction to this inhibiting affect, it exerts a positive and highly important influence upon the religious and moral nature of the individual.

Because of the barrier that sets the sacred apart from the profane, man can enter into close relations with sacred things only if he strips himself of what is profane in him. He cannot live a religious life of any intensity unless he first withdraws more or less completely from secular life. The negative cult in a sense is a means to an end; it is the precondition of access to the positive cult. Not confined to protecting the sacred beings from ordinary contact, it acts upon the worshipper himself and modifies his state positively.

[49]See above, p. 9.

[50]See above, p. 220.

After having submitted to the prescribed prohibitions, man is not the same as he was. Before, he was an ordinary being and for that reason had to keep at a distance from religious forces. After, he is on a more nearly equal footing with them, since he has approached the sacred by the very act of placing himself at a distance from the profane. He has purified and sanctified himself by detaching himself from the low and trivial things that previously encumbered his nature. Like positive rites, therefore, negative rites confer positive capacities; both can increase the religious zest of individuals. As has been rightly observed, no one can engage in a religious ceremony of any importance without first submitting to a sort of initiation that introduces him gradually into the sacred world.[51] Anointings, purifications, and blessings can be used for this, all being essentially positive operations; but the same results can be achieved through fasts and vigils, or through retreat and silence—that is, by ritual abstinences that are nothing more than definite prohibitions put into practice.

When negative rites are considered only one by one, their positive influence is usually too little marked to be easily perceptible; but their effects cumulate, and become more apparent, when a full system of prohibitions is focused on a single person. This occurs in Australia during initiation. The novice is subjected to an extreme variety of negative rites. He must withdraw from the society where he has spent his life until then, and from virtually all human society. He is not only forbidden to see women and uninitiated men,[52] but he also goes to live in the bush, far from his peers, under the supervision of a few old men serving as godfathers.[53] So much is the forest considered his natural milieu that, in quite a few tribes, the word for initiation means "that which is of the forest."[54] For the same reason, the novice is often decorated with leaves during the ceremonies he attends.[55] In this way, he spends long months[56] punctuated from time to time by rites in which he

[51]See [Henri] Hubert and [Marcel] Mauss, "Essai sur la nature et la fonction du sacrifice," in *Mélanges d'histoire des religions* [Paris, F. Alcan, 1909], pp. 22ff.

[52]Howitt, *Native Tribes*, pp. 560, 657, 659, 661. Not even a woman's shadow must fall on him (ibid., p. 633). What he touches must not be touched by a woman (ibid., p. 621).

[53]Ibid., pp. 561, 563, 670–671; Spencer and Gillen, *Native Tribes*, p. 223; Spencer and Gillen, *Northern Tribes*, pp. 340, 342.

[54]The word *jeraeil*, for example, among the Kurnai; *kuringal* among the Yuin and the Wolgat (Howitt, *Native Tribes*, pp. 518, 617).

[55]Spencer and Gillen, *Native Tribes*, p. 348.

[56]Howitt, *Native Tribes*, p. 561.

must participate. For him, this is a time for every sort of abstinence. He is forbidden a great many foods, and he is allowed only as much food as is strictly necessary to sustain life.[57] Indeed, rigorous fasting is often obligatory,[58] or he is made to eat disgusting food.[59] When he eats, he must not touch the food with his hands; his godfathers put it in his mouth.[60] In some cases, he must beg for his subsistence.[61] He sleeps only as much as is indispensable.[62] He must abstain from speaking unless spoken to and indicate his needs with signs.[63] He is forbidden all recreation.[64] He must not bathe;[65] sometimes he must not move. He remains lying on the ground, immobile,[66] without clothing of any kind.[67] The result of these multiple prohibitions is to bring about a radical change in the status of the neophyte. Before the initiation, he lived with women and was excluded from the cult. From now on, he is admitted into the society of men; he takes part in the rites and has gained a quality of sacredness. So complete is the metamorphosis that it is often portrayed as a second birth. The profane person that previously was the young man is imagined to have died, to have been killed and taken away by the God of initiation—Bunjil, Baiame, or Daramulun—and to have been replaced by an altogether different individual from the one who existed previously.[68] Thus we capture in the raw the positive effects of which the negative rites are capable. I do not mean to claim that these rites alone produce so profound a transformation, but they certainly contribute to it, and substantially.

In light of these facts, we can understand what asceticism is, what place it holds in religious life, and where the virtues that are widely imputed to it

[57]Ibid., pp. 633, 538, 560.

[58]Ibid., p. 674; Parker, *The Euahlayi Tribe*, p. 75.

[59][William] Ridley, *Kamilaroi [and Other Australian Languages*, Sydney, T. Richards, 1875], p. 154.

[60]Howitt, *Native Tribes*, p. 563.

[61]Ibid., p. 611.

[62]Ibid., pp. 549, 674.

[63]Ibid., pp. 580, 596, 604, 668, 670; Spencer and Gillen, *Native Tribes*, pp. 223, 351.

[64]Howitt, *Native Tribes*, p. 567. [This note and the phrase to which it is attached are missing from the Swain translation. Trans.]

[65]Ibid., p. 557.

[66]Ibid., p. 604; Spencer and Gillen, *Native Tribes*, p. 351.

[67]Howitt, *Native Tribes*, p. 611.

[68]Ibid., p. 589.

originate. In actuality, there is no prohibition whose observance is not to some degree like asceticism. To abstain from something that may be useful or from an activity that, because habitual, must meet a human need, is of necessity to impose restrictions and renunciations upon oneself. For there to be asceticism properly so-called, it is enough for these practices to develop in such a way as to become the foundation for a genuine system of life. The negative cult usually serves as barely more than an introduction to, and a preparation for, the positive cult. But it sometimes escapes that subordination and becomes central, the system of prohibitions swelling and aggrandizing itself to the point of invading the whole of life. In this way, systematic asceticism is born; it is thus nothing more than a bloating of the negative cult. The special virtues it is said to confer are only those conferred through the practice of any prohibition, though in magnified form. They have the same origin, for both rest on the principle that the very effort to separate oneself from the profane sanctifies. The pure ascetic is a man who raises himself above men and who acquires a special sanctity through fasts, vigils, retreat, and silence—in a word, more by privations than by acts of positive piety (offerings, sacrifices, prayers, etc.). History shows what heights of religious prestige are attainable by those means. The Buddhist saint is fundamentally an ascetic, and he is equal or superior to the gods.

It follows that asceticism is not a rare, exceptional, and almost abnormal fruit of religious life, as one might think, but quite the contrary: an essential element of it. Every religion has at least the seed of asceticism, for there is none without a system of prohibitions. In this respect, the only possible difference between cults is that this seed is more or less developed within them. And it is well to add that there probably is not even a single one in which this development does not at least temporarily adopt the characteristic traits of asceticism proper. This generally happens at certain critical periods, when a profound change in an individual's condition must be brought about in a relatively short time. In that case, in order to bring him more rapidly into the circle of sacred things with which he must be put in contact, he is abruptly separated from the profane world. This does not occur without increased abstinences and an extraordinary intensification in the system of prohibitions. Precisely this occurs in Australia at the time of initiation. To transform the youths into men, they are required to lead the life of ascetics. Mrs. Parker quite accurately calls them the monks of Baiame.[69]

[69]These ascetic practices may be compared to the ones used during a magician's initiation. Like the young neophyte, the apprentice magician is subjected to a multitude of prohibitions the observance of which helps him acquire his specific powers (see "L'Origine des pouvoirs magiques," in *Mélanges d'histoire des religions*, by Hubert and Mauss, pp. 171, 173, 176). It is the same for husbands on the eve of their mar-

Abstinences and privations are not without suffering. We hold to the profane world with every fiber of our flesh. Our sensuous nature attaches us to it; our life depends upon it. Not only is the profane world the natural theater of our activity; it enters us from every direction; it is part of us. We cannot detach ourselves from it without doing violence to our nature and without painfully clashing with our instincts. In other words, the negative cult cannot develop unless it causes suffering. Pain is its necessary condition. By this route, people came to regard pain as a sort of rite in itself. They saw it as a state of grace to be sought after and induced, even artificially, because of the powers and privileges it confers in the same right as those systems of prohibitions to which it is the natural accompaniment. To my knowledge, Preuss was the first to become aware of the religious[70] role that is ascribed to pain in the lower societies. He cites cases: the Arapaho who inflict torture upon themselves as protection from the dangers of battle; the Gros-Ventre Indians who submit to torture on the eve of military expeditions; the Hupa who swim in freezing rivers and afterward remain stretched out on the shore as long as possible, to ensure the success of their undertakings; the Karaya who periodically draw blood from their arms and legs with scrapers made of fish teeth, to firm their muscles; the men of Dallmannhafen (Emperor William's Land in New Guinea) who combat sterility in their wives by making bloody cuts on the women's upper thighs.[71]

But similar doings can be found without leaving Australia, especially in the course of initiation rites. Many of those rites involve the systematic infliction of suffering on the neophyte, for the purpose of altering his state and

---

riage or on the day after (taboos of fiancés and of newlyweds); this is because marriage also involves an important change in status. I confine myself to noting these briefly without lingering over them. The former concern magic, which is not my subject, while the latter belong to that system of juridico-religious rules that refer to commerce between the sexes; the study of those will be possible only in conjunction with the other precepts of primitive conjugal morality.

[70]True, Preuss interprets these facts by saying that pain is a means of increasing a man's magical power (*die menschliche Zauberkraft*); it might be thought, following this statement, that suffering is a magic rite and not a religious one. But as I have already pointed out, Preuss calls all anonymous and impersonal forces magic, without great precision, whether they belong to magic or to religion. There no doubt are tortures that serve to make magicians, but many of those he describes are part of authentically religious ceremonies. Hence their aim is to modify the religious states of individuals.

[71][Konrad Theodor] Preuss, "Der Ursprung der Religion und der Kunst," *Globus*, LXXXVII [1904], pp. 309–400. Preuss categorizes many disparate rites under the same rubric, for example, the sheddings of blood that act through the positive qualities ascribed to blood rather than through the sufferings they involve. I single out only those phenomena in which pain is the essential element of the rite and the source of its efficacy.

making him take on the distinguishing qualities of a man. Among the Larakia, while the youths are on retreat in the forest, their godfathers and overseers constantly assault them with brutal blows, without advance warning and for no apparent reason.[72] Among the Urabunna, at a given moment, the novice lies stretched out on the ground with his face down. All the men present beat him brutally; then they make a series of four to eight incisions on his back, down both sides of his spine, and one along the midline of his neck.[73] Among the Arunta, the first rite of initiation consists of tossing the subject; the men throw him into the air, catch him when he comes down, and then throw him again.[74] In that same tribe, at the end of a long series of ceremonies, the young man is made to lie down on a bed of leaves with live coals under it; and he continues to lie there immobile, in the midst of the heat and suffocating smoke.[75] The Urabunna practice a similar rite, but the initiate is beaten on the back as well.[76] So much are his exertions of this kind that he seems pathetic and half-dazed when he is allowed to resume ordinary life.[77] It is true that all these practices are often presented as ordeals to test the novice's worth and to make known his worthiness for acceptance into religious society.[78] Actually, however, the probationary function of the rite is but another aspect of its efficacy, for the manner in which the novice bears the ordeal proves that the rite has accomplished exactly what it was meant to: to confer on him the qualities that are its primary *raison d'être*.

In other cases, these ritual torments are applied not to the whole body but to an organ or a tissue, in order to stimulate its vitality. Among the

---

[72]Spencer and Gillen, *Northern Tribes*, pp. 331–332.

[73]Ibid., p. 335. A similar practice is found among the Dieri (Howitt, *Native Tribes*, pp. 658ff.).

[74]Spencer and Gillen, *Native Tribes*, pp. 214ff. From this example, we see that the rites of initiation sometimes have the characteristics of hazing. This is so because hazing is a true social institution that arises spontaneously whenever two groups that are unequal in their moral and social situations find themselves in intimate contact. In this case, the group that views itself as superior to the other resists the intrusion of the newcomers; it reacts against them in such a way as to make them understand how superior it feels. That reaction, which occurs automatically and takes the form of more or less severe torments, is also aimed at adapting individuals to their new life and assimilating them into their new milieu. It thus constitutes a sort of initiation. In this way, we can explain why initiation constitutes a sort of hazing. It does because the group of elders is superior in religious and moral status to that of the young, and yet the elders must take in the youths. All the conditions of hazing are present.

[75]Spencer and Gillen, *Native Tribes*, p. 372.

[76]Ibid., p. 335.

[77]Howitt, *Native Tribes*, p. 675.

[78]Ibid., pp. 569, 604.

Arunta, the Warramunga, and several other tribes,[79] at a certain moment during the initiation, delegated individuals plunge their teeth into the novice's scalp. This is so painful that usually the patient cannot bear it without crying out. Its purpose is to make the hair grow.[80] The same treatment is applied to make the beard grow. The rite of hair removal, which Howitt reports for other tribes, may well have the same *raison d'être*.[81] Among the Arunta and the Kaitish, according to Eylmann, men and women make small wounds on their arms with red-hot sticks so as to become skillful at making fire or gain the strength they need to carry heavy loads of wood.[82] According to the same observer, Warramunga girls amputate the second and third joints of the index finger on one hand, believing that the finger becomes more skillful at uncovering the yams thereby.[83]

It is not impossible that the extraction of teeth might sometimes be intended to bring about effects of the same kind. It is certain, in any case, that the purpose of such cruel rites as circumcision and subincision is to confer special powers on the genital organs. Since the young man owes special virtues to those rites, he is not allowed to marry until he has undergone them. What makes this *sui generis* initiation indispensable is the fact that, in all the lower societies, sexual union is endowed with a quality of religiousness. It is thought to bring into play awesome forces that man can approach without danger only if he has gained the requisite immunity through ritual procedures.[84] A whole series of positive and negative rites, of which circumcision and subincision are the forerunners, have this purpose. An organ is given sacredness by painful mutilation, for that very act enables it to withstand sacred forces that otherwise it would be unable to confront.

I said at the beginning of this work that all the essential elements of religious thought and life should be found, at least in seed, as far back as the most primitive religions. The foregoing facts reinforce that claim. If one belief is held to be specific to the most modern and idealistic religions, it is the

[79]Spencer and Gillen, *Native Tribes*, p. 251; Spencer and Gillen, *Northern Tribes*, pp. 341, 352.

[80]Consequently, among the Warramunga, the operation must be done by individuals favored with beautiful heads of hair.

[81]Howitt, *Native Tribes*, p. 675, which is about the tribes of Lower Darling.

[82][Richard] Eylmann, [*Die Eingeborenen der Kolonie Süd Australien*, Berlin, D. Reumer, 1908], p. 212.

[83]Ibid.

[84]Information on this question is to be found in my article "La Prohibition de l'inceste et ses origines" (*Année Sociologique*, vol. 1 [1898], pp. 1ff.) and in [Alfred Ernest] Crawley, *The Mystic Rose* [London, Macmillan, 1902], pp. 37ff.

one that attributes sanctifying power to pain. The rites just examined are based upon the same belief, which is variously interpreted, depending upon the historical period in which it is examined. For the Christian, pain is thought to act above all upon the soul—refining, ennobling, and spiritualizing it. For the Australian, it acts upon the body—increasing its vital energies, making the beard and hair grow, toughening the limbs. But in both cases, the principle is the same. In both, pain is held to be generative of exceptional forces. Nor is this belief unfounded. In fact, the grandeur of a man is made manifest by the way he braves the pain. Never does he rise above himself more spectacularly than when he subdues his nature to the point of making it follow a path contrary to the one it would take on its own. In that way, he makes himself unique among all the other creatures, which go blindly where pleasure leads them. In that way, he takes a special place in the world. Pain is the sign that certain of the ties that bind him to the profane world are broken. Because pain attests that he is partially emancipated from that world, it is rightly considered the tool of his deliverance, so he who is delivered in this way is not the victim of mere illusion when he believes he is endowed with a kind of mastery over things. By the very act of renouncing things, he has risen above things. Because he has silenced nature, he is stronger than nature.

Furthermore, that virtue is far from having only aesthetic value. Religious life as a whole presupposes it. Sacrifices and offerings do not go unaccompanied by privations that exact a price from the worshipper. Even if the rites do not require tangible things of him, they take his time and strength. To serve his gods, he must forget himself. To create for them the place in his life to which they are entitled, he must sacrifice some of his profane interests. The positive cult is possible, then, only if man is trained to renunciation, abnegation, and detachment from self—hence, to suffering. He must not dread suffering, for he can carry out his duties joyfully only if he in some measure loves it. If that is to come about, he must train himself to suffering, and this is where the ascetic practices lead. The sufferings they impose are not arbitrary and sterile cruelties, then, but a necessary school in which man shapes and steels himself, and in which he gains the qualities of disinterestedness and endurance without which there is no religion. In fact, if this result is to be achieved, it helps if the ascetic ideal is eminently incarnated in certain individuals who are specialized, as it were, in that aspect of ritual life, almost to excess. Those certain individuals amount to so many living models that encourage striving. Such is the historical role of the great ascetics. When we analyze in detail the things they do, we wonder what the useful point of those things could be. The contempt they profess for all that ordinarily impassions men strikes us as bizarre. But those extremes are necessary to maintain among

the faithful an adequate level of distaste for easy living and mundane plea-
sures. An elite must set the goal too high so that the mass does not set it too
low. Some must go to extremes so that the average may remain high enough.

But asceticism serves more than religious ends. Here, as elsewhere, religious interests are only social and moral interests in symbolic form. The ideal
beings to which cults are addressed are not alone in demanding of their servants a certain contempt for pain; society, too, is possible only at that price.
Even when exalting the powers of man, it is often brutal toward individuals.
Of necessity, it requires perpetual sacrifices of them. Precisely because society lifts us above ourselves, it does constant violence to our natural appetites.
So that we can fulfill our duties toward it, our conditioning must ready us to
overcome our instincts at times—when necessary, to go up the down stair-
case of nature. There is an inherent asceticism in all social life that is destined
to outlive all mythologies and all dogmas; it is an integral part of all human
culture. And, fundamentally, that asceticism is the rationale and justification
of the asceticism that religions have taught since the beginning of time.

III

Having determined what the system of prohibitions consists of and what its
negative and positive functions are, we must now uncover its causes.

In a sense, the very notion of the sacred logically entails it. Everything
that is sacred is the object of respect, and every feeling of respect is translated
into stirrings of inhibition in the person who has that feeling. Because of the
emotion it inspires, a respected being is always expressed in consciousness by
a representation that is highly charged with mental energy. Hence, it is armed
in such a way as to throw any representation that wholly or partly contradicts
it far away from itself. Antagonism characterizes the relationship the sacred
world has with the profane one. The two correspond to two forms of life
that are mutually exclusive, or at least that cannot be lived at the same time
with the same intensity. We cannot be devoted entirely to the ideals to which
the cult is addressed, and entirely to ourselves and our sensuous interests also;
entirely to the collectivity and entirely to our egoism as well. Herein are two
states of consciousness that are oriented toward, and that orient our behavior
toward, two opposite poles. Whichever is more powerful must push the
other out of consciousness. When we think of sacred things, the idea of a
profane object cannot present itself to the mind without meeting resistance,
something within us that opposes its settlement there. The idea of the sacred
does not tolerate such a neighbor. But this psychic antagonism, this mutual
exclusion of ideas, must necessarily culminate in the exclusion of the things

that correspond to them. If the ideas are not to coexist, the things must not touch one another or come into contact in any way. Such is the very principle of the prohibition.

Moreover, the world of the sacred is a world apart, by definition. Since the sacred is opposed to the profane world by all the features I have mentioned, it must be treated in a way that is appropriate to it. If, in our dealings with the things that comprise the sacred world, we used the actions, language, and attitudes that serve us in our relations with profane things, that would be to misapprehend the nature of the sacred world and confound it with what it is not. We may freely handle profane things, and we talk freely to ordinary beings. So we will not touch sacred beings or will touch them only with reserve, and we will not talk in their presence or not talk in the ordinary language. All that is customary in our dealings with one set of things must be excluded in our dealing with the other.

But while this explanation is not inaccurate, still it is inadequate. In fact, a good many beings that are objects of respect exist without being protected by strict systems of prohibitions, such as I have been describing. Doubtless, the intellect has a sort of general tendency to situate different things in different environments, especially when they are incompatible with one another. But the profane environment and the sacred one are not merely distinct but also closed to one another; there is a gulf between them. In the nature of sacred beings, there must be some special cause that necessitates this condition of unusual isolation and mutual exclusion. And voilà: By a sort of contradiction, the sacred world is as though inclined by its very nature to spread into the same profane world that it otherwise excludes. While repelling the profane world, the sacred world tends at the same time to flow into the profane world whenever that latter world comes near it. That is why they must be kept at a distance from each other and why, in some sense, a void must be opened between them.

What necessitates such precautions is the extraordinary contagiousness that sacredness has. Far from remaining attached to the things that are marked with it, sacredness possesses a certain transience. Even the most superficial or indirect contact is enough for it to spread from one object to another. Religious forces are so imagined as to appear always on the point of escaping the places they occupy and invading all that passes within their reach. The nanja tree in which an ancestral spirit lives is sacred for the individual who considers himself a reincarnation of that ancestor. But every bird that comes to light upon that tree shares in the same quality; so to touch the bird is forbidden as well.[85] I have already shown how the mere touch of a churinga is enough to

---

[85]Spencer and Gillen, *Native Tribes*, p. 133.

sanctify people and things.[86] More than that, all rites of consecration are founded upon this principle, the contagiousness of the sacred. Such, indeed, is the churinga's sacredness that it makes its influence felt at a distance. As we recall, this sacredness spreads not only to the cavity in which churingas are kept but also to the whole surrounding area, to the animals taking refuge there (which may not be killed), and to the plants growing there (which may not be plucked).[87] A snake totem has its center at a place where there is a water hole. The sacredness of the totem is passed on to the place, to the water hole, and to the water itself, which is forbidden to all members of the totemic group.[88] The neophyte lives in an atmosphere full of religiousness, and he himself is as though suffused with it.[89] As a result, everything he has and everything he touches is forbidden to women and withdrawn from contact with them, down to the bird he has struck with his stick, the kangaroo he has run through with his spear, and the fish that has struck his fishhook.[90]

But another side of it is that the rites he undergoes and the things that play a role in them have greater sacredness than he. That sacredness is passed on contagiously to everything that brings either to mind. The tooth that has been pulled from his mouth is regarded as very sacred.[91] Therefore, he cannot eat of animals that have prominent teeth, since they bring to mind the extracted tooth. The ceremonies of the Kuringal end with ritual washing.[92] Aquatic birds are forbidden to the novice because they evoke this rite. The animals that climb all the way to the tops of trees are sacrosanct to him as well, because they are too much the neighbors of Daramulun, the god of initiation, who lives in the heavens.[93] The soul of a dead man is a sacred being. We have already seen that the same property passes to the body in which that soul has lived, to the place where it is buried, the camp where the man lived

---

[86]See above, p. 120.

[87]Spencer and Gillen, *Native Tribes*, pp. 134–135; [Carl] Strehlow, [*Die Aranda- und Loritja-stämme in Zentral-Australien*, Frankfurt, J. Baer, 1907], vol. II, p. 78.

[88]Spencer and Gillen, *Northern Tribes*, pp. 167, 299.

[89]Apart from the ascetic rites of which I have spoken, there are positive ones whose purpose is to fill or, as Howitt says, to saturate the neophyte with religiousness (Howitt, *Native Tribes*, p. 535). True, instead of speaking of religiousness, Howitt speaks of magic powers, but we know that, for the majority of ethnographers, this word simply means religious virtues that are impersonal in nature.

[90]Howitt, *Native Tribes*, pp. 674–675.

[91]Spencer and Gillen, *Native Tribes*, p. 454. Cf. Howitt, *Native Tribes*, p. 561.

[92]Howitt, *Native Tribes*, p. 557.

[93]Ibid., p. 560.

his life (which is destroyed or abandoned), the name he had, his wife, and his relations.[94] It is as though they themselves are invested with sacredness, so one keeps at a distance from them and does not treat them as mere profane beings. In the societies studied by Dawson, their names, like that of the dead man, must not be spoken during the period of mourning.[95] Certain of the animals he ate may be prohibited as well.[96]

This contagiousness of the sacred is too well known a fact[97] for there to be any need to demonstrate its existence with numerous examples. I have sought only to establish that it is as true of totemism as it is of more advanced religions. Once noted, that contagiousness readily explains the extreme rigor of the prohibitions that divide the sacred from the profane. By virtue of that exceptional volatility, the slightest contact, the least proximity of a profane being, whether physical or simply moral, is enough to draw the religious forces outside their domain. On the other hand, since they cannot exit without belying their nature, a whole system of measures to keep the two worlds at a respectful distance apart becomes indispensable. This is why ordinary people are forbidden not only to touch but also to see or hear that which is sacred, and why these two kinds of life must not mingle in consciousness. Precautions to keep them apart are all the more necessary because they tend to merge, even while opposing one another.

At the same time as we understand the multiplicity of these prohibitions, we understand how they and the sanctions attached to them function. One result of the contagiousness inherent in all that is sacred is this: A profane being cannot violate a prohibition without having the religious force that he has improperly approached extend to him and take him over. But since there is antagonism between himself and that force, he finds himself subject to a

[94]See above, pp. 307, 310. Cf. Spencer and Gillen, Native Tribes, p. 498; Spencer and Gillen, Northern Tribes, pp. 506–507, 518–519, 526; Howitt, Native Tribes, pp. 449, 461, 469; Mathews, "Aboriginal Tribes of New South Wales and Victoria," RSNSW, vol. XXXVIII [1904], p. 274; Schulze, "Aborigines of . . . Finke River," p. 231; Wyatt, Adelaide and Encounter Bay Tribes, in Woods [The Native Tribes of South Australia], pp. 165, 198.

[95][James Dawson], Australian Aborigines, [The Languages and Customs of Several Tribes of Aborigines in the Western District of Victoria, Australia, Melbourne, G. Robertson, 1881], p. 42.

[96]Howitt, Native Tribes, pp. 470–471.

[97]On this question, see [William] Robertson Smith, [Lectures on] the Religion of the Semites [London, A. & C. Black, 1889], pp. 152ff., 446, 481; Frazer, "Taboo," in Encyclopedia Britannica; [Frank Byron] Jevons, Introduction to the History of Religions [London, Methuen, 1896], pp. 59ff.; Crawley, Mystic Rose, Chaps. 2–9; Arnold] Van Gennep, Tabou et totémisme à Madagascar [étude descriptive et théorique, Paris, E. Leroux, 1904], chap. 3.

hostile power, the hostility of which is inevitably manifested in violent reactions that tend to destroy him. This is why sickness and death are presumed to be the natural consequences of all such transgressions, and such are the consequences that are presumed to occur by themselves with a sort of physical necessity. The culprit feels invaded by a force that takes him over and against which he is powerless. Has he eaten the totemic animal? He feels it pervading him and gnawing at his entrails; he lies on the ground and awaits death.[98] Every profanation implies a consecration, but one that is dreadful to whoever is consecrated and whoever comes near him. Indeed the results of that consecration in part sanction the prohibition.[99]

Notice that this explanation of the prohibitions does not depend upon the varied symbols with whose help the religious forces can be imagined. It is of little consequence whether they are imagined as anonymous and impersonal energies or as personalities endowed with consciousness and feeling. To be sure, they are thought in the first case to react against profaning transgressions mechanically and unconsciously, whereas in the second they are thought to obey goadings of passion aroused by the offense. Fundamentally, however, these two conceptions (which, by the way, have the same practical effects) do no more than express one and the same psychic mechanism in two different languages. Both are based on the antagonism between the sacred and the profane, plus the remarkable capacity of the first to be passed on to the second. The antagonism and the contagiousness act in the same way, whether sacredness is imputed to blind forces or to consciousnesses. So authentically religious life is far from beginning only where mythical personalities exist, for we see in this case that the rite remains the same whether or not the religious beings are personified. This observation is one I will have occasion to repeat in each of the chapters to come.

IV

If the contagiousness of the sacred helps to explain the system of prohibitions, how is this contagiousness itself to be explained?

Some have thought they could account for it by the well-known laws

---

[98] See the references above, p. 128, n. 1. Cf. Spencer and Gillen, *Northern Tribes*, pp. 323, 324; Spencer and Gillen, *Native Tribes*, p. 168; Taplin, *The Narrinyeri*, p. 16; Roth, [possibly "Marriage Ceremonies"], p. 76.

[99] Bear in mind that when the prohibition violated is religious, these sanctions are not the only ones; there is, besides, either an actual punishment or a public stigma.

governing the association of ideas. Feelings evoked by a person or a thing spread contagiously, from the idea of that thing or person to the representations associated with it, and from there to the objects with which those representations become associated. The respect we have for a sacred being is thereby communicated to all that touches this being and to all that resembles it or calls it to mind. Of course, an educated man is not the dupe of such associations. He knows that the emotions result from mere plays of images, entirely mental combinations, and he will not abandon himself to the superstitions that those illusions tend to create. But, it is said, the primitive objectifies these impressions naively, without critiquing them. Does a thing inspire reverent fear in him? From the fear, the conclusion: A majestic and awesome force does indeed live in it, so he keeps his distance from that thing and treats it as if it was sacred, even though it is in no way entitled to be.[100]

To say this, however, is to forget that the most primitive religions are not the only ones that have ascribed to sacredness such an ability to propagate. Even the most modern cults have a set of rites based on this principle. Does not every consecration by anointing or washing transmit the sanctifying virtues of a sacred object into a profane one? Although that mode of thinking has no natural explanation or justification, still it is hard to see today's enlightened Catholic as a kind of backward savage. Moreover, the tendency to objectify every emotion is ascribed to the primitive quite arbitrarily. In everyday life, in the details of his secular occupations, he does not attribute to one thing the properties of its neighbor, or vice versa. To be sure, he is less infatuated with clarity and distinctness than we are. Even so, it is far from true that living in him is who-knows-what deplorable inclination to scramble everything, to run everything together. It is religious thought alone that has a marked inclination toward fusions of this sort. Clearly, then, it is not in the general laws of human intelligence that we must seek the origin of these predispositions but in the special nature of religious things.

When a force or a property seems to us to be an integral part, a constituent element, of whatever it inhabits, we do not easily imagine it as capable of detaching itself and going elsewhere. A body is defined by its mass and atomic composition; we do not imagine either that it can pass on any of these distinguishing properties by mere contact. On the other hand, if the force is one that has entered the body from outside, the idea that it should be

---

[100]See Jevons, *Introduction to the History of Religion*, pp. 67–68. I will say nothing about the (by the way, barely formulated) theory of Crawley (*Mystic Rose*, chaps. 4–7), in which the reason taboos are contagious is that certain phenomena of contagion are erroneously interpreted. That is arbitrary. As Jevons quite correctly observes in the passage to which I refer the reader, the contagiousness of the sacred is affirmed *a priori*, and not on the basis of improperly interpreted experiences.

able to escape from that body is in no way unimaginable, for nothing attaches it there. Thus, the heat or electricity that any object has received from outside can be transmitted to the surrounding milieu, and the mind readily accepts the possibility of that transmission. If religious forces are generally conceived of as external to the beings in which they reside, then there is no surprise in the extreme ease with which religious forces radiate and diffuse. This is precisely what the theory I have put forward implies.

Religious forces are in fact only transfigured collective forces, that is, moral forces; they are made of ideas and feelings that the spectacle of society awakens in us, not of sensations that come to us from the physical world. Thus, they are qualitatively different from the tangible things in which we localize them. From those things they may very well borrow the outward and physical forms in which they are imagined, but they owe none of their power to those things. They are not held by internal bonds to the various supports on which they eventually settle and are not rooted in them. To use a word I have used already and that best characterizes them,[101] *they are superadded.* Thus no objects, to the exclusion of others, are predisposed to receiving those forces. The most insignificant objects, even the most commonplace ones, can play this role. Chance circumstances decide which are the elect. Let us recall the terms in which Codrington speaks of mana: "It is a force *that is by no means fixed on a material object, but that can be carried on almost any sort of object.*"[102] Similarly, Miss Fletcher's Dakota portrayed wakan for us as a kind of moving force that comes and goes throughout the world, alighting here or there without settling anywhere once and for all.[103] The religiousness that is inherent in man is no different. It is true that, in the world of experience, no being is closer to the very source of religious life; none participates in it more directly, for human consciousness is the place where it develops. And yet we know that the religious principle that animates man, the soul, is partly external to him.

If the religious forces do not have a place of their own anywhere, their mobility becomes easy to explain. Since nothing binds them to the things in which we localize them, it is not surprising that they escape from those things upon the slightest contact—against their will, so to speak. Their intensity pushes them on toward diffusion, which everything facilitates. This is why the soul itself, though holding onto the body with entirely personal

---

[101]See above, p. 230.

[102]See above, p. 197. [I have rendered this passage by Codrington according to the two slightly different renderings by Durkheim. Trans.]

[103]See above, p. 201.

bonds, continually threatens to leave it; all the openings and pores of the body are so many channels through which it tends to spread and diffuse to the outside.[104]

But the phenomenon we are trying to understand will be explained better still if, instead of considering the fully formed concept of religious forces, we go back to the mental process from which it results.

We have seen that the sacredness of a being did not depend upon any one of its inherent characteristics. It is not because the totemic animal has this or that appearance or property that it inspires religious feelings. The causes of those feelings are entirely foreign to the nature of the object on which they eventually settle. What constitutes those feelings are the impressions of reassurance and dependence that are created in consciousness through the workings of society. By themselves, these emotions are not bound to the idea of any definite object. But since they are emotions, and especially intense ones, they are eminently contagious as well. Hence, they are like an oil slick; they spread to all the other mental states that occupy the mind. They pervade and contaminate especially those representations in which are expressed the various objects that the man at that very moment has in his hands or before his eyes: Totemic designs that cover his body, bull roarers that he causes to resonate, rocks that surround him, ground that he tramps underfoot, and so on. So it is that these objects themselves take on religious significance that is not intrinsic to them but is conferred on them from outside. Hence contagion is not a kind of secondary process by which sacredness propagates, once acquired, but is instead the very process by which sacredness is acquired. It settles by contagion; we should not be surprised that it is transmitted contagiously. A special emotion gives it the reality it has; if sacredness becomes attached to an object, that happens because the emotion has encountered the object on its path. It naturally spreads from the object to all the others it finds nearby—that is, to all that some cause has brought close to the first in the mind, whether physical contiguity or mere similarity.

Thus, the contagious quality of sacredness finds its explanation in the theory of religious forces that I have proposed, and that very fact serves as confirmation of the theory.[105] At the same time, it helps us understand a feature of primitive mentality to which I previously called attention.

---

[104]This Preuss clearly demonstrated in the *Globus* articles I cited previously.

[105]It is true that the contagiousness is not peculiar to religious forces, for those belonging to magic have the same property. And yet it is evident that those forces do not correspond to objectified social feelings. This is because the magic forces were conceived on the model of religious forces. I will return later to this point (see p. 366).

We have seen[106] how easily the primitive assimilates disparate kingdoms of nature and sees the most disparate things as identical—men, animals, plants, stars, and so forth. We now see one of the causes that contributed most to facilitating these fusions. Because religious forces are eminently contagious, a single principle is continually found to be animating the most disparate things. It passes among them as a result of mere physical nearness or mere similarity, even superficial similarity. So it is that men, animals, plants, and rocks are held to participate in the same totem: the men because they carry the name of the animal; the plants because they serve as food for the animal; the rocks because they stand where the ceremonies are conducted. The religious forces are considered the source of all that is powerful; as a result, beings that had the same religious principle must have seemed to be of the same essence and to differ from one another only in secondary characteristics. This is why it seemed entirely natural to put them in the same category and to view them as varieties within a single genus and as transmutable into one another.

Once established, this relationship makes the phenomena of contagion appear in a new light. By themselves, they seem alien to logical life. Do they not bring about the mingling and fusion of things, despite the natural differences of those things? But we have seen that these fusions and participations have played a logical role, and one of great utility: They have served to connect things that sensation leaves separate from one another. Thus, the sort of fundamental irrationality that we are at first led to impute to contagion, the source of that bringing together and mixing, is far from being its distinctive mark. Contagion prepared the way for the scientific explanations of the future.

[106]See above, p. 237.

CHAPTER TWO

THE POSITIVE CULT

The Elements of the Sacrifice

Whatever its importance and although it has indirectly positive effects, the negative cult is not an end in itself. It gives access to religious life but presupposes, rather than constitutes, that life. If the negative cult commands the faithful to flee the profane world, the point is to draw them closer to the sacred world. Man has never imagined that his duties toward the religious forces could be limited to abstinence from all commerce. He has always thought of himself as maintaining positive bilateral relations with them, which a set of ritual practices regulate and organize. To this special system of rites I give the name "positive cult."

For a long time, we were almost entirely ignorant of what the positive cult of totemic religion might include. We knew almost nothing beyond the initiation rites, and those inadequately. This gap in our knowledge has been partially filled by the studies of Spencer and Gillen on the tribes of central Australia, for which Schulze paved the way and which Strehlow has confirmed. There is one celebration in particular that these explorers were especially intent on describing and that seem to dominate the totemic cult: the one that, according to Spencer and Gillen, the Arunta call the Intichiuma. It is true that Strehlow disputes this meaning of the word. According to him, *intichiuma* (or as he spells it, *intijiuma*) means "to teach" and designates the ceremonies that are performed before the young man for the purpose of initiating him into the traditions of the tribe. He says that the feast I will describe bears the name *mbatjalkatiuma*, which means "to fertilize" or "to repair."[1] I will not try to settle this question of vocabulary, which is beside the point—all the more so, in that the rites to be discussed are also conducted during initiation. Be-

---

[1][Carl] Strehlow, [*Die Aranda- und Loritja-Stämme in Zentral-Australien*, Frankfurt, J. Baer, 1907], vol. I, p. 4.

sides, since today the word "Intichiuma" belongs to the common parlance of ethnography, to substitute another would seem pointless.[2]

The date on which the Intichiuma takes place depends largely on the time of year. In central Australia there are two clearly marked seasons: a dry season, which lasts a long time, and a rainy one, which by contrast is short and often irregular. As soon as the rains come, the plants spring from the ground as if by a spell, the animals multiply, and lands that were but sterile deserts the day before are rapidly covered again with luxuriant flora and fauna. The Intichiuma is celebrated at the precise moment when the good season seems at hand. But because the rainy season is quite variable, the date of the ceremonies cannot be set once and for all. It varies according to climatic conditions, which only the head of the totemic group, the Alatunja, is qualified to assess. On the day he judges to be appropriate, he informs his people that the time has come.[3]

Each totemic group has its own Intichiuma. Although the rite is found throughout the societies of the center, it is not the same everywhere. Among the Warramunga it is not the same as it is among the Arunta, and it varies not only by tribe but also by clan within the same tribe. Still, the various procedures in use are too akin to one another to be completely dissociable. There are probably no ceremonies that do not have several of those mechanisms, but quite unequally developed. What exists only as a seed in one case dominates elsewhere, and vice versa. Still it is important to distinguish them carefully. They constitute so many different ritual types that we must describe and explain separately—and only after that try to discern whether they all have a common origin. I will begin with those that are observed more specifically among the Arunta.

I

The feast has two successive phases. The series of rites that occur one after the other in the first phrase are intended to ensure the well-being of the animal or plant species that serves as the totem of the clan. The means used for this purpose are reducible to a few main types.

[2]The word designating that feast varies by tribe. The Urabunna call it *Pijinta* ([Sir Baldwin] Spencer and [Francis James] Gillen, *Northern Tribes* [of *Central Australia*, London, Macmillan, 1904], p. 284); the Warramunga, *Thalaminta* (ibid., p. 297), etc.

[3][Rev. Louis] Schulze, "Aborigines of the Upper and Middle Finke River," *RSSA*, vol. XIV [1891], p. 243; [Sir Baldwin] Spencer and [Francis James] Gillen, *Native Tribes* [of *Central Australia*, London, Macmillan, 1904], pp. 169–170.

Recall that the mythical ancestors from which each clan is thought to descend once lived on earth and left traces of their passage. In particular, those traces include stones or rocks that they are thought to have set down in certain places or that were formed at the places where they sank into the ground. The rocks and stones are considered to be the bodies or body parts of the ancestors whose memory they evoke and whom they represent. Since an individual and his totem are one, it follows that they also represent the animals and plants that were the totems of those same ancestors. Consequently, the same reality and the same properties are accorded to them as to the animals and plants of the same sort that live today. The advantage they have over these latter is to be immortal—to know neither sickness nor death. In this way, they constitute something like a permanent, unchanging, and always available stock of animal and plant life. And in a certain number of cases, it is this reserve that people draw upon annually to ensure the reproduction of the species.

Here, as an example, is how the Witchetty Grub clan, at Alice Springs, conducts its Intichiuma.[4]

On the day set by the chief, all the members of the totemic group gather at the main camp. The men of other totems retire a certain distance; among the Arunta, they are forbidden to be present at the celebration of the rite, which has all the characteristics of a secret ceremony.[5] Sometimes an individual of the same phratry but a different totem may be invited as a courtesy, but only as a witness. Under no circumstances may he take an active role.

Once the men of the totem have gathered, they depart, leaving only two or three of their number at the camp. Completely naked, without weapons, and without any of their usual ornaments, they walk single file, in profound silence. Their attitude and pace are marked with religious solemnity, because the act in which they are taking part is, in their eyes, one of exceptional importance. In addition, they must observe a rigorous fast until the end of the ceremony.

The land they cross is filled with mementos left by the glorious ancestors. Finally they reach a place where a large block of quartzite is stuck in the earth, surrounded by small, rounded stones. The block represents the witchetty grub in its adult state. The Alatunja hits it with a sort of small wooden plate, called an *apmara*,[6] while intoning a chant whose object is to invite the

---

[4]Ibid., pp. 170ff.

[5]Of course, the same obligation binds the women.

[6]The Apmara [Durkheim capitalized here. Trans.] is the only object he has brought from the camp.

animal to lay eggs. He does the same with the stones, which represent the eggs of the animal, and, using one of them, he rubs the stomach of each person in attendance. This done, they all descend a little lower, to the foot of a rock that the Alcheringa myths also celebrate, and at the base of which is found another stone that again represents the witchetty grub. The Alatunja strikes it with his apmara; the men accompanying him do the same with gum tree branches that they have gathered on the way, all this amid hymns repeating the invitation earlier addressed to the animal. Nearly ten different places, sometimes a mile apart, are visited one after the other. At each of them, in the back of a sort of cave or hole, is a stone that is said to represent the witchetty grub in one of its aspects or phases of life, and the same ceremonies are repeated on each of these stones.

The meaning of the rite is apparent. The Alatunja strikes the sacred stones in order to detach some dust from it. The grains of this very holy* dust are regarded as so many seeds of life, each containing a spiritual principle that, by entering an organism of the same species, will give birth therein to a new being. The tree branches that the participants carry are used to spread this precious dust in all directions; it goes forth in all directions to do its work of impregnation. By this means, they believe they have ensured the abundant reproduction of the animal species that the clan watches over, so to speak, and to which it belongs.

The natives themselves interpret the rite in this way. In the clan of the Ilpirla (a sort of manna), they proceed in the following way. When the day of the Intichiuma has come, the group meets at a place where a large rock, about five feet high, stands; a second rock that looks very much like the first rises on top of it, and smaller rocks surround this one. Both represent accumulations of manna. The Alatunja digs in the ground at the foot of these rocks and brings forth a churinga that is said to have been buried there in Alcheringa times and that itself is like the quintessence of mana. He then climbs to the top of the higher rock and rubs it first with this churinga, then with the smaller stones that are around it. Finally, using tree branches, he sweeps the dust that has collected on the surface of the rock. Each of the other participants does the same thing in turn. Now, say Spencer and Gillen, the thought of the natives "is that the dust thus dispersed will go and rest on the mulga trees and there produce manna." These operations are accompanied by a hymn sung by the participants that expresses this idea.[7]

The same rite is found, with variations, in other societies. Among the

---

* *Sainte.*

[7] Spencer and Gillen, *Native Tribes*, pp. 185–186.

Urabunna, there is a rock representing an ancestor of the Lizard clan; stones
are detached from it and thrown in all directions in order to obtain abundant
lizard births.[8] In this same tribe, there is a sand bank that mythological recol-
lection closely associates with the totem of the louse. There are two trees at
the same place—one called the tree of the ordinary louse, the other that of
the crab louse. The worshippers take some of the sand, rub it against those
trees, and throw it in all directions, being convinced that by this means many
lice will be born.[9] The Mara go about the Intichiuma of bees by spreading
dust that has been detached from sacred rocks.[10] A somewhat different
method is used for the plains kangaroo. They collect some kangaroo dung
and wrap it in a grass that the animal is very fond of and that therefore belongs to the kangaroo totem. They place the dung on the ground in the
wrapping, between two layers of the same grass, and then set fire to all of this.
With the flame that results, they light tree branches and then shake them, so
sparks fly in all directions. These sparks play the same role as the dust of the
preceding cases.[11]

In a number of clans,[12] the men mix some of their own substance with
that of the stone, in order to make this rite more efficacious. Young men
open their veins and let the blood gush onto the rock. This occurs, for example, in the Hakea Flower Intichiuma, among the Arunta. The ceremony
is held at a sacred place, around a stone that is also sacred and that, in the eyes
of the natives, represents hakea flowers. After several preliminary operations,
"the old man who is conducting the rite asks a young man to open his veins.
The young man obeys and lets his blood flow freely onto the stone, while
those present continue to sing. The blood flows until the stone is completely
covered with it."[13] The object of this practice is to infuse new life into the
virtues the stone contains and make it more powerful. Bear in mind that the
clansmen themselves are relatives of the plant or animal whose name they
bear. The same life-principle resides in them, especially in their blood. Naturally, then, this blood and the mystical seeds carried along by it are used to
ensure the regular reproduction of the totemic species. When a man is sick
or tired, it is common among the Arunta for one of his young companions

---

[8]Spencer and Gillen, *Northern Tribes*, p. 288.

[9]Ibid.

[10]Ibid., p. 312.

[11]Ibid.

[12]We will see below that these clans are much more numerous than Spencer and Gillen say.

[13]Spencer and Gillen, *Native Tribes*, pp. 184–185.

to open his own veins and sprinkle the ailing man with the blood to revive him.[14] If blood can thus reawaken life in a man, it is not surprising that blood can also serve to awaken life in the animal or plant species with which the men of the clan are identified.

The same technique is used in the Kangaroo Intichiuma at Undiara (Arunta). The setting for the ceremony is a water hole precipitously overhung by a rock. This rock represents an Alcheringa animal-kangaroo that was killed and set in this place by a man-kangaroo of the same period. For that reason, many spirits of kangaroos are thought to reside here. After a number of sacred stones have been rubbed against one another in the manner I have described, several of those present climb onto the rock and let their blood flow all along it.[15] "The purpose of this ceremony, according to what the natives say, is actually the following. The blood of the man-kangaroo is spilled on the rock in order to free the spirits of animal-kangaroos and scatter them in all directions; the effect must be to increase the number of kangaroos."[16]

There is even a case among the Arunta in which blood seems to be the active principle of the rite. In the Emu group, neither stones nor anything resembling stones are used. The Alatunja and certain of those with him sprinkle the ground with their blood. On the ground thus moistened, they trace lines of various colors, which represent the various parts of the emu's body. They kneel around this drawing and chant a monotonous hymn. From the fictive emu incanted in this way, hence from the blood used in doing so, life-principles come forth that will animate the embryos of the new generation and thus prevent the species from dying out.[17]

A clan among the Wonkgongaru[18] has a certain kind of fish as its totem; in the Intichiuma of this totem as well, blood plays the central role. After having painted himself ceremonially, the chief of the group enters a water

[14]Ibid., pp. 438, 461, 464; Spencer and Gillen, *Northern Tribes*, pp. 596ff.

[15]Spencer and Gillen, *Native Tribes*, p. 201.

[16]Ibid., p. 206. I use the language of Spencer and Gillen and say, as they do, that it is the spirits of kangaroos that come away from the rocks (*spirits* or *spirit parts of kangaroos*). Strehlow, *Aranda* (vol. III, p. 7), disputes the accuracy of this phrase. According to him, it is real kangaroos, living bodies, that the rite causes to appear. But quite like the dispute over the notion of ratapa (see p. 254–255 above), this one is without interest. Since the kangaroo seeds that escape from the rocks are invisible, they are not made of the same substance as the kangaroos our senses perceive. That is all Spencer and Gillen mean. It is quite certain, moreover, that these are not pure spirits as a Christian might conceive of them. Just like human souls, they have physical forms.

[17]Spencer and Gillen, *Native Tribes*, p. 181.

[18]A tribe living east of Lake Eyre.

hole and sits down in it. Then, using little pointed bones, he pierces his scrotum and then the skin around his navel. "The blood that flows from these various wounds spreads in the water and gives rise to fish."[19]

The Dieri believe they make two of their totems reproduce, the carpet snake and the woma snake (an ordinary snake), by a similar practice. A Muramura called Minkani is believed to live under a dune. His body is represented by fossil bones of animals or reptiles such as are found, Howitt tells us, in the deltas of the rivers that empty into Lake Eyre. When the day of the ceremony comes, the men assemble and go to the place where Minkani is to be found. There they dig until they reach a layer of damp earth, which they call "the excrement of Minkani." From then on, they continue to sift through the soil with great care until "the elbow of Minkani" is uncovered. Then two men open their veins and let the blood flow on the sacred stone. The songs of Minkani are sung while the participants, caught up in a veritable frenzy, strike one another with their weapons. The battle continues until their return to camp, about a mile away. There the women intervene and end the fighting. The blood that flows from the wounds is collected and mixed with the "excrement of Minkani"; the products of the mixture are sowed on the dune. Having carried out the rite, they are convinced that carpet snakes will be born in abundance.[20]

In some cases, the substance used as a vitalizing principle is the same one they are trying to produce. Among the Kaitish, a sacred stone representing the mythical heroes of the Water clan is sprinkled during the rainmaking ceremony. It is apparently believed that the productive virtues of the stone are by this means increased, just as they are with blood, and for the same reasons.[21] Among the Mara, the celebrant goes to draw water in a sacred hole, drinks some and spits some in each direction.[22] Among the Worgaia, when the yams begin to grow, the head of the Yam clan sends people belonging to the phratry to which he himself does not belong to harvest some of the plants; they bring him some and ask him to intervene so that the species will develop well. He takes one, bites it and throws pieces in all directions.[23]

[19]Spencer and Gillen, Northern Tribes, pp. 287–288.

[20][Alfred William] Howitt, Native Tribes [of South-East Australia, London, Macmillan, 1904], p. 798. Cf. Howitt, "Legends of the Dieri and Kindred Tribes of Central Australia," JAI, vol. XXIV [1885], pp. 124ff. Howitt believes that the ceremony is conducted by the people of the totem but is not in a position to certify this fact.

[21]Spencer and Gillen, Northern Tribes, p. 295.

[22]Ibid., p. 314

[23]Ibid., pp. 296–297.

Among the Kaitish, when (after various rites which I will not describe) a certain seed grass called erlipinna comes to full maturity, the chief of the totem brings a little to the men's camp and grinds it between two stones. The dust thereby obtained is piously collected, and several grains of it are placed on the lips of the chief, who blows, scattering them in all directions. Undoubtedly, the purpose of this contact with the mouth of the chief, which has a special sacramental virtue, is to stimulate the vitality of the seeds contained within these kernals and that, propelled to all points of the horizon, will spread their fertilizing properties to the plants.[24]

For the native, the efficacy of these rites is beyond doubt: He is convinced that they must produce the results he expects of them, and with a sort of necessity. If the outcome does not live up to his hopes, he merely concludes that they have been cancelled out by the evil deeds of some hostile group. In any case, it does not enter his mind that a favorable outcome might be obtained by other means. If, by chance, the vegetation grows, or if the animals multiply before he has carried out the Intichiuma, he assumes that another Intichiuma has been celebrated—under the earth, by the souls of the ancestors—and that the living reap the benefits of this underground ceremony.[25]

---

[24]Spencer and Gillen, *Native Tribes*, p. 170.

[25]Ibid., p. 519. The analysis of the rites just studied has been made only with the observations that we owe to Spencer and Gillen. After this chapter was written, Strehlow published the third installment of his work, which treats the positive cult and, in particular, the Intichiuma—or, as he says, the rites of *mbatjalkatiuma*. I have found nothing in this publication that obliges me to alter the preceding description, or even to make major amendments. Of greatest interest in what Strehlow teaches us on this subject is that the sheddings and offerings of blood are much more common than might have been suspected from the account of Spencer and Gillen (see Strehlow, *Aranda*, vol. III, pp. 13, 14, 19, 29, 39, 43, 46, 56, 67, 80, 89).

Incidentally, Strehlow's information on the cult must be used circumspectly, for he did not witness the rites he describes. He settled for collecting oral accounts, and in general these are rather sketchy (see vol. III, preface of Leonhardi, p. v). One can even ask whether he has not gone too far in assimilating the totemic ceremonies of initiation to those he calls mbatjalkatiuma. To be sure, he has not failed to make a laudable effort to distinguish them: indeed, he has brought out clearly two of their differentiating characteristics. First, the Intichiuma is always conducted in a consecrated place, to which the memory of some ancestor is attached, whereas the initiation ceremonies may be conducted anywhere. Second, offerings of blood are specific to the Intichiuma, which proves that they are part and parcel of what is most essential to these rites (vol. III, p. 7). In the description of the rites that he gives, we find mingled together information that refers indiscriminately to both kinds of rite. In fact, in the ones he describes for us under the name mbatjalkatiuma, the young men generally play an important role (see, for example, pp. 11, 13, etc.)—which is characteristic of initiation. Similarly, it even appears that the location of the rite is up to the participants, since they build an artificial stage. They dig a hole and go into it; throughout no reference is made to rocks or sacred trees and to their ritual role.

II

Such is act one of the feast.

Actually, there is no ceremony as such in the period that immediately follows, yet religious life remains intense. It reveals itself through a heightening in the usual system of prohibitions. The sacredness of the totem is somehow reinforced; there is less inclination to touch it. Whereas the Arunta may eat their totemic animal or plant in ordinary times, provided they do so with moderation, this right is suspended the day after the Intichiuma. The dietary prohibition is strict and unqualified. It is believed that any violation will neutralize the beneficial effects of the rite and arrest the reproduction of the species. Although the people of other totems who happen to be in the same locality are not subject to the same restriction, they are not as free at this time as they ordinarily are. They may not eat the totemic animal just anywhere—in the bush, for example—but are required to bring it to the camp, and only there may it be cooked.[26]

There is a final ceremony to bring these extraordinary prohibitions to an end and adjourn this long series of rites. Although it varies somewhat according to clan, the essential elements are the same everywhere. Here are two of the principal forms the ceremony takes among the Arunta. One refers to the Witchetty Grub and the other to the Kangaroo.

Once the caterpillars have reached full maturity and prove to be abundant, the people of the totem, as well as others, collect as many as possible. Everyone then brings those they have found to camp and cook them until they become hard and crisp. The cooked products are kept in a type of wooden container called a *pitchi*. Caterpillars can be harvested for only a very short time, as they appear only after the rain. When they begin to be less plentiful, the Alatunja summons everyone to the men's camp; at the Alatunja's invitation, each brings his supply. The outsiders place theirs before the people of the totem. With the help of his companions, the Alatunja takes one pitchi and grinds the contents between two stones. He then eats a little of the powder thus obtained, and the rest is given to the people of the other clans, who from now on may do what they want with it. The procedure is exactly the same for the supply the Alatunja has made. From this moment on, the men and women of the totem may eat some, but only a little. If they exceeded the permissible limits, they would lose the strength they need to celebrate the Intichiuma, and the species would not reproduce. But if they

---

[26]Spencer and Gillen, *Native Tribes*, p. 203. Cf. [Rev. A.] Meyer, *The Encounter Bay Tribe*, in [James Dominick] Woods, [*The Native Tribes of South Australia*, Adelaide, E. S. Wigg, 1879], p. 187.

ate none of it at all, and especially if the Alatunja totally abstained from eating any in the circumstances just mentioned, they would be stricken with the same impotence.

In the totemic group of the Kangaroo that has its center at Undiara, certain features of the ceremony are more obvious. After the rites on the sacred rock that I have described are done with, the young men leave to hunt the kangaroo and bring the game back to the men's camp. The elders, in the midst of whom stands the Alatunja, eat a little of the animal's flesh and with its fat anoint the bodies of those who have taken part in the Intichiuma. The rest is shared among the assembled men. Next, the men of the totem decorate themselves with totemic designs, and the night is spent in singing that recalls the exploits of the men- and animal-kangaroos in Alcheringa times. On the following day, the young men go hunting again in the forest, bringing back more kangaroos than they did the first time, and the ceremony of the previous night resumes.[27]

With variations of detail, the same rite is found in the other Arunta clans,[28] among the Urabunna,[29] the Kaitish,[30] the Unmatjera,[31] and the Encounter Bay tribe.[32] Everywhere it comprises the same basic elements. Several specimens of the totemic plant or animal are presented to the head of the clan, who solemnly eats some and is required to do so. If he did not fulfill this obligation, he would lose his power to celebrate the Intichiuma efficaciously—that is, to create the species each year. Sometimes the ritual eating is followed by an anointing done with the fat of the animal or with certain parts of the plant.[33] Generally, the rite is repeated afterward by the men of the totem, or at least by the elders. Once it is over, the special restrictions are lifted.

At present, there is no such ceremony among the tribes farther north, the Warramunga and neighboring societies.[34] Nonetheless, one still finds traces that seem to evidence a time when that was not unknown. It is true

[27]Spencer and Gillen, *Native Tribes*, p. 204.

[28]Ibid., pp. 205–207.

[29]Spencer and Gillen, *Northern Tribes*, pp. 286–287.

[30]Ibid., p. 294.

[31]Ibid., p. 296.

[32]Meyer, ["The Encounter Bay Tribe"] in Woods [*The Native Tribes of South Australia*], p. 187.

[33]I have already cited one case of this; others are to be found in Spencer and Gillen, *Native Tribes*, p. 205; Spencer and Gillen, *Northern Tribes*, p. 286.

[34]The Walpari, Wulmala, Tjingili, Umbaia.

that the head of the clan never eats the totem ritually and obligatorily. But in certain cases, the people who are not of the totem whose Intichiuma has just been conducted are required to bring the animal or plant to the camp and offer it to the head, asking him if he wishes to eat some. He refuses and adds: "I have made this for you; you may eat freely of it."[35] Thus the custom of presentation persists and the question asked of the chief seems to hark back to a time when ritual eating was practiced.[36]

III

What gives the system of rites just described its interest is that it contains all the principal elements, and in the most elementary form now known, of a great religious institution that was destined to become a foundation of the positive cult in the higher religions: the institution of sacrifice.

It is well known how much the works of Robertson Smith have revolutionized the traditional theory of sacrifice.[37] Until Smith, sacrifice was seen only as a sort of tribute or homage, either obligatory or freely given, and

---

[35]Spencer and Gillen, *Northern Tribes*, p. 318.

[36]For this second part of the ceremony, as for the first, I have followed Spencer and Gillen. On this point, Strehlow's recent volume confirms the observations of his predecessors, at least in essentials. He recognizes, indeed, that after the first ceremony (on p. 13 he says two months after), the head of the clan ritually eats a bit of the totemic animal or plant, and that they then proceed to the lifting of the prohibitions; he calls this operation *die Freigabe des Totems zum allgemeinen Gebrauch* (vol. III, p. 7). He even informs us that this operation is important enough to be designated by a special word in the Arunta language. True, he adds that this ritual consumption is not the only one, that sometimes the chief and elders also eat the sacred plant or animal before the initial ceremony, and that the celebrant in the rite does the same after the celebration. There is nothing implausible about this. Such acts of consumption are so many means used by the celebrants or the participants to confer on themselves the virtues they wish to acquire; it is not surprising that they should be multiple. None of that invalidates the account of Spencer and Gillen, for the rite they emphasize, not without reason, is the *Freigabe des Totems*.

Strehlow disputes the claims of Spencer and Gillen on only two points. In the first place, he declares that the act of ritual consumption does not always take place. That fact is beyond question, because some totemic animals and plants are inedible. But the fact remains that the rite is very common; Strehlow himself cites numerous examples of it (pp. 13, 14, 19, 23, 33, 36, 50, 59, 67, 68, 71, 75, 80, 84, 89, 93). In the second place, we have seen that (according to Spencer and Gillen) if the chief of the clan did not partake of the totemic animal or plant, he would lose his powers. Strehlow assures us that native testimony does not corroborate this assertion. But this question seems to me altogether secondary. The certain fact is that this ritual consumption is prescribed—hence that it is judged to be useful or necessary. Like all communions, its only purpose is to confer on the communicant the virtues he needs. It does not follow from the fact that the natives, or some of them, have forgotten that this function of the rite is not real. Must it be repeated that worshippers most often do not know the real reasons for the practices that they carry out?

[37]See [William Robertson Smith, *Lectures on*] *the Religion of the Semites*, 2d. ed., London, A. & C. Black, 1894], Lectures VI to XI, and the article "Sacrifice" in the *Encyclopedia Britannica* [Edinburgh, Adam & Charles Black, 1891].

analogous to those that subjects owe their princes. Robertson Smith was the first to draw attention to the fact that this traditional explanation did not account for two fundamental features of the rite. First, it is a meal; the substance of sacrifice is food. Second, it is a meal of which the faithful who offer it partake at the same time as the god to whom it is offered. Certain parts of the victim are reserved for the deity; others are conferred on the celebrants, who consume them. This is why, in the Bible, the sacrifice is sometimes called a meal prepared before Yahweh. In many societies, the meal is taken in common to create a bond of artificial kinship among the participants. Kin are beings who are made of the same flesh and the same blood. And since food constantly remakes the substance of the body, shared food can create the same effects as shared origin. According to Smith, the object of sacrificial banquets is to have the faithful and the god commune in one and the same flesh, to tie a knot of kinship between them. From this perspective, sacrifice came into view in an altogether novel way. Its essence was no longer the act of renunciation that the word "sacrifice" usually expresses, as was so long believed; it was first and foremost an act of alimentary communion.

In particular details, no doubt, this manner of explaining what sacrificial banquets achieve must be qualified. What they achieve does not result exclusively from the fact of sharing a common table. Man does not sanctify himself only because, in some sense, he sits down at the same table as the god, but principally because the food that he consumes in the ritual meal has sacredness. Indeed, as has been shown, a whole series of preliminary steps in the sacrifice (washings, anointings, prayers, and so on) transform the animal to be immolated into a sacred thing, the sacredness of which is thereafter communicated to the faithful who partake of it.[38] But it is no less true that alimentary communion is among the essential elements of sacrifice. Now, if we go back to the rite that ends the Intichiuma ceremonies, it too consists in an act of this kind. When the totemic animal is killed, the Alatunja and the elders solemnly partake of it. Thus they commune with the sacred principle that inhabits it, and they absorb that principle into themselves. The only difference in this context is that the animal is sacred naturally, whereas ordinarily it acquires sacredness only artificially in the course of the sacrifice.

Furthermore, the function of this communion is manifest. Every member of the totemic clan carries within himself a kind of mystic substance that makes up the higher part of his being: His soul is made from that substance. He becomes a person through it; the powers he ascribes to himself, and his

---

[38]See Hubert and Mauss, "Essai sur la nature et la fonction du sacrifice," in *Mélanges d'histoire des religions* [Paris, F. Alcan, 1909], pp. 40ff.

social role, come to him from it. So he has a vital interest in preserving it intact and in keeping it in a state of perpetual youth as much as possible. Alas, all forces, even the most spiritual, are worn away with the passage of time if nothing replenishes the energy they lose in the ordinary course of events: Herein lies a vital necessity that, as we will see, is the profound cause of the positive cult. The people of a totem cannot remain themselves unless they periodically renew the totemic principle that is in them, and since they conceive this principle in the form of a plant or an animal, they go to that animal or plant to seek the strength they need to renew and rejuvenate it. A man of the Kangaroo clan believes he is, and feels he is, a kangaroo. Through that quality he defines himself, and it determines his place in society. In order to maintain that quality, from time to time he causes a little flesh of that animal to pass into his own substance. A few bits are enough, in accordance with the rule that the part is as good as the whole.[39]

To make all the hoped-for results possible, however, it is important that this procedure not occur at just any time. The time when the new generation has just reached its full development is the most opportune, for that is also when the forces that animate the totemic species come into full bloom. They have just been extracted from the rich reservoirs of life that are the sacred trees and rocks. Besides, all sorts of means have been used to heighten their intensity, such being the purpose of the rites that have occurred in the first part of the Intichiuma. What is more, by their very appearance, the first fruits of the harvest make the energy they contain manifest. In those first fruits, the totemic god asserts himself in all the splendor of youth. This is why, throughout the ages, the first fruits have been considered very sacred food, reserved to very sacred beings. Naturally, therefore, the Australian uses them to regenerate himself spiritually. In this way, both the date and the circumstances of the ceremony are explained.

Perhaps it will seem surprising that such sacred food is eaten by mere profane beings, but there is no positive cult that does not move within this contradiction. All beings that are sacred stand beyond the reach of the profane, by reason of their distinguishing trait. On the other hand, they would lose their whole *raison d'être* if they were not placed in a relationship with those same faithful who must otherwise stay respectfully at a distance from them. There is no positive rite that does not fundamentally constitute a veritable sacrilege. Man can have no dealings with the sacred beings without crossing the barrier that must ordinarily keep him separate from them.

All that matters is that the sacrilege be carried out with mitigating pre-

---

[39]For an explanation of this rule, see above, pp. 230–231.

cautions. The commonest of those consist of preparing the transition and introducing the faithful into the world of sacred things slowly, and only in stages. Broken up and diluted in this way, the sacrilege does not strike the religious consciousness abruptly. Not felt as such, it vanishes. This is what is happening in the case before us. The effect of a whole sequence of ceremonies conducted prior to the moment when the totem is solemnly eaten has been gradually to sanctify the participants. It is essentially a religious period, which they could not go through without transformation of their religious state. Little by little, the fasts, the contact of sacred rocks and the churingas,[40] totemic decorations, and so forth, have conferred a sacredness on them that they did not have before and that permits them, without scandalous and dangerous profanation, to confront the dangerous and awesome food ordinarily forbidden to them.[41]

If the act by which a sacred being is offered up and then eaten by those who venerate it can be called a sacrifice, the rite just discussed is entitled to the same name. Moreover, the similarities it has with other practices found in many agrarian cults clarify its meaning. As it turns out, even among peoples who have attained a high level of civilization, a common rule is that the first products of the harvest are used as the substance of ritual meals, the paschal meal being the best-known example.[42] Since agrarian rites are at the very foundation of worship in its most advanced forms, we see that the Intichiuma of Australian societies is closer to us than its apparent crudeness might have led us to believe.

By a stroke of genius, Smith had an intuition of these facts without knowing them. Through a string of ingenious deductions (which need not be repeated here, since they are of only historic interest[43]), he came to believe he could establish that at the beginning the animal offered up in the sacrifices must at first have been considered as quasi-divine and as the close kin of those who offered it. Now, these are precisely the characteristics by which the totemic species is defined. Thus, Smith came to suppose that totemism must have known and practiced a rite very similar to the one we have just examined. Indeed, he tended to see this kind of sacrifice as the origin of the

[40]See Strehlow, *Aranda*, vol. III, p. 3.

[41]Besides, it should not be forgotten that among the Arunta, eating of the totemic animal is not forbidden altogether.

[42]See other examples in [James George] Frazer, *The Golden Bough*, 2d. ed. [London, Macmillan, 1894], pp. 348ff.

[43]*The Religion of the Semites*, pp. 275ff.

sacrificial institution as a whole.[44] At the beginning, sacrifice is instituted not to create a bond of artificial kinship between man and his gods but to maintain and renew the natural kinship that at the beginning united men. Here, as elsewhere, the artifice is born only to imitate nature. But in Smith's book, this hypothesis was presented as little more than a mental construct, which the facts then known did not at all adequately warrant. The few cases of totemic sacrifice that he cites in support of his thesis do not mean what he says they do, and the animals that figure in it were not real totems.[45] But today, one may say that this has been proved, on one point at least: We have just seen that totemic sacrifice, as Smith conceived it, is or was practiced in a large number of societies. Granted, we have no proof that this practice is necessarily inherent in totemism or that it is the seed from which all the other types of sacrifice have emerged. But if the universality of the rite is hypothetical, its existence can no longer be disputed. We must consider it established from now on that the most mystical form of alimentary communion is found as early as the most rudimentary religion now known.

IV

On another point, however, the new facts we have at hand undermine Smith's theories. According to him, communion was not only an essential element of sacrifice but also the only element, at least initially. He thought not only that it was a mistake to reduce sacrifice to a mere act of tribute or offering but also that the idea of offering was initially absent; that this idea made only a late appearance, influenced by external circumstances; and that, far from helping us to understand the true nature of the ritual mechanism, the idea of offering masked it. Smith believed that he detected too gross an absurdity in the very idea of sacrifice for it to be viewed as the profound cause of such a great institution. One of the most important functions that fall squarely upon the shoulders of the deity is to see that men have the food they need to live, so it would seem impossible that sacrifice should involve a presentation of food to the deity. It seems contradictory for the gods to expect their food from man, when it is by them that man himself is fed. How

[44]Ibid., pp. 318–319.

[45]See on this point Hubert and Mauss, *Mélanges d'histoire des religions*, preface, pp. vff.

could they need his help to claim their just portion of the things that he receives from their hands? From these considerations, Smith concluded that the combined idea of sacrifice-offering could have been born only in the great religions. In them once the gods were separated from the things with which they were originally merged, they were conceived as rather like kings, foremost owners of the land and its products. From then on, according to Smith, sacrifice was confounded with the tribute that subjects pay their prince in return for the rights conceded to them. In reality, however, this new interpretation was an alteration and even a corruption of the original idea. For when the notion that "the idea of property makes everything it touches material" becomes part of sacrifice, sacrifice is denatured and made into a kind of bartering between man and the deity.[46]

The facts I have set forth undermine that argument. The rites I have described are certainly among the most primitive ever observed. As yet, no definite mythical personality is seen to make its appearance in them; there are neither gods nor spirits as such, and only vague, anonymous, impersonal forces are at work. Yet the reasoning they presuppose is exactly the reasoning Smith declared impossible because of its absurdity.

Let us look again at the first act of the Intichiuma: the rites intended to bring about the fertility of the animal or plant species that serves as the totem of the clan. This species is the sacred thing. It incarnates what I was led to call, in a metaphorical sense, the totemic deity. But we have seen that it needs man's help to perpetuate itself. It is man who dispenses life to a new generation each year; without him, it would not see the light of day. If man stopped celebrating the Intichiuma, the sacred beings would disappear from the face of the earth. In a sense, it is from him that they have their being. In another sense, however, it is from them that he has his own. Once they have attained maturity, it is from them that he will borrow the strength needed for the maintenance and repair of his spiritual being. Hence it is man who makes his gods, one can say, or at least, it is man who makes them endure; but at the same time, it is through them that he himself endures. Thus he regularly closes the circle that, according to Smith, is entailed by the very notion of sacrificial tribute. He gives to sacred beings a little of what he receives from them and he receives from them, all that he gives them.

There is more: The offerings that he is required to make each year are not different in nature from those that will be made later, in sacrifices prop-

---

[46][William Robertson Smith], *The Religion of the Semites*, pp. 390ff.

erly so-called. The sacrificer offers an animal so that the life-principles within it separate from the organism and go forth to feed the deity. Similarly, the grains of dust that the Australian detaches from the sacred rock are so many principles that spread through space so that they will vitalize the totemic species and bring about its renewal. The movement by which this spreading is done is also the one that normally accompanies offerings. In certain cases, the resemblance between the two rites goes as far as the details of the movements made. We have seen that the Kaitish pour water on a stone in order to have rain; among certain peoples, the priest pours water on the altar for the same purpose.[47] The sheddings of blood, which are customary in some Intichiumas, are true offerings. Just as the Arunta or the Dieri sprinkle the rock or the sacred design with blood, so in the more advanced cults is the blood of the sacrificed victim, or the believer, in many cases poured out on, or in front of, the altar.[48] In this case, it is given to the gods, whose favorite food it is. In Australia, it is given to the sacred species. Thus there are no longer any grounds for the view that the idea of offerings is a recent product of civilization.

A document for which we are indebted to Strehlow brings out this kinship between the Intichiuma and sacrifice. It is a hymn accompanying the Kangaroo Intichiuma that describes the ceremony and states its hoped-for effects. A piece of the kangaroo's fat has been placed by the chief on a support made of branches. The text says that this fat makes the fat of the kangaroos grow.[49] In this case, therefore, they do not confine themselves to spreading sacred dust or human blood; the animal itself is immolated—one can say sacrificed, placed on a kind of altar—and offered to the species whose life it must maintain.

We see now in what sense it is permissible to say that the Intichiuma contains the seeds of the sacrificial system. In the form it takes when fully constituted, sacrifice comprises two essential elements: an act of communion and an act of offering. The faithful commune with the god by ingesting a sacred food and simultaneously make an offering to this god. We find these two acts in the Intichiuma as just described. The only difference is that

[47]R. Smith himself cites such cases, ibid., p. 231.

[48]See for example Exodus, 29:10–14; Leviticus, 9:8–11; the priests of Baal let their own blood flow on the altar (I Kings 18:8). [Compare Exodus 39:13 with Durkheim's discussion of special treatment given to the liver, fat, and other parts of sacrificed animals. In I Kings 18:28, we learn about the Baal priests' encounter with Elijah, where Durkheim's claim that "there are no religions that are false" is dramatically contradicted. Trans.]

[49]Strehlow, Aranda, vol. III, p. 12, verse 7.

they are done simultaneously or immediately after one another in sacrifice proper,[50] whereas they are separated in the Australian ceremony. In the first case, they are part of one indivisible rite; in the second, they occur at different times and may even be separated by a rather long interval, but basically the mechanism is the same. Taken as a whole, the Intichiuma is a sacrifice, but one whose parts are not yet joined and organized.

This comparison has the twofold advantage of helping us understand the nature of both the Intichiuma and sacrifice better.

We understand the Intichiuma better. Indeed, the conception put forth by Frazer, who made it out to be simply a magical operation devoid of any religious character,[51] now seems untenable. To place outside religion a rite that appears to be the herald of such a great religious institution is unimaginable.

We also understand better what sacrifice itself is. In the first place, the equal importance of the two elements that enter into it is henceforth established. If the Australian makes offerings to his sacred beings, there is no basis at all for supposing that the idea of offering was foreign to the original organization of the sacrificial institution and disturbed its natural harmony. Smith's theory must be revised on this point.[52] Sacrifice is certainly a process of communion in part. But it is also, and no less fundamentally, a gift, an act of renunciation. It always presupposes that the worshipper relinquishes to the gods some part of his substance or his goods. Any attempt to reduce one of these elements to the other is pointless. Indeed, the offering may have more lasting effects than the communion.[53]

In the second place, it seems that sacrifice in general, and in particular the sacrificial offering, can be made only to personal beings. The offerings we have just encountered in Australia do not entail any such notion. In other words, sacrifice is independent of the variable forms in which religious forces are thought of; it has deeper causes, which we will examine below.

It is clear, however, that the act of offering naturally awakens in people the idea of a moral subject that the offering is meant to satisfy. The ritual acts

---

[50]At least, when it is performed in its entirely; in certain cases it can be reduced to only one of these elements.

[51]According to Strehlow [*Aranda*] vol. III, p. 9, the natives "regard these ceremonies as a sort of divine service, in the same way as the Christian regards the practices of his religion."

[52]It might be well to ask whether the sheddings of blood and offerings of hair that Smith sees as acts of communion are not typical offerings. (See Smith, *The Religion of the Semites*, pp. 320ff.)

[53]The piacular sacrifices, of which I will speak more specifically in Bk. 3, chap. 5, consist entirely of offerings. They serve as communions only secondarily.

I have described become easier to understand when they are believed to be addressed to persons. Thus, even while only bringing impersonal powers into play, the practices of the Intichiuma paved the way for a different conception.[54] To be sure, they could not have been sufficient to produce the idea of mythic personalities straightaway. But once formed, the idea was drawn into the cult by the very nature of the rites. At the same time, it became less abstract. As it interacted more directly with action and life, it took on greater reality by the same stroke. Thus we can believe that practice of the cult encouraged the personification of religious forces—in a secondary way, no doubt, but one that deserves notice.

V

The contradiction that R. Smith saw as inadmissible, a piece of blatant illogic, must still be explained.

If sacred beings always manifested their powers in a perfectly equal manner, it would appear inconceivable that man should have dreamed of offering them favors. It is hard to see what they could have needed from him. But as long as they are merged with things and seen as cosmic principles of life, they are subject to its rhythm. That life unfolds through oscillations back and forth that succeed one another in accordance with a definite law. At some times, life affirms itself in all its splendor; at others, it fades so much that one wonders whether it will not end altogether. Every year, the plants die. Will they be reborn? The animal species tend to diminish through natural or violent death. Will they renew themselves in time, and as they should? Above all, the rain is uncertain, and for long periods it seems to have disappeared, never to return. What these weakenings of nature bear witness to is that, at the corresponding seasons, the sacred beings to which the animals, plants, rain, and so forth are subject pass through the same critical states, so they too have their periods of breakdown. Man can never take part in these spectacles as an indifferent watcher. If he is to live, life must continue universally, and therefore the gods must not die. He therefore seeks to support and aid them; and to do this, he puts at their service the forces he has at his disposal and mobilizes for that purpose. The blood flowing in his veins has fecundating virtues; he will

---

[54]This has caused these ceremonies often to be spoken of as though they were addressed to personal deities. (See, for example, a text of Krichauff and another of Kempe cited by [Richard] Eylmann, [*Die Eingeborenen der Kolonie Sud Australien*, Berlin, D. Reumer, 1908], pp. 202–203.)

pour it out. He will draw upon the seeds of life that slumber in the sacred rocks that his clan possesses, and he will sow them in the wind. In a word, he will make offerings.

In addition, these external and physical crises go hand in hand with internal and mental crises that tend toward the same result. The sacred beings are sacred only because they are imagined as sacred. Let us stop believing in them, and they will be as if they were not. In this respect, even those that have a physical form, and are known to us through sense experience, depend on the thought of the faithful who venerate them. The sacredness that defines them as objects of the cult is not given in their natural makeup; it is superadded to them by belief. The kangaroo is only an animal, like any other; for the Kangaroo people, however, it contains a principle that sets it apart from other beings, and this principle exists only in the minds that think of it.[55] If, once conceived, the sacred beings did not need men in order to live, the representations that express them would have to remain the same. This stability is impossible. In actuality, it is in group life that these representations are formed, and group life is by nature intermittent. Of necessity, then, they share the same intermittence. They achieve their greatest intensity when the individuals are assembled and in direct relations with one another, at the moment when everyone communes in the same idea or emotion. Once the assembly is dissolved and each person has returned to his own existence, those representations lose more and more of their original energy. Overlaid little by little by the rising flood of day-to-day sensations, they would eventually disappear into the unconscious, unless we found some means of calling them back to consciousness and revitalizing them. Now they cannot weaken without the sacred beings' losing their reality, because the sacred beings exist only in and through their representations.* If we think less hard about them, they count for less to us and we count less on them; they exist to a lesser degree. Thus, here again is a point of view from which the favors of men are necessary to them. This second reason to help them is even more important than the first, for it has existed from time immemorial. The intermittences of physical life affect religious beliefs only when religions are not yet detached from their cosmic magma. But the intermittences of social life are inevitable, and even the most idealistic religions can never escape them.

Moreover, it is because the gods are in this state of dependence on the

---

*This sentence is missing from the Swain translation.

[55] In a philosophical sense, the same is true of anything, for things exist only through representation. But as I have shown (pp. 228–229), this proposition is doubly true of religious forces, because there is nothing in the makeup of things that corresponds to sacredness.

thought of man that man can believe his help to be efficacious. The only way to renew the collective representations that refer to sacred beings is to plunge them again into the very source of religious life: assembled groups. The emotions aroused by the periodic crises through which external things pass induce the men witnessing them to come together, so that they can see what it is best to do. But by the very fact of being assembled, they comfort one another; they find the remedy because they seek it together. The shared faith comes to life again quite naturally in the midst of reconstituted collectivity. It is reborn because it finds itself once again in the same conditions in which it was first born. Once it is restored, it easily overcomes all the private doubts that had managed to arise in individual minds. The mental image* of the sacred things regains strength sufficient to withstand the inward or external causes that tended to weaken it. Despite the obvious failures, one can no longer believe that the gods will die, because they are felt to live again in the depths of one's own self. No matter how crude the techniques used to help the gods, they cannot seem unavailing, because everything happens as if they really were working. People are more confident because they feel stronger, and they are stronger in reality because the strength that was flagging has been reawakened in their consciousnesses.

It is necessary, then, to refrain from believing, with Smith, that the cult was instituted only for the benefit of men and that the gods have no use for it. They still need it as much as their faithful do. No doubt, the men could not live without the gods; but on the other hand, the gods would die if they were not worshipped. Thus the purpose of the cult is not only to bring the profane into communion with sacred beings but also to keep the sacred beings alive, to remake and regenerate them perpetually. To be sure, the material offerings do not produce this remaking through their own virtues but through mental states that reawaken and accompany these doings, which are empty in themselves. The true *raison d'être* of even those cults that are most materialistic in appearance is not to be sought in the actions they prescribe but in the inward and moral renewal that the actions help to bring about. What the worshipper in reality gives his god is not the food he places on the altar or the blood that he causes to flow from his veins: It is his thought. Nevertheless, there remains a mutually reinforcing exchange of good deeds between the deity and his worshippers. The rule *do ut des*,† by which the principle of sacrifice has sometimes been defined, is not a recent invention

---

*Durkheim said *image*, which here refers to a mental, rather than a physical, representation.

†I give in order that you might give.

by utilitarian theorists; it simply makes explicit the mechanics of the sacrificial system itself and, more generally, that of the whole positive cult. Thus, the circle Smith pointed out is quite real, but nothing about it offends the intelligence. It arises from the fact that although sacred beings are superior to men, they can live only in human consciousnesses.

But if, pressing the analysis further and substituting for the religious symbols the realities they express, we inquire into the way those realities behave within the rite, this circle will seem to us even more natural, and we will better understand its sense and purpose. If, as I have tried to establish, the sacred principle is nothing other than society hypostasized and transfigured, it should be possible to interpret ritual life in secular and social terms. Like ritual life, social life in fact moves in a circle. On the one hand, the individual gets the best part of himself from society—all that gives him a distinctive character and place among other beings, his intellectual and moral culture. Let language, sciences, arts, and moral beliefs be taken from man, and he falls to the rank of animality; therefore the distinctive attributes of human nature come to us from society. On the other hand, however, society exists and lives only in and through individuals. Let the idea of society be extinguished in individual minds, let the beliefs, traditions, and aspirations of the collectivity be felt and shared by individuals no longer, and the society will die. Thus we can repeat about society what was previously said about the deity: It has reality only to the extent that it has a place in human consciousnesses, and that place is made for society by us. We now glimpse the profound reason why the gods can no more do without their faithful than the faithful can do without their gods. It is that society, of which the gods are only the symbolic expression, can no more do without individuals than individuals can do without society.

Here we touch the solid rock on which all the cults are built and that has made them endure as long as human societies have. When we see what the rites are made of and what they seem to be directed toward, we wonder with astonishment how men could have arrived at the idea and, especially, how they remained attached to it so faithfully. Where could they have gotten the illusion that, with a few grains of sand thrown to the wind or a few drops of blood poured on a rock or on the stone of an altar, the life of an animal species or a god could be maintained? When, from beneath these outward and seemingly irrational doings, we have uncovered a mental mechanism that gives them sense and moral import, we have made a step toward solving this problem. But nothing assures us that the mechanism itself is anything but a play of hallucinatory images. I have indeed shown what psychological processes make the faithful think that the rite makes the spiritual forces they need come to life again around them; but from the fact that it can be explained psychologically does not follow that this belief has objective value. To have a sound basis for seeing the efficacy that is imputed to the rites as something other than offspring of a chronic delusion with which humanity deceives itself, it must be possible to establish that the effect of the cult is periodically to recreate a moral being on which we depend, as it depends upon us. Now, this being exists: It is society.

In fact, if religious ceremonies have any importance at all, it is that they set collectivity in motion; groups come together to celebrate them. Thus their first result is to bring individuals together, multiply the contacts between them, and make those contacts more intimate. That in itself modifies the content of the consciousnesses. On ordinary days, the mind is chiefly occupied with utilitarian and individualistic affairs. Everyone goes about his own personal business; for most people, what is most important is to meet the demands of material life; the principal motive of economic activity has always been private interest. Of course, social feelings could not be absent altogether. We remain in relationship with our fellow men; the habits, ideas, and tendencies that upbringing has stamped on us, and that ordinarily preside over our relations with others, continue to make their influence felt. But they are constantly frustrated and held in check by the opposing tendencies that the requirements of the day-in, day-out struggle produce and perpetuate. Depending on the intrinsic energy of those social feelings, they hold up more or less successfully; but that energy is not renewed. They live on their past, and, in consequence, they would in time be depleted if nothing came to give back a little of the strength they lose through this incessant conflict and friction.

When the Australians hunt or fish in scattered small groups, they lose sight of what concerns their clan or tribe. They think only of taking as much game as possible. On feast days, however, these concerns are overshadowed obligatorily; since they are in essence profane, they are shut out of sacred periods. What then occupies the mind are the beliefs held in common: the memories of great ancestors, the collective ideal the ancestors embody—in short, social things. Even the material interests that the great religious ceremonies aim to satisfy are public and hence social. The whole society has an interest in an abundant harvest, in timely rain that is not excessive, and in the normal reproduction of the animals. Hence it is society that is foremost in every consciousness and that dominates and directs conduct, which amounts to saying that at such times it is even more alive, more active, and thus more real than at profane times. And so when men feel there is something outside themselves that is reborn, forces that are reanimated, and a life that reawakens, they are not deluded. This renewal is in no way imaginary, and the individuals themselves benefit from it, for the particle of social being that each individual bears within himself necessarily participates in this collective remaking. The individual soul itself is also regenerated, by immersing itself once more in the very wellspring of its life. As a result, that soul feels stronger, more mistress of itself, and less dependent upon physical necessities.

We know that the positive cult tends naturally to take on periodic forms; this is one of its distinguishing traits. Of course, there are rites that man celebrates occasionally, to deal with temporary situations. But these episodic practices never play more than a secondary role, even in the religions we are studying in this book. The essence of the cult is the cycle of feasts that are regularly repeated at definite times. We are now in a position to understand where that impulse toward periodicity comes from. The rhythm that religious life obeys only expresses, and results from, the rhythm of social life. Society cannot revitalize the awareness it has of itself unless it assembles, but it cannot remain continuously in session. The demands of life do not permit it to stay in congregation indefinitely, so it disperses, only to reassemble anew when it again feels the need. It is to these necessary alternations that the regular alternation of sacred and profane time responds. Because at least the manifest function of the cult is initially to regularize the course of natural phenomena, the rhythm of cosmic life set its mark upon the rhythm of ritual life. Hence, for a long time the feasts were seasonal; we have observed that such was already a trait of the Australian Intichiuma. But the seasons merely provided the external framework of this organization, not the principle on which it rests, for even the cults that have exclusively spiritual ends have remained periodic. The reason is that this periodicity has different causes. Because the seasonal changes are critical periods for nature, they are a natural occasion for gatherings and thus for religious ceremonies. But other events could play, and have in fact played, the role of occasional causes. Yet it must be acknowledged that this framework, although purely external, has shown remarkable endurance, for its vestige is still found in the religions that are furthest removed from any physical basis. Several Christian feasts are bound with unbroken continuity to the pastoral and agricultural feasts of the ancient Israelites, even though they are neither pastoral nor agricultural any longer.

The form of this cycle is apt to vary from one society to another. Where the period of dispersion is long or the dispersion very great, the period of

congregation is prolonged in turn, and there are veritable orgies of collective
and religious life. Feasts come one after the other for weeks or months, and
ritual life sometimes rises to outright frenzy. This is true of the Australian
tribes and of several societies in the American North and Northwest.[56] Elsewhere, by contrast, these two phases of social life follow one another more
closely, and the contrast between them is less marked. The more societies
develop, the less is their tolerance for interruptions that are too pronounced.

[56]See Mauss, *Essai sur les variations saisonnières des sociétés Eskimos,* in *AS,* vol. IX [1906], pp. 96ff.

CHAPTER THREE

THE POSITIVE CULT (CONTINUED)

Mimetic Rites and the Principle of Causality

The techniques just discussed are not the only ones used to bring about the fertility of the totemic species. Others with the same purpose either accompany them or take their place.

I

In the same ceremonies I have described, various rites apart from blood or other sacrifices are often performed to supplement or reinforce the effects of those practices. They are composed of movements and cries intended to mimic the behavior or traits of the animal whose reproduction is hoped for. For this reason, I call them *mimetic*.

Among the Arunta, the Witchetty Grub Intichiuma involves more than the rites that are carried out on the sacred rocks, as discussed above. Once those have been completed, the participants start back toward the camp. When they are no more than about a mile away from it, they call a halt and decorate themselves ritually, after which they continue their march. Their adornment announces that an important ceremony is to come. And so it does. While the detachment was away, one of the elders left on guard at the camp has built a shelter out of long, narrow branches; it is called the *Umbana* and represents the chrysalis from which the insect emerges. All those who have taken part in the earlier ceremonies gather near the place where this structure has been put up; then they slowly advance, stopping from time to time until they reach the Umbana, which they enter. Immediately, all those who do not belong to the phratry to which the Witchetty Grub totem belongs (but who are on the scene, though at a distance) lie face down on the ground; they must stay in this posture until they are given permission to get up. During this time, a hymn rises from within the Umbana. It recounts the various phases the animal goes through in the course of his development and the myths concerning the sacred rocks. At the end of this hymn, the Alatunja glides out of the Umbana and, still crouching, slowly advances on the ground in front of it. He is followed by all his companions, who imitate his gestures. They apparently mean to portray the insect as it emerges from the chrysalis. The singing that is heard at the same moment, a kind of oral commentary on the rite, is in fact a description of the movements the animal makes at this stage of its development.[1]

In another Intichiuma,[2] celebrated à propos of another sort of grub, the unchalka[3] grub, this characteristic is even more pronounced. The participants in the rite adorn themselves with designs representing the unchalka bush, on which this grub lives at the beginning of its life; then they cover a shield with concentric circles of down that represent another kind of bush on which the adult insect lays its eggs. When these preparations are complete, everyone sits on the ground in a semicircle facing the principal celebrant. The celebrant alternately curves his body in two by bending toward the ground and rising on his knees; at the same time, he shakes his outspread arms, a way of representing the wings of the insect. From time to time, he leans over the shield, imitating the manner in which the butterfly hovers over the shrubs in which it lays its eggs. When this ceremony is over, another begins at a different place, to which they go in silence. This time, two shields are used. On one, the tracks of the grub are represented by zigzag lines; on the other are concentric circles of unequal size, some representing the eggs of the insect and the others the seeds of the eremophile bush, on which it feeds. As in the first ceremony, everyone sits in silence while the celebrant moves about, imitating the movements of the animal when it leaves the chrysalis and struggles to take flight.

Spencer and Gillen point out a few more practices from among the Arunta, which are similar but of lesser importance. For example, in the Intichiuma of the Emu, the participants at a given moment try to copy the gait and appearance of this bird in their own behavior;[4] in an Intichiuma of the

[1][Sir Baldwin Spencer and Francis James Gillen, The Native Tribes of Central Australia, London, Macmillan, 1899], p. 176.

[2][Sir Baldwin Spencer and Francis James Gillen, The Northern Tribes of Central Australia, London, Macmillan, 1904], p. 179. It is true that Spencer and Gillen do not say explicitly that the ceremony is an Intichiuma, but the context leaves no doubt about the meaning of the rite.

[3]In the index of names of totems, Spencer and Gillen spell it Untjalka (Northern Tribes, p. 772).

[4][Spencer and Gillen], Native Tribes, p. 182.

Water, the men of the totem make the characteristic cry of the plover, a cry that in their minds is associated with the rainy season.[5] But all in all, these two explorers noted rather few instances of mimetic rites. It is certain, however, that their relative silence on this point arises either from the fact that they did not observe enough Intichiumas or that they overlooked this aspect of the ceremonies. Schulze, on the other hand, was struck by the extremely mimetic character of the Arunta rites. "The sacred corroborees," he says, "are for the most part ceremonies that represent animals"; he calls them "animal tjurungas,"[6] and the documents Strehlow collected have corroborated his reporting. In Strehlow's work, the examples are so numerous that it is impossible to cite them all; there are virtually no ceremonies in which some imitative gesture is not noted. According to the nature of the totems whose feast is celebrated, they jump in the manner of kangaroos and imitate the movements kangaroos make when eating. They imitate the flight of winged ants, the characteristic noise the bat makes, the cry of the wild turkey and that of the eagle, the hissing of the snake, the croaking of the frog, and so forth.[7] When the totem is a plant, they gesture as though picking[8] or eating[9] it, for example.

Among the Warramunga, the Intichiuma generally takes a very unusual form (described in the next chapter) that differs from those studied up to now. Nonetheless, a typical case of a purely mimetic Intichiuma exists among this people: that of the White Cockatoo. The ceremony Spencer and Gillen described began at ten at night. All night long, the head of the clan imitated the cry of the bird with distressing monotony. He stopped only when he had used up all his strength and was replaced by his son; then he began again as soon as he felt a little rested. These exhausting exercises continued without break until morning.[10]

Living beings are not the only ones they try to imitate. In a large number of tribes, the Intichiuma of the Rain basically consists of imitative rites. That celebrated among the Urabunna is one of the simplest. The head of the

[5]Ibid., p. 193.

[6][Rev. Louis] Schulze, "Aborigines of the Upper and Middle Finke River," *RSSA*, vol. XIV [1891], p. 221; cf. p. 243.

[7][Carl] Strehlow, [*Die Aranda- und Loritja-Stämme in Zentral-Australien,* Frankfurt, J. Baer, 1907], vol. III, pp. 11, 84, 31, 36, 37, 68, 72.

[8]Ibid., p. 100.

[9]Ibid., pp. 81, 100, 112, 115.

[10][Spencer and Gillen], *Northern Tribes,* p. 310.

clan is seated on the ground, decorated in white down and holding a lance. He moves every which way, probably to shake off the down that is attached to his body and represents the clouds when they are dispersed in the air. In that way, he imitates the great Alcheringa man-clouds that, according to legend, had the habit of rising to the sky to form the clouds from which the rain then came back to earth. In short, the object of the entire rite is to depict the formation and ascent of the rain-bearing clouds.[11]

Among the Kaitish, the ceremony is much more complex. I have already noted one of the means employed: The celebrant pours water on the sacred stones and on himself. Other rites strengthen the effect this sort of offering has. The rainbow is thought to be closely connected to the rain. It is the son, the Kaitish say, and it is always in a hurry to come out and stop the rain. So if the rain is to fall, the rainbow must not appear. They think they can get this result in the following way. On a shield they draw a design representing the rainbow. They take this shield to camp, carefully keeping it hidden from all eyes. They are convinced that, in making this image of the rainbow invisible, they are preventing the appearance of the rainbow itself. Meanwhile, with a pitchi full of water at his side, the head of the clan throws tufts of white down, representing the clouds, in all directions. Repeated imitations of the plover's cry round out the ceremony, which seems to have special solemnity. For as long as it lasts, those who participate in it, whether as actors or as members of the congregation, must have no contact with their wives, not even to speak with them.[12]

The methods of depiction are not the same among the Dieri. The rain is depicted not by water but by blood, which men cause to flow from their veins onto those in attendance.[13] At the same time, they throw handfuls of white down, which symbolize the clouds. Into a hut that has been built ahead of time, they place two large stones that represent the banking up of clouds, a sign of rain. Having left them there for a time, they move the stones a certain distance away and place them as far up as possible on the tallest tree they can find. This is a way of making the clouds mount into the sky. Some powdered gypsum is thrown into a water hole, at the sight of which the rain

[11]Ibid., pp. 285–286. It may be that the movements of the lance are to pierce the clouds.

[12][Spencer and Gillen] *Northern Tribes,* pp. 294–296. On the other hand, interestingly enough, among the Anula, the rainbow is held to bring about rain. (Ibid., p. 314.)

[13]The same procedure is used among the Arunta (Strehlow, *Aranda,* vol. III, p. 132). True, the question arises whether this shedding of blood might not be an offering for the purpose of bringing forth the principles that produce rain. However, Gason says emphatically that it is a way of imitating the falling rain.

spirit immediately makes clouds appear. Finally everyone, young and old, come together around the hut and, with their heads down, rush toward it. They pass violently through it, repeating the movement several times, until the only part of the structure that remains standing is its supporting posts. Then they attack the posts as well, shaking and tearing at them until the whole structure collapses. The operation of piercing the hut all over is intended to represent the clouds parting; and the collapse of its structure, the falling of the rain.[14]

Among the tribes of the northwest studied by Clement,[15] which occupy the territory between the Fortescue and Fitzroy rivers, there are ceremonies conducted for exactly the same purpose as the Intichiumas of the Arunta and that seem in the main to be essentially mimetic.

Among these peoples, the name *tarlow* is given to piles of stones that are apparently sacred because, as we will see, they are the object of important rites. Each animal and plant—each totem or subtotem[16]—is represented by a tarlow, of which a specific[17] clan is the custodian. The similarity between these tarlows and the sacred stones of the Arunta is easy to see.

When kangaroos are scarce, for example, the head of the clan to which the tarlow of the kangaroos belongs goes to the tarlow with some of his companions. There they execute various rites. The principal ones consist of jumping around the tarlow as the kangaroos jump and drinking as they drink—in short, imitating their most characteristic movements. The weapons used in hunting the animal play an important role in these rites. They are brandished, thrown against the stones, and so forth. When it is a matter of emus, they go to the tarlow of the emus; they walk and run as those birds do. The cleverness that the natives display in these imitations is apparently quite remarkable.

Other tarlows are dedicated to plants—grass seeds, for example. In this

---

[14][S.] Gason, "The Dieyerie Tribe," in [Edward Micklethwaite Curr, *The Australian Race: Its Origin, Languages, Customs, Place of Landing in Australia and the Routes by Which It Spread Itself over That Continent*, Melbourne, J. Ferres, 1886–1887], vol. II, pp. 66–68; [Alfred William] Howitt (*The Native Tribes [of Southeast Australia*, London, Macmillan, 1904], pp. 798–800) mentions another Dieri rite to get rain.

[15][E.] Clement, "Ethnographical Notes on the Western-Australian Aborigines [with a Descriptive Catalogue of Ethnographical Objects from Western Australia]," in *Internationales Archiv für Ethnographie*, vol. XVI [1903], pp. 6–7. Cf. Withnal, *Marriage Rites and Relationship*, in [*Science of*] Man: [*Australasian Anthropological Journal*, vol. VI], 1903, p. 42.

[16]I assume that a subtotem can have a tarlow because, according to Clement, certain clans have several totems.

[17]Clement says *a tribal family*.

case, the techniques used in winnowing or milling those seeds are mimed. And since, in ordinary life, it is women who are ordinarily responsible for such tasks, it is also they who perform the rite amid songs and dances.

II

All of these rites belong to the same category. The principle on which they are based is one of those on which what is commonly (and improperly[18]) called sympathetic magic is based.

This principle may usually be subdivided into two.[19]

The first can be stated in this way: *Whatever touches an object also touches everything that has any relationship of proximity or solidarity with that object.* Thus, whatever affects the part affects the whole; any force exerted on an individual is transmitted to his neighbors, his kin, and everything with which he is united in any way at all. All these cases are simply applications of the law of contagion, which we studied earlier. A good or bad state or quality is transmitted contagiously from one subject to another that has any relationship with the first.

The second principle is usually summarized in this formula: *Like produces like.* The depiction of a being or a state produces that being or state. This is the maxim that the rites just described put into operation, and its characteristic traits can be grasped best when they occur. The classic example of bewitchment, which is generally presented as the typical application of this same precept, is much less significant. Indeed, the phenomenon in bewitchment is largely a mere transfer. The idea of the image is associated in the mind with the idea of the model. As a result, the effects of any action on the statuette are passed on contagiously to the person whose traits it mimics. In relation to the original, the image plays the role of the part in relation to the whole; it is an agent of transmission. Thus it is believed that one can obtain the same result by burning the hair of the person one wants to get at. The only difference between these two kinds of operation is that, in one, the communication is done by means of similarity, and in the other, by means of contiguity.

The rites that concern us are a different case. They presuppose not

---

[18]I will explain the nature of this impropriety below (p. 517).

[19]On this classification see [James George] Frazer, *Lectures on the Early History of Kingship*, [London, Macmillan, 1905], pp. 37ff.; [Henri] Hubert and [Marcel] Mauss, ["Esquisse d'une] théorie générale de la magie," [*AS*, vol. VII, 1904], pp. 61ff.

merely the passage of a given state or quality from one object into another but the creation of something altogether new. The very act of depicting the animal gives birth to that animal and creates it—in imitating the noise of the wind or the falling water, one causes the clouds to form and dissolve into rain, and so forth. In both kinds of rites, resemblance undoubtedly has a role but a very different one. In bewitchment, resemblance only guides the force exerted in a particular way; it orients a power that is not its own in a certain direction. In the rites just considered, it acts by itself and is directly efficacious. Besides, contrary to the usual definitions, what really differentiates the two principles of the magic called sympathetic and its corresponding practices is not that contiguity acts in some cases and resemblance in others, but that, in the first, there is merely contagious communication and, in the second, production and creation.[20]

Thus to explain the mimetic rites is to explain the second of these principles, and vice versa.

I will not tarry long over the explanation that the anthropological school has put forward, notably Tylor and Frazer. They call upon the association of ideas, just as they do to account for the contagiousness of the sacred. "Homeopathic magic," says Frazer, who prefers this term to that of "mimetic magic," "rests on the association of ideas by similarity, and contagious magic on the association of ideas by contiguity. Homeopathic magic errs by taking things that resemble one another as identical."[21] But this is to misunderstand the specific character of the practices under discussion. From one point of view, Frazer's formula could be applied somewhat justifiably to the case of bewitchment.[22] In that context, it actually is two distinct things—the image and the model it represents more or less schematically—that are assimilated to one another because of their partial resemblance. But only the image is given in the mimetic rites we have just studied, and as for the model, there is none, since the new generation of the totemic species is still no more than a hope, and an uncertain hope at that. Thus there can be no question of assimilation, mistaken or not; there is creation, in the full sense of the word, and how the association of ideas could ever lead one to believe in this cre-

---

[20] I say nothing about the so-called law of contrariety. As Hubert and Mauss have shown, the contrary produces its contrary only by means of its like (*Théorie générale de la magie*, p. 70).

[21] [Frazer], *Lectures on the Early History of Kingship*, p. 39.

[22] It is applicable in the sense that there really is an amalgamation of the statuette and the person bewitched. But this amalgamation is far from being a mere product of the association of ideas by similarity. As I have shown, the true determining cause of the phenomenon is the contagiousness that is characteristic of religious forces.

ation is not clear. How could the mere fact of representing the movements of an animal produce certainty that the animal will be reborn in abundance?

The general properties of human nature cannot explain such odd practices. Instead of considering the principle on which they rest in its general and abstract form, let us put it back into the moral milieu to which it belongs and in which we have just observed it. Let us reconnect it with the set of ideas and feelings that are the origin of the rites in which it is applied, and we will be in a better position to discern its causes.

The men who gather for these rites believe they really are animals or plants of the species whose name they bear. They are conscious of an animal or plant nature, and in their eyes that nature constitutes what is most essential and most excellent about themselves. When they are assembled, then, their first act must be to affirm to one another this quality that they ascribe to themselves and by which they define themselves. The totem is their rallying sign. For this reason, as we have seen, they draw it on their bodies, and they try to emulate it by their gestures, cries, and carriage. Since they are emus or kangaroos, they will behave like the animals of the same name. By this means, they witness to one another that they are members of the same moral community, and they take cognizance of the kinship that unites them. The rite not only expresses this kinship but also makes or remakes it, for this kinship exists only insofar as it is believed, and the effect of all these collective demonstrations is to keep alive the beliefs on which it rests. So although these jumps, cries, and movements of all kinds are bizarre and grotesque in appearance, in reality they have a meaning that is human and profound. The Australian seeks to resemble his totem just as the adherent of more advanced religions seeks to resemble his God. For both, this is a means of communing with the sacred, that is, with the collective ideal that the sacred symbolizes. It is an early form of the ὁμοίωσις τῷ θεῷ.*

Still, this first cause applies to what is most specific to the totemic beliefs, and if it was the only cause, the principle of like produces like would not have lived beyond totemism. Since there is perhaps no religion in which rites derived from it are not to be found, another cause must have combined with that one.

In fact, the very general purpose of the ceremonies in which we have seen it applied is not only the one I have just mentioned, fundamental though it is, for they also have a more immediate and conscious purpose: to bring about the reproduction of the totemic species. The idea of this neces-

*Imitation of God.

sary reproduction haunts the minds of the faithful; they concentrate the force of their attention and will on this goal. Now a single concern cannot haunt an entire group of men to that extent and not become externalized in tangible form. Since all are thinking of an animal or plant to whose destinies the clan is allied, this thinking in common is inevitably manifested outwardly by movements, and the ones most singled out for this role are those that represent the animal or plant in one of its most characteristic forms. There are no movements that as closely resemble the idea that fills consciousnesses at that moment, since they are its direct and almost automatic translation. The people do their best to imitate the animal; they cry out like it; they jump like it; they mimic the settings in which the plant is daily used. All of these processes of representation are so many ways of outwardly marking the goal to which everyone aspires and of saying, calling on, and imagining the thing they want to bring about.[23] Nor is this the need of any one era or caused by the beliefs of any one religion. It is quintessentially human. This is why, even in religions very different from the one we are studying, once the faithful are gathered together to ask their gods for an outcome that they fervently desire, they are virtually compelled to depict it. To be sure, speech is one means of expressing it, but movement is no less natural. Springing from the body just as spontaneously, it comes even before speech or, in any case, at the same time.

But even if we can thus understand how these movements found their way into the ceremony, we must still explain the power that is ascribed to them. If the Australian repeats them regularly at each new season, it is because he thinks they are required for the success of the rite. Where could he have gotten the idea that imitating an animal makes it reproduce?

Such an obvious error seems barely intelligible so long as we see in the rite only the physical purpose it apparently has. But we know that apart from its presumed effect on the totemic species, it has a profound influence on the souls of the faithful who take part. The faithful come away from it with an impression of well-being whose causes they do not see clearly but that is well founded. They feel that the ceremony is good for them; and in it they do indeed remake their moral being. How would this kind of euphoria not make them feel that the rite has succeeded, that it actually was what it set out to be, that it achieved its intended goal? And since the reproduction of the totemic species is the only goal that is consciously pursued, it seems to be achieved by the methods used, the efficacy of which stands thereby demonstrated. In this way, men came to ascribe creative virtues to movements that

---

[23]On the causes of this outward manifestation, see above, pp. 231ff.

are empty in themselves. The power of the rite over minds,* which is real, made them believe in its power over things, which is imaginary; the efficacy of the whole led men to believe in that of each part, taken separately. The genuinely useful effects brought about by the ceremony as a whole are tantamount to an experimental justification of the elementary practices that comprise it, though in reality all these practices are in no way indispensable to its success. Moreover, the fact that they can be replaced by others of a very different nature, without change in the final result, proves that they do not act by themselves. Indeed, it seems there are Intichiumas made up of offerings only and without mimetic rites; others are purely mimetic and without offerings. Nevertheless, both are thought to be equally efficacious. Thus if value is attached to these various manipulations, it is not because of value intrinsic to them but because they are part of a complex rite whose overall utility is felt.

We can understand that way of thinking all the more easily since we can observe it in our midst. Especially among the most cultivated peoples and milieux, we often come upon believers[†] [*croyants*] who, while having doubts about the specific power ascribed by dogma to each rite taken separately, nonetheless persist in their religious practice. They are not certain that the details of the prescribed observances can be rationally justified, but they feel that it would be impossible to emancipate themselves from those without falling into moral disarray, from which they recoil. Thus the very fact that faith has lost its intellectual roots among them reveals the profound causes that underlie it. This is why the faithful [*fidèles*] are in general left indifferent by the facile criticisms that a simplistic rationalism has sometimes leveled against ritual prescriptions. The true justification of religious practices is not in the apparent ends they pursue but in their invisible influence over consciousnesses and in their manner of affecting our states of mind. Similarly, when preachers undertake to make a convert, they focus less upon directly establishing, with systematic evidence, the truth of some particular proposition or the usefulness of such and such observance, than upon awakening or reawakening the sense of moral support that regular celebration of the cult provides. In this way, they create a predisposition toward believing that goes in advance of proof, influences the intellect to pass over the inadequacy of

---

*L'efficacité morale du rite, qui est réelle, a fait croire à son efficacité physique, qui est imaginaire. . . . Here the term "moral" refers to mind as opposed to matter.

†Durkheim here uses the term *croyants* in contrast with *fidèles*, used twice as often. Professor Douglas Kibbee was kind enough to give me an exact count, plus the exact contexts, using his database searcher. Personal communication, 4 May 1992.

the logical arguments, and leads it to go, as if on its own, beyond the propositions the preachers want to get it to accept. This favorable prejudice, this leap toward believing, is precisely what faith is made of; and it is faith that gives the rites authority in the eyes of the believer—no matter who he is, the Christian or the Australian. The Christian is superior only in his greater awareness of the psychic process from which belief results. He knows that salvation comes "by faith alone."

Because such is the origin of faith, it is in a sense "impervious to experience."[24] If the periodic failures of the Intichiuma do not shake the confidence the Australian has in his rite, it is because he holds with all the strength of his soul to those practices he comes to for the purpose of renewing himself periodically. He could not possibly deny them in principle without causing a real upheaval of his entire being, which resists. But however great that resistance might be, it does not radically distinguish the religious mentality from the other forms of human mentality, even from those other forms that we are most in the habit of opposing to it. In this regard, the mentality of the savant differs only in degree from the foregoing. When a scientific law has the authority of numerous and varied experiments, to reject it too easily upon discovery of one single fact that seems to contradict it is contrary to all method. It is still necessary to ensure that this fact has only one interpretation and cannot be accounted for without abandoning the proposition that seems discredited. The Australian does no differently when he puts down the failure of an Intichiuma to evildoing somewhere, or the abundance of a harvest that comes too soon to some mystic Intichiuma celebrated in the beyond.

He has even less grounds for doubting his rite on the strength of a contrary fact, since its value is, or seems to be, established by a larger number of facts that accord with it. To begin with, the moral efficacy of the ceremony is real and directly felt by all who take part; therein is a constantly repeated experience whose import no contradictory experience can weaken. What is more, physical efficacy itself finds at least apparent confirmation in the results of objective observation. It is in fact normal for the totemic species to reproduce itself regularly. Thus, in the great majority of cases, everything happens as if the ritual movements truly have brought about the hoped-for results. Failures are not the rule. Not surprisingly, since the rites, especially the periodic ones, demand only that nature take its regular course, it seems most often to obey them. In this way, if the believer happens to seem resistant to certain lessons from experience, he does so by relying on other experiences

[24][Lucien] Lévy-Bruhl, *Les Fonctions mentales dans les sociétés inférieures* [Paris, F. Alcan, 1910], pp. 61–68.

that seem to him more conclusive. The researcher does this more methodically but acts no differently.

Thus magic is not, as Frazer held,[25] a primary datum and religion only its derivative. Quite the contrary, the precepts on which the magician's art rests were formed under the influence of religious ideas, and only by a secondary extension were they turned to purely secular applications. Because all the forces of the universe were conceived on the model of sacred forces, the contagiousness inherent in the sacred forces was extended to them all, and it was believed that, under certain conditions, all the properties of bodies could transmit themselves contagiously. Similarly, once the principle that like produces like took form to satisfy definite religious needs, it became detached from its ritual origins and, through a kind of spontaneous generalization, became a law of nature.[26] To comprehend these fundamental axioms of magic, we must resituate them in the religious milieux in which they were born and which alone permits us to account for them. When we see those axioms as the work of isolated individuals, lone magicians, we wonder how human minds imagined them, since nothing in experience could have suggested or verified them. In particular, we cannot understand how such a deceptive craft could have abused men's trust for so long. The problem disappears if the faith men have in magic is only a special case of religious faith in general, if it is itself the product, or at least the indirect product, of a collective effervescence. In other words, using the phrase "sympathetic magic" to denote the collection of practices just discussed is not altogether improper. Although there are sympathetic rites, they are not peculiar to magic. Not only are they found in religion as well, but it is from religion that magic received them. Thus, all we do is court confusion if, by the name we give those rites, we seem to make them out to be something specifically magical.

Hence the results of my analysis strongly resemble those Hubert and Mauss obtained when they studied magic directly.[27] They showed magic to be something altogether different from crude industry, based on crude science. They have brought to light a whole background of religious conceptions that lie behind the apparently secular mechanisms used by the ma-

[25][James George Frazer], *Golden Bough*, 2d. ed. vol. I [London, Macmillan, 1894], pp. 69–75.

[26]I do not mean to say that there was a time when religion existed without magic. Probably, as religion was formed, certain of its principles were extended to nonreligious relations, and in this way, a more or less developed magic came to complement it. Even if these two systems of ideas and practices do not correspond to distinct historical phases, nevertheless there is a definite relationship of derivation between them. This is all I have set out to establish.

[27][Mauss and Hubert, *Théorie générale de la magie*], pp. 108ff. [Actually, pp. 131–187. Trans.]

gician, a whole world of forces the idea of which magic took from religion. We can now see why magic is so full of religious elements: It was born out of religion.

III

The principle just explained does not have a merely ritual function; it is of direct interest to the theory of knowledge. In effect, it is a concrete statement of the law of causality and, in all likelihood, one of the earliest statements of it ever to have existed. A full-fledged notion of the causal relation is implied in the power thus attributed to "like produces like." And because it serves as the basis of cult practices as well as the magician's technique, this conception bestrides primitive thought. Thus, the origins of the precept on which mimetic rites rest can explain how the principle of causality originated. The one should help us understand the other. I have just shown that the first arises from social causes. It has been fashioned by groups with collective ends in view, and collective feelings express it. Thus we may presume that the same is true of the second.

To verify whether this is indeed the origin of the elements from which the principle of causality is made, it is enough to analyze the principle itself.

First and foremost, the idea of causal relation implies efficacy, effective power, or active force. We usually understand "cause" to mean "that which is able to produce a definite change." Cause is force before it has manifested the power that is in it. Effect is the same power, but actualized. Humanity has always imagined causality in dynamic terms. To be sure, some philosophers deny this conception any objective basis; they see it only as an arbitrary construct of imagination that relates to nothing in things. For the moment, however, we do not have to ask ourselves whether it has a basis in reality; noticing that it exists and that it constitutes, and has always constituted, an element of ordinary thought (as is acknowledged even by those who criticize it) is enough. Our immediate purpose is to find out not what causality amounts to logically but what accounts for it.

It has social causes. The analysis of the evidence has already permitted us to show that, in prototype, the idea of force was mana, wakan, the totemic principle—various names given to collective force objectified and projected into things.[28] So the first power that men imagined as such does indeed appear to have been that which society exerts upon its members. Analysis later confirms this result of observation. Indeed, it is possible to establish why this

[28]See above, p. 205ff.

idea of power, of efficacy and of active force, could not have come to us from anywhere else.

It is obvious at first glance, and recognized by all, that external experience cannot possibly give us this idea. The senses show us only phenomena that coexist with or follow one another, but nothing they perceive can give us the idea of that constraining and determinative influence that is characteristic of what we call a power or a force. The senses take in only states that are realized, achieved, and external to one another, while the internal process that binds these states together eludes the senses. Nothing they teach us can possibly suggest to us the idea of something that is an influence or an efficacy. For just this reason, the philosophers of empiricism have seen these different ideas as so many mythological aberrations. But even supposing that there was nothing but hallucinations in all these, it would still behoove us to say how they came to be.

If external experience has no part in the origin of these ideas and if, on the other hand, it is inadmissible that they should have been given us ready-made, we must assume that they come to us from internal experience. In fact, the idea of force is obviously full of spiritual elements that could only have been borrowed from our psychic life.

It has often been thought that the act by which our will comes to a decision, holds our desires in check, and rules our bodies could have served as the model for this construction. In an act of will, it is said, we directly perceive ourselves as a power in action. Seemingly, therefore, once man came upon that idea, extending it to things was all it took for the concept of force to come into being.

As long as the animist theory passed for demonstrated truth, that explanation could seem confirmed by history. If the forces with which human thought at first populated the world really had been spirits—that is, personal and conscious beings more or less like man—we might believe that our individual experience was enough to furnish us with the elements from which the idea of force is made. Instead, we know that the first forces men imagined are anonymous, vague, diffuse forces, the impersonality of which resembles cosmic forces, and which therefore stand in the strongest contrast with the eminently personal power that is the human will. Hence they could not have been conceived in the image of the will.

Moreover, there is a fundamental characteristic of impersonal forces that would be inexplicable on that hypothesis: their communicability. The forces of nature have always been conceived of as being able to pass from one object into another, to mingle and combine with one another, and to change into one another. Indeed, that property is what gives them explanatory value. By virtue of that property, the effects can be joined to their causes without discontinuity. Now, the "I" is exactly opposite in character; it is incommunicable. It cannot change bases or spread from one to another. It spreads in only a metaphorical sense. The manner in which it arrives at and carries out its decisions cannot possibly suggest to us the idea of an energy that is communicated, that can even assimilate into others and, through those combinations and mixtures, give birth to new effects.

Thus, as implied in the causal relation, the idea of force must have a twofold character. First, it can come to us only from our inward experience; the only forces we can touch directly are of necessity moral forces. At the same time, however, they must also be impersonal, since the idea of impersonal power was constituted first. Now, the only forces that satisfy this twofold condition are those that arise from life in common: collective forces. In actuality, they are on the one hand wholly psychic, made exclusively of objectified ideas and feelings, and on the other hand, they are by definition impersonal, since they are the product of cooperation. Being the work of all, they are the property of no one in particular. So little do they belong to the personalities of the subjects in which they reside that they are never fixed there. Just as they enter subjects from outside, so are they always ready to detach themselves from those subjects. They have a spontaneous tendency to spread further and invade new domains. As we know, none are more contagious and hence more communicable.

Granted, physical forces have the same property, but we cannot have direct consciousness of them. Because they are external to us, we cannot even apprehend them as such. When I run against an obstacle, I have a sensation of confinement and discomfort; however, the force causing that sensation is not in me but in the obstacle and thus beyond the range of my perception. We perceive its effects but not the force itself. This is not the case with social forces. Since they are part of our interior life, we not only know the results of their action but see them in action. The force that isolates the sacred being and holds the profane ones at a distance is, in reality, not in that being; it lives in the consciousness of the faithful. Thus the faithful feel it at the very moment that it acts on their wills to prohibit certain actions and prescribe others. Because this happens entirely within us, we capture in action the constraining and necessitating influence that escapes us when it comes from an external thing. Of course, we do not always interpret that influence adequately, but we cannot fail to be conscious of it.

Furthermore, the idea of force bears the mark of its origin overtly. It in fact entails an idea of power that does not go without those of ascendancy, mastery, domination—and, correspondingly, of dependence and subordination. The relations that all these ideas express are eminently social. It is society that has classified beings as superior and subordinate, as masters who command and subjects who obey; it is society that has conferred on the first that singular property that makes command efficacious and that constitutes *power*. So everything tends to show that the first powers the human mind conceived are those that societies instituted as they became organized. It is in their image that the powers of the physical world were conceived. Thus man could not have arrived at the idea of himself as a force in charge of the body in which it resides without introducing concepts borrowed from social life into the idea he had of himself. In fact, he had to differentiate himself from his physical double and impute a higher sort of dignity to himself than to this double—in a word, he had to think of himself as a soul. In fact, it is in the form of the soul that he has always imagined the force that he believes he is. But we know that the soul is something altogether different from a name given to the abstract faculty to move, think, or feel. Above all, it is a religious principle, a particular aspect of the collective force. In sum, man feels he is a soul, and thus a force, because he is a social being. Although an animal moves its legs just as we do and has the same control over his muscles as we, nothing warrants our supposing that he has consciousness of himself as of an active and efficient cause. This is because it has no soul—or, more precisely, it does not impute a soul to itself. But if it does not impute a soul to itself, this is because it does not participate in a social life comparable to that of men. Among animals, nothing resembling a civilization exists.[29]

The idea of force is not all there is to the principle of causality. This principle consists in a judgment stating that a force develops in a definite manner and that its state at each moment of its evolution predetermines the succeeding state. The first is called cause; the second, effect; and the causal judgment affirms the existence of a necessary conjunction between these two moments of any force. Ruled by a sort of constraint from which it cannot free itself, the mind sets up this relation in advance of any proof. It postulates this relationship, as people say, *a priori*.

Empiricism has never succeeded in giving an account of that apriorism and that necessity. Never have the philosophers of that school been able to explain how an association of ideas reinforced by habit could produce anything other than a state of expectancy, a more or less strong predisposition on the part of ideas to call themselves to mind in a definite order. Now, the

---

[29]Of course, there are animal societies. Even so, the meaning of the word is by no means the same when applied to men and animals. The institution is the characteristic phenomenon of human societies; there are no institutions in animal societies.

principle of causality has an entirely different character. It is not simply an inherent tendency for our thought to unfold in a certain way; it is a norm external and superior to the flow of our representations, which it rules and regulates absolutely. It is endowed with an authority that binds the intellect and goes beyond the intellect; in other words, the intellect is not its creator. In this regard, it does no good to substitute hereditary for individual habit. The nature of habit does not change because it lasts longer than a man's life; it is only stronger. An instinct is not a rule.

The rites just studied enable us to discern a source of that authority that until now has been little suspected. Let us recall how the causal law that the mimetic rites put into practice was born. The group comes together, dominated by one concern: If the species whose name it bears does not reproduce, the clan is doomed. In this way, the common feeling that animates all its members is expressed outwardly in the form of definite movements that always recur in the same way in the same circumstances. And for the reasons set forth, it turns out that the desired result seems to be obtained when the ceremony has been conducted. An association is thereby formed between the idea of this result and that of the actions preceding it. This association does not vary from one subject to the other. Because it is the product of a collective experience, it is the same for all who take part in the rite. Nonetheless, if no other factor intervened, only a collective state of waiting would result. Having completed the imitative movements, everyone would wait, more or less confidently, to see the imminent approach of the hoped-for event. Even so, an imperative rule of thought would not come into being.

Because a social interest of premier importance is at stake, society cannot let things take their course, at the mercy of circumstances; hence it intervenes to regulate their course to suit its needs. Society requires this ceremony, which it cannot do without, to be repeated whenever necessary and, hence, the actions that are the condition of success to be regularly done. It imposes them as an obligation. Those actions imply a definite attitude of mind that, in response, shares the same quality of obligation. To prescribe that the animal or plant must be imitated to make them come to life again is to make "like produces like" into an axiom that must not be doubted. Opinion cannot permit individuals to deny this principle in theory, without at the same time permitting them to violate it in their conduct. It therefore imposes the principle, as it does the practices that derive from it, and in this way the ritual precept is reinforced by a logical principle that is none other than the intellectual aspect of the ritual one. The authority of both derives from the same source: society. The respect evoked by society passes into those ways of thinking and acting to which it attaches value. One cannot stand aside from either without meeting resistance from prevailing opinion. This is why the ways of thinking require the adherence of the intellect in advance of all examination, just as the ways of acting directly bring about the submission of the will.

Using this example, we can test once again how a sociological theory of the idea of causality, and the categories more generally, both diverges from the classical doctrines on this question and accords with them. Here, as in apriorism, causality retains the *a priori* and necessary character of the causal relation. The sociological theory does not simply affirm it but also accounts for it and yet does not, as in empiricism, make it disappear while ostensibly accounting for it. Besides, there can be no question of denying the part that belongs to individual experience. That the individual by himself notes regular sequences of phenomena, and in so doing acquires a certain *sensation* of regularity, is not to be doubted. But this sensation is not the *category* of causality. The first is individual, subjective, and incommunicable; we make it ourselves from our personal observations. The second is the work of the collectivity, which gives it to us ready-made. It is a framework in which our empirical observations arrange themselves and which enables us to think about them—that is, to see them from an angle that enables us to understand one another on the subject of those observations. To be sure, if the framework can be applied to the content, that is because it is not without relationship to that content, but the framework does not merge with what it contains. It transcends and dominates the content because it has a different origin. It is not simply a collection of individual memories; it is made, first and foremost, to satisfy the needs of life in common.

In sum, the mistake of empiricism has been to see the causal tie as only a learned construct of speculative thinking and the product of a more or less systematic generalization. Pure speculation can give birth only to views that are provisional, hypothetical, and more or less plausible, but views that must always be regarded as suspect. We do not know whether some new observation will invalidate them in the near future. Therefore an axiom that the mind does and must accept, without testing and without qualification, cannot come to us from that source. The demands of action, especially of collective action, can and must express themselves in categorical formulas that are peremptory and sharp and that brook no contradiction, for collective movements are possible only if they are concerted, and thus regulated and well defined. They preclude blind groping, which is the source of anarchy. They tend by themselves toward an organization that, once established, imposes itself upon individuals. And since action cannot do without the intellect, the intellect is eventually pulled along in the same way, adopting without argument the theoretical postulates that practice requires. The imperatives of thought and those of the will are probably two sides of the same coin.

It is far from my intention, however, to offer these observations as a complete theory of the concept of causality. That issue is too complex to be resolved in this way. The principle of cause has been understood differently in different times and places; in a single society it varies with social milieux, and with the realms of nature to which it is applied.[30] Therefore, one cannot possibly determine what causes and conditions lie behind it after considering only one of the forms it has taken historically. The views that have just been set forth must be regarded only as indicative; they will have to be tested and fleshed out. Nonetheless, since the causal law just considered is surely one of the most primitive in existence and since it has played an important role in the development of human thought and industry, it constitutes a choice experiment, and so it can be presumed that the observations it has allowed us to make are in some measure generalizable.

---

[30]The idea of cause is not the same for a scientist as for a man who is scientifically uneducated. Besides, many of our contemporaries understand the principle of causality differently depending on the phenomena to which it is applied—social or physicochemical. In the social realm, there is an idea of causality that is extraordinarily reminiscent of the one on which magic was based for so long. We might well ask ourselves whether a physicist and a biologist imagine the causal relation in the same fashion.

CHAPTER FOUR

THE POSITIVE CULT (CONTINUED)

Representative or Commemorative Rites

In the two preceding chapters, the explanation of the positive rites that I offered ascribes to them moral and social meaning, first and foremost. The physical efficacy ascribed to them by the faithful is an interpretation that hides their fundamental reason for being: They are deemed to have an effect on things because they serve to remake individuals and groups morally. This hypothesis enabled me to account for the facts, but it cannot be said to have been proved directly. Indeed, it seems at first glance to jibe rather poorly with the nature of the ritual mechanisms I have analyzed. Whether these mechanisms be offerings or mimetic practices, the actions that constitute them have purely physical ends in view. Their sole purpose is or seems to be to induce the rebirth of the totemic species. In that case, is it not surprising that their real function should be to serve moral ends?

It is true that their physical function may very well have been exaggerated by Spencer and Gillen, even in the cases where it is most clearly incontestable. In the view of those authors, each clan celebrates its Intichiuma in order to provide a useful foodstuff to the other clans. The whole cult supposedly involves a kind of economic cooperation among different totemic groups, each supposedly working for all the rest. But, according to Strehlow, this notion of Australian totemism is utterly foreign to the native mentality. He says: "If, while doing their utmost to multiply the animals or plants of the consecrated species, the members of a totemic group seem to be working for their fellow men of other totems, we must refrain from seeing this collaboration as the fundamental principle of Arunta or Loritja totemism. Never have the black men themselves told me that the point of their ceremonies was any such thing. Of course, when I suggested this idea to them and explained it, they understood and went along. But no one will blame me if I have a certain mistrust for responses obtained under these conditions." Strehlow observes, furthermore, that this way of interpreting the rite is contradicted by the fact that the totemic animals or plants are not all edible or useful; some have no use, and indeed some are dangerous. Thus the ceremonies that concern them cannot have nutritional ends in view.[1]

Our author concludes: "When the natives are asked the decisive reason for these ceremonies, they reply unanimously: It is because the ancestors have so instituted things. That is why we act in this way and not some other."[2] But to say that the rite is observed because it comes from the ancestors is to acknowledge that its authority is one and the same as the authority of tradition, which is eminently a social thing. It is celebrated to keep faith with the past and preserve the group's moral* identity, not because of the physical effects it can bring about. Thus, its profound causes can be glimpsed through the very manner in which the faithful explain it.

There are cases in which this aspect of the ceremonies is immediately obvious.

I

This aspect of the ceremonies is best observed among the Warramunga.[3] Among this people, each clan is held to be descended from a single ancestor who, although born in a definite place, spent his life on earth traveling the country in all directions. He it is who gave the land its present form during those travels, they say, and he who made the mountains and the plains, the water holes and the streams, and so forth. At the same time, along his route he sowed the seeds of life that came forth from his body and, through successive reincarnations, became the present-day members of the clan. The

*Note the term "moral," here used in the sense that encompasses *conscience collective* in its cognitive and normative meanings.

[1]Of course, these ceremonies are not followed by alimentary communion. According to Strehlow, they have a distinct generic name, at least when they involve inedible plants: They are called *knujilelama*, not *mbatjalkatiuma*. ([Carl Strehlow, *Die Aranda- und Loritja-Stämme in Zentral-Australien*] vol. III [Frankfurt, J. Baer, 1907], p. 96).

[2]Ibid., p. 8.

[3]The Warramunga are not the only people among whom the Intichiuma takes the form I will describe. It is also found among the Tjingilli, the Umbaia, the Wulmala, the Walpari, and even the Kaitish, although the Kaitish ritual is in some ways reminiscent of the Arunta one ([Sir Baldwin] Spencer and [Francis James] Gillen, *Northern Tribes [of Central Australia*, London, Macmillan, 1904], pp. 291, 309, 311, 317). I adopt the Warramunga as the type case because they have been very well studied by Spencer and Gillen.

purpose of the Warramunga ceremony, which corresponds exactly to the Intichiuma of the Arunta, is to depict and commemorate the mythical history of the ancestor. It involves neither sacrifice nor, with only a single exception,[4] mimetic practices. The rite involves remembering the past and making it present, so to speak, by means of a true dramatic performance [représentation]. This term is all the more appropriate in the present case, since the celebrant is by no means viewed as an incarnation of the ancestor he represents. He is an actor playing a role.

Here, as an example, is what the Intichiuma of the Black Snake consists of, as observed by Spencer and Gillen.[5]

The initial ceremony does not seem to refer to the past; at least, the description given us does not justify such an interpretation. It consists of running and jumping by two celebrants[6] adorned with figures that represent the black snake. When both at last fall exhausted to the ground, those in attendance run their hands gently over the emblematic designs that cover the backs of the two actors. This gesture is said to please the black snake. Only after that does the series of commemorative rites begin.

They act out the mythical history of the ancestor, Thalaualla, from the moment he came out of the ground to the moment he finally disappeared into it again. They follow him through all his travels. According to the myth, he conducted totemic ceremonies in each of the localities where he sojourned. These are repeated in the same order in which they are said to have taken place at the beginning. The movement that recurs most frequently is a sort of rhythmic and violent trembling of the entire body because, in mythical times, the ancestor shook himself in this way to bring out the seeds of life within him. The actors have their skin covered with down that comes off and flies away as a result of this shaking. This is a means of depicting the flight of the mystical seeds and their dispersion in the air.

We recall that among the Arunta, the place where the ceremony occurs is ritually determined. It is the site of the sacred rocks, trees, and water holes, and the faithful must go there to celebrate the cult. Among the Warramunga, though, the choice of site is arbitrary and a matter of convenience. Theirs is a conventional stage. The actual place where the events that are the theme of the rite occurred is represented by drawings. Sometimes these drawings are

[4]This is true for the Intichiuma of the white cockatoo; see p. 357 above.

[5]Spencer and Gillen, Northern Tribes, pp. 300ff.

[6]One of the two actors does not belong to the Black Snake clan but to the Crow. This is because the Crow is considered an associate of the Black Snake—in other words, its subtotem.

made on the bodies of the actors themselves. For example, a small circle colored in with red and painted on the back and stomach represents a water hole.[7] In other examples, the image is traced in the dirt. On ground previously dampened and covered with red ochre, they make curved lines from a series of white points, symbolizing a stream or a mountain. This is a rudimentary theatrical set.

In addition to the strictly religious ceremonies that the ancestor is said to have conducted in the past, simple epic or comic episodes of Thalaualla's earthly career are presented. Thus, at a certain moment, while three actors are busy on stage with an important rite, another hides behind a clump of trees some distance away. Hung around his neck is a packet of down representing a wallaby. As soon as the main ceremony has ended, an old man traces on the ground a line that leads to the place where a fourth actor is hiding. The others walk behind, with their eyes lowered and fixed upon this line as if they are following a path. When they discover the man, they act surprised, and one of them beats him with a stick. This entire mimicry portrays an incident in the life of the great black snake. One day, his son went off to hunt alone, bagged a wallaby, and ate it without giving any to his father. The father followed his tracks, surprised him, and forced him to vomit. This incident is alluded to in the beating that ends the performance.[8]

I will not state here all the mythical events that are presented one after the other. The foregoing examples are enough to show the character of these ceremonies. They are plays, but plays of a very particular kind. They act, or at least are thought to act, upon the course of nature. When the commemoration of Thalaualla is over, the Warramunga are convinced that black snakes cannot fail to increase and multiply. Thus these dramas are rites, and in fact rites that, by the way they work, are comparable in every respect to those that make up the Arunta Intichiuma.

Consequently, the two sets of rites can shed light upon one another. Indeed, comparing them is all the more legitimate because there is no radical discontinuity between them. Not only is the same goal pursued in both cases, but what is most characteristic of the Warramunga ritual is to be found in embryonic form in the other. As the Arunta generally practice it, the Intichiuma contains what amounts to a kind of implicit commemoration. The places where it is celebrated are, obligatorily, those that the ancestors made illustrious. The paths the faithful take in their pious pilgrimages are those

---

[7]Spencer and Gillen, *Northern Tribes*, p. 302.

[8]Ibid., p. 305.

traveled by the Alcheringa heroes; the places where they stop to conduct rites are those where the ancestors themselves sojourned, where they vanished into the ground, and so forth. Thus everything calls their memory back into the minds of those in attendance. Moreover, they quite often supplement the physical rites* with hymns recounting the ancestors' exploits.[9] Let those stories be acted out rather than told, and let them develop in this new form so as to become the essence of the ceremony, and we will have the Warramunga ceremony. More than that: From one standpoint, the Arunta Intichiuma is already a sort of play. The celebrant, in fact, is one and the same as the ancestor from whom he descends and whom he reincarnates.[10] The movements he makes are those the ancestor made in the same circumstances. To speak precisely, of course, he is not playing the ancestral personage as an actor might do; he is that very personage. In a sense, it is still the hero who is on the stage. To accentuate the representative character of that rite, all it takes is to accentuate the duality of the ancestor and the celebrant. This is precisely what happens among the Warramunga.[11] Indeed, there is mention of at least one Intichiuma among the Arunta, in which certain people are responsible for portraying ancestors with whom they have no mythical relation of descent and thus in which there are dramatic performances in the full sense. This is the Intichiuma of the Emu.[12] In this case, too, contrary to what usually happens among this people, it does seem that the theater of the ceremony is artificially set up.[13]

* *Rites manuels.* These stand in contrast to *rites oraux,* "oral rites."

[9] See Spencer and Gillen, *Native Tribes [of Central Australia,* London, Macmillan, 1889], p. 188; Strehlow, *Aranda,* vol. III, p. 5.

[10] Strehlow himself recognizes this: "The totemic ancestor and his descendant, that is to say the one who depicts him *(der Darsteller),* are presented in these sacred songs as one and the same" ([*Aranda*], vol. III, p. 6). Since this incontestable fact contradicts the thesis that ancestral souls are not reincarnated, Strehlow adds in a note, "During the ceremony, there is, properly speaking, no incarnation of the ancestor in the person who depicts him." If Strehlow means that incarnation does not occur during the ceremony, nothing is more certain. But if he means that there is no incarnation at all, I do not understand how the celebrant and the ancestor can merge.

[11] Perhaps this difference arises in part from the fact that, among the Warramunga, each clan is thought to descend from a single ancestor around whom the mythical history of the clan has gradually condensed. This is the ancestor commemorated in the rite; however, the celebrant is not necessarily descended from him. Indeed, we might ask whether these mythical chiefs, demigods of a sort, undergo reincarnation.

[12] In that Intichiuma, three participants depict ancestors "of considerable antiquity"; they actually play a role (Spencer and Gillen, *Native Tribes,* pp. 181–182). Spencer and Gillen add, it is true, that those are ancestors who came after the Alcheringa period. But they are nonetheless mythical personages, and they are portrayed during a rite.

[13] Indeed, we are not told of sacred rocks and water holes. The center of the ceremony is an image of an emu that is drawn on the ground and can be drawn anywhere.

That these two kinds of ceremonies have a certain air of kinship, despite the differences between them, does not mean that there is a definite relationship of succession between them, and that one is a transformation of the other. The resemblances observed may actually arise from their having the same origin—that is, from their being divergent forms of the same original ceremony. We will see, in fact, that this hypothesis is the most probable. But there is no need to take a position on that question, and the preceding is enough to establish that these are rites of the same kind. Thus we have a basis for comparing them and for using the one to help us understand the other better.

What is peculiar to those Warramunga ceremonies that I have just discussed is that not one movement is made for the purpose of helping or directly causing the totemic species to be reborn.[14] If we analyze the movements made together with the words said, we find nothing that reveals any intention of this kind. Everything takes place in dramatic performances* that have no purpose other than to make the clan's mythical past present in people's minds. But the mythology of a group is the collection of beliefs common to the group. How the society imagines man and the world is expressed in the traditions whose memory the mythology perpetuates; it is a morality and a cosmology at the same time as it is a history. Therefore the rite serves and can only serve to maintain the vitality of those beliefs and to prevent their memory from being obliterated—in other words, to revitalize the most essential elements of the collective consciousness and conscience. Through this rite, the group periodically revitalizes the sense it has of itself and its unity; the nature of the individuals as social beings is strengthened at the same time. The glorious memories that are made to live again before their eyes, and with which they feel in accord, bring about a feeling of strength and confidence. One is more sure in one's faith when one sees how far into the past it goes and what great things it has inspired. This is the feature of the ceremony that makes it instructive. The tendency of the whole ceremony is to act on minds, and on minds alone. But if it is believed to act on things at the same time, and to bring about the prosperity of the species, this can only be as a counterpart of the moral influence it exercises—and that moral influence obviously is the only one that is real. Therefore, the hypothesis I have proposed is verified by a revelatory experiment and is the more compelling

---

* *Tout se passe en représentations qui ne peuvent être destinées qu'à rendre présent aux esprits le passé mythique du clan.* The word *représentation* neatly joins two meanings: "dramatic performance" and "idea."

[14]I do not mean to say, however, that all the ceremonies of the Warramunga are of this type. The example of the white cockatoo, discussed above, proves that there are exceptions.

because, as I have just established, the ritual systems of the Warramunga and the Arunta do not differ fundamentally. The one simply brings out with greater clarity what we had already guessed about the other.

II

There are ceremonies in which this representative and ideal feature is even more pronounced. In the ceremonies just discussed, dramatic representation was not an end in itself; it was only a means to a completely mundane end, the reproduction of the totemic species. But there are others that are not particularly different from the preceding and yet from which interests of that sort are entirely absent. In those, the past is represented for the sole purpose of representing it and impressing it more deeply upon minds, with no expectation that the rite should have any particular influence upon nature. At the very least, the physical effects that are sometimes imputed to the rite are entirely secondary and unrelated to the liturgical importance it is given. This is notably the case of the feasts the Warramunga celebrate in honor of the snake Wollunqua.[15]

As I have already said, Wollunqua is a totem of a very special kind. It is not an animal or plant species but a unique being; only one Wollunqua exists. Furthermore, he is a purely mythical being. The natives imagine him as a sort of colossal snake, so tall that his head is lost in the clouds when he stands on his tail. He is believed to live in a water hole, called Thapauerlu, which is hidden deep in a lonely valley. But although Wollunqua differs in some respects from ordinary totems, still he has all the distinguishing features of one. He serves as a collective name and emblem for a whole group of individuals who see him as their common ancestor. And the relations they have with this mythical beast are identical to those that the members of other clans believe they have with the founders of their own respective clans. In Alcheringa times,[16] Wollunqua traveled the country in every direction. In the various localities where he stopped, he sowed spirit-children, spirit principles that continue to serve today as souls for living beings. Wollunqua is

[15]Spencer and Gillen, *Northern Tribes*, pp. 226ff. Cf. on the same subject certain passages of Eylmann that apparently refer to the same mythical being ([Richard] Eylmann, *Die Eingeborenen [der Kolonie Sud Australien*, Berlin, D. Reumer, 1908], p. 185). Strehlow also mentions a mythical snake among the Arunta (Kulaia, water snake), which may well be the same as Wollunqua (Strehlow, *Aranda*, vol. I, p. 78; cf. vol. II, p. 71, where Kulaia figures on the list of totems).

[16]So as not to complicate the terminology, I use the Arunta term. Among the Warramunga, this mythical time is called Wingara.

even regarded as a kind of preeminent totem. The Warramunga are divided into two phratries, one called Uluuru and the other Kingilli. Almost all the totems of the first are various species of snake. They are all considered to be descendants of Wollunqua; he is said to be their grandfather.[17] From this one can guess how, in all likelihood, the Wollunqua myth was born. To explain the presence of so many similar totems in one phratry, they were all imagined to be derived from one and the same totem; but of necessity, he had to be given gigantic form, so that, by his very appearance, he would fit the important role assigned to him in the history of the tribe.

Wollunqua is the object of ceremonies no different in nature from those we studied previously. These are performances in which the principal events of his mythical life are depicted; he is shown coming out of the ground and moving from one locality to the other; the various episodes of his life and his travels are acted out; and so forth. Spencer and Gillen were present at fifteen ceremonies of this kind, which occurred one after the other between 27 July and 23 August, following a prescribed order in such a way as to form a true cycle.[18] Thus, the details of the rites that make up this feast do not distinguish it from an ordinary Intichiuma among the Warramunga; that much is recognized by the authors who have described it for us.[19] But on the other hand, it is an Intichiuma that cannot possibly have the aim of ensuring the fecundity of an animal or plant species; Wollunqua is a species in himself and does not reproduce. He is; and the natives apparently do not feel that he requires a cult in order to go on being. Not only do these ceremonies not have the efficacy of the classic Intichiuma, but they do not seem to have material efficacy of any kind. Wollunqua is not a deity set over a definite range of natural phenomena, and thus no definite service is expected of him in exchange for worship.

True, it is said that if the ritual prescriptions are improperly observed, Wollunqua becomes angry, leaves his retreat, and avenges himself upon the faithful for their negligence. And when everything has been properly done, they tend to believe that all will be well and that some happy event will occur. But the idea of these possible sanctions was apparently born only after

[17]"It is not easy," say Spencer and Gillen, "to express in words that which is a rather vague feeling among the natives. But after having carefully observed the different ceremonies, we gained the quite distinct impression that, in the minds of the natives, Wollunqua corresponded to the idea of a dominant totem." (Spencer and Gillen, *Northern Tribes*, p. 248.)

[18]Among the most solemn of these ceremonies is the one I had occasion to describe above (pp. 219–220), during which an image of Wollunqua is drawn on a sort of mound that is later broken into pieces amid a general effervescence.

[19]Spencer and Gillen, *Northern Tribes*, pp. 227, 248.

the fact, so as to account for the rite. It seemed natural that, once born, the ceremony should have some purpose, and hence that to omit prescribed observances was somehow dangerous. But the rite was not instituted to prevent these mythical dangers or to bring about particular advantages. Incidentally, these dangers are conceived in the vaguest of terms. For example, when everything is done with, the elders announce that Wollunqua will send rain if he is satisfied. But they do not celebrate the feast for the purpose of having rain.[20] They celebrate it because the ancestors did, because they are attached to it as a very respected tradition, and because they come out of it with a sense of moral well-being. Other considerations play only a supplementary role; they can serve to strengthen the faithful in the conduct that the rite imposes, but they are not the *raison d'être* of that conduct.

Here, then, is a whole collection of ceremonies whose sole purpose is to arouse certain ideas and feelings, to join the present to the past and the individual to the collectivity. In fact, not only are these ceremonies incapable of serving other ends, but the faithful themselves seek nothing more from them. This is additional evidence that the psychic state in which the assembled group finds itself does indeed constitute the only solid and stable basis of what might be called the ritual mentality. So far as beliefs ascribing this or

[20]Here is how the terms used by Spencer and Gillen describe the proceedings in their only passage about a possible relationship between the Wollunqua and the phenomenon of rain. Some days after the rite that is celebrated at the mound, "the elders declare that they have heard Wollunqua speak, that he was satisfied with what happened, and that he would send rain. The reason for this prophecy is that they had heard, as we had, the thunder resounding some distance away." Rainmaking is so far from being the immediate aim of the ceremony that it was not imputed to Wollunqua until several days after the rite had been celebrated, and following accidental circumstances. Another fact shows how vague the ideas of the natives are on this point. Several lines further on, the thunder is presented as a sign, not of Wollunqua's satisfaction but of his annoyance. Despite the prognostications, continue our authors, "the rain did not fall. But some days later, thunder was again heard rumbling far away. The elders said that Wollunqua was rumbling because he was angry" about the way in which the rite had been conducted. Thus, the same phenomenon, the sound of thunder, is interpreted sometimes as a sign of favorable intentions and at others, of evil ones.

There is, however, a detail of the ritual that would have direct efficacy, if one accepted the explanation of it that Spencer and Gillen suggest. According to them, the mound is destroyed in order to frighten Wollunqua and, by magical means, prevent him from leaving his retreat. To me, this interpretation appears very suspect. As a matter of fact, in the circumstances just described in which it was announced that Wollunqua was angry, this anger was attributed to the fact that they had neglected to clean up the debris from the mound. Hence, this cleanup is far from being aimed at intimidating and coercing Wollunqua; Wollunqua himself demands it. This is probably no more than a special case of a more general rule in effect among the Warramunga: The cult instruments must be destroyed after each ceremony. Thus, when the rite has been completed, the ritual ornaments in which the celebrants are dressed are torn off forcefully. (Spencer and Gillen, *Northern Tribes*, p. 205.)

that physical efficacy to the rites are concerned, those are accessory and contingent matters, since they can be absent without change to the essence of the rite. Thus, even more markedly than the preceding, the Wollunqua ceremonies in a sense lay bare the positive cult.

If I have given special emphasis to those ceremonies, it is because of their unusual importance, but others are of the same character. Thus, the Warramunga have a "Laughing Boy" totem. Spencer and Gillen say that the clan of this name has the same organization as the other totemic groups. Like them, it has its sacred places (*mungai*) where the founding ancestor conducted ceremonies in mythical times and where he left behind spirit-children who became the men of the clan. The rites connected with this totem are indistinguishable from those related to animal or plant totems.[21] It is obvious, however, that the rites cannot possibly have physical efficacy. They are a series of four more or less repetitive ceremonies, their sole purpose being to amuse, to provoke laughter by laughter—that is, to cultivate gaiety and good humor within the group that more or less specializes in those traits.[22]

We find among the Arunta themselves more than one totem that has no other Intichiuma. In fact, among this people, the folds or depressions in the land that mark the place where some ancestor sojourned are sometimes used as totems.[23] To such totems are attached ceremonies that obviously cannot have physical effects of any kind. They can only be made up of performances whose purpose is to commemorate the past, and they can have no goal other than that commemoration.[24]

While these ritual performances help us understand the nature of the cult better, they also bring out an important element of religion: its recreational and aesthetic element.

I have already shown that they are closely akin to dramatic performances.[25] This kinship stands out even more clearly in the ceremonies just described. Not only do they use the same techniques as drama, but they have

---

[21]Ibid., pp. 207–208.

[22]Ibid., p. 210.

[23]See numbers 432–442, in the list of totems compiled by Strehlow ([*Aranda*], vol. II, p. 72).

[24]See ibid., vol. III, p. 8. Also among the Arunta, there is a *Worra* totem that greatly resembles the Warramungas' "Laughing Boy" totem (ibid. and vol. III, p. 124). *Worra* means "young men." The object of the ceremony is to make the young men take more pleasure in the game of *labara* (on this game, see ibid., vol. I, p. 55, n. 1).

[25]See above, p. 376.

the same sort of goal. Since utilitarian purposes are in general alien to them, they make men forget the real world so as to transport them into another where their imagination is more at home; they entertain. Sometimes they even go as far as having the outward appearance of recreation. We see those present laughing and openly having fun.[26]

The representative rites and the collective recreations are so close to one another that people move from one genre to the other without any sense of discontinuity. The trait of the specifically religious ceremonies is that they must be performed on consecrated ground, from which women and the uninitiated are excluded.[27] In others, this religious feature is somewhat obscured, although not gone completely. They occur away from the ceremonial ground, which shows that to some extent they are already secular; even so, the profane (women and children) are not admitted. Hence they straddle the boundary between two domains. In general, they relate to mythical personages that do not fit neatly into the scheme of totemic religion. The personages are spirits, most often evil ones, that are more connected with the magicians than with the ordinary faithful, and sorts of bogeymen in which men do not believe with the same degree of seriousness and firm conviction as they accord to properly totemic beings and things.[28] In step with the weakening of the tie that binds events and personages to the history of the tribe, both take on a more unreal appearance, and the nature of the corresponding ceremonies changes. In this way, we gradually enter into the domain of pure fantasy and pass from the commemorative rite to the ordinary corroboree, mere public rejoicing that is no longer religious in any way and in which everyone, without distinction, may take part. Indeed, perhaps certain of these performances that today are only for entertainment are ancient rites whose function has changed. In fact, the boundaries between these two kinds of ceremonies are so fluid that it is hard to say precisely to which group they belong.[29]

---

[26]An example of this kind is to be found in Spencer and Gillen, *Northern Tribes*, p. 204.

[27]Spencer and Gillen, *Native Tribes*, pp. 118 n. 2, 618ff.; Spencer and Gillen, *Northern Tribes*, pp. 716ff. However, there are sacred ceremonies from which women are not totally excluded (see, for example, ibid., pp. 375ff.); but that is the exception.

[28]See Spencer and Gillen, *Native Tribes*, pp. 329ff.; Spencer and Gillen, *Northern Tribes*, pp. 210ff.

[29]This is the case, for example, of the Molonga corroboree, among the Pitta-Pitta of Queensland and neighboring tribes (see [Walter Edmund] Roth, *Ethnological Studies among the North West Central Queensland Aborigines* [Brisbane, E. Gregory, 1897], pp. 120ff.). Information on these ordinary corroborees is to be found in Stirling [Sir Baldwin] Spencer, *Report [on the Work] of the Horn [Scientific] Expedition to Central Australia* [London, Dulau, 1896], Part IV, p. 72, and in Roth, *Queensland Aborigines*, pp. 117ff.

It is well known that games and the principal forms of art seem to have been born in religion and that they long maintained their religious character.[30] We can see why: while pursuing other goals directly, the cult has at the same time been a form of recreation. Religion has not played this role by chance or a happy coincidence but as a result of its inherent logic. Indeed, as I have shown, although religious thought is something other than a system of fictions, the realities to which it corresponds can gain religious expression only if imagination transfigures them. Great is the distance between society, as it is objectively, and the sacred things that represent it symbolically. The impressions really felt by men—the raw material for this construction—had to be interpreted, elaborated, and transformed to the point of becoming unrecognizable. So the world of religious things is partly an imaginary world (albeit only in its outward form) and, for this reason, one that lends itself more readily to the free creations of the mind. Moreover, because the intellectual forces that serve in making it are intense and tumultuous, the mere task of expressing the real with the help of proper symbols is insufficient to occupy them. A surplus remains generally available that seeks to busy itself with supplementary and superfluous works of luxury—that is, with works of art.

What is true of practices is true of beliefs. The state of effervescence in which the assembled faithful find themselves is translated outwardly by exuberant motions that are not easily subordinated to ends that are defined too strictly. They escape, partly without destination, displaying themselves merely for the sake of displaying themselves, and taking pleasure in what amount to games. Besides, to the extent that the beings to which the cult is addressed are imaginary, they are in no position to contain and regulate this exuberance; the weight of tangible and durable realities is needed to press activity into exact and harmonious adaptations. Therefore, we risk misunderstandings when, to explain rites, we believe an exact purpose and *raison d'être* must be assigned to each movement. Some serve no purpose; they merely satisfy the worshippers' need to act, move, and gesticulate. The worshippers are seen jumping, whirling, dancing, shouting, and singing, and they are not always able to assign a meaning to this turbulence.

Thus, religion would not be religion if there was no place in it for free combinations of thought and action, for games, for art, for all that refreshes a spirit worn down by all that is overburdening in day-to-day labor. That

---

[30]On that question, see especially the excellent work of [Stewart] Culin, "Games of the North American Indians," *Twenty-Sixth Report, BAE,* [Washington, Government Printing Office, 1907].

which made art exist makes it a necessity. It is not merely an outward adornment that the cult can be thought of as dressing up in, in order to hide what may be too austere and harsh about it; the cult in itself is aesthetic in some way. Because of the well-known connections mythology has with poetry, scholars have sometimes wanted to situate mythology outside religion.[31] The truth is that there is a poetry inherent in all religion. The representative ceremonies just studied make this aspect of religious life obvious, but there are virtually no rites that do not manifest it in some degree.

Obviously, it would be a grave error to see only this aspect of religion or to overstate its importance. When a rite serves only as entertainment, it is no longer a rite. The moral forces that religious symbols express are real forces that we must reckon with and that we may not do with as we please. Even if the purpose of the cult is not to achieve physical effects, but deliberately stops at acting upon minds, it exerts its influence in a different direction than does a pure work of art. The representations it works to arouse and maintain are not empty images that correspond to nothing in reality and that we call up for no purpose, merely for the pleasure of watching them appear and combine with one another before our eyes. They are as necessary to the good order of our moral life as food is to the nurture of our physical life. It is through them that the group affirms and maintains itself, and we know how indispensable the group is to the individual. Thus a rite is something other than a game; it belongs to the serious side of life.

But while the unreal and imaginary element is not the essence, it still plays a role that is far from negligible. That element enters into the feeling of comfort that the faithful draw from the accomplished rite. Recreation is one form of the moral remaking that is the primary object of the positive cult. Once we have fulfilled our ritual duties, we return to profane life with more energy and enthusiasm, not only because we have placed ourselves in contact with a higher source of energy but also because our own capacities have been replenished through living, for a few moments, a life that is less tense, more at ease, and freer. Religion gains thereby an appeal that is not the least of its attractions.

For this reason, the idea of a religious ceremony of any importance naturally elicits the idea of a festival. Inversely, every festival has certain characteristics of a religious ceremony, even if it is of purely secular origin. In every case, its effect is to bring individuals together, to put the masses into motion, and thus induce a state of effervescence—sometimes even delirium—which

[31]See above, p. 79.

is not without kinship to the religious state. Man is carried outside himself, pulled away from his ordinary occupations and preoccupations. We observe the same manifestations in both cases: cries, songs, music, violent movements, dances, the search for stimulants that increase vitality, and others. It has often been observed that popular festivals lead to excesses, causing people to lose sight of the boundary between the licit and the illicit;[32] there are also religious ceremonies that bring about a kind of thirst for violating those rules that ordinarily are widely obeyed.[33] To be sure, this is not because there is no basis for distinguishing between the two forms of public activity. Simple rejoicing, the profane corroboree, has no serious purpose, but when taken as a whole, a ritual ceremony always has a serious purpose. Once again, we must notice that there is no rejoicing in which the seriousness of life has no echo at all. Instead, the basic difference lies in the different proportions in which the two elements are combined.

III

As it happens, a more general fact confirms the preceding views. In their first work, Spencer and Gillen presented the Intichiuma as a perfectly circumscribed ritual entity. They spoke of it as if it was a process devoted exclusively to ensuring the reproduction of the totemic species; and it seemed that the Intichiuma must necessarily lose any sort of meaning beyond this single function. But in their *Northern Tribes of Central Australia*, the same authors use different language, perhaps without being aware of it. They recognize that these same ceremonies can just as well take place in the Intichiumas proper as in the initiation rites.[34] They serve just as well either to make animals and plants of the totemic species or to confer upon the neophytes the qualities it takes

---

[32]Notably, in sexual matters. Sexual license is common in the ordinary corroborees (see Spencer and Gillen, *Native Tribes*, pp. 96–97, and *Northern Tribes*, pp. 136–137). On sexual license in popular feasts generally, see [Alfred] Hagelstange, *Süddeutsches Bauernleben im Mittelalter* [Leipzig, Duncker & Humbolt, 1898], pp. 221ff.

[33]Thus, the rules of exogamy are obligatorily violated during certain religious ceremonies (see above, p. 218, n. 27). We probably should not seek precise ritual meaning in this license. It simply arises mechanically from the state of overexcitement provoked by the ceremony. It is an example of those rites that have no definite object in themselves but are merely discharges of activity (see above, p. 385). The native himself does not assign it a definite purpose; he says only that if this license is not committed, the rite will not produce its effects; the ceremony will be botched.

[34]These are the very words Spencer and Gillen use: "They (the ceremonies connected to the totems) are often, but not always, associated with those that concern the initiation of young men, or else they are part of the Intichiumas" (Spencer and Gillen, *Northern Tribes*, p. 178).

to become full members of the society of men.[35] From this point of view, the Intichiuma appears in a new light. No longer is it a distinct ritual mechanism based on principles that are peculiar to it but instead a particular application of more general ceremonies that can serve quite different purposes. This is why, before speaking of the Intichiuma and of initiation, they devote a special chapter of their new work to totemic ceremonies in general, apart from the various forms they may take depending on the purposes they serve.[36]

This inherent indeterminacy of the totemic ceremonies was only pointed to by Spencer and Gillen, and indeed rather indirectly, but it has been confirmed by Strehlow in the most explicit terms. He says, "When the young novices are passed through the various initiation celebrations, rites are performed one after another for them. Nevertheless, although these rites reproduce those of the cult proper, down to the most characteristic details (*Read: the rites that Spencer and Gillen term Intichiuma*), their purpose is not to multiply the corresponding totem and make it prosper."[37] So the same ceremony is used in both cases; only the name is changed. When its purpose is strictly the reproduction of the species, it is called Mbatjalkatiuma, and when it is a procedure of initiation it is given the name Intichiuma.[38]

In addition, among the Arunta, certain secondary characteristics distinguish these two kinds of ceremonies from one another. Although the structure of the rites is the same in both cases, the shedding of blood and, more generally, the offerings characteristic of the Arunta Intichiuma are lacking in their initiation ceremonies. Furthermore, whereas the Arunta Intichiuma is held at a place authoritatively set by tradition and to which people must pilgrimage, the stage on which the initiation ceremonies are held is purely conventional.[39] But when the Intichiuma consists merely of a dramatic performance, as is the case among the Warramunga, the lack of distinction be-

---

[35]I leave aside the question of what this trait consists in. That question would lead into a development that would be very long and very technical and, for this reason, would have to be handled separately. The question does not, however, affect the propositions that are established in the course of the present work.

[36]This is Chapter VI, titled "Ceremonies Connected with the Totems."

[37]Strehlow, *Aranda*, vol. III, pp. 1–2.

[38]The error with which Strehlow taxes Spencer and Gillen is explained in this way: They applied to one form of the rite the term that more especially suits the other. But in this instance, the error does not seem as grave as Strehlow makes it out to be.

[39]Indeed, it cannot have any other character. In fact, since initiation is a tribal feast, the novices of different totems are initiated at the same time. The ceremonies that occur one after the other in this way, at the same place, always refer to several totems, and consequently, they must take place outside the localities to which myth attaches them.

tween the two rites is total. The past is commemorated in both; the myth is put into action—performed—and cannot be performed in two markedly different ways. Thus, depending on the circumstances, one and the same ceremony fulfills two distinct functions.[40]

Indeed, it can lend itself to a good many other uses. As we know, since blood is a sacred thing, women must not see it flowing. Nevertheless, a quarrel may on occasion break out in their presence and end in bloodshed. A ritual infraction is thereby committed. Among the Arunta, in order to atone for this lapse, the man whose blood has flowed first must "conduct a ceremony that refers either to his father's or his mother's totem."[41] That ceremony bears a special name, *Alua uparilima,* which means "erasing of the blood." But, in and of itself, it is no different from those conducted during initiation or at the Intichiumas; it portrays an event of the ancestors' history. Thus it can serve equally well to initiate, to act upon the animal species, or to expiate a sacrilege. We will see below that a totemic ceremony can take the place of a funeral rite.[42]

Hubert and Mauss have already drawn attention to a functional ambiguity of the same sort in the case of sacrifice and, more specifically, Hindu sacrifice.[43] They have shown that the sacrifices of communion, expiation, oaths, and contracts were but variants of the same mechanism. As we now see, this phenomenon is far more primitive and by no means confined to the institution of sacrifice. There is perhaps no rite that does not display similar indeterminacy. The mass is used for marriages as well as for burials; it redeems the sins of the dead, ensures divine favor to the living, and so on. Fasting is an expiation and a penance, but it is also a preparation for communion; it even

---

[40]How it happens that I have nowhere studied rites of initiation in and of themselves will now be understood. They do not constitute a ritual entity but are a composite made from various sorts of rites. For example, there are prohibitions, ascetic rites, and representative ceremonies that are indistinguishable from those conducted during the Intichiuma. Thus I have had to take this composite system apart and separately treat each of the elementary rites that comprise it, classifying them with those similar rites with which they must be compared. In addition, we have seen (pp. 288–289) that initiation has served as the point of departure for a new religion that tends to move beyond totemism. But it was enough to show that totemism contained the seed of that religion; I did not have to pursue its development. Since the object of this book is to study the elementary beliefs and practices, I must stop at the moment they give birth to more complex forms.

[41]Spencer and Gillen, *Native Tribes,* p. 463. If the individual can, as he chooses, conduct a ceremony of either his father's or his mother's totem, that is because, for the reasons set forth above (p. 185), he belongs to both.

[42]See below, Bk. 3, chap. 5, p. 399.

[43]See [Henri Hubert and Marcel Mauss], "Essai sur [la nature et fonction du] sacrifice," in *Mélanges d'histoire des religions* [Paris, F. Alcan, 1909], p. 83.

conveys positive virtues. This ambiguity shows that the real function of a rite is not the specific, well-defined results it seems intended to reap and by which it is usually characterized. Instead, its real function is a general result, which can take different forms in different circumstances and yet remain always and everywhere the same.

The theory I have put forward presupposes exactly this. If the true function of the cult is to arouse in the faithful a certain state of soul, are of moral strength and confidence, and if the various effects imputed to the rites are only due to secondary and variable causes of this fundamental state, then it is not surprising that the same rite should seem to produce multiple effects while keeping the same components and structure. In every case, those mental dispositions that its permanent function is to bring about remain the same; they depend on the fact that the group is assembled, not on the particular reasons why the group is assembled. On the other hand, however, they are interpreted differently to fit the circumstances to which they apply. Is it a physical effect that one wants to obtain? The confidence felt will lead to believing that this result has been or will be obtained by the means used. Has one committed some lapse that one wants to erase? The same state of moral assurance will cause the same ritual movements to take on expiatory virtues. In this way, the apparent efficacy will seem to change, even though the real efficacy remains unchanging; and the rite will seem to fulfill disparate functions even though in fact it has only one, which is always the same.

Conversely, just as a single rite can serve several ends, several rites can be used interchangeably to bring about the same end. To ensure the reproduction of the totemic species, sacrifices, mimetic practices, or commemorative performances can be used equally well. This interchangeability of rites demonstrates once again—just as their plasticity demonstrates—the extreme generality of the useful influence they exercise. What matters most is that individuals are assembled and that feelings in common are expressed through actions in common. But as to the specific nature of these feelings and actions, that is a relatively secondary and contingent matter. To become conscious of itself, the group need not perform some acts rather than others. Although it must commune in the same thought and the same action, the visible forms in which this communion occurs hardly matter. The external forms probably do not come about by chance. They have their causes, but these causes do not go to the essence of the cult.

Everything brings us back, then, to the same idea. First and foremost, the rites are means by which the social group reaffirms itself periodically. And perhaps, beginning there, we can achieve a hypothetical reconstruction of the manner in which the first totemic cult must have been born. Men who feel united—in part by ties of blood but even more by common interests and traditions—assemble and become conscious of their moral unity. For the reasons I have set forth, they are led to conceive this unity as a very special kind of consubstantiality. They regard themselves as all participating in the nature of a certain animal. Under those conditions, there will be only one way for them to affirm their collective existence: to affirm themselves as animals of that same species—and this not only in the silence of consciousness but by physical doing. It is this doing that will form the cult, and obviously it can only be movements by which the man imitates the animal with which he identifies himself. Thus understood, the mimetic rites come into view as the primitive form of the cult. Some will find that this is to attribute a rather large historical role to practices that at first glance resemble childish games. But, as I have shown, these naive and gauche gestures, these crude modes of representation, express and nurture a feeling of pride, confidence, and reverence that is entirely comparable to the feeling expressed by the faithful of the most idealist religions when, gathered together, they proclaim themselves to be the children of the all-powerful God. In both cases, this feeling stems from the same impressions of security and respect that are aroused in individual consciousnesses by the great moral force that dominates them: the collective force.

In all likelihood, the other rites we have studied are no more than variations on this fundamental rite. Once the close union between animal and man was accepted, man strongly felt the need to ensure the regular reproduction of the totemic species, and that reproduction was made the principal object of the cult. In this way, those mimetic practices that probably had only a moral aim at the beginning found themselves subordinated to a utilitarian, material one, and he conceived of them as means of producing the desired result. But with further evolution in the mythology that at first identified the ancestor hero with the totemic animal, the ancestor figure became more distinct and personal, imitation of the ancestor replaced imitation of the animal, and the representative rites replaced or supplemented the mimetic ones. Finally, to become more certain of attaining the goal he was striving toward, man felt the need to bring into play all the means available to him. Having in hand reserves of life-forces accumulated in the sacred rocks, he used those; since the man's blood was of the same nature as the animal's, he used it for the same purpose, and he shed it. Inversely, because of that same kinship, the man used the animal's flesh for the purpose of remaking his own substance. Thence came the rites of sacrifice and communion. In the end, however, all these varied practices are variations on the same theme: Fundamentally, we encounter everywhere the same state of soul, differently interpreted according to the circumstances, historical moments, and inclinations of the faithful.

CHAPTER FIVE

THE PIACULAR RITES* AND THE AMBIGUITY OF THE NOTION OF THE SACRED

No matter how greatly the actions they involve may differ from one another, the various positive rites just reviewed have one feature in common: They are all carried out with confidence, joy, and enthusiasm. Although the wait for a future and contingent event is never without uncertainty, usually the rain falls when the season comes, and the animal and plant species reproduce on schedule. Repeated experience has shown that the rites generally bring about the hoped-for effect that is their *raison d'être*. They are celebrated with assurance, and with rejoicing in advance of the happy event they induce and announce. The actions contribute to that state of mind. To be sure, the seriousness that always attends a religious ceremony marks them, but that seriousness precludes neither high spirits nor joy.

Those ceremonies are joyful. But there are sad ceremonies as well, whose purpose is to meet a calamity or to remember and mourn one. These rites take on a distinctive form that I will characterize and explain. Since they reveal a new aspect of religious life, it is all the more necessary to examine them separately.

I propose to call ceremonies of this type "piacular." The advantage of the term "piaculum" is that while suggesting the idea of expiation, it nevertheless has a much broader meaning. Any misfortune, anything that is ominous, and anything that motivates feelings of disquiet or fear requires a piaculum

---

*Durkheim formulated this concept of rites conducted on the occasion of death, misfortune, or collective crisis that are not expressions of individual feeling. He introduced the term into the study of religion and ritual. See the *Macmillan Dictionary of Anthropology*, London, 1986.

and is therefore called piacular.[1] This word seems well suited to designating rites that are conducted under conditions of uncertainty or sadness.

I

Mourning offers us an initial, and important, example of piacular rites.

The various rites used for mourning must be distinguished. Some consist only of prohibitions: It is forbidden to pronounce the name of the deceased[2] or to remain at the place where the death occurred;[3] the relatives, especially the female ones, must abstain from all communication with outsiders;[4] the ordinary occupations of life are suspended, just as they are during feasts;[5] and so on. Since all these practices belong to the negative cult and are explained as rites of that sort, they need not concern us here. They arise from the fact that the deceased is a sacred being. As a result of contagion, everything that is or was in contact with him is in a religious state that precludes all contact with the things of profane life.

But mourning consists of more than prohibitions to be respected. Positive acts are required, and kin are both the agents and the objects of them.

These rites quite commonly begin as soon as death seems imminent. Here is a scene that Spencer and Gillen witnessed among the Warramunga. A totemic rite had just been celebrated, and the actors and spectators were leaving the sacred ground when suddenly a piercing scream arose from the

---

[1] *"Piacularia auspicia appellabant quae sacrificantibus tristia portendebant"* (Paul ex. Fest., p. 244, ed. Muller). [They used to call the auspices piacularia auspices, which portended sad things to the people sacrificing. Trans.] The word *piaculum* is even used as a synonym of misfortune. *"Vettonica herba,"* says Pliny [The Elder, *Natural History*], *"tantumque gloriae habet ut domus in qua sata sit tuta existimetur a piaculis omnibus"* (XXV, 8, 46). [The vetonica herb is so renowned that the house in which it is planted is considered safe from all piacula. I am indebted to Kathryn Argetsinger for these Latin translations.]

[2] [Sir Baldwin] Spencer and [Francis James] Gillen, *Northern Tribes [of Central Australia*, London, Macmillan, 1904], p. 526; [Richard] Eylmann, [*Die Eingeborenen der Kolonie Sud Australien*, Berlin, D. Reumer, 1908], p. 239. Cf. above, p. 310.

[3] [Robert] Brough Smyth [*The Aborigines of Victoria*], vol. I [Melbourne: J. Ferres, 1878], p. 106; [James] Dawson, [*Australian Aborigines; The Languages and Customs of Several Tribes of Aborigines in the Western District of Victoria, Australia*, Melbourne, G. Robertson, 1881], p. 64; Eylmann, *Die Eingeborenen*, p. 239.

[4] Dawson, *Australian Aborigines*, p. 66; Eylmann, *Die Eingeborenen*, p. 241.

[5] [Sir Baldwin] Spencer and [Francis James] Gillen, *Native Tribes [of Central Australia*, London, Macmillan, 1899], p. 502; Dawson, *Australian Aborigines*, p. 67.

encampment. A man was dying there. Immediately, the whole company began to run as fast as possible, and most of them began to scream even as they ran. "Between us and the camp," say these observers, "there was a deep stream on whose banks sat several men; scattered here and there, heads down between their knees, they cried and lamented."

> As we crossed the stream, we found the camp broken up, as required by custom. Some of the women, who had come from all directions, lay upon the body of the dying man; others stood or knelt all around it, pushing the points of their digging sticks into the tops of their heads, thereby causing wounds from which the blood ran down over their faces. They kept up a continuous wailing all the while.
>
> At this juncture, some men run up to the body, throwing themselves down upon it as the women get up; after a few moments, nothing is visible but a writhing mass of interlaced bodies. To one side, seated with their backs to the dying man, and still dressed in their ceremonial decorations, three men of the Thapungarti class let out piercing cries. After a minute or two, another man of the same class rushes onto the scene, screaming with pain and brandishing a stone knife. As soon as he reaches the camp, he makes such deep incisions across his thighs, into the muscles, that, unable to hold himself up, he finally falls on the ground in the midst of a group; two or three of his female relatives pull him away and apply their lips to his gaping wounds while he lies senseless.

The sick man did not die until late that evening. As soon as he had drawn his last breath, the same scene began again. This time, the moans were even more penetrating. Caught up in the same frenzy, men and women ran back and forth, cutting themselves with knives and pointed sticks; the women hit each other, with no one trying to fend off the blows. Finally, after an hour, a torchlight procession moved across the plain to the tree in whose branches the body had been placed.[6]

Whatever their violence, these displays are tightly controlled by etiquette. Custom designates the individuals who make bloody gashes on themselves; they must have specified kinship relations with the deceased. In the case Spencer and Gillen observed among the Warramunga, those who slashed their thighs were the maternal grandfather, maternal uncle, and wife's brother of the deceased.[7] Others are required to cut their whiskers and hair

---

[6]Spencer and Gillen, *Northern Tribes*, pp. 516–517.

[7]Ibid., pp. 520–521. The authors do not tell us whether these are tribal or blood relatives. The first hypothesis is the more likely.

and then cover their scalps with pipe clay. The women have especially rigorous obligations. They must cut their hair and cover their entire body with
pipe clay; furthermore, total silence is imposed on them for the period of
mourning, which can last up to two years. As a result of this prohibition, it
is not uncommon among the Warramunga for all the women of a camp to
be condemned to absolute silence. They become so accustomed to it that,
even after the period of mourning expires, they voluntarily give up spoken
language and prefer sign language (which they use with remarkable skill).
Spencer and Gillen knew an old woman who had not spoken for more than
twenty-four years.[8]

The ceremony I have described opens a long sequence of rites that occur one after the other for weeks and even months. It is repeated in various
forms over the days that follow. Groups of men and women sit on the
ground, crying, lamenting, and embracing one another at particular times.
These ritual embraces are repeated often over the period of mourning. The
individuals feel the need to come close to one another, it seems, and to commune intimately. They can be seen pressed together and entwined to the
point of forming a single mass that emits loud moans.[9] Meanwhile, the
women go back to lacerating their heads, and they go to the extreme of applying the ends of red-hot sticks to the wounds they make, in order to ag-
gravate them.[10]

Practices of this sort are common throughout Australia. Funeral rites—
that is, the ritual attention given the corpse, the manner in which it is buried,
and so forth—vary from tribe to tribe[11] and, within a single tribe, according
to the age, sex, and social rank of the individuals.[12] But the ceremonies of

[8]Ibid., pp. 525–526. Although only an abstinence, this prohibition against speaking, specifically
women's, has all the signs of a piacular rite, for it is a way of inconveniencing oneself. This is why I mention it here. Fasting also can be either a piacular or an ascetic rite, depending on the circumstances. It depends on the conditions in which the fasting occurs and the aim sought (see below, p. 400, on the
difference between these two sorts of rites).

[9]A plate in Spencer and Gillen, Northern Tribes, p. 525, illustrates this rite quite vividly.

[10]Ibid., p. 522.

[11]On the principal kinds of funeral rites, see [Alfred William] Howitt, Native Tribes [of South-East Australia, New York, Macmillan, 1904], pp. 446–508, for the tribes of the southeast; Spencer and Gillen,
Northern Tribes, p. 505, and Spencer and Gillen, Native Tribes, pp. 497ff., for the tribes of the center; [Wal-
ter Edmund] Roth, North Queensland Ethnography, Bull. 9, in RAM, VI, part 5, 1907, pp. 365ff. ("Burial
Ceremonies and Disposal of the Dead").

[12]See, for example, Roth, "Burial Ceremonies," p. 368; [Edward John] Eyre, Journals of Expeditions [of
Discovery] into Central Australia [London, T. and W. Boone, 1845], vol. II, pp. 344–345, 347.

mourning itself vary only in detail, repeating the same theme everywhere. Everywhere, there is the same silence punctuated by wailing,[13] the same obligation to cut the hair or beard[14] and cover the head with pipe clay, ashes, or even excrement;[15] everywhere, finally, there is the same frenzy of beating, lacerating, and burning oneself. In the center of Victoria, "when there is a death, the women cry, lament, and tear the skin of their temples with their fingernails. The relatives of the deceased lacerate themselves furiously, especially if they have lost a son. The father hits his head with a tomahawk and sobs bitterly. The mother, seated near the fire, burns her breast and abdomen with a stick reddened in the fire. . . . Sometimes, these burns are so cruel that death results."[16]

According to an account by Brough Smyth, here is what occurs in the southern tribes of the same state. Once the body is lowered into the grave,

the widow begins her funeral observances. She shears off the hair above her forehead, and, reaching outright frenzy, takes hold of red-hot sticks and applies them to her chest, arms, legs, and thighs. She seems to enjoy the tortures she inflicts on herself. It would be rash and, besides, useless to try to stop her. When she is so exhausted that she can no longer walk, she goes on trying to kick the ashes of the fire and throw them in all directions. Having fallen on the ground, she takes ashes into her hands and rubs her wounds with them; then she scratches her face (the only part of her body that the sticks passed through the fire have not touched). The blood that flows mingles with the ashes that cover her wounds and, still scraping herself, she laments and cries out.[17]

The description of mourning rites among the Kurnai that Howitt gives us is remarkably similar to the preceding. Once the body has been wrapped in opossum skin and enclosed in a bark shroud, a hut is built, and in it the relatives gather. "There, lying on the ground, they lament their fate, saying for example: 'Why have you left us?' From time to time, their grief is inten-

---

[13]Spencer and Gillen, *Native Tribes*, p. 500; Spencer and Gillen, *Northern Tribes*, pp. 507, 508; Eylmann [*Die Eingeborenen*], p. 241; Mrs. Langloh Parker [Catherine Sommerville Field Parker], *The Euahlayi Tribe* [London: A. Constable, 1905], pp. 83ff.; Brough Smyth, *Aborigines of Victoria*, vol. I, p. 118.

[14]Dawson, *Australian Aborigines*, p. 66; Howitt, *Native Tribes*, p. 466; Eylmann, *Die Eingeborenen*, pp. 239–240.

[15]Brough Smyth, *Aborigines of Victoria*, vol. I, p. 113.

[16]W. E. Stanbridge, *Transactions of the Ethnological Society of London*, n.s., vol. I, p. 286.

[17]Brough Smyth, *Aborigines of Victoria*, vol. I, p. 104.

sified by penetrating moans from one of them: The wife of the deceased cries, 'My husband is dead,' or the mother, 'My child is dead.' Each of those present repeats the same cry: Only the words change, depending upon the tie of kinship each has with the deceased. Using sharpened stones or toma-hawks, they beat and tear themselves until their heads and bodies stream with blood. The cries and moans continue through the night."[18]

Sadness is not the only feeling expressed during these ceremonies. A kind of anger is usually mingled with it. The relatives apparently need some-how to avenge the death suffered. They are seen throwing themselves upon and trying to wound each other. The attack is sometimes real and sometimes pretended.[19] There are even cases in which a kind of dueling is organized. Among the Kaitish, the hair of the deceased goes by right to his son-in-law. In turn, the son-in-law must go, together with a company of relatives and friends, to challenge one of his tribal brothers (that is, a man who belongs to the same marriage class as he and who, as such, could also have married the daughter of the deceased). The challenge may not be refused, and the two combatants inflict serious injuries upon one another's shoulders and thighs. When the duel is over, the challenger gives his adversary the hair he had con-ditionally inherited. The adversary leaves, in his own turn, to challenge and fight another of his tribal brothers to whom the precious relic is then trans-mitted, but always conditionally; in this way it passes from hand to hand and circulates from group to group.[20] Moreover, some part of these same feelings enters into the sort of rage with which each relative beats, burns, or slashes himself. A pain that reaches such great intensity does not go without anger. One cannot but be struck by the similarities of these customs to those of the vendetta. Both arise from the same principle: that death calls for the shedding of blood. The only difference is that the victims are relatives in one case and strangers in the other. Although we need not specifically discuss the vendetta, which falls under the domain of legal institutions, it is appropriate to show how it is connected to the mourning rites, whose end it announces.[21]

In some societies, mourning concludes with a ceremony whose efferves-cence matches or even surpasses that produced during the opening cere-monies. Among the Arunta, this rite of cloture is called Urpmilchima.

[18]Howitt, *Native Tribes*, p. 459. Similar scenes will be found in Eyre, *Journals of Expedition*, vol. II, pp. 255 n, 347; Roth, "Burial Ceremonies," especially pp. 394, 395; [George] Grey, [*Journal of the Two Expeditions in North Western and Western Australia*, London, T. and W. Boone, 1841], vol. II, pp. 320ff.

[19]Brough Smyth, *Aborigines of Victoria*, vol. I, pp. 104, 112; Roth, "Burial Ceremonies," p. 382.

[20]Spencer and Gillen, *Northern Tribes*, pp. 511–512.

[21]Dawson, *Australian Aborigines*, p. 67; Roth, "Burial Ceremonies," pp. 366–367.

Spencer and Gillen were present at two of these. One was conducted in honor of a man, the other of a woman. Here is the description they give of the woman's.[22]

They begin by making ornaments of a very special type, which are called Chimurilia by the men and Aramurilia by the women. Using a sort of resin, they glue small animal bones (which have previously been collected and stored) to locks of hair furnished by relatives of the dead woman. They attach these pendants to one of those headbands of the kind that women often wear, adding white cockatoo and parakeet feathers to it. When these preparations are complete, the women gather in their camp. They paint their bodies with different colors, according to the degree of their kinship with the deceased. After having held themselves in a mutual embrace for about ten minutes, wailing all the while, they begin to walk toward the tomb. At a certain distance along the way, they meet a blood brother of the deceased, who is accompanied by some of her tribal brothers. They all sit on the ground, and the wailing begins again. Then, a pitchi[23] containing the Chimurilias is presented to the older brother, who presses it against his stomach; this is said to be a means of lessening his pain. They bring out one of these Chimurilias, and the mother of the dead woman puts it on her head for a few moments. Then it is put back into the pitchi, which the other men take turns pressing against their breasts. Finally, the brother places the Chimurilias on the heads of the two older sisters, and they set out again for the tomb. En route, the mother throws herself on the ground several times, trying to slash her head with a pointed stick. Each time, the other women lift her up again and seem absorbed in preventing her from hurting herself. Once at the tomb, she throws herself on the mound and tries to destroy it with her hands, while the other women literally dance on top of her. The tribal mothers and aunts (father's sisters of the dead woman) follow her example. They, too, throw themselves on the ground, beating and tearing at one another. In the end, blood streams over their entire bodies. After a time, they are pulled away. The older sisters then make a hole in the earth of the tomb, into which they place the Chimurilias, which have previously been broken into pieces. Once again, the tribal mothers throw themselves on the ground and slash each other's heads. At this moment, "the crying and wailing of the women who have remained all around seemed to rouse them to the ultimate degree of excitement. The blood that flowed the length of their bodies, over the pipe clay

[22]Spencer and Gillen, *Native Tribes*, pp. 508–510.

[23]The small wooden vessel already described, above p. 338.

with which they were covered, gave them the appearance of ghosts. At the end, the old mother remained alone lying on the tomb, completely exhausted and groaning feebly." The others then lifted her up again, and removed the pipe clay in which she had been covered. This was the end of the ceremony and of the mourning.[24]

Among the Warramunga, the final rite has rather special features. Although the shedding of blood seems to have no place in it, the collective effervescence is expressed differently. Among this people, before the body is finally buried, it is laid out on a sort of platform in the branches of a tree and left there slowly to decompose until only the bones remain. The bones are then collected and, with the exception of one humerus, placed inside an anthill. The humerus is wrapped in a bark sheath that is decorated in various ways. The sheath is carried to the camp amid the shrieks and moans of women. In the days that follow, the Warramunga conduct a series of totemic ceremonies, which refer to the totem of the deceased and to the mythical history of the ancestors from whom the clan is descended. When all these ceremonies are over, they move on to the rite of cloture.

A trench one foot deep and fifteen feet long is made on the ceremonial ground. A totemic design has previously been drawn on the ground at a distance from it, the design representing the totem of the deceased and certain places where the ancestor sojourned. A small trench has been dug in the ground very near this design. Ten decorated men then advance, one after the other. With their hands crossed behind their heads and their legs apart, they stand astride the trench. When the signal is given, the women rush from the camp, in the deepest silence. When they are near, they get into single file, the last holding in her hands the sheath containing the humerus. Then they all throw themselves on the ground and, moving on their hands and knees between the spread legs of the men, crawl the full length of the trench. This scene marks a state of great sexual excitement. As soon as the last woman has passed, the sheath is taken away from her and carried toward the hole, near which stands an old man; he breaks the bone in one stroke, and the pieces are speedily buried. During this time, the women have remained farther away with their backs to the scene, which they are forbidden to watch. But when they hear the blow of the axe, they flee, shrieking and moaning. The rite is over; the mourning done.[25]

[24]Spencer and Gillen, *Native Tribes*, pp. 508–510. The other last rite that Spencer and Gillen attended is described on pp. 503–508 of the same work. It does not differ fundamentally from the one I have just analyzed.

[25]Spencer and Gillen, *Northern Tribes*, pp. 531–540.

II

These rites belong to a category very different from those I have constructed thus far. This is not to say that important resemblances between them cannot be found, and there will be occasion to note those; but the differences are perhaps more obvious. Instead of joyful dances, songs, and dramatic performances, which entertain and relax the spirit, there are tears and laments—in short, the most varied displays of anguished sorrow and a kind of mutual pity that takes up the entire scene. Although there certainly is shedding of blood in the course of the Intichiuma, that is an offering made out of pious enthusiasm. So although the actions resemble one another, the feelings they express are different and even opposite. Similarly, ascetic rites do indeed involve abstinences, prohibitions, and mutilations that must be borne with impassive firmness and a kind of serenity. But here, despondency, cries, and tears are the rule. The ascetic tortures himself in order to prove—in the eyes of his neighbor as well as his own—that he is above suffering. In mourning, people hurt themselves in order to prove that they are in the grip of suffering. All these signs are recognizable as characteristic traits of piacular rites.

How may these rites be explained?

One initial fact remains constant: Mourning is not the spontaneous expression of individual emotions.[26] If the relatives cry, lament, and beat themselves black and blue, the reason is not that they feel personally affected by the death of their kinsman. In particular cases, to be sure, the sadness expressed may happen to be truly felt.[27] But generally there is no relationship between the feelings felt and the actions done by those who take part in the rite:[28] If, at the very moment when the mourners seem most overcome by the pain, someone turns to them to talk about some secular interest, their faces and tone often change instantly, taking on a cheerful air, and they speak with all the gaiety in the world.[29] Mourning is not the natural response of a private sensibility hurt by a cruel loss. It is an obligation imposed by the group. One laments not simply because one is sad but because one is obli-

---

[26]Contrary to what [Frank Byron] Jevons says, *Introduction to the History of Religions* [London, Methuen, 1896], pp. 46ff.

[27]This is what leads Dawson to say that people mourn sincerely (*Australian Aborigines*, p. 66). But Eylmann declares that he has known only one case of wounding for sadness really felt (*Die Eingeborenen*, p. 113).

[28]Spencer and Gillen, *Native Tribes*, p. 510.

[29]Eylmann, *Die Eingeborenen*, pp. 238–239.

gated to lament. It is a ritual facade that must be adopted out of respect for custom, but one that is largely independent of the individuals' emotional states. Moreover, this obligation is sanctioned by mythic or social penalties. It is believed, for example, that when a relative does not properly carry out mourning, the soul of the deceased dogs his steps and kills him.[30] In other cases, society does not leave the punishment of the neglectful to religious forces but steps in to punish ritual lapses. If a brother-in-law does not carry out the funeral obligations he owes to his father-in-law, if he does not make the mandatory incisions on himself, his tribal fathers-in-law take his wife back and give her to someone else.[31] In order to do right by custom, therefore, sometimes they force tears artificially.[32]

Where does this obligation come from?

Ethnographers and sociologists have generally been satisfied with the natives' own answer to this question. The natives say that the dead man wants to be mourned, that he is offended if denied his rightful tribute of sorrow, and that the only way to prevent his anger is to conform to his wishes.[33]

But this mythological explanation merely changes the terms of the problem and does not solve it; we still need to know why the dead man imperatively demands mourning. It will be said that it is in the nature of man to want to be mourned and missed. But to use this feeling to explain the complex apparatus of rites that constitute mourning is to ascribe affective needs to the Australian that even the civilized man does not display. Let us grant something that is not self-evident *a priori*: that the idea of not being too quickly forgotten is naturally pleasing to the man who thinks of the future. Even if that was true, we would still need to establish that it has always had so large a place in the hearts of the living that an attitude based almost entirely on such a concern could reasonably have been ascribed to the dead. It seems especially improbable that such a feeling could have managed so completely to preoccupy and impassion men who just barely have the habit of thinking beyond the present. It is far from true that the desire to live on in the memory of the survivors must be regarded as the root of mourning. Rather, one begins to ask oneself whether it is not mourning itself, once instituted, that awakened the notion of and taste for posthumous lamentation.

If we know what primitive mourning is, the standard interpretation seems all the more untenable. It consists not merely of pious regrets accorded

[30]Spencer and Gillen, *Northern Tribes*, p. 507; Spencer and Gillen, *Native Tribes*, p. 498.

[31]Spencer and Gillen, *Native Tribes*, p. 500; Eylmann, *Die Eingeborenen*, p. 227.

[32]Brough Smyth, *Aborigines of Victoria*, vol. I, p. 114.

[33]Spencer and Gillen, *Native Tribes*, p. 510.

to the one who is no more but also of harsh abstinences and cruel sacrifices. The rite not only demands that one think of the deceased in a melancholy way but that one beat, bruise, lacerate, and burn oneself. We have even seen that people in mourning are so carried away in torturing themselves that they sometimes do not survive their wounds. What would be the dead man's reason for imposing such tortures upon them? Such cruelty on his part indicates something other than a desire not to be forgotten. For the deceased to find pleasure in seeing his own suffer, he would have to hate them and thirst for their blood. This ferocity will no doubt seem natural to those for whom every spirit is necessarily an evil and dreaded power. But we know that there are all kinds of spirits. How does it happen that the soul of the deceased should necessarily be an evil spirit? As long as the man is alive, he loves his kin and trades favors with them. Is it not strange that his soul should slough off his earlier feelings the instant it is freed from the body, so as to become a mean and tormenting genie? Yet generally, the dead man retains the personality of the one who lived; he has the same character, the same hatreds, and the same affections. So the metamorphosis is far from being self-evident and comprehensible. True, the natives implicitly concede that point when they explain the rite by the demands of the deceased; but the question precisely is to know from whence that idea came to them. Far from our being able to regard that metamorphosis as a truism, it is as obscure as the rite itself and, hence, inadequate to account for the rite.

Finally, although one may have found the reasons for this stunning transformation, one would still have to explain why it is only temporary, for it does not last beyond mourning. Once the rites have been done, the deceased once again becomes what he was in life: an affectionate and devoted relative. He places the new capacities he gains from his new condition at the disposal of his own.[34] From then on, he is seen as a good genie, always ready to help those he once tormented. From whence could these successive reversals have arisen? If the bad feelings ascribed to the soul arise only from the fact that it is no longer alive, then they ought to remain invariant. And if mourning derives from such feelings, then it ought to be without end.

These mythical explanations do not translate the rite itself but the idea the individual has of it. In order to confront the reality they do translate but distort, we can put them aside. While mourning differs from other forms of the positive cult, it resembles them in one respect: It too is made of collec-

---

[34]Several examples of this belief are to be found in Howitt, Native Tribes, p. 435. Cf. Strehlow, Aranda, vol. I, pp. 15–16 and vol. II, p. 7.

tive rites that bring about a state of effervescence in those who take part. The intense feelings are different; the wild intensity is the same. Presumably, therefore, the explanation of the joyful rites is applicable to the sad rites, provided their terms are transposed.

When an individual dies, the family group to which he belongs feels diminished, and it comes together to react to this diminishment. A shared misfortune has the same effect as the approach of a happy event. It enlivens collective feelings, which lead individuals to seek one another out and come together. In fact, we have seen this need affirm itself sometimes with special energy—people kissing and putting their arms around one another, pressing as close together as possible. But the emotional state in which the group finds itself reflects the circumstances it is then going through. Not only do the kin most immediately affected bring their personal sorrow to the gathering, but the society exerts moral pressure on its members, and they bring their feelings into harmony with the situation. If society permitted them to remain indifferent to the blow that strikes and diminishes it, it would be proclaiming that it does not hold its rightful place in their hearts. Indeed, it would deny itself. For a family to tolerate that one of its members should die without being mourned would give witness thereby that it lacks moral unity and cohesiveness: It abdicates; it renounces its existence.

For his part, when the individual feels firmly attached to the society to which he belongs, he feels morally bound to share in its grief and its joy. To abandon it would be to break the ties that bind him to the collectivity, to give up wanting collectivity, and to contradict himself. If the Christian fasts and mortifies himself during the commemorative feasts of the Passion and the Jew on the anniversary of Jerusalem's fall, it is not to give way to sadness spontaneously felt. In those circumstances, the believer's inward state is in disproportion to the harsh abstinences to which he submits. If he is sad, it is first and foremost because he forces himself to be and disciplines himself to to be; and he disciplines himself to be in order to affirm his faith. The attitude of the Australian in mourning is to be understood in the same way. If he cries and moans, it is not only to express individual sadness but also to fulfill a duty to the feeling—an obligatory feeling of which the society around him does not fail to remind him on occasion.

We know from elsewhere how human feelings intensify when they are collectively affirmed. Like joy, sadness is heightened and amplified by its reverberation from one consciousness to the next, and then it gradually expresses itself overtly as unrestrained and convulsive movement. This no longer is the joyful animation that we observed awhile ago; it is cries and shrieks of pain. Every person is pulled along by every other, and something like a panic of sadness occurs. When the pain reaches such a pitch, it becomes suffused with a kind of anger and exasperation. One feels the need to break or destroy something. One attacks oneself or others. One strikes, wounds, or burns oneself, or one attacks someone else, in order to *strike*, wound, or burn him. Thus was established the mourning custom of giving oneself over to veritable orgies of torture. It seems to me probable that the vendetta and head hunting have no other origin. If every death is imputed to some magical spell and if, for that reason, it is believed that the dead person must be avenged, the reason is a felt need to find a victim at all costs on whom the collective sorrow and anger can be discharged. This victim will naturally be sought outside, for an outsider is a subject *minoris resistentiae**; since he is not protected by the fellow-feeling that attaches to a relative or a neighbor, nothing about him blocks and neutralizes the bad and destructive feelings aroused by the death. Probably for the same reason, a woman serves more often than a man as the passive object of the most cruel mourning rites. Because she has lower social significance, she is more readily singled out to fill the function of scapegoat.

We see that this explanation of mourning leaves ideas of soul or spirit entirely out of account. The only forces really at work are of an entirely impersonal nature; these forces are the emotions that the death of a member arouses in the group. But the primitive does not know the psychic mechanism from which all these practices arise. Thus, when he tries to account for them, he has to forge a quite different explanation for himself. All he knows is that he must painfully mortify himself. Because every obligation arouses the idea of a will that obligates, he looks around him for the source of the constraint he feels. Now there is a moral power whose reality seems to him certain and altogether apt for this role—and that is the soul set at liberty by the death. For what could be more interested than the soul in the repercussions of its own demise for the living? Therefore, we imagine that if the living inflict unnatural treatment upon themselves, it is to give in to the soul's demands. The idea of the soul must therefore have entered the mythology of mourning after the fact. Moreover, since inhuman demands are attributed to the soul, we must on those grounds suppose that it abandoned all human feeling when it left the body it formerly animated. Thus is explained the metamorphosis that

*Less able to resist. This account of scapegoating, as a process by which society reaffirms itself in the face of loss, is closely analogous to Durkheim's 1899 account of anti-Semitism in France: "When society undergoes suffering, it feels the need to find someone whom it can hold responsible for its sickness, on whom it can avenge its misfortunes: and those against whom opinion already discriminates are naturally designated for this role. These are the pariahs who serve as expiatory victims." Quoted in Steven Lukes, *Emile Durkheim:* His Life and Work (London, Allen Lane, 1973), p. 345.

makes a dreaded enemy out of yesterday's relative. This transformation is not the genesis of mourning but rather its sequel. It expresses the change that has occurred in the emotional state of the group. The dead man is not mourned because he is feared; he is feared because he is mourned.

This change in emotional state can only be temporary. The rites of mourning both result from and conclude it. They gradually neutralize the very causes that gave them birth. The basis of mourning is the impression of enfeeblement that is felt by the group when it loses a member. But this very impression has the effect of bringing the individuals close to one another, putting them into closer touch, and inducing in them the same state of soul. And from all this comes a sensation of renewed strength, which counteracts the original enfeeblement. People cry together because they continue to be precious to one another and because, regardless of the blow that has fallen upon it, the collectivity is not breached. To be sure, in that case they only share sad emotions in common; but to commune in sadness is still to commune, and every communion of consciousnesses increases social vitality, in whatever form it is done.

The extraordinary violence of the displays that necessarily and obligatorily express the shared sorrow is evidence that, even at this moment, society is more alive and active than ever. In fact, when social feeling suffers a painful shock, it reacts with greater force than usual. One never holds so tightly to one's family as when it has just been tested. This excess of energy all the more thoroughly erases the effects of the crippling that occurred to begin with, and in this way the sensation of cold that death everywhere brings with it is dissipated. The group feels its strength gradually coming back to it; it begins again to hope and to live. One comes out of mourning, and one comes out of it thanks to mourning itself. But since the idea people have of the soul reflects the moral state of the society, that idea must change when the state changes. While the people were in the period of dejection and anguish, they conceived of the soul as having the traits of an evil being, interested only in persecuting men. Now that they again feel confidence and security, they must concede that the soul has recovered its original nature and its original feelings of tenderness and solidarity. Thus can be explained the very different ways in which it is conceived at different periods of its existence.[35]

---

[35]One may ask why repeated ceremonies are necessary to bring about the relief that follows mourning. First, it is because funerals are often very long, with multiple procedures that spread out over many months. In this way, they prolong and maintain the moral disturbance caused by the death (cf. [Robert] Hertz, ["Contribution à une étude sur la] représentation collective de la mort," *AS*, vol. X [1907], pp. 48ff.). Furthermore, death is a profound change, with wide and lasting repercussions for the group. It takes time for those effects to be neutralized.

Not only do mourning rites bring into being certain of the secondary characteristics ascribed to the soul, but perhaps, as well, the idea that the soul outlives the body is not alien to them. To be in a position to understand the practices to which he subjects himself when a relative dies, man has no choice but to believe that those practices are not a matter of indifference to the deceased. The shedding of blood that is so widely practiced in mourning is actually a sacrifice to the dead man.[36] It is done because some part of the deceased person lives on, and since what lives on is not the body, which is obviously not moving and is decomposing, that part can only be the soul. Of course, it is impossible to say for certain what role these considerations played in the origin of the idea of life after death. But probably the influence of the cult was in this case what it is elsewhere. Rites are easier to explain when they are thought of as being addressed to personal beings; in this way, men were prompted to extend the influence of mythic personalities in religious life. So that they could account for mourning, they extended the existence of the soul beyond the tomb. Here is a further example of the way in which rites react upon beliefs.

III

Death is not the only event that can unsettle a community. There are a good many other occasions for men to be saddened and become disquieted. And so we might anticipate that even the Australians know and conduct piacular rites other than those of mourning. It is noteworthy, however, that only a small number of examples can be found in observers' accounts.

One rite of this sort very closely resembles those just studied. Recall that, among the Arunta, each local group ascribes exceptionally important virtues to its collection of churingas. It is a collective palladium, whose fate is linked with that of the collectivity. Thus, when enemies or white men manage to uncover one of these religious treasures, the loss is deemed a public calamity. This misfortune is the occasion of a rite that has all the characteristics of mourning. Bodies are covered with white pipe clay, and at the camp two weeks are spent in wailing and lamentation.[37] This is further evidence that mourning is caused not by the manner in which the soul of the dead person

---

[36]In a case reported by Grey, based on an observation by Bussel, the rite is quite like sacrifice, with the blood being poured onto the corpse itself (Grey, *Journal of Two Expeditions*, vol. II, p. 330). In other instances, there is a sort of beard offering, in which the men in mourning cut off part of their beards, which they throw on the corpse (ibid., p. 335).

[37]Spencer and Gillen, *Native Tribes*, pp. 135–136.

is conceived but by impersonal causes, by the moral state of the group. Here, indeed, is a rite whose structure cannot be distinguished from mourning proper and yet does not depend upon any idea of spirit or evil demon.[38]

The distress in which society finds itself when the harvests have been insufficient is another circumstance that gives rise to ceremonies of this sort. "The natives who live in the environs of Lake Eyre," says Eylmann, "also try to conjure away the inadequacy of the food supply with secret ceremonies. But several of the ritual practices observed in this region are different from those previously discussed: They seek to act upon the religious powers or forces of nature not with symbolic dances, mimetic movements, and dazzling decorations, but with sufferings that the individuals inflict upon themselves. In the northern territories, as well, they strive to appease those powers that are ill-disposed toward men, by using tortures such as prolonged fasts, vigils, dances carried on until the dancers are exhausted, and physical suffering of all kinds."[39] The torments the natives undergo for this purpose sometimes leave them so worn out that they are unable to hunt for many days.[40]

These practices are used most of all to combat drought, since lack of water leads to general famine. They resort to violent means of remedying this evil. One of the means used is tooth extraction. Among the Kaitish, for example, an incisor is extracted from an individual and hung from a tree.[41] Among the Dieri, the idea of rain is closely associated with that of bloody incisions made on the skin of the thorax and arms.[42] Among the same people, when the drought is very severe, the grand council meets and summons the whole tribe. It is a genuinely tribal event. Women are sent forth in all directions to call the people together at a prescribed place and time. Once gathered, they are heard to groan, to scream in piercing voices about the miserable state of the land, and to ask the Mura-muras (mythical ancestors) to confer on them the power to make abundant rain fall.[43] In cases (very rare, however) when there has been too much, an analogous ceremony to stop the

---

[38]Of course, each churinga is considered to be connected with an ancestor. Still, lost churingas are not mourned in order to appease the spirits of the ancestors. I have shown elsewhere (pp. 121–122) that the idea of the ancestor entered into the idea of the churinga only in a secondary way, and after the fact.

[39]Eylmann, *Die Eingeborenen*, p. 207; cf. p. 116.

[40]Ibid., p. 208.

[41]Ibid., p. 211.

[42][Alfred William] Howitt, "The Dieri [and Other Kindred Tribes of Central Australia"], *JAI*, vol. XX (1891), p. 93.

[43]Howitt, *Native Tribes*, p. 394.

rain takes place. The old men then enter into a state of out-and-out frenzy,[44] and the cries made by the crowd are pathetic to hear.[45]

Spencer and Gillen recount a ceremony for us, under the name Intichiuma, that may well have the same purpose and origin as the preceding. Physical torture is used to make an animal species multiply. There is a clan among the Urabunna that has a kind of snake called *wadnungadni* as its totem. This is how the chief goes about "making sure that animal does not fail to reproduce." After decorating himself, he kneels on the ground, with his arms fully extended. A helper pinches the skin of the right arm between his fingers while the celebrant forces a pointed bone five inches long through the fold thereby formed. The left arm is treated in the same way. This self-mutilation is held to produce the desired result.[46] Among the Dieri, an analogous rite is used to make the wild chicken lay eggs: The celebrants pierce their scrotums.[47] In certain other tribes of Lake Eyre, the ear is pierced to make the yams produce.[48]

Partial or total famines are not the only disasters that can befall a tribe. Other events that threaten or seem to threaten the group's existence occur from time to time. This is the case, for example, of the southern lights. The Kurnai believe that it is a fire lit in the sky by the high god Mungan-ngaua. This is why, when they see the lights, they fear that fire will spread to earth and engulf them. The result is a great effervescence in the camp. The Kurnai shake the dried hand of a dead man, to which they ascribe an assortment of virtues, and they give out yells such as: "Send it back; do not let us burn." At the same time, by order of the elders, there are exchanges of wives, which always signals great excitement.[49] The same sexual license is reported among the Wiimbaio whenever some calamity appears imminent, and especially in times of epidemic.[50]

Under the influence of these ideas, mutilation and the shedding of blood are sometimes regarded as efficacious means of curing sicknesses. Among the

[44]Ibid., p. 396.

[45]Communication of [S.] Gason, ["Of the Tribes Dieyerie, Auminie, Yandrawontha, Yarawurka, Pilladapa, Lat. 31°S., Long. 138° 55′ "], *JAI.*, vol. XXIV (1895), p. 175.

[46]Spencer and Gillen, *Northern Tribes*, p. 286.

[47][S.] Gason, "The Dieyerie Tribe," in [Edward Micklethwaite] Curr, *The Australian Race: Its Origin, Languages, Customs, Place of Landing in Australia, and the Routes by Which It Spread Itself over That Continent*, vol. II, Melbourne, John Ferres, 1886–1887, p. 68.

[48]Ibid.; Eylmann, *Die Eingeborenen*, p. 208.

[49]Howitt, *Native Tribe*, pp. 277, 430.

[50]Ibid., p. 195.

Dieri, when a child has an accident, his relatives beat themselves on the head with sticks or boomerangs, until the blood streams down their faces. They believe they are relieving the child's pain thereby.[51] Elsewhere, people imagine they obtain the same result with an additional totemic ceremony.[52] These are analogous to the rite to erase the consequences of a ritual lapse, already considered.[53] To be sure, although in these last cases there are neither wounds nor blows nor physical sufferings of any kind, the rite does not differ in essence from the preceding ones. The point in all cases is to turn aside an evil or expiate a misdeed with extra ritual proceedings.

Such are the only piacular rites, other than rites of mourning, that I have managed to collect for Australia. In all likelihood, some must have escaped me, and we may surmise as well that others went unnoticed by the observers. Still, if only a few have been discovered up to now, the likely reason is that they do not count for much in the cult. Since the rites that express painful emotions are relatively few in primitive religions, we see how far those religions are from being daughters of apprehension and fear. No doubt, the reason is that although the Australian leads an impoverished existence compared to that of more civilized peoples, he by contrast asks so little of life that he contents himself with little. His only need is for nature to follow its normal course, for the seasons to move in regular succession, and for the rain to fall at the usual time, abundantly but not excessively. Great disturbances in the cosmic order are always unusual. Thus it was noteworthy that most of the regular piacular rites I reported above were observed in the tribes of the center, where droughts are frequent and constitute genuine public disasters. Still, it is surprising that piacular rites for the specific purpose of expiating sin appear to be almost entirely absent. Nonetheless the Australian, like any man, must commit ritual misdeeds that it would be in his interest to atone for. And so I raise the question whether the silence of the texts on this point may not be put down to inadequacies of observation.

Although the substantive evidence I have managed to call upon is sparse, it is nonetheless instructive.

When we study piacular rites in the more advanced religions, in which the religious forces are individualized, the rites seem to be closely connected

[51]Gason, *The Dieyerie Tribe*, vol. II, p. 69. The same procedure is used to redeem a ridiculous act. When, through clumsiness or otherwise, a person has made those near him laugh, he asks them to hit him on the head until the blood flows. Then things are restored and the person others were laughing at joins in the gaiety of those around him (ibid., p. 70).

[52]Eylmann, *Die Eingeborenen*, pp. 212, 447.

[53]See above, p. 389.

with anthropomorphic ideas. If the faithful impose privations on themselves and undergo tortures, they do so to disarm the malevolence that they impute to sacred beings to whom they think they are subject. To appease the hate or anger of those beings, the faithful anticipate their demands, striking themselves so as not to be struck by them. It seems, then, that these practices could only have been born when gods and spirits were conceived of as moral persons susceptible to passions like those of humans. For this reason, Robertson Smith believed he could assign expiatory sacrifices and sacrificial offerings to a relatively recent date. According to him, the shedding of blood that is characteristic of these rites was at first merely a process of communion: Man spilled his blood on the altar to tighten the bonds between himself and his god. The rite presumably did not take on a piacular and punitive character until its original meaning had been forgotten and until the new idea people had of the sacred beings enabled them to ascribe a different function to it.[54]

But since piacular rites go as far back as the Australian societies, they cannot be assigned so recent an origin. Moreover, with one exception,[55] all those I have just mentioned are independent of any anthropomorphic idea, for they involve neither gods nor spirits. Abstinences and bloodletting stop famines and cure sicknesses, acting on their own. The work of no spiritual being is thought to intrude between the rite and the effects it is thought to bring about. Hence it was only later that mythic personalities came onto the scene. They helped to make the ritual mechanism easier to imagine, once it was established, but they are not conditions of its existence. That mechanism was instituted for different reasons and owes its efficacy to a different cause.

It acts through the collective forces that it sets in motion. Does a misfortune threatening the collectivity seem imminent? The collectivity comes together, as it does in consequence of mourning, and a sense of disquiet naturally dominates the assembled group. As always, the effect of making these feelings shared is to intensify them. Through being affirmed, these feelings are excited and inflamed, reaching an intensity that is expressed in the equivalent intensity of the actions that express them. In the same way that people utter terrible cries upon the death of a close relative, they are caught up by the imminence of a collective misfortune and feel the need to tear and destroy. To satisfy this need, they strike and wound themselves and make their blood flow. But when emotions are as vivid as this, even if they are painful,

---

[54][William Robertson Smith, *Lectures on*] *the Religion of the Semites,* lect. XI [London, A. and C. Black, 1889].

[55]According to Gason, this is true of the Dieri invoking the water Mura-muras in time of drought.

they are in no way depressing. Quite the contrary, they point to a state of effervescence that entails the mobilization of all our own active energy and, in addition, a further influx from outside ourselves.

That this excitation has arisen from a sad event matters little, for it is no less real and not specifically different from the one observed in joyful feasts. As a matter of fact, it sometimes manifests itself through movements of the same kind. The same frenzy takes hold of the faithful, along with the same inclination to sexual debauchery—a sure sign of great nervous overexcitement. Robertson Smith had already noticed this curious influence of the sad rites in the Semitic cults. "In difficult times," he says, "when men's thoughts were usually somber, they turned to the physical excitements of religion, just as, now, they take refuge in wine. Among the Semites, as a general rule, when worship began with wailing and lamentation—as in the mourning of Adonis or in the great expiatory rites that became common in later times—a sudden revolution created an explosion of gaiety and rejoicing to follow the gloomy service with which the ceremony had begun."[56] In short, while the religious ceremonies start out from a disquieting or saddening fact, they retain their power to enliven the emotional state of the group and the individuals.

Simply by being collective, religious ceremonies raise the vital tone. When one feels life in oneself—in the form of painful anger or joyful enthusiasm—one does not believe in death; one is reassured, one takes greater courage, and, subjectively, everything happens as if the rite really had set aside the danger that was feared. This is how curative or preventive virtues came to be ascribed to the movements that the rite is made of: the cries uttered, the blood shed, the wounds inflicted upon oneself or others. And since these various torments necessarily cause suffering, in the end, suffering in itself is regarded as the means of conjuring away evil and curing sickness.[57] Later, when most of the religious forces had taken the form of personified spirits,* the efficacy of these practices was explained by imagining their purpose to be propitiation of a malevolent or angry god. But these ideas reflect only the rite and the feelings it arouses; they are an interpretation of it, not its determining cause.

A ritual lapse works no differently. It, too, is a menace for the collectivity. It strikes at the moral existence of the collectivity because it strikes at the

---

Personnalités spirituelles.

[56]Robertson Smith, *Religion of the Semites*, p. 262.

[57]It is possible, by the way, that the belief in the morally uplifting virtues of suffering (see above, p. 317) played some role in this. Since pain sanctifies and since it raises the religious level of the faithful, it can also uplift the faithful when they have fallen below the norm.

beliefs of the collectivity. But let the anger caused by a ritual misdeed be expressed openly and energetically, and the evil it caused is counteracted. If that anger is strongly felt by all, the reason is that the infraction committed is an exception, while the shared faith is still intact. Hence the moral unity of the group is not in danger. The pain inflicted as expiation is but a manifestation of this public anger and physical proof of its unanimity. In this way, the pain really does have the redeeming powers that people impute to it. Basically, the feeling at the root of the properly expiatory rites is no different in kind from the one we have found at the root of other piacular rites. It is a sort of angry sorrow, which tends to express itself through destructive acts. At times, this pain is relieved to the detriment of the very one who feels it; at times, it is at the expense of an outside third party. But the psychic mechanism is basically the same in both cases.[58]

IV

One of the greatest services Robertson Smith rendered to the science of religions is to have called attention to the ambiguity of the idea of the sacred.

Religious forces are of two kinds. Some are benevolent, guardians of physical and moral order, as well as dispensers of life, health, and all the qualities that men value. This is true of the totemic principle, which is spread out over the whole species, of the mythical ancestor, of the animal-protector, of civilizing heroes, and of tutelary gods in all their kinds and degrees. Whether they are thought of as distinct personalities or as diffused energies makes little difference. In both forms, they play the same role and affect the consciousness of the faithful in the same manner. They inspire a respect that is full of love and gratitude. The persons and things that are ordinarily in contact with them participate in the same feelings and the same quality. They are sacred persons and things. So, too, are the places consecrated to the cult, the objects used in the regular rites, the priests, the ascetics, and so on. On the other hand, there are evil and impure powers, bringers of disorder, causes of death and sickness, instigators of sacrilege. The only feelings man has for them is a fear that usually has a component of horror. Such are the forces on which and through which the sorcerer acts: those that come from corpses and from menstrual blood, those that unleash every profanation of holy [saintes] things, and so on. The spirits of the dead and the evil genies of all kinds are its personified forms.

Between these two categories of forces and beings, there is the sharpest possible contrast, up to and including the most radical antagonism. The good

[58]Cf. what I have said about expiation in my *Division du travail social*, 3d ed., Paris, F. Alcan, 1902, pp. 64ff.

and wholesome forces push far away from themselves those other forces, which negate and contradict them. Besides, the first are forbidden to the second. Any contact between them is considered the worst of profanations. This is the archetype of those prohibitions between sacred things of different kinds, whose existence I have mentioned along the way.[59] Since women during menstruation are impure, and especially so at the first appearance of the menses, they are rigorously sequestered at that time, and men must have no contact with them.[60] The bull roarers and the churingas are never in contact with a dead person.[61] A sacrilegious person is cut off from the society of the faithful and not allowed to take part in the cult. The whole of religious life gravitates around two opposite poles, then, their opposition being the same as that between the pure and the impure, the saint and the sacrilegious person, the divine and the diabolical.

But although opposite to one another, these two aspects of religious life are at the same time closely akin. First, both have the same relation to profane beings. They must abstain from all contact with impure things and with very holy [*saintes*] things. The former are no less forbidden than the latter, and they, too, are taken out of circulation, which is to say that they are also sacred [*sacrés*]. To be sure, the two do not provoke identical feelings. Disgust and horror are one thing and respect another. Nonetheless, for actions to be the same in both cases, the feelings expressed must not be different in kind. In fact, there actually is a certain horror in religious respect, especially when it is very intense; and the fear inspired by malignant powers is not without a certain reverential quality. Indeed, the shades of difference between these two attitudes are sometimes so elusive that it is not always easy to say in just which state of mind the faithful are. Among certain Semitic peoples, pork was forbidden, but one did not always know with certainty if it was forbidden as an impure thing or as a holy [*sainte*] thing.[62] And the same point can be applied to a very large number of dietary restrictions.

There is more: An impure thing or an evil power often becomes a holy thing or a tutelary power—and vice versa—without changing in nature, but

[59]See pp. 304–306 above.

[60]Spencer and Gillen, *Native Tribes*, p. 460; Spencer and Gillen, *Northern Tribes*, p. 601; Roth, [*Superstition, Magic and Medicine*], *North Queensland Ethnography*, Bull. 5 [Brisbane, G. A. Vaughn, 1903], p. 24. There is no need to multiply references in support of such a well-known fact.

[61]However, Spencer and Gillen cite a case in which churingas are placed under the head of the dead person (Spencer and Gillen, *Native Tribes*, p. 156). As they acknowledge, however, this is unique and abnormal (ibid., p. 157), and it is strenuously denied by Strehlow (*Aranda*, vol. II, p. 79).

[62]Robertson Smith, *Religion of the Semites*, p. 153, cf. p. 446, the additional note titled "Holiness, Uncleanness and Taboo."

simply through a change in external circumstances. We have seen that the soul of the dead person, at first a dreaded principle, is transformed into a protective genie when the mourning is over. Similarly the corpse, which at first inspires only terror and distance, is later treated as a venerated relic. Funeral anthropophagy, widely practiced in the Australian societies, is evidence of this transformation.[63] The totemic animal is archetypically the holy being, but for him who wrongfully consumes its flesh, it is a principle of death. The person guilty of sacrilege is, generally speaking, only a profane person who has been infected by a benevolent religious force. Changing its nature when it changes its habitat, this force pollutes rather than sanctifies.[64] The blood that comes from the genital organs of a woman, though it is obviously as impure as that of the menses, is often used as a remedy against sickness.[65] The victim immolated in expiatory sacrifices is saturated with impurity, because the sins to be expiated have been made to converge upon it. However, once it is slaughtered, its flesh and blood are put to the most pious uses.[66]

Inversely, although communion is a religious procedure whose function is ordinarily consecration, it sometimes has the same effects as a sacrilege. Individuals who have communed together are, in certain cases, forced to flee one another, like carriers of plague. It is as though they have become sources of dangerous contamination for one another. The sacred bond that joins them separates them at the same time. Communions of this sort are common in Australia. One of the most typical has been observed among the Narrinyeri and neighboring tribes. When a child comes into the world, its parents carefully preserve its umbilical cord, which is thought to contain some part of the child's soul. Two individuals who exchange umbilical cords preserved in this way commune by the very fact of this exchange; it is as though they exchanged souls. But by the same token, they are forbidden to touch one another, to speak to one another, and even to see one another. It is as though they were objects of horror for one another.[67]

[63]Howitt, *Native Tribes*, pp. 448–450; Brough Smyth, *Aborigines of Victoria*, vol. I, pp. 118, 120; Dawson, *The Australian Aborigines*, p. 67; Eyre, *Journals of Expedition*, vol. II, p. 257; [Walter Edmund] Roth, "Burial Ceremonies," p. 367.

[64]See pp. 324–325 above.

[65]Spencer and Gillen, *Native Tribes*, p. 464; Spencer and Gillen, *Northern Tribes*, p. 599.

[66]For example, among the Israelites, the altar is purified with the blood of the expiatory victim (Lev. 4: 5ff.); the flesh is burned, and the ashes are used to make a purifying water (Num.: 19.)

[67]Taplin, "The Narrinyeri Tribe," in [James Dominick Woods, *The Native Tribes of South Australia*, Adelaide, E. S. Wigg, 1879], pp. 32–34. When the two individuals who have exchanged their umbilical cords belong to different tribes, they are used as agents of intertribal commerce. In this case, the exchange of cords takes place shortly after their births and through the intermediary of their respective parents.

So the pure and the impure are not two separate genera but two varieties of the same genus that includes all sacred things. There are two sorts of sacred, lucky and unlucky; and not only is there no radical discontinuity between the two opposite forms, but the same object can pass from one to the other without changing its nature. The impure is made from the pure, and vice versa. The possibility of such transformations constitutes the ambiguity of the sacred.

But while Robertson Smith had a keen sense of this ambiguity, he never accounted for it explicitly. He confined himself to pointing out that since all religious forces are intense and contagious, in whatever direction their influence is exercised, the wise thing is to approach them with respectful precautions. It seemed to him that the family resemblance they all have could be accounted for in this way, despite the contrasts that otherwise distinguish them. But first of all, that only shifted the question. Still to be shown was how the powers of evil come to have the intensity and contagiousness of the others. Put differently, how does it happen that these powers are of a religious nature? Second, the energy and volatility common to both do not enable us to understand how, despite the conflict between them, they can transform themselves into one another or replace one another in their respective functions, or how the pure can contaminate while the impure sometimes sanctifies.[68]

The explanation of the piacular rites that I have just proposed enables us to answer this twofold question.

We have seen that the evil powers actually result from and symbolize these rites. When society is going through events that sadden, distress, or anger it, it pushes its members to give witness to their sadness, distress, or anger through expressive actions. It demands crying, lamenting, and wounding oneself and others as a matter of duty. It does so because those collective demonstrations, as well as the moral communion they simultaneously bear witness to and reinforce, restore to the group the energy that the events

---

[68]It is true that [William Robertson] Smith does not accept the reality of these substitutions and transformations. According to him, the expiatory victim could purify only because it was itself in no way impure. From the beginning, it was a holy thing; it was intended to reestablish, through communion, the ties of kinship that united the worshipper to his god, after a ritual lapse had loosened or broken them. For that operation, they chose an exceptionally holy animal, so that communion would be more efficacious and might remove the effects of the wrong more completely. Only when they had ceased to understand the meaning of the rite was the sacrosanct animal considered impure (*Religion of the Semites*, pp. 347ff.). But it is inadmissible that such universal beliefs and practices as those that we find at the basis of expiatory sacrifice should result from a mere error of interpretation. In fact, it is beyond doubt that the impurity of the sin was loaded onto the expiatory victim. Moreover, we have just seen that these transformations from pure to impure, or vice versa, are found in the simplest societies we know.

threatened to take away, and thus enables it to recover its equilibrium. It is this experience that man is interpreting when he imagines evil beings outside him whose hostility, whether inherent or transitory, can be disarmed only through human suffering. So these beings are nothing other than collective states objectified; they are society itself seen in one of its aspects. But we also know that the beneficent powers are not made any differently; they too result from and express collective life; they too represent society, but society captured in a very different posture—that is, at the moment when it confidently affirms itself and zealously presses things into the service of the ends it is pursuing. Since these two kinds of forces have a common origin, it is not surprising that, even though moving in opposite directions, they should have the same nature, that they should be equally intense and contagious—and hence, prohibited and sacred.

From precisely this fact, we can understand how they are transformed into one another. Since they reflect the emotional state in which the group finds itself, a change in that state is sufficient to make the forces themselves change direction. When the mourning ends, the household of the deceased has been calmed by the mourning itself; it gathers new confidence; the individuals are relieved of the painful pressure that was exerted upon them; they feel more at ease. It therefore seems to them that the spirit of the deceased has set aside its hostile feelings in order to become a benevolent protector. The other transmutations, examples of which I have cited, are to be explained in the same way. What makes a thing sacred is, as I have shown, the collective feeling of which it is the object. If, in violation of the prohibitions that isolate it, it comes in contact with a profane person, this same feeling will spread contagiously to that person and mark him with a special quality. However, when it arrives at that, it finds itself in a very different state from the one in which it was at the outset. Having been shocked and angered by the profanation entailed by this wrongful, unnatural extension, it becomes aggressive and inclined toward destructive violence; it is inclined to seek revenge for the trespass it has endured. For this reason, the infected subject is as though invaded by a virulent and noxious force, threatening to all that comes near him; thereafter, he inspires nothing but distance and repugnance, as though he was marked with a taint or stain. And yet the cause of this stain is the very psychic state that in other circumstances consecrated and sanctified. But let the anger thus aroused be satisfied by an expiatory rite, and it subsides, relieved. The offended feeling is propitiated and returns to its initial state. Thus, it again acts as it acted at first. Instead of contaminating, it sanctifies. Because it goes on infecting the object to which it has become attached, that object cannot become profane and religiously indifferent again. But the direction of the religious force that appears to occupy it has been inverted. From being impure it has become pure and an instrument of purification.

In summary, the two poles of religious life correspond to the two opposite states through which all social life passes. There is the same contrast between the lucky and the unlucky sacred as between the states of collective euphoria and dysphoria. But because both are equally collective, the mythological constructions that symbolize them are in their very essence closely related. While the feelings placed in common vary from extreme dejection to extreme high-spiritedness, from painful anger to ecstatic enthusiasm, the result in all cases is communion among individual consciousnesses and mutual calming. While the fundamental process is always the same, different circumstances color it differently. In the end, then, it is the unity and diversity of social life that creates at the same time the unity and the diversity of sacred beings and things.

This ambiguity is not peculiar to the idea of the sacred alone. Something of this same quality is to be found in all the rites studied. Of course, it was necessary to distinguish them. Treating them as one and the same would have been to misunderstand the multiple aspects of religious life. But however different they may be, there is no discontinuity between them. Quite the contrary, they are overlapping and even interchangeable. I have already shown that rites of offering and communion, mimetic rites, and commemorative rites often perform the same functions. One might think that the negative cult is more clearly separated from the positive cult, yet we have seen that the negative cult can nonetheless bring about positive effects identical to those of the positive cult. The same results are obtained through fasts, abstinences, and self-mutilation as through communions, offerings, and commemorations. Conversely, offerings and sacrifices imply privations and renunciations of all kinds. The continuity between ascetic and piacular rites is even more apparent. Both are made of sufferings, accepted or endured, to which similar efficacy is ascribed. Thus, the practices no more fall into two separate genera than the beliefs do. However complex the outward manifestations of religious life may be, its inner essence is simple, and one and the same. Everywhere it fulfills the same need and derives from the same state of mind. In all its forms, its object is to lift man above himself and to make him live a higher life than he would if he obeyed only his individual impulses. The beliefs express this life in terms of representations; the rites organize and regulate its functioning.

CONCLUSION

I said at the beginning of this book that the religion whose study I was undertaking contained within itself the most characteristic elements of religious life. The truth of that proposition can now be tested. However simple the system I have studied may be, I have nonetheless found within it all the great ideas and all the principal forms of ritual conduct on which even the most advanced religions are based: the distinction between sacred and profane things; the ideas of soul, spirit, mythical personality, national and even international divinity; a negative cult with the ascetic practices that are its extreme form; rites of sacrifice and communion; mimetic, commemorative, and piacular rites. Nothing essential is absent. Thus I have reason to be confident that the results achieved are not specific to totemism but can help us understand what religion in general is.

Some will object that a single religion, whatever its geographic spread, is a narrow basis for such an induction. It is by no means my intent to ignore what an expanded test can add to the persuasiveness of a theory. But it is no less true that when a law has been proved by a single well-made experiment, this proof is universally valid. If a scientist managed to intercept the secret of life in only a single case, the truths thus obtained would be applicable to all living things, including the most advanced, even if this case was the simplest protoplasmic being imaginable. Accordingly if, in the very humble societies just studied, I have managed to capture some of the elements that comprise the most fundamental religious ideas, there is no reason not to extend the most general results of this research to other religions. In fact, it is inconceivable that the same effect could be sometimes due now to one cause, now to another, according to the circumstances, unless fundamentally the two causes were but one. A single idea cannot express one reality here and a different one there unless this duality is merely apparent. If, among certain peoples, the ideas "sacred," "soul," and "gods" can be explained sociologically, then scientifically we must presume that the same explanation is valid in principle for all the peoples among whom the same ideas are found with essentially the same characteristics. Assuming that I am not mistaken, then, at least some of my conclusions can legitimately be generalized. The time has come to draw these out. And an induction of this sort, based on a well-defined experiment, is less reckless than so many cursory generalizations that, in their striving to reach the essence of religion in a single stroke without

418

grounding themselves in the analysis of any particular religion, are at great risk of floating away into the void.

I

Most often, the theorists who have set out to express religion in rational terms have regarded it as being, first and foremost, a system of ideas that correspond to a definite object. That object has been conceived in different ways—nature, the infinite, the unknowable, the ideal, and so forth—but these differences are of little importance. In every case, the representations—that is, the beliefs—were considered the essential element of religion. For their part, rites appeared from this standpoint to be no more than an external, contingent, and physical translation of those inward states that alone were deemed to have intrinsic value. This notion is so widespread that most of the time debates on the topic of religion turn around and about on the question of whether religion can or cannot be reconciled with science—that is, whether there is room alongside scientific knowledge for another form of thought held to be specifically religious.

But the believers—the men who, living a religious life, have a direct sense of what constitutes religion—object that, in terms of their day-to-day experience, this way of seeing does not ring true. Indeed, they sense that the true function of religion is not to make us think, enrich our knowledge, or add representations of a different sort and source to those we owe to science. Its true function is to make us act and to help us live. The believer who has communed with his god is not simply a man who sees new truths that the unbeliever knows not; he is a man who *is stronger.* * Within himself, he feels more strength to endure the trials of existence or to overcome them. He is as though lifted above the human miseries, because he is lifted above his human condition. He believes he is delivered from evil—whatever the form in which he conceives of evil. The first article of any faith is belief in salvation by faith.

But it is hard to see how a mere idea could have that power. In fact, an idea is but one element of ourselves. How could it confer on us powers that are superior to those given us in our natural makeup? As rich in emotive power as an idea may be, it cannot add anything to our natural vitality; it can only release emotive forces that are already within us, neither creating nor increasing them. From the fact that we imagine an object as worthy of being loved and sought after, it does not follow that we should feel stronger. Energies greater than those at our disposal must come from the object, and, more

---

* *Qui peut davantage.* Literally "who *is capable of* more." Durkheim italicized *peut.*

than that, we must have some means of making them enter into us and blend into our inner life. To achieve this, it is not enough that we think about them; it is indispensable that we place ourselves under their influence, that we turn ourselves in the direction from which we can best feel that influence. In short, we must act; and so we must repeat the necessary acts as often as is necessary to renew their effects. From this standpoint, it becomes apparent that the set of regularly repeated actions that make up the cult regains all its importance. In fact, anyone who has truly practiced a religion knows very well that it is the cult that stimulates the feelings of joy, inner peace, serenity, and enthusiasm that, for the faithful, stand as experimental proof of their beliefs. The cult is not merely a system of signs by which the faith is outwardly expressed; it is the sum total of means by which that faith is created and recreated periodically. Whether the cult consists of physical operations or mental ones, it is always the cult that is efficacious.

This entire study rests on the postulate that the unanimous feeling of believers down the ages cannot be mere illusion. Therefore, like a recent apologist of faith,[1] I accept that religious belief rests on a definite experience, whose demonstrative value is, in a sense, not inferior to that of scientific experiments, though it is different. I too think "that a tree is known by its fruits,"[2] and that its fertility is the best proof of what its roots are worth. But merely because there exists a "religious experience," if you will, that is grounded in some manner (is there, by the way, any experience that is not?), it by no means follows that the reality which grounds it should conform objectively with the idea the believers have of it. The very fact that the way in which this reality has been conceived has varied infinitely in different times is enough to prove that none of these conceptions expresses it adequately. If the scientist sets it down as axiomatic that the sensations of heat and light that men have correspond to some objective cause, he does not thereby conclude that this cause is the same as it appears to the senses. Likewise, even if the feelings the faithful have are not imaginary, they still do not constitute privileged intuitions; there is no reason whatever to think that they inform us better about the nature of their object than ordinary sensations do about the nature of bodies and their properties. To discover what that object consists of, then, we must apply to those sensations an analysis similar to the one that has replaced the senses' representation of the world with a scientific and conceptual one.

This is precisely what I have tried to do. We have seen that this reality—

[1]William James, *The Varieties of Religious Experience* [London, Longmans, 1902].

[2]Ibid. (p. 19 of the French translation).

which mythologies have represented in so many different forms, but which is the objective, universal, and eternal cause of those *sui generis* sensations of which religious experience is made—is society. I have shown what moral forces it develops and how it awakens that feeling of support, safety, and protective guidance which binds the man of faith to his cult. It is this reality that makes him rise above himself. Indeed, this is the reality that makes him, for what makes man is that set of intellectual goods which is civilization, and civilization is the work of society. In this way is explained the preeminent role of the cult in all religions, whatever they are. This is so because society cannot make its influence felt unless it is in action, and it is in action only if the individuals who comprise it are assembled and acting in common. It is through common action that society becomes conscious of and affirms itself; society is above all an active cooperation. As I have shown, even collective ideas and feelings are possible only through the overt movements that symbolize them.[3] Thus it is action that dominates religious life, for the very reason that society is its source.

To all the reasons adduced to justify this conception, a final one can be added that emerges from this book as a whole. Along the way, I have established that the fundamental categories of thought, and thus science itself, have religious origins. The same has been shown to be true of magic, and thus of the various techniques derived from magic. Besides, it has long been known that, until a relatively advanced moment in evolution, the rules of morality and law were not distinct from ritual prescriptions. In short, then, we can say that nearly all the great social institutions were born in religion.[4] For the principal features of collective life to have begun as none other than various features of religious life, it is evident that religious life must necessarily have been the eminent form and, as it were, the epitome of collective life. If religion gave birth to all that is essential in society, that is so because the idea of society is the soul of religion.

Thus religious forces are human forces, moral forces. Probably because collective feelings become conscious of themselves only by settling upon external objects, those very forces could not organize themselves without taking some of their traits from things. In this way, they took on a kind of

[3]See above, pp. 231ff.

[4]Only one form of social activity has not as yet been explicitly linked to religion: economic activity. Nevertheless, the techniques that derive from magic turn out, by this very fact, to have indirectly religious origins. Furthermore, economic value is a sort of power or efficacy, and we know the religious origins of the idea of power. Since mana can be conferred by wealth, wealth itself has some. From this we see that the idea of economic value and that of religious value cannot be unrelated; but the nature of these relationships has not yet been studied.

physical nature; they came to mingle as such with the life of the physical world, and through them it was thought possible to explain events in that world. But when they are considered only from this standpoint and in this role, we see only what is most superficial about them. In reality, the essential elements out of which they are made are borrowed from consciousness. Ordinarily, they do not seem to have a human character except when they are thought of in human form,[5] but even the most impersonal and most anonymous are nothing other than objectified feelings.

Only by seeing religions in this way does it become possible to detect their real meaning. If we rely on appearances, the rites often seem to be purely manual operations—anointings, purifications, meals. To consecrate a thing, one places it in contact with a source of religious energy, just as today a body is placed in contact with a source of heat or electricity in order to heat or electrify it. The procedures used in the two cases are not essentially different. Understood in this way, religious technique seems to be a kind of mystical mechanics. But these physical operations are but the outer envelope in which mental operations lie hidden. In the end, the point is not to exert a kind of physical constraint upon blind and, more than that, imaginary forces but to reach, fortify, and discipline consciousnesses. The lower religions have sometimes been called materialistic. That term is incorrect. All religions, even the crudest, are in a sense spiritualistic. The powers they bring into play are, above all, spiritual, and their primary function is to act upon moral life. In this way, we understand that what was done in the name of religion cannot have been done in vain, for it is necessarily the society of men, it is humanity, that has reaped the fruits.

It may be asked, Exactly what society is it that in this way becomes the substrate of religious life? Is it the real society, such as it exists and functions before our eyes, with the moral and juridical organization that it has toiled to fashion for itself over the course of history? But that society is full of flaws and imperfections. In that society, good rubs shoulders with evil, injustice is ever on the throne, and truth is continually darkened by error. How could a being so crudely made inspire the feelings of love, ardent enthusiasm, and willing self-sacrifice that all the religions demand of their faithful? Those perfect beings that are the gods cannot have taken their traits from such a mediocre, sometimes even base, reality.

Would it not be instead the perfect society, in which justice and truth reigned, and from which evil in all its forms was uprooted? No one disputes

---

[5]It is for this reason that Frazer and even Preuss set the impersonal religious forces outside religion, or at most at its threshold, in order to relate them to magic.

that this perfect society has a close relationship to religious sentiment, for religions are said to aim at realizing it. However, this society is not an empirical fact, well defined and observable; it is a fancy, a dream with which men have lulled their miseries but have never experienced in reality. It is a mere idea that expresses in consciousness our more or less obscure aspirations toward the good, the beautiful, and the ideal. These aspirations have their roots in us; since they come from the very depths of our being, nothing outside us can account for them. Furthermore, in and of themselves, they are already religious; hence, far from being able to explain religion, the ideal society presupposes it.[6]

But to see only the idealistic side of religion is to simplify arbitrarily. In its own way, religion is realistic. There is no physical or moral ugliness, no vice, and no evil that has not been deified. There have been gods of theft and trickery, lust and war, sickness and death. As uplifted as its idea of divinity is, Christianity itself was obliged to make a place in its mythology for the spirit of evil. Satan is an essential component of the Christian machinery; yet, even if he is an impure being, he is not a profane being. The anti-god is a god—lower and subordinate, it is true, yet invested with broad powers; he is even the object of rites, at the very least negative ones. Far from ignoring and disregarding the real society, religion is its image, reflecting all its features, even the most vulgar and repellent. Everything is to be found in it, and if we most often see good triumphing over evil, life over death, and the forces of light over the forces of darkness, this is because it is no different in reality. If the relationship between these forces was reversed, life would be impossible, whereas in fact, life maintains itself and even tends to develop.

But it is quite true that even if the mythologies and theologies allow a clear glimpse of the reality, the reality we find in them has been enlarged, transformed, and idealized. The most primitive religions are no different in this respect from the most modern and the most refined. We have seen, for example, how the Arunta place at the beginning of time a mythical society whose organization exactly replicates the one that still exists today. It is made up of the same clans and phratries, it is subject to the same marriage rules, and it practices the same rites. But the personages that comprise it are ideal beings endowed with capacities to which mere mortals cannot lay claim. Belonging to animality and humanity at the same time, their nature is not only higher but also different. The evil powers undergo a similar metamorphosis

---

[6][Emile] Boutroux, *Science et religion* [*dans la philosophie contemporaine*, Paris, E. Flammarion, 1907], pp. 206–207.

in that religion. It is as though evil itself undergoes refinement and idealization. The question that arises is where this idealization comes from.

One proposed answer is that man has a natural capacity to idealize, that is, to replace the real world with a different one to which he travels in thought. But such an answer changes the terms of the problem, neither solving nor even advancing it. This persistent idealization is a fundamental feature of religions. So to explain religions in terms of an innate capacity to idealize is simply to replace one word with its equivalent; it is like saying that man created religion because he has a religious nature. Yet the animal knows only one world: the world it perceives through experience, internal as well as external. Man alone has the capacity to conceive of the ideal and add it to the real. Where, then, does this remarkable distinction come from? Before taking it to be a primary fact or a mysterious virtue that eludes science, one should first have made sure that this remarkable distinction does not arise from conditions that can be determined empirically.

My proposed explanation of religion has the specific advantage of providing an answer to this question, since what defines the sacred is that the sacred is added to the real. And since the ideal is defined in the same way, we cannot explain the one without explaining the other. We have seen, in fact, that if collective life awakens religious thought when it rises to a certain intensity, that is so because it brings about a state of effervescence that alters the conditions of psychic activity. The vital energies become hyperexcited, the passions more intense, the sensations more powerful; there are indeed some that are produced only at this moment. Man does not recognize himself; he feels somehow transformed and in consequence transforms his surroundings. To account for the very particular impressions he receives, he imputes to the things with which he is most directly in contact properties that they do not have, exceptional powers and virtues that the objects of ordinary experience do not possess. In short, upon the real world where profane life is lived, he superimposes another that, in a sense, exists only in his thought, but one to which he ascribes a higher kind of dignity than he ascribes to the real world of profane life. In two respects, then, this other world is an ideal one.

Thus the formation of an ideal is by no means an irreducible datum that eludes science. It rests on conditions that can be uncovered through observation. It is a natural product of social life. If society is to be able to become conscious of itself and keep the sense it has of itself at the required intensity, it must assemble and concentrate. This concentration brings about an uplifting of moral life that is expressed by a set of ideal conceptions in which the new life thus awakened is depicted. These ideal conceptions correspond to the onrush of psychic forces added at that moment to those we have at our disposal for the everyday tasks of life. A society can neither create nor recreate itself without creating some kind of ideal by the same stroke. This creation is not a sort of optional extra step by which society, being already made, merely adds finishing touches; it is the act by which society makes itself, and remakes itself, periodically. Thus, when we set the ideal society in opposition to the real society, like two antagonists supposedly leading us in opposite directions, we are reifying and opposing abstractions. The ideal society is not outside the real one but is part of it. Far from our being divided between them as though between two poles that repel one another, we cannot hold to the one without holding to the other. A society is not constituted simply by the mass of individuals who comprise it, the ground they occupy, the things they use, or the movements they make, but above all by the idea it has of itself. And there is no doubt that society sometimes hesitates over the manner in which it must conceive itself. It feels pulled in all directions. When such conflicts break out, they are not between the ideal and the reality but between different ideals, between the ideal of yesterday and that of today, between the ideal that has the authority of tradition and one that is only coming into being. Studying how ideals come to evolve certainly has its place, but no matter how this problem is solved, the fact remains that the whole of it unfolds in the world of the ideal.

Therefore the collective ideal that religion expresses is far from being due to some vague capacity innate to the individual; rather, it is in the school of collective life that the individual has learned to form ideals. It is by assimilating the ideals worked out by society that the individual is able to conceive of the ideal. It is society that, by drawing him into its sphere of action, has given him the need to raise himself above the world of experience, while at the same time furnishing him the means of imagining another. It is society that built this new world while building itself, because it is society that the new world expresses. There is nothing mysterious about the faculty of idealization, then, whether in the individual or in the group. This faculty is not a sort of luxury, which man could do without, but a condition of his existence. If he had not acquired it, he would not be a social being, which is to say that he would not be man. To be sure, collective ideals tend to become individualized as they become incarnate in individuals. Each person understands them in his own way and gives them an individual imprint, some elements being taken out and others being added. As the individual personality develops and becomes an autonomous source of action, the personal ideal diverges from the social one. But if we want to understand that aptitude for living outside the real, which is seemingly so remarkable, all we need to do is relate it to the social conditions on which it rests.

But the last thing to do is to see this theory of religion as merely a refurbishment of historical materialism. That would be a total misunderstanding of my thought. In pointing out an essentially social thing in religion, I in no way mean to say that religion simply translates the material forms and immediate vital necessities of society into another language. I do indeed take it to be obvious that social life depends on and bears the mark of its material base, just as the mental life of the individual depends on the brain and indeed on the whole body. But collective consciousness is something other than a mere epiphenomenon of its morphological base, just as individual consciousness is something other than a mere product of the nervous system. If collective consciousness is to appear, a *sui generis* synthesis of individual consciousnesses must occur. The product of this synthesis is a whole world of feelings, ideas, and images that follow their own laws once they are born. They mutually attract one another, repel one another, fuse together, subdivide, and proliferate; and none of these combinations is directly commanded and necessitated by the state of the underlying reality. Indeed, the life thus unleashed enjoys such great independence that it sometimes plays about in forms that have no aim or utility of any kind, but only for the pleasure of affirming itself. I have shown that precisely this is often true of ritual activity and mythological thought.[7]

But if religion has social causes, how can the individual cult and the universalistic character of certain religions be explained? If it is born *in foro externo*,* how was it able to pass into the inner core of the individual and become ever more deeply implanted in him? If it is the work of definite and particular societies, how could it become detached enough from them to be conceived of as the common holding of all humanity?

Since, in the course of our study, we came upon the first seeds of individual religion and religious cosmopolitanism and saw how they were formed, we possess the most general elements of an answer to that twofold question.

I have shown that the religious force animating the clan becomes individualized by incarnating itself in individual consciousnesses. Secondary sacred beings are formed in this way, each individual having his own that is made in his own image, part of his intimate life, and at one with his fate. They are the soul, the individual totem, the protecting ancestor, and so forth.

---

*In the external world.

[7]See above, pp. 382ff. Cf. my article on the same question: "Représentations individuelles et représentations collectives," *RMM*, vol. VI, 1898 [pp. 273ff.].

These beings are the objects of rites that the worshipper can conduct on his own, apart from any group, so it is actually a primitive form of the individual cult. Of course, it is still only a very undeveloped cult, but that is because the cult expressing the individual personality could not be very well developed, given that the individual personality is at that stage still marked very slightly, with little value attributed to it. As individuals became more differentiated and the value of the person grew, the corresponding cult itself took on a larger role in religious life as a whole, at the same time more completely sealing itself off from the outside.

The existence of individual cults does not therefore imply anything that contradicts or complicates a sociological explanation of religion. The religious forces they address are merely collective forces in individualized forms. Even where religion seems to be entirely within the individual, the living source that feeds it is to be found in society. We can now judge the worth of the radical individualism that is intent on making religion out to be a purely individual thing: It misconceives the fundamental conditions of religious life. And if that radical individualism has remained in the state of unrealized theoretical aspiration up to now, that is because it is unrealizable in fact. A philosophy can very well be worked out in the silence of inward meditation, but not a faith. A faith above all is warmth, life, enthusiasm, enhancement of all mental activity, uplift of the individual above himself. Except by reaching outside himself, how could the individual add to the energies he possesses? How could he transcend himself by his own strength? The only hearth at which we can warm ourselves morally is the hearth made by the company of our fellow men; the only moral forces with which we can nourish our own and increase them are those we get from others. Let us even grant the existence of beings more or less like those the mythologies depict for us. If they are to have the useful influence over souls that is their *raison d'être*, we must believe in them. The beliefs are at work only when they are shared. We may well keep them them going for a time through personal effort alone, but they are neither born nor obtained in this way, and it is doubtful that they can be preserved under those conditions. In fact, the man who has a genuine faith feels an irrepressible need to spread it. To do so, he comes out of his isolation, he approaches others, he seeks to convince them, and it is the ardor of the convictions he brings about that in turn reinforces his own. That ardor would speedily dissipate if left alone.

What is true of religious individualism is true of religious universalism. Far from being exclusively the trait of a few very great religions, we have found it in the Australian system—not at its base, to be sure, but at its pinnacle. Bunjil, Daramulun, and Baiame are not mere tribal gods, since each is recognized by a number of different tribes. Their cult is in a sense international. So this conception is quite close to the one found in the most modern theologies. As a result, and for that very reason, certain writers have felt duty bound to deny its authenticity, even though its authenticity cannot be denied. But I have been able to show how this conception was formed.

Tribes that neighbor one another and are of the same civilization cannot help but have ongoing relationships with one another. All kinds of circumstances provide the occasion for contact. Apart from business, which is still rudimentary, there are marriages; international marriages are very common in Australia. In the course of these contacts, men naturally become conscious of the moral kinship that unites them. They have the same social organization, the same division into phratries, clans, and marriage classes; they conduct the same or similar initiation rites. The effect of mutual borrowings or agreements is to consolidate the spontaneous similarities. The gods to which such obviously identical institutions were attached could hardly remain distinct in people's minds. Everything brought them together; and in consequence, even supposing that each tribe had worked out its own notion of them independently they must as a matter of course have had a tendency to amalgamate. Furthermore, the likelihood is that the gods were first conceived in these intertribal assemblies, for they are gods of initiation, first and foremost, and various tribes are usually represented at the initiation ceremonies. Thus if sacred beings unconnected with any territorially defined society were formed, it is not because they had an extrasocial origin. Rather, it is because above these territorial groupings are others with more fluid boundaries. These other groupings do not have fixed frontiers but include a great many more or less neighboring and related tribes. The very special social life that emerges tends to spread over an area without clear limits. Quite naturally, the corresponding mythological personages are of the same character; their sphere of influence is not definite; they hover above the individual tribes and above the land. These are the great international gods.

Nothing in this situation is peculiar to Australian societies. There is no people, and no State, that is not engaged with another more or less undelimited society that includes all peoples and all States* with which it is directly or indirectly in contact; there is no national life that is not under the sway of an international collective life. The more we advance in history, the larger and the more important these international groupings become. In this way, we see how, in some cases, the universalistic tendency could develop to

*Durkheim capitalized "Church" and "State."

the point of affecting not only the highest ideas of the religious system but also the very principles on which it rests.

II

Thus there is something eternal in religion that is destined to outlive the succession of particular symbols in which religious thought has clothed itself. There can be no society that does not experience the need at regular intervals to maintain and strengthen the collective feelings and ideas that provide its coherence and its distinct individuality. This moral remaking can be achieved only through meetings, assemblies, and congregations in which the individuals, pressing close to one another, reaffirm in common their common sentiments. Such is the origin of ceremonies that, by their object, by their results, and by the techniques used, are not different in kind from ceremonies that are specifically religious. What basic difference is there between Christians' celebrating the principal dates of Christ's life, Jews' celebrating the exodus from Egypt or the promulgation of the Decalogue, and a citizens' meeting commemorating the advent of a new moral charter or some other great event of national life?

If today we have some difficulty imagining what the feasts and ceremonies of the future will be, it is because we are going through a period of transition and moral mediocrity. The great things of the past that excited our fathers no longer arouse the same zeal among us, either because they have passed so completely into common custom that we lose awareness of them or because they no longer suit our aspirations. Meanwhile, no replacement for them has yet been created. We are no longer electrified by those principles in whose name Christianity exhorted the masters to treat their slaves humanely; and besides, Christianity's idea of human equality and fraternity seems to us today to leave too much room for unjust inequalities. Its pity for the downcast seems to us too platonic. We would like one that is more vigorous but do not yet see clearly what it should be or how it might be realized in fact.

In short, the former gods are growing old or dying, and others have not been born. This is what voided Comte's attempt to organize a religion using old historical memories, artificially revived. It is life itself, and not a dead past, that can produce a living cult. But that state of uncertainty and confused anxiety cannot last forever. A day will come when our societies once again will know hours of creative effervescence during which new ideals will again spring forth and new formulas emerge to guide humanity for a time. And when those hours have been lived through, men will spontaneously feel the need to relive them in thought from time to time—that is, to preserve their memory by means of celebrations that regularly recreate their fruits. We have already seen how the [French] Revolution instituted a whole cycle of celebrations in order to keep the principles that inspired it eternally young. If that institution quickly perished, it is because the revolutionary faith lasted only briefly, and because disappointments and discouragements quickly replaced the first moment of enthusiasm. But although that work miscarried, it helps us to imagine what might have come to be under other conditions; and everything leads us to believe that the work will sooner or later be taken up again. There are no immortal gospels, and there is no reason to believe that humanity is incapable of conceiving new ones in the future. As to knowing what the symbols will be in which the new faith will come to express itself, whether they will resemble those of the past, whether they will better suit the reality to be expressed—that is a question that exceeds human faculties of prediction and that, moreover, is beside the point.

But feasts and rites—in a word, the cult—are not the whole of religion. Religion is not only a system of practices but also a system of ideas whose object is to express the world; even the humblest have their own cosmologies, as we have seen. No matter how these two elements of religious life may be related, they are nonetheless quite different. One is turned toward action, which it elicits and regulates; the other toward thought, which it enriches and organizes. Since they do not rest on the same conditions, then, there is reason to ask whether the ideas correspond to needs as universal and as permanent as the practices do.

When we impute specific traits to religious thought and believe its function is to express, by its own methods, a whole aspect of the real that eludes both ordinary knowledge and science, we naturally refuse to grant that the speculative role of religion could ever be overthrown. But it does not seem to me that analysis of the facts has demonstrated this specificity of religion. The religion we have just studied is one of those in which the symbols used are the most unsettling to reason. Everything about it seems full of mystery. At first glance, those beings that simultaneously participate in the most disparate kingdoms, multiply without ceasing to be one, and break up without diminishing, seem to belong to an entirely different world from the one in which we live. Some have even gone so far as to say that the thought that built it was totally ignorant of the laws of logic. Never, perhaps, has the contrast between reason and faith been so pronounced. If ever there was a moment in history when the difference between them must have stood out plainly, then that truly was the moment.

But I have noted, contrary to such appearances, that the realities to which religious speculation was applied then are the same ones that would later serve as objects of scientists' reflection. Those realities are nature, man, and society. The mystery that appears to surround them is entirely superficial and fades upon closer scrutiny. To have them appear as they are, it is enough to pull aside the veil with which the mythological imagination covered them. Religion strives to translate those realities into an intelligible language that does not differ in nature from that used by science. Both attempt to connect things to one another, establish internal relations between those things, classify them, and systematize them. We have even seen that the essential notions of scientific logic are of religious origin. Of course, science reworks those notions in order to use them. It distills out all sorts of extraneous elements and generally brings to all its efforts a critical spirit that is unknown in religion; it surrounds itself with precautions to "avoid haste and bias" and to keep passions, prejudices, and all subjective influences at bay. But these improvements in method are not enough to differentiate science from religion. In this regard, both pursue the same goal; scientific thought is only a more perfected form of religious thought. Hence it seems natural that religion should lose ground as science becomes better at performing its task.

There is no doubt, in fact, that this regression has taken place over the course of history. Although the offspring of religion, science tends to replace religion in everything that involves the cognitive and intellectual functions. Christianity has by now definitively sanctioned that replacement, in the realm of physical phenomena. Regarding matter as a profane thing par excellence, Christianity has easily abandoned knowledge to a discipline that is alien to it, *tradidit mundum hominum disputationi*.* So it is that the sciences of nature have, with relative ease, succeeded in establishing their authority and in having that authority acknowledged. But Christianity could not let the world of souls out of its grip as easily, for it is above all over souls that the god of the Christians wishes to rule. This is why the idea of subjecting psychic life to science long amounted to a kind of profanation; even today, that idea is still repugnant to many. Today, experimental and comparative psychology has been created and must be reckoned with. But the world of religious and moral life still remains forbidden. The great majority of men continue to believe that there is an order of things that the intellect can enter only by very special routes. Hence the strong resistance one encounters whenever one attempts to treat religious and moral phenomena scientifically. Yet these efforts

---

*It abandoned the world to the disputes of men.

persist despite opposition, and that very persistence makes it foreseeable that this last barrier will give way in the end, and that science will establish itself as mistress, even in this preserve.

This is what the conflict of science and religion is about. People often have a mistaken idea of it.* Science is said to deny religion in principle. But religion exists; it is a system of given facts; in short, it is a reality. How could science deny a reality? Furthermore, insofar as religion is action and insofar as it is a means of making men live, science cannot possibly take its place. Although science expresses life, it does not create life, and science can very well seek to explain faith but by that very fact presupposes faith. Hence there is conflict on only a limited point. Of the two functions originally performed by religion, there is one, only one, that tends more and more to escape it, and that is the speculative function. What science disputes in religion is not its right to exist but its right to dogmatize about the nature of things, its pretensions to special expertise for explaining man and the world. In fact, religion does not know itself. It knows neither what it is made of nor what needs it responds to. Far from being able to tell science what to do, religion is itself an object for science! And on the other hand, since apart from a reality that eludes scientific reflection, religious speculation has no special object of its own, that religion obviously cannot play the same role in the future as it did in the past.

However, religion seems destined to transform itself rather than disappear.

I have said that there is something eternal in religion: the cult and the faith. But men can neither conduct ceremonies for which they can see no rationale, nor accept a faith that they in no way understand. To spread or simply maintain religion, one must justify it, which is to say one must devise a theory of it. A theory of this sort must assuredly rest on the various sciences, as soon as they come into existence: social sciences first, since religious faith has its origins in society; psychology next, since society is a synthesis of human consciousnesses; sciences of nature finally, since man and society are linked to the universe and can be abstracted from it only artificially. But as important as these borrowings from the established sciences may be, they are in no way sufficient; faith is above all a spur to action, whereas science, no matter how advanced, always remains at a distance from action. Science is fragmentary and incomplete; it advances but slowly and is never finished; but life—that cannot wait. Theories whose calling is to make people live and make them act, must therefore rush ahead of science and complete it prema-

---

*This sentence is missing from Swain.

turely. They are possible only if the demands of practicality and vital necessities, such as we feel without distinctly conceiving them, push thought beyond what science permits us to affirm. In this way, even the most rational and secularized religions cannot and can never do without a particular kind of speculation which, although having the same objects as science itself, still cannot be properly scientific. The obscure intuitions of sense and sensibility often take the place of logical reasons.

Thus, from one point of view, this speculation resembles the speculation we encounter in the religions of the past, while from another, it differs from them. While exercising the right to go beyond science, it must begin by knowing and drawing inspiration from science. As soon as the authority of science is established, science must be reckoned with; under pressure of need, one can go beyond science, but it is from science that one must start out. One can affirm nothing that science denies, deny nothing that science affirms, and establish nothing that does not directly or indirectly rest on principles taken from science. From then on, faith* no longer holds the same sway as in the past over the system of representations that can continue to be called religious. There rises a power before religion that, even though religion's offspring, from then on applies its own critique and its own testing to religion. And everything points to the prospect that this testing will become ever more extensive and effective, without any possibility of assigning a limit to its future influence.

III

If the fundamental notions of science are of religious origin, how could religion have engendered them? It is not obvious at first glance what the points of contact between logic and religion might be. Indeed, since the reality that religious thought expresses is society, the question can be posed in terms that bring out the difficulty more clearly, as follows: What could have made social life such an important source of logical life? Nothing predisposed society for this role, it would seem, since it is obvious that men did not come together for the purpose of satisfying speculative needs.

Some will think it reckless of me to broach a problem of such complexity here. For the treatment it deserves to be possible, the sociological conditions of knowledge would have to be better known than they are. We can only begin to discern a few of those conditions. However, the question is so

---

*The first edition says la foi—"faith"; the second says la loi—"law."

important and so directly implied by everything that has gone before that I must make an effort not to leave it without an answer. Perhaps, moreover, it may be possible to set forth even now a few general principles of a kind that may at least shed light on the solution.

The basic material of logical thought is concepts. To try to discover how society could have played a role in the genesis of logical thought therefore amounts to asking how it can have taken part in the formation of concepts.

If we see the concept only as a general idea, as is most usually the case, the problem seems insoluble. By his own means, the individual can indeed compare his perceptions or images and sift out what they have in common; in other words, he can generalize. So it is not easy to see why generalization should be possible only in and through society. But, first of all, it is inadmissible that logical thought should be characterized exclusively by the wider scope of the representations that constitute it. If there is nothing logical about the particular ideas, why would the general ones be any different? The general exists only in the particular; it is the particular, simplified and stripped down. The general, then, cannot have virtues and privileges that the particular does not have. Inversely, if conceptual thought can be applied to genus, species, and variety, however small, why could it not extend to the individual, that is, to the limit toward which the idea tends in proportion as its scope narrows? As a matter of fact, there are a good many concepts that have individual objects. In every kind of religion, the gods are individualities distinct from one another; they are nevertheless conceived, not perceived. Each people imagines its historical or legendary heroes in a certain fashion, which is historically variable, and these representations are conceptual. Finally, each of us has a certain notion of the individuals with whom he is in contact—their character, their appearance, and the distinctive traits of their physical and moral temperaments. Such notions are true concepts. No doubt, they are in general rather crudely formed; but even among scientific concepts, are there many that are perfectly adequate to their objects? In this regard, our own concepts and those of science differ only in degree.

Therefore, the concept must be defined by other traits. The following properties distinguish it from tangible representations of any sort—sensations, perceptions, or images.

Sense representations are in perpetual flux; they come and go like the ripples of a stream, not staying the same even as long as they last. Each is linked with the exact moment in which it occurs. We are never assured of retrieving a perception in the same way we felt it the first time; for even if the thing perceived is unchanged, we ourselves are no longer the same. The concept, on the other hand, is somehow outside time and change; it is shielded from all such disturbance; one might say that it is in a different region of the mind, a region that is calmer and more serene. The concept does not move on its own by an internal, spontaneous development; quite the contrary, it resists change. It is a way of thinking that at any given moment in time is fixed and crystallized.[8] To the extent that it is what it has to be, it is unchangeable. If it does change, change does not come about because of its nature but because we have discovered some imperfection in it, because it needs to be rectified. The system of concepts with which we think in everyday life is the one the vocabulary of our mother tongue expresses, for each word translates a concept. Language is fixed; it changes but slowly, and, hence, the same is true of the conceptual organization it translates. The scientist finds himself in the same position vis-à-vis the special terminology used by the science to which he is committed, and consequently vis-à-vis the special system of concepts to which that terminology corresponds. He may innovate, of course, but his innovations always do a certain violence to established ways of thinking.

At the same time as being relatively unchangeable, a concept is universal, or at least universalizable. A concept is not my concept; it is common to me and other men or at least can be communicated to them. It is impossible for me to make a sensation pass from my consciousness into someone else's; it is closely dependent on my body and personality and cannot be detached from them. All I can do is invite another person to set himself before the same object as I and open himself to its influence. By contrast, conversation and intellectual dealings among men consist in an exchange of concepts. The concept is, in essence, an impersonal representation. By means of it, human intelligences communicate.[9]

Defined in that way, the nature of the concept bespeaks its origins. It is common to all because it is the work of the community. It does not bear the imprint of any individual intellect, since it is fashioned by a single intellect in which all the others meet, and to which they come, as it were, for nourishment. If it has greater stability than sensations or images, that is so because collective representations are more stable than individual ones; for while the

---

[8]William James, *The Principles of Psychology,* I [New York, Macmillan, 1890], p. 464.

[9]This universality of the concept must not be confused with its generality. The two are very different things. What I call universality is the property the concept has of being communicated to a number of minds and indeed to all minds, in principle. That communicability is altogether independent of its scope. A concept that applies only to a single object, one whose scope is therefore minimal, can be universal in the sense that it is the same for all minds: The concept of a deity is of this sort.

individual is sensitive to even slight changes in his internal or external environment, only quite weighty events can succeed in changing the mental equilibrium of society. Whenever we are in the presence of a *type*[10] of thought or action that presses uniformly on individual intellects or wills, that pressure on the individual reveals the intervention of the collectivity. Further, I said before that the concepts with which we routinely think are those deposited in the vocabulary. It is beyond doubt that speech, and hence the system of concepts it translates, is the product of a collective elaboration. What it expresses is the manner in which society as a whole conceives the objects of experience. The notions corresponding to the various elements of language are therefore collective representations.

The very content of these notions testifies in the same way. Indeed, there are scarcely any words, even among those we most commonly use, whose meaning does not to some degree go beyond the limits of our personal experience. Often a term expresses things we have never perceived and experiences we have never had or never witnessed. Even when we know certain of the objects to which the term refers, we know them only as particular examples that serve to illustrate the idea but that would never have been enough to form it by themselves. There is a whole science condensed in words then, a science that is more than individual; and it so far surpasses me that I cannot even make all the results my own. Who of us knows all the words of the language he speaks and the full meaning of each word?

This point enables me to define the sense in which I say that concepts are collective representations. If they are common to an entire social group, it is not because they are a simple average of the corresponding individual representations; if they were that, they would be of poorer intellectual content than individual representations, whereas they are in fact replete with knowledge surpassing that of the average individual. Concepts are not abstract things that have reality only in particular circumstances. They are representations just as concrete as any the individual can make of his own environment, for they correspond to the way in which the special being that is society thinks about the things of its own experience. If, in fact, concepts most often are general ideas, if they express categories and classes rather than partic-

---

[10]Some will object that, in the individual, ways of acting or thinking often become fixed and crystallized as habits that resist change, through the effect of repetition alone. But habit is only a tendency to repeat an action or an idea automatically whenever the same circumstances reactivate it; habit does not imply that the idea or action is constituted in the state of exemplary types, proposed or imposed on the mind or will. It is only when a type of this sort is preestablished—that is, when a rule or norm is instituted—that the workings of society can and must be presumed.

ular objects, that is because individual and variable characteristics of beings are rarely of interest to society. Because of its very scope, society can hardly be affected by any but their most general and lasting properties. Hence it is this general aspect that bears society's attention. It is in the nature of society most often to see things in large masses and in the form they take most generally. However, that generality is not indispensable; and, in any case, even when these representations have the generic character that is most usual for them, they are the work of society and are enriched by its experience.

This, furthermore, is what makes conceptual thought valuable to us. If the concepts were merely general ideas, they would not greatly enrich knowledge, for as I have already said, the general contains nothing more than the particular. But if they are collective representations, first and foremost, they add to what our personal experience can teach us all the wisdom and science that the collectivity has amassed over centuries. To think with concepts is not merely to see the real in its most general characteristics but to turn upon sensation a beam that lights, penetrates, and transforms it. To conceptualize a thing is to apprehend its essential elements better and to place it in the group to which it belongs. Each civilization has its own ordered system of concepts, which characterizes it. Before this system of ideas, the individual intellect is in the same situation as the νοῦς of Plato before the world of Ideas. He strives to assimilate them, for he needs them in order to deal with his fellow men, but this assimilation is always incomplete. Each of us sees them in his own way. Some escape us completely, remaining beyond our range of vision, while others are glimpsed in only some of their aspects. There are some, and indeed many, that we distort by thinking them. Since they are by nature collective, they cannot become individualized without being added to, modified, and consequently distorted. This is why we have so much difficulty understanding one another, and why, indeed often, we lie to one another unintentionally. This happens because we all use the same words without giving them the same meaning.

We can now begin to see society's share in the origin of logical thought. Logical thought is possible only when man has managed to go beyond the fleeting representations he owes to sense experience and in the end to conceive a whole world of stable ideals, the common ground of intelligences. To think logically, in fact, is always, in some measure, to think impersonally; it is also to think *sub specie aeternitatis*.* Impersonality and stability: Such are the two characteristics of truth. Logical life obviously presupposes that man knows, at least confusedly, that there is a truth distinct from sense appear-

---

*Under the aspect of eternity.

ances. But how could he have arrived at any such idea? People proceed most often as though logical life must have appeared spontaneously, as soon as man opened his eyes upon the world. But there is nothing in direct experience to suggest it; indeed, everything opposes it. Thus, children and animals have not even a clue of it. History shows, furthermore, that it took centuries to emerge and take shape. In our Western world, only with the great thinkers of Greece did logical life for the first time become clearly conscious of itself and of the consequences it implies. And when the discovery came, it provoked wonderment, which Plato expressed in magnificent language. But even if it was only then that the idea was expressed in philosophical formulas, it necessarily existed before then as a vague awareness. Philosophers sought to clarify this awareness; they did not create it. To have been able to reflect upon and analyze it, they must have been given it, and the question is where this awareness came from, that is, on what experience it was based. The answer is collective experience. It is in the form of collective thought that impersonal thought revealed itself to humanity for the first time, and by what other route that revelation could have come about is hard to see.

Solely because society exists, there also exists beyond sensations and images a whole system of representations that possess marvelous properties. By means of them, men understand one another, and minds gain access to one another. They have a kind of force and moral authority by virtue of which they impose themselves upon individual minds. From then on, the individual realizes, at least dimly, that above his private representations there is a world of type-ideas according to which he has to regulate his own; he glimpses a whole intellectual world in which he participates but which is greater than he. This is a first intuition of the realm of truth. As soon as he became aware of that higher intellectuality, he set about scrutinizing its nature, trying to find out how these preeminent representations came by their prerogatives. And to the extent that he thought he had discovered their causes, he undertook to put those causes to work himself and, by himself, to draw the conclusions they lead to; that is, he gave himself the right to make concepts. In this way, the faculty of conceptualization individualized itself. But to understand the origins of that faculty, it must be linked to the social conditions on which it depends.

Some will object that I am presenting the concept in only one of its aspects—that its role is to ensure not only agreement among minds but also, and even more, their agreement with the nature of things. A concept would seem not to fulfill its *raison d'être* unless it was true—that is, objective—and its impersonality to be only a consequence of its objectivity. It is in things conceived as adequately as they can be that minds should communicate. I do not deny that conceptual evolution moves partly in this direction. The concept that is at first held to be true because it is collective tends not to become collective unless it is held to be true: We demand its credentials before giving it credence. But first, we must not lose sight of the fact that, even today, the great majority of the concepts that we use are not methodically constructed; we come by them from language, that is, from common experience, and without subjecting them to any prior critique. Concepts that are scientifically wrought and criticized are always in a very small minority. Second, there are only differences of degree between those concepts and the ones that draw all their authority only from the fact of being collective. A collective representation, because it is collective, already presents assurances of objectivity. Not without reason has it been able to generalize and maintain itself with such persistence. If it was in disagreement with the nature of things, it would not have succeeded in acquiring broad and prolonged dominion over minds. Fundamentally, what makes scientific concepts inspire confidence is that they can be tested methodically. A collective representation necessarily undergoes a test that is repeated indefinitely. The men who adhere to a collective representation verify it through their own experience. Thus it cannot be wholly inadequate to its object. Certainly it may explain that object with imperfect symbols, but scientific symbols are themselves never more than approximate. The method I follow in the study of religious phenomena is based on exactly this principle. I regard it as axiomatic that, strange though religious beliefs may sometimes be in appearance, they contain their own truth, which must be uncovered.[11]

Inversely, even when constructed in accordance with all the rules of science, concepts are far from taking their authority from their objective value alone. To be believed, it is not enough that they be true. If they are not in harmony with other beliefs and other opinions—in short, with the whole set of collective representations—they will be denied; minds will be closed to them; as a result, they will be and yet not be. If bearing the seal of science is usually enough today to gain a sort of privileged credibility, that is because we have faith in science. But that faith is not essentially different from religious faith. The value we attribute to science depends, in the last analysis, upon the idea we collectively have of its nature and role in life, which is to say that it expresses a state of opinion. The reason is that everything in social life rests on opinion, including science itself. To be sure, we can make opinion an object of study and create a science of it; that is what sociology principally consists in. Still the science of opinion does not create opinion, but

[11]From the very fact that a representation has a social origin, we see how far it is from being without objective value.

can only clarify it and make it more conscious of itself. In this way, it is true, science can lead opinion to change, but science remains the product of opinion even at the moment it seems to rule opinion; for as I have shown, science draws the strength it takes to act upon opinion from opinion itself.[12]

To say that concepts express the manner in which society conceives of things is also to say that conceptual thought is contemporaneous with humanity. Therefore, I refuse to see them as the product of more or less modern culture. A man who did not think with concepts would not be a man, for he would not be a social being. Limited to individual perceptions alone, he would not be distinct from an animal. It has been possible to uphold the contrary thesis only because the concept has been defined by features that are not fundamental to it. The concept has been identified with the general idea[13]—and with the clearly delimited and circumscribed general idea.[14] In that case, the lower societies could appear to be ignorant of the concept properly so-called, for they have only undeveloped processes of generalization, and the notions they use are generally not well defined. Yet most of our present concepts also lack clear definition; we can barely force ourselves to define them except in debate, and when we are operating as scientists. Besides, we have seen that conceptualizing is not the same as generalizing. To think conceptually is not merely to isolate and group the features common to a certain number of objects. It is also to subsume the variable under the permanent and the individual under the social. And since logical thought begins with the concept, it follows that logical thought has always existed; there has been no historical period when men lived in chronic confusion and contradiction. Certainly, the different features of logic in different historical periods cannot be overemphasized; logic evolves as societies themselves evolve. But however real, the differences should not cause us to miss the similarities, which are no less fundamental.

IV

We can now take up a final question, which was set out in the Introduction[15] and has remained more or less implicit throughout this book. We have seen

[12]Cf. above, p. 210.

[13][Lucien] Lévy-Bruhl, *Les Fonctions mentales dans les sociétés inférieures* [Paris, F. Alcan, 1910], pp. 131–138.

[14]Ibid., p. 446.

[15]See above, p. 12.

that at least certain of the categories are social things. The question is where they got this trait.

No doubt, since they are themselves concepts, we easily understand that they are the work of the collectivity. Indeed, no concepts display the distinguishing marks of a collective representation to the same degree. Indeed, their stability and impersonality are such that they have often been taken to be absolutely universal and immutable. Besides, since they express the fundamental conditions of understanding between minds, it seems obvious that they could only have been fashioned by society.

Yet the problem is more complex, insofar as the categories are concerned, for they are social in another sense and, as it were, to a higher degree. Not only do they come from society, but the very things they express are social. It is not only that they are instituted by society but also that their content is various aspects of the social being. The category of genus was at first indistinct from the concept of human group; the category of time has the rhythm of social life as its basis; the space society occupies provided the raw material for the category of space; collective force was the prototype for the concept of effective force, an essential element in the category of causality. Nevertheless, application to the social realm is not the only function of the categories; they extend to reality as a whole. Why is it, then, that the models on which they were built have been borrowed from society?

The answer is that these are preeminent concepts that have a preponderant role in knowledge. Indeed, the function of the categories is to govern and contain the other concepts. They form the permanent framework of mental life. But to encompass such an object, they must be modeled on a reality of equally wide scope.

Doubtless the relations they express exist, implicitly, in individual consciousnesses. The individual lives in time and, as I have said, has a certain sense of temporal orientation. He is at a definite point in space, and it has been possible to hold, with good reason, that all sensations have a spatial aspect.[16] He has a sense of similarity. Similar representations attract one another and come together within him, and the new representation formed by their coming together has a certain generic quality. We also have the sensation of a certain regularity in the order of succession in phenomena; even the animal is not incapable of that. But all these relationships are personal to the individual who is involved with them, and hence the notion he can gain from them can in no case stretch beyond his narrow horizon. The generic images

---

[16]James, *Principles of Psychology*, vol. I, p. 134.

that form in my consciousness through the coming together of similar images represent only those objects that I have perceived directly; nothing is there to give me the idea of a class, that is, a framework able to encompass the *whole* group of all possible objects that fulfill the same criterion. I would still need to have the idea of group beforehand, an idea that the mere unfolding of our inner life cannot be sufficient to arouse in us. Above all, there is no individual experience, no matter how broad or prolonged, that could make us even suspect the existence of a whole genus embracing the universality of beings, and in which the other genera would be only species coordinated among, or subordinated to, one another. This notion of the *whole*, which lies at the basis of the classifications I have cited, cannot come to us from the individual himself, who is only a part of the whole and never comes in contact with more than an infinitesimal part of reality. And yet there is perhaps no more fundamental category. Since the role of the categories is to encompass all the other concepts, the category par excellence would indeed seem to be the very concept of *totality*. The theorists of knowledge usually postulate totality as if it is self-evident, but in fact it goes infinitely beyond the content of each individual consciousness, taken separately.

For the same reasons, the space I know through my senses, where I am at the center and where everything is arranged in relation to me, could not be the space as a whole, which contains all the individual spaces and in which, moreover, those individual spaces are coordinated in relation to impersonal reference points common to all individuals. Similarly, the concrete duration that I feel passing within and with me could never give me the idea of time as a whole. The first expresses only the rhythm of my individual life; the second must correspond to the rhythm of a life that is not that of any particular individual, but one in which all participate.[17] In the same way, finally, the regularities that I can perceive in the way my sensations follow one another may very well have value for me; they explain why I tend to wait for the second when the first of two phenomena whose constant conjunction I have experienced is given to me. But that state of personal expectancy cannot be assimilated to the conception of a universal order of succession that imposes itself on all minds and all events.

Since the world expressed by the whole system of concepts is the world society conceives of, only society can provide us with the most general no-

[17]Space and time are often spoken of as if they were only concrete extension and duration, such as individual consciousness can experience them, but impoverished through abstraction. In reality, they are representations of an entirely different kind—constructed out of different elements, following a very different plan, and with ends in view that are different as well.

tions in terms of which that world must be conceived. Only a subject that encompasses every individual subject has the capacity to encompass such an object. Since the universe exists only insofar as it is thought of and since it is thought of in its totality only by society, it takes its place within society; it becomes an element of society's inner life, and thus is itself the total genus outside which nothing exists. The concept of totality is but the concept of society in abstract form. It is the whole that includes all things, the supreme class that contains all other classes. Such is the underlying principle on which rest those primitive classifications that situated and classified beings of all the kingdoms, in the same right as men.[18] But if the world is in the society, the space society occupies merges with space as a whole. As we have seen, each thing does indeed have its assigned place in social space. But what brings out the extent to which that total space differs from those concrete expanses that our senses cause us to perceive is the fact that localization is wholly ideal and in no way resembles what it might be if it was dictated to us by sense experience.[19] For the same reason, the rhythm of collective life governs and contains the various rhythms of all the elementary lives of which it is the result; consequently, the time that expresses it governs and contains all the individual times. It is time as a whole.

For a long time, the world's history was only a different aspect of society's history. The one begins with the other; the periods of the world are determined by the periods of the society. Measuring that impersonal and global duration and setting reference points in relation to which it is divided and organized are society's movements of concentration or dispersal—or, more generally, the periodic need for collective renewal. If those critical moments are most often attached to some physical phenomenon, such as the regular reappearance of a certain star or the alternation of the seasons, it is because objective signs are needed to make that essentially social organization tangible for all. Similarly, the causal relation becomes independent of any individual consciousness from the moment it is collectively established by the group; it hovers above all the minds and all the individual events. It is a law having impersonal validity. I have shown that the law of causality seems to have been born in just this way.

There is another reason why the constituent elements of the categories must have been taken from social life: The relationships they express could

---

[18]In all probability, the concepts of totality, society, and deity are at bottom merely different aspects of the same notion.

[19]See "Classifications primitives" [Emile Durkheim, "De Quelques formes primitives de classification," *AS*, vol. VI, 1903], pp. 40ff.

not become conscious relationships except in and through society. Even if, in a sense, they are immanent in the life of the individual, the individual had neither reason nor means to grasp them, think about them, make them explicit, and build them up into distinct notions. To orient his individual self in space and to know at what times to satisfy various physical needs, he had no need for a conceptual representation of time or space, once and for all. Many animals know how to find their way back to the paths leading to places familiar to them; they return there at the right time yet without their having any category at all; sensations are enough to guide them automatically. These would be sufficient for man as well if his movements had to satisfy individual needs alone. In order to recognize that one thing resembles others with which we are already acquainted, we need not arrange them in genera and species. The way in which similar images call one another forth and merge are enough to create the feeling of resemblance. The impression of *déjà vu*, of something already experienced, implies no classification. In order to differentiate between those things we must seek after and those we must flee, we have no need to join the effects of both to their causes with a logical link, if individual convenience alone is at stake. Purely empirical sequences, strong connections between concrete representations, are equally sure guides to the will. Not only does the animal have no others, but our own individual practice quite often presupposes nothing more. The wise man is one who has a very clear sense of what he must do but one that he would usually be unable to translate into a law.

It is otherwise with society. Society is possible only if the individuals and things that make it up are divided among different groups, which is to say genera,* and if those groups themselves are classified in relation to one another. Thus, society presupposes a conscious organization of itself that is nothing other than a classification. That organization of society is naturally passed on to the space it occupies. To forestall conflict, a definite portion of space must be assigned to each individual group. In other words, the space must be divided, differentiated, and oriented, and these divisions and orientations must be known to all. In addition, every call to a feast, hunt, or military expedition implies that dates are fixed and agreed upon and, therefore, that a common time is established that everyone conceives in the same way.

---

*Here and later in the paragraph (as well as twice previously in this chapter), Durkheim shifts to the word *classe*. Since the English term "class" can imply economic differentiation, which would move the argument out of its present context, I have used the term "genus" throughout. Nonetheless, what the economic sense of "class" would add or subtract should be kept in mind—for example, in the end of the last sentence in this paragraph.

Finally, the collaboration of several in pursuit of a common goal is possible only if there is agreement on the relation between that goal and the means that make its achievement possible—that is, if a single causal relation is accepted by all who are working together in the same enterprise. It is not surprising, then, that social time, social space, social genera [*classes*], and collective causality should be the basis of the corresponding categories, since it is in their social forms that they were first conceived with any degree of clarity by human consciousness.

To summarize, society is by no means the illogical or alogical, inconsistent, and changeable being that people too often like to imagine. Quite the contrary, the collective consciousness is the highest form of psychic life, for it is a consciousness of consciousnesses. Being outside and above individual and local contingencies, collective consciousness sees things only in their permanent and fundamental aspect,* which it crystallizes in ideas that can be communicated. At the same time as it sees from above, it sees far ahead; at every moment, it embraces all known reality; that is why it alone can furnish the intellect with frameworks that are applicable to the totality of beings and that enable us to build concepts about them. It does not create these frameworks artificially but finds them within itself, merely becoming conscious of them. They express ways of being that are met with at all levels of the real but that appear with full clarity only at the pinnacle, because the extreme complexity of the psychic life that unfolds there requires a more highly developed consciousness. Therefore, to attribute social origins to logical thought is not to denigrate it, diminish its worth, or reduce it to no more than a system of artificial combinations—but is, quite the contrary, to relate logical thought to a cause that naturally implies it. Assuredly, this is not to say that notions worked out in that way could be directly adequate to their objects. If society is something universal as compared to the individual, it is still an individuality, having its own form and idiosyncrasies; it is a particular subject and, consequently, one that particularizes what it thinks of. So even collective representations contain subjective elements, and if they are to become closer to things, they must be gradually refined. But crude as these representations might have been at first, it remains true that with them came the seed of a new mode of thinking, one to which the individual could never have lifted himself on his own. The way was open to stable, impersonal, ordered thought, which had only to develop its own special nature from then on.

*Note the similarity between this formulation about *conscience collective* as "a permanent and fundamental" aspect of society and a similar one about religion as a "fundamental and permanent aspect of humanity" in the Introduction (above, p. 1).

Moreover, the factors that have brought about this development seem to be no different in kind from those that brought it forth originally. If logical thought tends more and more to jettison the subjective and personal elements that were launched with it, the reason is not that extrasocial factors have entered in but far more that a new kind of social life gradually developed: international life, whose effect even then was to universalize religious beliefs. As that international life broadens, so does the collective horizon; society no longer appears as the whole, par excellence, and becomes part of a whole that is more vast, with frontiers that are indefinite and capable of rolling back indefinitely. As a result, things can no longer fit within the social frames where they were originally classified; they must be organized with principles of their own; logical organization thus differentiates itself from social organization and becomes autonomous. This, it seems, is how the bond that at first joined thought to defined collective entities becomes more and more detached and how, consequently, it becomes ever more impersonal and universalizes.* Thought that is truly and peculiarly human is not a primitive given, therefore, but a product of history; it is an ideal limit to which we come ever closer but in all probability will never attain.

Thus, the sort of antimony that has so often been accepted, between science on one hand and religion and morality on the other, is far from the case. In reality, these different modes of human activity derive from one and the same source. This Kant well understood, and therefore he considered speculative reason and practical reason to be two different aspects of the same faculty. According to him, what joins them is that both are oriented toward the universal. To think rationally is to think according to the laws that are self-evident to all reasonable beings; to act morally is to act according to maxims that can be extended without contradiction to all wills. In other words, both science and morality imply that the individual is capable of lifting himself above his own point of view and participating in an impersonal life. And, indeed, herein we undoubtedly have a trait that is common to all the higher forms of thought and action. But what Kantianism does not explain is where the sort of contradiction that man thus embodies comes from. Why must he do violence to himself in order to transcend his individual nature; and inversely, why must impersonal law weaken as it becomes incarnate in individuals? Will it be said that there are two antagonistic worlds in which we participate equally: the world of matter and sense, on the one hand, and on the other, that of pure and impersonal reason? But that is to repeat the ques-

---

*This sentence was omitted from the Swain translation but is in both French versions of *Formes*.

tion in terms that are barely different: for the point precisely is to know why we must* lead those two lives concurrently. Since the two worlds seem to contradict one another, why do they not remain separate from one another, and what makes it necessary for them to interpenetrate, despite their antagonism? The hypothesis of the Fall, with all its attendant difficulties, is the only explanation of that singular necessity that has ever been offered—and it need not be recited here.

On the other hand, the mystery dissolves once we have acknowledged that impersonal reason is but collective thought by another name. Collective thought is possible only through the coming together of individuals; hence it presupposes the individuals, and they in turn presuppose it, because they cannot sustain themselves except by coming together. The realm of impersonal aims and truths cannot be realized except through the collaboration of individual wills and sensibilities;† the reasons they participate and the reasons they collaborate are the same. In short, there is something impersonal in us because there is something social in us, and since social life embraces both representations and practices, that impersonality extends quite naturally to ideas as well as to actions.

Some will be astonished, perhaps, to see me connecting the highest forms of the human mind with society. The cause seems quite humble as compared to the value we attribute to the effect. So great is the distance between the world of the senses and appetites on the one hand, and the world of reason and morality on the other, that it seems the second could have been added to the first only by an act of creation. But to attribute to society this dominant role in the origin of our nature is not to deny that creation. Society does indeed have at its disposal a creative power that no observable being can match. Every creation, unless it is a mystical procedure that escapes science and intellect, is in fact the product of a synthesis. If the syntheses of particular representations that occur within each individual consciousness are already, in and of themselves, productive of novelties, how much more effective must societies be—these vast syntheses of entire consciousnesses! A society is the most powerful collection of physical and moral forces that we can observe in nature. Such riches of various materials, so highly concentrated, are to be found nowhere else. It is not surprising, then, that a higher life develops out of them, a life that acts on the elements from which it is made, thereby raising them to a higher form of life and transforming them.

---

*The second edition says *Il nous fait* instead of *il nous faut,* surely a typographical error.

†The phrase "and sensibilities" does not appear in Swain.

Thus, it seems the vocation of sociology is to open a new way to the science of man. Until now, we stood before these alternatives: either to explain the higher and specific faculties of man by relating them to lower forms of being—reason to sense, mind to matter—which amounted to denying their specificity; or to connect them with some reality above experience that we postulated but whose existence no observation can establish. What placed the mind in that difficulty is that the individual was taken to be *finis naturae.** It seemed there was nothing beyond him, at least nothing that science might discover. But a new way of explaining man becomes possible as soon as we recognize that above the individual there is society, and that society is a system of active forces—not a nominal being, and not a creation of the mind. To preserve man's distinctive attributes, it is no longer necessary to place them outside experience. Before drawing that extreme conclusion, at any rate, it is best to find out whether that which is in the individual but surpasses him may not come to him from that supraindividual, yet concretely experienced, reality that is society. To be sure, it cannot be said at this moment how far these explanations can be extended and if they can lay every problem to rest. Equally, however, it is impossible to mark in advance a limit beyond which they cannot go. What must be done is to try out the hypothesis and test it against the facts as methodically as possible. This is what I have tried to do.

---

*The culmination of nature.

INDEX

449